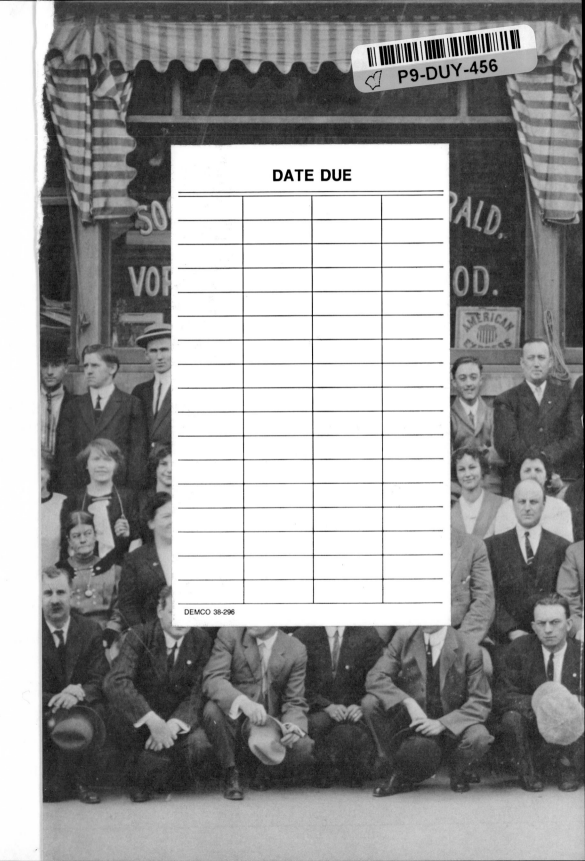

The Family Letters of Victor and Meta Berger

The Family Letters of Victor and Meta Berger

1 8 9 4 – 1 9 2 9

MICHAEL E. STEVENS
Editor

ELLEN D. GOLDLUST-GINGRICH
Assistant Editor

Center for Documentary History
STATE HISTORICAL SOCIETY OF WISCONSIN
Madison: 1995

The family letters of Victor
and Meta Berger, 1894-1929 *erese*

LIBRARY OF CONGRESS CATALOGING IN PUBLICATION DATA
The family letters of Victor and Meta Berger, 1894–1929.
Michael E. Stevens, editor.
Ellen D. Goldlust-Gingrich, assistant editor.
Illustrated. Includes bibliographical references and index.

ISBN 0-87020-277-4
1. Berger, Victor L., 1860–1929—Correspondence.
2. Berger, Meta Schlichting, 1873–1944—Correspondence.
3. Socialists—United States—Correspondence.
4. Socialism—United States—History—Sources.
5. United States—Politics and government—1865–1933—Sources.
6. World Politics—1900–1918—Sources.
7. World Politics—1918–1932—Sources.
I. Berger, Victor L., 1860–1929. II. Berger, Meta Schlichting, 1873–1944. III. Stevens, Michael E. IV. Goldlust-Gingrich, Ellen D. V. State Historical Society of Wisconsin.

HX86.F35 1995   335'.0092'273—dc20
[B]   94-43793 CIP

Endpapers: The staff of the Social-Democratic Publishing Company in front of Brisbane Hall, Milwaukee, ca. 1912–1913. In the second row, below the word "Vorwaerts," are Elizabeth Thomas, Meta Berger, and Victor Berger. *Photo courtesy of the Milwaukee County Historical Society.*

Contents

Illustrations follow pages 154 and 282.

Introduction

Congressman, newspaper editor, and co-founder of the Socialist Party of America, Victor Luitpold Berger was the most successful politician in his party's history.[1] Berger's well-organized political machine engineered his election to the U.S. House of Representatives six times and remained influential in Milwaukee through much of the first quarter of the twentieth century. With the help of his wife, Meta Schlichting Berger, who held state and local offices as a Socialist for three decades, he demonstrated that the Socialist Party could compete effectively in American politics. Although he believed ardently in the necessity of social and economic change, he regularly found himself in the Socialist Party's right wing. Whereas his more radical colleagues hoped for change through revolution, Berger believed in evolutionary socialism. Indeed, he preferred the term "social democrat" to "socialist," and the Wisconsin branch of the party used the former name until World War I tarnished the label by linking it with the German Social Democratic Party.[2]

Berger preached the gospel of social democracy, and although he envisaged the eventual arrival of the cooperative commonwealth, he worked for a set of immediate demands that would ameliorate the conditions of the working class. Ironically, his persecution by the federal government for his opposition to American involvement in World War I aided his political career and made him a symbol for civil libertarians during the 1920s. Tagged a radical early in his career, by the time Berger left the U.S. House of Representatives in 1929, Congressman Fiorello La Guardia (R-N.Y.) called him "a pioneer, popularizing ideas of political and social reform long before they are accepted by the many."[3]

* * *

1. The outline of Berger's public life is drawn from three excellent works that are indispensable for any student of his career: Sally M. Miller, *Victor Berger and the Promise of Constructive Socialism, 1910–1920* (Westport, Connecticut, 1973); Edward J. Muzik, "Victor L. Berger, A Biography" (Ph.D. diss., Northwestern University, 1960); and Frederick I. Olson, "The Milwaukee Socialists, 1897–1941" (Ph.D. diss., Harvard University, 1952).

2. To avoid confusion stemming from the differing names of the national and state parties, the editors use the term "Socialist Party" in the introduction and in the annotation to the letters to refer to Berger's party after 1901.

3. Speech by Fiorello La Guardia, March 4, 1929, *Congressional Record*, 70th Cong., 2d sess., 5236.

Born to Ignatz and Julia Berger on February 28, 1860, in Nieder-Rehbach in Austria-Hungary, Victor was the eldest of seven children (two boys and five girls) in a comfortable Jewish family that prized education. Victor's parents sent him to a local Lutheran minister for tutoring and later to schools in Budapest and Vienna, although he never completed his studies or received a college degree. Throughout his life he remained an avid reader, and he eventually accumulated one of the largest private libraries in Milwaukee. The threat of conscription into the Austro-Hungarian army led to Victor's emigration to America in 1878; his family followed shortly thereafter. After living briefly in New York City, his parents and siblings settled in Bridgeport, Connecticut, where they earned a good living by retailing shoes and leather goods and later by investing in real estate.

After his arrival in the United States, Victor traveled around the country, holding odd jobs ranging from repairing wash boilers to punching cattle. He eventually learned the trade of metal polishing before moving to Milwaukee in 1881. He became a naturalized citizen five years later. The large German-speaking community in Milwaukee provided ample opportunities for his talents, and he soon became active in German-American organizations and wrote for the German-language press as a drama critic. For nearly ten years beginning in the fall, 1883, he taught German and other subjects in the city's public schools.[4]

Although an adequate teacher, Berger preferred life in the public arena, where he could indulge his passion for politics. Throughout the 1880s, he became increasingly engaged with the great social issues of his time—questions of the role of capital, the organization of labor, and the ways in which a humane society could be constructed in the new industrial era. With its active Turnverein (social and athletic clubs that promoted free thinking), Milwaukee provided Berger with an intellectual atmosphere in which he could imbibe the latest socialist thought imported from Germany. His service as secretary and president of Milwaukee's South Side Turn Society helped him develop his organizational and political skills. Embracing socialism, Berger became active in local labor politics, joined the Knights of Labor, and briefly belonged to the Socialist Labor Party.

4. Biographical material on Berger's early life is sparse and at times contradictory. For an early biographical sketch probably drafted by Berger, see Independent Order Knights of Labor, *Official Historical Handbook* (Jersey City, 1898), n.p. Family traditions about Berger can be found in Meta Berger's autobiography (hereafter cited as Meta Berger autobiography) and in an incomplete manuscript biography of Berger by his daughter, Doris Berger Welles Hursley, (hereafter cited as Hursley biography), both in the Victor L. Berger Papers at the State Historical Society of Wisconsin (hereafter cited as SHSW). Berger's naturalization certificate and teaching certificate are also in the Berger Papers.

In December, 1892, Berger left the school system and purchased a German-language labor newspaper, the *Milwaukee'r Volkszeitung*, renaming it the *Wisconsin Vorwärts* (Forward). He ran the paper as a daily from January, 1893, until August, 1898, when financial setbacks forced him to scale it back to a weekly, called simply the *Vorwärts*.[5] From the beginning, Berger sought to tie his publishing efforts to the labor movement. The *Wisconsin Vorwärts* served as the official newspaper of the Wisconsin State Federation of Labor and of the Milwaukee Federated Trades Council, thus forging the links between organized labor and Berger's political machine that later served his cause so well. Berger moved quickly from state labor politics to the national arena. Starting in 1898, he attended the annual conventions of the American Federation of Labor (AFL), where he regularly locked horns with Samuel Gompers, who opposed Berger's efforts to tie the labor movement to the socialist cause.

Berger's involvement with labor politics was inextricably linked to his desire to form a political party that would serve the cause of social democracy and in which he would play a major part. During the 1890s, Berger dabbled with Populism, serving as a delegate to the People's Party's 1894 Wisconsin convention and to the party's 1896 national convention, where he attempted to secure the presidential nomination for Eugene V. Debs, leader of the American Railway Union. The party's endorsement of William Jennings Bryan ended Berger's interest in the Populists, and he staked his future on Debs's ability to generate a new political movement.

Berger first met Debs in 1895, while the latter was in jail in Woodstock, Illinois, for his role in the Pullman strike the previous year. Debs later recalled how Berger had given him an inscribed copy of Karl Marx's *Das Kapital* and "delivered the first impassioned message of socialism I had ever heard—the very first to set the wires humming in my system."[6] Although the friendship between the two men eventually soured over ideological and personality differences, each remained indispensable to the other—and to the party. New York Socialist Morris Hillquit, who frequently sided with Berger in party disputes, described Debs as the party's St. John—its "inspired prophet, preacher, and poet." Berger was its St. Paul—the "practical propagandist and builder."[7]

5. Berger had published the Sunday edition of *Wisconsin Vorwärts* under the name *Vorwärts* since January, 1893, and simply continued the latter paper after halting the daily edition. He also published *Die Wahrheit* (The Truth), another German-language weekly, from January, 1893, until June, 1910.

6. Eugene V. Debs, "How I Became a Socialist," *The Comrade* 1 (April, 1902), 147–148.

7. Morris Hillquit, *Loose Leaves from a Busy Life* (New York, 1934), 51–52.

Berger envied the popular adulation showered on Debs, but Berger's stiff public demeanor prevented him from winning public acclaim. Whereas Debs would greet a comrade on the street with a bear hug, Berger would offer a discourse on socialist theory.[8]

Although Debs refused to follow Berger's urging and run for president in 1896, the two men worked together a year later to convert the remnants of the American Railway Union into the Social Democracy of America. In 1898 Berger convinced Debs to bolt from his own organization and form the Social Democratic Party, a move that led in 1900 to the first of Debs's five runs for the presidency. The Social Democrats merged with Morris Hillquit's dissenting faction of the Socialist Labor Party, and in 1901 the two groups created the Socialist Party of America. Berger remained a leader of that organization for the remainder of his life.

While Berger was attempting to create a new political party, he married Meta Schlichting, who would become his political confidante and adviser, and began a family. Born in Milwaukee to Bernhard and Mathilde Schlichting on February 23, 1873, Meta was the second of five children. Her parents were natives of Germany; Bernhard came to Wisconsin in 1847 at age nine, and Mathilde immigrated in 1852, when she was five. The Schlichtings took an interest in politics in their adopted country, and both Meta's father and his brother served in the Wisconsin legislature as Republicans. Thirteen years younger than Victor, Meta recalled seeing him nervously coming to a job interview with her father, who was then serving on the Milwaukee school board, and she later studied German under her future husband. Following Bernhard's death in 1883, Victor frequently dined at the Schlichting house, as Meta's mother tried to raise money by providing meals for teachers. Although the family had lost its principal wage earner, Meta insisted on getting an education and earned a teaching degree from the Milwaukee State Normal School in 1894. Following graduation, she taught in the Milwaukee public schools, yielding her position when she married Victor on December 4, 1897.[9]

Meta became pregnant within weeks of their marriage and gave birth to a daughter, Doris, on September 29, 1898. Victor quickly rebounded from his initial disappointment at having a daughter rather than a son, saying, "This will be a woman's world. She will do her part."[10] Eighteen months later, on March 26, 1900, Meta gave birth to a second daughter, Elsa. After two pregnancies within a little more than

8. Hursley biography. For a description of the relationship between Debs and Berger, see Nick Salvatore, *Eugene V. Debs: Citizen and Socialist* (Urbana, Illinois, 1982), 163–165, 167–168, 247–251, 259–261.

9. Meta Berger autobiography.

10. Ibid.

two years, Meta started "brooding on how not to have more children."[11] Unbeknownst to her husband, she obtained a diaphragm. Victor "never knew the reason for no more pregnancies."[12]

Meta found herself torn between her desire to be a model, submissive wife and her will to use her considerable talents in the public arena. Victor at first tried to continue the role of teacher, regularly instructing Meta on what to read and how to think. For instance, a year prior to their marriage, he urged her to read a novel about the struggle between labor and capital and sent along his "annotations for your sake because I could not expect you to understand the hints and suggestive remarks."[13]

Meta initially accepted Victor's supposed superiority, although with some reluctance. She was to "keep the home calm, quiet, good meals on the table & keep the children as healthy as possible & to be as sympathetic as possible."[14] She recalled that their early marriage was a difficult "period of adjustment & readjustment," as Victor tried to remake her according to his own ideas. Prior to their marriage, she would stand "in the shadow of a building or a tree," trying to understand socialist debates, which were "in German, way above my head & hard to follow." After their marriage, she attempted to read the books he recommended, but she called them "Dry stuff!" Her mind was on "whether or not the baby's bottle was too hot or too cold," and she found that she learned little from the readings.[15]

Despite Meta's initial indifference, Victor continued to try to interest her in politics, and she attended her first Socialist Party convention in 1904. There, she found herself inspired by the debates and became committed to her husband's work in the socialist and labor movements, but she chafed at the personal and family costs of Victor's political activity.[16] As late as 1907, she questioned "whether the rabble, the very gang at the [AFL] convention and all the others are worth the sacrifices you make for them. I don't think so and never never will."[17]

Victor repeated with his children the patterns he had seen in his own relationship with his mother and father. He acutely felt and strongly resisted the domination of his parents, even into adulthood. When he announced his intention to marry a non-Jew, his mother visited Milwaukee and tried to persuade him to call off the marriage by

11. Ibid.
12. Elsa Berger Edelman, "The Second One," unpublished memoir, Berger Papers.
13. Victor to Meta, August 20, 1896, printed below.
14. Meta Berger autobiography.
15. Ibid.
16. Ibid.
17. Meta to Victor, November 20, 1907, printed below.

offering him half of her business.[18] Victor similarly tried to mold his children, even attempting to control their choice of spouses, and, like Victor, they resisted parental domination. When they were young, he set down rules for them—no candy, no meat until the age of seven, each to learn how to ride, hunt, shoot, and swim. At first Meta carefully enforced Victor's dictates, but eventually there was "a show-down between us as parents," after which Victor's rules began to be set aside.[19]

With a family established, Berger threw his energies into both national and local politics. Factional disputes racked the Socialist Party from its very beginning. Berger fought furiously to retain control of the organization's machinery, and although his faction of right-wing Socialists lost their share of party battles, they usually maintained firm control of the party's apparatus. Despite charges of bossism, Berger remained popular with the party's rank and file and regularly won reelection to the party's governing National Executive Committee. Like other Socialists, he believed that the cooperative commonwealth would inevitably arrive, but he was among those who departed from Marxist orthodoxy by denying that it would come about through revolution. According to Berger, "Just as feudalism followed the ancient customs of slavery, so will Socialism follow capitalism," although he conceded that the changes might take centuries.[20] The party's left wing frequently targeted him for criticism, and in 1905 Berger was removed from the National Executive Committee for endorsing a non-Socialist in a local election. (He later regained his seat following a party referendum.)

His standing in the national party depended substantially on the disciplined party organization that he had created in Milwaukee. With the help of local labor unions and Berger's publishing operations, the party long remained influential in city politics. Although Milwaukee's Socialists reached the high point of their success in 1910, they nonetheless controlled the mayor's office for all but four years between 1910 and 1940.

Socialists in Milwaukee offered candidates for office as early as 1898, the year after Berger established the first local branch of the Social Democracy of America. Building on criticism of municipal

18. Hursley biography.
19. Meta Berger autobiography.
20. "Victor L. Berger's Eastern Tour," *Social-Democratic Herald,* June 11, 1910. Berger never systematically set out his political philosophy, although his views can be found in his newspaper writings and his published speeches. His editorials and speeches were collected and published in Victor L. Berger, *Berger's Broadsides* (Milwaukee, 1912) (reprinted under the title *Broadsides* in second and third editions in 1912 and 1913) and in Victor L. Berger, *Voice and Pen of Victor L. Berger: Congressional Speeches and Editorials* (Milwaukee, 1929).

corruption, Berger's party became a serious contender in local politics by 1904, when the Socialists elected nine city aldermen, four county supervisors, five state assemblymen, and one state senator. Berger himself ran for mayor in the spring of that year, finishing third with 25 percent of the vote. He ran for Congress in the fall, finishing second with 28 percent of the vote. Encouraged by her husband, Meta Berger ran for the Milwaukee school board in the spring of 1909 on the Socialist ticket. To her surprise, she was elected, thus beginning her career in Wisconsin educational politics. She served on the board for thirty years, winning reelection in 1915, 1921, 1927, and 1933.

Encouraged by their success in 1909, the Socialists continued to hammer away at governmental corruption in Milwaukee and swept the spring election in 1910. The party won majorities on the city council and the county board and carried all major city offices, with Victor Berger winning election as an alderman-at-large. Further victories occurred that fall, as the party gained seats in the state legislature and Berger became the first Socialist elected to the U.S. House of Representatives.

Berger quickly won national recognition as the political strategist who helped organize the Socialist victory. The party's "bundle brigade" blanketed Milwaukee with 150,000 pieces of literature (published in a dozen different languages to appeal to the city's varied ethnic groups) during the six weeks before the election.[21] Berger's own publishing efforts played a significant role in the growth of Socialist strength in Milwaukee. But while Berger retained the editorship of the *Vorwärts* until 1911 as well as a financial stake in the paper for the remainder of his life, he realized that restricting himself to the German-language press would limit his influence in Milwaukee and the nation. Consequently, in 1901 he acquired the weekly Chicago-based *Social-Democratic Herald* and moved the paper to Milwaukee, where he published it until 1913. (Berger also established a weekly Polish-language newspaper, *Naprzod*, in 1909.) Although the *Herald* was supposedly national in scope, its Wisconsin edition provided thorough coverage of Milwaukee Socialist politics. Still, a weekly paper could not hope to compete with the English-language dailies that criticized socialism as a dangerous doctrine. Two days after Berger's election to Congress, Milwaukee's Socialists began their formal efforts to establish a daily newspaper. A year later, on December 7, 1911, the *Milwaukee Leader* first appeared.

The *Leader* always stood on shaky financial ground and depended on the contributions of labor unions and thousands of members of the rank and file who were persuaded to part with their cash by advertising that often overstated the soundness of the investment. Berger also

21. *History of the Milwaukee Social-Democratic Victories* (Milwaukee, 1911), 9, 14–22, 40–41, 45–46.

sought investors throughout the country, winning his most substantial support from a popular writer for the Hearst newspaper chain, Arthur Brisbane. Although the *Leader* usually failed to show a profit, it provided Berger with a living and a pulpit from which he could preach his ideas. Organized labor also provided Berger with funds to finance the *Leader* and to build Brisbane Hall, which served as headquarters for the *Leader* and the party.

In developing his publishing operations, Berger learned from his earlier mistakes. Financial losses at the *Vorwärts* had saddled him with a substantial private debt, and he established various legal entities to control his business ventures. By incorporating multiple bodies, he protected his personal assets, and in the event of a legal judgment against one corporation, the assets of the others remained protected. Thus, in 1902 Berger founded the Milwaukee Social-Democratic Publishing Company, which published the *Social-Democratic Herald* and later all of Berger's newspapers. By January, 1911, the business employed sixty-four people, and its receipts had grown from $3,000 to more than $56,000 in less than ten years.[22] In 1906 Berger established the Vorwärts Publishing Company, which published Berger's German-language newspapers.[23] The Co-operative Printery, which provided printing services for the party and the newspapers, was created in 1905, and the People's Realty Company, established in 1909, owned Brisbane Hall and rented space to the Milwaukee Social-Democratic Publishing Company and to the party.

Berger retained a leading role in all of these ventures, serving as president of the People's Realty Company and of the Vorwärts Publishing Company and as vice-president of the Milwaukee Social-Democratic Publishing Company. Each of these firms had further links to other organizations that Berger dominated. For example, when the Social-Democratic Publishing Company decided it needed a building for its operations, it named a committee with members from several organizations: the publishing company, the Milwaukee County Socialist Party, the executive board of the state party, the Vorwärts Publishing Company, and the Milwaukee Federated Trades Council—all organizations in which Berger had significant influence.[24]

While trying to launch a newspaper and run the party machine in Milwaukee, Berger began his career in Congress during the special

22. Ibid., 19.
23. The Milwaukee Social-Democratic Publishing Company acquired the assets of the Vorwärts Company in 1909 in exchange for stock in the former company.
24. Information on Berger's financial operations must be reconstructed from various sources. Corporation charters and annual reports of the Milwaukee Social-Democratic Publishing Company and of the People's Realty Company can be found in the Records of the Secretary of State, Corporation Divi-

session that convened in April, 1911. As the sole member from what seemed to be an up-and-coming party, Berger attracted substantial press attention and used the opportunity to promote social democracy. He viewed himself as the representative of all workers and claimed that only 3 percent of his congressional correspondence came from his district. During his first term, Berger gained national publicity for his old-age pension bill, the first of its kind introduced in Congress. He also secured a congressional investigation into the 1912 textile strike in Lawrence, Massachusetts, and initiated impeachment proceedings that led to the resignation of a federal judge who revoked the naturalization papers of a member of the Industrial Workers of the World (IWW).

Although Berger and his comrades thought that their party was on the upswing and that their success would recur throughout the country, the party in Milwaukee had in fact reached its apex. Even though Berger won election to Congress five more times and Socialist Daniel Webster Hoan held the mayor's office from 1916 to 1940, Berger's machine never repeated its 1910 successes. The party remained a force in Milwaukee politics, but future victories increasingly represented personal triumphs rather than the success of a movement. A coalition of Democrats and Republicans swept the Socialists from office in Milwaukee in the spring of 1912 and defeated Berger in the fall.

Berger failed to regain his congressional seat in 1914 and 1916, losing the 1914 campaign to a candidate who charged Berger with being unsympathetic to the German cause in the European war. In fact, like many residents of Milwaukee, Berger's sympathies lay with Germany, although he had little use for the Kaiser and was proud that the German Social Democrats initially had resisted Germany's involvement in the war. In accord with Socialist ideology, Berger opposed American intervention in World War I, maintaining that capitalist interests were earning money at the expense of the lives of America's working class. He argued for American neutrality, believed that the United States should cut off trade with all belligerents, and participated in the founding meeting of William Howard Taft's League to Enforce Peace. Berger's stance cost him dearly, initially with the pro-German voters of

---

sion, Incorporation Papers, Domestic, series 356, files P865 and M1290, SHSW. Financial reports on the publishing company are in the Records of the Milwaukee Social-Democratic Party at the Milwaukee County Historical Society and in the Berger Papers. The minutes of the Vorwärts Publishing Company, 1906–1909, and of the Milwaukee Social-Democratic Publishing Company, 1905–1935, both at the SHSW, provide sketchy but important details about the business decisions of the companies. See also *History of the Milwaukee Social-Democratic Victories* for information on the Co-operative Printery and Socialist publishing efforts in Milwaukee.

Milwaukee and later with self-appointed patriots who supported the Allied cause.

While Victor struggled to regain office, Meta's career flourished as she became increasingly active in local educational and suffrage politics. After winning a one-year term as president of the Milwaukee school board in 1915, she was appointed by Governor Emanuel Philipp in 1917 to a two-year term on the Wisconsin Board of Education. She took an active part in the state's suffrage movement, serving as a vice-president of the Wisconsin Woman Suffrage Association (WWSA) from 1914 until 1917. She attended the convention of the National American Woman Suffrage Association for the first time in 1915 and found it "full of interest & all, but nothing compared to a Socialist convention."[25] Two years later she resigned from the WWSA because it was "not nearly courageous & radical enough to suit me."[26] She then joined the National Woman's Party, whose members were regularly being arrested for picketing the White House.

Victor's and Meta's lives changed forever when the United States declared war on Germany on April 6, 1917. In an emergency convention that opened the next day, the Socialist Party condemned American involvement, a decision that set the party on the road to destruction. Prowar Socialists abandoned the party, and those who remained loyal to it became objects of repression. The war, however, revitalized Berger's flagging political career; he became the rallying point for opponents of the war and later a symbol for civil libertarians. Berger openly opposed the war and organized a local branch of the antiwar People's Council, although he attempted to walk a careful editorial line in the *Milwaukee Leader*. Nonetheless, on October 3, 1917, the *Leader* lost its second-class postal permit, effectively banning it from the mails.

Because a substantial number of subscribers lived outside of Milwaukee, this loss of mailing rights nearly destroyed the paper. In addition, revenue declined when patriotic organizations pressured local businesses to drop their advertising. Furthermore, the post office opened Berger's personal mail throughout the summer of 1918 and refused to deliver any mail to the *Leader* starting in August of that year. Berger appealed the postal-permit case to the U.S. Supreme Court, eventually losing on March 7, 1921, with Justices Oliver Wendell Holmes and Louis D. Brandeis dissenting. Not until May 31, 1921, did the Harding administration restore the *Leader*'s mailing privileges.

The fall of 1917 propelled Meta into a more active role in her husband's career. Elsa joined her sister, Doris, at the University of Wisconsin in September, freeing Meta from some of her responsibilities at

25. Meta to Victor, December 15, 1915, printed below.
26. Meta to Doris and Elsa, October 7, 1917, printed below.

home. In addition, Meta found herself increasingly embroiled in controversies over the war. An event in November, 1917, proved a significant turning point in her own sense of self-esteem and her realization of the extent of popular support for herself and her husband. During the convention of the Wisconsin Teachers' Association, Patrick Henry Martin, a Green Bay attorney who was considered a candidate for the U.S. Senate, delivered an "abusive & bitter tirade" against Victor and his supporters, denouncing them as "slimy snakes in the grass." Meta was seated on the stage during Martin's speech and was scheduled to speak next for the National Woman's Party on behalf of a women's suffrage resolution. The chairman of the convention, fearing the reaction of the audience, asked Meta if she wanted to postpone her remarks until the next day. Meta refused to relinquish her spot on the program and approached the podium with trepidation. To her surprise, "The whole house broke into a tremendous applause and each time the applause threatened to die down it broke forth greater than ever. . . . It was the biggest ovation any woman ever got."[27] This public display of support seemed to give Meta a new confidence, as she realized, "I was not alone."[28]

With a strengthened belief in herself as well as in her husband, Meta assumed a more public role in Victor's political activities. In the past she had served primarily behind the scenes as her husband's adviser. For instance, when Victor's career suffered in 1914 because he had not sufficiently embraced the German cause in the war, she urged him to "play politics now for all your [*sic*] worth." When opposing newspapers printed news that aided their cause, she suggested to Victor, "If I were you I'd get into the game & play it too especially since all news is unreliable. You too could put that construction on the war situation that would best help your cause for it undoubtedly is quite as reliable."[29] By 1917 Meta openly took an active part in her husband's work, regularly visiting the *Leader* offices and working on the newspaper.

Because he kept the *Leader* operating despite the loss of its postal permit with the help of donations from party members in Wisconsin, Berger soon found himself subject to prosecution. Federal officials indicted him in Wisconsin and Illinois, charging him with conspiracy to violate the Espionage Act of 1917, which prohibited publications that hindered the war effort.

Despite the charges (or perhaps because of them), Berger found himself increasingly popular at the polls. When he ran for the U.S. Senate in an April, 1918, special election, newspapers refused to print his

27. Ibid., November 3, 1917, printed below.
28. Meta Berger autobiography.
29. Meta to Victor, August 8, 1914, printed below.

advertising, vandals defaced his billboards, and he was unable to rent halls for meetings outside of Milwaukee. In addition, federal indictments against Berger were announced less than a month before the election. Meta later recalled that she and Victor decided that the "campaign committee needed push and energy as nothing was being done so Miss [Elizabeth] Thomas & I were appointed." Meta organized a team of volunteers and managed the campaign's mass mailings.[30] Berger received 26 percent of the popular vote in the three-way race and finished first in eleven of Wisconsin's seventy-one counties and second in another five. His showing represented a substantial increase over the 7 percent won by the Socialist Party in the 1916 senatorial election, when its candidate failed to carry a single county and finished second only in Milwaukee County. In the fall of 1918, Berger sought to regain his seat in Congress. A week before the general election, the federal government announced additional charges against him; nonetheless, the people of Wisconsin's Fifth Congressional District sent Berger to the U.S. House of Representatives with 43 percent of the popular vote.

Berger had little time to savor his victory. Beginning on December 9, he and four other Socialists—J. Louis Engdahl, Adolph Germer, William F. Kruse, and Irwin St. John Tucker—stood trial in Chicago before Judge Kenesaw Mountain Landis on charges of conspiracy to violate the Espionage Act. Lawyers for the five Socialists accused Landis of bias against the defendants, citing his statement that "one must have a very judicial mind, indeed, not to be prejudiced against German Americans in this country. Their hearts are reeking with disloyalty."[31] (After the trial, the judge said that he regretted that the law did not permit him to "have Berger lined up against a wall and shot.")[32] Landis ruled against the request for a change of venue and during the trial overruled most defense objections. The jury brought in a verdict of guilty on January 8, 1919. On February 20 Landis sentenced Berger and the others to twenty years in federal prison and refused to set bail.

The defendants immediately appealed their convictions, and bond was set at $500,000 for the five men. Meta Berger and Mary O'Reilly, a teacher and one of the founders of the Chicago Teachers Federation, spent the evening giving speeches in union halls throughout Chicago and raised the full amount of the bond in a single day. The U.S. Supreme Court eventually heard the case and overturned

30. Meta to Doris and Elsa, March 23, 1918, printed below.
31. *Hearings before the Special Committee Appointed under the Authority of House Resolution No. 6 Concerning the Right of Victor L. Berger to Be Sworn in as a Member of the Sixty-sixth Congress,* 2 vols. (Washington, D.C., 1919), 2:77.
32. "Landis Regrets He Could Not Sentence Berger to Be Shot," *New York Times,* December 30, 1919.

the conviction by a vote of six to three on January 31, 1921, ruling that Landis had acted improperly when he denied the defendants' request for a change of venue. The U.S. Department of Justice formally dropped the case on January 8, 1923, ending threats of legal action against Berger.

Berger's conviction raised questions about whether the House of Representatives would seat him. He maintained that until the courts decided on his appeal, he was eligible to sit in the House, but when he appeared on May 19, 1919, Speaker Frederick H. Gillett (R-Mass.) refused to permit him to take the oath of office and appointed a special committee to consider his eligibility. The hearings dragged on through September, 1919, and the committee eventually concluded that Berger could not be seated because he had given aid and comfort to the enemy. On November 10, the House declared Berger's seat vacant by a vote of 311 to 1, with Edward Voigt, a Republican from Wisconsin, casting the sole vote for Berger.

Milwaukee's Socialists immediately renominated Berger, while local Democrats and Republicans united behind Henry H. Bodenstab, a noncontroversial former state legislator. In the special election of December 19, 1919, Berger achieved the greatest electoral victory of his life, winning more than 55 percent of the popular vote. Berger appeared in the House with his credentials on January 10, 1920, but that body again refused to seat him, this time by a vote of 330 to 6. The Socialist Party nominated Berger for a third time, but Governor Emanuel Philipp refused to call yet another election. Consequently, Wisconsin's Fifth Congressional District remained unrepresented for the remainder of the Sixty-sixth Congress.

While trying to stay out of prison, Berger had the added responsibility of two college-age daughters. Because of financial problems at the *Leader,* Berger's sisters helped to pay Doris's and Elsa's tuition at the University of Wisconsin. Furthermore, both girls were ostracized by their schoolmates because of their father's notoriety.[33] Victor worried about the effect his wartime stance would have on his children. As early as November, 1917, he tried to console Doris, warning her that "if I should have to go to *prison* for my principles—you must not consider that a disgrace." At the same time, he assured her that he would do all he could to avoid imprisonment, as he was well aware of the burden that it would place on his family. As he told Doris, "You can readily see

---

33. Meta Berger autobiography. University of Wisconsin President Edward A. Birge denied that Berger's daughters were ostracized but admitted that they were unpopular because of their father's views. See Merle Curti and Vernon Carstensen, *The University of Wisconsin: A History, 1848–1925,* 2 vols. (Madison, Wisconsin, 1949), 2:142.

that I do not believe in playing martyr, if martyrdom can be avoided without doing greater injury to one's better self or to the movement which a man represents."[34]

As his daughters matured, Victor hoped to influence their career choices. After her graduation from the University of Wisconsin in 1920, Victor hoped that Doris would follow in his footsteps and take over the *Milwaukee Leader*. She had inherited her father's temperament, however, and the two consequently often ran into conflicts in which Meta served as mediator. Later that summer, partly to get away from Victor's heavy hand, Doris married Colin Welles, a doctoral candidate in botany at the university, despite her parents' initial opposition. Doris and Colin lived in the Philippines while Colin taught at the University of Manila during 1921 and 1922, and after their return to the United States the couple lived north of Milwaukee on a fox farm owned by Victor. Colin taught science at the Milwaukee Vocational School, Doris worked as an attorney in Milwaukee after receiving a law degree from Marquette University in 1926, and both Colin and Doris occasionally contributed articles to the *Leader*. The couple divorced in 1935, and in the following year Doris married Frank Hursley, an English professor at the University of Wisconsin's Milwaukee Extension. She worked as an unemployment compensation examiner for the state of Wisconsin from 1936 to 1941 and then began writing for radio with Frank during World War II. In 1946 the couple moved to California, where they had successful careers as radio and television scriptwriters. In the decade before her death in 1984, she turned again to the biography of Victor that she had begun writing with Meta in the 1930s, although with her health failing, she was unable to complete the manuscript.[35]

Elsa, the Bergers' younger daughter, also resented her father imposing his standards on her. Yet Victor encouraged her to attend medical school at a time when relatively few women had the opportunity to do so. When she told him that she wanted to spend her life helping the ill, he advised, "It is much better to be the person who orders an enema than to be the person who gives one."[36] Elsa received her undergraduate degree from the University of Wisconsin in 1921 and an M.D. from the University of Pennsylvania in 1923. Following additional study in Austria at the University of Vienna, in 1927 she married Jan Edelman, a native of Holland, despite Victor's initial opposition. Elsa

34. Victor to Doris, November 15, 1917, printed below.

35. Meta Berger autobiography; Hursley biography; clippings, Berger Papers; alumni records in Marquette University Archives and University of Wisconsin–Madison alumni office; Wisconsin Bureau of Personnel, State Employee Roster Cards (series 2198), box 45, SHSW.

36. Edelman, "The Second One," Berger Papers.

began practicing medicine in Massachusetts later that year and in 1930 returned with her husband to Milwaukee, where she worked as a physician almost continuously for the next thirty years. In her only foray into politics, she ran unsuccessfully for a seat on the Milwaukee school board in 1945. A year after Jan's death in 1963, she moved to California, where she lived until her death in 1984.[37]

In the immediate postwar years, the Socialist Party splintered. By September, 1919, the organization had divided into separate Socialist, Communist, and Communist Labor Parties, with Berger and his allies controlling the remnants of the Socialist Party.[38] Berger distanced himself from communism, stating that "socialism is not Bolshevism. Socialism is the collective ownership and democratic management of the social means of production and distribution—steel industry, oil wells, coal mines, railroads &c.—but Bolshevism is an autocratic communism based upon a super-State supported by terror."[39] Berger again ran for Congress in the fall of 1920 and received 45 percent of the vote, but he lost to a fusion candidate in a Republican landslide year.

The rise to power of the Republican administration of Warren Harding proved fortuitous for Berger. The Post Office Department restored mailing rights to the *Milwaukee Leader,* the Department of Justice announced that it would not prosecute Berger after the Supreme Court overturned his conviction, and President Harding met with him to discuss the release of Eugene Debs from prison. Berger also won the next three elections to the U.S. House of Representatives, gaining 53, 42, and 49 percent of the vote, respectively. He felt vindicated on being returned to Congress and joked about being a party of one, noting that "when I want to have a caucus I could have one in a telephone booth."[40] During his six years in Congress following World War I, he won the respect of his non-Socialist colleagues. In addition to such standard socialist causes as the nationalization of railroads and of telegraph and telephone companies, he advocated civil liberties legislation,

37. Victor to Jan, July 28, 1926, printed below; Wisconsin Board of Medical Examiners, Applications (series 1606), box 30, SHSW; interview with Deborah Hardy, September 3, 1992; Edelman for School Board literature, Berger Papers.

38. Once outside the Socialist Party, the leaders of the two communist parties continued to battle each other. In 1920 a faction of the Communist Party merged with the Communist Labor Party to create the United Communist Party. In the following year the Communist Party and the United Communist Party, under orders from Moscow, merged and formed the Workers Party, which changed its name to Workers (Communist) Party in 1925 and to Communist Party, U.S.A. in 1929.

39. "Berger Defends His War Record; Sees New Fascisti in Ku Klux Klan," *New York Times,* December 3, 1922.

40. Berger, *Voice and Pen of Victor L. Berger,* 16.

repeal of Prohibition, antilynching laws, and the rehabilitation of Germany. Berger realized that his bills would all die in committee, but he told a constituent that "I propose through these bills and my speeches to make propaganda for Socialism."[41]

Although Berger remained a Socialist for the rest of his life and served as the party's national chairman from 1927 until his death, he realized that the party was dead except in Wisconsin and cooperated with efforts to create a new national reform party. He convinced Wisconsin's Socialists not to oppose Robert M. La Follette's candidacy for the U.S. Senate in 1922 and attended an organizational meeting of the Conference for Progressive Political Action that year. Two years later, he persuaded the national party not to nominate a presidential candidate but instead to offer its slot to La Follette. The failure of La Follette's campaign to develop into a new party disappointed Berger, who had hoped that the Socialists would take part in a new national coalition.

Meta continued her increasingly public activities during the 1920s. She served on the national committee that ran La Follette's presidential campaign in 1924. When radio became a vehicle in politics, she, not Victor, made public addresses in the new medium during his campaigns. Local party leaders felt her wrath when they did not meet her standards. For instance, in 1925, when the state Socialist Party failed to launch a campaign for its senatorial candidate during Victor's absence in Europe, Meta met with the party leaders and (as she put it) "scolded" them for running an inadequate campaign.[42] By the end of Victor's career, Meta felt free to warn him against political pitfalls or to rebuke him when he voted against her wishes.[43] She also gained increasing recognition in state educational politics; Governor Fred Zimmerman appointed her to the Wisconsin Board of Regents of Normal Schools in 1927 and to a six-year term on the University of Wisconsin Board of Regents in 1928.

Victor lost his final campaign in 1928 by about seven hundred votes in an election marred by charges of voting fraud. Following his defeat, Berger hoped to retire from the newspaper business and sought a purchaser for the *Milwaukee Leader*. Before he could dispose of the paper, however, he was seriously injured in a streetcar accident on July 27, 1929. He died on August 7. His body lay in state in Milwaukee's city hall, where more than 100,000 mourners came to pay their last respects.

Following Victor's death in 1929, Meta was named to his seat on the National Executive Committee of the Socialist Party. Many party

41. "Memoirs of William George Bruce," *Wisconsin Magazine of History*, 18 (1934–1935), 48.
42. Meta to Victor, September 26, 1925, printed below.
43. Ibid., January 10, 1927, February 7, 1928, printed below.

members expected her to run for Congress in 1930, but her employment of nonunion workers on the family's farmhouse north of Milwaukee cost her the nomination.[44] Two years later, she was considered for the vice-presidential nomination at the Socialist Party convention but withdrew her name.[45] In the years following Victor's death, Meta became increasingly sympathetic toward communism, a position in stark contrast to Victor's beliefs.[46] In 1919 she shared Victor's critical view of American communists, writing that "The trouble is these radicals do not believe in *political action* but want *direct* action at once. They think they can get hold of all industries by a revolution *now*. Poor fools! They can't even get a strike up much less a revolution."[47] By the 1930s, Meta became enamored of communism, especially after her 1935 trip to Russia. Although her critics pointed out the discrepancy between Victor's strident anticommunism and her own sympathetic views, she insisted that she did not feel "bound by any attitudes he took under different circumstances," because he lived before fascism had become a world threat. In 1936, when asked if Victor would have maintained his old attitudes toward Russia, she replied, "I don't think there is any use in that sort of speculation. We all claim the angels for our side."[48]

Milwaukee Mayor Daniel Hoan forced her off his campaign committee in 1936 because of her public procommunist stance, but despite her affiliation with various communist-front organizations, the Socialist Party tolerated her membership out of respect for her position as the widow of the party's former leader. By 1940, however, the party's national leadership lost its patience and requested that Meta withdraw from the front organizations. She refused and resigned from the Socialist Party. Because of ill health, she remained politically inactive until her death on June 16, 1944.

* * *

44. Olson, "Milwaukee Socialists," 477–478.
45. *Milwaukee Leader,* May 23, 1932.
46. For background on Meta Berger's move to the left and her departure from the Socialist Party, see Olson, "Milwaukee Socialists," 537–538, 560–561. See also Meta's correspondence during the 1930s and 1940s in the Berger Papers; Peggy Dennis, "Meta Berger: The Velvet-Fisted Radical, 1873–1944," unpublished manuscript, Eugene and Peggy Dennis Papers, SHSW; and Peggy Dennis to Doris Hursley, July 9, 1983, also in the Dennis Papers.
47. Meta to Doris and Elsa, April 26, 1919, printed below.
48. Interview with Meta Berger by Doris Berger Hursley, September, 1936, Berger Papers. Hursley published an abbreviated version of the interview under a pseudonym in a Popular Front communist magazine. See Judith Post, "I Say What I Think," *The Woman Today* 1 (October, 1936), 14, 30.

As an editor and politician, Victor Berger took stands on public issues in his writings, speeches, and campaign documents. His correspondence with Meta, however, offers insight into how his private life affected his public career and into the relationship of this politically active couple. Temperamental, egotistical, caustic, and quick to anger, Victor nonetheless won the deep friendship, respect, and admiration of many who praised his commitment to social justice. His friends noted his personal integrity and his generosity, and even his political opponents described him as an "affable, courteous, and congenial" man who "never failed to meet his political enemies as cordially as he met his friends."[49] His longtime friend and colleague Morris Hillquit described Berger as "sublimely egotistic, but somehow his egotism did not smack of conceit and was not offensive. It was the expression of deep and naïve faith in himself."[50]

Berger's elder daughter described him as "a magnificent contradiction. He is soft-hearted as he is iron-willed."[51] He himself was aware early in life of the dual sides of his personality. In a remarkably introspective 1895 letter to Meta, he described his inner tensions, claiming "I am 'made up' of two entirely different *moods*," although it was not "as bad as with poor 'Dr. Jekyl' in the story."

> One V.L.B is a well educated and unusually well read man. He is pretty conscientious, ambitious and all that, but queer and unsociable to the extreme. You know the man, you have met him often. Although he styles himself a Socialist, he is proud and aristocratic. And since he is dissatisfied with the world and himself he is either saying nothing at all, or sharp and disagreeable things. The man has no friends, except probably his books. He is not practical a bit, and if it wasn't for me (the other V.L.B, who writes this letter) he would have a hard time of it. Under the pretext of fighting for humanity, he is always making trouble for me and for all those whom I love. . . .
>
> The other V.L.B *you* also know, dear Meta. Say it yourself,— am I not always lighthearted, good natured, *conceited* and lovable? I will admit that I am extremely silly at times, that I am liable to take Annie Hartmann to the show, flirt with every pretty girl etc.[52]

49. For the recollections of a friend of Berger's, see Oscar Ameringer, *If You Don't Weaken: The Autobiography of Oscar Ameringer* (New York, 1940), 286, 293–299. The quotations are from "Memoirs of William George Bruce," 47.
50. Hillquit, *Loose Leaves from a Busy Life,* 53.
51. Hursley biography.
52. Victor to Meta, August 14, 1895, printed below.

When financial pressures or frustration at being thwarted hung heavy on his shoulders, Victor could become cranky and mean-spirited. In his letters to Meta, he allowed himself to vent his feelings freely, expressing criticism of fellow Socialists that he could not put in such strong terms in public. For instance, Victor thought Upton Sinclair and his followers "a lot of weakly, well-meaning but impossible crazy chickens," and Eugene Debs had "learned nothing in 15 years and is repeating parrotlike the same old speech." Berger characterized Morris Hillquit as a "bright fellow but he has constituted himself as the party pope," and Dan Hoan as "a good hand-shaker" who "proves his radicalism by eating with his knife,— and by stamping with his foot, whenever he wants emphasis."[53]

When he felt threatened, Berger could be fierce in person with his colleagues in the socialist movement. In 1911 Elizabeth Thomas, his longtime aide, printed a story in the *Social-Democratic Herald* against his wishes and then called him a traitor to the movement. He responded by giving her "a calling down like I never gave to any woman in my life. . . . I told her there was *nothing* I could commit treason to, *except* the *fifth congressional* district,—that was the most important thing in the Milwaukee movement, because the rest had no brains and *did not make good,* and that included her. And I told her that if she ever interfere[d] in my editorial policy again, she would have to go."[54]

Although Berger verbally blasted both his friends and opponents, he could also be remarkably cordial on a personal level, even with his ideological rivals. Berger and AFL President Gompers disagreed deeply over the future of the trade union movement, yet prior to the 1907 AFL convention, Berger stayed up drinking with Gompers until two o'clock in the morning. Victor reported to Meta that "I had to drink some too, no matter how much I hate it. Sam grew to be rather confidential and loving, but of course he was not in a condition for serious business."[55] As a member of Congress, Berger often got along better with conservative presidents such as William Howard Taft, Warren Harding, and Calvin Coolidge than with liberals who shared some of his political beliefs. Although he could cooperate with Progressives such as Robert M. La Follette Sr., he reserved his most bitter attacks for those who shared some of his goals, "very much prefer[ring] an honest reactionary to such political swindlers."[56]

53. Victor to Meta, July 14, 1911, January 1, 1910, February 2, 1929, February 2, 1928, printed below.
54. Ibid., July 23, 1911, printed below.
55. Ibid., November 14, 1907, printed below.
56. Ibid., January 25, 1924, printed below. For Berger's relations with Republican presidents, see Victor to Meta, December 10, 1912, December 16, 1921, November 25, 1922, January 22, 1928, February 18, 1928, printed below.

Berger also vacillated between extreme optimism and feelings of depression about the socialist movement, his newspapers, and his likelihood of success. After his first election to the U.S. House of Representatives, he told Meta that he hoped some day to serve in the U.S. Senate or to be named secretary of state in a Socialist administration.[57] At other times, he would report that "with all this (what some would call success) I feel very depressed and lonesome."[58] Meta likened Victor to a rubber ball, rebounding when hit, but during the last decade of his life, Victor feared that "the rubber got old and dry."[59]

Victor usually recovered from setbacks quickly, but the persecution that he suffered during the war deeply affected his confidence. Meta long had doubts about Victor's sacrifices for the movement, but by the fall of 1919, he told her that he had begun "to think as you do i.e. that I am a fool who to a certain extent has thrown his life away on a 'mirage.'" He no longer was "as cock-sure as I used to be about *my own belief* in Socialism." Wartime repression "gave us a good taste of the all-powerful state—of the politician in control of opinions." Although he denounced Woodrow Wilson as a "vainglorious liar and hypocrite," he would not trust leaders of the American Left in the same position in a socialist commonwealth. According to Berger, "Capitalism is bad and is daily becoming more impossible," but "Communism would mean a new form of *slavery*." Although he hoped for the gradual socialization of industry, it was important at the same time to "guaranty certain *fundamental liberties* for every *individual*."[60]

Despite his dread of revolutionary upheaval, Berger became increasingly pessimistic in his later years about the possibility of peaceful change. At a party held two months before his death in 1929, he told a dinner companion, "Now I'm of the right wing and all my life I have been preaching change by evolutionary methods but I do not believe that it will come that way. When it comes we will have a violent revolution. It will not come in my lifetime, maybe not in yours, but it will come with violence."[61]

In addition to vacillating between aggressiveness and charm and between optimism and pessimism, Victor also felt a tension between his political ideals and his desire to make money. Although it lost money, his publishing business provided him with a salary as editor,

57. Victor to Meta, November 23, 1910, printed below.
58. Ibid., July 23, 1912, printed below.
59. Ibid., December 3, 1927, Berger Papers.
60. Ibid., September 21, 1919, printed below.
61. Notes (filed under Berger), June 4, 1929, Irma Hochstein Papers, SHSW.

and his congressional seat gave the family additional income. The Bergers lived comfortably in rental housing in Milwaukee until 1912, when they purchased a house in a middle-class neighborhood, expecting that he would be reelected to Congress. The Bergers also bought a cottage in northern Wisconsin, where Meta and their two daughters spent the summers while Victor remained in Milwaukee, and in 1921 the family purchased a farm in Ozaukee County, just north of Milwaukee. Nonetheless, despite the family's comfortable status, the Bergers regularly seemed to spend whatever cash they had, which meant that they routinely deferred one creditor to pay another.[62]

Victor and Meta's desire to live well, however, conflicted with Victor's reluctance to give up political activity and plunge wholeheartedly into business. Even as a young man, he felt he could "make lots of money, if the book-spirit was not in my way."[63] Victor's concern with moneymaking resulted partly from family pressures; his mother advised him to drop his newspaper and get into another line of work, "real-estate preferred." For all his bluster, Victor felt intimidated by his parents, who did not agree with their son's radical politics. Even at the age of forty, he had "to be rather meek" with his mother, because she "hate[d] socialism and socialists."[64]

Not only did he have to deal with parental expectations, but Victor also found himself frequently at odds with Meta over her desire for greater financial security. In 1904 Meta told Victor that she planned to attend all future party conventions. When he asked where he would get the money, she responded, "That is your affair Darling!"[65] Money (or rather the lack of it) remained a constant worry throughout their marriage. In 1910, after Meta herself had become a Socialist officeholder, she admitted to Victor that "the time was when I thought that if you gave up your work and devoted yourself to money making I would be happy."[66] Yet despite this disavowal, financial security remained important to her, and she had legitimate reason for concern—Victor continued to accumulate debts. In 1905, after Victor sold the *Vorwärts* for $6,000 worth of stock in a corporation he formed, he remained indebted to the estate of Meta's parents for $8,250 and to his father for another $3,340.[67] Even as late as 1929, Meta chafed under the need to budget her funds carefully: "I really want to live comfortably & without so many restrictions."[68]

62. Details about the Bergers' financial difficulties can be found throughout their correspondence printed below. See also Meta Berger autobiography.
63. Victor to Meta, August 14, 1895, printed below.
64. Ibid., January 23, 1900, printed below.
65. Meta Berger autobiography.
66. Meta to Victor, May 30, 1910, printed below.
67. Minutes of the Vorwärts Company, May 23, 1906.
68. Meta to Victor, June 26, 1929, printed below.

Knowing his wife's worries, Victor promised Meta "that I will try to make some money even if I have to let a good deal of the movement slip out of my hands."[69] Nonetheless, whenever he found himself having "almost made up my mind to quit the movement, go into some business and also make money," he was torn by not knowing "how I can go out honorably before I have achieved certain things which I have started out to do."[70] Yet financial responsibilities limited Victor's political independence. In the summer of 1916, he told Meta of his wish to leave the Socialist Party and call a convention to form a new third party, but "I cannot afford to do so just now—the Leader is evidently making a coward of me."[71]

Only at the end of his life, when he saw the Socialist Party in ruins, did he lament "that I feel like a sinner at times—since I had the natural ability to make money in any business, and thus having had the gift easily to secure a comfortable and care-free old age for my wonderful wife and for myself—and to leave some wealth for my children—that I missed these opportunities by spending my life in a thankless movement."[72] Throughout the 1920s, Victor believed that he had to make up for lost opportunities. He bought land in Wisconsin and elsewhere, acquired stock in several companies, and intended to use his "wits in a rather *ruthless fashion* to dispose of [the *Milwaukee Leader*] and secure our old age."[73] He planned to take the proceeds from the sale of the paper and build a winter home in Florida, where he and Meta could spend their time "boating, fishing and bathing" and "grow oranges, figs and grapefruits."[74]

Victor's concern over money not only stemmed from the expectations of others but also represented personal freedom for him. He feared becoming dependent and in 1917 advised Doris to be careful with her funds:

Under our present economic system—the capitalist system— money, wealth and capital are the means of a certain very necessary *freedom* for you when *you* have the money, wealth or capital. They become the means of intolerable slavery and inhuman exploitation very often when the other person has

69. Victor to Meta, November 29, 1907, printed below.
70. Ibid., January 16, 1904, printed below.
71. Ibid., July 24, 1916, printed below.
72. Ibid., February 2, 1929, printed below.
73. Ibid. Victor had acquired 5,750 shares of the liberal *Madison (Wisconsin) Capital Times*, which Meta sold for $12,000 in 1932. See Meta Berger to William T. Evjue, July 8, 1932, and memorandum of sale, William T. Evjue Papers, SHSW.
74. Victor to Meta, February 19, 1929, printed below.

them and you have none. Therefore, darling child, always look out, and look out ahead, that you always have at least enough to secure a certain amount of freedom for yourself and for those whom you love and who are dependent upon you.[75]

Despite conflicts over finances, a warm and deep friendship marked the relationship between Victor and Meta. Meta not only received her early political education from Victor but often equated his happiness with her own. Writing in 1910, she told him, "I find that I can only be happy when you are happy, I can only be content when I know that you are the same and strange to say I believe I can only be well when you are well."[76] She recognized his influence over her, telling him, "You can mold my character according to your desires, you can make or unmake me. When I was only a little girl, my thoughts were always 'Does he approve?' You know it & so I needn't go all over the ground again. But that's the way a woman lives."[77] In turn, Victor recognized his own emotional dependency on Meta, repeatedly lamenting their separation when they were apart. In one revealing note, he explained that when he was alone he felt "like a child that is yelling for mamma."[78]

Victor and Meta's devotion to each other, however, survived rocky times. In her autobiography, Meta obliquely referred to Victor's interest in other women, and Doris, in her unfinished biography of her father, implied that Victor's relationship with Inez Milholland, a feminist and suffragist, went considerably beyond platonic friendship. Victor and Meta apparently had words over his friendship with Milholland, and at one time he promised Meta that he would not call on the other woman.[79] On another occasion, he conceded to Meta, "As to 'flirtation', I have had a very severe lesson, as you know."[80]

75. Victor to Doris, February 1, 1917, printed below.
76. Meta to Victor, May 30, 1910, printed below.
77. Ibid., October 27, 1909, printed below.
78. Victor to Meta, September 9, 1925, Berger Papers.
79. Ibid., May 8, 1914, June 6, 1914, printed below. In her autobiography, Meta claims that a number of women found Victor attractive, although she denies that he was a womanizer. Doris Berger Hursley, on the other hand, cites one case of Victor's infidelity about which Meta knew and also implies that he had been intimate with Milholland and possibly with other women. Doris also states that she and Elsa burned a considerable number of Victor's love letters following his death. Irma Hochstein, a friend of Meta's, wrote a memorandum following a dinner party at which Meta discussed in Victor's presence "the trials of being married to a man in public life—so many women fell in love with him." Meta also told of finding gifts and letters from various women to Victor. See Meta Berger autobiography; Hursley biography; notes (filed under Berger), June 4, 1929, Irma Hochstein Papers.
80. Victor to Meta, August 30, 1911, printed below.

Victor's "flirtations" and Meta's awareness of them did not represent for them a rejection of middle-class values, for neither Victor nor Meta agreed with the revolution in mores and social thought that was occurring in some circles. According to Doris, Victor had a streak of prudishness about him on questions relating to sex and disapproved of birth control.[81] Socialism did not mean identification with working-class culture for either of the Bergers. Upright, reserved, always nattily dressed, Victor could be persuaded to campaign in saloons only with great reluctance.[82] According to Doris, "Brotherhood was an ideal— and a little abstract for Papa. For Papa, it meant equality of opportunity, not back-slapping and chumminess."[83]

Meta also maintained her bourgeois standards and placed a high premium on appearances. In 1918, while attending the mass trial of IWW defendants, she was surprised by how they looked: "I guess I expected to see a rather tough hard unclean looking group. On the contrary! They were well washed, clean shaved with clean linen & looked very respectable & intelligent."[84] Although she called for political, economic, and social equality for women, she disliked many whom she met in the Socialist Party. "The women socialists are surely no good, morally mentally or any other way. I've no use for them, not one!"[85] Like Victor, she did not believe that social institutions such as the family or marriage should change. In 1928 when the University of Wisconsin prohibited Dora Russell, the wife of British philosopher Bertrand Russell, from speaking on campus, Meta criticized her "philosophy of free-love, several trial marriages, or affairs etc." Meta thought that Russell should not "preach her doctrine to the half baked co-eds at Madison" but found it difficult to take a public stance against the speech because Victor was "fighting for the teeth in the 1st Amendment."[86]

Although the war created adversity for the Bergers, it simultaneously made their marriage more of a partnership and led to an ever-greater mingling of their public and private existences. They understood how their lives were intertwined and sought to protect each other from the consequences of their actions. After Meta had denounced American involvement in World War I in the presence of a Milwaukee lawyer, Victor warned her not to talk openly about the subject because "you know that the only place where I can be hurt at all is

81. Hursley biography.
82. Ameringer, *If You Don't Weaken*, 296.
83. Hursley biography.
84. Meta to Doris and Elsa, May 8, 1918, Berger Papers.
85. Meta to Victor, May 29, 1911, printed below.
86. Ibid., February 20, 1928, printed below.

through my wife and children."[87] She likewise was angered by the treatment Victor received from federal authorities and told him that "I am not at all reconciled that you should be victimized by a cruel selfish inhumane society. Sometimes I become inwardly so rebellious that I am really dangerous & get frightened at my own thoughts."[88]

The war also caused Meta and Doris to resent the failure of the American Left to recognize Victor's sacrifices for the movement. Doris complained that "Unlike Eugene Debs, [my father] is not made of the stuff of martyr, and yet he belligerently courted what he had stern reason to believe might very well mean his death in the penitentiary. This while he was denied even the compensatory comfort of martyrdom. Other men who have made smaller and safer sacrifices in a feebler cause, have been placed by public approval in high seats. But he was too brusque for politics, too honest for compromise for security, too proud to wear an obvious mantle of bravery."[89]

Victor himself rankled at the adulation showered upon his imprisoned colleague, Eugene Debs, who received a ten-year sentence for criticizing the war effort. Berger thought that "nobody seems to think much of the twenty years the rest of us received—in fact, some so called radicals tacitly seem to approve the sentence."[90] He failed to see that his own personality made him a poor symbol for those who wished for a romantic revolutionary hero. After his conviction, his friends tried to offer consolation by comparing him to past heroes who had been imprisoned for their ideas. Berger replied, "That's all very fine, but I don't want to go to jail!"[91]

Berger's alienation from the American Left continued in the postwar years. Although he remained "a Socialist—a Social Democrat, if you please," he harshly criticized the Left's belief in imminent revolution. Denigrating the overblown rhetoric of the Socialist Party's left wing, he warned, "In this game of would-be radical phrases the one who can play the game the hardest will naturally win. And the emptier the barrel the louder the sound."[92] Berger's pragmatic politics, which permitted his election to public office during the 1920s, remained too conservative for many of his colleagues. Berger himself would plead guilty to the charge of conservatism, arguing that socialism was "the

87. Victor to Meta, July 14, 1917, printed below.
88. Meta to Victor, July 31, 1918, Records of the Milwaukee Social-Democratic Party, Milwaukee County Historical Society.
89. Hursley biography.
90. Berger to Morris Hillquit, August 20, 1919, Morris Hillquit Papers, SHSW.
91. "Berger, a Socialist Who Fascinated Americans," *Literary Digest*, August 31, 1929, 29.
92. Berger to Hillquit, August 20, 1919, Hillquit Papers.

greatest conservative world force," saving what was best from capitalism while bringing about a new, humane order.[93]

His party did not achieve the success it sought, but viewed from the perspective of mainstream American politics rather than by standards of Marxist purity, Berger was far from a failure. By keeping social and civil liberties issues in the public eye, he helped transform the debate over what was politically possible. His congressional service provided a degree of respectability that social democracy had previously lacked because of its association in the public mind with violence and anarchism. His fight for free speech chipped away at a narrow interpretation of the First Amendment. Many of the once-radical ideas he advocated, such as unemployment compensation and federal old-age pensions, have become commonplace—but only after they shed the taint of socialism. Repudiated by the Left, Victor L. Berger and his social democracy also faded from the memory of the American mainstream. As fellow Socialist Upton Sinclair put it, "the American people will take Socialism, but they wont take the label."[94]

93. "Berger Defends His War Record; Sees New Fascisti in Ku Klux Klan," *New York Times,* December 3, 1922.

94. Upton Sinclair to Norman Thomas, September 25, 1951, Norman Thomas Papers (microfilm), Series I, General Correspondence, reel 22, frame 1018.

Acknowledgments

Many people have contributed to the success of this volume. The granddaughters of Victor and Meta Berger—Deborah Hardy, Polly Keusink, and Bridget Dobson—made this project possible through their donation of the Berger family correspondence to the State Historical Society of Wisconsin. Their cooperation and assistance have been invaluable. In addition, Deborah Hardy and Polly Keusink supplied information on their family's history, provided photographs from their private collections, and offered encouragement at every stage of the project. I am deeply grateful for their personal interest.

Victor Berger's grandnieces and grandnephews—Judith Greene, Alan Loewenthal, Robert Mock, Susan Nurock, Miriam Peck, Helenrose Schwab, and Roger Steck—assisted the project by providing information on Victor's siblings and their families. Susan Nurock also generously supplied photographs from her family's collection and a copy of the tape-recorded reminiscences of Victor's niece. Likewise, Meta Berger's grandniece and grandnephew, Gail Anderson Patout and Robert Schweers, offered information about Meta's family.

Staff at various archives and libraries have consistently assisted with all stages of the research. Myrna Williamson and Virginia Fritzsch, who processed the Berger Papers at the State Historical Society of Wisconsin, regularly pointed out useful documents. Judith Simonsen at the Milwaukee County Historical Society and Virginia C. Schwartz at the Milwaukee Public Library helped at their respective institutions. David Fischer, secretary of Eintracht Cemetery Association in Bridgeport, Connecticut, and Mary Witkowski, librarian at the Bridgeport Public Library, compiled information on Victor Berger's Bridgeport relatives. The Milwaukee County Historical Society and the Tamiment Institute Library at New York University kindly allowed us to print photographs from their collections.

This volume builds on the scholarship of the historians whose works are cited in the introduction and the editorial procedures and has benefited from the assistance of scholars who offered advice and comments. I am especially grateful to Sally Miller, Frederick I. Olson, and David Zonderman, who read the text prior to publication and offered useful suggestions. John Kaminski offered counsel concerning editorial decisions. Paul Hass, as always, provided invaluable guidance in bringing this book into print.

This project could not have been completed without generous financial support from several donors. I would like to thank the William T. Evjue Foundation, Deborah Hardy, Polly Keusink, and Kenneth L. Smith for their gifts to the project.

A book of this type is a collective work, and many individuals have worked conscientiously to bring it to fruition. Borghild Kelly and Waltraud Tepfenhardt transcribed Victor's sometimes difficult-to-read German script and provided all the translations in this volume. Denise Ready coped with Victor's and Meta's handwriting and made the initial transcriptions of their English-language letters. Sean Adams helped with the proofreading of the text and researched various aspects of Victor Berger's career and Socialist politics. Ellen Goldlust-Gingrich assisted at every stage of this edition; the high quality of her work is reflected throughout this volume.

Finally, I would like to thank Therese, Elisabeth, Martha, and Emily for their support. They patiently listened to far too many stories about Victor and Meta over the dinner table.

MICHAEL E. STEVENS

Editorial Procedures

In 1990 the granddaughters of Victor L. and Meta Berger donated their grandparents' papers to the State Historical Society of Wisconsin. This extensive collection consists of professional correspondence, campaign materials, speeches, writings, photographs, and various other documents. Most significantly, the collection contains approximately twenty-five hundred letters that Victor and Meta Berger wrote to each other and to their daughters, Doris and Elsa, between 1894 and 1929. The Bergers were politically active and took a vital interest in the world around them; consequently, their letters are filled with commentary on the politics and issues of their time. This edition offers 260 letters selected to illuminate the public and private lives of this politically active couple. (Researchers interested in the entire Berger collection, including all known family correspondence, should consult *The Victor L. Berger Papers*, microfilm edition with guide, published by the State Historical Society of Wisconsin and distributed by Scholarly Resources, Inc., 1994.)

The letters in this volume were chosen to illustrate Victor and Meta's political activities; Victor's congressional career and his newspaper publishing business; Meta's involvement in the suffrage movement; the Bergers' views on the major political and social issues of the era; and their association with key figures in the labor, socialist, suffrage, peace, and civil liberties movements. In addition, the selected correspondence depicts Meta and Victor's evolving relationship and their family life. Because World War I and the Red Scare that followed are crucial to understanding the couple's lives, more than a third of the letters printed here are from the period 1914–1920, providing a comprehensive account of the Bergers' views on the war, Victor's trial and conviction under the Espionage Act, and his subsequent exclusion from the U.S. House of Representatives in 1919 and 1920.

Only one of Meta's letters prior to the Bergers' marriage in 1897 is extant, and the first surviving letter written by her after their marriage dates from 1905. As a result, the couple's early years are depicted almost exclusively through Victor's letters. During certain key periods of their lives, such as the Chicago war trial and the hearings on Victor's exclusion from the House, Victor and Meta were together and consequently did not correspond with each other. Letters to their daughters have been used from these times. Additional letters to Doris and Elsa and two letters to Jan Edelman, Elsa's future husband, were chosen to depict the parents' relationship to their children. All the letters printed here are recipients' copies found in the Victor L. Berger Papers at the State Historical Society of Wisconsin, with the exception of Victor's letter of July 28, 1926, to Jan Edelman, which is a retained carbon copy from the same collection.

Headings noting the author and the recipient have been supplied for each letter. The place and date of composition have been standardized; dates and place names supplied by the editors have been enclosed in brackets. Letterhead has not been transcribed because the Bergers frequently borrowed each other's stationery or used outdated letterhead for their personal correspondence. Some original documents have notations and dates added by Doris Berger Welles Hursley, who had custody of the letters between 1944 and 1984, although in many cases her dating is in error. These notations have not been transcribed.

The letters have been rendered into type as literally as possible without sacrificing readability. The editors have not corrected the Bergers' spelling, punctuation, or grammar. Punctuation has been silently added at the end of sentences, to numbers larger than three digits, and occasionally elsewhere to clarify meaning. Hyphens, dashes, and ampersands have been left as written. Underlined words are printed in italics. Missing words or letters supplied by the editors appear in brackets; the editors have also noted in brackets places where parts of manuscripts are missing or illegible. Interlineations have been brought down to the line and treated as part of the text. The Bergers used deletions to correct spelling and grammatical errors; these have not been noted. All ellipsis points appearing in the text are those of the letter writer and do not indicate omitted material.

Nearly all the letters are written in English, although many contain German phrases or words. Such text has been reproduced literally, with translations appearing in the endnotes. No translations have been provided for frequently used nicknames, such as *Schatzl* or *Schnuckie,* which are included in the list of abbreviations and nicknames. Letters written entirely in German have been printed only in English translation and have been marked as such. (The original German versions are available in the microfilm edition of the Berger Papers.) All translations from the German were done by Borghild Kelly and Waltraud Tepfenhardt.

Typewritten letters and telegrams provide special problems because of keyboarding and transmission errors. Keyboarding errors, which abound in typewritten letters, have been silently corrected. Telegrams have been printed in small capital letters, and spelling errors made by the telegrapher have been silently corrected. The word PERIOD, used to indicate terminal punctuation, has been rendered as a period.

The editors have attempted to identify all persons mentioned in the text, a task that required the use of a variety of sources, particularly for less prominent individuals. The following sources proved especially valuable in preparing the biographical notes: *Biographical Directory of the*

United States Congress, 1774–1989 (Washington, D.C., 1989); Mari Jo Buhle, Paul Buhle, and Dan Georgakas, eds., *Encyclopedia of the American Left* (New York, 1990); J. Robert Constantine, ed., *Letters of Eugene V. Debs,* 3 vols. (Urbana and Chicago, 1990); Solon De Leon, ed., *The American Labor Who's Who* (New York, 1925); *Dictionary of American Biography* (New York, 1937–); *Dictionary of Wisconsin Biography* (Madison, Wisconsin, 1960); Gary M. Fink, ed., *Biographical Dictionary of American Labor* (Westport, Connecticut, 1984); Gary M. Fink, ed., *Biographical Dictionary of American Labor Leaders* (Westport, Connecticut, 1974); Bernard K. Johnpoll and Harvey Klehr, eds., *Biographical Dictionary of the American Left* (Westport, Connecticut, 1986); *Who Was Who in America* (Chicago, 1963–).

The editors also made extensive use of U.S. census records; the *Wisconsin Blue Books;* the minutes and annual reports of the Milwaukee Board of School Directors; the minutes of the Milwaukee Common Council; alumni records of the University of Wisconsin, Marquette University, and the University of Pennsylvania; State Employee Roster Cards (series 2198) at the State Historical Society of Wisconsin; the Social Security Death Index available at the genealogical libraries of the Church of Jesus Christ of the Latter Day Saints; the Research Libraries Information Network (RLIN); the *New York Times;* and birth and death records at the state of Wisconsin's Bureau of Vital Statistics. In addition, obituary or clipping files at the State Historical Society of Wisconsin, the Milwaukee County Historical Society, the Milwaukee Public Library, the Chicago Historical Society, and the Bridgeport, Connecticut, Public Library all proved valuable.

The sources of photographs have been noted in the captions, with the exception of photographs identified with WHi negative numbers, which are from the collections of the State Historical Society of Wisconsin.

Chronology

1860   Victor L. Berger (VLB) born in Austria-Hungary (February 28).

1873   Meta Schlichting (MB) born in Milwaukee, Wisconsin (February 23).

1878   VLB immigrates to New York.

1881   VLB moves to Milwaukee.

1883   VLB appointed Milwaukee public school teacher (September 4).

1892   VLB submits resignation from teaching position (December).

1893   VLB becomes editor and publisher of *Wisconsin Vorwärts* (January 1).

1894   MB graduates from Milwaukee State Normal School (June 27) and appointed Milwaukee public school teacher (June 28).

1896   VLB attends People's Party national convention (July 22–25).

1897   VLB and Eugene Debs establish Social Democracy of America (June); MB leaves teaching position (November 6); VLB and MB marry (December 4).

1898   Social Democrats run first candidates for public office in Milwaukee (April 5); VLB and Eugene Debs break from Social Democracy of America and form Social Democratic Party (June 11); *Wisconsin Vorwärts* discontinued as a daily because of financial problems (August 17); Doris Berger born (September 29).

1900   Elsa Berger born (March 26); VLB serves on committee negotiating merger of Social Democratic Party with dissenting faction of Socialist Labor Party (March).

1901   Social Democratic Party merges with faction of Socialist Labor Party and forms Socialist Party of America (July 29); VLB acquires *Social-Democratic Herald* and moves it to Milwaukee (August).

1902   VLB incorporates Milwaukee Social-Democratic Publishing Company (May 1).

1904   VLB defeated in election for mayor, but Socialists win nine seats on Milwaukee Common Council (April 5); VLB defeated in election for U.S. House of Representatives, but Socialists win six seats in Wisconsin legislature (November 8).

1908   VLB defeated in election for Wisconsin Assembly (November 3).

1909   MB elected to Milwaukee school board (April 6); VLB visits Europe (September 25–November 25) and attends planning meeting in Brussels for International Socialist Congress (November 6–8).

1910   Socialists win control of Milwaukee city and county governments and VLB elected alderman (April 5); VLB visits Europe (August 10–September 18) and attends International Socialist Congress in Copenhagen (August 28–September 3); VLB elected to U.S. House of Representatives (November 8).

1911   VLB takes office as a member of U.S. House of Representatives (April 4); first issue of *Milwaukee Leader* published (December 7).

1912   Socialists lose Milwaukee local elections (April 2); VLB defeated for reelection to U.S. House of Representatives (November 5).

1914   VLB defeated in election for U.S. House of Representatives (November 3) and criticized for not sufficiently supporting German cause in World War I.

1915   MB reelected to Milwaukee school board (April 6) and elected board president (July 6).

1916   Socialist Daniel W. Hoan wins first of seven consecutive terms as Milwaukee mayor (April 4); VLB defeated in election for U.S. House of Representatives (November 7).

1917   MB appointed to Wisconsin Board of Education (June 25); *Milwaukee Leader* loses mailing permit because of antiwar editorials (October 3).

1918   Announcement of VLB's indictment under Espionage Act (March 9); VLB receives 26 percent of vote in election for U.S. Senate (April 2); additional indictments of VLB announced (October 28); VLB wins election to U.S. House of Representatives (November 5); trial of VLB and four other Socialists begins in Chicago (December 9).

1919   VLB convicted (January 8), sentenced to twenty years in prison, and released on bond (February 20); U.S. House of Representatives refuses to seat VLB (May 19) and declares seat vacant (November 10); VLB wins special election to fill vacant seat (December 19).

1920   U.S. House of Representatives refuses to seat VLB and declares seat vacant (January 10); Doris Berger marries Colin Welles (July 17); VLB defeated in election for U.S. House of Representatives (November 2).

1921   U.S. Supreme Court overturns VLB's conviction (January 31) but upholds denial of *Milwaukee Leader*'s mailing permit (March 7); MB reelected to Milwaukee school board (April 5); Harding administration restores *Milwaukee Leader*'s mailing rights (May 31); MB departs for trip to Philippines, Japan, China, and Korea (September 27) and visits Colin and Doris Welles.

1922   MB returns to U.S. (April 25); VLB elected to Congress (November 7).

1923   U.S. Justice Department drops case against VLB (January 8); VLB and MB tour Europe (May–August) and VLB serves as delegate to International Socialist Congress in Hamburg (May 21–25); U.S. House of Representatives seats VLB without objection (December 3).

1924   VLB and MB attend Conference for Progressive Political Action convention (July 4); MB appointed to La Follette national presidential campaign committee (July 6); VLB reelected to U.S. House of Representatives (November 4).

1925   VLB and MB visit Panama and Haiti (February); VLB visits Europe (July–September) and serves as delegate to International Socialist Congress in Marseilles (August 22–27).

1926   VLB reelected to U.S. House of Representatives (November 2).

1927   MB appointed to Wisconsin Board of Regents of Normal Schools (January 17); Elsa Berger marries Jan Edelman (February 1); MB reelected to Milwaukee school board (April 5); Deborah Welles born (November 2).

1928   MB appointed to University of Wisconsin Board of Regents (February 1); VLB defeated for reelection to U.S. House of Representatives (November 6).

1929   VLB injured in streetcar accident (July 16); VLB dies (August 7).

1930   MB fails to win Socialist nomination for Congress.

1933   MB reelected to Milwaukee school board (April 4).

1935   MB visits Europe (April–June) and tours Soviet Union.

1939   MB declines to run for sixth term on Milwaukee school board.

1940   MB resigns from Socialist Party (May 2).

1944   MB dies from heart disease (June 16).

The Berger and Schlichting Families

Children of Ignatz (1830–1925) and Julia Berger (1837–1915):

Victor (1860–1929)
    married: **Meta Schlichting** (1873–1944)
    children: Doris (1898–1984); Elsa (1900–1984)
Rose (1861–1928)
    married: Sigmund Morganstern (d. ca. 1893–1900)
    children: Edith (1886–1950); Hilda (1887–1942); Sidney
                (1893–1971); Milton (1893–1918)
Mathilde (1863–1957)
    married: Hyman Weingarten (1854–1940)
    child: Edna (1894–1992)
Anna (1866–1950)
    married: William Gorman (1863–1918)
    children: Sybil (1892–1968); Helen (1895–1911); Edna
                (1897–1966)
Rebecca (1868–1936)
    married: ? Leverthal (divorced); Alexander Gottlieb
                (1873–1922)
    children: Richard G. Berger (1893–1977) (child of Rebecca's
                first marriage; originally named George Leverthal and
                later adopted by Ignatz and Julia Berger); Leah
                (1901–1982); Ruth (1902–1983)
George (1871–after 1929)

Children of Bernhard (1838–1883) and Mathilde Schlichting
(1847–1905):

Paula (1871–1902)
    married: Archibald Anderson (1861–1936)
    child: Jack (1899–1970)
Meta (1873–1944)
    married: **Victor Berger** (1860–1929)
    children: Doris (1898–1984); Elsa (1900–1984)
Hedwig (Hattie) (1874–1959)
    married: Frank Schweers (1868–1948)
    stepchildren: Franklin (Hi) (1896–1948); Edwin (b. 1898); Kermit
                   (1901–1974); Carl (1904–1959); Marie (b. 1905)
    child: Harriet (b. 1913?)
Ernst (1876–1920)
    married: Arline Warnke (b. 1899)
Walter (1883–1898)

Abbreviations and Nicknames

AFL	American Federation of Labor
Betty	Elizabeth Thomas, president of the Milwaukee Social-Democratic Publishing Company and assistant to Victor Berger
Co, Coie, or Colin	Colin Welles, first husband of Doris Berger
Debby	Deborah Welles, elder daughter of Colin and Doris Berger Welles
Dod, Doddie, Doris, Dudd, or Duddie	Doris Berger (Welles) (later Hursley), daughter of Victor and Meta Berger
Elsa	Elsa Berger (Edelman), daughter of Victor and Meta Berger
Hattie	Hedwig (Hattie) Schlichting (Schweers), sister of Meta Berger
Hearings	*Hearings before the Special Committee Appointed under the Authority of House Resolution No. 6 Concerning the Right of Victor L. Berger to Be Sworn in as a Member of the Sixty-sixth Congress* (Washington, D.C., 1919), 2 vols.
IWW	Industrial Workers of the World
Jack	Jack Anderson, nephew of Meta Berger, who lived with the Berger family
Jan	Jan Edelman, husband of Elsa Berger
Josie	Josephine Rudkowsky Skobis, housekeeper for the Bergers
Schatzl	"Little darling," literally "little treasure." Term of affection used by Victor and Meta Berger for each other
Schnuckie/Schnucks	"Little darling," literally "small sheep." Term of affection used by the Bergers for their daughters, Doris and Elsa; after 1919 used exclusively for Elsa
SHSW	State Historical Society of Wisconsin
Stedy	Seymour Stedman, Socialist attorney from Chicago

The Family Letters of Victor and Meta Berger

Victor to Meta

Milwaukee, Wisconsin
August 24, 1894

My Dear Little Meta:—

I had expected a letter from you earlier and I was just trying hard to get angry at you, when your lead-pencil "epistula" came. Under the circumstances I will have to forgive once more.

Told you beforehand that you would—in the sweet by-and-by—miss my charming company. Who never wanted to believe it? Miss Meta Schlichting. Who is in back-woods now doing nothing? Miss Meta Schlichting. Who is sighing and wishing for Milwaukee? Miss Meta Schlichting.

By the way, I am shocked to hear that you are getting fat and lazy. Wenn ein Mädel nicht einmal sein eigen Bett mehr macht, so ist es Zeit, daß es bald nach Hause kommt.[1]

Not because I miss you so very much. Oh, no! In fact, I have a lovely time with Hattie[2] and "Lärle" and my Watertown-girl who happens to be here on a visit just at the right time, to see her again and to invite her to the "show" for to-night, was naturally one and the same thing. But to my deepest sorrow and her unlimited consternation I will have to back out of my invitation. V.L.B. must address a meeting in the 7th Ward to-night. . . .

Well, I will try and take the poor girl to the Matinee to-morrow.

The play in the Academy is far above the average. "The Lost Paradise" is adapted from the German ("Das verlorene Paradies" von Fulda),[3]—it is a sort of a sentimental semi-socialistic play. Hattie liked it extremely well.

Last week I spent three days in Sheboygan. Spoke in several meetings to very large crowds. The "Peoples Party" will no doubt carry Sheboygan.[4]

The "Federated Trades Council" in its meeting last night voted to take 500 dollars worth of stock in the "Vorwärts Company."[5] The vote stood 50 "yes" to 1 "no".

I am very glad of it. It isn't so much on account of the money, my dear little Meta, as on account of the *moral effect* of the vote that I am glad of. For the moral effect this vote will have on the paper is simply immeasurable. Not only will the 46 Unions represented in the "Trades Council" have to "follow suit", but from now on Socialism will be preached to the working classes of Milwaukee with the official and financial aid of Unions of Milwaukee. The edition of the "Vorwärts" will be tripled within a year, and our influence will grow in geometric progression to it.

Und ich . . . . . werde schließlich in den Stand gesetzt werden, mich ebenfalls zu verheiraten, wie andere Narren auch.[6]

Have also made arrangements with the "Davidson Theatre" for advertising. Meine verschiedenen Schätze können also wieder in das Theater gehen, vorausgesetzt natürlich, daß Du die Sache nicht *monopolisieren* willst.[7]

If you let me know the day and the train on which you intend to return, I may run up to Green Bay and escort you home.

Walter[8] is all right and getting stronger and better every day. When I saw him last, he was writing a long love-letter to you. Your "Ma"[9] claims that she is not a bit tired, and Hattie has appearently not lost one pound of her stately weight.

And therefore:—while I, as a matter of fact, cannot for the life of me see, what you can be doing Gescheidtes[10] in the wilderness without me, I still think it my duty to advise you to stay there as long as possible. You have had a hard year of it, little Meta, and a still harder "vacation". And a hard year is also in store for you, von wegen Deiner Dummheit,[11] you know. Therefore you ought to get rested before school begins, thoroughly rested.

But you must write more often to your

V.L.B.

1. If a girl doesn't even make her own bed anymore, it is time for her to come home soon.
2. Hedwig "Hattie" Schlichting (1874–1959) was Meta's younger sister. After marrying Frank Schweers in September, 1909, she moved to Shawano, Wisconsin, where she taught music and served on that city's school board.
3. "The Lost Paradise" by Fülda. Berger attended an English-language performance of an 1892 drama by German playwright Ludwig Fulda (1862–1939) in which an industrialist steals an invention from the superintendent at his factory. The workers at the factory strike for higher wages, and the superintendent supports their cause. After the industrialist's daughter falls in love with the superintendent, the workers' demands are met, and all is resolved.
4. Berger attended the July, 1894, convention of the Wisconsin People's (Populist) Party and soon thereafter joined the party, serving as secretary of its central committee from August, 1894, until August, 1896. Fred C. Runge, the Populist candidate in Wisconsin's Fifth Congressional District, received 23 percent of the vote in Sheboygan that fall, compared to 11 percent in districtwide voting.
5. Berger purchased the German-language labor newspaper *Milwaukee'r Volkszeitung* in December, 1892, renamed it *Wisconsin Vorwärts,* and began publishing it as a daily in January, 1893. The paper received financial support from the Milwaukee Federated Trades Council (a citywide organization of trade unions) and served as the official German-language organ of the Wisconsin State Federation of Labor. Although Berger halted the daily edition in August, 1898, he continued editing the weekly edition, entitled *Vorwärts,* until 1911,

when Heinrich Bartel became editor. The paper continued to be published by Berger's Milwaukee Social-Democratic Publishing Company until 1932.

6. And I . . . . . will finally be put in the position to get married, too, just like other fools.

7. Thus my various sweethearts can go to the theater again, provided, of course, that you don't want to *monopolize* things.

8. Walter Schlichting (1883–1898), Meta's brother.

9. Meta's mother, Mathilde Krak Schlichting (1847–1905), was born in Germany and came to the United States in 1852. She married Bernhard Schlichting (1838–1883), who emigrated from Germany with his family in 1847 and later settled in Milwaukee, where he worked as an accountant. He served as a Republican member of the Wisconsin Assembly, 1875–1876, and on the Milwaukee school board, 1878–1882.

10. that makes any sense.

11. because of the foolish thing you did.

Meta to Victor

Casco, Wisconsin
July 31, 1895

My Dear Dear Friend,

After I left you yesterday afternoon, it was as I expected. I felt so very lonesome that I had hard work to control myself. The journey seemed endless and I did not arrive in Casco until 5.30 o'clock. You see it takes longer than an hour from Green bay to Casco. Once there, Tony, Clara, the Dr.[1] and another lady were at the depot to meet me. They gave me a very cordial welcome indeed. When asked about my journey up here & about meeting any acquaintances on the way, I of course replied that I had met no one that I knew which was of course true. But some how they mistrusted my statement. I finally admitted that I had company to Green bay. Clara & the doctor were very much put out that you didn't come way up & felt rather hurt. You know these people are very very sensitive in such matters and they think you think yourself above them. But I explained matters all right.

Today is a beautiful day and after having a good talk with the people up here Tony and I took a ramble in the woods. It is beautiful here and I think I could be quite content if I only had some one up here with me; for no matter where I go or what I do my thoughts are always with him. I have not yet talked with the doctor concerning myself but will do so presently.

Next Monday the Dr. is going to preform a very important operation on a man and he said I could come into the room and watch him do it. He says he don't think the man will pull thro' & told him so and sent him home to make his will. It is very very sad isn't it? The man has a tumor which is located near his bowels & consequently in a very dangerous place.

I wish, Victor that you could be up here drinking in this pure fresh air instead of worrying and bothering and working in your dingy office. You see, you told me to put down my thoughts no matter how foolish they are. Well I have done so and here is the one which to me is the most prominent one. I love you more than I can say and if you don't write me a long long letter as soon as you get this one I shall be very likely to return to Milwaukee to see whether any one else has stolen your heart from me. But you will write, I feel sure of that for you said you would.

What did your partner[2] say when you arrived the next morning? Now don't go to the opera or exposition too often with other girls; will you? And above every thing else tell me all about your self when you write.

I can't write any more now because the people are all around me dictating what I should write all though they don't know to whom I am writing but they are only guessing.

mit herzlichem Gruß, Deine[3]

Meta

1. Antoinette "Toni" Belitz (Lammers) (b. 1872), her sister, Clara Belitz Hipke (1868–1938), and Clara's husband, Dr. Gustave Hipke (1867–1954). Antoinette and Clara were Meta's first cousins. The Hipkes were active in health issues in Milwaukee during much of the early twentieth century. Clara, a women's health and rights advocate, organized the Milwaukee Maternity Hospital and Dispensary Association in 1906 and was a founding member of the National Woman's Party. Gustave practiced medicine in Casco, Wisconsin, prior to moving in 1902 to Milwaukee, where he worked as an obstetrician until 1946.

2. Valentine Raeth (1857–1935) was the manager of the *Milwaukee'r Volkszeitung* when Berger purchased the paper in 1892. The paper continued under the name *Wisconsin Vorwärts,* and Raeth served as its business manager and was part owner until about 1896, when he sold his interest to Berger. Raeth later became a game warden, working for the state of Wisconsin from 1905 until his death.

3. Sincerely yours.

Victor to Meta

Milwaukee, Wisconsin

August 13, 1895

My Dear Meta:—

The step which we are contemplating to take, compells me to give you once more, what I believe to be a correct picture of my inner self.

It is true, you think, you know *me* better than any other person knows me, excepting perhaps my mother.[1] And as a matter of fact you *do* know me better than even my mother, who has seen very little of me since I have grown up to manhood. And yet even *you* do not know me.

Dear Meta:—There is an evil spirit lingering about me, of which *I* only know, and whom I cannot master. Whenever I get *enraged,* my blood seems all to rush towards my head, and I (who otherwise can control my actions to an unusual extent,) lose control over myself entirely. During these fits of madness I am *capable* of committing murder, and while I hope and expect that such will never be the case, I on the other hand fear that this fault of temper may end with *insanity.*

For instance, last Thursday when I again had serious trouble with my "partner",[2] (he lifting a chair against me after calling me a "Juddebub"[3] etc.) there, all of a sudden, was a red veil before my eyes, and I felt that I could have killed him, had he not dropped the chair and ran out on the street, when I made a rush for him. And now mind you, I cannot keep any *hatred,* not even against that man, for 5 minutes, and he was perfectly safe after he came in again, and he knew it. But the mere fact that I do not harbor any hatred before or afterwards, shows these spells to be *insane* spells. And a man like that is not a safe man for *you* to marry, my little darling Meta.

Consider further that my eyes are in a pretty poor condition, and that my business does not permit me to save them much. And I am also troubled with Hemorrhoids, an ailment, which makes me very erratic, eccentric and morose at times. Now is such a man a fit subject for *you* to marry?

Your "sickness" you see, has no right to bother me much. In fact, if you would be all "perfect", I suppose you would not have me under any circumstances. But not being strong bodily, you my little Meta, ought to weigh and consider things double as much as any other girl,—it is not your lover, it is your dear old friend who writes to you at this moment, and asks you to stop and think—what will become of you and . . . well, of your children . . . . if things should take an unnfortunate, an unexpected turn?

Dear little Meta! I feel that I have possibly undertaken to lift a bigger load than I can carry. Shall you, my darling, also be crushed beneath it? I feel heavy of heart and depressed in mind when I think of the home I could offer you *just now*. . . . . You are very well able to take care of yourself at the present time, and be tolerably happy. Now, what wrong have *you* little darling ever done to me, that I should destroy your happiness, possibly for ever. . . .

I have pictured the dangers before you, my girl, as they are constantly entering my mind. They are only dire spooks now, and I hope, *spooks* only they will remain for ever.

And you need not think that I am trying to "get out". I *love* you, and I have told all this, *because* I love you.

You are a better girl than I could ever hope to get anymore. And *I* will surely take you for my wife, if you will only risk to take *me* for your husband. And I will try to do all in my power to make you happy.

And in case you should decide otherwise I will truly remain your "best friend". I will help you, advise you, take you out as often and be with you as much, as *you,* the so-called propriety and my own moral code will permit.

It is therefore for *you,* my dear little Meta, to decide, whether, when we meet the next time, we shall meet as a bethroted couple or—as *good friends* who can and do *trust* each other in *everything.*

But remember, dear Meta, I shall always remain

Your

Victor

1. Berger's parents, Ignatz (1830–1925) and Julia (1837–1915), emigrated from Austria-Hungary to New York City in the late 1870s. Sometime after 1880 they moved to Bridgeport, Connecticut, where they retailed leather goods and invested in real estate. Victor was not living with the family at the time of the 1880 census.
2. Valentine Raeth.
3. Jew-boy.

Victor to Meta

Milwaukee, Wisconsin

August 14, 1895

My Dear Little Meta:—

I beg your pardon a thousand times for having scared you so in my last letter. But you know well enough, my dear, that I am "made up" of two entirely different *moods.* While it isn't as bad as with poor "Dr. Jekyl" in the story, still I am a sufferer in *some* degree.

One V.L.B is a well educated and unusually well read man. He is pretty conscientious, ambitious and all that, but queer and unsociable to the extreme. You know the man, you have met him often. Although he styles himself a Socialist, he is proud and aristocratic. And since he is dissatisfied with the world and himself he is either saying nothing at all, or sharp and disagreeable things. The man has no friends, except probably his books. He is not practical a bit, and if it wasn't for me (the other V.L.B, who writes this letter) he would have a hard time of it. Under the pretext of fighting for humanity, he is always making trouble for me and for all those whom I love. That malcontent super-wise book-spirit wrote you the letter last Sunday.[1]

The other V.L.B *you* also know, dear Meta. Say it yourself,—am I not always lighthearted, good natured, *conceited* and lovable? I will admit that I am extremely silly at times, that I am liable to take Annie Hartmann to the show, flirt with every pretty girl etc.—but *you* know that I sit on the porch until 1 o'clock A.M. with *one* girl only,—and that is the reason why I do not mind the Gewissensbisse[2] of the other V.L.B.

I am the fellow who has all the spunk; I went into business for myself.
And while it is true the I am the V.L.B who makes the debts, I am also
the V.L.B to pay them. As a matter of fact, I would even make lots of
money, if the book-spirit was not in my way. . . .

Now, dear Meta, you understand the simile. I have only told you,
what you already knew. Which of the two *moods* do *you* like best? Com-
monsense, the enemy of all genius, tells me to suppress them both. So
far, I have not been able to do it; I hope you will help me, and your love
will show you the right way to do it.

I have been out with the Summer Girls 4–5 times,—told them,
i.e. to one of them (to a tall well developed blonde) that I had a girl
for *good*. Did so, last Monday. Just now, I got a letter—written with
perfect penmanship—that she is very sorry, but she cannot go out
with me to-night, because . . . . . . I have hurt her feelings! So, there
you have it, Metie. I will have to go out either alone, or advertise for
a summer girl.

Excuse my penmanship, darling, the pen is miserable, and that is
the reason why I will have to close this letter.

Take good care of yourself and do all the eating, sleeping, exercis-
ing etc., you can possibly do. I don't know whether I will be able to call
for you as far as Casco,—but I will surely meet you in Green Bay.

Good by, kleine[3] Meta!

Yours, waiting for an answer
V.L.B.

1. If Victor wrote Meta on Sunday, August 11, 1895, the letter is no longer
extant; however, he probably was referring to his letter of August 13, 1895,
above. Berger also erred in dating his letter of August 14, writing "Thursday,
Aug. 14, 1895," although August 14 was a Wednesday.
   2. guilty conscience.
   3. little.

Victor to Meta

Milwaukee, Wisconsin
August 22, 1895

My Dear Girl:—

Enclosed please find a new R.R ticket (which you must sign in *ink*
on the back) and also my picture. I am in a hurry, you see, for I want
my letter *every* second day.

I will meet you in Green Bay at the Northwestern Depot (12 o'clock
noon) on Saturday, Aug 31st, provided that date suits you.

Leave your satchel at the St. Paul depot, (where you arrive) until I
call for it, in your company.

If you should be lonesome in Green Bay until I come, then walk just right up into Küstermann's Music store, and tell Mr. Küstermann[1] that you want to wait for me there.

The picture you get, is not the size you expected, I suppose;—but it is probably a good measure of how much I *shriveled* mentally because you are away. . . . See!

To-morrow I shall go to Chicago. I want to get an English speaker for our Unions on "Labor Day". In case I should not visit Mr. Debs in Woodstock jail,[2] I will return on the same day,—otherwise I will return on Saturday.

I am writing this letter during business hours (stealing my time so to say, in order to be able to do so), you must therefore, my little girl, excuse my brevity.

At home everything is all right. But you know that, I suppose, for you get "all kinds" of letters from home.

My Cincinnati summer girl, the one with the excellent penman-ship, has reconsidered her resolution not to go with me, because I have a girl. She went to Whitefish Bay with me the other day. Although she was invited out that night, we stayed in Whitefish Bay until 11.15 P.M. on account of the moonshine, the lake and the stars etc. . . . Went home with the steamer and then I took her up to the "party" which had been arranged in her honor, and where they had given her up for lost. Things appear to be rather serious when one considers, that she has also invited me to the "Heart of Gesu" church (the new Jesuit church on Grand Ave which you admired so much) for next Sunday, in order to hear her sing a "solo". The girl is a Catholic you know.

Now I wonder whether I would not better get *your permission* first. . . .

At any rate, sweet Meta, you would better write as soon as possible (Meine Briefe zeigst Du aber keinem Menschen)[3]

to your loving
V.L.B.

1. Gustave Küstermann (1850–1919) served as postmaster of Green Bay, Wisconsin, 1892–1896, where he operated a stationery and musical instrument store, and as a Republican congressman, 1907–1911.

2. Eugene V. Debs (1855–1926) was the best-known American socialist of the twentieth century and the Socialist Party's presidential candidate in 1900, 1904, 1908, 1912, and 1920. As president of the American Railway Union, Debs was arrested for defying an injunction during the Pullman strike of 1894 and spent six months in the Woodstock jail in Illinois. Berger's visit to Debs at the jail became legendary. Seven years later Debs recalled how "Victor L. Berger—and I have loved him ever since—came to Woodstock, as if a providential instru-ment, and delivered the first impassioned message of socialism I had ever heard—the very first to set the wires humming in my system. As a souvenir of that visit there is in my library a volume of 'Capital,' by Karl Marx, inscribed with the compliments of Victor L. Berger, which I cherish as a token of priceless

value" (Eugene V. Debs, "How I Became a Socialist," *The Comrade* 1 [April, 1902]: 147–148).

3. But don't show my letters to anybody.

Victor to Meta

Milwaukee, Wisconsin
August 25, 1895

My Dear Girl:—

I did not go to Catholic church to-day. The reason? Well, I did not have the permission of Miss Meta. . . .

But the summer girl will be in Milwaukee next Sunday yet. If *you* want to hear her sing, I will gladly escort *you* to the "Heart of Gesu" church. . . .

The "Davidson Theater" opens next Thursday with the "Cotton King", i.e, the real opening will take place of Monday Sept. 2nd with Julia Marlowe[1] in Shakespeare's historic drama "Henry IV." Julia herself will take the part of young Prince Harry. If it so pleases you, my dear Miss, I shall take the liberty to accompany you to the theater on that evening.

I am always complaining to your folks that you do not write often enough, and that is true, you don't write half as often as you should. But certainly I could not tell them how *many* letters you wrote me,—few enough—but *they*, i.e the folks, only know of *two* letters so far. . . .

You know, dear Meta, I hate to make an exhibition of my love, (or of anything that belongs to my inner self) and that explains my conduct on a good many occassions.

But in spite of my love for you, or in fact: for *that very reason,* I would advise you, dear girl, *not* to marry me, if you can possibly help it. . . . But pardon me, I don't want to broach that subject again.

Knowing that you take interest in all that concerns me, I send you a clipping from this mornings (Sunday) "Sentinel."

As you know, I am a member of the "Committee of One Hundred" for the semi-centennial celebration,—and so are 3 or 4 more representatives of the labor-unions. Ex-Governor Peck[2] who is also a member wants to invite the militia of the whole state for that occassion, in order to make "a grand military display", as he says.[3] Now if the Peck-idea prevails, we *all* will resign in a body, (I mean the representatives of the labor element.) The clipping will tell you what I said to a "Sentinel" reporter on this subject. Here it is:[4]

OPPOSITION TO THE MILITIA. Victor L. Berger Explains the Attitude of Some of the Labor Unions.

Asked last night why the labor unions were opposed to inviting the militia of the state to take part in the semi-centennial celebration Victor L. Berger said:

"All progressive laboring people are opposed to all militarism as far as military display is concerned, although it was the laboring people of the country who fought all the great battles and died on the field for good or bad issues, in order to win glory, fame and wealth for others. Still as things are now we must have some military organizations, but these must be by the entire people and for the entire people, such as they have in Switzerland. The present organization is simply a uniformed rank of Pinkertons kept by the state for the benefit of the capitalists. We look upon the militia displays, since there is no outside enemy to fight, simply as a demonstration against those who are dissatisfied with the present order of things. We are dissatisfied with the present condition of things, and we are going to change them in spite of the militia. But we certainly do not think it advisable to give any helping hand to any military display."

Let me know in time, sweet girl, when you want to come home, so that I can make arrangements and also may know the time and the place where to *meet* you.

You have received my picture, by this time, I suppose. Grottkau[5] is making a crayon of it—¾ life size,—you shall have that, if you want it.— Grottkau will also give me a large picture each of *himself,* Gov. *Altgeld,*[6] & of Karl Marx.

I am in bad humor again to-day. Did not sleep any at all last night,— went to the Turkish bath last night, after I got through with my work, and *my eyes* hurt me bad all day. I don't intend to read any more to-day.

While I am writing this, a delegate of the "Trades Council" is here asking me to *preside* on labor day and also to act as "master of ceremonies" in general. I have kept him waiting now for over half an hour.

I am glad you are getting along so finely, my sweet little girl. Write soon, to your cranky

V.L.B.

1. Julia Marlowe (1866–1950) was a popular English-born actress known for her roles in Shakespearean plays between 1887 and her retirement in 1916.
2. George Wilbur Peck (1840–1916), a humorist and journalist, served as the Democratic governor of Wisconsin, 1891–1895.
3. Milwaukee celebrated its fiftieth anniversary on October 16–17, 1895, and, despite labor opposition, six hundred National Guardsmen marched in the October 16 parade marking the event.
4. The following three paragraphs are from a clipping from the *Milwaukee Sentinel,* August 25, 1895, that Berger pasted here.
5. Paul Grottkau (1846–1898), a labor leader and socialist journalist, came to Milwaukee in 1883 and edited the *Milwaukee Arbeiter Zeitung.* Grottkau moved to San Francisco in 1889 but visited Milwaukee in 1895 and 1898 to aid socialist campaigns.

6. John Peter Altgeld (1847–1902) served as the Democratic governor of Illinois, 1893–1897. Altgeld granted clemency to the men who had been convicted in the Haymarket riot of 1886 and opposed President Grover Cleveland's use of federal troops to quash the 1894 Pullman strike.

Victor to Meta

St. Louis, Missouri
July 21, 1896

My Dear Little Meta:—

Although I am tired and sleepy I must write this note to you to-night, for I promised to write to you on Tuesday. But, alas! I cannot mail it until to-morrow, i.e. I will put into the box to-night but it will not go until to-morrow.

Well, little Meta, I tried hard to get up an anti-Bryan combine.[1] Succeeded, because circumstances helped me. Telegraphed for Debs. He promised to come, but hasn't so far. Henry D. Lloyd[2] also one of our radical leaders and prominently mentioned in connection with the nomination has just left me. He is rather disgusted with the leaders of the People's Party. Whether Bryan will be nominated or not, I do not know. He is certainly very popular personally. And the leaders seeing the party break up on account of the "silver question", tried to "sneak under" in the *new* Democratic Party. But the rank and file of our party, the so-called "Middle of the Road" people stood it, like a stone wall so far; they don't want to hear anything about Bryan. Now, you can about imagine how Silverites and the Democ[r]ats work day and night. If the People's Party puts up its own candidate it means certain defeat to Bryan. If we endorse him, or rather if we *also* nominate him, it means certain victory. But it also means the surrender of all our principles and the death of the People's Party.

I do not play as big a role in this convention as you probably imagine, little Meta,—although my name gets into the papers every day. I am young and rather new in national affairs,—this being the first national convention of a political party, which I have ever attended.

But then I am talking too much politics, Meta, and you do not like politics. And you would like it still less if you would know, how hot it is here, in spite of the frequent rains. Oh, I do wish, I was in Milwaukee again and not only on account of Milwaukee's lovely cool breezes. You know why. . .

Dear little Meta; if you want to answer my letter, you must do it right away, otherwise I will not get it. I will stay here until Saturday only.

How is Walter?[3] Is Paula[4] feeling any better? Did Hattie write? Give my regards to all of them and to Ma.

Cannot write any more, I am too tired. Tell you all the rest, when I get to Milwaukee.

Answer instantly

Your loving
Victor L.

1. Berger served as a delegate to the People's (Populist) Party convention that met July 22–25, 1896, in St. Louis. Berger promoted the nomination of Eugene V. Debs for the presidency through the *Wisconsin Vorwärts*, but Debs ended his candidacy when he sent a telegram to the convention declining to run. William Jennings Bryan (1860–1925), who had served as a Democratic congressman from Nebraska from 1891 to 1895, received his party's presidential nomination earlier in July and eventually also won the Populist nomination. Bryan was the Democratic presidential candidate again in 1900 and 1908 and served as U.S. secretary of state, 1913–1915.

2. Henry Demarest Lloyd (1847–1903), a muckraking journalist and author of *Wealth Against Commonwealth* (1894), quit the Populists after the nomination of Bryan and subsequently supported socialist candidates, but he did not join the Socialist Party until 1903.

3. Walter Schlichting, Meta's brother.

4. Paula Schlichting (Anderson) (1871–1902), Meta's older sister.

Victor to Meta (translation)

Milwaukee, Wisconsin
August 20, 1896

My dear little Meta!

I really am so tired that my eyes are almost closing, but since I promised you two letters each week, and the week actually is nearly over, I must hurry and quickly write you a few lines.

I wasn't a bit pleased by your dream, because it suggests an *overheated* imagination. Above all you must eat sensibly, then you won't dream such nonsense. Dreams come from the stomach and have *no* meaning *whatsoever*—neither "contrary" nor any other.

But I do not want to scold.

You have, no doubt, already received the books. The two novels you may leave there, but the "Dogs and the Fleas"[1] you may bring back as soon as the doctor[2] has read it. I provided my annotations for your sake because I could not expect you to understand the hints and suggestive remarks. It, of course, would read much better if the reader had to discover the similes and satires *by himself*. By the way, the book is already outdated, it was written in 1892, shortly after the big strike in the Carnegie Steel Works, in Homestead (near Pittsburgh).

Since you left I have been in "Schlitz Park" only once. There I met Mrs. Hickler and her sister (an old maid) and played the chaperon. Mr. Hickler[3] has accepted a well-paid position as editor of the "Wächter und Anzeiger" in Cleveland and already is in his new position. The "Wächter und Anzeiger" is a "gold-democratic"[4] newspaper.

Next week the "Mikado" will be shown here. It would actually make me happy if you were here and it is not only because of the opera. . . However it is best that you remain where you are, that is, as long as feasible because the fresh, fragrant forest air will do you good. For your affliction of the throat,—by the way, you could consult Dr. Hipke about it sometime—it would probably be better if you could teach in the Casco School next year. I would then go to see you every month.

How is Paula?[5] I was at your mother's last Sunday to see how things were there and to find out what you had written home. Walter[6] was quite well and alert.

Do not read at night when the light is bad and also prevent Paula from doing so. Don't sit on the damp grass either, you two.

On *Labor Day* I shall speak in Oshkosh. They also wanted me in Milwaukee and Sheboygan. The Milwaukeans went so far as to write to the Oshkosh Trades Council asking them to absolve me from my promise. But that did not go over well at all. . . .

However, all this is of little significance. The big question for us is: Do you love me? As far as I know you did not tell me so in your letter with the least little word. And just as important, yes, even more important to me, is the question of your health. I want you to take care of yourself, dear girl, so that you will get well. If you think it is too crowded or too hospital-like at Hipke's, then better go to Cedar Lake to "Rosenheimer's" for a week. I would gladly get you your tickets and also pay for your board.

By the way, do not do anything that could somehow make the Hipkes angry with you. They are such dear people.

Give them my regards, also to Tony[7] and Paula and write soon to

your
Victor L.

1. [Frederic Scrimshaw], *The Dogs and the Fleas, by One of the Fleas* (Chicago, 1893) satirized the American economic system, using dogs and fleas to symbolize labor and capital, respectively.
2. Dr. Gustave Hipke.
3. Simon Hickler had recently left his position as a reporter for the Milwaukee German-language daily *Der Herold* to become editor of the Cleveland *Wächter und Anzeiger,* a conservative Democratic paper.
4. Gold Democrats were conservative party members who supported the gold standard and opposed the presidential candidacy of William Jennings Bryan. They formed the National Democratic Party, whose presidential candidate, John M. Palmer, received only about 130,000 votes in 1896.

5. Paula Schlichting (Anderson), Meta's sister.
6. Walter Schlichting, Meta's brother.
7. Antoinette Belitz (Lammers).

Victor to Meta

Milwaukee, Wisconsin
November 18, 1897

Mein kleines Schatzl![1]

See by the letter you wrote to your mother that there is Diphteria in Casco. The condition of your throat is such that you are inclined to all kinds of throat-diseases. Now, I don't want to be a widower before I am married[2] and, therefore Schatzl I came to the conclusion that you are best taken care of at my side, or in my arms. Please Schatzl, schnür your Bündelz,[3] make it as diplomatic to Clara and the Doctor[4] as possible and let me know immediately when I am to meet you in Green Bay. We will get married this month yet.

Give my love to all. I will make out a list of books for Alfred[5] in my next leisure hour, I only hope that he will like the list.

I may go to hear Nansen[6] to-night. I did not attend the German theater last night, but did lead in discussion in the Social Science Club[7] on the topic of: "Are Strikes Ever Justifiable?" Was just ready to go to the theater when I saw in the paper that I was on the program. And since I had disappointed them once before,—when I went to the Davidson with you—I had to go this time. For next Wednesday I am to deliver a lecture there on the "Concentration of Wealth"—so would better come before Wednesday.

You are not writing many letters this time. This is my third. I had so far *one* from you. If you don't make up, by writing (a letter or two) every day from now on, each 16 pages long, I will not write to you any more.

Darum bessere Dich, Schatzl, bessere Dich![8]

With many kisses
your
V.L.B.

1. My dear little darling!
2. Victor and Meta married on December 4, 1897.
3. pack your bags.
4. Clara and Gustave Hipke.
5. Probably Dr. Alfred Belitz (1866–1953), the brother of Clara Belitz Hipke and Meta's first cousin. Belitz practiced medicine in Chicago and several western states between 1895 and 1918 and in Pepin, Wisconsin, from 1918 until his death.

6. Fridtjof Nansen (1861–1930), a Norwegian professor of zoology and Arctic explorer, lectured in Milwaukee on November 18. Nansen later became a diplomat and won the Nobel Peace Prize in 1922.

7. The Sociological Club, a small educational group that met weekly in Milwaukee.

8. Therefore mend your ways, little darling, mend your ways!

Victor to Meta (translation)

Chicago, Illinois
June 8, 1898

My sweet little darling!

This is the slowest, most boring and weirdest convention, I ever saw. The whole convention has been dragged into the battle of the parties on the executive board, which for a long time had been waged in secret, and in fact without either side having issued a proper declaration of war. The battle cry is: Here Colony, there *political* Action![1] I am regarded as one of the leaders of the "political Action," or rather as *the* leader, although that is not what I want. The main battle was about the committee for the drafting of the platform, or expressed more correctly, about the election of the members thereof. The opposition had offered me a compromise, which I simply rejected, although thereby I would have been elected *unanimously*. I was elected in spite of it but with a very small majority. Because of the colony swindle it could easily come to a split tomorrow, in which case however Eugene V. Debs will obviously go along with us.[2]

Stay with your mother tomorrow, Thursday, little darling, for if I don't come at 10:30 p.m. I won't arrive before Friday morning.

Many greetings to everybody and even more kisses (in spirit) for you. Take good care, that you are well and cheerful when your darling arrives.

As always yours
Victor

1. The national convention of the Social Democracy of America, held in Chicago on June 7–11, 1898, was marked by a split between the "colonization" faction and the "political action" faction. The colonizers hoped to migrate to a western state, where they would achieve power through elections, establish public ownership of the means of production and distribution, and then spread the socialist message to the rest of the country. The political action faction called for immediate efforts against the status quo through a formal political party and trade unionism.

2. Berger was a member of the platform committee, which wrote a report favoring political action; the minority report supported colonization. Debs

spoke to the convention on June 10 in support of colonization but later that evening reversed himself and supported Berger's report. The convention adopted the procolonization report, and Berger and his supporters bolted from the party. The next day, Berger, Debs, and others met at Hull House and formed the Social Democratic Party.

Victor to Meta

Boston, Massachusetts
January 19, 1900

My Dear Wife!

I have just returned from Haverhill where I received both of your letters at the same time. And that happened in the following way.

I left New York on Tuesday, going to Boston. At that time your letter adressed to the Gross-New Yorker Arbeiter-zeitung[1] had not arrived as yet and I gave directions to forward the same to Haverhill. I arrived in Boston late on Tuesday night, and went to Brockton the next morning, where I was the guest of the mayor[2] and the chief of police and put up at the best hotel the town affords—it is a place of about 40,000 inhabitants, i.e. somewhat larger than Racine. From Brockton I returned to Boston had a conference with our representatives at the "State House" (the Capitol) and left for Haverhill, where I arrived Thursday evening. They had a mass meeting and a public reception in my honor in Haverhill,[3] and they will have a similar affair to-night at Boston. I have not had a spare minute in four days—up every night until 3 A.M. "Talking it over" with the different comrades in the different cities. This letter I am writing at the office of Dr. Konikow[4] waiting for his return. It is the first free half an hour, I have had.

Let me thank you, my dear Schatzl, for your sweet and fine letters. Especially the last one was a picture of your *noble* and *beautiful soul*. You are the *greatest* and *best* thing in *my life; you* are *more* to *me* than even the labor-movement which is my religion, as you seem to think. Don't you think for a moment that I love our little girlie[5] more than I do you, it is only, the girlie being so little and so helpless, I simply cannot help *showing* my feeling more.

I am very happy to know you are showing my picture to little Doris every day, but do not let her kiss it, please, the photographers use all kind of poisonous substances in making the photographs, you know. I am sorry she does not get her *two* naps every day, but considering that she gets up so very *late,* I do not think the affair will amount to much. Just give her every morning and every evening a half a dozend kisses extra for her Papa. Thats all she would get from me, you know.

The movement here is simply splendid, and within a few years we will be the *second* party in Massachussetts, ie. the Democratic party will be wiped out. As to Margaret Haile,[6] I only saw her once, but I will see more of her to-night at the meeting and at the reception that is to follow. I also intend to make a short call at her home in Roxbury, one of the leaders of the Boston movement wants to take me out. Margaret Haile looks fearfully old and wrinkled,—I think she looks *much* older than she did two years ago—she dresses shabbily to the extrem, her gray felt hat, ancient and spotted and with two rooster feathers on it, is a sight, and when she took off her old brown cloak—the same evidently that she had worn for many years—I noticed that the lining was torn in a dozend different places. I understand that she has *lost* the good place she has had, or that she has given it up, in order to be able to give more time to the movement, and that she is working as a typewriter in a lawyers office. The pay there cannot be very much, I suppose, and she has to support herself and child. Will tell you more about her, after I have made, my call there.

I am going to leave for Bridgeport to-morrow.[7] Please, send your next letter there. I hope to be home again before the end of next week. I feel a queer longing to see you and the baby again and as soon as possible. When in Bridgeport, I will dismiss all thoughts of the movement and do nothing but eat and sleep and sing the praises of my dear sweet darling wife, and that little chip of the same block called Doris.

But the Doctor has just came in and I must close. Please, give my love to all, and tell especially Ma and Hattie that I appreciate their kindness. With a thousand kisses your loving husband

Victor L. Berger

1. The *New York Arbeiter-Zeitung* was a Yiddish-language socialist newspaper published in New York City from 1890 until about 1902.

2. Charles H. Coulter, a Social Democrat, served as mayor of Brockton, Massachusetts, 1899–1901.

3. Like Brockton, Haverhill was a center of Social Democratic strength in Massachusetts, and by 1900 the city's party could boast a mayor (John C. Chase), a representative in the state legislature (James F. Carey), and a weekly newspaper, the *Social Democrat.*

4. Morris J. Konikow was a Boston physician. From 1891 until 1908 he was married to Antoinette Buchholz Konikow (1869–1946), a prominent physician, Socialist activist, and birth-control advocate.

5. The Bergers' first daughter, Doris, was born on September 29, 1898.

6. Margaret Haile, a journalist, advocate of women's rights, and secretary of the Massachusetts Social Democratic Party, supported Berger on the platform committee in the 1898 convention of the Social Democracy of America and helped to found the Social Democratic Party.

7. Berger's parents and several of his siblings lived in Bridgeport, Connecticut.

Victor to Meta

Bridgeport, Connecticut
January 23, 1900

My Dear Wife:—

I am in Bridgeport since Sunday. Found things somewhat different than I expected. Mother and Annie and Beckie[1] still have flats near each other and mother is taking care of all the children. Mother is doing a great deal more in other ways than she ought to. Will tell you about it when I get home.

Told mother about our baby not sleeping nights, i.e. waking up so often. She put on a very sober face and said Doris ought to sleep all night, and about four hours every day besides. She advised that you should arrange meals so that Baby does not get anything two hours *before* she goes to bed. Mother thinks a full stomach will put Baby to sleep for a *little while*, but will inconvenience her and give her *bad dreams*. I see here that Annie's child[2] (2½ years old) is still sleeping twice every day. Mother puts the child into an alcove and sternly tells it to go to sleep and—the child sleeps. But then, children are so different, you know.

I went to Ansonia to see my other sister,[3] who has a store there. She does fairly well and supports her four children in good style. Besides two good-looking girls who attend high-school, she calls a pair of beautiful boys (twins) her own.[4]

Mother has more than forgiven my marriage and she told me that after the description I gave of *you* and *your ways,* she loves *you* as much as any of her *own daughters.* She admonishes me day and night to take *good care* of *you* and to get *some wealth* for you and the *children.* She does not advise me to drop the paper suddenly, but she wants me to slowly work into some other business,—real-estate preferred. And as is usual with people of her age and her business—she hates socialism and socialists. I have to be rather meek, in order not to excite her.

I intend to be home Saturday or Monday next. You can hardly write any more letters to me—this time, I am the boss letter writer.

Give *my* regards to all and also the greetings of my family. With many kisses for you and little Doris

Your loving husband
Victor L. Berger

1. Anna Berger Gorman (1866–1950), the wife of a Bridgeport, Connecticut, clothier, and Rebecca Berger (Gottlieb) (1868–1936), a milliner, were two of Victor's sisters.
2. Edna Gorman (Mock) (1897–1966).
3. Rose Berger Morganstern (1861–1928), one of Victor's sisters, was the widowed mother of four children and an Ansonia, Connecticut, women's clothing merchant.

4. Edith Morganstern (Lehman) (1886–1950), Hilda Morganstern (Loewen-thal) (1887–1942), Sidney Morganstern (1893–1971), and Milton Morganstern (1893–1918). Milton died while serving in the U.S. Army in World War I.

Victor to Meta (translation)

Indianapolis, Indiana
March 8, 1900

My dear little darling:

I hope that this letter will find you in good health. I feel guilty that I have been so heartless to not have found the time to write you a letter every day, because of the business matters which overburdened me at this convention. How is our sweet baby? I was glad to hear that Doris is feeling better. But you must be sure to get enough sleep, sweet little darling, or else what will become of you?

Concerning the convention: this time I saved the party in the literal meaning of the word. We are going to unite with the New York S.L.P, but the name of the *united party* will be *Social Democratic Party*. E. V. Debs will function as the candidate for the presidency, the candidate for the presidency of the S.L.P will be our vice-presidential candidate.[1] The party will probably cast one million votes in the *next* election.[2]

I, however, will withdraw after the election: that is now absolutely certain. Through the unification the party is becoming independent and strong enough to continue.

I hope to be in your arms Friday evening, my little darling, to kiss our baby, and to tell you more.

With many greetings and kisses
your V.L.B.

1. Berger served as a delegate to the Social Democratic Party convention held in Indianapolis on March 6–9, 1900. The convention debated merger with a faction of the Socialist Labor Party, which had previously nominated Job Har-riman and Max Hayes for president and vice-president at a convention held in Rochester, New York. At the Indianapolis convention, the Social Democrats nominated Eugene Debs for president and Harriman for vice-president and appointed a committee that included Berger to negotiate the merger. An acri-monious dispute over the name of the new party delayed full union, with Berger's faction insisting on "Social Democratic Party" and the Socialist Laborites arguing for "United Socialist Party." Additional confusion ensued in July, 1900, when the Socialist Labor faction claimed to be the legitimate Social Democratic Party and established headquarters in Springfield, Massachusetts, while the original Social Democrats, with which Berger was aligned, maintained their headquarters in Chicago. The two parties finally merged in 1901, when they agreed on the name "Socialist Party of America," although the Wisconsin party remained the Social-Democratic Party until 1916.

2. In 1900, the ticket of Debs and Harriman received more than 95,000 votes, or 0.7 percent of the national vote. Four years later, Debs and vice-presidential

candidate Benjamin Hanford received more than 386,000 votes, or almost 3 percent of the vote.

Victor to Meta

Girard, Kansas
March 30, 1900

My Dear Schatzl:

I am writing this in Waylands[1] office, one of the queerest and oddest edifices I have ever been in. He has built it especially for the Appeal with all modern conveniences to get out his paper—the Appeal. He employs about 35 people—and is the best customer of Uncle Sam in the entire state of Kansas,—on account of *his* mail the salary of the postmaster of Girard had to be more than doubled and the post-office raised to the rank of a second class post-office. Wayland is solid with us, he will support the Social Democratic Party to the exclusion of any other party whether it calls itself "socialistic" or otherwise.

So much of business,—since you always claim that I do not tell you enough about it. By-the-way, Wayland is also going to print a Milwaukee or rather a Wisconsin edition of the Appeal.[2] He has also encouraged me to put down the price of the "Wahrheit"[3] to 50 cents a year, and try to work up a big edition. He is going to give me a free "Ad" in his paper for a time. He even wants [us] to come down to Girard and have it printed in his office; he figured out, we could live much cheaper here, and make some money out of the paper. But certainly you understand that I am in no special hurry to jump at *this* proposition.

I hope, my dear Schatzl, you are well and getting stronger every day. I furthermore hope that you took my advice and got a nurse for the time of my absence. I feel guilty that I have left you so soon after your confinement[4] and can, therefore, hardly wait for the time, when I will again see you and the babies. Down here everything is nice and green,—I do not think spring has advanced as far as this in our northern climate, but I have good reason to expect that you had fair and warm weather, and that it helped to get you cheerful and into good spirits.

I will be home Sunday. Until then, my dear Schatzl, good-by.

With many kisses for yourself and babies

Your loving husband
Victor L. Berger

1. Julius Augustus Wayland (1854–1912) founded the weekly socialist newspaper *Appeal to Reason* in Kansas City, Missouri, in 1895 and two years later moved his publishing operation to Girard, Kansas. The *Appeal* reached a paid circulation of more than 100,000 in 1900 and more than 760,000 in 1913. It

printed sensational articles as well as important original works, such as the first publication of Upton Sinclair's *The Jungle*.

2. Wayland published an edition of the *Appeal to Reason* that contained a Wisconsin page for several months in 1900.

3. Berger assumed control of the weekly German-language *Die Wahrheit* at the time he began publishing *Wisconsin Vorwärts* in 1893. *Die Wahrheit* halted publication in June, 1910.

4. Meta gave birth to a second daughter, Elsa, on March 26, 1900.

Victor to Meta

Boston, Massachusetts
December 6, 1900

My Dear Schatzl:

Have arrived in Boston to-day after a long tedious journey and my first business—even though it is late at night—is to write to you. I have put up at a very fine hotel which has the advantage of being opposite the depot and to cost no more than a "cheap hotel" would. I do not like it that they put me up on the 9th floor, but then the hotel is *absolutely fire proof*. The first thing I did (i.e. after washing) I sat down into a fine new mahogony chair—something like the one we had at home, only upholstered—leaned back to get a good rest and *broke* it. The back split right into two in a similar way as ours did at home. I am wondering now whether they will try to make me pay [for] it,—if they do they will have the hardest job of their life.

I read in the Boston Globe that our party was snowed under in the election held last Tuesday in the towns of Massachussetts. John C Chase and three aldermen were defeated in Haverhill,[1] and only two councilman elected. The Social Democratic mayor of Brockton[2] got there by the skin of his teeth—a plurality of 35. McCartney[3] and some of the others who received me at the depot expressed satisfaction about it— Margaret Haile I haven't seen yet, will see her to-morrow—they expressed satisfaction because Haverhill had gone over to the N.Y. faction and had played the part of a socialist Mecca to the detriment of the movement of this country. But I take a different view of the matter. I am afraid of the loss of prestige for our party—besides, I would rather have seen Carey[4] who is a conspirator and a mischief maker defeated and Chase elected. As it is the real guilty person has been elected to the assembly in November, while Chase who simply went with him because he did not dare to go against him, was defeated. However this may be one thing is sure: the prestige of Haverhill, Brockton etc. has been diminished in this election while that of Milwaukee has grown considerably: I am not selfish enough though to be glad of that, as long as the movement at large has not grown to my expectation.

But that is politics and I suppose you care for it only for my sake. I intend to leave here Saturday and spend Sunday in Bridgeport, Monday in Ansonia, and I may visit my sister[5] in Springfield on Tuesday, for I have never been to see her since she is married. Have seen a cap of *Alaska seal* in the show window of one of the large stores here, the cap is to cost only 5 dollars. I intend to buy one for my father, only I am afraid it is made up of so many little pieces that it is not going to last long.

How are the babies, Schatzl? Does little Doris ever ask for her papa? Does she sleep better? Do *you* get more sleep at night? Do *you* follow my advice about sleeping during day time? All of these questions I want you to answer in your next letter which you are to send to me to Bridgeport. And a good many other things I want you to tell me,—for you know everything that concerns you or the babies is of the greatest interest to me, far more than even the movement.

Give my love to all our relations with many kisses for you and the babies

Your loving husband
Victor L.B.

1. John C. Chase, a shoemaker, was elected mayor of Haverhill as a Social Democrat in 1898 and 1899. In 1900 he and three Social Democratic aldermen were defeated in their bids for reelection.
2. Charles H. Coulter, a plumber and local union president, was reelected mayor of Brockton, Massachusetts, as a Social Democrat by only twenty-three votes. He was soundly defeated the following year.
3. Frederic C. MacCartney (1864–1903) was a Unitarian minister in Rockland, Massachusetts, who resigned his pastorate in 1899 to become an organizer for the Social Democrats. MacCartney served four terms in the Massachusetts legislature (1899–1903) and died in office.
4. James F. Carey (b. 1867), a Social Democratic trade unionist from Haverhill, served in the Massachusetts legislature, 1898–1903.
5. Rebecca Berger Gottlieb.

Victor to Meta

Chicago, Illinois
January 17, 1901

My Dear Schatzl:

I know I am a base wretch for leaving my sweet wife and my darling babes for three days without any information about papa, but enclosed clipping will show you that I am very busy. I am as you can see the chairman of two committees; but I am a member of two other committees *besides*. Had very little rest at nights, I dont believe I slept five hours on an average. The convention[1] is a very hot one, all kinds of propositions of "unity" and re-organization are in the air and I am bitterly opposed by some of my "best friends",—Corinne Brown[2] for instance. Your prediction that I may be forced out of the movement may come true.

But leaving politics aside,—how is my Schatzl? Does Doris [*portion of letter missing*]

The convention will last till Friday, I suppose, but I hope to be home on Friday night. Please send me a letter at once and also the babies and your pictures, which I forgot to take along. I ought to have these pictures in my watch.

With love to you all
I am ever your
Victor L.

1. Berger was a delegate to the convention of the Social Democratic Party (Chicago headquarters) held in Chicago on January 15–18, 1901. The convention agreed to poll its members about calling a unity convention, which led to the creation of the Socialist Party of America in July, 1901.
2. Corinne Stubbs Brown (1849–1914) was elected to the National Executive Board of the Social Democratic Party (Chicago headquarters) in January, 1901. She worked as a teacher and principal in the Chicago public school system before marrying Frank E. Brown, a Chicago banker.

Victor to Meta

St. Louis, Missouri
January 25, 1902

My Dear Schatzl:

This is my first free minute since I am in St. Louis. Besides attending the meetings of the National Board[1] I have been on three committees: committee on Rules, comm. on nominations and comm on organization and agitation. To-night the other members attend the big meeting at Music Hall where Ben Tillett[2] (from England) Job Harriman[3] and a couple of others will blow off their steam while the members of the National Committee will sit on the stage and try to look important. I thought I could improve my time a great deal better by writing to you Schatzl and writing for my paper.

Your letter has duly arrived this afternoon and was the first pleasure I had since I arrived in St. Louis. I am glad to hear the babies are so good and I did not mean to "lecture" you. On the contrary I can hardly wait until I get home,—which will be Monday evening, no matter whether the committee gets through or not. We have state autonomy now and the more is left to the states the better.

As to my safety you need not worry—I have travelled a great deal all my life and I am fully able to take care of myself and others if necessary. Railroad accidents are a very rare occurence, there is about as much chance to be struck by lightning when at home, as by an accident on the railway. So do not worry, please.

Kiss the babies, Doris and Elsa, for their papa, who yearns to be again in the arms of their sweet mama.

Yours always
V.L.B.

1. Berger was attending the meeting of the Socialist Party's National Committee, at which he adamantly argued for the independence of local branches of the party. The National Committee, originally consisting of one member from each state, was nominally the ruling body of the Socialist Party, although by 1910 most power was held by the smaller National Executive Committee, which was elected by the party's membership.

2. Benjamin Tillett (1860–1943), an influential British trade unionist, helped direct successful dock strikes in 1889 and 1911. Tillett served as a Labour Party member of Parliament, 1917–1924 and 1929–1931.

3. Job Harriman (1861–1925), a California lawyer, was the Social Democratic nominee for vice-president in 1900 and ran as a Socialist for mayor of Los Angeles in 1911.

Victor to Meta

Hurley, Wisconsin
April 25, 1902

My Dear Schatzl:

You will not complain this time I hope, you get a letter from me every day. We arrived in Hurley, Wis this afternoon, after a trip though the iron region of Michigan—a country where the woods were murdered in about the same way as in Wisconsin. The Americans are the most wasteful people on earth, and the next generations will have to suffer for it, I suppose.

We are going to Manitowish (Iron County) to-night at 8.30. The land which we want to see is in Carson right on the station, but there is no place to stop over night in Carson. The next station to Carson is Mercer, a place that is not much better. So we have to go four miles south to Manitowish, which is quite a fishing resort. It is raining pitchforks and I suppose we will have to swim through the woods, which are supposed to be quite level a lowlands. Conrad got a letter of recomendation from the bank president in Hurley to the proprietor of the Hotel in Manitowish and we hope to get a good guide—they call them "cruisers" up here.

Do not speak to Josie[1] or anybody else for what purpose I went up here, I do not want people to think that I am a millionaire or a landshark who is bu[y]ing up land.

The country up here is full of iron and I hope we will strike something that may be good for something else, besides farming.

I was quite lame this morning after the exploring trip of yesterday, but now I am all right and feel good.

Hope you and the babies are well. With best wishes and kisses for you all

Your loving husband
V.L.B.

1. Josephine Rudkowsky (Skobis) (b. 1873) worked as a housekeeper for the Bergers from approximately 1898 to 1920.

Victor to Meta

Appleton, Wisconsin
July 18, 1902

My Dear Schatzl:

I am still in Appleton, where we had no organization before. We will try to organize to-night and I believe we will have success. The movement here will be entirely in the hands of Americans—whether it will be a very "class conscious" movement, I doubt very much, especially since we were not able to get into touch with the trade-union element of the town. The movement in Green Bay will be of an entirely different nature. There the trades-union men and the Federated Trades Council took the matter into their hands—and they expect 150 people at the conference to-morrow afternoon and a great success for the mass meeting on Monday.

We had also very good success in Neenah last night, where we started a branch after a well attented and interesting meeting.

Please do not show any of my letters to Miss Thomas,[1] nor tell her anything about them,—for I have not answered her letter as yet—did not have the time—and she might feel slighted, the good soul.

I do not think you can send me any more letters. I will be in Green Bay to-morrow and in Fond du Lac Monday,—and it is a bare possibility that I may drop in on you on *Monday* night, but I do not want to go to any meetings and therefore I do not want this to be known, especially since I am expected to attend the meeting of the County Committee on Tuesday evening and to go right on to Racine on Wednesday.

I am very glad to hear that you and the babies are doing so well. Do not fear that I will overwork myself—on the contrary: in spite of the constant hustle I am getting heavier—when I weighed myself on the Depot I found that I have gained a few pounds—which is no doubt due to the three heavy meals one gets at the hotels. My sleep is not much better than usual, I ought to quit smoking, but the temptation on the road is considerably greater than at home. To-day I have smoked but one cigar, and I will smoke no more.

Sometimes I do wish I could take you with me on a weeks trip like this. For you it would be a great novelty and I am sure you would enjoy it. We may try it some day when our children have grown up a little.

With many kisses for my Schatzl and the babies

Your loving husband
V.L.B.

1. Elizabeth H. Thomas (1856–1949) ably served the Milwaukee socialist movement as a party official, editor, and financial supporter. Born to a New York Quaker family, the independently wealthy Thomas worked at Hull House in Chicago prior to moving to Milwaukee in 1900. Thomas became a principal stockholder in the Milwaukee Social-Democratic Publishing Company and served as the firm's president from 1902 until 1929. She played an indispensable role in the day-to-day operations of the *Social-Democratic Herald* and the *Milwaukee Leader* and served as state secretary of the Wisconsin Socialist Party, 1901–1919, and as a member of the Milwaukee school board, 1915–1921. She resigned from the party following the defeat of the conservative Old Guard faction at the 1936 national convention.

Victor to Meta

Green Bay, Wisconsin
July 20, 1902

My Dear Schatzl:

While eating dinner at the Beaumont to-day I thought it might have been a wise trick to meet me at Green Bay to-day (at noon) and to have gone home together by the way of Fond du Lac to-morrow. On the other hand I am glad I did not do it. It was raining pitch forks all last night and nearly all day to-day; it is cold and disagreeable to such a degree that I have been buying a warm woolen shirt yesterday, in order to keep warm—and I do not feel comfortable in spite of it, whenever I am in the free air. In the future I will always take some warm woolen underclothing as a *reserve*, whenever I leave for longer trip than 3 days.

The conference this afternoon was a failure as a consequence of the heavy rain. We will try to again to-night. Got acquainted with a very fine young man, a lawyer and an Irishman by the name of Macmillan[1] whom the Democrats boom for the congressional nomination this fall, but who has decided socialistic leanings. The conference was held in his office, and since the few people who finally showed up were rather late on account of the rain, we had quite a conversation or "heart to heart talk" as he called it. I evidently made a very deep impression on him, but whether this impression will outweigh his political ambition remains to be seen. Besides, I did not try to capture him and used rather drastic colors in describing the difficulties of man who devotes his life to the propaganda of socialistic ideas. Certainly, I would not expect him to do more than to come out openly and declare himself a member of our party—at the most. I will send him literature, as soon as I get to Milwaukee.

It is now pretty certain that I will be home to-morrow (Monday) night. I want to take a bath first, therefore, please tell Josie to have the warm water ready.

I am rather anxious this time to see you and the babies. This anxiety of mine will cut business rather short in Fond-du-Lac.

With many kisses for you and the babies and kind regards for Josie, Ernst[2] and other friends

Your loving husband
V.L.B.

1. Berger probably meant James H. McGillan (1870–1935), a former city attorney, district attorney, and municipal judge in Marinette, Wisconsin, who had moved to Green Bay in 1900. The Democrats did not nominate McGillan for Congress in 1902, although he later served as mayor of Green Bay, 1927–1929, and unsuccessfully ran for Congress as a Democrat in 1928.

2. Ernst Schlichting (1876–1920), Meta's brother.

Victor to Meta

New York, New York
November 1, 1903

My Dear Schatzl:

Have arrived here safely after a rather tedious and uninteresting trip. Lost half a day by playing the "true Knight" to a Norwegian maiden all alone and forlorn who could speak little or no English nor German and who went back to the land of the Midnight-Sun. Looked up the Millionaire Socialist[1] and Margaret Haile yesterday—both were very glad to see me, especially Margaret. Was invited to a Fifth Ave restaurant for lunch—one of the most expensive restaurants in town. Ate very little lunch cost $3.60. Like your or Josie's cooking fully as well or better. Still the restaurant is so well patronized that we could hardly find a seat. Wilshire is loosing money and losing it rapidly. He told me he lost $3,200 last month on the magazine, and that he would soon reach bottom. He wants to move his office back to Canada, in order to save expenses. His paper is still printed there, you know, because he cannot get it entered in the U.S. he claimed. I could not see the reason, why not, since the S.D. Herald[2] and hundred of Socialist papers, and even quite a number of Anarchist papers get "second class" postal rates. The final outcome of the discussion was that I promised him to go [to] Washington D.C. with him this week and get the paper entered. He is to pay all my expenses. So I will have to shorten my visit in Connecticut considerably, in fact, I can only stay a day at my parents, and only a few hours at the other places. And I will not go to Boston at all. Wilshire wants to move his paper to Milwaukee and publish it there. Please, keep the whole business secret, and speak to nobody about it.

So much about my affairs. Now, please, write me how you and the babies are getting along. I am sorry I did not take a picture of you and the babies along for my personal and private benefit, I have always done so in the past. Kiss little Doris and little Elsa three times a day for their papa, and have them kiss their sweet mama for me.

My next address I will let you know by telegraph, for I do not know it myself at this time.

Is Miss Thomas with you? And how do you like it? Give her my regards.

Give also my regards to Grandma and Hattie and Josie.

Schatzl, ich habe dich lieb und wenn ich nach Hause komme, werde ich Dich arg viel lieb halten.[3]

Otherwise I am feeling well only I have lost a great deal of sleep of late. But then, I did not sleep much at home either.

By-the-way, Hillquitt[4] received me with exceeding cordiality. He invited me to dinner to his house, to lunch from his business place,— but I accepted neither. But this afternoon (Sunday) I will spend at his house owing to his very pressing invitation.

I hope you are all getting along very nicely, and now I will close my letter, (the longest you have received in a quite a while) with many kisses and embraces as your Schatzl

V.L.B.

1. Henry Gaylord Wilshire (1861–1927), an affluent California real estate speculator, published *Wilshire's Magazine* between 1901 and 1915 in Ontario, Canada; New York; and California. The periodical sought to popularize socialism for a middle-class audience and in 1905 had a circulation of nearly 300,000. Wilshire moved to England in 1910 and on his return to the United States in 1914 took an active prowar stance.

2. The *Social-Democratic Herald* was a weekly newspaper founded in 1898 in Chicago as the organ of the Social Democratic Party. In 1901 Berger moved the paper to Milwaukee, where it served as the mouthpiece of the Milwaukee branch of the party in its efforts to reach an English-speaking audience. Publication ceased in September, 1913, its role having been preempted by Berger's daily *Milwaukee Leader.*

3. Little darling, I love you and when I come home, I will hold you so very lovingly.

4. Morris Hillquit (1869–1933), a Latvian-born labor lawyer, became a prominent author and spokesman for socialist causes in the United States. A member of the Socialist Labor Party since 1888, Hillquit led dissenting members out of that party in 1899 and eventually joined with Berger's Social Democratic Party to form the Socialist Party. He frequently sided with Berger in factional party disputes. Hillquit ran unsuccessfully for mayor of New York twice and for Congress five times.

Victor to Meta

Washington, D.C.
November 9, 1903

My Dear Schatzl:

I am in Washington D.C. to-day and will try to see senators Spooner and Quarles,[1] representatives Otjen and Stafford;[2] postmaster-general Payne,[3] and "his excellency" the President,[4] if neccessary. Do not know what success I will have, but *hope* the best. Wilshire is with me.

At home I found everything all right, only very much involved. Just think of it, my parents have *16* tenants. Will tell you all about it when I get home.

Start from here to New-York sometimes to-morrow. Must go back to New York, because my ticket reads from New York. Am very desirous and impatient to see you, my Schatzl and my sweet babies again. Feel very tired and exhausted, cannot travel as easily as of yore. What knocks me is that I do not sleep as I ought. But otherwise I am all right.

Hope that you are all well at home. (I am sorry that I forgot to leave you a check for the land-lord, but I suppose that he will wait without a murmur).

You can expect me home by Thursday. The worst of it is that I will have to take a train the next day for Omaha. Such is the Socialist movement.

With many kisses and embraces for you and the babies

Your loving
V.LB.

1. John C. Spooner (1843–1919) and Joseph V. Quarles (1843–1911) were Republican senators from Wisconsin. Spooner served 1885–1891 and 1897–1907; Quarles served 1899–1905.
2. Theobald Otjen (1851–1924) and William H. Stafford (1869–1957) were Republican congressmen representing the Milwaukee area. Otjen served 1895–1907; Stafford served 1903–1911, 1913–1919, 1921–1923, and 1929–1933. Berger succeeded Stafford, who lost the Republican primary in 1910, as the representative from Wisconsin's Fifth Congressional District. The two men faced each other nine times in general elections for the seat.
3. Henry Clay Payne (1843–1904), a prominent Republican businessman and railroad executive from Milwaukee, served as U.S. postmaster general from 1902 until his death.
4. Theodore Roosevelt (1858–1919) served as president of the United States, 1901–1909.

Victor to Meta

Omaha, Nebraska
November 14, 1903

My Dear Schatzl:

You are going to get a letter every day this time if I can possibly manage it. (I hope you have received my epistle from the train.) All I have to tell you is that I safely arrived in Omaha after a sleepless night, and with great effort managed to concentrate my thoughts during the three very tiresome sessions we held to-day—although I was very near the point of falling asleep several times.[1] I blankly refused to participate in a session after supper, and so now after 9 o'clock I am a free American citizen who has the right to sit in the rotunda and watch some other citizens spit "Terbacco"-juice into the spittoons. The "Paxton" is a good old and very large hotel—I have a room with bathroom on the fourth floor near the fire-escape and it is the intention of the management (since I live on the American plan i.e.—take all my meals in the hotel) to fine me $3.50 daily. This is too steep and, therefore, I am going to be an European again after to-night, i.e. take my meals outside and thereby save mammon. But, then, all of this will be of little interest to you, yet, the endless report of Mailly[2] on the organization of the party in the organized and the unorganized states would be of still less interest to you.

In the next letter which I hope to find in the national office on Monday I suppose you will in turn inform whether you and the babies are well, whether they have slept well (and with open windows), whether they were in the open air much, and have taken their "Turnübungen",[3] and even whether they had done their duty as to "jobs" etc.

I suppose "Tante Thomas"[4] is there as last time and is good company to you. Will try and be home on Wednesday, I am rather tired of being away from home so much.

Am played out so thouroughly that I intend to go to bed within an hour, provided my colleagues do not come here to bother me. The fact that I have smoked two cigars to-day also lays heavily upon my conscience, because I know that I ought *not* do it,—for your sake and the babies sake.

With many kisses and embraces

Your loving
V.L.B.

1. Berger was in Omaha to attend a meeting of the National Committee of the Socialist Party.

2. William Mailly (1871–1912) served as secretary of the Socialist Party, 1903–1905. He had previously worked as a labor organizer, party official, and

journalist in Alabama, Massachusetts, New York, and Tennessee. After 1909 he
worked as a drama critic for mainstream magazines.
   3. exercises.
   4. "Aunt Thomas," a reference to Elizabeth Thomas.

Victor to Meta

[en route to Omaha, Nebraska]
[January 16, 1904]

My Dear Schatzl:
   Just to show you what good husband I am I am writing this note
aboard of the train to Omaha. I left Milwaukee on the 1.45 and had just
time enough to order stencils and other utensils in Chicago for our
addressing machine.
   Dinner I took on the train—turkey, pie and milk—tasted well but
cost too much money. For supper I only had a ham-sandwich and a bottle of beer in the buffet-car—I didn't go into the diner at all. Still I do
not know whether I did wise in taking beer.
   Made up my mind that the next time I go on a trip like this I will
take you along. Have your tickets in my pockets and they are not used.
While it is true that I must use the tickets *sparingly* I ought *not* to save
the mileage where *you* are concerned, and I am not going to. Only do
not tell Miss Thomas about it because she even refused a 500 mile
ticket this year on the grounds that I was hard up for mileage last year.
   Seeing how other people travel, live and enjoy life I have almost
made up my mind to quit the movement, go into some business and
also make money. Yet I do not know how I can go out honorably before
I have achieved certain things which I have started out to do. . . .
   Hope your new dress is all right and do not worry about the bill. I
have always taken good care of you and the babies and will do so in
future. With many kisses and embraces for you and the Darlings

Your loving
VL.B.

Victor to Meta

Omaha, Nebraska
January 16, 1904

My Dear Schatzl:
   Now don't you say that I am not "lieb"[1]—here is the second letter
and have not been away longer than one day. We have hardly started

work as yet—this morning we went over the referendum on the amendment to the constitution—tell Miss Thomas it carried with 5,591 against
2,037.[2]

Kindly also tell Miss Thomas to send a marked copy containing my
article on the "Revisionists" to the Chicago Socialist with the request to
copy it since I have accused of "mud slinging", ask Miss Thomas to sign
the request in her own behalf or have Bistorius[3] sign it.

With love to you and the babies and my best regards to Miss
Thomas, Grandma Hattie and all our friends

I am your liebes Schatzl[4]
V.L.B.

1. nice.
2. The amendment changed voting on the National Committee of the
Socialist Party from one vote for every organized state to one vote for every one
hundred members in each state, thereby shifting power to states that had large
memberships, such as Wisconsin.
3. Herman W. Bistorius (b. 1874) served as business manager and secretary-treasurer of the Milwaukee Social-Democratic Publishing Company from
1902 until his resignation in 1914. He ran for Congress in Wisconsin's Fourth
District as a Socialist in 1902 and received 15 percent of the vote.
4. dear sweetheart.

Victor to Meta

Pittsburgh, Pennsylvania
November 13, 1905

My Dear Schatzl:

The Convention[1] was opened this morning—and this afternoon
Samuel Gompers[2] read a report so ungodly in lenght that it took him
three hours and a half to read it. He flayed the Socialists unmerci-
fully—telling the *delegates* that unbeknown to them and behind their
backs, the Socialists in a convention held in Chicago last June legislated
the American Federation of Labor out of existence, but that no doubt
most of the delegates present never heard of it. He kept that up for
about fifteen minutes, and of course most of the delegates looked at
me—although I had opposed the so-called Industrial Workers of the
World, which by-the-way most of them did not seem to know.[3]

I secured a room jointly with Barnes.[4] We went to a sort of a cheap
boarding-house, where we occupy the parlor, and take breakfast also. I
hope that there no bugs in the place—the lady promised me five dollars for every one that we can find—but I would rather not find any.
You know I did not sleep the last night when I was home, and in the
sleeper—I had an upper berth and could not open any window—I did
not sleep at all. So if there should be bugs in this place I would be an

unhappy man indeed. As a *precaution* I am going to buy Persian insect-powder before I retire.

I cannot do very much at this convention and I really wish it was over. Barnes and I will try to soldier a few *sessions* and see Pittsburg and vicinity. Yet I can hardly wait for the time when I back in Milwaukee with my Schatzl and my Schnuckies.

And I hope you are getting along nicely. Would rather see it if Hattie slept there, only I am sorry that she cannot stand an open window. Hattie as a Schlichting ought to make a special effort to sleep with an open window. See to it, my dear Schatzl that the window in the room of our babies is always kept open.

I will try to write you a letter about every second day. Send your letters to the Convention Hall, American Federation of Labor—especially since I do not know whether we will stay in this boarding house another week.

Please do not forget to tell Mrs. Lietzau that if she wants a place as a second cook on an excursion train running to San Francisco she must write Mr. R. Matters, Superintendent of Dining and Parlor Car Service, Northwestern Railway, Chicago Ill.

And now my sweet Schatzl—good by! I must make a little copy for my paper, which I intend to send with the same mail. Kiss the babies for me and consider yourself embraced by your loving husband.

V.L.B.

Best regards to Hattie.

1. Berger represented the International Typographical Union at the AFL annual convention.

2. Samuel Gompers (1850–1924) served as president of the AFL, 1886–1895 and 1896–1924. Throughout their careers, Berger and Gompers held each other in mutual contempt.

3. A group of socialists and labor leaders, including Bill Haywood, Daniel De Leon, and Eugene V. Debs, participated in a convention in Chicago in June and July, 1905, that resulted in the formation of the IWW. The IWW attacked the AFL and craft unionism and attempted to create a structure that would organize both skilled and unskilled labor in a single union. Berger declined an invitation to attend the January, 1905, meeting that planned the convention, and he later publicly and privately criticized the IWW.

4. John Mahlon Barnes (1866–1934), a longtime officeholder in the Cigar Makers' International Union and a vigorous critic of Samuel Gompers, served as the Socialist Party's national secretary from 1906 until 1911, when he resigned because of corruption and morals charges. Barnes directed Eugene Debs's 1908 and 1912 presidential campaigns.

Meta to Victor

Milwaukee, Wisconsin
November 21, 1905

My Darling Papa

I need hardly tell you how delighted both the children & I were to get you[r] dear letters. I especially since I have missed you more than I care to tell. We have been so patient with each other & gotten along so splendidly that now I miss you very very much. I am awfully sorry to hear that you are not feeling well. Just take care of yourself first and of the A.F. of L. afterwards. No matter about the resolutions, they would have been killed any way only as a matter of course. Barnes or some one should have been there. What's the use of presenting resolutions that are so antagonistic to Gompers & his clique.[1] They only make things hard for *you* at the convention & no good is achieved anyway. Why don't you go slower, be politic with yourself & after you have gained favor, then present those resolutions. It may take a while but then you can do something in the end. You & you alone can do absolutely nothing in that body but create bitter feelings for yourselve. Do as the others do, think of yourself a little more & let the Socialist end take care of itself which it will do if you take care of the "Father & founder of the Party".

But enough of preaching. It is easier to preach a good deal than to practice. Now as to home news. Both children have been quite ill with the "Grippe." But [they] are getting better now. It was a pretty good thing I didn't go with you. As for me, I am extremely nervous, having had no night's rest since you left & no chance to get out into the fresh air. I am simple a bundle of nerves, which every-body seems to rub the wrong way. I must & will get out & do something besides having two cross cross children after me. I have done little else but sew doll's clothes read stories & amuse them. Of course the end is in view & I am glad of it. Yes I went to Mrs. Lietzow. Will tell you more when you get home.

What do you think the Fair Committee did? Raffled out the work of the Fair & the Dining Room fell to the U.S. Woman's Club. Nice prospects for me? But, come home as soon as you can as I am also more than anxious to embrace you & hold you "lieb."[2] I think the loss of your companionship does a great deal to make me nervous. I read the papers eagerly for news, but such as it is, is scant & unpleasant. With lots of love from the children & kisses too I am

Yours as ever
Meta

1. Berger introduced an unsuccessful resolution condemning Samuel Gompers as an ally of the interests of capital, but Berger was absent because of

illness when the resolution came before the convention. Berger also introduced resolutions relating to old-age pensions, state militias, AFL legal services, creation of a universal union label, industrial unions, relations with German trade unions, organization of working women, state insurance systems, and state labor federations.

2. lovingly.

Victor to Meta

New York, New York
March 4, 1906

My Dear Schatzl:

Had a very fine time at Noroton[1]—got acquainted with a new lot of people—William Kent[2] a radical wealthy reformer in Chicago, Peter Dunne[3] ("Mr. Doole") and Mr. Ridgeway[4] (publisher of Everybody's) were about the most interesting. Hope to meet some of them again.

Senator La Follette, Gov. Folk, Mayor Tom. Johnson[5] (Cleveland) were not there. Of course that was a little setback but the discussion was very lively anyway.

To my best knowledge I am going to leave here on Wednesday night—so you can confidently expect me on Friday.

Will leave for Bridgeport to-morrow. I do not expect to stay more than one day in my fathers house—in fact I have already engagements for both Tuesday & Wednesday.

Hope that you are well and the babies also. Have not received any letters from you—but I suppose they will not get there until Monday—the post office being locked on Sunday,—but I left there to-night (Sunday) and I am staying in New York with Hunter.[6] Told them in Noroton to forward letters to New York in charge of Brisbane.[7]

I am exceedingly tired Schatzl and that accounts for the dreary letter. "Aber ich habe Dich lieb"[8] and therefore you will forgive me.

With many kisses for you and babies

Your
V.L.B.

Best regards to Hattie

1. Berger attended a meeting of about twenty-five reformers at the summer home of Anson Phelps Stokes near Noroton, Connecticut. The meeting and Berger's role in it are described in Morris Hillquit, *Loose Leaves from a Busy Life* (New York, 1934), 56–59.

2. Chicago businessman William Kent (1864–1928) made a fortune in real estate and livestock before moving to California in 1907. He later served as a Progressive Republican and independent U.S. representative from California, 1911–1917, and on the U.S. Tariff Commission, 1917–1920.

3. Finley Peter Dunne (1867–1936), a journalist and humorist, worked for a number of Chicago newspapers prior to 1900, when he moved to New York

City. Dunne received national attention for his fictional character, Mr. Dooley, who commented on current affairs in a thick Irish brogue.

4. Erman J. Ridgeway (1867–1943) was president of the Ridgeway Company, which published *Everybody's Magazine*.

5. Robert M. La Follette Sr. (1855–1925), Joseph Wingate Folk (1869–1923), and Tom L. Johnson (1854–1911) were politicians known for their advocacy of progressive reforms. La Follette, a Republican, served as governor of Wisconsin, 1901–1906, and as a U.S. senator, 1906–1925. Folk, a reformist attorney, served as Democratic governor of Missouri, 1905–1909. Johnson, a Democrat and successful inventor and businessman, served as a U.S. representative from Ohio, 1891–1895, and as mayor of Cleveland, 1901–1909.

6. Robert Hunter (1874–1942), an affluent social worker and writer, declared himself a Socialist in 1905 and ran for governor of Connecticut on the Socialist ticket in 1910. He served on the party's National Executive Committee from 1909 to 1912 but resigned from the party in 1914 after war broke out in Europe.

7. Arthur Brisbane (1864–1936), a popular New York journalist who wrote for the Hearst newspaper chain from 1897 until his death, provided financial support for the *Milwaukee Leader* through loans and the purchase of stock. Berger named Brisbane Hall, the home of the *Leader,* after Arthur's father, utopian agrarian Albert Brisbane.

8. But I love you.

Victor to Meta

[en route to Colorado Springs, Colorado]
August 13, 1906

My Dear Schatzl:

I forgot to tell you in my other letter[1] that I received a very nice letter from Brisbane—with a clipping from the N.Y. Evening Telegram where a goodly portion of my last weeks editorial was quoted in the dispatches with a big three column title.[2] I was not aware that my editorials were wired to New York and I was rather surprised.

In his letter Brisbane tried to defend his position against my attacks—at the same time stating two–three times that if he had his choice he would rather be with me than with Hearst.[3] Of course he claims that Hearst is doing good work for the present, while I am doing good work for the future.

A representative of the *Saturday Evening Post* of Philadelphia (you remember we used to keep that paper some years ago) came to Milwaukee to interview me. The Post is going to run a series of interviews (*one* every week) and mine is to be one of them. The other men are to be Roosevelt, Bryan, Hearst, etc. You see I am beginning to get on in the world—if I only had a little more money. By-the-way I had to give the last photo I had of myself to the Herald.

I hope to find a long letter from you when I arrive in Colorado Springs. Ich habe Dich sehr lieb Schatzl[4] and I love to read your letters. Please kiss the babies for me. Ich umarme Dich im Geiste.[5]

Yours ever
V.LB.

Give my regards to the friends.

1. This was the second letter that Victor wrote to Meta while traveling to the International Typographical Union convention, held August 13–18, 1906, in Colorado Springs.
2. Berger criticized William Randolph Hearst for his opposition to socialism and praised Hearst editorial writer Arthur Brisbane in "Declares Hearst Runs Counter to His Papers," *New York Evening Telegram,* August 7, 1906.
3. William Randolph Hearst (1863–1951) built a national chain of newspapers and magazines and served as a Democratic congressman from New York, 1903–1907.
4. I love you very much, little darling.
5. I embrace you in spirit.

Victor to Meta

Minneapolis, Minnesota[1]
November 12, 1906

My Dear Schatzl:

Arrived here this morning after a tedious and dusty ride—my windows were open all night and my bed sheets had half an inch of dust on them,—and I am sorry to say, my overcoat also got "initiated".

I stop at a brand new hotel and pay for a nice and clean little room with bath 1.50 per day. The room is not an outside room, but the window is overlooking a house which is a story *lower,* so that it is *almost* as good as an outside room, it is facing the street. Barnes is stopping in the same hotel and has a similar room, and so has also Basenberg,[2] the delegate of the Milwaukee Federated Trades Council,—who *changed his ticket* at the depot from the "Pionier Limited" to the Wis. Central, in order to be able to *travel with me.* Poor fellow! I was sorry for him—he claimed that he "bumped the bumps" from Rugby Junction (near Milwaukee) to Minneapolis.

Sam Gompers read the longest report in his "carriere" this afternoon. It took him over three hours. He covered up the miserable failure of his "political action" very smoothly. But newspaper gossip has it, that he is facing defeat, and that John Mitchell[3] is to be his successor. I do not believe it. Gompers has his machine of well paid "general organizers" very much in evidence at this convention. And Mahlon Barnes saw Mitchell so fearfully *drunk* in a saloon this afternoon that he (Barnes) had to telephon for a cab to take Mitchell home. And while Gompers also gets very drunk often, he knows enough to keep sober when his scalp is in danger.

And now you know enough about the convention—for one day. If you want to know more read the Journal—that paper wired me to send them 200 words every day.

The comrade who came with me from Milwaukee told me that his little girl just got over the whooping cough. He told me that *elderberry* jam and *elderberry wine* (*non* alcoholic) very effectively relieved his little girl. You might try to get both at Steinmeyer's. He also recommended Blackberry cordial (non alcoholic) and as much fresh air as possible.

If Doris gets any worse do not fail, please, to *get* a *nurse* for night service. Get one that will know how to get into Doris' favor. Don't be stingy. I would rather spend every cent I have, and every cent I can borrow, than have you get sick too.

I am writing this letter in my room at night. I am very tired not having slept much last night. Someway-another I do not think so much of these conventions as I used to,—I find more or less the same lot of egotistic and selfseeking "labor leaders" at every convention. There are very few idealists among them. And what they do and what they say is of very little importance, although they nominally represent two million organized wage-workers.

If Brisbane should write a letter please forward it to me. You can send your letters either to the convention hall (Normanna Hall) or to the Hotel Majestic.

I wonder how things will get along in the office during my absence. Miss Thomas is very nervous—I believe she is on the verge of a collapse. I am very glad that she is going on a long vacation as soon as I return.

And as for you, my sweet Schatzl, I wish *you* could go on a *long vacation* too. Sometimes I think I ought to send you and the babies down South, even if I have to borrow the money. Then again I think it would be just as good to take you East to my folks—only this is their busiest season. We will talk that over when I get home.

Schatzl, ich hab Dich lieb![4] My love to the babies and Hattie.

Yours always
V.L.B.

1. Berger represented the Wisconsin State Federation of Labor at the AFL annual convention held in Minneapolis, November 12–24, 1906.

2. Edward H. Basenberg (b. 1870), a Milwaukee molder.

3. John Mitchell (1870–1919) served as president of the United Mine Workers Union, 1898–1908, second vice-president of the AFL, 1900–1914, and chairman of the New York Industrial Commission, 1915–1919.

4. Little darling, I love you!

Victor to Meta

Minneapolis, Minnesota

November 18, [1906]

My Sweet Schatzl:

I spoke in a Socialist meeting this afternoon—about 500 being present—and they all claimed that I made a very good speech. Owing to the splendid showing we made in Milwaukee I am the hero of the hour as far as the Minneapolis Socialists are concerned and although I took up more time than anybody else I was overwhelmed with applause.

Three of my resolutions came up Saturday forenoon, while I was absent from the hall. Duncan[1] had told me that none of them would be taken up before Monday or Tuesday. Queerly enough the committee reported in *favor* of all three, but they butchered the preamble of one of them.[2] Of course they did not improve the resolution any and there was a hot fight between the Socialists and the reactionary element. Especially Barnes pitched in with main and might. Needless to say that the report of the committee was adopted.

I hope the Schnuckies are a little better. Try and get some sleep during day-time as long as you have no nurse. Take a walk in the fresh air every day and take the children with you. If the lamp you spoke of does the children good, use it, and try to give them as much fresh air as possible during day-time. Off and on you might leave the lamp out so as not to injure your and the babies lungs.

I have had many sleepless nights since I am in Minneapolis. I am up late at night (often until 2 and 3 o'clock in the morning) and then I can't sleep. Expect a hot time next week when about a dozen of my resolutions will come up.

My standing in the convention is better than it was ever before. Only Gompers and his main lieutenants hate me *personally*. We have about 20 members of the party here, but we can count on twice that number as sympat[h]izing with our ideas.

Don't bother about not being able to read books. You keep up wonderfully. With the broken nights you have other people could not do one half of what you are doing. That is the reason why I want you to get a nurse—I do not [want] to wreck my sweet and good wife. I know that you are infinitely better than I am.

I will try and get home Sunday morning even if they do have a night session on Saturday. We have lost a good deal of time last week—simply with the mutual admiration of the would be big bugs.

You did not tell me whether Hattie sleeps over at our place and whether the babies are very cross? Tell Doris to write me all about it, but let her write the letter herself.

With love and kisses for all you and especially for *you,* my better half

I am yours ever
V.L.B.

1. James Duncan (1857–1928), served as first vice-president of the AFL, 1900–1928, and held various offices in the Granite Cutters' National Union.
2. Berger introduced resolutions calling for the popular election of judges, adoption of a graduated income tax and an inheritance tax, and the gathering of labor statistics by states. The convention approved all three resolutions but removed language referring to class conflict from the preambles of the first two.

Victor to Meta

Milwaukee, Wisconsin
July 22, 1907

My Dear Schatzl:

This was a busy week for me. I was way behind with my work, had to get out my papers and attend a convention[1] besides.

Well, you have seen that they have re-elected me a delegate to the convention of the American Federation of Labor. After one of the delegates—Handley[2] from the Machinist union—had made a speech claiming that while he was satisfied with my work, it was time to elect another man, else it would be said that the working men of Wisconsin had only one man capable of representing them,—I withdrew my name although I had been nominated by many unions. But the convention unanimously refused to permit me to withdraw. And I was re-elected with a big majority over both opponents—one of them a Milwaukee Social Democrat and supervisor of the 20th Ward (Jeske)[3]—having considerable more votes than both of them combined.

Well I am *not* proud of the achievement. I virtually had to pull myself together when I got there last Thursday—yet the Milwaukee Sentinel of last Sunday says that the spirit of Victor L. Berger ruled the convention and was particularly visible in every resolution.

But I am proud that I made the best and wittiest speech at the banquet and made it without any preparation.

Our picnic was absolute failure. It rained pitchforks all day and particularly in the afternoon and evening. Mr & Mrs. Stokes[4] were here, and so was Mr & Mrs Lloyd[5] who came from Chicago in an automobile. We had an automobile ride to Whitefish Bay in the evening where the company were my guests. They all stopped at the Pfister— Lloyds paying their own expenses of course,—while the hotel expenses of Stokes will be paid by the party, although he protested like a lawyer. He made a donation of $500 to the campaign-fund though which came very handy, since a note we owed the Machinist Union was due and the picnic a failure.

The picnic will be tried again on August 18th and I hope we will have good weather then.

I am glad to hear that the cottage[6] and the lot are in fairly good shape now. As to chairs—they will need *more than one* application of carbolineum—and that has to be done in a shady place, where the sun light does not strike the people using it. I would advise you to buy some cheap gloves in Shawano for that purpose. I would also suggest that you use the little can that had not been opened—because the other stood open to[o] long and it rained into it, I noticed that the carpenters did not even cork it up again.

Am very glad to hear that the babies can swim now. Now keep them in good practice until they will be as much in their element in water as they are on dry land.

I will send you a marked copy of the Racine Journal containing the report of the last days proceeding—you get the Sentinel anyway—and you can look up the Sunday edition.

I understand you were somewhat disappointed in the boat and so was I—when I got to Milwaukee and found a letter stating that "they did not know what I meant by a lazy back cane seat"—after they had offered to add it to the equipment of the boat—and although their catalogue contains it—not for this kind of a boat, of course.

Sweet Schatzl, it is getting dark and I want to go a meeting, and take this letter along and mail it down-town.

Hast Du mich lieb, süßes Schatzl?[7] With many kisses for you and babies dear Schatzl and my best regards to all I am always

Your Victor L.

1. The annual convention of the Wisconsin Federation of Labor met in Racine, July 17–20, 1907.

2. John J. Handley (1876–1941) worked as an organizer and business manager for the machinists union in Milwaukee, 1904–1910, served as secretary-treasurer of the Wisconsin State Federation of Labor, 1912–1941, and was a member of the Milwaukee Park Commission, 1918–1936.

3. Charles Jeske, a member of the stationary engineers union, served on the Milwaukee County Board of Supervisors, 1904–1910. The state convention elected Jeske as an alternate delegate to the 1907 AFL convention.

4. James Graham Phelps Stokes (1872–1960) and Rose Harriet Pastor Stokes (1879–1933) were prominent "millionaire socialists." Rose Pastor, an immigrant cigar maker and journalist who grew up in poverty, married the affluent Stokes in 1905. The couple joined the Socialist Party in 1906 but left it in 1917 because of its antiwar stand. Rose Stokes changed her mind about the war in 1918, rejoined the party, and left it again in 1919 to help found the Communist Party. The couple divorced in 1925.

5. William Bross Lloyd (1875–1946) and Lola Maverick Lloyd (1875–1944). William, millionaire son of Henry Demarest Lloyd, had been a member of the

Socialist Party since 1905. In February, 1919, he posted $125,000 of the $500,000 bond needed to free Berger and his four codefendants. Lloyd helped to form the Communist Labor Party in September, 1919. He was convicted on charges of sedition in 1920, but his one- to five-year sentence was commuted in 1922 after he served only eight days in prison. Lloyd became disillusioned with communism after his release from prison and within a decade became a conservative Republican. Lola was a peace and women's rights activist and a co-founder of the Women's International League for Peace and Freedom. The couple married in 1902 and divorced in 1916.

6. The Bergers purchased a cottage and boat in Shawano in northeastern Wisconsin, and Meta and their daughters spent much of each summer at the cottage.

7. Do you love me, sweet little darling?

Victor to Meta

Milwaukee, Wisconsin
August 20, [1907]

My Dear Schatzl:

Just got back from the convention—yesterday.[1] Left there on Friday at 1:30 PM. but a bridge was burned and they took our train all over Arkansas in order to bring it to Memphis. There we had missed the connection with the New Orleans train and the next New Orleans train was 4½ hours late, with the result that I did not get into Milwaukee until 5 PM. on Sunday. I just got into the park to see one of the biggest crowds we had ever gathered here—about 20,000 people. I missed Haywood's[2] speech, of course, he was just finishing it, when I got in, and I did not get within a block anyway, the crowd was too big.

I did not meet Haywood until to-day, when I took dinner with him at the hotel. He [is] a nice simple fellow who does not put on any airs on account of the great celebrity he has achieved on account of his trial.[3]

I will try to come next Saturday if I can make it possible. Sonbron promised to come next week—if he makes good I will be there.

You did not write me whether you had spoken to Walrich.[4] If you did not then leave the matter to me. I will fix it up when I get there.

Gertrude Breslau-Hunt[5] is here as the guest of Miss Thomas. And David Coates,[6] former Lieutenant-governor of Colorado came with Haywood. So there is [no lack] of prominent guests here at present.

I have missed about 100 hours sleep last week and I am very nervous. Therefore I must ask you to excuse my scribbling.

I am very glad to hear that the babies are making such good headway in swimming. I hope when I get there they will teach me.

Kiss the children for me and remember that I am ever my Schatzl's

V.L.B.

Dear Friend and children.

I am enjoying the hospitality of the "Berger" Flat wish I could have had the pleasure of meeting you, will leave for home in a day or two, with regrets at leaving Milwaukee come West and visit with your friend and comrade in Denver, With love to you all

Wm. D. Haywood "Bill"[7]

1. Berger had been in Little Rock, Arkansas, where he represented the Newspaper Writers Union at the annual convention of the International Typographical Union.

2. William Dudley "Big Bill" Haywood (1869–1928) was one of the founders of the IWW and became its leading spokesman. He served as an officer of the Western Federation of Miners and as a member of the Socialist Party's National Executive Committee until his removal in 1913 because of his advocacy of industrial sabotage. Because of his opposition to World War I, Haywood was arrested in September, 1917, convicted in August, 1918, and sentenced to twenty years in prison. In March, 1921, while free on bail, he fled to Russia, where he lived until his death.

3. Haywood had been acquitted the previous month of the murder of former Idaho governor Frank Steunenberg.

4. Michael J. Wallrich (1857–1941), a Shawano, Wisconsin, attorney and businessman, served as a Republican member of the Wisconsin Assembly, 1903–1905, and as mayor of Shawano, 1900–1906.

5. Gertrude Breslau Hunt was a Socialist and women's rights activist.

6. David C. Coates (1868–1933), a newspaper editor and union official, served in the Colorado House of Representatives, 1897–1899, and as the state's lieutenant governor, 1901–1903. After leaving Colorado in 1904, Coates published newspapers in Idaho, Washington, and North Dakota.

7. The postscript is in Haywood's hand.

Meta to Victor

Milwaukee, Wisconsin
November 12, 1907

Dear Papa:—

It is very late & I just got home from seeing "The Man of the Hour"[1] with Miss Thomas. And as you know what a consciencious girl I am, I could not go to bed without writing only a few words to you, dear, in place of my goodnight kiss.

Miss Thomas enjoyed the play immensely & said she was going to try & have the office force go too. I even enjoyed it again.

Miss Thomas said that you & the publishing company were threatened with another libel suit. She said she would write you the particulars. She said you would know if I mentioned it in my letter. It does not refer to the "Court article."

This morning the Sentinel had a cartoon of you & Gompers.[2] It wasn't exactly a thing of joy so I didn't show it to the children. And what do you think happened? At noon when little Doris came home from school she asked first thing for the Sentinel. I asked her why & she said some of the children in school told her that there was something in about her papa. Of course she didn't understand even after I had tried to explain the situation & only said that that was the poorest picture of you & why couldn't they make a better one.

You see dearie you will have to begin to be very careful what they bring of you in the papers.

The journal has brought nothing so far that you could have sent.

Elsa is still coughing & so is Jack[3] & myself but of course every thing takes time.

Now papa I want you to send all the postal cards & letters you can to me or the children or Hattie but you needn't send them to my neighbors. Their husbands are never attentive to me either. Besides you should think only of the girls and your devoted

Meta.

1. *The Man of the Hour* was a play by George H. Broadhurst (1866–1952) that told the story of a young mayor's efforts to combat corruption within a city's political machine. It was inspired by Lincoln Steffens's *The Shame of the Cities* (1904) and was based on New York's Tammany Hall.

2. The *Milwaukee Sentinel*, November 12, 1907, ran a front-page cartoon portraying Gompers and Berger as perspiring boxers with the caption "Victor L. Berger Had a Long Conference With Samuel Gompers but no Definite Conclusion Was Reached.—NEWS ITEM."

3. Jack Anderson (1899–1970), the son of Meta's sister, Paula Schlichting Anderson, lived with the Bergers from around the time of Paula's death in 1902 until about 1918. He later studied animal husbandry and held various positions with the federal and Louisiana state governments.

Victor to Meta

Norfolk, Virginia
November 14, 1907

My Sweet Schatzl:

These were strenuous days since Sunday. This afternoon (Thursday) I finally got all my resolutions[1] in. I put in seven, Hayes[2] took two, Feely 1, Schwab 1, Finger (N.Y.) 1, Grout (Cincinnati) 1,[3] etc. There were altogether nearly 20 of them.

The resolution pertaining to the restoration of the Brewery Workers I gave to Walker[4] of the Mine Workers, thereby I hope to line up the mine-workers delegation in favor of it.

I have never received as much attention in the press as this time. And not only in Norfolk. I was shown a Philadelphia paper with my picture in it,—I casually picked up a Richmond sheet, and there was my "photo" (and a very old one) side by side with the picture of Gompers.

The Norfolk Dispatch asked me this afternoon to go to a photographer to have my picture taken. I did so but told the artist not to expect that I will buy any.

The long conference with Gompers (which the Milwaukee papers reported as you say) actually took place on the steamer coming from Washington. It lasted until 2 o'clock in the morning and Gompers drank more whisky on that occassion than two average men could stand without getting delirium tremens. Needless to tell you that I had to drink some too, no matter how much I hate it. Sam grew to be rather confidential and loving, but of course he was not in a condition for serious business.

Yet the upshot of the matter was that I wrote a resolution[5] based upon his presidential report, and upon his pet idea that every international union is sovereign and has full control over its own affairs. The logical conclusion of this principle is that the American Federation of Labor has no right to co-erce any international union when it does not carry out the decision of the A. F of L.

I have taken a similar stand ever since the controversy started, and therefore it was easy for me (and at the same time very apropos) to quote from Gompers' report in my resolution.

I tell you all this because you seemed to be eager to know it, yet after all: it is small potato business. I have to help the Brewers because they are a progressive organization, and because there seems to be nobody here capable to take charge of their case.

And now tell me how sweet little darling Elsa feels? Of course from your letter I have learned that there is no danger, yet at the same time we have to be very careful. I wish sometimes I could send you all to Florida for the winter. If neccessary I will have to borrow the money to do so.

I am still walking around here without any over-coat. There were some rainy and chilly days here, yet many flowers are still in bloom and there [are] acres after acres planted with lettuce, and other green stuff. They tell me they send all these vegetables North. Virginia has a lovely climate.

I want you to take care of yourself sweet Schatzl. Do it for the children's sake, do it for my sake, and do it for your own sweet sake. You are my guardian angel, sweet Schatzl,—if I should lose *you,* I would not know what to do.

I will write you more often after this, but I was probably the busiest man in the convention until now. Tell the Schnuckies I will answer them separately. With kisses and love to *all*.

> Your
> V.L.B.

1. Berger, representing the Wisconsin Federation of Labor at the AFL annual convention, introduced resolutions regarding child labor, militia service, federal public works programs, old-age pensions, political action, women workers, and local trade unions.

2. Max S. Hayes (1866–1945), a delegate from the Cleveland United Trades and Labor Council at the convention and a member of the Socialist Party, edited the *Cleveland Citizen,* a weekly labor newspaper, from 1892 to 1939. He unsuccessfully challenged Gompers for the AFL presidency in 1912. Hayes left the Socialist Party in 1919 and was the vice-presidential candidate of the Farmer-Labor Party in 1920.

3. Thomas Feeley of Milwaukee (Milwaukee Federated Trades Council), William Schwab of Milwaukee (Iron Molders' Union), George Finger of New York City (Brotherhood of Painters), and A. B. Grout of Cincinnati (Metal Polishers, Buffers, Platers, and Brass Workers Union).

4. John H. Walker (1872–1955), a Socialist union leader from Illinois, served as a United Mine Workers of America district president, 1905–1913 and 1930–1933, and as president of the Illinois Federation of Labor, 1913–1930. Walker introduced a resolution drafted by Berger that restored the charter of the United Brewery Workmen, which had been revoked because of a jurisdictional dispute with the engineers', firemen's, and teamsters' unions. The convention adopted a substitute resolution, introduced by Samuel Gompers, that accomplished the same end.

5. Berger is referring to John Walker's resolution mentioned above.

Meta to Victor

> Milwaukee, Wisconsin
> November 14, 1907

Dear Papa—

Hattie has gone to a concert & I am home alone. The house is dreadfully quiet since you left, the telephone particularly is conspicuous for its silence. Today I spent about 3 hours at the dentist's office, also went to Dr. Hipke again and of course tonight I'm rather tired myself. I haven't even the patience to read the newspaper. That reminds me, yesterday, the Sentinel stated that you were sudpoenad (I don't know how to spell it) to appear as a witness to testify as to the character of Chas. Pfister.[1] I was very glad indeed that you were out of town & that they couldn't find you. It wouldn't have been very pleasant to testify in that case. Your party would surely expect you to tell of his crookedness. Yet strange to say, not one person has been found to say that he was a briber. David Rose[2] was on the stand today & under fire. But he is smooth & wouldn't be trapped. I'll save you the papers.

The papers say little about the convention. Is there nothing doing?

The children still cough altho' I think it is lessening some now. My throat tonight feels like a new attack of tonsilitis, altho' I've been very careful. Wish you were home to baby me a bit. The children love me to be sure but they never show it. At least not in a way to be appreciated by me.

Doris got a nice little german letter from your mother. Be sure to go there as she is expecting you. She says we are all to come to the golden wedding but I don't see how we are going to do it. It costs so dreadfully much.

Both children are looking for a letter. You should see how disappointed they were when cards & no letter came for them. I am sorry you lost your pen, but better that than your health. With lots & lots of love

Meta

1. Charles F. Pfister (1859–1927), an influential Milwaukee businessman, owned the *Milwaukee Sentinel* from 1900 until 1924 and used it to support conservative Republican causes. Pfister won $15,000 in damages in a libel suit against the *Milwaukee Free Press,* which had charged that he had bribed city officials.
2. David Rose (1856–1932), a flamboyant and controversial lawyer and Democratic politician, served as mayor of Milwaukee, 1898–1906 and 1908–1910. Although Rose avoided prosecution, charges of graft during his administration led to the Socialist victory of 1910.

Victor to Meta

Norfolk, Virginia
November 18, 1907

My Dear Schatzl:

To-day was one of my "bad" days. The resolution pertaining to political action[1] was ruled out of order by Gompers and my resolution asking union men to refrain from service in the militia was voted down[2]—and only one—the old age pension resolution[3] was accepted conditionally that is it was referred to the Executive Council for action with the instruction to report a plan at the next convention.

By my championship of the Brewers I have earned the displeasure of the Irish labor leaders favoring the Engineers, Firemen and Teamsters who want to cut pieces out of Brewers International union. Some of them were drunk and they enjoyed themselves with all kind of noises while I spoke. But Gompers did not see it fit to call them to order.

But enough of that. On Saturday night I will leave for Philadelphia and from there to New York. Someway-another I feel that I ought to cut my visit as short as possible and go back to Milwaukee to my babies and my sweet Schatzl who is lonesome. And sitting here in my room and working over a speech for to-morrow—because some more of my resolutions will come up—I feel very lonesome too. I have never been made to feel that I am a fool for working with these people and for these people so much, as I was this time. May be—I am getting tired and sore.

I notice the Milwaukee papers are saying very little about the convention. It seems the Associated Press is inclined to boycott the affair, and I do not blame the capitalist press.

Well, sweetheart, you and my mother may have been right in more than one thing, but I simply did what I thought I ought to do. Yet, I have also made up my mind firmly to take care of you and the babies before I die—and I am going to do it.

Just look out for your health and for the Schnuckies—I will surely make good with you—even if I could not make good with the movement as I intended.

With many kisses
V.L.B.

1. Berger introduced a resolution calling on the AFL to organize politically along class lines. Gompers ruled the resolution out of order because the AFL constitution forbade partisan activity.
2. See Meta to Victor, November 20, 1907, below.
3. In the conventions of 1902, 1904, 1905, and 1906, Berger introduced and the AFL rejected resolutions calling for federal old-age pensions. The convention endorsed the idea in 1907 and instructed the executive council to report a plan for obtaining legislation.

Meta to Victor

Milwaukee, Wisconsin
November 20, 1907

Dear Papa:—

Just a few lines to let you know that my thoughts as well as my sympathy & love are with you for I see by the paper that you have had a hard time of it with your fire-arms resolution.[1] I put the paper away so that Hattie, Josie & the children didn't see it. For myself I don't care.

But the question arose in my mind for the —th time whether the rabble, the very gang at the convention and all the others are worth the sacrifices you make for them. I don't think so and never never will. And

I believe in Socialism too, only it can't be hurried into or forced down people's throat before they are ready for it.

I got another love-missive from the Shawano Lumber Co. in which they threaten to draw a draft against you. Perhaps you had better write them or is it all-right. My letter & their last one crossed each other. So they know now you are east.

Miss Kluckow[2] is here sewing for Hattie & Carl Sch.[3] will be up tonight. The children of course are glad of it.

They all cough a little yet. Elsa is getting better while Doris seems to be getting worse. I didn't go to the German theatre tonight as I don't care to see Magda by the leading lady of the Pabst Co. So this week I'll stay at home all week, fighting & loving the kids by turns. I might make one exception & go to Ferrullo Friday provided I can get Arch[4] to accompany Hattie & myself. This is there last week here.

I suppose my next letter I can address to New York c/o of Arthur Brisbane. I'll be glad to as that means the time is near where my poor poor papa will be back home with us again. Please don't forget to write oftener when the convention is over. With love & kisses from us all I am your

Meta.

1. The *Milwaukee Journal*, November 19, 1907, ran a front-page story headlined "Fun with Berger," which reported that AFL convention delegates ridiculed Berger by popping paper bags when he presented his resolution calling on union members not to serve in the militia.

2. Emma Kluckow, a Milwaukee dressmaker.

3. Carl Schweers (1904–1959) became the stepson of Meta's sister, Hattie, following her marriage to Frank Schweers. Carl later worked as a funeral director in Shawano, Wisconsin.

4. Archibald Anderson (1861–1936), a Milwaukee salesman, was the widowed husband of Meta's sister, Paula. Anderson's son, Jack, lived with the Bergers.

Victor to Meta

Norfolk, Virginia
November 21, 1907

My Schatzl:

By this time you will probably know that all of a sudden and within 24 hours I changed from being the most hated man of the convention into the most popular. And without any fault of mine either. I simply used the psychological moment to set the socialist position right and I did it without mental reserve or diplomacy. Just on the spur of the moment. It would be impossible for me to describe the scene. They cheered like maniacs for about six minutes and I could not have made a speech if I had tried.

The Brewery workers got their charter back this afternoon and I got a great deal of credit for it, because I really worked hard for them, although my resolution was not adopted, but a substitute introduced by Sam Gompers.

However I am tired of the convention, although there [are] four more of my resolutions that will come up to-morrow and Saturday. I intend to leave here Saturday night, provided we have no night session.

By-the-way, it may interest you that I have not seen the Fair at all so far, but I do intend to steal away to-morrow afternoon and spend the afternoon and evening out there. A reporter of an evening paper here who took a great liking to me on account of my fearless stand in the convention, will act as my guide.

I have not found time yet to write to my sweet Schnuckies (or anybody in Milwaukee) excepting you. I am afraid you sent Elsa to school too soon, if she is still coughing, but you must judge that for yourself best.

I had a very nice letter from Mr Edmond Kelly[1] which had gone to Milwaukee and was sent to me by Miss Thomas. I will answer that letter tomorrow and I will also write a letter to Brisbane and to Miss Thomas.

I have sent you a few papers that were lying around here. As I told you I have received more attention from the press this time than ever before.

My sweet Schatzl, I want you to take good care of yourself, so that you can go with me next time. This convention you would have enjoyed more than any other before, just think of it—there were several men who came to me to tell me that they felt "like hugging" me.

And the only person that I felt like hugging was far, far away.

My love to all.
V.L.B.

1. Edmond Kelly (1851–1909) was a New York lawyer, political reformer, and author.

Victor to Meta

New York, New York
November 29, 1907

My Dear Schatzl:—

This letter I write at Kelly's.[1] Had luncheon here and am going to stay for dinner. They have invited quite a party in my honor. His wife seems to be a very sweet woman.

But the truth of the matter is—I am very tired. I have not had much sleep since I left home. My nights are abominable.

After I left Norfolk, I stopped in Philadelphia—found there was very little of any party and what there is has a strong "impossibilistic"[2] tinge.

Find the same thing in New York. Only they are also fighting like cats and dogs among themselves. There is an uproar against the Mailly-Hilquit ring.

Brisbane received me very cordially. I stayed at Hempstead since Wednesday evening i.e. I came in yesterday and had lunch and a talk with Alexander Jonas.[3] Found Jonas very much of the same opinion as I am, but the man is 74 years old, and cannot do very much anymore.

This morning I came into town and took a room at the Manhattan Hotel—just one night. Telephoned to both Stokes and Hunter—who are in Connecticut. Hunter was out, but Stokes will come to town to-morrow and we will lunch together i.e. Brisbane, Strobell,[4] Hunter, Weeks[5] and possibly some more if they happen to run up against me.

Tell Miss Thomas that I hunted up Miss O'Reilly[6] on thanksgiving day, but found her out. But Mrs. Thursby[7] (Brisbane's sister) is going to invite her out to dinner to-morrow. So I will meet her at Hempstead and possibly also at the opera tomorrow, for which Brisbane wants to provide a box.

So you see I am going some.

On the other hand I must say my comrades here are a most discouraging lot. Just think of it—while the convention at Norfolk was the biggest ever held and the first where the Socialists ever made friends with the "pure and simplers" the Socialist press—including N.Y. Worker, Volkszeitung and Chicago Socialists—joined in the "conspiracy of silence" instituted by the Associated press.

And there is no excuse for it as far as the Worker is concerned because I know that two copies of the local Daily papers were sent to John Chase every day.

But enough of that. With all the dining and wining I will be a very happy man when I get home again—with my sweet Schatzl and my dear children. I will have lots to tell you and also promise you that I will try to make some money even if I have to let a good deal of the movement slip out of my hands.

Sunday I will go to Connecticut and stay there all afternoon night and part of the forenoon and then leave them about noon on Monday. I will tell them that my *next* visit will be devoted to the family—at least mainly so.

I hope to find you and all the folks in the best of health. Will write you another letter from Bridgeport although I hardly think that you will have time to answer this one.

Take good care of yourself darling, and remember that in all my travels I have not found a woman that is in any way your equal—taking it all in all

With great deal of love
Your
V.L.B.

1. Berger was writing from the home of Edmond and Edith Thuresson Kelly.

2. *Impossibilist* was a term of derision applied to Socialists who opposed political action and believed that the party should restrict its activities to the circulation of propaganda.

3. Alexander Jonas (1834–1912), a New York journalist and socialist activist, founded the *New Yorker Volkszeitung* in 1878 and served as its editor until 1889.

4. George H. Strobell (1854–1925), a jewelry manufacturer and the brother-in-law of Henry Demarest Lloyd, helped to finance the Intercollegiate Socialist Society following its establishment in 1905.

5. Rufus Wells Weeks (1846–1930), an actuary with New York Life Insurance Company, helped to finance the Intercollegiate Socialist Society.

6. Leonora O'Reilly (1870–1927) was a New York labor leader who taught at the Manhattan Trade School for Girls and served on the board of the National Women's Trade Union League. She became a Socialist in 1910.

7. Alice Brisbane Thursby (1860?–1953), the widowed sister of Arthur Brisbane, lived with her brother prior to his marriage in 1912.

Victor to Meta

Milwaukee, Wisconsin
July 13, 1908

My Dear Schatzl:

I stayed over in Chicago until yesterday (Sunday) and thus I received three of your letters at the same time. I had quite a treat reading them.

Debs is going to have a special train for sixty days in this election, made up of a private car, a day coach, a dining car and a baggage car.[1] The train will stop at 3 or 4 places every day and will cost about $30,000. A music band will be on the train, also a secretary, a manager and some newspaper correspondents.

I came up with Debs from Chicago to the picnic. You probably know by this time that the affair was a great success—there were over 25,000 paid admission tickets passed in.

Lincoln Steffens[2] was here to interview Debs for Everybodys Magazine. He (Lincoln Steffens) took lunch with me at Blatz park—the interview was gotten up in our house and was practically as much of an interview with me as with Debs. Mrs. Heath[3] who came in with Fred Heath[4] was so kind to go down to Uebelhacks and prepare a lunch for the company. Steven Reynolds[5] and Margaret Haile were also here. The entire crowd left this morning. In one way I was glad that you were not here to have all that extra work.

So much for the Picnic.

There is a little hitch in the sale of the lot. You see, Schatzl, I have the lot on a land contract, and I agreed to furnish the deed and receive the money on July 20th. Now Mr. Brown[6] is absent from the city on a vacation;—he is in Maine and they do not expect him to return before July 25th. I went to [the] agent (Mr Green)[7] who consumated the deal and told him about that—at the same time offering to release the other party, since I am not anxious to sell the lot for $6,000. But he said that the five days more or less would not make any difference to his client who is anxcious to get the lot. However I wrote to Mr Brown and his secretary sent him a blank to fill out for a deed—so there will [be] no trouble anyway because I believe we will get the deed here before the 20th of this month.

Miss Thomas will leave here on Wednesday noon. I will buy the book on birds and send it along with her. You are not to speak to her about the sale of our lot.

I will collect your rents in person this month and devote part of to-morrow to that duty. Next month Koll[8] can do it.

I may not be able to go up to Shawano until July 25th in case the deed is not made out before that time. Then I will also pay the Wolf River Paper Co for the brick.

The cottage I consider a very good investment and not only because we will get a good price for it when we should decide to sell it. It is an excellent investment because it will build up the good health of my Schatzl and my babies,—and I believe it is an excellent thing for Hattie, Jack and Ernst[9] also. By-the-way, I have seen or heard nothing from Ernie since my return from Shawano.

Annie preserved some more fruit. She takes good care of the rooms now.

I have no time to be home-sick. The last four days of this week I am expected to spend in Fond du Lac where the annual convention of the State Federation of Labor will be in session. I doubt however whether I can spare so much time from my papers.

I am very glad to hear that Zachow's[10] and Wallrich's[11] are so friendly to you. We will have to be good to Margaret Zachow when she will be in town.

Do not worry a bit about me. Now since the big lot is sold and most all of our debts will be paid—we will both have it considerably nicer.

You did not say a word about money. Will send you a check for $25 by the end of this week.

I hope the children will continue to enjoy their vacation and the lake. Have they improved any in their swimming?

We had some very hot days here. Especially the two days and three nights in Chicago were scorchers. To-night it is cooler.

Within ten days or so I hope to be in Shawano again. Und dann will ich mein Schatzl auch so recht lieb halten.[12]

With love to all
Your
V.L.B.

1. Socialist Party presidential candidate Eugene V. Debs visited more than three hundred communities in thirty-three states between late August and election day on a chartered train called the Red Special. Debs received more than 420,000 votes in the election, an increase of only about 18,000 over his showing in 1904.

2. Lincoln Steffens (1866–1936), an independently wealthy free-lance journalist, wrote muckraking works for popular magazines. After 1917 he became an advocate for Soviet Russia, although he never joined the Communist Party. His interview with Berger and Debs appeared in "Eugene V. Debs on What the Matter Is in America and What to Do about It," *Everybody's Magazine* 19 (October 1908): 455–469. The article contrasts Debs's views with those of the more conservative Berger.

3. Elizabeth H. Dorethy Heath (1873–1958), the wife of Frederic F. Heath.

4. Frederic F. Heath (1864–1954), a Milwaukee journalist and Socialist politician, worked as an artist for the *Milwaukee Sentinel*, 1888–1900, and the *Milwaukee Journal*, 1900–1901; edited the *Social-Democratic Herald*, 1902–1913; and served as a reporter and editorial writer for the *Milwaukee Leader*, 1913–1933. Heath held several local offices, including alderman, 1904–1906, school board member, 1909–1910, and county supervisor, 1910–1948.

5. Stephen Marion Reynolds (1849–1948), a Terre Haute, Indiana, attorney, served on the Socialist Party's National Executive Committee in 1905.

6. James P. Brown (b. 1860), a Milwaukee real estate agent.

7. Nathanael Greene (1872–1945), a Milwaukee real estate agent.

8. Fritz Koll (b. 1857), a Milwaukee bill collector.

9. Ernst Schlichting, Meta's brother.

10. William C. Zachow (1857–1939), a Shawano, Wisconsin, banker and business leader, his wife, Mary (b. 1866?), and their daughter, Margaret (Rollman) (b. 1889).

11. Michael J. and Gertrude Wallrich (b. 1866) of Shawano, Wisconsin.

12. And then I will hold my little darling so very lovingly.

Victor to Meta

Milwaukee, Wisconsin
August 30, 1908

My Dear Schatzl:

I am very much surprised to hear that you have received no let-ters—I have written you two and I do not understand why you should not get them. One of the letters I took to the post office myself—on Wednesday I believe.

Now my busy time commences—we are only eight weeks from elec-tion. And I will have to divide my energies between the national, state and county campaigns. Have written one national leaflet already and I expect to write two state and six local leaflets. In the meeting this morn-ing I was given charge of the literature-department but practically I will have to manage the campaign as usual.

You no doubt have seen my interview in last Saturday's Journal giv-ing McGovern[1] credit for what he has done as district attorney. This is a very unusual performance right on the eve of a primary election—and doubly so coming from a Social Democrat. But McGovern deserves the praise and we have no special interest in a primary election—having nominated our Ticket by a referendum. Besides I distinctly say that I will vote our ticket and that I expect every member of our party to do the same.[2] However we have many thousand voters who are not party-members in the strict sense of the word and it may help him with those, in fact I am sure it will help him. And in spite of all that I do not believe that he will get the nomination, Stephenson[3] the biggest money bag will in all probability get it. However he may carry Milwaukee county at the primary—and the radical half-Breeds being turned down in the state will be very sore. They will give a willing ear to our propaganda, especially after I had proven my good will towards them as I did.

But I will not bother you with politics.

I do not know Schatzl, whether our house, particularly the north side of it, can stand another winter without being painted. Hemlock must be kept well in paint or it will rot. Of course when I say paint I mean creozot stain. We will decide this when I come up.

As to the bears—a bear never attacks a man unless he believes him-self threatened or he has cubs. But it is wiser not to let the children go into the woods alone (from every point of view), because they might lose their way or eat something they ought not to eat.

Judging from the samples of leaves you have sent me, the woods must be beautiful indeed. What a pity that the place is not nearer

Milwaukee so that I could go out every Friday night. Someday we will have to sell or trade our cottage anyway for that reason.

What you told about Walrich is rather interesting, because Zachow is interested in Walrich's railroad and a director I believe.[4] Well, they will become the best of friends again when there will be some chance to make a deal together.

I am being written up in the magazines in great style and I expect every day that some of them will ask me for articles. And then we will begin to make a little money, Schatzl.

By-the-way, I was put up for assembly in our district and this time I will see to it that I am elected.[5]

Otherwise there is not much news here. Kiss the babies for me and remember that you are my sweet Schatzl. My love to Hattie.

Ever yours
V.L.B

1. Francis McGovern (1866–1946), a progressive Republican, successfully prosecuted corrupt government officials while serving as Milwaukee County district attorney, 1905–1909. He served as governor of Wisconsin, 1911–1915.
2. Berger chose his words carefully in the interview, having been removed from (and later restored to) his seat on the Socialist Party's National Executive Committee in 1905 because of his endorsement of a Republican candidate in a Milwaukee judicial election. For Berger's interview, see "Berger on M'Govern," *Milwaukee Journal*, August 29, 1908.
3. Isaac Stephenson (1829–1918), a wealthy Wisconsin Republican lumberman, served as a U.S. representative, 1883–1889, and as U.S. senator, 1907–1915. As Berger predicted, Stephenson won the Republican senatorial primary in 1908.
4. Meta had written to Victor about a lawsuit involving Shawano businessmen Michael Wallrich and William Zachow. See Meta to Victor, August 23, 1908, Berger Papers, SHSW.
5. Berger finished second in his campaign for the Wisconsin Assembly, receiving 1,668 votes to 1,722 for Republican Peter F. Leuch and 1,206 for Democrat Gerhard Ausen.

Meta to Victor

[Milwaukee, Wisconsin]
February 4, 1909

My dear Papa:

When I arrived home after seeing you off at the train I put my bundles down & Josie unwrapped my parcel with Steffen's address on it & of course it got lost. I'm so sorry. But you see I'll chance it & hope that the letter will reach you anyhow. I went to the theatre in the evening, & while there noticed how care-free, happy, & chatty the other young women were & compared them with me. I made up my mind not to grow old before my time & to force myself too, to be chatty etc. But going home I was again taken dreadfully sick, got out & walked & vomited etc. All my good resolutions I gave up too. I've come to the conclusion that that trouble saps all my energy, my ambition & keeps me the tired, sleepy in animate thing that I am.

Well now tell me how did your speech come off? Did you do it well? Were the others interested? How were the other speakers? It seems only where you are concerned am I really ambitious. I want you always to make use of every such opportunity. How I wish I could have been with you. Those are the only real pleasures I've had. The theatre you know is only a passing show. But your successes are real true pleasure & gratification. You sometimes think I'm not interested but that shows how little men & busy men think of women or understand them. The one thing that has been a sort of compensation for all and an inspiration has been your success & from now on you must never never pass up good opportunities whenever you can possibly make use of them.

Please tell Mr. & Mrs Steffen's[1] how sorry I am not to have been able to see them this time. If you see Mrs D'Orsay[2] remember me kindly to them.

With my very best regards to your host & hostess & with lots & lots of love for you dearie

I am

Your very proud

Meta.

Give my love to your parents too.

1. Josephine Bontecou Steffens (1856?–1911) married Lincoln Steffens in 1891.
2. Harriet D'Orsay was a Socialist organizer from Lynn, Massachusetts.

Victor to Meta

Boston, Massachusetts

February 6, 1909

My Dear Schatzl:

These were busy days for me. I had three times as many invitations as I could possibly accept and the Steffens'es were simply lovely to me.

My lecture came off all right. There was only one difficulty. On Friday evening I was invited by Prof. Emily G. Balge[1] (Wellesly College) who seemed to be behind the entire affair, to a little dinner at some woman's club, where I met Dean Hodge[2] and John Spargo[3] and Prof. Vida Scudder.[4] There I was told by the dean—he is the dean of Harvard University that I would have to cut my lecture down to thirty minutes. Now just imagine—give the history of Socialism in this world in thirty minutes. And I only had ten minutes time to re-arrange the lecture. Well I simply had to slash things—but I explained to audience the difficulties under which I was laboring and I must say I met a very responsive and appreciative crowd. I was told afterwards that the audience was made up mainly of well-to-do people and hardly any socialists among them.

Today I had lunch at the Twentieth Century Club and dinner in Longwood at the home of Miss Perkins[5]—the lady who had invited me to stay at their house.

Russell,[6] Hillquit, Irvine[7] and Spargo have spoken here besides me—and altogether the affair seems to be considered a great success, although the press is *not* responsive. One paper even remarked that I looked like "one of the men whom Lincoln called the plain people" and that I had a strong German accent.[8] However I seemed to have taken with the audience, because they have swarmed around me all day, telling me how much they have enjoyed my speech.

To-morrow, Schatzl, or rather today (for it is two o'clock in the morning) I shall leave for Bridgeport; expect to get there about 3 o'clock in the afternoon. I have to close this letter because my pen is running dry, and I am so sleepy that I *can hardly keep my eyes open.*

Kiss the babies for me and take good care of yourself,—always remember that you and the babies are after all the only valuable possessions I have in this world.

With lots of kisses
Your loving
VLB

1. Emily Greene Balch (1867–1961) taught economics at Wellesley College until 1918, when she lost her position because of her opposition to World War I. She later became active in the Women's International League for Peace and Freedom and received the Nobel Peace Prize in 1946.

2. Rev. George Hodges (1856–1919) had been dean of the Episcopal Theological School at Cambridge, Massachusetts, since 1894. Berger mistakenly thought that the school was part of Harvard University.

3. John Spargo (1876–1966), a British socialist who emigrated to the United States in 1901, wrote extensively about socialism and child poverty and served on the Socialist Party's National Executive Committee. Spargo resigned from the party in 1917 because of its opposition to World War I and eventually became a Republican.

4. Julia Vida Dutton Scudder (1861–1954), a Christian socialist, taught English at Wellesley College from 1887 to 1928.

5. Probably Agnes Frances Perkins (1875–1959), a women's rights supporter who taught English at Wellesley College, 1906–1944.

6. Charles Edward Russell (1860–1941), a muckraking journalist, joined the Socialist Party in 1908 and ran for office four times on its New York ticket. Russell supported American involvement in World War I and left the party in 1917, but he remained active in reform causes.

7. Alexander Fitzgerald Irvine (1863–1941) was a New York Congregational minister who lost his post in 1910 because of his socialist views.

8. Berger and John Spargo were the principal speakers at a conference on "Socialism as a World Movement" that opened on February 5. See the *Boston Globe*, February 6, 1909, for the reference to Berger's appearance and accent.

Victor to Meta

London, England
[October 5, 1909]

My Sweet Schatzl:

I found your very welcome letter in the office of "Justice". Also a letter from Brisbane and one from Miss Thomas.

Schatzl—you have no idea how much of a blessing you are to me, I just devour your letters—wish you were with me when I am awake and dream of you at night time.

And what a place London is![1] I have never seen anything like it. While there may be more rush in New York or Chicago—London is simply unique in its way.

I met the national secretary[2] of the "Independent Labour Party of Great Brit." this morning and he took me around this morning for a few hours. Tomorrow I will hire a "taxi-cab" for six hours and both of us are going to see London—he is a born Londoner you know and, therefore he is just as anxious as I—he claims that he does not know much about London and that he is glad of the chance to learn something about it.

He made dates for me to meet the Labor members of Parliament— some odd fifty—tomorrow. For Thursday I have an appointment with Hyndman.[3] Everybody here in Socialist circles seems to know me by name and reputation—however they seem inclined to ascribe the success of the Milwaukee movement to the fact that the "city is German".

I am glad to hear that my Schnuckies are well and that my sweet darling Schatzl is busy. You must diet Jack—don't give him much meat.

With love to all and especially to *my sweet Schatzl*

V.LB.

1. Berger traveled to Europe to attend the Brussels meeting (November 6–8) of the International Socialist Bureau, which prepared the agenda for the 1910 Copenhagen Congress of the Second International. During his two-month stay, Berger also visited Great Britain, Austria-Hungary, France, and Germany.

2. Probably Francis Johnson, who served as general secretary of the Independent Labour Party beginning in 1903.

3. Henry Mayers Hyndman (1842–1921), an English socialist journalist, founded the Democratic Federation (later the Social Democratic Federation), which merged with other organizations to form the British Socialist Party in 1909.

Victor to Meta

Berlin, Germany
October 13, [1909]

My Sweet Schatzl:

Had tooth ache today and went to a dentist with Kautsky.[1] Before that I attended a meeting of the "Vorstand" (Executive Board) of the German Social Democracy—or rather that meeting was suspended for about half an hour in order to give the members a chance to meet me. I am invited to Bebel[2] for to-morrow (Thursday) night and to dinner to Kautsky on Friday. Had lunch with Mr. & Mrs. Kautsky[3] to day. Saturday I will spend with Bernstein.[4]

Met Bebel, Singer, Molkenbuhr, Pfannkuch[5] and all the big men of the German Social Democracy of course. Kautsky acted as my guide all day and will do so again to-morrow. Also met the members of the editorial staff of the Berlin Vorwaerts.

I have not prepared a single line for my speech on Friday night. However I feel that I will make a *howling success* of it, if I get rid of my tooth ache. Of course, I am in a rather delicate position, since there seems to be a sort of a soreness between the big trade unions leaders of Germany and, the party leaders because Gompers had been invited to speak. The trades union leaders admit their mistake, only they don't want to "have it rubbed in" on them. Will see the chief of the trades unions of America tomorrow at 11 o'clock.

But enough of all this. I am tired enough to drop—and while I am lionized and made very much of, I wish I had my sweet Schatzl with me. I feel in the evening that I want to go home to my mamma and to my Schnuckies—and the only substitute I get is an occassional letter from my Schatzl—i.e. to day I got two of them at the same time from London.

What good, dear, noble and sweet woman you are. You did right in telling Doris what you did tell her, and since you had to tell Doris, you were of course also compelled to tell Elsa. I have no doubt that you found the proper form and words for the occassion—you *always* do.

So far I have not written a line to anybody in Europe or America— excepting to my Schatzl. However I feel that I owe at least twenty five letters and I shall have to go to it. I also feel that I owe something to my paper and to the noble comrades in Milwaukee who helped me to make this trip. Therefore I have quite made up my mind that I shall devote the first rainy day to letter writing and letter writing exclusively.

Kiss my Schnuckies and Jack for me, and imagine yourself kissed by your Schatzl a hundred times.

VLB

1. Karl Kautsky (1854–1938), a leading theorist of the German Social Democratic Party, edited the Marxist journal *Die neue Zeit*. He defended orthodox Marxism against the revisionist wing led by Eduard Bernstein.

2. August Bebel (1840–1913) was one of the co-founders of the German Social Democratic Party. He served in the German Reichstag almost continuously from 1867 until his death.

3. Luise Ronsperger Kautsky (1864–1944) was the second wife of Karl Kautsky. They married in April, 1890, and had three sons, two of whom were later imprisoned by the Nazis. Luise, a Jew, died in Auschwitz.

4. Eduard Bernstein (1850–1932) was the leader of the revisionist or evolutionary wing of the German Social Democratic Party, which rejected revolutionary Marxism in favor of moderate constitutional reform.

5. Paul Singer (1844–1911), Hermann Molkenbuhr (1851–1927), and Wilhelm Pfannkuch (1841–1923) were prominent members of the German Social Democratic Party.

Victor to Meta

Dresden, Germany
October 19, 1909

My Sweet Schatzl:

I am in Dresden and expect to stay here until to-morrow night.

These were memorable days I lived in Berlin. To begin with I made a *bigger hit there* than I made anywhere or at any time. I spoke without notes—i.e. I referred to them only for dates and figures—and the speech took finally. The hall was over-crowded, but whenever anybody dared to whisper a remark to a friend there was an indignant pst! all around him. I did not notice it, being taken up with my speech, but my friends so reported. This also goes to *prove* that my friends the unusual interest the people took in my remarks.

So much for the speech—a copy of which you will no doubt have in Milwaukee by this time, because I told the manager of the Berlin Vorwaerts to send you a copy of the paper. Besides Kautsky (they call him the "pope" of socialism) told me that the *entire Socialist press* of Germany will reprint the speech.

However my reception by the leaders was even more remarkable. Both Kautsky and Bernstein—the first the "theoretical exponent" or rather the standard bearer of the radicals in the Social Democratic party—, and Bernstein, the foremost writer of the "Revisionists" (so called because they want to "revise" some of the doctrines of Karl Marx)—vied with each other in their attentions to me. As it happened I was in the main the guest of Kautsky who had arranged the lecture for me.

I was invited to a dinner at August Bebel who is suffering from heart disease and does not go out much any more, being 70 years besides being sick. He felt very spry that night and drank some wine in honor of his American guest to whom he took a great liking—as I was told by Kautsky. The old man also gave me his picture with his signature.

I met all the leaders of the German party—or at least all those that were in Berlin at the time. However most of them I met only for a few minutes, like Singer for instance.

Kautsky has a very nice wife—a lady about my age who writes—and also translates books from English and French into German. Two of her sons attend the University of Berlin and since she fell in love with the *pictures* of *our Schnuckies,* she proposed that they marry her sons. She sends a little present for each of the Schnuckies and also sends her best regards to you.

I left Berlin on Monday morning and spent last night and to-day until 4 o clock P.M. in looking over Leipsic. Enclosed find a picture of the Volkshaus in Leipsic—a sort of a trade-union office building with a restaurant, a big hall and various small halls a cafe—and a "herberge" (a cheap boarding house for union-men traveling from place to place). Everything very nice and very clean—the building cost them in Leipsic over 1,000,000 Mark—the building in Hamburg was still more expensive. I have no idea what the "Gewerkschafts Haus"[1] in Berlin is valued at.

This is the first time that I was really "snubbed" in Germany and of course it was done by my country-men—the Americans. When I got into Dresden to-night I decided to leave my things at the depot and to take the next hotel on the way. It happened to be very swell place, although I pay only 4M.50pf.—that means about a dollar for the room.

However when I got into the dining room the girlies were dressed in white and the men in full dress—and one of the sweet creatures (she looked too sweet to live all paint and powder) rather audibly remarked to her young man in English that I (meaning me) looked like a coach-man. I was mean enough, not to take notice the general consternation, but to look very happy and smiling and after a while I also asked the waiter in *English* all about the location of Socialist papers in Dresden, incidentally dropping the remark that the party had been making terrific progress of late in America.

All of this is very funny—but I wish I were home with my sweet Schatzl and my Schnuckies. For go where I may—I have not seen or met a woman like my sweet Schatzl, so good, so lady-like, so sweet and so exceedingly fitted to be the mate of me. Does distance lend enchantment? Answer your

V.L.B.

1. union hall.

Meta to Victor

Milwaukee, Wisconsin
October 27, 1909

My darling Papa:—

Just after I mailed my letter to you, telling you I was disappointed in your little letters, I received your nice long letter from Berlin, telling me all about Kautzke, Bernstein, Bebel, Singer, etc etc. That's the kind I like & furthermore you were loving to me in it. God knows I need it. If you want me to stay sweet & noble & etc. you are the one that can make me be it & stay it. You are in fact responsible for myself & my whole disposition. You can mold my character according to your desires, you can make or unmake me. When I was only a little girl, my thoughts were always "Does he approve?" You know it & so I needn't go all over the ground again. But that's the way a woman lives.

Last night I attended the committee meeting.[1] The regular chairman was absent & I being the next ranking member acted as *chairman*. My very first time. I don't think I was a discredit to you dearie. At least after it was thro' I felt as tho' I had conducted the meeting properly. Heath said so anyway. I gathered up all my nerve & went & did it.

After our meeting adjourned we went into the tradeschool committee meeting where they were discussing my resolution. It was creating quite a turmoil. Of course I defended it & think I did it tolerably well as my fighting blood & courage were up. The committee couldn't come to any discision & adjourned to meet again Thursday. I'm afraid however it will be lost. The resolution relates to changing the vice-principles to principle of tradeschools with the present salary. That is to safeguard the continual increase of salary asked for.

I also am asked to address about 200 teachers at a banquet Nov. 4th. Do you think I can do it? I'm going to try. Of course I shall try to remember that my husband is of world renowned reputation & must therefore do him credit.

Now darling you can see how much, how very very much I'm doing all because I love you so; surely not because of any ambition on my part.

I really do think you owe the comrades & the S.D.H.[2] a nice long letter. They are anxiously waiting for one. I don't care so much about any other personal letters. People ought not to expect you to write just now; but the comrades & comradesses (that's good) here have a certain right. I'll be watching for it in the paper.

When you come back here you will find some changes in the neighborhood. Schomberg's[3] are moving this week. Harlands[4] bought Schomberg's flat & expect to move into the upper one.

The children are well go to school regularly, practice irregularly, quarrel regularly & are lovely generally. Do you know that since I've enlightened the girls concerning the origin of the races, they have never once asked me any thing concerning it, & I don't think they have even thought about it much if any either. The curiosity seems to have died out or be satisfied. I'm very glad indeed I told them.

Hattie seems to be very lonesome & to have very much work. She wanted me to come up to see her. I told her at present I couldn't see my way clear whereupon she even went so far as to offer to pay my fare if only I would come. I guess she misses me very very much. I don't think I shall go while you are gone as I now carry the entire responsibility concerning the children. I wouldn't feel right about leaving them until you are back.

And now sweetheart, don't let my letters lie around tear them up or burn them. They are meant only for your own dear eyes. I won't feel at liberty to tell you that Ich Dich lieb halten will[5] if you are not careful. With a thousand kisses I am always

Your Meta.

Please tell me when you are coming home & by what boat.

1. Meta Berger had been elected to the Milwaukee school board in April, 1909. She served as a board member until 1939.
2. The *Social-Democratic Herald.*
3. Otto H. Schomberg (1864–1927), vice-president of the Schomberg Hardwood Lumber Company, and his wife, Ida (b. 1866).
4. Frank W. Harland (b. 1865), manager of the Park Amusement Company, and his wife, Jean (b. 1875).
5. I want to hold you lovingly.

Victor to Meta

Paris, France
November 12, 1909

My Sweet Mama-Schatzl:

This is to let you know that I am going to sail tomorrow (Saturday) from Boulogne-sur-Mer (France) with the Holland-America Line (which starts at Rotterdam) to join my sweet Schatzl and my darling Schnuckies— and that I am very glad of it. The name of the steamer is *Rydam* and I am going to travel first class and have an *outside cabin* all to *myself* for $90.00. The steamer is due in New York on Monday November 22nd. I shall have to spend the 23rd and the 24th in New York to tend to *business*—however I expect to take the fastest train I can possibly get and arrive in Milwaukee on Thursday (Thanksgiving) night. I will wire from New York so that you can meet me in Chicago—however do not give the date of my arrival away, so that I do not have trouble about the Neacy[1] suit, until I had rested for a day and gotten acquainted with the situation.

Had a very fine time in Paris—the people here treated me gloriously. Had dinner with Longuet[2] (the grandson of Karl Marx) yesterday and also spent a half a day with Jaures[3] in the Chamber of Deputies. Today I interviewed Jaures and was in turn interviewed by Longuet for Humanitè the French Socialist daily of Paris.

Well, sweetheart Mamma I have a few more appointments to-night and I can only tell you daß ich Dich sehr lieb halten werde,[4] when I get home, and that I can hardly—*Wait* for *the Time.*

Ever your lover
V.L.B.

1. Thomas J. Neacy (1848–1926), an Irish-born Milwaukee businessman, became known as "Injunction Tom" as a result of his frequent legal battles on behalf of what he considered the public good. After Neacy threatened an injunction to halt subsidized school lunches for poor children, Berger called him a "briber of public officials," "ignorant, stupid and greedy," and the "Devil's Best Friend" in the *Social-Democratic Herald,* September 18, 1909. Neacy sued Berger and the Milwaukee Social-Democratic Publishing Company for $10,000 and eventually won a retraction.

2. Jean Frédéric Laurent Longuet (1876–1938), a French socialist politician, wrote about foreign affairs for the socialist daily newspaper *L'Humanité* and served in the National Assembly, 1914–1919 and 1932–1936.

3. Jean Jaurès (1859–1914), the leading French socialist politician of his time, edited *L'Humanité,* which he helped to establish in 1904, and served in the National Assembly, 1885–1889, 1893–1898, and 1902–1914.

4. that I will hold you very lovingly.

Victor to Meta

[en route to New York]
[ca. January 1, 1910]

My Sweet Mama:

It is a drizzling disagreeable day—and so far I have not even succeeded in concentrating my mind on my speech. Yet I feel that a great deal depends upon it—my future standing in the party, and also the future standing of that party itself.[1] Debs has gone to pieces entirely—he has learned nothing in 15 years and is repeating parrotlike the same old speech. If I can build up a following in New York—and the chances to do so are very favorable, then I do believe that this party will amount to a great deal within five years or so.

I feel that I can do it and I will do it. I feel that I can repeat the tremendous successes of Berlin and Vienna—I intend to let rethoric and fine language go to the winds and let myself go entirely. If my personality, my knowledge and my good judgement are only half of that what they are renowned to be, I ought to win out easily.

Have read the last issue of Collier's on the train. It is a remarkably *radical* magazine. I am rather curious to know where it is going to land—for so much is clear: it is attacking the Republican party viciously and it has only contempt for the Democratic party. I am going to subscribe for the paper when I am in New York—and I shall also keep up the acquaintance (and the friendship if possible) of both Robert Collier the owner, and Norman Hapgood the editor.[2]

I wish you were with me, sweet Schatzl. You do realize how much you have grown on me and how much of my life you have become. I wish I could show you in some way—not only by getting that home for you, for that you will get if I stay well and healthy and get this year,—no I wish I could show you in some other way.

We are just getting into Toledo, and I will have to close this note Schatzl, ich hab Dich sehr lieb[3]—take good care of yourself and the sweet Schnuckies.

Your V.L.B.

1. Berger delivered a speech at Cooper Union in New York City on January 3, 1910, entitled "A Labor Party in America." According to the *New York Call*, January 4, 1910, Berger's speech was "keen, incisive and witty" and "the applause was long continued." Berger rebutted William English Walling's charges that Berger, Algie Simons, John Spargo, Morris Hillquit, and Robert Hunter planned to transform the Socialist Party into a labor party.
2. *Collier's Weekly* was an influential popular magazine that advocated progressive causes. Robert Joseph Collier (1876–1918), the magazine's publisher, served as editor, 1898–1902 and 1912–1913. Norman Hapgood (1868–1937), a progressive journalist, edited the magazine, 1902–1912. During the 1890s, Hapgood worked as a writer and drama critic for the *Milwaukee Sentinel*.
3. little darling, I love you very much.

Victor to Meta

[en route to New York]
[May 30, 1910]

Sweet Schatzl:

A fine train—but writing is difficult indeed. I ought to have a little typewriter with me and know how to use it.

Getting to be well known in Chicago and so forth even personally. The railway clerk at the depot to whom I paid the excess fare asked me whether I was the "Victor" Berger from Milwaukee—when boarding the train I was again pointed out by some elderly gentlemen in a semi-audible sort of a way. Both the Chicago Tribune and the Inter-Ocean had editorials this morning on the Stokes incident in which I got decidedly the best of the argument.[1]

By-the-way, sweetheart, don't forget to telephone to the Hermann Miller the photographers not to print the Seidel[2]-Berger picture. We will come there some other time—tell him—to have our picture taken together. Nobody likes the prove he gave me—and you liked it least. Take good care of your self, Schatzl—and of the babies. But more so of yourself, because if you manage to keep your health another 15 years— and I manage to keep mine—and I *also* manage to keep *your love*—then I feel confident that you will bring up our children in a way that we will have the model family of Milwaukee.

With lots of love for all.

your V.LB.

1. J. G. Phelps Stokes, a New York millionaire Socialist, called Milwaukee's Socialists "mere reformers" after they won the April, 1910, election. Berger replied by chiding Stokes for living off his father's wealth. Both editorials mentioned by Berger criticized Stokes; see "Waiting, Pleasantly, for the Millennium," *Chicago Daily Tribune,* May 30, 1910, and "The Money of Comrade J. G. Phelps-Stokes," *Chicago Inter Ocean,* May 30, 1910.

2. Emil Seidel (1864–1947), a patternmaker by trade, served as Milwaukee's first Socialist mayor, 1910–1912, as a Milwaukee alderman, 1904–1908, 1909–1910, 1916–1920, and 1932–1936, and as the state party secretary, 1920–1923. He ran for vice-president on the Socialist ticket in 1912.

Meta to Victor

[Milwaukee, Wisconsin]
May 30, 1910

My Darling Papa:—

I wonder and wonder how you can stand the long summer weeks when we are up at Shawano and you are here alone. I find consolation in the thought that your life is so full, your thoughts so busy with the world's doing, and your evenings so occupied with meetings. When you go away from home, the day is empty for me. There is a certain peculiar feeling comes over me about this time 6 P.M. which tells me how dreadfully I would miss you should something happen to you. Darling papa for my sake, for the girl's sake take care of yourself. The time was when I thought that if you gave up your work and devoted yourself to money making I would be happy. That time is past. Fortunately it didn't last long. Now in a riper judgement I find that I can only be happy when you are happy, I can only be content when I know that you are the same and strange to say I believe I can only be well when you are well. So you see darling how much, how very very much I need my own big papa. Money is after all a very small thing; and if we both retain our health and our love for each other and the babies I can wish for nothing better. So take care darling, take care of my very life, for you are that.

I received a letter from Clara Hipke saying she was leaving New York Tuesday so you do not need to look her up.

Give my love to your mother & Rosie[1] and all and be sure to telephone to Rose so that she will be in Bridgeport when you are there.

Hast Du mich auch so sehr sehr lieb?[2]

Your own Meta.

My best regards to your friend Mr. Brisbane. Do not antagonize the Stokes more than need be.

Meta.

1. Victor's sister, Rose Berger Morganstern, lived in Ansonia, Connecticut.
2. Do you also love me so very very much?

Victor to Meta

New York, New York
[June 7, 1910]

My sweet Schatzl:

My meeting last night was a great success—the hall was packed to its utmost capacity.[1] However *I* was not satisfied with my speech, I did not do as good as in Philadelphia. I feel that I *must* practice speaking a great deal more than I do. Nevertheless even Debs could get no more applause than I did.

Tomorrow I intend to steal a few hours to run to Bridgeport—if I should be unable to do it tomorrow, I cannot do it before Friday and that would of course mean, that I could not get home before Sunday.

There is a stenographer waiting for me to take a statement therefore, sweet Schatzl, I cannot write you a long letter this time.

Kiss the babies for me and Jack also. And always remember that you are the best part of me, of my life, darling.

Ever your
V.L.B

1. The *New York Call,* June 7, 1910, reported that Berger "in a calm yet passionate manner held the rapt attention of an audience which packed Lyric Hall to the doors last night" and that "storm after storm of applause greeted him." Berger's New York speech was part of an eastern speaking tour that received substantial press coverage, including a full page in the *New York Times,* June 5, 1910.

Victor to Meta

[Milwaukee, Wisconsin]
July 6, 1910

My Sweet Mama:—

Have promised you a letter every second day—and I will live up to my promise. By this time you have probably learned from the papers that John Puelicher[1] was elected president of the school board. He evidently expected the election, because he had his speech all prepared and I understand the papers even had it. I congratulated him the next day and he thanked me very much.

I was nominated for congress in the Fifth district with 360 against 47 for Welch.[2] While the majority is big enough to be rather decisive—the mere fact that Welch got 47 votes against me the founder, the leader and the "brains" of the party, is rather significant. Do not give these figures to anybody.

It is also significant that our aldermanic caucus selected Welch and Riess[3] as [delegates] to the convention of League of Wisconsin municipalities to be held in Fond du Lac next week—the other three are Republicans and Democrats—although I as the chairman of the *legislative committee* should be considered the natural delegate to that convention.

Well, I start to shoot at the crowd in this weeks Herald, picking out a particularly asinine and anti-socialist act of three of them at the last meeting of the common council.[4]

There was almost a hitch in the building of our corner. You see we thought that the trust company would let us have the money at once—as it is they only want to let us have it to finish the building. The concrete contractor demanded $3,400 at once for work done—and there was no money. We had a special meeting of the board of directors last night and finally I was asked to see Uhlein[5] so that the Second Ward bank would let us have $1,700 for 90 days—until some stock is sold—while Hübschman[6] volunteered to get the other $1,700 from the trust company.

Thus the danger seems to be averted. I hope that these situations will not repeat themselves too often. By-the-way Joe invited me at his house to-morrow (Thursday) night. He will call for me at the office with his automobile. He is a mighty nice fellow and I am going to keep on good terms with him.

Now I have written you a long letter and have told you lots of news. You should write to me every day. I am incredibly busy, because I shall use my evenings to work on my aldermanic[7] duties and to go to some meetings of branches and also to get the situation in the party well in hand again.

Take good care of the Schnuckies and be especially good to Doris, don't excite her. I wish she and Elsa could go way, just with you alone, for about a six months trip to California next winter and do nothing but play. Of course I realize that such is impossible next winter. Besides, what would become of me?

I am in ill humor always and growl at everybody. I do not sleep well and take my meals rather irregularly. However I am going to put in a stock of victuals of all kinds into my ice box and will also have the milk man bring me a pint of milk every day. That will make me independent of the restaurants.

Have ordered the Social Democratic Herald to be sent to you. Hope you will read it—semi-occassion[ally].

Habe mich imer recht lieb Schatzl[8]—think of me nicely and kiss my babies for me. Also Jack and Hattie and little Marie.[9] Give my best regards to the Schweers family and tell Josie that I am going to see her folks today.

Ever your
V.L.B.

1. John H. Puelicher (1869–1935), a banker, served on the Milwaukee school board, 1907–1911.
2. Albert J. Welch, a Socialist, served as a Milwaukee alderman, 1910–1914.
3. John Reisse (b. 1858), a Socialist, served as a Milwaukee alderman, 1910–1912.
4. See Victor to Meta, July 12, 1910, note 5, below.
5. Joseph E. Uihlein Sr. (1875–1968) was the son of August Uihlein, who served as president of Second Ward Savings Bank and headed the family that owned the Joseph Schlitz Brewing Company. The younger Uihlein served as the bank's president (1911–1928) and as the brewery's general manager (1906–1919) and vice-president (1912–1919 and 1933–1945). In 1910 Socialist mayor Emil Seidel appointed Uihlein as Milwaukee commissioner of the public debt, a position he held until 1911.
6. Adolph Huebschmann (1859–1921), a Milwaukee lawyer.
7. Berger served as an at-large alderman on the Milwaukee Common Council from April, 1910, to April, 1911.
8. Love me dearly all the time, darling.
9. Marie Schweers (b. 1905), the stepdaughter of Meta's sister, Hattie.

Meta to Victor

[Shawano, Wisconsin]
[July 8, 1910]

My darling papa:—

I just got your long and interesting letter. I do think you will have to use a great deal of tact and some strategy to get the situation well in hand again. I so thoroughly dislike the socialists which make up the bulk of the party. They are all so narrow, so jealous of you & so hateful. But your very superiority will have to win over their measley minds. I have all kinds of faith in you and know everything will come out O.K. if you will keep in close touch and a sharp watch on them *all.*

Now papa dear I want you to [give] Strehlow[1] *hell!!!* He hasn't begun to put on the second coat so I am informed by letter and the tenants are kicking like sixty because they cannot put on their screens. It is a shame the way he is treating me. If he doesn't want to finish it let him say so and we will give it to some one else. He needs a raking over the coals. Be sure to do this for me. If I knew Strehlow's address I'd write him myself.

Next winter darling, we won't want to go to California. It will be Washington you know, I am planning on my new dress now already.[2] So you see how sure I feel about it.

The Bank here hasn't yet sent me my insurance papers and I'm going in tomorrow again to see about it. With all the forest fires around I feel worried about it. Every body is so slow around here.

Yesterday I wrote Miss Thomas a few lines in answer to her card. Now sweetheart, before all things take care of yourself especially with regular meals and eat slowly. Sleep as much as you can and love me more & more & more always more.

Ever your own
Meta.

1. Possibly August Strehlow (1867–1943), a Milwaukee house painter and contractor and Socialist politician who served in the Wisconsin Assembly, 1905–1906, and on the Milwaukee Common Council almost continuously from 1906 until 1940.
2. Berger ran for Congress in 1910.

Victor to Meta

Milwaukee, Wisconsin
[July 12,] 1910

My Sweet Schatzl:

I have a busy time of it. I am using at least some of my evenings to get back full control over the organization, in which I will undoubtedly succeed. The three aldermen who voted with Corcoran[1] and Carney[2] in the meeting of the Common Council (Arnold,[3] Mikkelsen[4] and Reisse) gave me a very good text for an editorial in the S.D. Herald—and in the last meeting of the Central Committee I had decidedly the upper hand.[5] Besides I will keep the whip of the paper over the central committee where the office-grafting spirit seems to be still rampant. I have a good mind to abolish the big and unwieldy Central Committee—which is a sort of a convention in permanence and has a paralyzing influence on doing things—and run the party through a small executive committee, with the help of the referendum.

I am still very much worried about the forest fires—although I know that the prevailing winds are from the South which gives safety to the cottages. However, Schatzl I know that you are a very deliberate person, and that you will not lose your head in case of any danger.

Schatzl, darling, there is not an hour in the day, when I do not think of you. Ich habe Dich sehr lieb![6]

With love to all and especially to my Schatzl, I am ever your

V.L.B.

1. Cornelius L. Corcoran (1864–1936), a typesetter, small businessman, and Democratic politician, served on the Milwaukee Common Council, 1892–1936, and as the council's president, 1898–1906, 1908–1910, 1912–1932.

2. Joseph P. Carney (1871–1941), a Milwaukee printer and proofreader, served as city treasurer, 1912–1916, and as a member of the Common Council, 1908–1912, 1918–1922, and 1924–1932. Carney ran as a Democrat for Congress in 1918 and, after finishing second behind Berger, unsuccessfully tried to claim the position when the House refused to seat Berger.

3. Louis A. Arnold (1872–1958), a Socialist, served as a Milwaukee alderman, 1908–1911, city tax commissioner, 1912–1915 and 1922–1939, and state senator, 1915–1923.

4. Martin Mikkelson (1870–1948), a Milwaukee realtor, served as a Socialist alderman, 1910–1912.

5. At the June 20, 1910, meeting of the Milwaukee Common Council, a letter from the Manhattan Lodge of the Brotherhood of Machinists that contrasted the Socialist administration with the "former regime of the Democratic and Republican boodlers" was entered into the council's record. Alderman Carney offered a resolution on July 5 to expunge the letter from the minutes. Carney's resolution was defeated eighteen to fourteen, with Socialist aldermen Arnold, Mikkelson, and Reisse voting in the minority. In an editorial in the *Social-Democratic Herald,* July 9, 1910, Berger accused the three dissenting aldermen of destroying party unity.

6. I love you very much!

Victor to Meta

Copenhagen, Denmark
September 3, [1910]

My dear Schatzl:

I am glad the congress[1] is over—and that I am going to America again. For to-morrow (Sunday forenoon) I am invited to take a round trip with the mayor to see the city.

As for actual work the congress has accomplished very little. Most of the time was taken up with the settlement of petty disputes among petty "parties" in petty countries. Even America had a squabble of that kind—the question of representation in the bureau and the question of votes in the congress. The first of these—the question of ousting De Leon[2] from the bureau—was postponed for another year. The question of votes was settled by a decision which gave our party 13 and the SLP *one* vote of the 14 to which America is entitled. Until now he *still* had 3½ of the 14. That was probably the most important business as far as America is concerned.

However I have fully made up my mind that in future congresses (if I should attend any) I will not go on any committee again. Sit in smoky and stuffy [rooms] until midnight to listen to uninteresting perorations on uninteresting subjects—when one could employ one's time much better in sleeping talking or anything else is not to my taste.

Mrs. Dietzgen[3] was here for two days and she sends her best regards. I was invited to the home of a Danish (wealthy) comrade for dinner last night, but could not go *until* 9.30 P.M. on account of the evening session.

I am thinking of you a hundred times every day—and will not go to any future congress without my sweet Schatzl. Kiss the babies for your loving

Papa

1. Berger was a delegate to the congress of the Second International in Copenhagen, August 28–September 3, 1910.
2. Daniel De Leon (1852–1914) was the leader of the Socialist Labor Party and the founder of the Socialist Trades and Labor Alliance. De Leon's opposition to the established trade unions and his rigid control over the party led to the secession of the faction that joined with Berger's Social Democratic Party to create the Socialist Party in 1901.
3. Probably the wife of Eugene Dietzgen, a Chicago Socialist and businessman.

Meta to Victor

Milwaukee, Wisconsin
September 3, 1910

My darling Papa:—

First of all, altho' it is weeks yet before you land, I'm going to say Hello papa hast du mich lieb?[1] I want to be the very first to greet you when you near American soil.

We came home from the lake today and to tell the truth I was loathe to come back. There was no papa here to welcome us home. It really didn't seem like a home coming at all. The house is strangely small, very empty & painfully quiet. Several times I went out on the porch because I couldn't stand it in the house. Therefore this letter at this time to you. Of course, it will be continued every time I have some thing really important to say to you.

Mr. Seidel refused to serve on the reception committee for Roosevelt[2] and now he is being roasted to a finish. The Sentinel called him a "peanut" & otherwise abused him in strong language. I am writing this to you so you can be ready with a reply when the newspaper men come to you. Seidel's letter I thought very dignified but he is certainly getting it in all papers by all kinds of citizens. I'll look up some of them & save them for you.

Next Mr. Taege[3] just now asked me if I would give him your invitation cards issued by the Press Club for the Roosevelt reception. I told him I would look thro' your mail tomorrow when I got it from Schoknechts.[4] If they were there, I saw no reason why he shouldn't use them. The country, no the world seems to be Roosevelt-mad.

Thirdly:—At this date in the primary fight it looks like Cochems[5] but will write you later in the same letter.

On the whole I think I feel slightly better for having had this much of a chat with you.

Hast du mich lieb?[6] And goodnight papa mine.

1. do you love me?
2. Mayor Emil Seidel declined to serve on a committee that welcomed former president Theodore Roosevelt to Milwaukee because of Roosevelt's attacks on socialism.
3. August W. Taege (b. 1861), a salesman, and his wife, Christina (b. 1868), shared a duplex with the Bergers on Milwaukee's north side.
4. Christian Schoknecht (b. 1845), a mason-contractor, and his wife, Bertha (b. 1855), were the Bergers' landlords and next-door neighbors.
5. Henry F. Cochems (1875–1921), a progressive Milwaukee lawyer, won the Republican primary in 1910 for the Fifth Congressional District but lost to Berger in the general election. Cochems later represented Berger during the *Milwaukee Leader* mailing-rights case, the Espionage Act trial, and the congressional hearings over Berger's seating.
6. Do you love me?

Victor to Meta

St. Louis, Missouri
November 23, 1910

My Dear Schatzl:

The convention is dragging along with endless jurisdiction fights. I was glad to see James Lynch[1] of the International Typ[o]graphical Union being dragged into one. A "solicitor's union" had been formed in San Francisco and since the daily papers there did not came to an agreement with it, one of them the San Francisco Call a big daily of the Sentinel type and carrying the "allied printing label" was boycotted by the "solicitors u[n]ion." Whereupon Lynch appealed to the Executive

Council of the A. F. of L. and had the charter of this 2 by 4 local union revoked. Gompers was not going to have a fight with the ITU and allied trades on account of a handful of fakirs. But the delegate of the San Francisco central body, a noisy Irishman by the name of Gallagher,[2] made a fearful outcry and accused the San Francisco publishers that they have paid the traveling expenses of two delegates and also hinted at dark influences behind Gompers. This made Gompers get up and "holler". He won out of course, because the action of the Executive Council was right in this case and because he has the votes anyway.

Well, Schatzl, all of this does not interest you. But it might interest you that it is just possible that I will not stay until the end of the convention but try and be home for Sunday. However I do not want to tell the papers or even my office anything about it—I want to have the Sunday for my family.

I have had two or three interviews in the papers since you left. But with the exception of one evening when I took supper with Gompers, Duncan, and the reporters of the Chicago Tribune I have been home every night. I will have to do something for that rash as soon [as] I get home.

Otherwise Schatzl, I hope you feel good and are not worried about the numberless editorials which are written all over the country on account of the new Housewife's union proposed by you. The latest one I saw was written by Arthur Brisbane and was rather friendly.[3] Though one could see that he tried hard to be serious. Well, Schatzl, such is fame!

Hast Du mich lieb?[4] And do you realize that you are the wife of the first Socialist congressman in the United States of America?[5] Now I do hope that they will make me United States Senator and Secretary of State—*you* deserve it all, even if I don't.

Take good care of the Schnuckies and kiss them for me. And always remember that I consider you my good angel—this is my father's expression for you—and the better part of me.

V.L.B.

1. James M. Lynch (1867–1930) served as president of the International Typographical Union, 1900–1914 and 1924–1926, and as a member of the New York Industrial Commission, 1914–1921.

2. Andrew J. Gallagher (1878–1966), a photoengraver and three-term San Francisco city supervisor, represented the San Francisco Labor Council at the AFL convention.

3. Following the 1910 AFL convention, Meta Berger was quoted as saying "Women have social equality with men now, and political equality is coming, but we must also have economic equality. A housewives' union would be a good means to this end. It would do for a start now." She went on to argue that women were entitled to half of their husbands' income. Meta later claimed that the housewives' union story was created out of thin air by a reporter. See

"Dangers of Proposed Union of Housewives," *Washington Times*, November 17, 1910; "Union Men Deserve Party of Their Own," *Milwaukee Free Press*, November 26, 1910 (both articles in 1910 scrapbook, Berger Papers, SHSW). For Brisbane's tongue-in-cheek editorial, see "'A Union of Housewives' Is Suggested by Mrs. Victor Berger," *New York Evening Journal*, November 21, 1910.
    4. Do you love me?
    5. Berger was elected to the U.S. House of Representatives from Wisconsin's Fifth District on November 8, 1910. He received 38 percent of the vote compared to 37 percent for Republican Henry F. Cochems and 24 percent for Democrat Joseph P. Carney.

Meta to Victor

Milwaukee, Wisconsin
May 1, 1911

Mine lieber Papa:—[1]
    May-day, a snow-storm and mine papa without an over-coat! What a mistake that was to pack your coat. I hope you had the good sense to go and buy a good spring coat, especially when I think of your dress-suit the evening-chills and no coat. I certainly worried about that today. Tell me what you did about it. Also about the meetings in Boston & New York and all your triumphs; which fate decides I shall only share with you at great distances.
    The day was so miserable here that I decided to stay at home and nurse myself, so after sitting around on each chair awhile with no ambition to work I finally laid down and slept 2 hours. Then my trunk came home and I had to pay $1.10 excess baggage and $.75 for delivery on account of it being so heavy. Well I unpacked things and tried to find a place to place things again which wasn't so easy as Josie has occupied both closets and bureau drawers. That's the worst of having her so close to me and makes me nervous.
    Last night (Sunday) Miss Thomas came up as usual and we had a nice visit together until Hipke's came. They came to see me & see if they could do any thing for me. Miss Thomas doesn't like them & shows it quite plainly. While the discussion was going on the facts came out that that Mr. Phillips[2] is back here working hand in hand with Beffel, (Mrs) Van Vyke & Patek[3] in order to get the Baby work[4] started. Beffel takes the *credit* for the fact that *Berger* got the Council to vote $4,000 for that work. Hipke's simply sounded a warning that that combination would not work for the best interests of the city. At this point Miss Thomas who had shut up like a clam rose to go. I ask[ed] her what she thought of the situation where upon she said she didn't care & wasn't concerned at all that that wasn't part of her work etc etc. I said aren't you interested in whatever the administration does for the kids and she said that no one was working more for the kids than she was, etc. It was

quite embarrassing. I don't understand her at all. She seems to be all tired out & worn out with the fearful newspaper campaign waged against us. She said every one was enraged at the Mil. papers & that's why she was working so hard for a Daily. Well after she was gone I didn't know whether she went away mad or not, but one thing is sure; she wasn't nice to my guests who came to see how I was getting on.

Did you succeed in getting any support for a daily paper in the East. I do hope so, as we need it badly.

Today I tried to get acquainted again with my school work by telephoning to different teachers. Refused to see all book-agents and reporters, but one got me on the telephone. He wanted to know what I considered most important in Washington at the opening of Congress. I told him the historic event of the first Socialist taking his seat in the national body. Then he said he heard I was going to resign right away. I told him I had no intentions of resigning at all. He seemed so surprised at that. Well dearie, the kids are all O.K. and a nice healthy noisy saucy bunch.

Elsa seems to be happiest that I am back as she comes oftenest to kiss me. I really don't know how I am going to stand it so long without you. I need your companionship almost as I need fresh air. There is no one here to talk to, to love & to love me back again. I will write you every day sweetheart and will continue this tomorrow when I have seen Seidel. It was pretty hot here I mean during the campaign. Mr. Augustyn[5] said too, that everyone is disgusted with the newspapers. Well good night sweet heart mine and please please dearie, love me, write to me & love me, love me, love me.

Wednesday [May 3, 1911] A.M. I simply begin where I left off and demand that you still love me. And now to report what I've been doing since Monday evening. Tuesday I visited Seidel at the City Hall and had a fine talk with him. Also met Stroesser[6] and Rehfeld[7] Grass,[8] Strehlow and another socialist Alderman whose name I've forgotten in the Mayor's office. All admit that the papers here have been most contemptible and lying and that the result has been to solidify the party more then ever. The party spirit is fine to be sure and Seidel thinks our recent defeat[9] the best thing that could have happened to us. Now as to the Park Proposition;[10] our aldermen are standing like one man for it so far, but I fear they have made a mistake to concede to *any kind* of an appraisel. Some people want the State Fair Board to appraise, others a real estate Board to appraise & so forth. Mr. R. Uehlein[11] was just here this minute to see if I had heard these things. The only thing I really did hear from the alderman was that they expected to choose their *own* men who would give them a square deal in the matter to do the appraising. If you have any suggestions to make concerning the matter perhaps you had better write to Welch or some one. Mr. Grass said that you had handed him "his package" in a fierce letter which he was keeping as a souveniere. He seemed to enjoy it but said he never had "cold feet."

Then Mr. Uehlein also wanted to know if I knew whom the administration was to appoint in the place of Building Inspector Koch.[12] I said I did not. Whereupon he pleaded that the administration please put in a "big broadminded" man even if he were not a Socialist rather than a Socialist who didn't know his business like this Meiseroff.[13] I told him that I would write you and then you would confer with the proper people. It seems the time is short so you had better take that under consideration. I really don't know of any architect outside of Fink[14] who is a Socialist and it would surely be a dreadful mistake if the comrades would insist upon his name at the caucus. Don't neglect this.

Now another thing in which I want your help. Mrs. Whitnall[15] resigned last night from the School Board. Some of the members are anxious *not* to fill her vacancy until after that new Catholic board[16] takes its seat. That would mean that another Roman Catholic would be elected which we surely don't want. The present members are willing I understand to stand for one of the retiring members (Pieplow, Mowry, Puehlicher, Tadduch)[17] if the vote came off next June. Now we two socialist[s] (Raasch[18] & I) can not elect a socialist and by standing out for one we will in all probability prevent an election of a successor to Mrs. Whitnall until after July 1. which we must avoid I think. In canvassing the situation last night Mr. Aarons[19] said that he would stand for either Puelicher or Mowry but was just as willing to wait if that seemed to be the wish of the board. Now both Raasch & I talked it over & we don't want that to happen. We have in a joking way in the past told Puelicher we would stand for him when the socialist[s] were elected. Raasch said he doubted if Puelicher would stand but if he did he would vote for him. I think he is infinitely more fair than Mowry not to mention the team work which would go on if another Catholic came in. Augustyn declare[d] that he would "bet his hat" that that was going to be done and that for the first time "politics would be the watchword." Write me what you think dearie and then I think we will have to do the best we can in the June board meeting. To be frank I don't want Rubin[20] in the board and besides he wouldn't have the ghost of a show.

I telephoned to Mr. Sell[21] yesterday to inquire how Doris was getting on in school and he said "Fine." She is giving good work and assured me that we made no mistake in the step we took. And yet with the highest words of praise for Doris from him, I still feel nervous lest she fails when it comes to the final showdown. Elsa is the finest kind of a little girl as far as her work goes. At present she has a "cold" but it isn't any thing serious. It is really very cold up here with a light frost every evening.

Now darling, here is where I am at a disadvantage again with every body else because I must come down to the materialistic again. But the fact is that my $60. is like a drop in the bucket and when you have drawn your pay I wish you could help here quite generously this month. When I got here I had to pay nearly $2 for the trunk, 6.50 for Espenhain whose man came several times, $20 for rent; $8 to Josie for wages and money she advanced until I cashed this check; also a telephone bill of $12.00 and Shawano long distance bill of $2.00. There is $50 gone before I am home 4 days. Then Chapman's have sent their collector & their bill is about $88. And a few others reaching close on to $150. I thought sweet heart I'd tell you this all at once and get it done with as I am really getting nervous when it comes to money matters as that seems to be the bone of contention. But from now on I hope to make things go better as we won't need to let things pile up on us so.

Today, this P.M. I expect to call for the girls at school and go down town with them for hats & shoes, they are still wearing their winter hats.

Now Schatzl please have lots of patience with me. I think I'm worth it because of my great immense & intense love for my illustrious husband. I am watching the papers eagerly for any reports that come from New York and Boston; and can hardly wait to get my first letter from you with your own account of it. Someway this life here in Mil is empty without you and it istn't only I that miss you, but every body; the comrades, the capitalists & yes even the Newspapers. Last night two of the reporters came up to me & shook hands & told me that they always liked you & missed you a good deal. You can see what a big place you filled in this community. Every body here is also asking how it is, what magnetic power you exercised to use the Washington press to such an extent and all agree that it must be a sort of genius in you. Now dearie isn't that fine.

And now darling mine, I'll close this or else I won't get it all in to one envelope. Today I am feeling much better and so I hope I'll be O.K. again in a day or two. Be good to yourself, take the best of care of yourself if you love me for you are the very life of your own loving

Mama.

1. My dear Papa.
2. Wilbur C. Phillips (1880–1969), the secretary of the New York Milk Committee, became secretary of the Milwaukee Child Welfare Commission in May, 1911.
3. John M. Beffel (1867–1927) was a physician who ran unsuccessfully as a Republican for Milwaukee mayor in 1910. Katherine Van Wyck (b. 1857) was a Milwaukee philanthropist. Arthur J. Patek (1868–1950), a Milwaukee physician, served as president of the Medical Society of Milwaukee County in 1911.
4. On March 27, 1911, in the Milwaukee Common Council Berger moved to appropriate $4,000 to create a Child Welfare Division in the city's Health Department. On May 8, 1911, the council established the Child Welfare Commission to combat infant mortality and protect children's health.

5. Godfrey William Augustyn (1872–1944) worked for the National Exchange Bank (later the Marine–National Exchange Bank), rising from the rank of messenger in 1890 to bank president in 1929. He served on the Milwaukee school board, 1899–1905 and 1909–1921, and as the board's president, 1900–1901 and 1913–1914.

6. Walter P. Stroesser (1874–1978) served as secretary to Milwaukee mayor Emil Seidel.

7. Ferdinand Rehfeld (1872–1921) served as a Socialist member of the Milwaukee Common Council, 1910–1912, and as business manager of the *Milwaukee Leader*, 1916–1921.

8. Max A. Grass (1876–1949), a brewery machinist, served as a Socialist member of the Milwaukee Common Council, 1906–1912, 1914–1918, and 1919–1920, and as a member of the Milwaukee Fire and Police Commission, 1932–1943.

9. Milwaukee's Socialists lost races for school board, alderman-at-large, and several judgeships in the April 4, 1911, election.

10. Berger introduced a resolution in the Milwaukee Common Council on March 27, 1911, to spend more than $350,000 to acquire land along the Milwaukee River for a city-owned park.

11. Robert A. Uihlein Sr. (1883–1959), a member of the family that owned the Joseph Schlitz Brewing Company, worked for the brewery for more than fifty years, eventually becoming its vice-president and secretary.

12. Edward V. Koch (1861–1931) served as Milwaukee building inspector, 1904–1911.

13. Joseph A. Mesiroff (b. 1873) served as Milwaukee city engineer, 1911–1914.

14. Charles A. Fink (1859–1922) was a Milwaukee architect.

15. Annie Gordon Whitnall (b. 1858), the first wife of Charles B. Whitnall, joined the Socialist Party in 1909 and served on the Milwaukee school board, 1907–1911. Charles filed for divorce in 1910, and the final decree was granted in 1912.

16. The 1911 nonpartisan election for the Milwaukee school board was marked by debate over religion. Socialists claimed that there was a Catholic ticket, but Catholics argued that church leaders had not endorsed a set of candidates and that the charge was a ruse to divide the anti-Socialist vote. Three of the four Catholic candidates were elected.

17. William L. Pieplow (1875–1959), Duane Mowry (1853–1933), John H. Puelicher, and John J. Tadych (b. 1877) served on the Milwaukee school board. Pieplow served 1902–1905 and 1906–1919, holding the presidency of the board, 1908–1909 and 1917–1919; Mowry and Puelicher served 1907–1911; and Tadych served 1904–1911.

18. Henry C. Raasch (1866–1957), a Milwaukee businessman and Socialist, served on the city's school board, 1907–1919.

19. Charles L. Aarons (1872–1952), an attorney, served on the Milwaukee school board, 1903–1905 and 1908–1912, and as a Wisconsin circuit court judge, 1926–1950.

20. Jacob H. Rubin (1870–1946), a Milwaukee Socialist, was the manager of the Provident Loan Society. In 1919 Rubin went to the Soviet Union, where he hoped to establish a Russian-American chamber of commerce, but he returned to Milwaukee in 1921, disillusioned with communism.

21. William F. Sell (1860–1933) served as a Milwaukee public school principal from 1894 until his death.

Meta to Victor

Milwaukee, Wisconsin
May 10, 1911

My Darling Papa:—

Your nice long enthusiastic letter reached me yesterday. How glad I am you had such fine enthusiastic receptions. You certainly must have made a hit according to the papers. A man by the name of McSweeny was here in the city looking up the socialists here. He told me he was to your meeting in Boston & that you were the only one that said any thing worth listening to & because of what you said he came out here to see for himself. It seems he is a newspaper man from Boston. He told Jacobs all those things even before he told them to me so I guess he was sincere. I am so sorry I can't be there to hear your "maiden speech." I feel that in some ways you will electrify the Congress & of course the nation by some of the light you will shed. Be sure to send me all the papers.

You didn't mention one word of your home-folks in your letter which of course goes to show how much of a success the meetings were. Did you find them all well? And did you see them all? Did you get my letter there? Did you see Brisbane? My how I wish I could talk to you now. The movement here is just as it was in my last letter to you. I am still deeply disappointed at the stand the aldermen took about the park.[1] But I notice Melms[2] went to Oklahoma so he didn't introduce that resolution yet. I hope your telegram will do some good. Since that decision was reached the newspapers are even quite with a few editorials excepted. You know of course that Ringer[3] is the new Building Inspector & I guess it is a wise joice. No opposition at all. Then Seidel appointed the Infant Mortality *Commission* consisting of Beffel, Patek, Hipke, Pereles[4] & Mrs Boyd.[5] I think they would have liked to freeze Hipke out & put a Catholic in his place only I told Seidel that in that event the administration wouldn't even have *one* man even friendly to us. You see they were trying to build up a commission which would be popular regardless of politics and they nearly succeeded in cutting Hipke. By they I mean Seidel's advisors who were Phillips, Jacobs, Patek, Beffel, Mrs. Van Vyke etc. etc. Phillips is completely hypnotized by Beffel. He told me so yesterday. Well perhaps Seidel played good politics there as the "minority" was won over & even enlarged the $4,000 you wanted to $5,000. So they share in the glory their. Seidel says he doesn't want credit nearly as much as he wants the work done. But we must have credit if we expect to be elected again.

Yesterday I went to the South Side to collect rent. Miss Straka now owes us $101.00 and Archie[6] wanted me to have a notice served on her. I told him I didn't want to put her out because I wouldn't have another lying newspaper report about "How Mr. V.L.B. puts people out" Whereupon he said he'd appear in behalf of the Schlichting Estate. I consented to this & made out a statement to take to the Justice of the Peace but before I got there I had "cold feet" & didn't do it. I have now decided that I'll turn the whole thing over to Archie July 1., the collecting etc etc & if he then wants to proceed why all right. I do not wish to appear in the matter at all. We now have an empty place which will need lots of attention so I'll have to hunt up Hassman & Strehlow again. I told all the tenants to submit the bill to me of the cleaning they wanted done, each tenant to do his own work, hire his own man & I would simply allow the money on the next month's rent. In that way I hope to avoid trouble with the unions.

Your hats will go out tomorrow. Mary will take them to Chapman's & have them do them up properly. Also the shoes.

I didn't take the babies picture home with me. It must be among your papers. How did mine turn out at Harris & Ewing's. Send me them if you can.

Your check was fine & I expect to make it go as far as possible. Of the things I must pay are those who are sending the collectors Chapman's 88, Bunde & Upmeyer 24.50, the rent 20, The Boston store I do not remember just now, but I'll surely be wise in spending it.

And now darling write me another nice long letter. Home really isn't home without our papa. It is simply a place to stay always looking for something, expecting something, missing something; a sort of an uneasy place. I have had another light attack at the back of my head & am going to see Hipke. Have already telephoned him about it.

The kiddies are O.K. and it does one's heart good really to see the interest they take in their gardens. I hope they will always be as happy as they are now. Write daily to your loving & homesick

Mama.

1. On May 8, 1911, the Milwaukee Common Council deferred Berger's proposal to acquire land for a city park by requiring an appraisal.

2. Edmund T. Melms (1874–1933), the secretary of the Milwaukee County Socialist Party for twenty-five years, served on the Milwaukee Common Council, 1904–1912, as the council's president, 1910–1912, and as Milwaukee County sheriff, 1915–1917. Melms developed the "bundle brigade," which rapidly distributed Socialist literature in as many as twelve languages around Milwaukee. He ran for Congress three times, losing by less than seven hundred votes in 1922.

3. Carl F. Ringer Sr. (1851–1939) served as Milwaukee building inspector, 1911–1912.

4. Nathan Pereles Jr. (1882–1967), a Milwaukee attorney. Neither Pereles nor Patek were among those appointed when Mayor Seidel announced the composition of the commission on May 11, 1911. Instead, Seidel appointed

William N. Fitzgerald (1862–1934), a businessman, and Lorenzo Boorse (1859–1931), a physician specializing in children's diseases.

5. Sarah M. Boyd (1849–1924) became president of the Shadbolt and Boyd Iron Company of Milwaukee after her husband died in 1901. In 1907 she founded and became the first president of the Visiting Nurse Association of Milwaukee, serving until her death.

6. Archibald Anderson, the widower of Meta's sister, Paula.

Victor to Meta

Washington, D.C.
May 18, 1911

My Sweet Schatzl:

I know you have a right to be angry with me—but you know my old failing as a letter writer seems to have grown worse in the heat of Washington. The thermometer stood 104 to-day and there were nine prostrations reported by the evening papers.

The debate on the admission of the Territories (Arizona and New Mexico) into statehood, is most uninteresting. I could break in on the Recall[1] which [is] the point in debate, but I dont want to. I know that the united Republicans and Democrats of my district would recall me any moment if they had the recall in Wisconsin, especially now under the leadership of the Jesuits and the holy Roman church. These democratic propositions—meaning democracy in its broadest sense—are a blessing only in very enlightened commonwealths.

Mrs. Willert[2] invited me to lunch last Sunday. I met there the first secretary of the Russian embassy—Nabakoff[3]—and an attache of the Norwegian legation Mr Morgenstierne.[4] Also the representative of the N.Y. Tribune.

Have met Mrs McCormick[5] after all in the Willard casually when I went there to meet a delegation of farmers which protested against the Canadian reciprocity. Mrs Willert and Mrs. McCormick were there taking tea—and I had to promise that I would look over the boarding houses for girls which Mrs. McCormick—who is a daughter of the late senator Mark Hanna[6]—is erecting—or rather fixing up—in Washington. A girl can get room and good board in these houses for three or four dollars—and as low as $2.25 a week. This will not solve the social question, of course, and I told the good lady so, but it will make [things] easier for a few working women in Washington. By-the-way Mrs McCormick is a cousin (or married a cousin) of Joe Medill Patterson[7] and seemed to know all about me.

Now I have done very little last week except trying to keep cool which was no easy job. Have given out a long interview on the supreme court decision[8]—and have prepared a sort of a brief for the McNamara case,[9] which is going to be taken up by the committee this week or early next week. Have also prepared a bill for an Old [Age] pension law[10] which will go in next week.

My interview about conditions in Washington you have no doubt seen in the papers. I am going to follow it up by another interview today. By-the-way, the editor-owner of the Star, Mr Noyes,[11] invited me to his house last Tuesday and talked an arm off me, on account of it.

Enclosed, please, find a letter to com[rade] Reuter,[12] the letter carrier. It will answer his grievance, I hope. Please, send it to him.

Do not worry about the Cardinal-Searchlight.[13] If I did not amount to anything—these curs would not be growling at me.

Do not worry away. If I live, you will have a bright future. And so will the children. Therefore just take care of the Schnuckies darling. And always remember, that you do not think one half as much of me, as I do of the noblest and sweetest woman in America, of my darling Schnuckie-Mamma.

Kiss the babies for me. Ich hab' Dich sehr lieb[14] darling and I almost go broke on day letters and other wire messages. However I feel that you are entitled to my messages either by mail or by wire. Auf baldiges Wiedersehen[15] sweetheart.

V.L.B

1. The Arizona constitution permitted the recall of judges, a provision that was cited by President Taft when he vetoed the statehood bill passed by Congress in 1911.
2. Ethel Florence McKay Willert (1875?–1955), the wife of London *Times* Washington correspondent Sir Arthur Willert.
3. Konstantin Dmitrievich Nabokov (1875–1929) served as first secretary of the Russian embassy in Washington, 1910–1912.
4. Wilhelm Thorleif Munthe Morgenstierne (1887–1963), an attaché at the Norwegian embassy in Washington, 1910–1912, held a number of diplomatic posts in the United States between 1929 and 1957, eventually serving as ambassador, 1942–1957.
5. Ruth Hanna McCormick (1880–1944), the wife of Joseph Medill McCormick, worked on behalf of women's suffrage, minimum wage, and child labor legislation. She served as a Republican representative from Illinois, 1929–1931.
6. Marcus Alonzo Hanna (1837–1904) served as a Republican senator from Ohio, 1897–1904.
7. Joseph Medill Patterson (1879–1946), the son of the *Chicago Tribune*'s publisher, joined the Socialist Party in 1906 and served on its National Executive Committee. Patterson became disillusioned with socialism by 1910 and turned his attention to publishing, serving as co-editor and co-publisher of the *Tribune*, 1910–1925, and publisher and editor of the *New York Daily News*, 1919–1946.
8. On May 15, 1911, the U.S. Supreme Court upheld a lower court ruling requiring the Standard Oil Company to dissolve.

9. In April, 1911, John J. McNamara (1876?–1941) was arrested in Indiana and extradited to California, where he was charged with the murder of twenty-one men killed in two explosions at the printing plant of the *Los Angeles Times.* Labor leaders and Socialists rallied around McNamara and his brother, James B. McNamara (1882–1941), who were portrayed as victims of a campaign to implicate the International Association of Bridge and Structural Ironworkers in the incident. Berger introduced a resolution in the House on April 15, 1911, calling for a federal investigation of McNamara's extradition. The rules committee held hearings on Berger's proposal but tabled the resolution. The McNamaras stunned the nation on December 1, 1911, when they appeared in court and pleaded guilty.

10. Berger introduced his old-age pension bill on July 31, 1911, and delivered a speech explaining it on August 7, 1911. The bill, which died in committee, would have provided a pension of up to four dollars per week for poor workers over the age of sixty provided they had been U.S. citizens for at least sixteen years.

11. Theodore Williams Noyes (1858–1946) joined his father's newspaper, the *Washington Evening Star,* as associate editor in 1887 and served as editor-in-chief from his father's death in 1908 until 1946.

12. Louis F. Reuter (b. 1865?) was a Milwaukee postal worker.

13. On May 13, 1911, Meta wrote to Victor about the *Searchlight* (formerly the *Cardinal*), a weekly anti-Socialist newspaper published in Milwaukee beginning in early 1911. Meta reported that the paper was "the vilest thing I ever saw. Every week they print an article signed by *Vigdor L. Bergie* (supposedly from you) that is fierce." Berger Papers, SHSW.

14. I love you very much.

15. See you soon.

Meta to Victor

Milwaukee, Wisconsin
May 20, 1911

My darling Papa:—

Only a few lines so as not to disappoint you in your daily letter. Every body here is about exhausted from the continued hot spell. It was so sudden that we feel it so much more. I don't suppose tho' it measures up with your long hot spell in Washington. Write & tell me about yourself. What do you do to keep cool? Where do you get your turkish baths? Are those other Wis. representatives home? What do you do evenings? Why don't you answer some of the personal things in which I am so interested. I suppose you had a fine talk with Seidel and in that way found out some of the home affairs. Miss Thomas says that you are doing splendid propaganda work for the nation but that Milwaukee as the centre isn't getting the good out of it, she should. In other words, do some thing for Mil. for Mil. needs it most and Mil. will send you back again. What have you done if any thing for the "Daily Paper." People here in the newspapers are beginning to ridicule the idea of the Socialists having a daily paper. That means of course they are afraid of it.

What are the chances of your coming home by the middle or end of June. Doris expects to graduate June 23. It would be too bad if her papa couldn't be here.

I am feeling some better again only not well yet. The dizzy spells come occasionally. Hipke says he thinks it is a case of auto-intoxication.

Did you see what Sandburg wrote in the Herald about me?[1] I am sorry I let him talk to me about it as I could have done better writing it out myself. It would have been less dis-jointed & more logical. Now dearest papa, you probably can see by the character of its letter that there isn't much to write about. We all (kiddies & mama) send the bestest kind of love to our own papa darling.

Write soon to your own

Meta.

1. Carl Sandburg (1878–1967), a poet and folklorist, began working as a Socialist organizer in Wisconsin in 1907 and served as private secretary to Milwaukee's Socialist mayor, Emil Seidel, 1910–1912. Sandburg frequently wrote for the *Social-Democratic Herald* and the *Milwaukee Leader* prior to moving to Chicago in 1912. An article entitled "What I Saw in Washington," based on Sandburg's interview with Meta Berger, appeared in the *Herald* on May 20, 1911. The piece noted that Victor Berger and socialism had stirred up considerable attention in the capital, commented on the undesirable influence of special interests, and included general observations about Washington.

Victor to Meta

Washington, D.C.
May 21, 1911

My Dear Schatzl:

It is still very hot, darling—in fact there is no sign of a let up of this equatorial wave. Got a letter from George[1] for you—but it is at home—while I am writing this in the office. It is cooler here, the capitol and the office building are on a hill, more over I have an electric fan going. Besides I like to be alone occassionaly, someway another I feel more alone here, when I am alone in this big building than at the Farragut—and I do not believe that besides the watchman there is anybody else in this great big building.

I often wonder how you stand the heat in Milwaukee. While it [is] nothing like we had it here—for three days about 105°—yet you got a taste of summer in Wisconsin. In your place I would pack up and go to Shawano. There is very little prospect for my getting home before the middle of July or even the end of July—and some of the Democratic leaders are talking about extending the session until October.

You see the case is this way: the Democrats control the house, while the Republicans rule the Senate.

This session was called by Taft[2] because the former congress had failed to pass the reciprocity treaty with Canada.

The Democratic house passed the Canadian treaty bragging that a Republican president was compelled to adopt a Democratic free trade policy. And bragging that a Republican president was compelled "to go down on his knees" and ask a Democratic house to do it for him.

Now the Democratic leaders—because the rank and file has nothing to say—put's it up to the Republican senate.

The Senate must decide either in *favor* of the reciprocity treaty, or *against* it.

Should the Senate decide in favor of it, then the Democrats will go home and crow that they settled the question in this extra-session.

Should the Senate decide against it, then the Democrats will go home and complain that the Republican Senate kept them from doing the work and that Democratic President and a Democratic Senate must be elected in order to make the people happy.

Therefore, no matter how the Senate may decide, the Republican party will get worst of it.

You understand now, Schatzl, why the Senate would like to adjourn tomorrow without being compelled to decide the question. But it takes the *concurrence* of the house for an adjournment and the Democrats will not adjourn, if they have to keep us here until into the next session, unless the Senate votes either "yes" or "no" on the "Reciprocity with Canada" and on the so-called "Farmer's Free List."

Do you understand the situation! It may just be possible that the hot weather will soften the tough old Senators, otherwise I may just lose my vacation in Shawano. Lord Percy[3] wrote me a nice letter today. He wants me to dine with him tomorrow (Monday) but alone, if I do not object. Of course, I will accept, because I like the fellow.

Will introduce my Old Age Pension bill next week, and probably my first three District bills, the week after. I may also have a rather elaborate insurance scheme for workingmen—old age, sickness, accident and out of work. And this will finish the new business for the extra-session. However I shall begin to push the bills I have introduced with main and might and I have an idea that I will get a hearing on every one of them.

This letter "got long" again. But I know you do not mind it. You see I am trying to make up for the brevity of the "night letters" and day-telegrams. But it is up to you to encourage me by sending me missives just as elaborate and verbose as mine.

And you might also tell me, wie lieb Du mich hast.[4] Because, if you do not love me dann geb' ich gar nichts um all den Ruhm.[5]

Take good care of the babies and tell the little imps to write. Jack hasn't written to me once.

With love and kisses
Ever your
V.L.B.

1. Probably George Berger (b. 1871), Victor's brother.
2. William Howard Taft (1857–1930), U.S. president, 1909–1913, called Congress into special session to consider the Canadian reciprocity bill, which would lower some tariffs on Canadian imports under the new Payne-Aldrich Act. The House passed the bill 268 to 89 on April 21, with Berger voting with the majority; the Senate approved the bill 53 to 27 on July 22. The Canadian government later rejected the agreement.
3. Lord Eustace Percy (1887–1958), a politician and educator, served as a diplomat at the British embassy in Washington, 1910–1914, and as a Conservative member of the House of Commons, 1921–1937.
4. how much you love me.
5. then all the fame does not matter to me.

Victor to Meta

Washington, D.C.
May 29, [1911]

My Dear Schatzl:

Before Mrs. Whitnall left she took out her friends and me for an automobile ride which cost her $10.00. I tried to be as nice to her as I could, and her friends the Folkmar's[1] felt highly honored to have a congressman at their house.

My speech before the committee on rules on the McNamara case was a great success and this will be the first bill reported back from that committee ie. they will not report in favor of appointing a special committee to investigate but they will report the testimony to the house and ask that it be turned over to the judiciary committee.

Of course, they mean thereby to make it appear that they did something but in reality do nothing. But I shall not let them go as easily as all that.

In first place I will get at least 50,000 copies of the hearing with my two statements and the statements of Ryan[2] (the president of the Iron workers) and their attorney Rappaport[3] printed and spread broadcast. This will help to create a favorable sentiment for McNamara and will also be good propaganda.

And second, I will frame up a bill tomorrow defining the crime of "kidnapping" and make it a felony, and introduce it.[4] They will have to take a stand on this.

By-the way, Rappaport and his wife may be up in Milwaukee for the Saengerfest[5] towards the end of June. *Should you still be* in town, then I want you to be friendly to them.

Kiss the babies and remember that I have only one Schatzl, only one sweet Schatzl.

V.L.B.

1. Daniel C. Folkmar (b. 1861), a Washington, D.C., clerk, and his wife, Elnora (b. 1863), a physician.
2. Frank M. Ryan served as president of the International Association of Bridge and Structural Ironworkers from 1905 to 1914, when he began a seven-year prison term in connection with the *Los Angeles Times* bombing. President Wilson pardoned him in 1918, and Ryan became an organizer for the union.
3. Leo M. Rappaport was an attorney for the International Association of Bridge and Structural Ironworkers who participated in the defense of the McNamara brothers.
4. On May 31, 1911, Berger introduced a bill that guaranteed additional federal rights to individuals in extradition proceedings, but the bill died in the Judiciary Committee.
5. A German music festival.

Meta to Victor

Milwaukee, Wisconsin
May 29, 1911

My dearest Papa:—

I hope it is as cool in Washington as it is here in Mil. While the cold weather is refreshing, yet the quick & sudden changes are hard to bear. Many people are suffering with the so-called colds.

Yesterday (Sunday) after I had mailed my letter, Dr. Kissling[1] stopped a moment to talk to me while I was on the porch. He is having a patient across the street at Urbans.[2] Of course the matter discussed was the next Presidency of the Board. Richardson[3] and Augustyn are the candidates. I told the Dr. that if I was in town, which I really doubted that I would be glad to support Augustyne. He said that made nine votes, so it looks like Pres. Aug. for next year. He will be fair to us, as well as to me and my position in case I am absent a lot next year.

This morning I had occasion to go to the South Side and as I kept Elsa out of school I took her along. We had our dinner at Krez, then went to the oratorical contest in the Fifth No. I. Elsa was there while I spoke a few words to the class. I wonder what she thought. The little rascal never said a word, not even to criticize me. From there we shopped and I bought each of the girls a graduating sash. The dress I shall not buy until I am pretty sure that all is well.

This evening I attended the trade-school committee in order to obtain a month's vacation instead of two weeks for the girl's trade school. That was passed unanimously and then I returned home Mrs. Kander[4] & I going to the car together. We were at home by 9 P.M. And now dearest, I am writing my daily letter altho' it will be mailed too late to go out tonight. By this evening's paper (Journal) I saw where a woman socialist orator by the name of Squires[5] was going for you because a New York paper reported that you had criticized both Jefferson & Lincoln. Read it dear. Tomorrow I'm going to hunt that ——— fool up and tell her where to get off at. Nice kind of a socialist she is to come here in your absence and give the papers another chance to rap the Socialists. The women socialists are surely no good, morally mentally or any other way. I've no use for them, not one!

Miss Thomas says she wrote you about the big victory we socialists had won on the street-paving proposition. Just what it is I must inform myself on; so she asked me to get the details from Briggs.[6] When I do I'll let you know. She thinks it was the best thing yet that happened.

I also see that Congress will not investigate the McNamara Case. Well that was to be expected wasn't it? Are you reading the news about McLenegan?[7] He is surely in a fix; altho' the Library board will probably sustain him no matter if he had done wrong. But I guess he doesn't like the notoriety of it all. Now sweetheart, write and tell me about your personal self. How are you feeling? Do you smoke? What do you do evenings & Sundays? It is just torture not to know & not to be with you. I still feel like packing up & going down. If you can stand the heat, why so can we. I don't like the Sundays or evenings here. Six o'clock, seven & eight P.M. are pretty lonesome hours for me. Ich hab Dich so lieb.[8] Do you understand how much I wonder. With love kisses & embraces from all your

Meta

1. Charles L. Kissling (1859–1917), a physician, served on the Milwaukee school board from 1907 until his death.
2. Hans Urban (b. 1878), a railway supervisor, and his wife, Alice (b. 1882), were neighbors of the Bergers.
3. Emmet Lee Richardson (1870–1960), an attorney, served on the Milwaukee school board, 1908–1909 and 1910–1914. He won the board's presidency in 1911 and served a one-year term.
4. Lizzie Black Kander (1858–1940) served on the Milwaukee school board, 1909–1919. Called the "Jane Addams of Milwaukee," Kander became active in settlement house work and wrote the *Settlement Cookbook*, which had twenty-three editions before her death.
5. Mary Squires, a Socialist suffragist from Oregon, criticized Berger for stating that American slaves were freed for political reasons. "She Raps Berger," *Milwaukee Journal*, May 29, 1911.
6. Harry E. Briggs (b. 1875?) served as Milwaukee commissioner of public works, 1910–1912. Milwaukee's Socialists claimed that they had uncovered graft

in street paving contracts, which restricted the work to a few select companies. By changing the contract specifications to permit more competition, the city lowered the cost from $2.40 per yard to $1.40. See "Paving Graft Smashed! Social-Democrats Break Contractors' Ring," *Social-Democratic Herald,* May 27, 1911.

7. Charles E. McLenegan (1858–1920) served as head of the Milwaukee Public Library, 1910–1920. Following complaints from city librarians, the library's board of trustees reprimanded McLenegan for his "discourtesy" to his employees.

8. I love you so much.

Victor to Meta

Washington, D.C.
June 9, [1911]

My Dear Schatzl:

Enclosed please find a check for another hundred dollars—which is to make it possible for you to buy the groceries etc for Shawano. Towards the end of the month (i.e in two weeks) I will send you another hundred which is to pay your moving expenses and start you in house keeping in Shawano. I hope this will be satisfactory.

Will try to pay off the cottage this summer, also our share on the launch with interest.

It is getting to be very hot in Washington again, but there is not the slightest sign of an adjournment. Nevertheless I shall slip away quietly as often as I can. For instance I am booked to speak at the Sagamore Sociological Conference near Boston at the *end of this month,*—speak there with Seidel on the things accomplished in Milwaukee. May also take in New York on that occassion and speak to a few of the larger unions in order to get money for the daily.

Have bought a ready made linen suit today—could not stand my heavy blue suits any longer.

Had dinner with Lord Percy last night. Mr.—I forget the name—the secretary of the British legation and Mr. Morganstierne, a Norwegian Attache were also there. We had a delightful time. Percy complained that everybody in Washington (in his circles) calls him a Socialist and a disciple of Berger. I told him that was a great honor. He wants to write for the S.D. Herald, but not under his name, but under some nome du plume. I encouraged him to do so.

Our boys in Milwaukee work in a sort of hap-hazard headless fashion. By the way, what became of the park? Ask Seidel, Miss Thomas, Chas Whitnall[1] and Melms and tell me what each of them said.

Have you tended to the note at Marshall & Ilsley's? Puehlicher might just as well go to a sanitarium. The case of Stephenson[2] will follow the Lorimer case[3] and is going to furnish material for another national scandal. It is very probable that both Lorimer and Stephenson will lose their seats in the senate—the latter may be saved by his old age. But with all this our friend Bob La Follette is slowly but surely killing himself in the Republican party—the Insurgent movement has gone to pieces entirely during this extra session and Taft is in the saddle again, as far as his party is concerned. By forcing the issue on the Reciprocity bill with Canada he has demolished the Insurgents (who could not vote for it, on account of the mouthings of the farmers in their states, and yet the leaders of these farmers admitted that their expenses was paid [by] the lumber trust)—while on the other hand these same Progressives (Insurgents etc.) had preached against the tariff and the high cost of living in the last national and state campaign.

Well, Schatzl, I am not going to talk politics to you—it is too hot. I just want to tell you, that we are preparing an old age pension bill—which I will introduce next week.

I expect to break into the debate next week. It is a very dry subject (Schedule K—the tariff on wool) however I will give a short explanation of our entire Socialist philosophy on that occassion and especially make clear our position towards all tariffs.[4]

I have been attacked by a letter from branch Wilmington Del. claiming that the local tried to secure me from the Coit Lecture Bureau for a speech in Wilmington and was held up for $250 per lecture. It seems that the rascally bureau went up in price without telling me any thing about it. I explained that I am going to speak for the party free of charge but that whenever I speak outside of the party I shall make them pay all I can,—especially since I have subscribed $4,000 stock for the paper as you know. Of course I did not tell them or anybody the sum.

Well Schatzl—this is all the news I know—and the letter got to be very lenghty indeed.

Don't be afraid of storms. Only one death of 200,000 is caused by lightning i.e only 1/2000 of a per cent.

Take good care of yourself, Schatzl. Don't worry. Have patience with the Schnuckies. And think of me often. Because, your thoughts are like angels that beware me of pitfalls and are with me in the thick of the battle.

Good night, sweet Schatzl. I must work on my speech now.

Kiss the Schnuckies for me.

V.LB.

1. Charles B. Whitnall (1859–1949), a Milwaukee banker, urban planner, and Socialist, served as city treasurer, 1910–1912, and as a member of the Milwaukee Public Land Commission, 1912–1943, and the Milwaukee County Park Commission, 1907–1947.

2. The Wisconsin legislature reelected Isaac Stephenson to the U.S. Senate in 1909 following a 1908 primary campaign in which he had spent more than $100,000. A subsequent session of the legislature challenged Stephenson's election, but the Senate refused to remove him from office.

3. William Lorimer (1861–1934), a Republican representative from Illinois, 1895–1901 and 1903–1909, and U.S. senator, 1909–1912. The Senate declared his seat vacant in 1912 because of corrupt election practices.

4. Berger made his first major speech in Congress on June 14, 1911, and received favorable press attention. More than 800,000 copies of the speech were eventually distributed.

Victor to Meta

New York, New York
July 2, [1911]

My Sweet Mamma:

The day was so ungodly hot in New York that I dread the night in the sleeper and the day in Washington tomorrow. New York may be hot *but* the asphalt pavements of Washington of which that city has several hundred miles and wide expanses at that—surely beat anything this side of Hades.

Schatzl, I have a good mind to run away some of these days—say nothing to anybody and simply run to Shawano to my Schnuckie-Mamma and my Mamma-Schnuckies. If I only dared—but I must stay until the middle of the month at least.

Emil Seidel was here with me all this time. This afternoon he went to a Saenger Picnic in Brooklyn, and I did not go with him—first because I have to go to Washington this evening and I might miss my train; Second because it is so confoundedly hot. And since [they] do not expect me, but they expect him, why push my attendance upon them?

I hope you and the Schnuckies have a nice time in Shawano. I am glad you have Nettie[1] up there since she seems to be the [most] sympathetic to you of the entire club.

Do not bother about Doris' watch. May be I will bring one home to her, but don't tell her anything about it.

My answer to Mr. Dennis McCarthy[2] the editor of the Sacred Heart Magazine in Boston (at the Sagamore Beach conference) was the *feature* of that convention—by a unanimous vote, Schatzl. It would have done your heart good and a *thrill* went through the meeting which was still the talk of the entire crowd when we left. Mr. McCarthy asked me—I had to answer the question you see—"whether there was *punch* enough left in the Socialist party (—this is a pugilistic expression)—to come back next spring?"

I told that if the Roman Church was not going to quit politics and the holy alliance of grafters, contractors, prostitutes and capitalists in Milwaukee,—that the Roman church would soon find out how much punch there was in this fist (making a fist) and that the Roman church would undergo a new Reformation which would do much more thourough work of it than did Luther, Calvin and Knox. Then I explained that the Roman church in this country was ruled by an old Italian ignorant peasant, who was pope[3]—and who transplanted the hatred of the church against the European Socialists—who fought for free schools and for the emancipation of the state from Roman church domination—to this country, where the church has never ruled this country and never can, without having a 30 years war like the church caused in Europe in the XVII century. Then I gave a short survey of the history of the Roman church in the past and of her aspirations for the future—Schatzl, all in five minutes and it was great.

Mr. Dennis McCarthy did not have punch enough left to come back, but simply explained that he did not mean anything wrong by his question. But the scene itself cannot easily be described.

Well, Sweetheart, it is very hot, the letter is getting very lenghty and I will close.

But remember—as soon as the babies get a little older, so that they can take care of themselves a little better, you must go with me every where, because *I will not go without you.* You have so far not witnessed a single one of my successes—expect probably the meeting at the auditorium on the Sunday before election.

With many kisses, your
V.L.B.

1. Annette Rosenthal (Gould) (b. 1874) graduated from Milwaukee State Normal School in 1894 with Meta Berger, and they remained friends thereafter. She taught at the normal school from 1911 until 1918, when she began teaching in the Milwaukee public schools.

2. Denis Aloysius McCarthy (1870–1931), a Boston journalist and poet, served as associate editor of the *Sacred Heart Review,* a Catholic periodical, from 1900 to 1916.

3. Pius X (1835–1914) (born Giuseppe Melchior Sarto) served as pope from 1903 until his death.

Victor to Meta

Washington, D.C.
July 14, 1911

My Sweet Schatzl:

Have not written to you for two days—partly because I was on my way from Philadelphia—where my speech was a great success, but did not bring the Daily a penny only cost me money—and partly because I felt a queer dizziness in my head for two or three days, which may have been the result of either a spoiled stomach or of the excessive heat or of both.

I am feeling better to-day—and I am going to take a train this afternoon for Columbus O. where I am to speak at a picnic tomorrow afternoon with Strickland[1] and that Mrs. Bloor[2] which you met here. From there I am to go to Dayton O. and return here by Monday.[3]

Since it is pretty thouroughly settled that Congress will adjourn no later than Saturday, Aug. 5th I shall stay to the end of the session. But if by some unexpected complication the session should be extended then I will go home anyway, no matter what the papers may say.

I intend to push the matter of the letter carriers—will see the President next Monday and put in a bill if neccessary.[4]

As for the house I have to leave that matter in the hands of Chas Nesbit[5] who seems to be a very nice fellow, bears an excellent reputation in *all* circles and is a great admirer of V.L.B. Before leaving Washington I shall go around with him for half a day so as to give him an idea what I want and also get an idea of the price. Enclosed, please find our "ad" in today's Times.

My Old Age pension bill I had to work over to make as reasonable as possible. Therefore it will not get in before next week.

When on my way to Philadelphia I got acquainted—(or rather closer acquainted) with Upton Sinclair,[6] his wife[7] and coterie. They live in a Single Tax Colony in Delaware called Arden. What a lot of weakly, well-meaning but impossible crazy chickens they are! Will tell you all about them—spent an afternoon there and they came in to my lecture in Philadelphia.

I am tired of the business around here and want to see my Schatzl and my Schnuckies. If I get there by the 5th of Aug. then I will be just right; darling, will I? Und kein "rubber-neck", nicht wahr?[8] I was real sorry to hear that my little Doris is suffering from poison ivy. She never had it before. It seems that they are more apt to catch these things since they eat meat—I mean fish, chicken and sweet meat.

Otherwise Schatzl, I do not know of any news. I have ordered the Washington papers for you and I hope that you get them.

The demand for my speech is still growing;—and so does the editorial comment on the speech.

Ich hab' Dich lieb, Schatzl![9] Think of me as much as you can, for you are my good angel and thus the good angel of the entire movement and to no small extent of the entire country.

V.L.B.

1. Rev. Frederick Guy Strickland, one of the founders of the Social Democratic Party, served as associate editor of *Social Forum,* the journal of the National Christian Citizenship League.
2. Ella Reeve Bloor (1862–1951) worked as an organizer for the Socialist Party and for various labor unions. She joined the Communist Labor Party in

1919 and served on the Central Committee of the Communist Party, U.S.A., 1932–1948.

3. After speaking in Columbus, Berger changed his plans and traveled to Wisconsin. On July 16, he made an impromptu speech before a crowd of 25,000 at a Socialist Party picnic in Milwaukee, and he then visited his family in Shawano.

4. Berger met with President Taft to request a change in work rules requiring postal workers to wear coats year round, even in hot weather. See William Howard Taft to Victor L. Berger, July 28, 1911, Berger Papers, SHSW. See also Victor to Meta, July 9, 1913, below.

5. Charles Francis Nesbit (1867–1934) was a Washington, D.C., insurance agent and adviser to several labor organizations.

6. Upton Sinclair Jr. (1878–1968), a muckraking journalist and novelist, became famous for *The Jungle* (1906), which exposed unsanitary practices in the Chicago meat packing industry. Sinclair joined the Socialist Party in 1902 but left it in 1917 because of its opposition to World War I. Rejoining the party after the war, Sinclair ran as a Socialist for public office several times in California between 1920 and 1930. He won the Democratic nomination for governor of California in 1934 but lost the general election.

7. Meta Fuller (1880–1964) married Upton Sinclair in 1900. Sinclair sued his wife for divorce in August, 1911, and a divorce was granted early in 1913.

8. And no "rubber-neck", all right?

9. I love you, little darling!

Victor to Meta

Chicago, en route to Wheeling, West Virginia
[July 23, 1911]

My Sweet Schatzl:

This is a sort of a penitent note—penitent because all felt like a *sinner* all day yesterday and to-day for having been grouchy while at the lake with my Schatzl. And yet—you know and I know that there is nobody in the world like my sweet Schatzl for me, and that you are not only sweet and noble and good—but also brighter than most of the women I have ever met. And that while I have married you fourteen years ago for sake of love pure and simple, I would marry you three times over now, because you are not only lovely and sweet but also bright and pure and good. And on top of it all a much better politician than I ever dared to be.

Now, sweetheart have I made up for the two days? Say, yes darling, for I had Gewissensbisse[1] on the train.

But Miss Thomas made me fearfully angry and I gave her a calling down like I never gave to any woman in my life. You see I had given strict orders not to attack Nieman[2] personally and even to mention the Journal as little as possible. The Journal was never a Socialist paper and we had no business to attack Nieman, as if he were a renegade from the Socialist party.

Instead of obeying my orders Miss Thomas deliberately *forced* copy upon Heath (mainly from Sandburg and Seidel) which made the last issue one contin[u]ous attack upon "Lute" Nieman, even dragging in his wife.[3]

Miss Thomas when I asked her about it, told me that by my absence I had "forfeited my leadership" and that my going to the Journal "looked like treason" to her etc.

I thought the woman was insane. I told her there was *nothing* I could commit treason to, *except* the *fifth congressional* district,—that was the most important thing in the Milwaukee movement, because the rest had no brains and *did not make good,* and that included her. And I told her that if she ever interfere[d] in my editorial policy again, she would have to go.

Well, Schatzl I am not over it yet. I called up Nieman and told him that I was not responsible for having his wife dragged in and that I did not approve of it. He thanked me and was very nice about it.

Gave Ernie[4] six dollars and told him to go Shawano *today.* I suppose he is there and will tell you his tale of woe himself.

With many kisses
Your cross
VL.B.

1. a guilty conscience.
2. Lucius "Lutie" Nieman (1857–1935) served as editor, 1882–1935, of the *Milwaukee Journal,* an independent paper that generally supported Democratic candidates.
3. The *Social-Democratic Herald,* July 22, 1911, contained a lengthy article attacking Nieman that twice referred to his "millionaire wife," Agnes Wahl Nieman (1870–1936), who was the daughter of a wealthy Milwaukee industrialist.
4. Ernst Schlichting, Meta's brother.

Meta to Victor

[Shawano, Wisconsin]
July 25, 1911

Papa! Darling!

You know how I worship you! What's the use of talking about it any more. The only thing that worries me is that I always think I'm over being so dreadfully nervous and then all of a sudden I find I'm not. Nettie[1] said after you left that never before did she realize how fearfully high-strung my nerves are. She said I was a completely changed individual. Now isn't that just dreadful to be changed for the worst when the one I love the best in all the world visits me? I can't understand & it must be changed. But how?

What you tell me of Miss Thomas doesn't surprise me in the least. All along I've told you that Miss Thomas was different, changed and not to your benefit, but just what it was I couldn't describe. Now you've seen it yourself. She is very intimate with the Sandburgs.[2] The Herald gave Carl Sandburg a berth and I wouldn't be surprised if he was trying to dictate the policy of the paper a bit now.

Keep your eyes on the Mil. situation dearest, don't let lo[o]se for a minute for even your best & most loyal people are not to be trusted especially now since they have had a taste of office holding and such success as that brings with it. Their ambition is stronger than their loyalty. Sometimes I wish you might have remained to have made this administration the success it ought to and would have been.

The days have been so cold and rainy that we have had a fire in both the kitchen stove and grate from morning until night. The sun is shining this morning however and things look brighter again.

Take good care of yourself my brown bear; with out you life would indeed be dull and uninteresting, hopeless. With lots of love & kisses I am always

your devoted
Meta

1. Annette Rosenthal (Gould).
2. Elizabeth Thomas had introduced Lilian Steichen (1883–1977), a Socialist schoolteacher, to Carl Sandburg late in 1907. The couple married in June, 1908.

Victor to Meta

Washington, D.C.
August 6, [1911]

Sweet Schatzl:

Just now it is hard to tell when we are going to adjourn. Underwood[1] told yesterday that he did not believe we could adjourn before Sept. 1st—Champ Clark[2] told me the same. On the 11th I shall be in Milwaukee however, although we have a meeting at the headquarters in Chicago on the morning of the same day.

My Old Age Pension bill has created more attention than anything I have done so far. And this is only the beginning, because we shall begin a nation-wide agitation for a constitutional convention and for the Old Age Pension bill—in every union, in every lodge and in every society.

I have moved from the Farragut to the Congress Hall hotel. My month expired the 5th of the month and I did not feel like paying for a full month's rent when I wasn't going to stay longer than a few days. At the hotel I pay four dollars a day for a room (nice corner room on the fifth floor) with bath and three meals. This is the "congressional rate", otherwise it would be a dollar more—this is the first time that anybody in Washington suggested that a congressman pays less than other people. Usually the contrary is the case. Your letters sent to the old address will reach me, however. I expect no letter in answer to this, because in order to be in time for the preliminary hearing in Chicago in the Barnes matter,[3] I may have to leave here on Wednesday—will find out how the New Yorkers go.

We have a very ugly and deplorable mess in the national office in Chicago. I shall tell you all about it when I get home.

I hope the Schnuckies are all right and good and obedient to their Schuckie-Mamma. Otherwise I shall take my Schnuckie-Mamma alone to Washington and send the girlies to some boarding-school, where they will learn to wash dishes, cook and obey.

With many kisses to all

Ever your
Papa.

Expect to be received by Schatzl on the 11th.

1. Oscar W. Underwood (1862–1929), a Democrat, served as a representative from Alabama, 1895–1896 and 1897–1915, and as a U.S. senator, 1915–1927. Underwood was the party's floor leader in the House, 1911–1915, and Senate minority leader, 1920–1923.
2. James Beauchamp "Champ" Clark (1850–1921) was a Democratic representative from Missouri, 1893–1895 and 1897–1921. Clark served as House minority leader, 1907–1911 and 1919–1921, and Speaker of the House, 1911–1919.
3. The Socialist Party's National Executive Committee held hearings in August, 1911, concerning charges of corruption and sexual misconduct against the party secretary, J. Mahlon Barnes. The committee accepted Barnes's resignation and replaced him with John M. Work.

Victor to Meta

Washington, D.C.
August 30, [1911]

My Sweet Mamma-Schatzl:

This time you have a right "to kick" because I did not write, although my night- and day-messages kept you fairly well informed about my where-abouts.

To begin with my speech in Baltimore:—that was a great success! The biggest meeting our party ever had there, with the possible exception of

Debs meeting on the occassion of the "Red Special". However this is to be said for my meeting: It rained cats and dogs between 6 and 8 o'clock—yet the crowd was so big at the park that hardly one-fifth of those present could hear me. My entrance was the usual—the people stood in line on both sides about ten deep and cheered. A band preceded the committee and me—the band playing the "Marseillaise"? Oh no! The band played "Oh Maryland, my Maryland"—the same tune as "O Tannanbaum, o Tannanbaum"! The committee *had* ordered the former, but the band didn't have the notes, so the "Tannanbaum" had to do.

You gave me a pretty bad scare about the typhoid at Shawano Lake. Moreover I believe that the wells cannot be dug too deeply there—with the loose sand-soil and the numerous water-closets and stables. The trouble is that the Shawano crowd is too stingy and too ignorant to give any attention to sanitation. I am glad you offered to go half on the ice-house proposition, sweetheart.

By this time you know that Huebschmann wired me that the Neacy suit will not come up this week. However it may come up next week, in which case I shall have to miss some of my New York dates.

I want you to come to New York about the 15th, if you can. I shall work out the details later and let you know. However I am going to have *four* dates in Connecticut (19th–22nd) beginning in Bridgeport on 19th, which date I hope will be a day of *joy* and *glory* for *my old parents*. I want *you* to be there also, because to you, your love and unselfish devotion, I owe more than to any other human being, except my mother,—and if this movement should ever achieve real success through my humble efforts, a great share of the credit belongs to *you*, sweet Schatzl.

As to the Sinclair affair[1]—that is of course very disagreeable and even painful to me because the entire movement (including myself) will have to bear some of the odium, but don't let that bother you any further. And so much is sure: *As long as you are the kind of wife you have been* to me during the fourteen years we have been married—*no woman can ever come between us.* I may laugh and joke with this or the other—but there is no woman living like my Schatzl. And even as to "flirtation", I have had a very severe lesson, as you know.

Therefore, Mamma-darling, you just take good care of your love for me, and of your two Schnuckies—and your grandchildren, if you ever have any, will bless your memory. As for me—I am and always will be (as far as character is concerned) what *you* make of me. As I have told you once before—from Europe if I am not mistaken—every loving thought of yours is a guardian angel for me. So much for teleopathy. Otherwise you need not worry: V.L.B. protected by the infinite and indescribable Genius of humanity is absolutely fearless and well able to take of himself as a rule.

And I do hope and wish that I shall live another fifteen years and keep to my health, intelligence and energy to take care of my family—to educate my children, and to secure the old age of my Schatzl. Because the movement will very soon be able to care for itself, even without my aid and interference.

However, Schatzl—this letter is again one of those that someway-another got to be sentimental—which is not to my taste.

Goodbye, Sweetheart. Kiss the babies for me. I shall soon see you in New York.

Ever your
V.L.B.

1. Socialist Upton Sinclair sued his wife, Meta Fuller Sinclair, for divorce on August 28, 1911, naming Harry Kemp, a poet, as the co-respondent. The Sinclairs and Kemp met with the press and amicably discussed trial marriage, free love, and the economic emancipation of women, causing embarrassment for conservative Socialists such as Berger. See "Sinclair Sues Wife, But They're Friends," *New York Times,* August 29, 1911.

Victor to Meta

[Milwaukee, Wisconsin]
March 16, 1912

My Sweet Schatzl:

Busy is no name for it—I am a sort of a Chief Justice all day long, and a field marshall besides. The enthusiasm of our crowd is so great that I do not dare to go to any meeting any more because they yell themselves hoarse as soon as I am recognized. My first official appearance will take place at the great mass meeting at the Auditorium Monday March 18th. After that I shall speak at two more meetings both at the Auditorium—one of them at the night of election. The comrades finally got sense enough not to book me at all sorts of dinky halls—even the turner halls are not considered to be big enough for me.

If the *size* of the meetings—especially compared with the meetings of the enemy—is to be any criterion at all, there is simply an unheard of victory in sight. Our comrades do not understand however that there is a tremendous crowd on the other side that never goes to meetings but is accostumed to vote their old party tickets and, therefore, I warn them not to be over-confident. But considering that we will get more Polish votes than ever—and that holds good of all foreign nationalities as far as they can vote—there can be no question that we poll a terrific vote.[1]

Now that is the situation. The only trouble is that all the papers are fighting us tooth and nail. The Leader[2] is gaining so rapidly however, that the time is not far distant when we shall have as much local circulation as all the other papers combined.

Well Schatzl, sweetheart I hope to have you here soon and have you in my arms soon. As it is I lead a very dreary and excited life, drawing a great deal of fire from the enemy—on account of my "yacht" and my "country home."[3] The affair has been overdone so much in the past however that really works as a boomerang. It is a very bitter campaign, but it will not be as ugly as it was in the past—as far as I am personally concerned. In fact the Sentinel has written some very respectful editorials about me since I am here—even a warm "Wilkommen to the great and famous comrade," and that is surely something considering that election takes place, two weeks from Tuesday.

Kiss the babies for me, sweetheart mine. And remember, that you are my good fairy, who holds at least one of the "three gold hairs" which God has given me to make me beloved by men, women and children—in spite of my ugly temperament.

Ever your,
[V.L.B.]

1. The Socialists suffered a major defeat in the Milwaukee election of April 2, 1912. A fusion ticket of Democrats and Republicans won control of the Common Council and County Board and defeated the incumbent Socialist mayor, treasurer, and comptroller.

2. The daily *Milwaukee Leader* began publishing on December 7, 1911. Berger served as the paper's editor until his death and was one of the principal stockholders in the Milwaukee Social-Democratic Publishing Company, which published the paper.

3. Berger's political opponents criticized his standard of living, including his summer cottage and boat on Shawano Lake in northeastern Wisconsin.

Victor to Meta

Washington, D.C.
[June 30, 1912]

My sweet Schatzl:

I slept late—after having talked it over with Democratic congressmen until 2 o'clock in the morning last night—i.e. talked over the situation in Baltimore.[1] If we Socialists had a party as we should have and a different candidate than Debs—we could take advantage of the situation. As it is—I may be the only Socialist [in] congress again next time—and in a way this may be the best thing for the party, which is in an academic and puerile condition still.

I took a long walk this morning—Prof. Thomas Will,[2] a former employee of the Forestry department, in whose church I spoke last winter—came to see me and we took a walk together. He told me of his troubles with the impossibilists in Kansas seven years ago. They not only took away everything he had but tried to land him in prison for criminal libel. The Appeal crowd in Girard standing sponsor for a great deal of the attacks against him. Will is a Christian socialist—but not of the Carr[3] type, thinks a great deal of Thompson[4] and Gaylord[5] and would like to work for the national party during the campaign or—*become my secretary.* He was willing to take the job right-a-way since Ghent[6] had resigned, but I told him that to begin with Ghent is going to draw Salary for an additional month. I shall need a man for my campaign in Milwaukee however, and I may use [him] during August, September and October—shall think the matter over thoroughly however, before I make any promises to him or anybody. If I could possibly do it, I would rather keep that salary during the three months and give it to the party in Milwaukee. On the other hand—if I have a man on the job as my private secretary, doing nothing else than promoting my election, that is also a great and decided advantage. Let me know *your* opinion in this matter Schatzl.

I still have a very desolate and lonesome feeling—a feeling as if I were all alone here, with nobody in particular taking any interest in me. Am I beginning to get old? I want to go home as soon as I can, but before I go I hope to do *something worth while* during the next two weeks.

Well don't worry! Take it easy in Shawano. Don't forget Schatzl, that your nerves have become a part of my nervous system.

Kiss the babies for me
V.L.B.

I am writing this in a very awkward position, so please excuse the penmanship.

1. The Democratic National Convention, which had been meeting in Baltimore since June 25, remained deadlocked over the nomination of a presidential candidate.
2. Thomas Will (b. 1861) was a college professor and president, newspaper editor, and U.S. Forest Service employee between 1891 and 1906, when he became president of the American Forestry Association and editor of its magazine. Will resigned in 1908 and pursued a career as a lecturer.
3. Rev. Edward Ellis Carr (b. 1865?) was editor of the Chicago-based *Christian Socialist.*
4. Carl D. Thompson (1870–1949), a Congregational minister, served as a Socialist member of the Wisconsin Assembly, 1907–1909, and director of the Information Department of the Socialist Party, 1911–1915. He spent the last thirty-five years of his life organizing and writing on behalf of the public ownership of utilities.
5. Winfield Gaylord (b. 1870) was a Congregational and Methodist minister until 1902, when he became a lecturer for the Socialist Party. Gaylord served

in the Wisconsin Senate, 1909–1913, and ran unsuccessfully for Congress five times between 1904 and 1916, losing by fewer than five hundred votes in 1910 and fewer than four hundred votes in 1914. Gaylord left the party in 1917 because he supported American involvement in World War I.

6. William James Ghent (1866–1942) became Berger's congressional secretary in 1911 but resigned the following year because he had contracted tuberculosis. A Socialist Party member since 1904, Ghent served as secretary, 1906–1909, and president, 1909–1911, of the Rand School of Social Science. He left the Socialist Party because of its opposition to World War I and in his later years wrote about the history of the American West.

Victor to Meta

Washington, D.C.
[July 2, 1912]

My Sweet Schatzl:

Enclosed, please, find a check for one hundred and fifty dollars so that you [will] be in a position to feed my Schnuckies on something else than fish and pine nuts—at least for a while. Deposit the check as usual in the bank and draw checks on it.

For the month of June there are quite a number of household bills to pay in Washington. I shall also send a check for sixty dollars to Schoknecht which will pay our rent until July 1st.—whether I will be able to meet the Gimbel and the Boston bills this month may depend on circumstances, but I hope so.

By this time you undoubtedly know all about the Democratic nominations. I should like to have seen a less "progressive"[1] nominated by the Democrats—on the other hand this nomination in all probability disposes of Teddy as a third party candidate and at the same time it has created such extreme bitterness in the Democratic camp that I cannot see how he can carry even his own home state of New Jersey, especially since Hearst is fighting him most bitterly. In New York Tammany will dispose of him.

I have to write out an interview tonight and so my letter must by necessity be short. Take special good care of yourself now, because you are getting older. Don't worry about anything—by-the-way I have written a nice letter to Miss Thomas—and remember you must live another thirty years because you will have to take care of your Schnuckies and see to it that they are happily married or otherwise well started in life.

Moreover I can hardly tell you how much I miss you. I never felt so lonesome before in my life and I am counting the days for this session to be over. With many kisses

Ever Your
V.L.B.

1. Woodrow Wilson (1856–1924), the governor of New Jersey, 1911–1913, received the Democratic presidential nomination on July 2, 1912, and served as U.S. president, 1913–1921.

Victor to Meta

Washington, D.C.
July 23, 1912

My Sweet Mamma-Darling:

My speech will appear in today's record and I shall send you a copy of course. It was well received and widely advertised—although by the very nature of the speech I could not get the applause I received for my other speeches. Expect to make one more speech—on the trusts. Expect to get a chance next week.

As for the Leader I have quite made up my mind to "fire" three–four of the men working there as soon as I get to Milwaukee. I don't know whether Bistorius will resume his position or not—he has [not] notified me. In fact nobody seems to tell me anything—the paper is simply drifting along. Bistorius is not a "genius", but he has a plodding and patient mind and he knows a great deal about machinery, the engine of the Thetis notwithstanding.

I am sending this letter to Milwaukee in care of Schoknecht's—as I did another letter before. Hope you will get them in time.

Congress will not adjourn before Aug 15th but I will. I have made up my mind to be home by the 10th and I expect to keep my promise to myself.

Today I was all alone—because Harris[1] was sick. Mail seems to be pouring in again in great shape—and I may have to get extra-help next week.

You have probably by this time heard about the great victory I have achieved in the Hanford case—Judge Hanford resigned his position by wire while being under fire.[2] There were only two Federal judges removed since the foundation of the republic—Hanford is the third and Judge Archbald[3] if he is found guilty *may be* the fourth.

Yet with all this (what some would call success) I feel very depressed and lonesome. There is an ugly fight in the party by the Haywood-Kerr[4]-Carr forces against Barnes, which now took the shape of an attack against Hillquitt and also against the entire Executive Committee, especially against me. Eugene V. Debs has joined in the attack, has had an almost personal encounter with Hillquitt and has issued a "manifesto" wherein he (Debs) claims that I had formed a "combination" against him. All of this just before election—isn't he contemptible?[5]

There can be no question that this party will have to get rid of the Haywood crowd and we will throw Debs after them.

I don't want to bother you with all this, sweet Schatzl—I only want to tell you that you [are] just as far above every woman I know, as—well comparisons are odious. Just now I am angry at some of the women in Ohio, especially one, Margaret Prevey,[6] who is using the state organization to turn Ohio into the hands of the impossibilists.

Tell me darling, whether you had a pleasant time at the committee meetings and where you are staying or whom you have at the flat with you, because I don't want you to be there all alone.

Kiss the babies for me—or convey my kisses—you can do it sweetheart.

V.L.B.

1. George H. Harris replaced William Ghent as Berger's congressional secretary in 1912. Harris forged Berger's signature on several checks during the fall of 1912, but Berger declined to prosecute him.

2. Cornelius H. Hanford (1829–1926) served as a federal judge in Washington state, 1890–1912. On June 7, 1912, Berger introduced a resolution in the House calling for Hanford's impeachment because of the judge's misbehavior, including his illegal revocation of the citizenship papers of an IWW member. Hanford resigned before hearings on the charges could be completed.

3. Federal judge Robert W. Archbald (1848–1926) of Pennsylvania was impeached and removed from office in January, 1913, because of conflicts of interest in his business dealings.

4. Charles H. Kerr (1860–1944) founded and directed the Chicago socialist publishing house of Charles H. Kerr and Company and published the *International Socialist Review* from 1900 until its suppression in 1918. Kerr, a left-wing Socialist, supported William D. Haywood and the IWW.

5. At the 1912 Socialist Party convention, Morris Hillquit won the appointment of J. Mahlon Barnes as campaign manager for the upcoming election. Barnes had lost his job as the party's national secretary the previous year because of charges of sexual immorality, and his choice in 1912 triggered opposition from Christian socialists, such as Edward Ellis Carr, who were outraged by Barnes's private behavior, and from members of the left-wing faction of the party, such as William Haywood and Charles H. Kerr, who saw an opportunity to attack the Hillquit and Berger faction. Although Eugene Debs joined those who called for the removal of Barnes, the party's leadership refused to do so.

6. Marguerite Prevey (1874–1925), an Ohio Socialist lecturer and organizer, was one of the original members of the Socialist National Woman's Committee.

Victor to Meta

Washington, D.C.
July 30, [1912]

My Sweet Mamma-Darling:

I received your letter dated last Sunday today. I am not quite clear what you went to Milwaukee for—since your school board meeting is not until Aug. 6th (Tuesday) and you *cannot* leave the children alone in Shawano that long. By your letter I see that you intend to return by Fri-

day, July 2nd,[1] so it was evidently a meeting of your committee that you
wanted to attend. That's all right enough, but is the light worth the candle, sweetheart? Your trip will cost you a lot of money.

However, I am very thankful for the flowers you sent me. And for
the letter accompanying the same. That I am needed very much in Milwaukee goes without saying. I shall stay there only a day or so, on my
way to Shawano, however, because I want to spend a week with my family at the lake before I do anything else.

If you can hardly wait, sweetheart,—then what shall I say? Because
after all you have the Schnuckies, and all I have is your letters—your
sweet refreshing letters, each of them giving me a mental bath (per-
fumed with your wonderful love) when I receive it in the office in the
morning. And I am always inclined to be cross and ugly whenever there
isn't a letter from you in the pile—Harris knows it and, therefore, he
invariably puts your letter on top of the heap. From this you can judge
the importance of having a love-message from you every day. You see I
am getting worse as I am getting older.

Moreover darling I am getting stout and nervous and sometimes I
think I would be best for me to undergo a hunger cure like Upton Sinclair for 30 days or so. It is a heroic remedy but I have seen a girl whom
the doctors had given up on account of a goiter—cure her goiter in
that way. Furthermore after the starvation cure she gained wonderfully
and she was a regular female giant when I saw her at Arden last year.

At any rate I must do something for my nervousness which is gaining on me and which puts me into a rather unfavorable [position] on
the eve of a hot campaign.

Of course, darling, there will be two and possibly three candidates in
the field against me. They cannot possibly unite—because by doing so
they would deliberately turn over the state to the Democrats—something
which McGovern cannot possibly permit, because he is running for governor on the Republican ticket.

Their chief difficulty however, is that they have no daily paper in
Milwaukee—out of sheer hatred for the Leader and because the Milwaukee gang of politicians wants the county offices, all of the Milwaukee dailies are for fusion. Of course, the Sentinel and the Milwaukee
Merchants & Manufacturers know of no party lines within capitalism,
and they are through with the sham battle—Wilson and Democrats
look as good to them as Taft and the Republicans.

This is a golden opportunity for the Leader, only my people in Milwaukee do not seem to know how to take care of it. The only one who
seems to come near it is *Howe*,[2] but he lacks the elementary force which
God has given me as a birthday present.

Therefore, sweetheart-schatzl mine, I shall have a big job on hand
when I get home. And more than ever will I depend on your love, your

advice, and your sweet magnetism—to brace me up, uphold me and help me to victory.

Kiss the babies for me and always remember: that dear as my cause is to me—the only real valuable achievement of my life *is* my Schnuckie-Mamma,—*will be* my Schnuckies, if they pan out to be like their Mamma.

With kind regards to all and thousand kisses to you

V.L.B.

1. Berger meant Friday, August 2.
2. James R. Howe (1868–1917) served as the editorial writer for the *Milwaukee Leader* from 1911 until his death.

Victor to Meta

Milwaukee, Wisconsin
August 11, 1912

My Sweet Mamma-Schatzl:

At home again—and it was high time that I should come. The editorial rooms of the Leader are getting to be disorganized—Rhodes[1] the cartoonist is also leaving them, getting three times the salary in Chicago he had here.

The conference this morning came to naught—the Leader employes having their first annual picnic. I did not go out to Lake Muskego, having two big propositions on hand for today and tomorrow—an article for the American Magazine[2] which must be there Wednesday, and a speech for the Congressional Record on Trusts—for the first time and may be for the last time I asked "leave to print" because I could not get the time in the House when I wanted it and I could not stay over for this week. We want something to send out for the campaign under my "frank" on the Trusts, however and that is what I am going to do with the speech I am writing now.

The weather was delightful in Washington the last few days and nobody appreciated this more than I—because I am practically all in. Expect to take the train on Tuesday evening for Shawano, if anything should develop suddenly so that I could not go, I shall call up Frank Schweers[3] by telephon and let you know. It may just come to pass, sweetheart, that you may have to come to Milwaukee to see me, although I would of course a thousand times rather go up to Shawano.

Conditions in Chicago—I mean in the National office are very deplorable—but the anti-sabotage clause seems to have won with a good majority.[4] I am not quite so sure about the referendum to recall Barnes.[5] We may lose out there. I wish the impossibilists would leave the party and take Debs with them.

But, darling, I should not bother you with party matters at this time. As for my re-election, the local situation is such that with a little *intelligent* work I will win with a bigger majority then I ever won in my life before.

Good-by, sweetheart, until Tuesday night, unless I let you know otherwise.

Kiss the Schnuckies for me, and remember, always remember, you and the babies are my most precious achievements and you even more than the babies.

With thousand kisses
V.L.B.

1. Clarence D. "Dusty" Rhodes (1878?–1929) served as a cartoonist, photographer, and special assignment reporter for the *Milwaukee Leader* from December, 1911, until August, 1912, when he left to work for the *Chicago World*.

2. Berger's essay, urging progressives to vote the Socialist ticket, was part of a series of articles on the 1912 presidential election by Jane Addams, Herbert Croly, Herbert Quick, and Charles E. Townsend under the heading, "The Progressive's Dilemma." See Victor L. Berger, "Socialism, the Logical Outcome of Progressivism," *American Magazine* 75 (November, 1912): 19–21.

3. Frank D. Schweers (1868–1948) married Meta's sister, Hattie, in 1909. He was a Shawano, Wisconsin, hardware dealer, machine shop owner, and automobile dealer and served on the Shawano County Board, 1938–1946.

4. The 1912 Socialist convention adopted an amendment to the party constitution calling for the expulsion any member who advocated sabotage, a clause that was used to drive William Haywood from the party in 1913. The membership adopted the amendment in a referendum by a vote of 13,000 to 4,000.

5. The referendum on the retention of J. Mahlon Barnes as campaign manager passed by a vote of 19,000 to 11,500. See Victor to Meta, July 23, 1912, above.

Victor to Meta

Washington, D.C.
December 2, 1912

My dear Schatzl:

This letter is to convey my sincerest congratulations to the new house and to your wedding anniversary. It is also the first letter that I send to 980 First street—the Red House—the Berger homestead.

And you are of course entitled to a wedding present. Enclosed please find fifty dollars which I want you to spend on your blue suit which should be ready for Christmas—and if you go to the tailor at once it will be ready. Whatever is left over, I want you to spend for Christmas presents for the children.

The situation here is not quite so bad as I feared. The national office owes me over 300 dollars—and the National owes me over fifty dollars for printed speeches which were delivered—I owe nearly $400 to the Public printer—therefore that will about square it.

Everybody here seems to be sorry that I was defeated[1]—even the Standpatters.[2] I tell them that if I live and everything goes well with me, I am not going to stay away from the halls of Congress long.

I can about imagine how the house looks just now. I hope the workmen—carpenters and painters—are out by this time. Please do not overwork. Get help. Your nerves,—your health—is of infinitely more importance to me than a few dollars. It is *cheaper* not to have these little worries.

Please get my little brown bank book of the Metropolitan National bank and send it to me. It is in the old black walnut book case with the other bank books.

Kiss the babies for me. And don't worry! Don't work too hard! Think lovingly of me.

V.L.B.

1. Although Berger received more votes (14,025) in 1912 than he did in 1910 (13,497), he nonetheless lost his bid for reelection to Congress to Republican William H. Stafford, who ran as a fusion candidate on the Democratic ticket. Stafford received 41 percent to Berger's 36 percent and nonfusing Republican James F. Trottman's 21 percent.
2. A name of derision coined by progressive or insurgent Republicans for their conservative opponents in the party.

Victor to Meta

Washington, D.C.
December 10, [1912]

My dear Schatzl:

I broke into the record yesterday with a short speech—will send you the issue of that day. I didn't expect to speak—was practically forced to do so, by some of the "laborites"—Buchanan[1] in this case.

Had an interesting visitor today—an editorial writer from the New York World who wants me to give him a short article (4–500 words) for a Christmas symposium on "international peace".[2] He stayed in my office until almost 11. PM. We talked about everything under the sun— he was formerly Mr. Pulitzers private secretary—is an Englishman by the name of Allain Ireland[3]—and quite well read on history and political economy.

Circumstances are such that I have to attend the sessions in the · house and can do little work, except evenings. The mornings are taken up with business in the departments or with visitors in my office.

I haven't told you about my visit to Mr. Taft. Went there to get a pardon for a Milwaukee soldier boy[4]—the son of Mr. Ohde, superinten-

dent of the Diamond Ink Co—who had sold whisky to his fellow soldiers. It was the next thing to muriatic acid—fearful stuff—and he
charged them two dollars for it. He was employed as a cook and he sold
the whisky to the soldiers doing duty in the kitchen.

Bringing whisky to the reservation and selling it to other soldiers—
is considered a great crime. Moreover it was miserable stuff which
added to his guilt. So he got off *easily*, when he was sentenced to a *year*
in the penitentiary at hard labor.

But he also lied under oath when on the witness stand on his own
behalf. This was proved on him, he was court-marshalled again two
weeks later, and did a wise thing when he pleaded guilty of "lying under
oath"; because thus he got off with *one* additional year at hard labor—
otherwise it would have been "perjury" and *three* years additional.

And the boy is only 19 years old. His father suffers from diabetes
and cannot live long any more. He came to see me at my office when I
was home. And so did the mother who was almost insane with grief.

Under the circumstances I tried to do my best. Mr Taft was very
friendly. He expressed his regret about my defeat and said "we both
went down together." "Yes" said I, "but with this difference, my party is a
coming party, while the Republican party is going and going fast." He
was inclined to agree with me there. Then he inquired about you and
whether you were in Washington. I told him, you had to stay home and
take care of the family, while I was trying to take care of the country. He
laughed and told me that his wife[5] was also very glad that his public
cariere was over. He told me that he would never run for president
again; and I believed him, considering the showing he had made—carrying two states, Utah and Vermont—of course I didn't say anything.

I asked him what he was going to do after the 4th of March—and
he told me in absolute confidence—*and I don't want you to tell it to anybody*—that he intends to lecture at Yale university on constitutional law
for $5,000 or 6,000 a year and also practice law "as a counsel" in New
Haven. He hopes to make also about $20,000 a year from his practice. I
asked him whether he had saved any money? He told me frankly that
his wife had saved about $100,000, out of his four years salary—which is
practically about $135,000 a year with all other expenses paid—and that
she had inherited about $45,000 and he had $25,000—so that they had
a total of $170,000, which of course is enough in itself to keep the wolf
from their door, although he will never be in the millionaire class.

We talked about many things and he got [to] be rather confidential. He is very bitter against Roosevelt—whom he considers the biggest
faker in America.[6]

Yet with all this, you ought to have seen his face drop—when I told
him in a very serious and dry voice, that I wasn't so friendly to him for
nothing, and that I also wanted my reward and wanted it right-a-way.

"Well, all right! What is it please?" he said in a rather downcast manner. Then I told him that I wanted the pardon of this boy, whom I had never seen, and whose father and mother I had only met once when they came to beg me to plead for their son's release. Taft even hardly looked at the papers, so glad was he. He rang the bell for his private secretary and dictated the letter to secretary of war, because I insisted that he should do it then and there—and although he first wanted to keep him in the pen until the first year was over, he yielded when I demanded his freedom as a Christmas present. He still had his arm around me when we left the inner room and I suppose some of the people in reception room must have been rather shocked at the familiarity.

But enough of that. After all is said and done, I feel incredibly lonesome here at times, because I don't seem to have any friend here, to whom I can talk about the things that are nearest to my heart. And for that reason alone it is a great thing to have you with me, because you are a part of me,—even if we do not always agree and I do call you a "Schafsnas'"[7] I never mean it.

Your furniture will be probably there when this letter reaches you. Just tell the men taking up to be careful and not to mark the walls and the wood work.

That you are not quite used to your new home, is natural enough. In the first place it is not as yet furnished. It will look differently when your carpets and chairs will be there. By-the-way—you did not tell me, what you got for the stairway? And whether you got your pneumatic carpet cleaner?

Well Schatzl, tell me all of these things and also what the bills are for the house? And above all things tell me always how much you love me—because this new fine home is nothing without your love, Schatzl—my Schnuckie-Mamma.

With thousand kisses
V.L.B.

By-the-way, I sent you some souvenir plates which I got very cheaply— they *guaranteed* their safe arrival in Milwaukee, therefore tell me whether any of them were broken.

    1. Frank Buchanan (1862–1930), a bridge builder and structural iron-worker from Chicago, served as a Democratic congressman from Illinois, 1911–1917. Berger spoke on behalf of a budget amendment providing $15,000 for the Bureau of Standards to investigate the dangers involved in the transmission of electricity.
    2. Berger's essay, "Strikes Will Prevent War," appeared in the *New York World*, December 22, 1912. Berger argued for universal military training and

claimed that organized labor and the international socialist movement could preserve peace by calling general strikes whenever war was declared.

3. Alleyne Ireland (1871–1951), a journalist and author, worked for the *New York World*, 1912–1915. Ireland previously had been the Far East correspondent for the *Times* of London and had lectured at a number of American universities.

4. Harold A. Ohde (b. 1893) was the son of Albert W. (b. 1872) and Augusta Ohde (b. 1871).

5. Helen Herron (1861–1943) married William Howard Taft in 1886.

6. Taft finished third in the presidential election of 1912 behind Democrat Woodrow Wilson and Theodore Roosevelt, who ran as a Progressive. After the completion of his term, Taft taught law at Yale University, 1913–1921, and served as chief justice of the U.S. Supreme Court, 1921–1930.

7. sheep's nose—i.e., a naive, simple-minded, unreasonable person.

Meta to Victor

[Milwaukee, Wisconsin]
January 8, 1913

My honorable Husband:—

You asked me in your day-letter today to tell you what kind of plants I wanted. If I am to have my choice I would like ferns or palms that stay with me the year round, good hardy kind. I do not care for plants that look pretty for a few days and then make your heart sad for weeks while they are drooping until you finally have the courage & heart to discard them. I like ferns of all kinds, but consult the florist and be sure to have them well packed. This is not a good time I fear for shipping plants.

Yesterday Bistorius telephoned me asking about flats. They are going to move again because they cannot stand the noise & the land lord says if they don't like it they can move. I advised them to do what we did & they were willing only where to find a house in such a short time. I told them of Frey's[1] bungalo 2 blocks east of us, so Bistorius telephoned over but found that the house was sold, Frey, getting between 8 & 9 thousand dollars for that little house & lot. Think of it!

Just now Mrs. Cantrovitz[2] rang me up to ask me to go tomorrow morning to the Pfister Club Room to listen to a discussion by the Merchants & Manufacturers against the law shortening the hours of laboring girls.[3] I shall go because it certainly will be interesting.

The children are all seated around me doing homework. I don't believe I've ever felt so comfortable before, except for the great big love I'm missing in your absence. But I do take such comfort & pleasure in our home. Have no desire even to go out.

I bought a McClure's to see what our friend Nan[4] did in her article. I was very much disappointed for not once did she mention the suffrage from a Socialist view point. Purely moral & nothing else. I hope she will do better in her dep't.[5] Others here were equally disappointed. She eulogizes Miss Adams[6] too much considering the unfair attitude Jane took in regard to the Socialist Party, but the pictures are fine. The Suffragists are surely going to do a parade in Washington aren't they?

The day-letter sort of tells me that I won't be getting a letter again for a day or more on account of the slowness of mail. Please don't fall behind darling. My letter to you must be written daily. It is as important as my meals and then some. Can't you get the habit too?

I'm anxious to hear of the surprise you may have for me. I hope it is some thing real good. But your coming home is as good as I want any thing just now.

Du Racker, ich hab Dich so schrecklich lieb![7]

With tender & deep love I am always

Your own
Schnukie Mama!

1. Probably Benjamin Frey, a Milwaukee real estate agent.
2. Bella Cantrovitz (b. 1870?) served on the Milwaukee school board, 1911–1917.
3. According to the *Milwaukee Journal*, January 10, 1913, Meta Berger participated in a meeting of Milwaukee clubwomen regarding enforcement of the state's law mandating a fifty-five-hour work week for women and argued against the granting of exemptions.
4. Inez "Nan" Milholland (Boissevain) (1886–1916), a Socialist lawyer, actively worked on behalf of women's suffrage and women's labor issues and helped found the National Woman's Party. Milholland and Wallace Irwin wrote an article entitled "Two Million Women Vote," *McClure's Magazine* (40 [January, 1913]: 241–251) that described the 1912 convention of the National American Woman Suffrage Association.
5. Beginning with the February, 1913, issue, Inez Milholland wrote "The New Department for Women" in *McClure's Magazine*.
6. Jane Addams (1860–1935), a feminist and social reformer, founded Hull House in Chicago in 1889. She became active in the women's peace movement during World War I and served as president of the Women's International League for Peace and Freedom from its founding in 1919 until her death.
7. You rascal, I love you so terribly!

Victor to Meta

Washington, D.C.
January 24, [1913]

My sweet Mamma-Schatzl:

How time flies—have been trying all evening to find a way by which congress could interfere in the garment worker's strike in New York—which in one sense is a purely local affair—but which I want investigated. I finally framed a somewhat labored resolution showing that the low wages make healthy surroundings and a decent standard of living impossible—and that clothing is being manufactured in filthy and unsanitary places saturated with germs of consumption small pox and scarlet fever—which clothing by getting to the people through *interstate* traffic becomes a menace to the health and welfare of all. Therefore it is the duty of congress to interfere and investigate.[1]

I am not quite sure whether my deduction will work this time—there [are] only five weeks more left for the present congress—and I am a "lame duck"—however I will try.

One of the most foolish things I did was to permit myself to be appointed on that investigation committee—which has nailed me down tight for a month, with very little profit to myself or the movement.[2] I have been staying away occassionally of late, or I could not have done any work at all.

Well sweetheart—this is midnight and my eyes hurt me today—therefore I will close. I shall put on a special delivery stamp on this letter—so that my Schatzl can get my "love-vibration" on Sunday. Ich hab' Dich lieb![3]

With thousand kisses
V.L.B.

1. Members of the International Ladies' Garment Workers Union in New York City voted on January 14, 1913, to go on strike. The union reached a tentative agreement on January 18, although an additional two weeks passed before final settlements were reached with all the city's manufacturers. Berger introduced a resolution on January 27 calling for an investigation into the New York garment industry, but the resolution died in the Rules Committee.

2. Berger served on a subcommittee of the House Committee on the District of Columbia that investigated the district's superintendent of insurance as well as several fire insurance companies doing business in the district.

3. I love you!

Victor to Meta

Washington, D.C.
February 7, 1913

My dear Schatzl:

You surely have no complaint to make this time as to the quantity of the letters you receive—because you *do* get one every day, but m[a]y have a kick coming as to the quality. For some reason which I cannot explain the investigation committee holds no session tonight—I found the district room dark and locked when I got there—therefore I hurried down to my office to write you a letter.

In reality I ought to prepare myself for the house tomorrow. It seems I must make a speech tomorrow because the Committee on rules brought in a *special rule* for the consideration of the Webb bill, which is designed to restrict the interstate shipment of intoxicating liquor into "dry" territory. This means that the members of the House must face a vote on one phase of the prohibition question—and it also means that Victor Berger must make a speech, if he can get the time. The bill knocks the Milwaukee brewers.

In itself the measure is rather tame. It merely provides that intoxicating liquors cannot or may not be shipped into states and be sold where such sale is forbidden by *state* law. But it would not forbid a person in a prohibition state for his personal use—but the danger is that the radical advocates of prohibition like Hobson[1] will force more drastic amendments. At any rate I am against the bill of course.

The bill contains no penal clause, not even a provision for confiscation—all that is left to the legislation of the individual states. It is a bill without teeth, but it is a sneaky affair.[2]

While I am writing this a special delivery letter is brought in from some cranky woman in Chicago who sends me one almost every day. It contains clippings from Chicago papers and disconnected hallucinations of a spiritualist character. As a rule I throw the stuff into the waste basket without looking at it—any further.

Well, sweetheart, I am glad that you have your vacuum cleaner all installed and your house in tolerable order. I shall concentrate all my efforts now in trying to pay for the home during the next two years—although I will not neglect the Leader of course. Because after all the Leader is the big thing for us, sweetheart.

By the way, sweetheart, I have ordered a full set of topographical maps—over 2,000 maps—cost price about $300.00, because the government also sells these maps—to be sent to the North Division High School. I also wrote Mr. Krug[3] a nice letter. Don't tell Doris anything about it—let Mr. Krug after he gets the maps.

That's all I can tell you to night. I must take a walk—because I feel that I don't get enough exercise.

Im übrigen hab' ich Dich sehr lieb.[4] Kiss the babies for me, and remember I am ever

Your
V.L.B.

1. Richmond Pearson Hobson (1870–1937), a Spanish-American War hero, served as a Democratic representative from Alabama, 1907–1915, and was a leading advocate of the prohibition of alcoholic beverages.
2. Congress eventually enacted the Senate version of the Webb Bill (the Kenyon-Sheppard Bill) over President Taft's veto. Berger spoke against the Webb bill, arguing that drunkenness was an economic problem.
3. Richard E. Krug (1865–1927) served as principal of Milwaukee's North Division High School, 1903–1927.
4. By the way, I love you very much.

Victor Luitpold Berger, ca. 1920s.

Victor Berger's extended family, ca. 1904. Standing, left to right: *Edna Gorman, Helen Gorman, Hyman Weingarten, Hilda Morganstern, Richard Berger, George Berger, Meta Berger, Victor Berger, Milton Morganstern, Edith Morganstern, Anna Gorman, Doris Berger, William Gorman, Rebecca Gottlieb.* Seated in chairs: *Mathilde Weingarten, Ignatz Berger, Julia Berger, Rose Morganstern.* Seated on grass: *Edna Weingarten, Sybil Gorman, Elsa Berger, Sidney Morganstern, Alexander Gottlieb, Ruth Gottlieb, Leah Gottlieb.* (Photo courtesy Susan Nurock.)

Victor Berger and his mother, Julia, ca. 1890s.

Meta Schlichting Berger, ca. 1897.

Above: *The duplex at 1218–1220 Second Street, Milwaukee, where the Bergers lived from 1903 until 1912. Meta and Victor are on the porch.* Below: *Victor and Doris Berger in his Milwaukee study, 1903.* (Photo courtesy Polly Keusink.)

At Home 1903

Above: *Meta Berger, Victor Berger, Jack Anderson, Elsa Berger, and Doris Berger at their cabin in Shawano, Wisconsin, ca. 1908.* (Photo courtesy Polly Keusink.) Below: *Elsa and Doris Berger, ca. 1930.*

*Doris Berger, Jack Anderson, Victor Berger, Meta Berger, and Elsa Berger,
ca. 1910.*

Hattie Schlichting Schweers and Frank Schweers, Meta's sister and brother-in-law, ca. 1909.

Jan Edelman, ca. 1930. (Photo courtesy Deborah Hardy.)

Meta Berger with her granddaughter,
Deborah Welles, 1928.

Doris Berger Welles and Colin Welles,
ca. 1925.

Victor to Meta

Washington, D.C.
February 20, 1913

My sweet Mamma-Schatzl:

I am driven rather hard just now—unexpectedly had to make a two minute speech on the Immigration question in favor of upholding the veto of the President—which speech took so well that some of them claim that it carried the day.[1] I am not conceited enough to think so— the bill failed only by five votes—and I know that there was defection in the Democratic ranks, but not on account of my speech. However, at least two members of the house—one of them a Democrat and the other a Republican—told me that they changed their votes on account of my speech.

Enclosed, please, find another check for fifty dollars—I want you to pay Hassmann and other house bills (I mean repair bills) that may be pressing.

Moreover I got a lovely red cedar chest from the government for you—I told the custos that the other one we had received was not much good—and I also ordered plants for you, two boxes full because we had not received our quota last year—these boxes are small, of course, but each of them is supposed to contain one hundred young plants—I selected mainly blooming shrubbery, since we own so fine a lot.

I dread my trip to Pittsburg, Allentown and Rochester N.Y.—the distances are not only far apart but leaving Pittsburg at 11.00 PM I get into Harrisburg at 4.30 A.M. and have to wait there until 8 A.M. for a train to Allentown Pa. where I speak in the afternoon.

Clara Hipke has not shown up as yet. I suppose she is visiting New York, Philadelphia etc. and will make her triumphant entry into Washington with "gen" Rosalie Jones and the suffragist "hikers".[2]

Was invited by the Press Club to be one of the speakers at "Lame Duck Night"—together with Cannon[3] and a few others—our friend Clifford Berryman,[4] the cartoonist, is to act as "lame duck chaser". The affair will take place next Saturday, however, and I shall be in Pittsburg on that night. Expect to write a letter instead.

Well, sweetheart, this is about all the personal news I have to tell you—except that I got it from good authority that President Taft seriously considered my name for the Industrial Commission which he appointed but which came to naught because the Democrats would not allow the appropriation.[5] At any rate I would *not* have accepted a position of that kind—ten dollars a day and expenses—when the commission would be in session. However that he seriously considered me— with a view of representing the Socialist view on the commission—I consider a compliment both to me and the Socialist party.

I will have a few very hard days—possibly also a hard week in the House next week because the Senate tagged a temperance bill to the District appropriation[6]—and you must think very lovingly of me.

Remember: Ich habe meine vierzig Jahre alte Frau sehr lieb![7] Kiss the babies for me. And furthermore remember no one in the world has ever, or could ever, appreciate you like your

                                                                        V.L.B.

Please telephon to H. Bistorius to send me by special delivery about half a dozen of the "Anti-Socialist Voices about V. L. Berger in Congress".[8] There [are] plenty of these pamphlets in the dark library room next to my office.

1. President Taft had vetoed an immigration bill because it included a literacy test. In his speech, Berger supported the veto, arguing that America had been built by "illiterate immigration." The Senate overrode the veto, but the House sustained the president.

2. General Rosalie Gardiner Jones (1883–1978) of New York led a self-styled "suffrage army" on a march from Newark, New Jersey, to Washington, D.C., to present a women's suffrage petition to Woodrow Wilson just prior to his inauguration.

3. Joseph G. Cannon (1836–1926), a Republican representative from Illinois, 1873–1891, 1893–1913, and 1915–1923, and Speaker of the House, 1903–1911.

4. Clifford Berryman (1869–1949) worked as an editorial cartoonist for the *Washington Post,* 1896–1907, and for the *Washington Evening Star,* 1907–1949.

5. On December 17, 1912, President Taft announced his appointments to the Commission on Industrial Relations, which was created to investigate industrial conflict, but Senate Democrats filibustered and refused to approve the nominees, thus allowing President Wilson to make the appointments.

6. Berger opposed a Senate amendment to an appropriations bill for the District of Columbia that would have reduced the number of saloons in the district. Congress adopted a modified version of the proposal, and the bill was signed by the president.

7. I love my forty-year-old wife very much!

8. *Some Anti-Socialist Voices of the Press on Victor L. Berger Representative of the Fifth Wisconsin District and His Work in Congress* (Milwaukee, [1912]) was a sixty-four-page pamphlet designed as a campaign document. It reprinted editorials, news stories, and cartoons from the non-Socialist press about Berger's first term in Congress.

Victor to Meta

                                                            Somewhere in Ohio
                                                            [April 19, 1913]

My sweet Schatzl:

I don't want to roll into my berth—can't sleep in these coffin-like contrivances, at best it is an irregular and uneasy slumber after I am good and tired. Therefore want to make use of my time—I am in the so-called club-car now where men smoke and drink (i.e. they do not drink since we are in Ohio)—to write you a letter which will reach you on Monday. I intend to send another one from the train which is to reach you on Tuesday—thus you will get a letter every day except on Sunday when you got two. Beat that if you can.

But as for news I would be hard up because I haven't spoken to a soul except to a buyer of Chas Stevens & Bros the "silk store" in Chicago who is going to New York to buy millinery and who told me confidentially that Nell-Rose hats are played out—that Stevens & Bros. are selling them out below cost, because *white* hats will be all the style this year, with an occassional green hat if one wants dark colors—and he the buyer will even take a chance on Panamas this season. But outside he evidently has no more ideas than Jackie, Graf's dog.

As for Mr. Baker[1]—he showed me the report of the stock market and told me most of the stock brokers were broke—and that he was more fortunate but not in any position to make investments. He wished me luck and thought I was doing good work, but good wishes will neither pay the paper bills, nor the type-setters. If ever—I will have to show my genius in financing the Leader. And I am going to do it.

When I am alone and thinking the matter over—then it always comes to me again that I *don't want* either you or my children to take a prominent part in public life. It is a losing game and the light is never worth the candle. Moreover, it has a tendency to destroy family life and family happiness—at least in most cases. *You* are not adapted to it at all,—although (I am sorry to say) that you have acquired a little taste for it through your work in the school board. When your term is over I don't want you to run again. But I will try to have you wind up your school board carriere as president of the board,—for the satisfaction it will give *you, not* me, because of all men in Milwaukee, I need *least* the lustre of my wife—noble and fine woman as she is—in order to shine myself.

As for our children—I am afraid Doris has inherited my native *ambition* to be one of the foremost of whatever crowd I may be in and where ever I may be. But Doddie does not like to work hard—I did. She doesn't take any advice from the folks who are her natural protectors—I always did. Moreover Doddie hasn't the self-reliance and self-confidence I had from childhood on. She is always running after others instead of having others pattern after her, which would be much easier for her than it was for me—considering the social and political standing her papa and mamma have acquired in the community. Doris is still young of course and her mode of thinking and her *future* actions can still be very largely influenced by you—and by you more than by anybody else—although I realize that she is not an easy child to handle. If I could re-build her, I should want her to be exactly like you.

As for Elsa I am less worried. All I ask of her is that she should be moderate in her eating and watch herself when she sits, stands and walks—I want her to sit, walk and stand straight. Sometime I wonder whether it wouldn't be a good idea to send the child to Lachenmaier.[2] I would rather do that now than later. I hope that she will pass this summer—Elsa is large-sized and if any re-peating is necessary, I would rather have her repeat a semester or even a year in high school than in the common school. Ask Miss Hall[3] if Elsa needs any help in her studies—and in which studies. I shall be glad to have her take private lessons from some teacher.

Well, sweetheart, this letter got to be almost an essay and considering the fact that the motion of the car has turned my penmanship into hieroglyphics (I really don't even know whether I have spelled the word right) you have enough reading for half-a-day.

Don't forget to have your letter for the Free Press *type written,*—printers and editors much prefer type-written copy. And don't go there before three o'clock (because Myrick[4] is not there) nor much after 5 o'clock, if you want the letter in the next day.

Und hab' mich lieb[5]

V.L.B.

1. Probably Alfred L. Baker (1859–1927), a wealthy Chicago lawyer, stockbroker, and bank president.
2. William Lachenmaier (1859–1933) founded and operated Lachenmaier's School of Health in Milwaukee.
3. Marcella Hall (b. 1865) served as vice-principal (1906–1925) of Milwaukee's Third Street School.
4. Harry P. Myrick (1857–1916) founded the *Milwaukee Free Press,* a progressive Republican newspaper, and served as its editor, 1901–1916.
5. And love me.

Victor to Meta

New York, New York
May 1, 1913

My sweet Mamma-Schatzl:

Life is a series of disappointments—but as far as I am concerned Arthur Brisbane is one of the worst of them. Went out to Hempstead to dinner yesterday and stopped there over night. Arthur had sold his old place to Mrs. Emily Cary (his present mother in law) about three years ago—and he and his brother and sister[1] lived in an old house near-by which he had remodeled. Now he lives in same house again which he had [sold] to the Carys—as I understand it, the house was given to Mrs. Brisbane, who expects an interesting event to take place within two weeks.[2]

Arthur told all about his wealth and his innumerable investments also about the $22,000 deficit he had in Allaire, his big estate in New Jersey last year. Incidentally he also mentioned that he had borrowed $150,000 the same day in order to pay debts, and that he intended to keep a cash balance of $50,000 in the bank always in order to pick up any good thing that might come along—but he declined to buy any bonds of the Leader because he was too poor. If I needed any money personally, he would help me—which is really adding insult to injury.

Mr. Little[3] the owner and publisher of Pierson's Magazine did much better. I had dinner with him at Delmonico's tonight and Allan Benson[4] (who had braught us together) broached the subject. I had copies of the Leader with me and explained all about it. He said that he had no ready cash because his fathers estate—his father died about three years ago—is still unsettled but that he would let me have two pages advertising in his magazine for three months to explain the proposition to the readers of Pierson's Magazine—he to get a certain percentage of bond sales in lieu of the advertising. I am not sure that I will accept the proposition because he wants the advertising to be done *over my signature*—and I don't feel that it would be right to use my name, prestige and reputation for that purpose.

At any rate sweet, Schatzl, this is a hard world to live in, and it still harder to change it. The only person who has never disappointed me is *you,* and I would become violently insane if you ever did. As for New York,—it is a hell hole which should be abolished, and undoubtedly will be abolished some day, if the May day parade and the number of red flags carried in the procession today mean anything at all. It took about six hours for the parade to pass a given point—I was told.

This evening I walked alone on Broadway (after dinner) and to me the "great white way" is simply a continuous carnival of male and female prostitutes, and fools and criminals.

Well, Schatzl, I am not in a very good humor and my letter may, therefore, not be very pleasant reading. But all of this will have one good result as far as we are concerned—I am going to look out for ourselves in the future, before I consider anybody else.

I leave here tomorrow, Friday night by way of Detroit where I am going to stop over to see a wealthy farmer to whom I have a letter from Benson. I don't expect too much, and if all of these exploits will result in $5,000 cash for bonds I shall be satisfied.

Good-by, mamma-sweetheart. Kiss the babies for me and always remember that you are the best part of me and as sweet as I am sour.

V.L.B.

1. Fowell Brisbane and Alice Brisbane Thursby.
2. Phoebe Cary (1890–1967), the daughter of Seward (1862?–1948) and Emily Cary, married Arthur Brisbane on July 30, 1912. She gave birth to the couple's first child, Sarah (1913–1979), on May 6, 1913.
3. Arthur W. Little (1873–1943), a New York printer, began managing *Pearson's Magazine* in 1902.
4. Allan L. Benson (1871–1940), a journalist and writer, was the Socialist candidate for president in 1916. Benson resigned from the party in 1918 because of its opposition to World War I.

Victor to Meta

Charleston, West Virginia
May 21, 1913

My Sweet Schatzl:

Landed in Charleston at last—and had a consultation with Debs, Germer[1] and the officials of the Miner's Union.[2] It is a rather mixed situation—a governor[3] who not only put a lot of our members into jail—apparently without any regular process of law but also some of the mine owners and superintendents,—a "feudist" by temper and family connection, he is a nephew of the Hatfield who was finally hanged in Kentucky on account of his bloody activity in the feud with the McCoys. He is a physician by profession—not bad, but exceedingly high strung and arbitrary. Moreover he doesn't seem to know the first thing about the labor movement.

He threatened in an interview to clap us all into jail—particularly also the ex-congressman. That would be the most stupid thing he could do now, of course, with an congressional investigation hanging over his head and he is not going to do it. We expect to see him tomorrow and I haven't the faintest doubt that I can show him the "error" of his ways in short order.

Well Schatzl—a reporter of the Citizen is waiting to interview me and I shall have to cut this letter short.

Don't worry—everything will come out all right. Send your letters to the General Delivery until otherwise notified.

With thousand kisses

Your
V.L.B.

1. Adolph Germer (1881–1966), a coal miner since the age of eleven, held a number of offices in the United Mine Workers of America and served as national secretary of the Socialist Party, 1916–1919. Germer, along with Berger and three others, was found guilty in 1919 of violating the Espionage Act and was sentenced to twenty years in prison, although the conviction was later overturned by the U.S. Supreme Court.

2. The Socialist Party appointed a committee consisting of Berger, Debs, and Germer to investigate the Paint Creek–Cabin Creek coal miners' strike in West Virginia, one of the most violent labor disputes in American history. The governor of West Virginia declared martial law, and the mine operators brought in Baldwin-Felts detectives to crush the strike.

3. Henry Drury Hatfield (1875–1962), a Republican, served as governor of West Virginia, 1913–1917, and as a U.S. senator, 1929–1935.

Victor to Meta

Charleston, West Virginia
May 22, 1913

My sweet Schatzl:

We had a conference with the governor of W. Virginia this after-noon—and found a man as ignorant of the labor movement as the man in the moon. He is not an ill-disposed fellow, however, and this morning (before we saw him) released *every prisoner* (including John W. Brown,[1] editor & organizer; H. W. Thompson[2] editor whose forms had been smashed and "pied" by the militia; and even half-crazy Fred Merrick)[3]— and thus made it much easier for us to negotiate with him. Most of the men had been imprisoned since February 12th and the governor claimed that he had prove and evidence enough to send over a dozen of them to the penitentiary for long terms for murder and man-slaughter, but since this had been "war", he did not intend to press any of the cases. The governor furthermore declared that he had kept up the mar-tial law in these mining districts, in order to prevent the private army of Baldwin thugs (who did the slugging and murdering for the mine oper-ators) from continuing their business. By the 24th of this month the law permitting the mine owners to hire private troops and to swear them in as "deputy-sheriffs" will go out [of] existence—and he will repeal the martial law. Tom Haggerty[4] who has charge of the United Mine Workers in West Virginia corroborated the governor's statement.

That's all well and good so far and especially Debs surprised me, outdoing me in conservatism three hundred per cent—especially at the interview with the governor. We have practically accomplished every-thing we came for in short order. More over tonight's papers report that the U.S. Senate adopted the Kern resolution[5] ordering an investi-gation—thus it doesn't seem necessary for us to go to Washington unless we are invited by the Senate Committee.

The great trouble seems to be this. A large part of W. Virginia is owned by foreign corporations who have fenced in entire counties. They cannot have any more deputy sheriffs but they have applied to the courts which the corporations own absolutely for permission to arm their guards and watchmen. The old story about slugging, black jacking and "beating up" of union men and organizers will be repeated—I am afraid—only under a different label. Of course, these watchmen have *no* police power,—but on the other hand the corporations claim every where "private property rights" (even on the roads which are their private roads) and also the right to order anybody off their private property. It is an impossible condition, full of great dangers, especially since the middle class of this state is also incredibly ignorant.

Well, Schatzl, next Saturday we are going to leave for the mines on Paint Creek, New River etc.—the seat of the trouble. The governor said, we are at liberty to go anywhere we please. It is hardly necessary for me to assure you that there is absolutely no danger of any kind connected with this trip, especially after the governor coming out with the assertion that we are gentlemen scholars and his friends. Moreover there are no more Baldwin thugs in that district since the governor put a price of $300 per head for the arrest of the last two of them. But the trip will be unpleasant to the extreme—there are no hotels in the mountains—we will have to sleep in cabins—and we will be in the enemies country—in the midst of a cowed population. We expect to stay there for two days and I hope to learn a good deal.

And after that, we will come back to Charleston—write our report and then hurry home, at least I will, Debs may possibly stay here a while longer.

And the first report I have written to you, Schatzl,—you may have to read it in instalments.

With love to all and kisses to my sweetheart and my Schnuckies

Your V.L.B.

1. John W. Brown was a national organizer and speaker for the Socialist Party.
2. Wyatt H. Thompson (1885–1969) worked for a number of newspapers before becoming the editor of the *Huntington (West Virginia) Socialist and Labor Argus* in 1912. On May 9, 1913, the state militia arrested Thompson and destroyed the paper's presses by order of Governor Hatfield.
3. Frederick H. Merrick became temporary editor of the *Charleston (West Virginia) Labor Argus* in March, 1913, after its editor was arrested. Merrick himself was arrested on May 2, 1913, and the presses were destroyed by order of Governor Hatfield.
4. Thomas T. Haggerty (1865–1940), a national organizer and member of the executive board of the United Mine Workers Union, negotiated a settlement of the West Virginia coal strike with Governor Hatfield. The union removed Haggerty from his position in 1916 on learning that he owned stock in a West Virginia coal mine.
5. The U.S. Senate adopted a resolution offered by Senator John Kern of Indiana calling for an investigation of the West Virginia strike. The final report strongly criticized the state government.

Victor to Meta

Charleston, West Virginia
May 24, [1913]

My sweet Schatzl:

Just a few lines before going out into the hills to visit the mining camp—the secretary of the governor is going with us. The entire affair would be (at least temporarily) settled, if it was not for the exceedingly bitter feeling of some of the miners and non-miners who had been in bull pens and jails. We had a stormy session with the local socialist crowd last night—the local is in a poor condition (only about 20 dues paying members left here) but these are extremely revengeful, suspicious and venemous. If they knew that the governor had offered us a special train to visit the mines and mining camps at the expense of the state—our offer which we had rejected of course—there would have been something doing, because the governor is one of their pet aversions.

But from all that you can see Schatzl, that the question is not so simple of solution. The common people here have been treated shamefully and they are revengeful and suspicious. Moreover the miners (or at least some of them) do not trust the officials of the United Mine Worker's union. You can see however from all this that nothing is going to the committee, if the governor and the state of W. Virginia, can prevent it. And as far as our crowd,—that is fanatically loyal at least to us.

I hope sweetheart everything is all right at home. With thousand kisses

Yours.
V.L.B.

Victor to Meta

Charleston, West Virginia
May 25, 1913

My sweet Schatzl:

Another very busy day—we have tramped about 12 miles in the mountains from one mining camp to the other, viewing the scenes of several battles, where miners and Baldwin-Feltz detectives (mine guards) were killed—and where the so-called "Bull-Moose" train, an armored train loaded with deputy sheriffs and armed with machine guns came stealthfully in the dead of night with the lights of the locomotive turned out, and firing at random and without discrimination at the houses and tents of the miners in the various villages the train passed. Saw a woman who was shot and crippled for life while she was

pressing her three children to the chimney in order to protect them—
and another woman whose husband was shot dead while she and three
children were in the cellar. Saw many houses with the bullet marks still
on them. I do not believe that anything like that be possible in any
other country except Russia or China. And this happened before the
martial law had been declared—the armored train was in charge of
the sheriff.

We also took a picture of a miniature fort built of steel at Mucklow.
The armed detectives have all left this region, but there are still nine
men militia left there—who were exceedingly polite and friendly, of
course,—and it seems they were so by order of the governor, whose
private secretary was our chaperone. We did all we could to allay the
existing bitterness, but, Schatzl—this part of the country will be socialist
by an overwhelming majority for the next thirty years to come—even
last November we polled 4,000 votes in that district, and I was told, that
the number of Socialists has more than doubled since. They are all—or
at least 95% of them, native West Virginians, simple mountaineers but
very intelligent. They are great hero worshippers and Gene Debs was
treated like a little God, of course, although I also came in for a very
friendly reception.

I insisted tonight that we send a *telegram* to the U.S. Senate urging
the acceptance of the Kern resolution to have an investigation of the
conditions that prevail—and in some districts are still prevailing in West
Virginia. We sent a night lettergramm containing one hundred words.

Tomorrow we will go to New River coal fields where about six hundred men struck yesterday, that field contains about 20,000 miners who
are very dissatisfied. On the other hand there Baldwin-Felts detectives
[are] "thicker than trees" according to the governors own secretary. He
will accompany us because otherwise we would be sure to be slugged.
We demand of the governor that the employment of armed guards by
private persons or private corporations be forbidden—but the governor
doubts whether he has the power to do so under the present laws of the
state. By the time you receive this letter you will have a night telegramm
telling you that we are all right, so that you needn't worry.

You see, sweetheart, there is nothing I can tell you except what per-
tains to my work here because that is all I am doing here—unless in
spare moments I am worrying about the Leader. Sometimes I think that
I should go to Noroton Conn. from here and put it up to Hunter. May
be I will wire to Bistorius and Miss Thomas and put it up to them. It
would not cost so much as going from Milwaukee.

At any rate, Schatzl, don't send any more letters to me to
Charleston after you receive this one—because they will not find me

here. We expect to leave here Wednesday, and if I don't go to see Hunter—I will be home by Thursday with my Mamma.

With thousand kisses to you and the Schnuckies

Your
V.L.B.

Victor to Meta

[Milwaukee, Wisconsin]
July 9, 1913

My sweet Schatzl:

Your welcome letter reached me today. Tomorrow I leave for Evansville where I speak next Friday. On Saturday evening I will be in Chicago and attend the meeting of the National Executive Committee until Tuesday,—please send your letters in care of National Secretary Socialist Party 111 North Market street—i.e letters which *you* write Friday, Saturday and Sunday.

Will mail you a check for one hundred dollars in tomorrows letter, also your bank book.

Was disappointed and ill-natured all day, because my editors (and particularly Smith)[1] do not know what news is. Had received a letter from the First Assistant Postmaster General telling that he had taken up the coat-question at once and by wire with the Milwaukee postmaster upon receiving my telegram—and that Owen[2] immediately promised to rescind his former order.

Now this letter of the Postmaster General is official (and not confidential) and may be published. And this letter when printed knocks into a cocked hat the claim of the Journal [that] its interviewing a few business men on Sunday had the effect on Monday.

I gave the letter to Engdahl[3] to publish. Nothing was done until Wednesday (today) when I asked Smith about it and told him to give it a prominent place. But it was hidden on the third page with a small head and directly under our Ad booming our advertising.

I felt like telling Smith to quit his job. He saw I was very angry and made all sorts of silly excuses, that it had been set up the day before and overlooked etc.

Nor is this all. I had asked Engdahl to save the letter for me. Any other paper would have photographed the letter. In the Leader office nobody knew what had become of the letter. Engdahl claimed that he had given it to the office boy to bring it down to me. The boy did not know what had become of it. One of the reporters had seen it the night before on some table. Finally they fished around in several waste baskets and found the letter in one of them all crumbled up. It was lucky that the waste basket had not been emptied for two days.

Now I don't like that kind of business and for the first time I let the entire editorial force know that I was the "boss" in that office.

Well, Schatzl these are all small affairs, but just such things are of great importance to my paper. The addition of Simons[4] and Engdahl is good, but I shall make more thorough changes next fall.

I shall also double the number of original editorials in every issue. Take it all in all, we have comparatively little editorial matter, only it is printed in big type. With Howe, Simons and Berger writing editorials it ought be easy to have an excellent editorial page.

And that is all I know tonight except that ich Dich sehr lieb hab'[5] and that I hate, positively hate to be away from you so much sweetheart. With thousand kisses

your VLB.

1. Osmore R. Smith (b. 1886) worked as an editor for the *Milwaukee Journal* until about 1911 and then joined the staff of the *Milwaukee Leader*. By the early 1920s he was again working for the *Journal.*

2. David C. Owen (1864–1932) was postmaster of Milwaukee. On June 30, 1913, the *Milwaukee Journal* ran a front-page story claiming credit for Owen's reversal of his order requiring letter carriers to wear coats year round, even in hot summer weather. The *Milwaukee Leader* waited until July 9, 1913, to print a letter from the Post Office Department indicating that the policy change resulted from Berger's efforts, and the article appeared on page 3, underneath a large advertisement for the *Leader.*

3. J. Louis Engdahl (1884–1932) worked as labor editor and field correspondent for the *Milwaukee Leader* in 1913. He edited the *Chicago Daily Socialist* from 1910 to 1912 and the *American Socialist* from 1914 until its suppression in 1917. Engdahl, along with Berger and three others, was found guilty in 1919 of violating the Espionage Act and was sentenced to twenty years in prison, although the conviction was later overturned by the U.S. Supreme Court. Engdahl joined the Workers Party in 1921, co-edited the Communist *Daily Worker* from 1924 to 1928, and headed the International Labor Defense from 1928 until his death.

4. Algie M. Simons (1870–1950) edited the *International Socialist Review*, 1900–1906, the *Chicago Daily Socialist*, 1906–1910, and the *Coming Nation*, 1910–1913. Between 1913 and 1916, Simons worked on the editorial staff of the *Milwaukee Leader*. He was expelled from the Socialist Party in 1917 because of his support of American participation in World War I, and he became an organizer for the rabidly prowar Wisconsin Defense League (later the Wisconsin Loyalty Legion). After the war, Simons researched and wrote on scientific management and industrial psychology.

5. I love you very much.

Victor to Meta

en route in Colorado
August 12, 1913

My sweet Schatzl:

This is the seventh letter—to say the least—I have written on this train. They are still on this train (which is supposed to be the fastest the Santa Fe has in the direction of Chicago) and in possession of the porter who cannot even mail them until we get to Kansas City because this train does not get a mail car until then—not all trains carrying mail. For all useful purposes, therefore, I could have written one letter instead of eight—and saved effort and postage. Moreover by this time at least the men on the train know me although I have not spoken to them—and even the porter is beginning to wonder *why* I am writing so many letters to my wife, since one long one would do the same service and get there the same time. And the worst is—my Schatzl may think the same.

But this is the reason—I just want to talk to my Schatzl. That's why I write all these letters. I might put them all into one envelope of course—but that would not look like so many conversations, at least not to my Schatzl. And even the difficult penmanship adds to the "reality"—because with all the noise of the train it would be just as difficult to understand each other speaking, as it is now writing.

But I am hard up for real live news on this train. The only thing I found here that might be of interest to you is a feature article on Inez Milholland in the Los Angeles Examiner "proving" that although a "suffragette" she is a "woman" after all.[1] How silly! You will get the article under separate cover.

The most interesting man I have met on this trip is Fremont Older,[2] the editor of the San Francisco Bulletin. You remember the two ladies who came to our house in Washington D.C. to interview me on the I.W.W? One the ladies was his wife,[3] the other was a Miss Somebody, a sister-in-law to Rudolph Spreckles[4] of San Francisco. I have not met the ladies this time—they weren't in the city. And I didn't particularly care whether I met them again or not, to me they looked like "faddists". But Fremont Older is worthwhile. He is not Socialist—and I don't think he knows much about it—but he is getting out the most progressive non-Socialist paper in the country. He told me that after I had made my first speech in congress and he had seen excerpts from it, he sent for it and published the entire speech in his paper verbatim.

Just now he is stirring up San Francisco on the question of prostitution. He is publishing the autobiographies of prostitutes and some of them are incredibly *shocking*—I use the term in the proper sense, I mean the articles are giving a real shock to the community.

Big capitalists and priests have already written to the postal authorities and to the government in general to stop him from publishing this stories or to revoke the second class mailing privilege for his paper. The Assistant United States District Attorney has written him a letter telling him to come to see him. Older received the letter while I was there and I advised him to wire at once to Bill Kent, to Postmaster General Burleson[5] and to President Wilson. The trouble is that I am afraid President Wilson is a small potato. Burleson a good fellow but a typical southern politician—and Bill Kent may not be able to do very much under such circumstances. I offered him my assistance in case of necessity—he thanked me but didn't think he would need it.

Well, Schatzl, aber sonst hast Du mich doch noch lieb, wie?[6] Don't let the girls go home before I get there, I also want to have the pleasure of their company for a few days. But you, Schatzl, are the company of all company for your

VLB.

1. Suffrage activist Inez Milholland married F. E. Boissevain in July, 1913. "Only a Woman After All!" *Los Angeles Examiner,* August 10, 1913, ridiculed Milholland's efforts on behalf of women's rights in light of her recent marriage.

2. Fremont Older (1856–1935), a Wisconsin-born journalist, worked as managing editor of the *San Francisco Bulletin,* 1895–1918, editor of the *San Francisco Call,* 1918–1929, and editor of the *San Francisco Call-Bulletin,* 1929–1935. Older advocated a variety of progressive causes, including prison reform and the abolition of capital punishment, and often wrote favorably about radical causes in the American West.

3. Cora Miranda Baggerly Older (1875–1968), the author of several books, was interested in industrial and political affairs and prison reform.

4. Rudolph Spreckels (1872–1958) was a San Francisco businessman and reformer who with Fremont Older and Lincoln Steffens organized the prosecution of graft in that city between 1906 and 1909.

5. Albert Sidney Burleson (1863–1937) served as postmaster general, 1913–1921, and as a Democratic representative from Texas, 1899–1913. Burleson's vigorous enforcement of the Espionage Act during World War I led to the exclusion from the mails of numerous socialist periodicals, including the *Milwaukee Leader.*

6. but otherwise you still love me, don't you?

Victor to Meta

en route near Dodge City, Kansas
August 12, 1913

My sweet Schatzl:

I just got a copy of the Chicago Record-Herald of Monday and see that the Roman Catholics have their annual convention in Milwaukee—5,000 Knights of Columbus in line, with 8,000 members of the

Catholic Forresters and at least 2,000 women. With Cardinal Gibbons[1] on the reviewing stand were 5 archbishops, twenty bishops and ten monsignores.

Gibbons singled out that "splendid organization, the Knights of Columbus. They are our joy and crown," he is reported to have said "They are the glory of Jerusalem. They are the joy of Israel. They are the honor of our people. Where ever calumny raises its foul head, they are ever ready, like true Knights to smite the enemy".

Archbishop Keane[2] of Dubuque made a real "non-partisan" speech—and a Jesuitical at that. He said

"Though I hold no brief to defend the aims of this assembly (Roman Catholic Societies) I know *it can have no political* programme. Catholics in this country are a cosmopolitan body, professing and defending every form of political creed save Socialism." And then they went to work immediately not only to formulate a political programme, but to ask for a division—of the school funds.

Well I shall answer as soon as I get home. I shall answer by making the taxation of churches and of church-property a part of *our* programme.

The Roman church is the one great danger—the only menace—this country has to face. Even the social question—the question of the next civilization—might find a peacable solution, if it wasn't for the Roman Catholic church. Some day after a terrific war, it will have to be forbidden in this country as it was forbidden for many hundred years in the Scandinavian countries. That church is really not a church it is the political machine of darkness, ret[r]ogression, cruelty and hell. It appeals to all the base, sensual and primeval passions of man even negatively in their celibacy and self-torture—very much in the same spirit as did the worshippers of Molock and do the Buddhists.

Well this seat here is write a long letter. But if [it] had not been for men who have given their lives in dungeons and at the faggot in opposition to that church of Hell, the Roman Catholic church—we could not be sitting in an observation car, fanned by electricity—because the holy fathers and the priests looked upon all inventions as the work of the devil—and killed the inventors. There is one cause for which [I] might take up arms and—that is, if this country would be in danger of becoming Catholic.

With love to you and the babies
Your VLB.

1. James Gibbons (1834–1921) served as the Roman Catholic archbishop of Baltimore, 1877–1921, and held the rank of cardinal after 1886. Gibbons was active in mobilizing the American church against socialism.

2. James John Keane (1857–1929) served as the Roman Catholic bishop of Cheyenne, Wyoming, 1902–1911, and as archbishop of Dubuque, Iowa, 1911–1929.

Victor to Meta

Hancock, Michigan
January 7, 1914

My dear Schatzl:

Have arrived here this morning and put up at the Hotel Scott. We had hardly arrived when some of the Finnish comrades came up and we had to look over the plant—it is rather remarkable.[1]

After lunch we went over to Houghton (which is just across the bridge) and made an engagement with Gov. Ferris[2] for Tomorrow (Thursday) afternoon at 1.30 P.M. Had also a private interview with a man by the name of O'Rourke—a supervisor of the county—and the only one who is favorable to the workmen being a reader of the Leader. He gave me some names of men who saw the mob that assaulted and deported Moyer.[3] The information will be submitted to the governor and also published in the Leader.

Stedy[4] then went to the courthouse to copy a *list* of the stockholders of the Hecla mine—on file there. We went to interview people—particularly also storekeepers and drifted into a "curio store", where we met a cigar-agent who had a citizens *alliance button* on his coat.[5] I wanted to buy one of these buttons and was told that they were not for sale but that he would give one—and I accepted it at once because it might be of some use in getting information.

Tonight we shall go over some affidavits—but I will try to get to bed early because I haven't slept a wink last night.

As for our safety you needn't worry—so long as the governor is here because just now the Citizens Alliance wishes that Moyer hadn't been assaulted. The majority of the gun men has left—there were of 1,600 of them in this county alone.

This letter is being written under great difficulties—comrades coming to see *me* and to shake hands with me—and Stedy babbling continually and expecting answers to his childish prattle. He accuses me of writing essays to you, each of them of several volumes.

Well, Schatzl it impossible to write any longer. Shall try again tomorrow when I am alone.

With thousand kisses
V.LB.

1. The Socialist Party appointed Berger, Seymour Stedman, and Charles E. Russell to investigate the beating and shooting of Western Federation of Miners' president Charles Moyer during a strike in Michigan's Upper Peninsula. Thousands of copper miners walked off their jobs in July, 1913, and the governor of Michigan responded by calling out the National Guard. Berger appeared before a congressional committee that held hearings on the strike in February and March, 1914.

2. Woodbridge Nathan Ferris (1853–1928), a Democrat, served as governor of Michigan, 1913–1917, and as a U.S. senator, 1923–1928.
    3. Charles H. Moyer (1866–1937) served as president of the Western Federation of Miners (later the International Union of Mine, Mill, and Smelter Workers), 1902–1926. He helped found the IWW in 1905 but led his union out of that organization in 1908. An anti-union mob beat and shot Moyer and then drove him from Michigan's Upper Peninsula in December, 1913.
    4. Seymour Stedman (1870–1948), a Chicago attorney, helped found the Social Democratic Party in 1898 and ran for vice-president in 1920 on the Socialist ticket. Stedman helped to represent Berger and the other defendants during the Espionage Act trial of 1918–1919.
    5. Businessmen in Hancock formed the Citizens' Alliance to halt the strike and distributed buttons to the organization's members. After seventy-four people, mostly children of striking workers, died during a stampede at a Christmas party, union leaders claimed that a man wearing a Citizens' Alliance button gave the false alarm that started the panic.

Victor to Meta

Chicago, Illinois
May 8, 1914

My dear Schatzl:
    I owe you a full report of the day spent in New York and the one spent in Washington D.C.
    Arriving in New York on Monday I was met by Edith, Will and Milton and taken to the hospital in an automobile, where Hilda showed me the smallest boy baby I have ever seen.[1] He only weighs five pounds but he is otherwise perfectly normal. At the hospital I also met Will's father—a friendly German Jew.[2]
    I took lunch with Hillquit and afterwards went down Broadway to look at the "Silent mourners" of the "Free Silence league" walking up and down before 26 Broadway, where the offices of the Standard Oil Company are located. Upton Sinclair is in his glory, because never before did he receive so much newspaper notoriety, otherwise the affair is asinine. Rockefeller is no worse than any other capitalist—and the Standard Oil company controls only a few of the mines in Colorado. It is taking advantage of the petty-bourgeois prejudice against the multi-millionaire.[3]
    Afterwards I made the costumary call on the Volkszeitung and the Call,[4] but with this result, that the Volkszeitung editors stuck to me until 11.45 P.M.—during that time I partook in a half a dozen schoppens of Rhine wine and several steins of beer, and discussed the social question in general and the Socialist party of America in particular. Edward Ziegler[5] dropped in on us at about 11 o'clock. He is just now doing business in New York.

Got up late the next day and tried to get into touch with some of the leaders of the German and the Hebrew trades—because the English speaking unions in New York will do nothing for a Socialist publication—being dominated entirely by the Irish and the Roman Catholic church. The nearest to any tangible result was that Hebrew trades particularly the Cloak makers would arrange for meetings next month, if I let them know before hand, and what is of more importance—the Jewish Vorwärts[6] would also call a special meeting for that purpose and give Hillquit and me a hearing. Hillquit who knows them well of course, thinks we can get $5,000 from the Vorwaerts, because they have offered the like sum to the Call if they should appoint Charles Edward Russell editor.

In the evening I call[ed] up the Benedicts (Crystal Eastman)[7] and tried to call up Elsie Cole Phillipps[8] but to my regret I heard that she was confined to the Red Cross Hospital on account of an operation for appendicitis. I did not see Mrs. Inez Milholland, nor did I call her up because I felt that you would *not* like to have me do so.[9] Tuesday evening I left for Washington.

In Washington I made a bee line for the House Office building. Looked up Cooper[10] and Kent. The latter was in a committee and could not give me much time—although he was evidently very glad to see me, as was seemingly everybody else. Afterwards I went over to the House and shook hands with everybody including Mann,[11] Underwood and Clark. Many of the Democrats and some of the Republicans wished I was there instead of Stafford who is not at all popular. Had also a conference with La Follette who is going to oppose the Non-Partisan movement[12] strenuously. In the evening I left for Chicago and here I am— after my first night's decent rest.

My reception in the National Executive Committee was not very friendly this morning—Maurer[13] taking sides with Goebel[14] against me—and giving me to understand that I am not such a big man after all. I shall not accept a re-nomination for the national executive committee under any circumstances. I am disgusted with the small potatoes around me.

Well, Schatzl I have again written you a long, long letter without really telling you very much news. The main thing, Sweetheart, is after all whether you love me and whether our children will pan out well— any satisfaction with my work I must otherwise find *within* myself. My room number in the Sherman House is 224—in case you want to call me up. The telephon-number of the National Office is Haymarket 5660.

With thousand kisses for you and the babies

V.LB.

1. Edith Morganstern (Lehman), William Loewenthal (1877–1973), Milton Morganstern, and Hilda Morganstern Loewenthal. Edith, Milton, and Hilda were the children of Victor's sister, Rose. William, a New York city manufacturer of women's hats, was Hilda's husband. The infant was William and Hilda's son, Alan, who was born on April 21, 1914.

2. Andrew Loewenthal (b. 1846) was a New York City manufacturer of women's hats.

3. Upton Sinclair and the Free Silence League set up a silent picket in front of the New York office of John D. Rockefeller Jr. (1874–1960) to protest the Ludlow mine massacre of April, 1914, in which two women and eleven children died when the Colorado National Guard attacked a tent village set up by striking miners. Rockefeller ran the Colorado Fuel and Iron Corporation, which was the largest company involved in the strike. The Socialist Party refused to call a nationwide protest, maintaining that the fault lay in the system, not with individuals such as Rockefeller.

4. The *New Yorker Volkszeitung*, a daily German-language newspaper, served as the organ of the Socialist Labor Party. The *New York Call* was a daily English-language newspaper that supported the Socialist Party.

5. Edward Ziegler (1865–1941), a Socialist, served on the Milwaukee city service commission, 1911–1915, and as business manager of the *Milwaukee Leader*, 1914–1917.

6. The Jewish *Vorwärts* (better known as the *Jewish Daily Forward*) was a Yiddish-language socialist newspaper founded in New York in 1897.

7. Crystal Eastman (1881–1928), the sister of Max Eastman, was a lawyer, social reformer, and feminist. In 1911 she married Wallace Benedict, a Milwaukee insurance salesman; they divorced in 1916. Although Eastman spent little time in Milwaukee, she served as campaign manager for the Political Equality League, which directed the unsuccessful 1912 effort for women's suffrage in Wisconsin. She was active in the peace movement during World War I and from 1918 to 1922 co-edited the *Liberator*, a magazine that supported the Russian Revolution.

8. Elsie La Grange Cole Phillips (1879?–1961), a New York Socialist and union leader, was the wife of Wilbur C. Phillips, the former secretary of the Milwaukee Child Welfare Commission.

9. In her unpublished biography of her father, Doris Berger Welles Hursley stated that Inez Milholland Boissevain was "unapologetically chummy with papa. There was something special in their relationship." Hursley added that Meta Berger "didn't even try to guess *how* friendly Papa was with Miss Mulholland [*sic*]. But he went often to New York and she must have figured that he probably saw Inez sometimes." See Hursley biography, chapter 8, Berger Papers, SHSW.

10. Henry Allen Cooper (1850–1931), a progressive Republican from Wisconsin, served as a U.S. congressman, 1893–1919 and 1921–1931.

11. James R. Mann (1856–1922), an Illinois Republican, served as a U.S. congressman, 1897–1922, and as his party's floor leader in the House, 1911–1919. Mann was one of only six representatives who voted to seat Berger in 1920.

12. Berger was referring to the movement to abolish partisan elections in Wisconsin. In the 1912 Milwaukee municipal election, Democrats and Republicans agreed to run a fusion ticket against the Socialists. Later that year, the state legislature enacted a law requiring nonpartisan municipal elections, a measure that the Socialists argued was aimed at their party. Bills were introduced in the legislature in 1913 and 1915 to extend nonpartisan elections to the county and state levels, but these measures were not adopted.

13. James Hudson Maurer (1864–1944) served as president of the Pennsylvania Federation of Labor, 1912–1928, and was elected to the Pennsylvania legislature in 1910, 1914, and 1916. He was first elected to the Socialist Party's National Executive Committee in 1904 and was the party's nominee for vice-president in 1928 and 1932. Maurer resigned from the party in 1936.

14. George H. Goebel (1876–1943), a New Jersey lecturer, served several terms on the Socialist Party's National Executive Committee.

Victor to Meta

New York, New York
June 6, 1914

My sweet Schatzl:

Arrived at New York—tired and dirty and my first care will be a thoro cleaning. Some [way] another I have never learned how to sleep in a berth and I have practically lost the last night. Shall go to bed early and call up Hillquit tomorrow.

To judge from the papers—Sinclair has gone over to the anarchists entirely and is trying to break into the papers in company with Alexander Berkman[1] (the man who shot Frick in 1893 on account of the Homestead strike and has served 14 years in the state penitentiary), with Leonard D. Abbot,[2] a former socialist, and the I.W.W.

There seems to be no Socialist movement here—only a few anarchistic literary men and some more or less anarchistic Russians. I really do not know what is to become of this party.

By the way, sweetheart, I shall not call up or look up our friend Inez.[3] Will call up Hilda and her husband[4] instead—will do so either tomorrow (Sunday) or Monday. Will try to arrange to run over to Bridgeport on Tuesday—but that will depend on circumstances.

And now Schatzl sweetheart good by for today. Always [remember] that *you are* the greatest achievement of my carriere—no matter what other things I may achieve—and also remember that it is my greatest hope and sincerest wish that my girls should grow up to be like you and be worthy of you.

With thousand kisses
your
V.L.B.

1. Alexander Berkman (1870–1936), a Russian-born anarchist, attempted to assassinate industrialist Henry Clay Frick (1849–1919) during the 1892 Homestead strike and was imprisoned until 1906. He later spent two more years in prison because of his opposition to World War I and was deported to Russia upon his release.

2. Leonard Dalton Abbott (1878–1953) served as associate editor of *Current Literature*, 1905–1925, and as president of the Free Speech League,

1910–1914. He was one of the founders of the Intercollegiate Socialist Society and of the Rand School.

3. Inez Milholland Boissevain.

4. Victor's niece, Hilda Morganstern Loewenthal, and her husband, William.

Victor to Meta

[Milwaukee, Wisconsin]
July 13, 1914

My sweet Schatzl:

So much is decided now that I shall not go to the coast before going to Europe.[1] They want no meetings on the coast before September—and I cannot blame them. I will communicate this news to my friend tomorrow morning.

On the other hand I am personally well satisfied with this outcome because I dreaded the trip very much. The only bad side of it is that I will be needed here in September but I believe that I can make up in the last few weeks for lost time.

I have been in Chicago yesterday and heard that Duncan,[2] mayor of Butte, is being held responsible by the Western Federation of Miners for all the trouble in Butte. Duncan is the sponsor and abettor of the I.W.W and of the new so-called Industrial Union in Butte. The trouble for him arrived when one of the crazy Finns wanted him to deport Altoonen[3] (whom you have seen at the convention in Chicago)—also a Finn, but sane and a national committee-man from Michigan. Altoonen had gone to Butte to ask aid for the Tyomes—The Finnish daily in Hancock, which opposes the I.W.W. Now it was not within the power of Duncan to deport Altoonen from Butte, as much as he might like to do it,—but, therefore, the crazy Finn tried to kill him. There was a great deal of "nemesis" in the entire performance. As soon as Duncan gets on his feet again I shall start a movement to recall him from the Executive Committee. He is a sneak and a snake.

Well, sweetheart, I expect to send Josie up on July 23rd or July 24th (Thursday or Friday.) If I had my way—she would go right-a-way.

Mary is here all the time—she does her sewing in your little room during day time and sleeps with Josie at night—so, you see, we have a boarder here although the fare is exceedingly simple except evenings, when there is something that looks like a meal.

I have not forgotten the taxes have looked out for them. They will be paid promptly. And I will also pay my life insurance before I leave for Europe. One instalment is due some time in September.

That is about all the news I can tell you—except that the Republicans and the Democrats have a beautiful cat and dog fight among themselves—I have never seen the old parties split up so fearfully before.

Kiss the babies and [tell] them that I expect them to do some swimming and some rowing every day. And I would rather have them go to bed early and rise early. And I want them both to learn all they can about machinery of the boat, because some day (if I live) I will get a good automobile and I want them to be able to run it. If they get thoroughly acquainted with the engine of the launch—they will easily learn the mechanism of the automobile.

I have noted what you have said about the dates—but I dont know how to arrange it—unless I go up on Friday the 24th—and stay there until the 27th, to take leave from the children and then take you with me to Milwaukee for a week. Well Schatzl let me know what you think of that?

With many kisses

Your V.LB.

1. See Victor to Meta, July 30, 1914, below.
2. Lewis J. Duncan (1857–1936), a Unitarian minister and a Socialist, served as the mayor of Butte, Montana, 1911–1914. Following the bombing of a mine office in Butte, the governor of Montana placed the city under martial law, and Duncan was removed from office for his failure to quell the violence.
3. Frank Aaltonen was an organizer for the Western Federation of Miners and a spokesman for the Finnish Socialist Federation in Michigan. On July 3, 1914, Eric Lantala, a supporter of the IWW, demanded that Mayor Duncan "deport" Aaltonen from Butte. When Duncan refused, the two men fought. Lantala stabbed Duncan, and the mayor shot his assailant, who died three days later.

Victor to Meta

Milwaukee, Wisconsin
July 22, 1914

My sweet Schatzl:

The Büch-Koch[1] matter will come up in tonights meeting of the central committee—it has been bungled up considerably because that "democratic bunch" making up the Executive Committee always waits for the Central Committee before anything is undertaken. Büch has declared that he would not accept the position any more, but we cannot, of course, permit Mr. Bading[2] to decide who is to be the representative and the trusted agent of the Social Democratic Party in the election commission.

I am on the look-out for somebody to become business-manager. I very much doubt the ability of Ziegler in that respect.

Had the occassion to turn down the offer of a $5,000 bribe these days. *This is strictly confidential!* Schatzl. But I was offered $5,000 in spot cash, if the Leader would change its position on the question of the "affidavit saloons" under the Baker laws.[3] I was told that the question was *not* a matter of principle, nor even of policy for our party, and that any Socialist could have any view he chose, on that point. I turned the man down cold,—or rather the men—because they were three. This is the first time in a long while that anybody dared to offer me a bribe— and I felt sore because I thought I had passed the stage where anybody in Milwaukee would think that I could be reached through money even if no principle or party policy was concerned. But again I say—this is strictly confidential, because I promised these lawyers to keep it so.

Well, sweetheart, I will leave for Shawano, next Friday at 8 PM. If you want to be at the depot at 12.50 AM—(which means *one o'clock at night* and sometimes a quarter of an hour later) then of course I shall be *more than pleased,* to have you with me that night—but I think, it is foolish to spoil *your night* like that. Just ask Frank[4] to leave the key to his house with the boy running the "buss", and I will come up to the lake on Saturday morning—and you will be rested.

I am glad to hear that Doris takes to sewing—so long as she gets sufficient exercise. I like swimming and rowing a good deal *better* for Doris and Elsa than anything that keeps them confined to one place.

Well darling I shall see you within less than three days, therefore, with many kisses—addio, carissima mia![5]

V.LB.

1. Robert Buech (1870–1949), a Socialist, served as a Milwaukee alderman, 1906–1908, election commissioner, 1911–1917, sheriff, 1919–1921, and county supervisor, 1932–1936. Mayor Gerhard Bading replaced Buech with William Koch as the Socialist member of the election commission, but the party refused to ratify the appointment on the grounds that Koch was no longer a party member. Buech regained his post through a successful appeal to the Wisconsin Supreme Court.

2. Gerhard A. Bading (1870–1946), a physician, served as Milwaukee health commissioner, 1906–1910, and mayor, 1912–1916. A Republican, Bading ran on a fusion ticket that defeated Socialist incumbent Emil Seidel in 1912. From 1922 to 1930, Bading held a number of diplomatic positions, including that of ambassador to Ecuador.

3. Wisconsin's Baker law restricted the number of saloons that could operate legally but permitted those in business prior to June 30, 1907, to remain open. Prohibitionists on the Milwaukee Common Council attempted to shut down more than one hundred "affidavit saloons"—taverns that operated with an affidavit showing that they were grandfathered under the law. The *Milwaukee Leader* opposed both the Baker law and local efforts to shut down the saloons.

4. Frank Schweers, Meta's brother-in-law.

5. goodbye, my little darling.

Victor to Meta

en route to New York
July 30, 1914

My sweet Schatzl:

This is my first letter—it is written only few hours after we parted and I don't know much news except what I have read in the papers. Some way another it seems to me that the great European conflagration will not come at this time—from what I have noticed from England, I am satisfied that England will never fight—surely not for France. Almost funny looked the report from Japan that that country would go to war to defend its "ally" England—and incidentally also Russia—with which England has the "entente"—when Great Britain did nothing absolutely nothing during the Russian-Japanese war to help Japan.

It is possible, of course, that Russia and Germany would get into war—and I believe that would be a good thing because it would hurt both the Czar and the Kaiser—and surely hurt the cause of monarchy and absolutism in Europe, especially if the Czar should get licked—a consumation devoutly to be wished.

I cannot see how France can go to war, with a rebellious anti-militaristic working class in the rear. The slightest mishap of the war may result in a second edition of the Paris Commune. And it also speaks volumes that there were immense protest meetings against war in Berlin and that the Kaiser did not dare to use the army or the police against the demonstrants.

From this point of view I believe that the French government—at the head of which just now is Viviani,[1] a former member of the Socialist party of France and socialist deputy not so very long ago—will not interfere with the International Congress,[2] if he is wise, but rather use it as a means "to get out from under."

But let's drop politics, I absolutely made up my mind, Schatzl, that this is the last time that I shall ever go to Europe without you, if we are both healthy and well, when I get the chance again. Now, you have my promise "black on white," darling, and you can hold me to it. Moreover I really need you more as I get older—and parting from you is harder for me than having a tooth pulled. Now don't smile—it is a fact which is telling on me all day.

There is a young fellow from Milwaukee on the train who serves in the navy. It is the man who stood near the train when I took leave of you. That is about all the news so far.

Schatzl remember that *you* are the best part of your

V.L.B.

1. René Viviani (1863–1925), a Socialist, served as French premier and minister of foreign affairs from June, 1914, through October, 1915.

2. Berger planned to attend the meeting of the International Socialist Congress, which was scheduled for Vienna and relocated to Paris because of the outbreak of war in Europe. Morris Hillquit, Emil Seidel, George E. Lunn, Oscar Ameringer, and Berger were ninety miles out at sea before news arrived that the meeting had been cancelled and they turned back.

Victor to Meta

[Milwaukee, Wisconsin]
[August 6, 1914]

My dear Schatzl:

There can be no question, but that Shawano is too far from Milwaukee, and too inaccessible—to make it really enjoyable for you and me.

Therefore, if we could get "our price" for the cottage, I am willing to sell. But all things and especially lumber, have gone up fearfully of late. And with the government printing a billion dollars worth of greenbacks (in order to help the bankers and businessmen) and thus still farther limiting the *buying power* of the dollar to that extent, everything is bound to go up still higher and to stay up. And you have the best cottage on the beach and you could not replace it today for less than $2,000. The lot ought to be worth $500, and your furniture $250—a total of $2,750. Now, no one is going to pay you that just now, although the chances are that they will pay you more than that amount in two or three years from now.

And as it is I don't want to sell the cottage for less. We get far more than the interest on $3,000 in health and enjoyment for our children.

Well, Schatzl, if I had a flying machine I would fly to you every evening—as it is I shall try to make a "home run" on Friday, Aug. 14th.

I have my trouble with my crowd[1] up-stairs on this war. They are thouroughly pro-English which in this case means also pro-Russian and pro-French and—anti-German. The news all comes by the way of London and is colored that way anyhow. Now, the majority of our readers are of German descent and are protesting. Moreover, it seems that the *insane* Kaiser has made a bad mess of it.

In short, I wish, the cruel war was over.

With thousand kisses,
Ever your
VLB.

1. Berger was referring to the editorial staff of the *Milwaukee Leader,* especially Algie Simons.

Victor to Meta

[Milwaukee, Wisconsin]
August 7, 1914

My sweet Schatzl:

The war gives me troubles of all kinds—so many comrades and readers of the paper believing that the Leader is anti-German because we print news unfavorable to the German side. As a matter of fact *there is no other news* to print,—all the news is coming from London, Paris and Brussels and naturally is anti-German. Germany and Austria seemed to be cut off entirely from the rest of the world.

We got a hold of some editions of Socialist papers however— including the Berlin Vorwaerts—printed just before the war was declared and it really makes me feel proud of the German Social Democratic party. That manifesto in face of almost certain court martial and death, will live in history.

The Free Press attacked me bitterly this morning (Friday) as a sort of a traitor to the German race because I do not sufficiently adore the German Kaiser.[1] As an answer I printed the manifesto of the German Social Democracy on the first page of the Leader today.[2] The Free Press had claimed in its editorial that the German party had unanimously supported the Kaiser and the Germania[3] claimed the same thing. By-the-way—all the Milwaukee papers claim now German victories in the *headlines* when there is not a line in the news to substantiate it. They must think the Germans very stupid.

Well, Schatzl, that is about all I know of news in this town. The other thing daß ich Dich sehr lieb hab'[4]—I must say it in German—is getting to be an old thing, and yet it is always new.

With love
VLB.

Enclosed a letter for Doddie. I want her to answer it.

1. The *Milwaukee Free Press*, August 7, 1914, published an editorial entitled "As for Mr. Berger" claiming that Berger had "set himself up as the original prophet of ill-omen for the German cause in Europe" and that his criticism of the German war effort had the "palpable purpose to arouse prejudice against the German emperor, the defender of western civilization."

2. The *Milwaukee Leader*, August 7, 1914, reprinted a statement of the German Social Democratic Party of July 25, 1914, opposing Germany's entry into the war on the side of Austria-Hungary.

3. *Germania* was a German-language weekly newspaper published in Milwaukee from 1873 until September, 1918, when its name was changed to the *Milwaukee America*. Prior to American entry into World War I, the paper advocated U.S. neutrality.

4. that I love you very much.

Meta to Victor

[Shawano, Wisconsin]
[August 8, 1914]

My dear Schatzl:—

I saw the article in the Free Press attacking you[1] and I couldn't see, even by the wildest stretch of the imagination, how he could attribute to you the motives he did from the interview you granted them. That's what you get in return for giving them any interview at all. The papers are surely playing politics with a vengeance; dirty politics and if I were you I'd get into the game & play it too especially since all news is unreliable. You too could put that construction on the war situation that would best help your cause for it undoubtedly is quite as reliable, even more so than the stuff one reads in the other papers. I have always found that your interpretation is much more correct than any one else's. Play politics now for all your worth.

I feel very very sorry for Pres. Wilson. I think perhaps she'd[2] been alive today but for politics & social responsibilities. Politics saps the life's blood out of some people you see.

Every body here is well especially the children. I could [be] better but think after this week will be O.K again. The weather continues to be warm & I only hope that when you make that home-run it will be cool enough to enjoy the woods. Arrange your affairs so you can stay a little longer time for I fear you won't be coming again this season.

With oceans of love I am

Ever your own

Meta

1. See Victor to Meta, August 7, 1914, above.
2. Ellen Louise Axson Wilson (1860–1914), the first wife of President Woodrow Wilson, died on August 6, 1914.

Victor to Meta

[Milwaukee, Wisconsin]
August 10, 1914

My sweet Schatzl:

It is not so easy to "play politics" when the fact is more and more established every day that the Social Democrats of all countries bitterly opposed this war—and especially did the Social Democrats of Germany, Austria and Hungary oppose it.

Moreover, this war is bound to become very unpopular with the Germans as soon as some of the facts are known—I only hope that they will be known before [the] election.[1] About the end of September would be the psychological moment. Just now it is pretty hard on us because the Socialism of many of German followers is only skin deep.

I have also some other troubles—mainly of a financial nature—however, I feel sure that the paper will pull through in excellent shape. But whether it will be possible for me to leave this Friday for Shawano has become a great question again. Ziegler has accepted the position[2] and Thursday night we will have a special meeting to have him appointed. Now I feel that it would not be fair if I leave for Shawano the day after (because that would also mean Saturday and Monday). I therefore wondered, whether it would not be a better plan to go to Shawano after Ziegler had been in Office at least a week—then I could also stay away a day or two longer.

Just let me know what you think of the idea, Schatzl.

Tell the babies to stick to their promise, I will stick to mine.

Hope you have a nice time up there, darling. It was incredibly hot in Milwaukee, during the last three days.

With thousand kisses
your V.LB.

1. Berger failed to reclaim his seat in Congress in November, 1914, receiving 35 percent of the vote against 47 percent for incumbent Republican William Stafford, who ran as a fusion candidate, and 18 percent for Democrat Lawrence McGreal. Berger was attacked during the campaign for not being sufficiently pro-German.
2. Edward Ziegler had agreed to become business manager of the *Milwaukee Leader*.

Meta to Victor

[Shawano, Wisconsin]
August 15, 1914

Papa Darling:—

Am sorry you didn't surprise us. If you would like me to come to Mil. write me at once & I'll come next Wednesday & stay as long as you like. If you say the word I'll bring the family & break up camp. On the other hand, I do really think the few days you do get do you some good at least. It is the only time you get anything out of this place. The days have been perfect, cool enough to thoroughly enjoy the tramps thro' the woods. And the nights are the finest kind for sleeping. This morning we tramped thro' the woods for a couple of hours hunting blackberries & birds. We certainly saw lovely flocks of beautiful birds.

Mrs. Oakland & Mary Rudkowski[1] left this morning. I shall let a long long time lapse before Mary comes up again. She is a disagreeable girl. Today for she suffers mostly herself.

Next Wed., all my other guests go with perhaps the exception of Ella.[2] She & the girls get along so well that if she will stay, she will be welcome.

I do wish the Leader will get on a safe financial basis soon. Do you think the war situation will effect you any? And how about the political situation? It is almost overshadowed by the European news. But the soaring prices in food stuffs & supplies is good campaign material. I see by the paper that you discredit the report that the German Socialists are shot. I hope you are correct. It would be terrible if that were true. I can't begin to tell you how glad I am you are not there now. Surely you would have been a mark for some one if not from over there, then for some [kind] of American thug hired to do it. Besides, I believe this Congress will be held as soon as the war situation is cleared up. Then there will be need of an international Congress to gather up the remnants. Think of the worry I am saved for I would not be able to get the news from abroad.

Well Papa, all things work out in some way & I hope our future will work itself out right for us & the children. I only hope that the children will be able to stand on their own feet & have certain ideals to work for.

And now sweetheart-mine, write me if I am to come to Mil. Wednesday or if you will be with us Sat. morning or Friday night. I am counting the days until you embrace me once more. Your embrace gives new life & desire. Ever your

Meta.

1. Elizabeth Ehrler Oakland (b. 1848) of Milwaukee and Marie Rudkowsky (Weaver) (b. 1883), the sister of the Bergers' longtime maid, Josephine Rudkowsky.
2. Ella Stuckert (b. 1896) was the daughter of Rudolph Stuckert, a public school janitor, and Matilda Stuckert, a librarian.

Victor to Meta

[Milwaukee, Wisconsin]
August 17, 1914

My dear Schatzl:

Your letter suggesting that you break up camp and come home on Wednesday was some temptation, I admit,—but after all, what do we have that cottage for, if the children and you are not to get their full share of fresh forest air and plenty of exercise on the lake and otherwise—in place of interest on the money invested. I shall go there next Friday night,—or early on Saturday morning—will let you know in a day or two—and spend a few days with you.

Ed Ziegler has taken possession of his new job today. No one can tell of course, whether he will like it, or not.

I have started to write a series of articles on the war for the Leader. The first article is done, but I don't like it because it is too dry. Will possibly re-write it tomorrow morning. I want everybody to read them and to like them.

I am suffering somewhat from a "falling arch" on my feet. And now I went to work to buy a certain kind of a shoe, which I will have to get used to, if it is to do my feet any good. So far the remedy seems to be worse than the evil.

Politics seem to be entirely overshadowed just now by the war. But I expect a reaction within a day or two. There can be no doubt that the war will make millions of Socialists—but whether the war will make them before the fall election, is questionable. With all this I feel more certain of my election than I ever did in my life before.

Kiss the babies for me and always remember that you are my Mamma-Schatzl und daß ich Dich lieb hab![1]

V.L.B.

1. and that I love you very much!

Victor to Meta

Milwaukee, Wisconsin
August 30, 1914

My sweet Schatzl:

Your letter had reached Archie Anderson the next day because he happened to be in town. And he also sent a check for $150.00—I should have appreciated, if he had sent just the exact sum of the bill. Of course, it might be said however, that we have advanced Jack's board so long that we can accept the advance for a few months.

At any rate I enclose you a check for $50.00—and I will also tend to [the] matter of paying interest on the mortgage. In September an item of paying $123.00 life insurance falls due which I cannot afford to overlook.

I have my dire troubles and tribulations with Simons who now openly admits that he hates everything German and tries to sneak in some venemous head-lines, or (what is just as bad) headlines that claim ridiculous victories.[1] He offered his resignation two or three times yesterday, and some day I will accept and Simons will get the same experience as Bistorius.[2]

I have also struck a plan which will help us out for at least a year—in other words permanently because after a year or so we shall need no more help.

Tonight I am going to Merill Wis.—I try to return by Tuesday. We hope to be able to turn the attention of the people to internal affairs— otherwise the most reactionary element of our society will get the benefit of the wholesale murder in Europe. On the other hand, of course, it getting to be an axiom with people not yet Socialists—that after all is said and done, we are the only party of progress.

With thousand kisses
Your VL.B.

1. Algie Simons eventually broke with Berger because of their differences on the war and resigned as managing editor of the *Milwaukee Leader* in December, 1916.
2. Herman W. Bistorius was forced to resign as business manager of the Milwaukee Social-Democratic Publishing Company in 1914 because he employed nonunion labor to build his house.

Victor to Meta

[Milwaukee, Wisconsin]
September 1, [1914]

My sweet Schatzl:

I just got your letter—all right I shall expect you on Thursday, at 2 PM.

The vote at this Primary is exceedingly light—there seems to be no other interest than the war. With the old parties there is at least a contest between the various candidates for office on the same ticket. We select our candidates by referendum and there is practically no personal interest involved. I will be satisfied if we get 4,000 votes in Milwaukee county.[1] We must have between 2,500 and 2,600 to get on the ticket. If we should not get enough votes, we would have to go on by petition and that would be a disgrace.

Such is war.

It might also interest you that the 21st Ward—Simon's ward— passed a vote of censure against the Leader on account of its "anti-German" and un-Socialistic attitude. Simons was not there, of course, when it was done. My fights were mainly with Simons on the head lines—even last Saturday, he offered to resign two or three times. However that crowd in 21st ward wants to find fault with me—if it wasn't on this, it would be for something else. I will make open war on them and have the branch re-organized.

Have you seen my interview in Monday's Sentinel?[2] The Evening Sentinel only had a little part of it and therefore I believe you didn't.

Well Schatzl, forgive me for telling you all these unpleasant things, but they are on my mind and therefore they get into the pen. Es wird schließlich doch alles gut werden.[3]

With thousand kisses
VLB.

1. The Socialists received more than 9,500 votes in Milwaukee County in the September, 1914, gubernatorial primary election.
2. "Socialists Prepare for War Protest," *Milwaukee Sentinel,* August 31, 1914. In the interview, Berger stated that no winners would emerge from the war in Europe and called for the United States to halt all trade with warring nations.
3. But everything will be all right in the end.

Victor to Meta

en route to New York, New York
November 23, 1914

My sweet Schatzl:

Have attended the Finnish convention last night and today until 4.20 P.M—and had to hustle like a good fellow to make my train. Got the train in good time, all right—but with all the excitement and my job as judge—or rather as presiding judge—I did not get the opportunity to call you up by telephon today as I had intended to do.

The trouble among the Finns is the old fight between the "sane" and "insane",—between the so-called "Radicals" and the Constructive—between I.W.W and the real Socialists etc. Only it is aggrevated in this case by some so-called "intellectuals" seeking jobs on the Finnish papers and trying to destroy not only these papers but to split up the organization because they did not get these jobs.[1]

Seymour Stedman will take my place tomorrow and I am sure he is just as qualified as I am to judge the situation.

But enough of that.

Coming to think of it: I left thirty dollars with you for the kids—why not use part of that money to get a cloak for Dodie, if you can find something prize-worthy that she likes. Look around in the various stores and get it from any advertiser. But if you cannot get something that is worth while and not too expensive, you will have to wait until after Christmas, of course. Only I don't [like] the idea of having my girl walk around in shabby cloak on Sunday,—"as her very best". Use your own judgement however.

With thousand kisses
Your
V.L.B.

1. The Finnish Socialist Federation was the largest of the Socialist Party's foreign-language groups, all of which maintained a great deal of autonomy from the national party. In 1914, the federation suffered a schism, with the right-wing faction maintaining control of the federation offices as well as of *Työmies,* its Superior, Wisconsin, newspaper. The pro-IWW faction established a rival newspaper, *Socialisti,* in nearby Duluth, Minnesota.

Victor to Meta

en route near Pittsburgh, Pennsylvania
[February 18, 1915]

Sweet Schatzl:

This will be a short one—simply to show you that I think of you before I go to bed. My previous letters on this trip were too business like—speaking mainly of the Leader and of our two Schnuckies. This one is to be devoted to you, darling.

To begin with, sweetheart, I want to see you elected this time and I will go to considerable lenght to accomplish this. And if you are elected I will at once launch a campaign to make you president.[1] Of course, I will *not* appear personally in either campaigns, but there are many roads leading to Washington.

Your election is *very probable* because you will—besides the Social Democratic votes—get many outsiders, even more so than either Zabel[2] or Melms. Many honest Non-Socialists will try to prove their non-partizanship by voting for you. Moreover, you will appear also on the Sentinel ticket, and the Journal and Evening Wisconsin—and even the Free Press—will not fight you.

Should you [be] defeated, however,—contrary to all expectation and contrary to common sense and public welfare—but simply in order to stop the awful waste of my evenings then in order to give you a field for your administrative ability I will try to get you appointed to the Board of Regents for the State University or to the Committee that shall take its place.

Im Übrigen, Schatzl, hoffe ich daß Du mich im̄er noch lieb hast.[3]

Write about Monday and send letter to the Hotel Martinique, Broadway & 32nd ok.

Mit thausend Küssen[4]
VL.B.

By-the-way, sweet Schatzl, while waiting for the other sheet to dry—the blotter is out of commission—I may just as well, speak to my sweet Schatzl, some more.

I would suggest, darling that Doris invite one of the Augustin girls up to Shawano. I believe Doris did so last year, but the girl for some reason did not go. May be she will come this year,—and if she does not, well, then Doris had at least invited her. If the Augustin girl should accept, that shall be an extra guest and not be counted in the list already made up—if such a list has been made up by our girls.

This is simply a suggestion—if you don't like it, then don't tell Doris anything about it.

Let me know, Schatzl, as soon as possible, whether you are going to the lake before I get home, or whether you will stay over until election.

And be careful, darling, to write your return address on the envelope, so that the letter is returned, in case it should miss me.

The weather has suddenly changed and while it was cool in the morning, it is now very warm and sultry. I expect some very hot days in Philadelphia and New York.

Mit vielen Küssen Dein[5]
V.L.B.

1. Socialists won four out of five open seats on the Milwaukee school board on April 6, 1915, and Meta Berger won reelection to her seat, receiving more votes than any other candidate in the at-large election. The board formally chose her as its president on July 6, 1915, and she held the post for one year.

2. Winfred C. Zabel (1877–1948) served as Milwaukee district attorney, 1911–1913 and 1915–1923. Zabel won election to the post as a Socialist but switched to the Republican Party in 1919.

3. By the way, little darling, I hope that you still love me.

4. With a thousand kisses.

5. With many kisses.

Victor to Meta

Washington, D.C.
February 19, [1915]

My sweet Schatzl:

Had a very kind reception at the house this morning—as usual everybody was glad to see me and many expressed their regret that I was not a member any longer. Barthold[1] of St. Louis, the great Pan-German made a speech today expressing his American patriotism and he and I and Bill Kent had lunch together at Congress Hall—and Barthold and Kent spoke together for the first time in three years (in my honor of course)—until now they had been bitter enemies. Tonight I am invited to take dinner at Kent's house on 19th and F N.W.

In the morning I ran around the capitol and immediate vicinity like a school boy looking at the sights. And the following little funny episode happened. I just came out of the new post office (near the station) which is a wonderful three million dollar building when a colored young man offered his services to act as a guide. He told me that he knew all the historical facts connected with the city, since the days of George Washington. The offer amused me and I said: "What all the historical facts since George Washington? Aren't you promising too much?"—"No sir," said he, "I could even show you the house where Victor Berger, the great Socialist lived, when he was in Congress." "Where?" said I—"At the Congress Hall hotel",—he answered promptly "and you are Mr. Berger." Of course, I felt terribly chesty for [a] moment, but he took the conceit out of me by adding—"And I was a waiter in the New Varnum the hotel nearby"! Well Schatzl I had to laugh and gave him a tip.

Well, sweetheart I also visited with Lenroot[2] and met La Follette on the street. Tomorrow I shall try to see Redfield in the morning.

As to my mission—I will consult with Kent tonight, from what he let me understand, I shall have to let him alone this time anyhow.[3]

Will tell you more about it in my next letter.

With kisses to you all—und Dich hab' ich lieb, Schatzl[4]—always, your

V.L.B.

1. Richard Bartholdt (1855–1932) served as a Republican representative from Missouri, 1893–1915.
2. Irvine L. Lenroot (1869–1949) served as a Republican representative from Wisconsin, 1909–1918, and as a U.S. senator, 1918–1927.
3. Berger was attempting to raise funds for the *Milwaukee Leader* by selling Social-Democratic Publishing Company bonds.
4. and you I love, little darling.

Meta to Victor

[Milwaukee, Wisconsin]
June 14, 1915

Dearest Papa,

Please answer this letter right away. Mabel Search[1] has been very kind in the past as we both know. Last Sat. I am told she had a short article in the Journal boosting my candidacy for Pres.[2] Today (Monday) she rang me up to ask me to announce my own candidacy saying that then she would have a better right to go ahead to boost. I told her that a certain feeling of diffidence or modesty or whatever you choose to call it forbad me from doing that even tho' I knew the Free Press was trying to create public opinion against me. She said "Well that's just what we want to overcome. Any one getting the endorsement you got & leading the ticket should go in unopposed." I asked her to let me think about *announcing myself* for a few days, promising her that if I got ready to talk I would give her the first story. She was satisfied with that & thus

I have a few days time to get word to you & a reply from you. So be sure to write me concerning this at once. Personally I think it much more becoming in me to be quiet & let the others do the talking. She (Mabel S.) said if I didn't talk, why then she'd get Dr. Kissling[3] to talk & that's more to my liking. She furthermore said Augustyn had told her he would stand for me, so she said "you have a clear cinch Mrs. Berger". Still I'm holding off from doing any of it myself. Don't you think I'm write?

Am sorry your journey was hot & unpleasant. It has been real cold here right along. Am anxious to hear from you again. Was in bed last night at 9 P.M. With oceans of love I am always your

Meta.

1. Mabel Search (1891–1955) was a reporter for the *Milwaukee Journal* until 1918, when she joined the staff of the *Milwaukee Leader*. In 1924 she moved to New York, where she worked as an editor for *Good Housekeeping, McCall's, Delineator,* and the *Pictorial Review.*

2. "Woman May Head School Directors," *Milwaukee Journal,* June 12, 1915, reported that Meta Berger would probably be elected president of the Milwaukee school board.

3. Charles L. Kissling (1859–1917), a physician, served on the Milwaukee school board from 1907 until his death.

Victor to Meta

Philadelphia, Pennsylvania
June 15, 1915

My sweet Schatzl:

I must thank you for the nice letter you wrote me and I am especially glad that our little Doddie did so well. Was sorry I could not be there.

Have spent the day to very good advantage. Went to see Mayor Blankenburg[1] and some of the newspapers and got a very fine reception everywhere. Blankenburg is an old man of 74 who has not the energy any more that would be required to rule a rotten town like Philadelphia in a real decent manner.

Tonight I have dinner with an editor and also lunch tomorrow with another. But I use all this for a purpose as you may well guess. I have not seen Mr. Taft as yet, he will not be here until tomorrow.

My mission here is very important, of course—the Peace conference[2] is simply a side show, as far as I am concerned. However I use the

Peace conference to get prestige for the other thing. I expect to amend Mr. Taft's three propositions by adding that in case of war a general embargo be put by all nations on export of war material and ammunition while all countries should be absolutely free to furnish and sell food stuffs and clothing to the fighting parties. In order words they should be forbidden to sell the means of killing while everybody be free to furnish the means of living.

My amendment will not be accepted of course, although I cannot see, what objections they can make against it.[3]

What you told me about the Free Press and its attempt to create a public sentiment against you disquitens me only in as much as it *might* influence Mrs. Kander. If I were in Milwaukee *now*, I would get the Sentinel and the Journal to come out for you. But these things cannot very well be arranged for by mail. Do you think I could suggest to Dr. Kissling in a letter to see Henry Campbell and Mr. Johnson?[4] Don't *you* do it. To morrow night is the banquett. I found out that the out-of-town delegates are the guests of the committee and that our plates are free. I suppose listening to these speeches will in itself amount to a considerable fine.

It is incredibly hot in this town and still hotter in my room. But in all this heat I find comfort in the thought that my work here may help my Schatzl and my babies in the near future.

Schatzl, ich hab' Dich sehr lieb![5] Kiss the babies for me.

V.L.B.

1. Rudolph Blankenburg (1843–1918), a German-born businessman and reformer, served as mayor of Philadelphia, 1912–1916.
2. Berger was a delegate to the organizational meeting of the League to Enforce Peace, a group dedicated to promoting a league of nations after the end of the European war. William Howard Taft served as the league's president; Berger was one of many honorary vice-presidents.
3. Berger proposed an amendment to the league's charter that would have prevented nonbelligerents from selling munitions to combatants but would have permitted the sale of foodstuffs. As he predicted, the convention defeated his amendment.
4. Henry Colin Campbell (1862–1923) worked for the *Milwaukee Journal* from 1894 until his death, serving as assistant editor from 1913 onward. Edward G. Johnson (1852–1934) became chief editorial writer for the *Milwaukee Sentinel* in 1901 and served as the paper's editor from 1918 until 1921.
5. Little darling, I love you very much!

Victor to Doris

New York, New York
June 19, 1915

My dear little girl:

According to our dear Mamma's letter you did so well at the recital (when you received your certificate for elocution) that I felt that I must send you a few lines of appreciation. I also want to tell you that I very much regretted the unfortunate circumstance that I had to start on my journey on that very day. However, Mamma, Elsa and Jack were there, and were proud of you. And so am I. I even bought a little present, which I shall give you in person when I get to Shawano this summer. And the other children shall have no reason either to feel neglected.

Mamma's plan to send you children to Shawano under the friendly guidance and supervision of our old stand-bys, Matta and Laura,[1] has my full approval. Otherwise you children might have very little of any outing this year. On account of our Mamma becoming the president of the School Board, we may have to come to town earlier than usual.[2]

Sometimes I wonder whether you girls sufficiently prize the fact that your mother is the first woman in *America* who has ever achieved the honor of being elected president of a school board. And the first Socialist president at that,—man or woman.

You will value this honor still more when I tell you that she is the first woman—and the first Socialist—*of any country,* upon whom such honor was bestowed, so far as I know.

Of course, I don't want you girls to speak to anybody about this. That would be in bad taste and might be considered bragging.

But I want you children to understand the situation and to be as proud of your mother as I am.

You girls can show this best by worrying her as little as possible. The presidency of the School Board will *add* to her burdens and responsibilities. You girls can do a thousand and one little things at home, which only loving daughters can do for their mother.

With love to all, your
Papa.

1. Matta Soik (b. 1868) was a teacher in the Milwaukee public schools from 1895 to 1938. Laura F. Duggan (1878–1962) taught in the Milwaukee public schools from 1908 until 1916 and worked for the system's administrative offices from 1916 to 1948.
2. Although Meta Berger was not formally elected president of the Milwaukee school board until July 6, 1915, she apparently had lined up by June 15, 1915, the five Socialist and three nonpartisan votes she needed for election. On that date, she wrote Victor that Godfrey William Augustyn, a fellow board member, had told her "that it was settled & nothing could change it" (Berger Papers, SHSW). The *Milwaukee Free Press* also reported that morning that the Socialists had sufficient votes to win the board's presidency ("Socialists Are Out to Control Schools").

Victor to Meta

Milwaukee, Wisconsin
December 15, 1915

My sweet Schatzl:

I feel like a sinner for not having written you any letter before— although the children have written and I have not received a letter from you until this morning. I was in Chicago Monday afternoon and Tuesday morning. It might interest you to hear that the initiative for the National Executive Committee which closed last Saturday at midnight gave me the highest number of nominations of anybody. I received the nominations of 368 locals, Germer is next and Hillquit the third in the number of nominations. I was also nominated for president by 38 locals, and even a larger number want me for vice-president—these good people do not know, of course, that I wasn't born in this country.

As for home affairs—Dod and I get along beautifully. I had dinner at Cantrowitzes[1] last night, Mr & Mrs Potter[2] were there also. We had ribs of Venison. After dinner we all went to school board office and I tried to keep from falling asleep while the Derse fire exploration committee[3] decided to have another session with the fire department officials to adopt a set of rules for the school houses. Then Mr. Potter took us all home in his machine—I invited them all up but they did not accept my invitation, of which I was very glad because I was tired and to judge from Mr. & Mrs. Cantrowitz—so were they.

The papers say very little about the Suffrage convention.[4] On[e] morning paper had an item tha[t] Mr. Byrne[5] of South Carolina wants to investigate the suffrage association to find out who is paying the expenses of the delegates—to "find out who is a lady and who is not"— in other words: to find out who has money, and who has not. Well, I believe that so far they are all of them ladies, according to Byrnes' standard, because they all pay their own expenses.

I am sorry you had such a bad ride down to Washington. As for the return trip see whether you can find nine more ladies to take the Pennsy. to Chicago with you—in order to get the reduced fare for all ten. But if you should not succeed in getting the ten, then you get your ticket on the Pennsylvania anyway. I have reserved lower 5, in car 75, for you on the train that leaves Washington at 6.04 P.M. on Saturday. That train will get you to Chicago at 2 P.M on Sunday and I will be on hand there.

By the way, if you go to ticket office of the Pennsylvania when you get this letter you might *also* reserve the upper berth (which is anyway 20% less than the lower) to some place where you get at 9 o'clock in the morning and thus have an entire section again coming home. I would rather have you do so.

With *love from all ever your*
V.L.B.

1. Solomon M. Cantrovitz (b. 1857?), a Milwaukee businessman, and his wife, Bella.

2. Milton C. (1873–1972) and Camilla P. Potter (1875–1962). Milton Potter served as Milwaukee superintendent of schools, 1914–1943.

3. James H. Derse (1862–1944), an educator and insurance agent, served on the Milwaukee school board, 1911–1923, and held its presidency, 1922–1923. In 1915–1916 Derse chaired a board committee that investigated fire hazards in the city's schools.

4. Meta Berger was a delegate to the annual convention of the National American Woman Suffrage Association, which met in Washington, D.C., on December 14–19, 1915.

5. James F. Byrnes (1879–1972) served as a Democratic representative from South Carolina, 1911–1925, U.S. senator, 1931–1941, associate justice of the U.S. Supreme Court, 1941–1942, U.S. secretary of state, 1945–1947, and governor of South Carolina, 1951–1955.

Meta to Victor

Washington, D.C.
[December 15, 1915]

Dear Papa:—

Today's convention was full of interest & all, but nothing compared to a Socialist convention. Of course all they talked of was campaign methods, literature, funds etc. But the interesting thing was in the personel. Mrs. Carrie Chapman Catt[1] is certainly a wonderful woman, strong, pretty logical eloquent. No wonder she is a leader. Dr. Shaw[2] of course is a leader to[o] but she is so arrogant & arbitrary. She can over look any one much better than Sam Gompers. Then I met Miss Blackwell[3] and all the others. Zona Gale[4] is especially nice to me and so is Mrs. Nelson.[5] I used to think I was a pretty good mixer but find I can't mix at all. Perhaps I am not within my own crowd but really I am glad I came because I can understand so much better many things and I am truly grateful to you darling for giving me this chance. Met Congressman Browne[6] from Waupaca today. He is a perfect stick. Also saw Kahn[7] from Cal. Telephone[d] Mrs Davis[8] & will have lunch with her Thursday. Also telephoned Mrs Stone.[9] She is ill, so is her baby & her husband.

Went to the White House shook hands with Wilson. When the name Mrs V. Berger was mentioned, a gleam of recognition came into his face & he gave me an extra squeeze of the hand.

The convention was in session until 10.30 P.M. & now it is 11.30 P.M. So will say good night to the bestest man in the wide world. With lots of love to you & the girls I am always

Your
Meta

Did you wire for my birth for the 6.15 P.M. train Sat. or Shall I?

1. Carrie Chapman Catt (1859–1947) served as president of the National American Woman Suffrage Association, 1900–1904 and 1915–1920, and as honorary president of the League of Women Voters, 1920–1947.

2. Anna Howard Shaw (1847–1919), a minister, physician, and activist, served as vice-president (1892–1904) and president (1904–1915) of the National American Woman Suffrage Association.

3. Alice Stone Blackwell (1857–1950), the daughter of women's rights activist Lucy Stone, was a socialist (although not a party member) and women's rights journalist. She served as assistant editor (1883–1909) and editor (1909–1917) of the *Woman's Journal.*

4. Zona Gale (1874–1938), a Pulitzer Prize–winning author from Portage, Wisconsin, was active in progressive causes and served as a member of the University of Wisconsin Board of Regents, 1923–1929.

5. Thea Johanna Stondall Nelson (1867–1946), a temperance and women's suffrage activist, was the wife of John Mandt Nelson (1870–1955), a progressive Republican congressman from Wisconsin, 1906–1919, 1921–1923.

6. Edward Everts Browne (1869–1945), served as a progressive Republican representative from Wisconsin, 1913–1931.

7. Julius Kahn (1861–1924) served as a Republican representative from California, 1899–1903 and 1905–1924.

8. Probably Emma Haven Davis, the wife of Charles Russell Davis, a Republican representative from Minnesota.

9. Probably Genevieve Francis Stone, the first wife of Claude Ulysses Stone, a Democratic representative from Illinois.

Victor to Meta

Milwaukee, Wisconsin
December 16, 1915

My sweet Schatzl:

Didn't I always tell you that we [are] best taken care of at home, or at least whenever you have your fierce, but far-seeing and circumspect Männele[1] with you. You must learn how to stand on your own feet, however, and to rely on your own resources. Therefore, I am very glad, you had this trip to Washington, D.C.

I have not met Mrs. Medill McCormick often and she meets very many people. Now that she did not seem to remember me very vividly I am almost sorry that I asked you to look her up. I don't like to run after anybody—on the contrary, I want them to run after me. And you and I are one.

The friendship of these middle class women from the state (like Mrs Hooper[2] for instance) for you, will not last long. They soon will get the viewpoint of the Milwaukee middle class women. Zona Gale, being an authoress, an artist and bohemian, may possibly keep up the friendship with you,—Mrs McCreery[3] being a proletarian, surely will—but as for the rest I have not much hope. You might get some of them on the grounds of personal friendship, if you entertain them at your home. And that will be all.

Hillquit told me that Meyer London[4] is a shallow ass. Hillquit may be a little prejudiced because both of them are lawyers and live in the same town—Hillquit is the successor of London as the attorney for the cloak-maker's union of New York—but on the whole I fear he is right and that I am going to shine in congress at least as much by my absence then by my presence, on account of comparison. As for you Schatzl, you have no reason to feel bitter. I would ten times rather have the Leader on a paying and safe basis than five more terms in Congress.

Well, Schatzl, this is probably the last letter, although I will send you one more night letter sweetheart. The regular mail cannot very well reach you in Washington on Saturday with a letter written tomorrow.

The children behaved beautifully—Dod even volunteered to clean the snow from the front steps last night.

We all went to the theater on Wednesday—the girls went with me to the German show and Jack went to the Majestic.

Let me know, please, whether you got your berth, and whether you also secured the upper—a few dollars more or less make no difference to me whenever your comfort is in question.

All in all, I hope this little trip with its novel experiences and impressions has benefited you and that you will come home so much better, stronger and riper for it, and *love more than ever* your busy and lonely, Schatz,

V.L.B.

1. hubby.
2. Jessie Annette Jack Hooper (1865–1935), an Oshkosh, Wisconsin, civic reformer, worked on behalf of women's and children's rights. She won the Democratic nomination for the U.S. Senate in 1922 but lost to Robert M. La Follette Sr. in the general election.
3. Maud Leonard McCreery (1883–1938) was a journalist and reformer who was active in the women's suffrage and peace movements. During the 1930s she edited a women's page for the *Milwaukee Leader* and worked as a labor organizer in Wisconsin.
4. Meyer London (1871–1926) served as a Socialist congressman from New York, 1915–1919 and 1921–1923. A Jewish immigrant from Russian Poland, London came to New York City in 1891 and frequently represented trade unions after his admission to the New York bar in 1898. As a congressman, he voted against American entry into World War I and opposed the Espionage Act, but he angered his fellow Socialists by refusing to vote against military appropriations during the war.

Victor to Meta

Milwaukee, Wisconsin
July 14, 1916

My sweet Schatzl:

We had a long and tedious director's meeting last night—and when I finally got home I was so tired that I fell asleep on Doris' bed last night; Doris' room being the coolest in the house. That is the reason I wrote you no letter last night.

Enclosed, please, find some matter from Mrs Youmans.[1] The meeting of your national council has been postponed until September. If you want to go—I may find it possible to arrange it that you make the trip. But so long as they propose to make "voiceless speeches" at fairs, your movement will stay in the freak class.

It is a little cooler here today and the outlook for the preparadness parade is improving.[2] All the Gimbel girl's will march, and so will the Boston store girls and the Schuster girls and the various candy factory girls. The men in the shops and offices have also received their marching orders and every one of them will march "voluntarily" or lose his or her day's wages. See? They do not dare to go so far as to tell them that they will lose their jobs if they don't march, but there can be no doubt that many of the employee's so understand it.

Incidentally it may interest you that I have also been elected a member of the "citizens committee" for the "preparadness parade" and had a badge duly sent to me. I shall not use the badge—but I will not return it either.

Well, sweet Schatzl—I am writing this in the office and I am interrupted every little while. By-the-way—I have called up Frank Harbach[3] and have told him that I am ready. He will commence with the concrete and cement work at-once, however I have asked him to employ *union men* exclusively, even if it does cost more. I don't want a repetition of the Bistorius business. Of course, the carpenter work can be done in the Trade School, no one will be able to object to that.

With thousand kisses for you and the babies

Your V.LB.

1. Theodora Winton Youmans (1863–1932) served as president of the Wisconsin Woman Suffrage Association, 1913–1920. She assisted her husband, Henry Mott Youmans, in editing the *Waukesha Freeman* and was active in Republican politics.

2. Milwaukee's Socialist mayor, Daniel Hoan, agreed to lead a war preparedness parade on July 15, 1916, after the sponsors agreed to change its name to a "National Civic Demonstration." In his proclamation, Hoan stated that participants were not "committing themselves to any specific kind of preparedness." Hoan's fellow Socialists criticized him for his participation.

3. Frank M. Harbach (b. 1868) served on the Milwaukee school board, 1899–1905, and as the board's secretary, 1904–1938.

Victor to Meta

Milwaukee, Wisconsin
July 16, 1916

My dear Schatzl:—

I write this in the room of our candidate for vice-president, George Kirkpatrick[1]—who made a pretty good speech only a little lenghty. The crowd while very numerous was not quite as large as in former years. We will have to find other means to raise funds since the monster-carnevals and mammoth picnics are beginning to lose their charms.

The preparadness parade was a frost. If you take out the employees of the public service corporations (street car, gas, telephone etc), the city employees, the department store girls and the letter carriers—there was not much left except the Greeks and Slavonians of Pfister & Vogel and of Trostel.[2] It really and truly was a frost although the Sentinel claims 30,000 and the Journal 28,000 including musicians and news-boys, and play ground children.

It is fearfully hot in Milwaukee and I am still glad you are in Shawano just now. Will send you the Sunday papers also.

With love to all

your V.L.B.

1. George Ross Kirkpatrick (1867–1937), a Socialist lecturer, author, and educator, ran as the party's vice-presidential candidate in 1916.
2. Pfister and Vogel Leather Company and Albert Trostel and Sons Company (tanners and curriers), both of Milwaukee.

Victor to Meta

Fond du Lac, Wisconsin
July 20, [1916]

My sweet Schatzl:

The convention[1] is so commonplace and routin-like—I did not get here until today and was not appointed on any committee, of course—that I shall go home again tomorrow where my presence is more necessary.

The strike of the machinists[2]—as you see by the papers is spreading and with it also the strike in the knitting works,[3] particularly in Hole-proof Stocking factory, where the girls are shamefully underpaid and are miserably treated.

I am afraid the next few years will be very stormy years in the labor movement of the country—especially if the European *war* should soon come to an end. Workingmen have received comparatively good wages of late and they will resist any reduction of hours or wages after the war. Strikes, boykotts and blacklists will be the result—the A. F of L. will show its impotence and some organization of the I.W.W type will take its place. In the end a purified and sane Social Democratic party will become the great political factor in our country. Whether I will be still young enough and vigorous enough to be one of its national leaders, I very much doubt however.

I write this late at night, Schatzl,—simply, in order to show you, that I did not forget you in all the turmoil and "hubub" of the convention. And now I am real tired and must bid you adieu—with many kisses.

V.L.B.

1. Berger served as a delegate of the Newspaper Writers Union at the annual convention of the Wisconsin State Federation of Labor held in Fond du Lac on July 19–22, 1916.

2. On July 18, 1916, the machinists union went on strike against the Allis-Chalmers Manufacturing Company in West Allis, Wisconsin, demanding a reduction of the workday from ten to eight hours with no loss in pay. The strike spread and within a week more than 2,500 machinists at ten plants in the Milwaukee area had left their jobs. Milwaukee Mayor Daniel Hoan and Wisconsin Governor Emanuel Philipp unsuccessfully sought to mediate the strike. The machinists returned to work eight weeks later without winning their demands.

3. Textile workers at Milwaukee's Holeproof Hosiery Company and Phoenix Knitting Company went on strike in July, 1916, demanding an eight-hour day, higher wages, and improved working conditions. They ended their strike in late July after agreeing to a wage increase, a nine-hour day, and the promise of improved sanitary conditions.

Victor to Meta

Milwaukee, Wisconsin
July 22, [1916]

My sweet Schatzl:

It a positive determination on my part—unless I am prevented by sickness—to leave here for Shawano (on the machine) on Saturday, July 29th with the understanding that we are to leave for Merill no later than Monday morning.

In order to console our girls who cannot go with us on this trip—I may bring a friend of theirs along, Evelyn Rippe[1] or some other girl—to stay there that week. Please let me know what you think of the idea.

The machinist strike will probably be settled by tonight—since there is only a difference of *30 minutes* working time *a week* between the two contending parties. The Machinists went out pretending to fight for the 8 hour day (with the old 10 hours pay), which would mean a raise of about

13 per cent in wages. Until a short time ago they worked 55 hours per week. An 8 hour day as they demanded—would mean 48 hours per week.

From the beginning, however, the Machinists were willing to accept 50 hours working time per week. And the manufacturers (being afraid of the Leader and trouble) some weeks ago *voluntarily reduced* the working time to 52½ hours per week. I told the machinists to stand pat on 50 hours as the minimum concession.

But the Machinists appointed a committee consisting of Rubin's[2] assistant cashier in the Onion Bank, John J. Handley—and the general organizer Emmett Adams[3] a professional labor leader,—and William Aldridge,[4] formerly a machinist and now a Social Democratic alderman and a muddlehead—to conduct the negociations. And these three individuals of course, accepted at once W. B. Rubin's offer of services. In fact John Handley suggested Rubin.

The first thing the committee did then, is to propose a 52 hour week to the governor[5]—who was undoubtedly surprised himself, because the manufacturers had granted 52½ hours some weeks ago. But when the governor went to the Metal Trades Association asking for the "30 minutes concession per week" there was only one vote in over 40 in favor of granting the "demand"—and that was Otto Falk's[6] vote. All the others naturally saw in this kind of a "demand" the weakness of the Machinists union—or Bill Rubin's successful attempt to "onionize" the Milwaukee trades union movement—to do business on an onion as profit like the Polish Jews do—and they rejected with scorn the pleadings of Gov. Phillip to "give him at least a little something to take back to the laboring men".

Even the capitalist papers however see that the Manufacturers really have no basis for a defense at all in this strike. And therefore, they urge peace and the granting of the "30 minutes" per week.

It is a comtemptible performance because the workingmen really get almost nothing even when they get the "30 minutes" less working-time per week. I am not in a position however, just now to show up the performance. Just now the Leader is very hard up and could not stand any "rocking of the boat". So I have to sit by quietly and simply boost the "30 minutes" strike. Well, if they do not get much out of it, they at least get a few days *vacation* in this beastly hot weather—and that is good for their health.

It is very hot here and I am glad you are in Shawano. Only I should like to have you near me at Oconomowoc or some other *good* Waukesha lake. Nevertheless I shall take the first opportunity to do the Shawano beachers the favor to report the Shawano Pulp mill steal to the commission. If these Shawano cokroaches cannot do business in at least an honest capitalistic way—then they ought to be put out of business.

Now, Schatzl, this is a long, long letter—and I hope that you will not have to take a day off to read it. Give my love to both Schnuckies and to Hattie, and tell Josie that our wash woman is keeping the house very clean, and Jack that I give the squirrel fresh water and nuts every day. It eats out of my hands.

With thousand kisses Ever
your VLB

1. Evelyn Rippe (b. 1895) taught in the Milwaukee public school system from 1915 to 1919.
2. William B. Rubin (1873–1959), a Russian-born labor lawyer, began practicing law in Milwaukee in 1897. He served as chief counsel for organized labor in the Pennsylvania steel strike of 1919 and represented the New York Actors Equity Association in its strike of the same year.
3. Emmett L. Adams served as a delegate of the Washington, D.C., Central Labor Union at the 1910 AFL convention and worked as a paid organizer for the AFL during the 1920s.
4. William Alldridge (1879–1942), a Socialist labor activist and attorney, served in the Wisconsin Assembly, 1905–1909, and as a Milwaukee alderman, 1910–1922.
5. Emanuel L. Philipp (1861–1925), a businessman and stalwart Republican politician, served as governor of Wisconsin, 1915–1921.
6. Otto H. Falk (1865–1940) served as president (1913–1932) and chairman of the board (1932–1940) of the Allis-Chalmers Manufacturing Company.

Victor to Meta

Chicago, Illinois
July 24, 1916

My sweet Schatzl:

Chicago is nice, sweet place to live in—at this temperature. It seems to me one could boil eggs on the side-walk, or at least bake them.

Goebel analyzed the seconds that came in of the total of 5,761—the so-called English branches. 2,147 (Russian Jews in Brooklyn that conduct their business in the English language)—Finns 2,042—Letts 1,377—German 45—Slavic (West Allis, Wis) 36—German 45—Jewish (Kings Co N.Y. again) 60—and Scandinavian 17. In the main, it is a *foreign* vote with a *very slight* admixture of Americans and Germans.

I am very sorry, darling, that I cannot come up next Saturday, but under the circumstances it is imperative that I attend the next meeting of the National Executive committee which begins its work next Saturday.

If it was not for the Leader and the election to congress I would tell the national party right now to go to ——— and call a special convention of Wisconsin and other states to organize a political party without the hoodoos, crooked foreigners and criminal fanatics. But I cannot afford to do so just now—the Leader is evidently making a coward of me.

As things are now I expect to leave Milwaukee on Saturday Aug. 5th, go to Merill on the Monday following—leave for Rhinelander on Wednesday, return to Shawano on Thursday, and go home on Friday or Saturday Aug. 11th or 12th.

Kindly let me [know] whether my telegram reached you in time for Frank and Hattie[1] to change their vacation date.

Well, sweetheart—the national office is not the place for me to write long letters. I just want to tell you, daß ich Dich sehr lieb hab'.[2]

With love to all and especially my Schnuckies and thousand kisses for you

always your V.LB.

1. Frank and Hattie Schweers, Meta's brother-in-law and sister.
2. that I love you very much.

Meta to Doris

Milwaukee, Wisconsin
October 1, [1916]

Darling Girl:—

Today is just beautiful & I am wondering if Madison is as pretty as I think it ought to be with its lakes, its trees & the beautiful campus.[1] Yesterday the day was so fine & papa & you being gone, I took Miss Thomas, Elsa, Josie, Matta, Nettie & Laura[2] for a picnic at the County park. We had our noon-day meal there & left about 3 P.M. as the wind from the lake blew a little too cold for us. In the evening we all went to hear Meyer London the Socialist Congressman talk. Each time I go to a Socialist meeting I am impressed with the sincereity & really the profound knowledge & wisdom that these Socialist leaders possess. Comparing the difference between our party & the old parties, we can't help but acknowledge that they speak two different languages. I should like you to affilliate yourself with the Socialist groupe out at the U. when you get time.

Wednesday night of this week I & Mr. Potter are to be the guests of honor at the Teacher's association's home-coming. We two are each to make short talks & the rest of the evening is to be spent in renewing old acquaintances. My subject will be "The good Old Times" & I shall try to weave in the different phases of woman's life leading up to her splendid opportunities of the present day. I've got the idea in my head & now it's got to be worked out.

Your two last letters were so nice that I mailed them on to papa at Chicago.

Elsa will write today. She has been getting bugs for her Zoology & has a nice collection all fixed up in a fine box Jack made for her with a glass top. It looks quite fine & scientific.

Jack is the same old kid as always and Hi[3] didn't show up as I tho't he would.

Miss Schmidt telephoned me & gave me your message of love & of course I am sending one back to you. Be good & faithful to yourself & your cause dear and you will always go right & please your own

Loving & devoted
Mother.

1. Doris Berger enrolled as a freshman at the University of Wisconsin in Madison for the fall semester, 1916.

2. Elizabeth H. Thomas, Elsa Berger, Josephine Rudkowsky (Skobis), Matta Soik, Annette Rosenthal (Gould), and Laura F. Duggan.

3. Franklin "Hi" Schweers (1896–1958) was the stepson of Meta's sister, Hattie. He worked as mechanic in the Schweers family's automobile repair business in Shawano, Wisconsin.

Meta to Doris

[Milwaukee, Wisconsin]
[November 4, 1916]

Doris darling:—

Your letter relieved me so much, I can't begin to tell you how much. I also feel a little better about your so-called episode because I know I can rely upon you.

Papa is over-worked & high strung. He is out every night, not only to speak but also to read proof for his political "adds." Then too the end of a long siege is drawing near & the doubts, hopes & guesses are a little nerve-racking to say the least. You never saw so many doubtful people. Old time party men say that they don't know whom to vote for. Hughes[1] or Wilson. You see the sporting blood in every man wants to have his candidate get the *office & win* and so he overlooks the platforms & principles at stake. All of the newspapers of course have been talking personalities—not platforms. The Socialist party is the only party offering a really *constructive* programe. But I predict that the *"old time party man"* will be governed by his traditions & conventions as of yore; so I'm not letting my hopes go too high. I only hope papa will gain over his vote of two years ago.[2] Papa as always is optimistic. We will surely let you know results but as the ballots are on paper, the counting will be slow.

The teachers convention is over & I'm glad because I've been burning to[o] much.

Next week we are going to clean house. The boys took down the summer house & are now busy chopping up the wood.

Elsa will write you all about the game. now sweetheart good night—lots & lots of love from your own

Mama

1. Charles Evans Hughes (1862–1948), a Republican, unsuccessfully challenged Woodrow Wilson for the presidency in 1916. Hughes served as governor of New York, 1906–1910, U.S. Supreme Court justice, 1910–1916 and 1930–1941, and U.S. secretary of state, 1921–1925.

2. Republican William Stafford was reelected to Congress with 45 percent of the vote to 37 percent for Berger and 17 percent for Democrat Lyman H. Browne. Berger's vote increased from 11,674 in 1914 to 15,936 in 1916.

Victor to Doris

Milwaukee, Wisconsin
February 1, 1917

My dear Dod:

Enclosed, please, find check for twenty dollars—fifteen for your fees and five for your pocket money.

I say your *"pocket money,"* darling—it is such only while it is in *your* pocket. The moment you spend it, it wanders into somebody else's pocket or bank account. Women are apt to call it "pin money"—it seems to prick them, so that they try to get rid of it, as soon as possible.

Under our present economic system—the capitalist system—money, wealth and capital are the means of a certain very necessary *freedom* for you when *you* have the money, wealth or capital. They become the means of intolerable slavery and inhuman exploitation very often when the other person has them and you have none. Therefore, darling child, always look out, and look out ahead, that you always have at least enough to secure a certain amount of freedom for yourself and for those whom you love and who are dependent upon you.

Be saving, darling, especially also in little things.

Rather deny yourself *luxuries voluntarily* while you have money, than be *compelled* to deny yourself *necessities* because you must do so on account of not having any money.

But I hate preaching and I am in danger of making my letter sound sententious. You have inherited *good brains* and I want you to use them and do so with common sense. And I also want you to take *plenty* of *good exercise*—especially walking—and—to get all the fresh air you can during day and night by keeping your windows open.

And *don't* ever *open* your young *heart* to anybody except your mother and father. Be honest with everybody but don't tell them all you

know or feel. *Reserve* is one of the greatest powers of the individuality—
it is the greatest power of your sweet mother.

Well, good-by, Dod. I may see you in Madison next week.

Papa.

Victor to Meta

St. Louis, Missouri
April 7, [1917]

My dear Schatzl:

The convention has started and the first vote shows the Impossibilists in such numbers that I have some *doubts* whether I will be elected
on the committee on War and Militarism.[1] You need not be at all afraid
that I will make radical utterances that might get me in bad with the
government—on the contrary, I must contre-balance the insane radicalism of the other side by taking an extra-ordinarily conservative attitude.

With all this however I believe that constructive side which com-
prises all the older leaders has a safe majority on the main questions
and that we will be able to steer the party through all the difficulties.

So much for the convention. I was exceedingly sorry to hear that
your teeth bothered you so much. I do wish you could be here—especially since Mrs Hillquit[2] is here also. Of course, I am not sure whether I
will be able to stay during the entire convention—The Leader is always
uppermost in my mind.

Please write to me every day. I need your letters and your encouragement [*two words illegible*] my daily bread.

They are calling me to go to the meeting—I refused to speak in
order not to have so many German speakers on the program.

With love to all
V.L.B.

1. The Socialist Party opened its emergency convention in St. Louis on
April 7, 1917, the day after the United States declared war on Germany. The
convention elected fifteen members to the committee on war and militarism
and Berger finished fourteenth in the balloting. The convention's report, signed
by Berger, called for "continuous, active, and public opposition to the war."

2. Vera Levene Hillquit (1879–1949), the wife of New York Socialist Morris
Hillquit.

Meta to Victor

[Milwaukee, Wisconsin]
[April 8, 1917]

Dear Papa.

Easter Sunday and a bright sunny tho' cold day. However I do not expect to go out yet as the swelling is not entirely gone down and my ambition is not back yet. I am feeling much better tho' and am watching the papers eagerly for the news from St Louis.

You must be having hot times down there. Only do please be careful. I saw by the paper the Katterfelt motion[1] & was glad it was voted down. Now that I am feeling better again, I wish I were with you.

Gerhard Bading has enlisted. His stock is going up again just now. But pity the boys under his charge.

I was told yesterday by Mrs. Roberts,[2] that the secret service men wanted to see her. I am anxious to hear what they had to say to her. Rumor also has it th[at] Albert Trostel[3] must report at the Federal building each morning. They say also that Milwaukee is full of secret service men. Well dear, the whole war makes me really sick. I wonder just what I would do if called upon to serve.

The boys went down to the Arcade last night. I believe Jack would enlist with a little encouragement. If I was sure he wouldn't be sent to Europe but would remain here in the army as a reserve, I'd let him go for the army discipline which he really needs.

Doris will be here Tuesday. She is going to bring Helen Brown[4] with her for a day or two. Miss Heip will also be here to get Doris served up for the spring. So I guess I'll be busy.

Remember to be careful & remember dear papa, that you are the life & heart of *this here family*.

With oceans of love I am your own
Mama

1. Ludwig E. Katterfeld (1881–1974) served on the staff of the Socialist Party in several capacities and was a leader of the left-wing faction of the party. During the St. Louis convention, Katterfeld moved that all candidates for the committee on war and militarism be asked to answer whether they opposed all wars, offensive and defensive, except those of the working class against the capitalist class. The motion was defeated ninety-nine to sixty-six. In 1919 Katterfeld helped to organize the Communist Labor Party.

2. Annette Jacobi Roberts (1883–1986), a peace and women's rights activist, later became one of the founders of the Women's International League for Peace and Freedom and served as president of its Milwaukee branch.

3. Albert O. Trostel Sr. (1866–1936), the son of a German immigrant, was a wealthy Milwaukee industrialist who headed a tanning company.

4. Helen Browne (Hobart) (1896–1978), a student at the University of Wisconsin, was the daughter of Wisconsin Congressman Edward Everts Browne. She later married Dr. Marcus H. Hobart, an Illinois surgeon.

Meta to Doris

[Milwaukee, Wisconsin]
April 28, [1917]

Dear Dudd!

This morning I gave Ernie[1] a lesson in driving the car & then Elsa. Elsa is a pretty good driver now and used rare presence of mind today when she avoided colliding with another car. Really she did excellently & her stock went up 100%. Just now we are having a blow-out & a puncture fixed.

My guest Miss Murtaugh[2] has gone. I am glad too because really it isn't much fun to entertain guests in this house. There is the expense to consider besides Josie, Papa, the boys, etc etc etc. I hope the time will come when things will be so that there will not be so [many] "considerations".

Papa just telephoned me that a "Press Dispatch" says that Pres. Wilson was considering sending one socialist with Elihu Root[3] to Russia to help democratize Russia & that his name was the only one mentioned. That is a nice compliment, but I don't believe the President will do it. If he really wanted to, many enemies will try to prevent it. Besides its just a "Press dispatch." I wonder how much is in it anyway. Don't talk about it until we know more about it.

Nettie[4] has broken up her home now. She is living with Mrs. Perry[5] while her father[6] is rooming on the West Side. I think that is very sad, but I guess there was nothing else to do. Besides Nettie wanted to get rid of her brother[7] which is a good thing.

Well dear, I think I've told you such news as might interest you. Eva[8] is coming up this P.M. to be with Elsa. You see Elsa misses your companionship & therefore looks for other friends.

Write & tell me all about yourself, also your financial status. And be a good girl. My trust & faith in you is absolute. With much love I am Ever your own

Mama

1. Ernst Schlichting, Meta's brother.
2. Probably Agnes Murtaugh (b. 1886), the business manager of a paper mill in Merrill, Wisconsin, that did business with the *Leader*.
3. Elihu Root (1845–1937) served as U.S. secretary of war, 1899–1904, as U.S. secretary of state, 1905–1909, and as a Republican senator from New York, 1909–1915. In April, 1917, President Wilson appointed Root as head of a mission to Russia, which had just begun its revolution, although the president later ignored the commission's recommendations. Charles E. Russell, who supported the war, was the only Socialist on the commission.
4. Annette Rosenthal (Gould).
5. Probably Caroline B. Perry, who rented furnished rooms in Milwaukee.
6. Julius Rosenthal (b. 1849) was a department manager in a Milwaukee dry goods store.

7. Irving Rosenthal (b. 1880).

8. Eva Kurz (Filtzer) (1895–1961) was a stenographer with the Milwaukee public schools and later taught in the system from 1925 through 1956. She married Robert L. Filtzer in 1927.

Victor to Meta

[en route to Washington, D.C.]
May 24, [1917]

My sweet Schatzl:

In Chicago I was met by Germer who submitted to me a protest by Boudin[1] a Russian-Jewish lawyer enemy of Hillquits—against the designation of Hillquit, Lee[2] and myself as delegates to the Stockholm conference.[3] He calls this action "unauthorized and scandalous". He says that "Berger is a German imperialist of the worst type; Hillquit a Scheidemann[4] tool; Lee, Hillquit's man Friday."

Now I am just getting tired of this. I shall bring charges against Boudin, and demand that he bring one iota of proof, or one line that I have ever written, which could be construed that I am a "German imperialist of the worst type" or of any type—or if he can't bring proof I shall demand his expulsion as a liar and a scoundrel—and incidentally also as a thief, because as Hillquit told me Boudin is on record in the criminal court for absconding money in his younger days.

Moreover I shall sue Mr Boudin who is fairly well off, for fifty thousand dollars damages—just to give that crowd a good lesson. I will take up the matter with Hillquit when I see him.

Tomorrow, darling I shall try to make an appointment with Lansing,[5] if I can. I don't believe, we shall be able to change matters.

With oceans of love to all

your own
VLB.

1. Louis Boudin (1874–1952) was a left-wing Socialist lawyer and theoretician. During the 1917 emergency party convention, Boudin authored a minority report that opposed the war but charted no course of action. Boudin left the Socialist Party in 1919, participated in and then bolted from the convention that formed the Communist Labor Party, and subsequently gave up politics to work as a labor lawyer.

2. Algernon Lee (1873–1954) edited a number of socialist newspapers, including the *New York Worker* and its successor, the *New York Call,* and served as educational director of the Rand School from 1909 until his death. He was elected as a New York City alderman in 1917 and 1919.

3. Berger was a member of the Socialist Party's delegation to an international socialist peace conference to be held in Stockholm, Sweden; however, the U.S. Department of State refused to issue passports.

4. Philipp Scheidemann (1865–1939), who later became the first chancellor of the German republic, was a German Social Democrat who supported his country's war effort.

5. Robert Lansing (1864–1928) served as U.S. secretary of state, 1915–1920.

Victor to Meta

Washington, D.C.
May 25, 1917

My sweet Schatzl:

Arrived in Washington on schedule time this morning (Friday)—and put up at the Congress Hall hotel. Went to see Kent—but found out that he was not a congressman any more but a member of the Tariff Commission at $7,500 per annum. Got Mr. Cooper to make an appointment for me with Mr. Lansing—which was easy since Cooper is on the Committee on Foreign Affairs. I cannot see Lansing before Monday, however, since his time every minute of it—is occupied, he claims, until then. I can clearly see the possibility of our delegation going over to Stockholm vanish—by Lansings delay's even [if] he should change his mind, which is not probable in face of the position of the American press which is owned body and soul by the bankers, munition makers and pro-Allies. I can see this very plainly everywhere and especially in this "National" press club.

Kent is very friendly. He had lunch with me and invited me to lunch at his house tommorrow (Saturday). Two of his sons have joined the army—one as a flyer. He is not enthusiastic at all about this war—although he tries to excuse it "with the Kaiser". He thinks, however, that our foreign policy was crazy from the beginning.

I spent part of the afternoon in the house where I met with an exceedingly friendly reception—Republicans and Democrats received me about equally well. I also made the acquaintance of our "congress-lady"[1] and promised to look her up in her office. She is a rather oldish girl with a very liberal sprinkling of gray hair, but very pleasant.

Tomorrow (Saturday) I shall look up Bob La Follette. Will let you know what transpires.

I hope you are well sweetheart and that everything is all right. Did our sick neighbor call for the receipt I left with you?

With love to *all* and especially to my only "bestest" darling

V.L.B.

1. Jeannette Rankin (1880–1973), served as a Republican representative from Montana, 1917–1919 and 1941–1943. Rankin was the first woman elected to the U.S. House of Representatives and was the only member of Congress to vote against declaring war both in 1917 and in 1941.

Victor to Meta

Washington, D.C.
May 27, [1917]

My sweet Schatzl:

Tomorrow Monday, I shall see Mr. Lansing in the forenoon and Mr. Burleson in the afternoon. I have little hope of convincing Lansing who is an ignorant and conceited country lawyer. If he had any brains, he would, in view of the European situation, not only make no trouble but shower honors and attentions upon us, thus not only get the good will of the European Socialists, especially the Russians, but even lessen any influence that we may have, by making it appear that we work hand in hand with our government. But Lansing is a cheap little fourth rate corporation lawyer who happened to marry the daughter of a former secretary of state (John W. Foster)[1] and who by luck and perseverance sneaked into the secretary [of] state office when Bryan left. The Morgan[2] clique wanted a man like him in that position and he was right handy, being the "legal adviser" of the department. If there is to be a reversal of the stupid order, it will have to come from Woodrow Wilson.

But Washington is just now swimming in blood lust and "patriotism." Of course, most every congressman I talked with is against the war and is very apprehensive of the dangerous autocracy we are establishing at home. But none dares to say that his soul is his own—they are all afraid of the press and of the organized "patriotic" mob spirit at home.

I want to see post master general Burleson,—who while he is a great politician and the president's mouth piece—has more brains than the rest of the cabinet, I believe—about the status of the socialist press, in case the espionage bill[3] should pass, and with it the censorship provision.

Tonight I am to have dinner at Kent's. I had a very interesting interview with Bob La Follette and also with his wife[4] in the Senate office building. Will tell you more about it when I get home.

Tuesday, I expect to leave for New York—where I intend to stay, about three days—by that time that conference on Long Branch will be over of course.

Well Schatzl—that is about all so far, except that I love you very, very much. Hast Du dein Schatzl immer noch lieb?[5]

VLB

1. In January, 1890, Robert Lansing married Eleanor Foster (1867–1934), daughter of John Watson Foster (1836–1917), who served as U.S. secretary of state, 1892–1893.

2. John Pierpont "Jack" Morgan (1867–1943) headed a firm that served as sole purchasing agent in the United States for Great Britain and France during World War I. Between 1915 and the American entry into the war in 1917, the Morgan firm handled more than $3 billion worth of war supplies at a commission of 1 percent.

3. The Espionage Act, which became law on June 15, 1917, provided penalties of up to twenty years in prison and a $10,000 fine for activities that obstructed the war effort. The legislation permitted the postmaster general to ban seditious materials from the mail.

4. Belle Case La Follette (1859–1931), the wife of U.S. Senator Robert M. La Follette Sr., was an advocate of women's suffrage and rights and was the first woman to receive a degree from the University of Wisconsin Law School.

5. Do you still love your sweetheart?

Meta to Victor

[Shawano, Wisconsin]
July 12, [1917]

Dearest Papa,

Today I spent helping the girls and before I knew it the 4 o'clock boat had gone away without your letter; so you will not get this promptly as I might have wished.

Mr. Bennett, the Milwaukee attorney and his wife[1] called today to congratulate me on the new office.[2] They are camping here for two weeks.

We got into a war argument. I told them that I was opposed to this war. They said "yes but now we are in it, now we can't help ourselves." Whereupon I replied, "Oh yes you can. If you gave voice to the things that are in your heart & in every body's heart, popular opinion would soon turn the tide. The trouble is, all are afraid that they will be considered unpatriotic. That patriotism must mean something more than the drum & fife patriotism and that if I had a son I would do all I could to keep him home!" Then Mrs. Bennett said, "Would you say that very loud?" Oh yes, I replied, "all people know where we stand." It seemed so queer for her to say that to me.

Well, I got my Leader today and enjoyed it so much. One misses the paper if one has been used to it. The Leader is good but you, my Leader, are my heaven to me. Love me darling man and keep well and safe. Sometimes I wish I could get the consolation that real prayer must bring to those who believe in prayer. I must content myself with hope & longing for your safety & love.

Ever your
Mama

1. John P. (b. 1877) and Nellie M. Bennett.
2. Governor Emanuel L. Philipp had appointed Meta Berger to the Wisconsin Board of Education, a position she held until 1919.

Victor to Meta

Milwaukee, Wisconsin
July 14, 1917

My sweet Schatzl:

I just returned from Chicago where I attended a meeting of the smaller publishers looking toward the establishment of a co-operative paper mill. While I do not believe that the mill will ever realize—I may get a fine chance to get Canadian paper at $2.50 through the confidential agent of the American Publishers Association whose acquaintance I made at that gathering.

I shall look over your desk tomorrow for the sketch of Mrs. Youman's.

As to the indictment in Oklahoma you need not worry—I don't believe that the government will press suits against us—on the contrary I believe that they will summon me to Washington.

However I want *you* to be careful, what you are saying to strangers. Bennett is no friend of mine. I don't want them to arrest you. I have troubles enough as it is. Moreover, I don't want them to make use of your expression as *additional* prove of my "disloyalty". You know that the only place where I can be hurt at all is through my wife and children. I am *personally* almost invulnerable. Therefore Schatzl be careful, please.

I want this letter to go tonight yet—and we will take it down to the post office in our machine.

Will send a few more books for Doris and Elsa to read, but above all I want them to have plenty of exercise, especially *swimming* and *rowing*.

With love to all and especially to my *better half,* I am as always your

V.LB

Meta to Victor

Shawano, Wisconsin
July 17, [1917]

Dearest!

Got your nice letter today. I believe that you analyze the progress in European troubles better & clearer than any one else. I read La Follette's article in the Leader with interest.[1] Doris read it aloud to her friends. On the war, these girls seemed to agree pretty well.

Both Elsa & Doris have written to another friend, a Theresa Stalls who will come here Saturday. The[y] wrote & asked her to come in order to keep Eva[2] here a little longer. I am willing that they should have their friends here for it keeps them quite contented. There is no hankering for boys & the things that other girls do.

We get along very well with the work. Elsa & Eva cook one day, & Evaline[3] & Doris the next day & so they alternate. Of course I have to stand by & help a little. Sometimes I think it would be quicker & easier work for me to do it all, but I realize that for the first time our girls are really using their hands.

No, I am not afraid of indictments. Yet I want The Leader to escape censorship which would bar it from the mails. But the last few editorials were not strong nor dangerous.

I shall expect you Friday some time. Write & tell me when to meet you. And don't forget the sheets & hot water bag.

With oceans of love I am always

Your own
Meta.

1. Robert M. La Follette, "The Right to Oppose War," *Milwaukee Leader,* July 14, 1917.
2. Eva Kurz (Filtzer).
3. Evelyn Rippe.

Victor to Meta

Milwaukee, Wisconsin
July 18, [1917]

My Sweet Schatzl:

Just got through reading the Leader and getting a fit of anger because my orders are not obeyed "to a tee" as I want them obeyed. And we pay the best wages in town to those SOB's.

Of course, I cannot go to Shawano tomorrow or Friday although I would very much like to go. Hillquit just send me a copy of a cablegram stating that the International Socialist Conference will re-assemble in Stockholm, August 15th and the American delegates are wanted in particular. I don't know whether our stupid and autocratic Morgan government in Washington will permit us to go, or not. That law of 1798[1] which Lansing dug *out* has *not* been dug *in* again—as yet, ridiculous as the thing is.

Had also a letter from Redfield[2] who evidently has become a great statesman and super-diplomat, since he holds the post of secretary of Commerce. He refuses to help me—although he "admires me very much"—because I am very prominently associated with men who are "not patriotic". In other words, he will not help me because I am a Socialist.

Kent sent me a telegram stating that it would be useless to go [to] Washington now because the clique would never permit me to have an interview with the president. They are evidently afraid I might tell him a few things they don't want him to know.

Burleson has not written me as yet. Nevertheless I can see from the correspondence sent by Engdahl to the Leader (tonight's Leader) that my letter had an immense influence on our friend Burleson. He told the committee of Socialist and labor attorneys: "It is the right of editors to advocate a repeal of the draft law. It is their right as American citizens." He also repeated that he had no prejudice against the Socialist press.[3]

Well, he should have none. He is a reader of the Milwaukee Leader, which goes to his private residence every day.

And there is also the print paper situation. I had a letter again from Binkhorst[4] today, assuring me that McIntire will immediately furnish me paper at $2.50 per hundred. I am expecting a letter or an offer for a contract from McIntire (who is a Canadian but whose office is in New York) every day. It would not be right for me to leave here, my dear Schatzl.

You better come down to see me Schatzl—let's say Saturday, July 28th. That will give you some vacation in Shawano and at the same time not make it so hard on me. Will send Josie up on the day you come—or the day before.

The girls can invite all the girl friends they want up there—provided they have no more than *two* or *three at the same time*. In fact I want them to show appreciation of their friends (who are loyal to them) in that way. It is a generous way. And I also want our Schnuckies to invite their student friends—so as to have up there good and wholesome company. The sole condition is—I want all of them to *row* and *swim* as much as possible, and Doris is also to practice on her *type-writer* a little every day.

As for other news, my dear Schatzl, I dont know any, except what you can read in the newspapers. As I have predicted from the beginning of the Russian revolution—they will have their up's and downs there for the next 30 years to come. We must not forget that 79 per cent of the Russian population can neither read nor write. It is hard to maintain the republican form of government with such a population—and next to impossible to have Socialism as the ruling political and economic creed. Unfortunately, the Socialists seem to be the only thinking part of that population—they surely were the only part that has fought for freedom under the most adverse circumstances for many years. And therefore, they are on top now, but how long will they stay on top?

Of course, there is *one* good circumstance connected with that: No matter how often the Socialists of Russia will be overthrown,—after this, the Russian populus will always come back to them again and again; until after a generation or so the people will be sufficiently educated to have and retain considerable Socialism in their economies and in their administration.

Last night we had a *special* meeting of the library board to consider the Lutie Stearns charges.[5] The report you will see in tonight's Leader.

I am glad to hear that the girls are contended to stay up there and get exercise and ozone. I also hope that instead of playing cards they will in their leisure hours in the evening *read* some of the nice books which you took up. I am willing to send Doris a fine book on *Socialism,* if she promises to *read* it.

Well, that's all for tonight. Und sonst hast Du mich doch noch lieb, Schatzl? Wie Sehr?[6]

V.L.B.

1. The Logan Act of 1799 prohibited American citizens from dealing with foreign governments regarding controversies involving the United States.

2. William C. Redfield (1858–1932) served as secretary of commerce, 1913–1919. Redfield had previously served with Berger in Congress as a Democratic representative from New York, 1911–1913.

3. A delegation of Socialists and civil libertarians, including Seymour Stedman, Morris Hillquit, and Roger Baldwin, met with Postmaster General Albert S. Burleson in July, 1917, to protest the suppression of the *American Socialist* and other radical publications. For the article mentioned by Berger, see J. L. Engdahl, "'Press Has Right to Ask Repeal of Draft,' Burleson," *Milwaukee Leader,* July 18, 1917. See also Victor to Meta, July 22, 1917, below.

4. Dingeman Binkhorst, a Kalamazoo, Michigan, broker.

5. Berger served on the Milwaukee Public Library Board of Trustees from 1916 until 1918. The board heard charges raised by Lutie Stearns (1866–1943) against city library director Charles E. McLenegan concerning poor labor relations, the library's public school program, and the waste of library funds. Stearns served on the library's staff from about 1888 to 1897 and on the Wisconsin Free Library Commission from 1897 to 1914. See "Outside Man to Make Survey of Library System," *Milwaukee Leader,* July 18, 1917.

6. And otherwise you still love me, don't you, little darling? How much?

Victor to Meta

Milwaukee, Wisconsin
July 19, [1917]

My sweet Schatzl:

Tonight's Journal contains a leading editorial against our party with veiled threats and insin[u]ations against the Milwaukee Leader.[1] It is just possible that they got an inkling that the Washington government may try to bother us. Well let them try. There is absolutely nothing that we have ever done that is unlawful.

I have written to Mr. Putnam and told him to fix a night when I could take him and his wife[2] out for a ride—since my better half is out of town. I received a very friendly a[n]swer promptly, inviting me to dinner at his house tomorrow (Friday), after which we will [go] out riding. I shall ask Franklin[3] to call for us at 7 P.M.

By-the-way, I had only two rides with Franklin so far—the third will be tonight, he is just waiting while I am writing this letter. I will try to reach Mrs Howe[4] by telephon before I call for her and her little girl. Last Saturday I called, they were not home and I took their neighbors (the Johnston's—Daisy Day)[5] out riding.

Next Sunday, I have an important state board meeting, and then I may take out the Zieglers for an airing.

Otherwise—there is not much news—outside of the war news in the papers. During day time I am very busy—but evenings I am a bit lonely at times, getting old I suppose. It does me good, however, to be alone—I think of you, sweet Schatzl and of the babies and try to pierce the dark veil of the future,—and what the party and the whole movement will amount to in the next ten years—and someway-another I feel wonderfully strong, hopeful and self-reliant. I do not fear imprisonement—if it will do the movement and the Leader good, I almost wish it; although I would not say this to anybody because that might sound like idle phrase monging.

Never mind, don't worry. It will never happen.

Have sent you the articles you asked for except one. Next week I hope to see you here my sweet Schatzl.

Franklin is getting impatient and has asked me whether he is to get the car ready. I shall close with my best wishes for my sweet Schatzl and my Schnuckies.

V.L.B.

1. The *Milwaukee Journal,* July 19, 1917, ran a lead editorial entitled "This Kind of Thing" that criticized the antiwar stance of Milwaukee's Socialists and warned that "public opinion, which is now suppressing itself, will burst forth some day and take judgment into its own hands. There is a limit even to patience."

2. Frank A. (1867?–1949) and Mabel Putnam. A poet and newspaperman, Frank Putnam worked for the Milwaukee Electric Railway and Light Company at this time.

3. Franklin Schweers, the stepson of Meta's sister, Hattie.

4. Laura E. Howe (b. 1872), the widow of *Milwaukee Leader* editorial writer James R. Howe, who died in May, 1917.

5. Griffith W. Johnstone (b. 1865), a Milwaukee machine shop superintendent, and his wife, Daisy Day Johnstone (b. 1865).

Meta to Victor

[Shawano, Wisconsin]
[July 20, 1917]

Dearest Papa,

Miss Jacobi[1] & Mrs. McCreery have gone & I am back at the lake. Have just finished that vicious & insinuating editorial of the Journal. Do they really mean mischief & trouble for The Leader? Be careful. That is all I ask. No good can come of it if you should go to jail. For a while sympathy would be yours & a few socialists might be added to our numbers. But the Leader can't afford to have you in jail. So be careful.

This is my second letter to you today altho' it probably won't reach you any earlier for all that.

I suppose you are wondering where I permitted Maud McCreery to sleep. Well, I got Jack's cot and Mattress down from his room. We are just about thro' with that out fit any way. She slept on the porch. Then I gave her all of those quilts which *we* have never used. At present the quilts are on the line, the mattress & pillow are sunning on the upper porch.

The girls are not a bit anxious to spoil Josie's vacation. They are doing very well with cooking. So we are going to consider whether or not Josie will come this summer or not. It would cost $8 to get her here & back again & for that she could stay at home & do pickling etc. for us. However we'll see. The girls will not be left alone. I'll see to that.

With oceans of love I am always your

Meta.

1. Etelka Jacobi (b. 1882), the sister of Annette Jacobi Roberts, was a Wisconsin suffragist.

Victor to Meta

Milwaukee, Wisconsin
July 22, [1917]

My sweet Schatzl:

You have a right to scold because I have sent you no letter since Friday—Saturday I was in Chicago however, hearing the report of the lawyers sent to Washington (Darrow[1] & Stedman) and that report sounded very differently from what Engdahl sent, in the correspondence to the Leader. According to Stedman our friend, Mr. Burleson, is an oily, slippery Southern politician who made no promises whatsoever, and who is bound to do all the damage he can to the Socialist press and the Socialist propaganda. Burleson made all the use he could of an obscure little Western Socialist paper[2] in order to get through Congress the provision of the law giving him the power to exclude "seditious literature"—and it is only due to the fact that great metropolitan papers (like the New York World) do not like to see the postal department get such extra-ordinary powers, which may ruin any publication—that the department has not as yet used this power against any daily. Well, we must wait and see. I have more confidence in Burleson.

I have heard nothing further about cheaper paper—than that Mr. McIntire wrote to the business manager asking him questions about the size of the rolls and the tonnage we use. I expect an answer any day.

Miss Thomas has returned and has called me up this morning. I have not as yet seen her. She seemed to be happy—to judge her by the conversation.

I took out Mrs. Ziegler, Gretchen and Elsie[3] today. We went to Racine and got caught in a rain. Franklin[4] and I had supper at Ziegler's.

My sister Mathilde[5] wrote, offering me $200.00 to pay interest on my mortgage—and also to buy anything in the clothing line wholesale for you, if you give her the size and the style you desire. She suggests that you clip the style of the garments out of some of the woman's magazines. She also informed me that my father and brother George are in Mount Clemens Mich.,—which means that we may expect their visit shortly—and that mother has willed me $5,000 etc. The latter is, of course, a mistake—she willed us only $4,000, and I don't know whether Mathilde simply wanted to make it a little unpleasant for George, by compelling him to explain that it is only $4,000 or whether the sum really grew some in her vivid financial imagination.

At any rate, by the time you come home, father and George may also be here. They will write to me first, of course, and I will at once either wire or telephon to Schweer's Hardware store. If they should come, I will want you here, darling.

While here, I also want you to give the People's Council[6] movement an impetus. I wonder whether we could not employ our friend Maud[7] as an organizer? It would give her an entrance into the Socialist party also.

Stedman told me th[at] Robert La Follette spoke in the very highest terms of me and also of the party in Wisconsin. If he is ready to come in, I will welcome him.

This is about all the news I know—except that I must tell you that ich Dich sehr lieb hab'[8] that is an old story, of course, doch bleibst Du mir ewig neu.[9] Kiss the babies for me.

V.L.B.

Don't ever show my letters to stranger[s] darling.

1. Clarence Darrow (1857–1938), a lawyer and reformer, headed the delegation that met with Postmaster General Burleson in July, 1917, to protest wartime press censorship. See Victor to Meta, July 18, 1917, above.
2. Berger probably was referring to the *Halletsville (Texas) Rebel*, a socialist newspaper suppressed in June, 1917, by Postmaster General Burleson after Congress enacted the Espionage Act but before the act was signed by President Wilson.
3. Rosa Ziegler (b. 1861), the wife of *Milwaukee Leader* business manager Edward Ziegler, and the couple's daughters, Gretchen (1897–1970) and Elsa (1900–1970).
4. Franklin Schweers, the stepson of Meta's sister, Hattie.
5. Mathilde Berger Weingarten (1863–1957), Victor's sister, ran a ladies' clothing store in Bridgeport, Connecticut.
6. The People's Council of America for Democracy and Peace opposed the war, supported free speech, and called for a negotiated peace. Because of governmental harassment and the excesses of self-appointed patriots, the council effectively ceased to exist by late 1917. Berger organized a Milwaukee branch of the council on July 30, 1917.
7. Probably Maud McCreery.
8. I love you very much.
9. yet you remain forever new to me.

Victor to Meta

Milwaukee, Wisconsin
August 23, [1917]

My sweet Schatzl:

Under separate cover I send you some cards and a letter from George[1]—who addresses now all mail to you and the girls.

Have called up Etelka Jacobi. She told me that in her opinion there is no doubt that you will be elected a delegate from the Peace society and that your expenses will be paid.

Was in Kenosha yesterday to address a meeting of *party members*. The meeting was very successful. They told me that for the first time in the history of the party Lutheran and Catholic farmers en masse— declare that they are through with both of the old parties and that they would vote the Socialist ticket in future. The boys claim that they will carry the county, which would be next to a miracle, in my estimation. The backbone of the movement in Kenosha County are the Scandinavians.

I have read the editorial in the Sentinel. That kind of article will not do us any harm.

Simons, Spooner,[2] Bloodgood[3] Gaylord & Co have started a "loyal legion"[4] in Wisconsin. A good name indeed. "Loyalists" was [the] name of the English Tories in America that fought George Washington and the American Revolution.

Gompers, Simons, Spargo, Russell and Gerard are going to have convention in Minneapolis at the same time as we.[5] That will give our convention so much more prominence.

Dont worry about money. Take all the rest you possibly can. This is the wish of your loving

V.L.B.

1. George Berger, Victor's brother.
2. Willet Main Spooner (1872–1928), the son of former U.S. senator John Coit Spooner, was a Republican lawyer from Milwaukee who advocated American participation in World War I.
3. Wheeler Peckham Bloodgood (1871–1930), a Milwaukee lawyer who had served on the national committee of the Progressive Party in 1912, headed the Wisconsin Defense League and later the Wisconsin Loyalty Legion.
4. The Wisconsin Loyalty Legion, a voluntary association that existed from the summer of 1917 until March, 1919, sought to identify and punish opponents of the war, promote Liberty Bond sales, and conduct educational programs on war aims. It succeeded the Wisconsin Defense League, which had been formed in March, 1917.
5. The AFL formed the American Alliance for Labor and Democracy to counter the efforts of the antiwar People's Council of America for Democracy and Peace. The alliance attempted to stop a meeting of the People's Council planned for September 1, 1917, in Minneapolis by renting every available hall in that city.

Victor to Meta

Milwaukee, Wisconsin
August 24, 1917

My sweet Schatzl.

The meeting in Minneapolis will have to be held in a tent—but should it be forbidden entirely, we will adjourn either to Fargo, N.D. or to Milwaukee Wis., where the state governors have not entirely abolished "the right to peaceably assemble".[1]

I shall probably leave here Wednesday night—since we meet on Thursday (i.e. the National Executive Committee.) If you want me to— I will reserve a birth for you for Friday night—ie I will reserve a section for you—and be on hand when the train arrives in Minneapolis.

I am glad to hear that Doris is reading the book I gave her. I want her to read it two–three times and discuss it with you and Elsa.

It was so cool here last night that I looked for more covers.

Kindly return the five gallon can of green paint to Samuel Cabot 24 W. Kinzie street Chicago, Ill. with a note of explanation—if possible a few words also tied to the cans.

Was in Kenosha Wednesday,—and may have to go to Chicago tomorrow (Saturday) or Monday. The Leader is slowly, but steadily and surely getting out the woods. If the government lets us alone for the next six months—your paper will be one of the most important propositions in the country. If the government should interfer—that would bother us, of course, but we expect to pull through even then.

Lovingly
V.L.B.

1. The People's Council of America for Democracy and Peace met in Chicago on September 1, 1917, after the governors of Minnesota and Wisconsin prohibited it from meeting in those states. Chicago police broke up the group after it had met for three hours, and Frank O. Lowden, the governor of Illinois, called up troops to prevent the council from meeting.

Meta to Victor

Wisconsin, Milwaukee
[September 23, 1917]

Dearest!

Your telegrams sound re assuring and you say the people are friendly. That I presume is due to their diplomatic training. The secretary of State was also friendly when the pass-ports were refused. But I shall hope & pray for the best.

We all went to hear Lincoln Steffens Friday night. He gave a very very good talk & reported correctly the facts about the Russian revolution. It was most interesting & just like a story. He kept his audience until after ten and that was late for he is not a good *speaker.*

He asked Carl Haessler[1] to be sure to tell me to wait until after the lecture as he wanted to see me. He was the same cordial Lincoln Steffens that he was years ago & was so friendly & sorry that you were not here. I felt again as the war had not changed him. He declared himself to be a radical, not a Socialist, but his talk was an indictment on the present system & he declared the only remedy was an industrial democracy.

His was a pure socialist talk all woven around the Russian revolution. Francis McGovern, Frank Hoyt,[2] Willet Spooner & any number of "patriots" were in the audience. This was *not* a pure socialist audience by any means.

McGovern tried to smear honey around Steffens after the lecture by telling him that he (Steffens) did more than any one other person to abolish graft from municipal & State government. Steffens laughed & said "If I had done it all, I wouldn't have done much for it is all there yet! It is the system McGovern & not the people". McGovern said "Well I like your old ideas better."

Steffens did us good, much more than Bigelow[3] did.

Today Betty is coming up for dinner & if the car works we will take her for a drive. The day is ideal & the sunshine and fresh air ought to cleanse our souls of the poison & hatred in us.

I wish you had the machine with you down there. It would do you more good than it does us.

I have sent a mere note to New York.

Tomorrow I pack the girls things for they leave Tuesday on the 9:50 A.M. train.[4]

I hope they will make good. If they don't I shall be nearly broke hearted. Well schatzl, take time enough if you can & feel like it after you hear results of your hearing to go & see grandpapa. Also look up George[5] in New York for a few minutes.

And now papa, my letter wouldn't be natural if I didn't again make you a passionate declaration of love & devotion. I love you more each & every day. It is the one & only beautiful thing that helps make life worth while but would me[an] nothing to me if you didn't love me in return. Love me Darling love me & all will be well.

Ever your own
Meta

1. Carl Haessler (1888–1972) taught philosophy at the University of Illinois from 1914 until 1917, when he lost his job because of his opposition to World War I. During 1917 and 1918 he worked for the *Milwaukee Leader* as a writer and mail circulation manager. In 1918 he was court-martialed for his refusal to be drafted and received a sentence of twelve years in prison, although he was released in 1920. From 1920 until 1956, Haessler worked for the Federated Press, a labor news wire service that he eventually headed.

2. Frank Mason Hoyt (1853–1934), a Milwaukee attorney and member of the Wisconsin Loyalty Legion.

3. Herbert Seely Bigelow (1870–1951) was a Socialist Congregationalist minister from Cincinnati who opposed the war. He served as a Democrat in the Ohio House of Representatives, 1913–1914, and in the U.S. House of Representatives, 1937–1939. Bigelow delivered an antiwar address in Milwaukee on September 7, 1917.

4. Elsa Berger enrolled as a student for the 1917 fall semester at the University of Wisconsin, where Doris was a sophomore.

5. George Berger, Victor's brother.

Victor to Meta

[Washington, D.C.]
September 23, [1917]

My sweet Schatzl:—

Enclosed, please, find the galley proof of an editorial for the Washington Times, which Arthur Brisbane wrote in my behalf.[1] As I told you in my last letter, the editorial was set up and is held subject to Brisbane's order. It will depend upon the action of the President, to whom Brisbane sent a copy with a short letter of explanation, whether the editorial will be printed.

Brisbane believes that the editorial proof sheet will do the business without further efforts. I believe he is mistaken and I have, therefore started a number of other things. At any rate, kindly *preserve this proof sheet for me*—it is a rather interesting testimonial for the future, if nothing else.

I have also already made my plans for the future—if the Leader should be surpressed entirely *during* the *war*. You and I will not starve and the babies will keep on with their school, even then—although we may have to be rather saving.

Looking over my contract with the Hotel Chelsea in New York—I find that the contract is *not* good for 4 months, the month of September among them. That is tough and now I am almost glad that you did not go with me *this* time.

I have spent considerable time in La Follette's office—which serves as a sort of headquarter for me. That crowd is very bitter against the war-fans—including Wilson, Russell etc.

Today was a sort of a gray, dreary day in Washington, although it did not rain. I slept for several hours in my room.

H. C. Campbell is a stupid toad. He is the proper tool for Lute Niemann. In your place I would not take any notice of him at all when I meet him.

Remember, darling, these days may appear to be dark and dangerous—but you just *love me* as you *always* did, and we will win out as sure as my name is

Victor L.B.

1. Berger enclosed a proof of an editorial entitled "Would It Be Wise to Suppress Victor Berger's Milwaukee Newspaper?" in which Brisbane argued that suppression of the *Milwaukee Leader* would strengthen the IWW and the German cause. Berger was in Washington, D.C., to attend a U.S. Post Office Department hearing concerning the revocation of the *Milwaukee Leader*'s second-class mailing privileges on the grounds that it encouraged disloyalty to the United States. The *Leader* lost its mailing privileges on October 3, 1917, and, following a lengthy appeal process, the U.S. Supreme Court upheld the post office on March 7, 1921, with Justices Louis D. Brandeis and Oliver Wendell Holmes dissenting. The Harding administration restored mailing rights to the *Leader* on May 31, 1921.

Victor to Meta

Washington, D.C.
September 24, [1917]

My sweet Schatzl:

The Senate this afternoon passed the "Trading with the Enemy" bill with the "joker" in it, which makes it impossible to *publish carry* or *dis-*

tribute, any paper which has lost its second class mailing privilege even in the state where it is printed. In other words, if we lose our second class mailing privilege—we are not permitted to send it out by automobile wagon or carrier, and are not permitted to publish it at all.

They expect to put this thing out of the bill by a "point of order" because it is *new* legislation inserted by the conference committee[1] to avoid: a re-approachement between Russians and Germans, with the possibility of a separate peace, especially since our government forbade Berger, Hillquit and Lee to attend a Socialist conference but at the same time sent Root, the sworn enemy of the Russian revolutionists, as "ambassador plenipotentiary" to Russia.

It seemed to dawn upon Lansing that he had made a mistake, but he said that it had been given out to the press and abroad that passports would not be granted and he could not now change his decision. He was very friendly and polite throughout the interview—seemed to know all about me, and several times expressed his regret, and finally his hope that I would give him credit for sincerity—as he is giving credit for sincerity to me.

He is a small potato—if he were a big man, he would not hesitate to change his decision, the moment he found that he has made a mistake.

Kent and postmaster general Albert S. Burleson will try to arrange an interview with President Wilson for me but I don't know whether I care for it at all. I am tired and somewhat discouraged.

Shall leave for New York tomorrow.

With thousand kisses your
V.LB.

1. The Trading with the Enemy Act made it illegal to publish or distribute any newspaper that could not be mailed under the Espionage Act. As Berger predicted, Socialist Congressman Meyer London raised a point of order about this clause on September 25, 1917, but he was overruled by House Speaker Champ Clark. Congress passed the bill, and President Wilson signed it into law on October 6, 1917.

Victor to Meta

New York, New York
September 25, 1917

My sweet Schatzl:—

The Manhattan was crowded and when I got there they expected to get *five* dollars a *day* for a front room *without* a bath. Whereupon I got angry and came to this old rat-hole. There is so much travel in New York with the ammunition and war business (uniforms, chemicals, food etc.) that the speculators and contractors have the best time they have ever had—and they seem to be on a perpetual spree. A dollar in New York looks about the size of a 10 cents–piece in Milwaukee.

Hillquits chances of election are very good—since there is sure to be a four-cornered fight—provided he can get a good manager for the campaign.[1] A man who could [win] the respect and the confidence of the newspapers could easily run a campaign that would land Hillquit. To begin with:—the war is the *issue*, and on that issue he could rally the Jews, the Germans and about half of the Irish around his ticket—*besides* the Socialists. That would elect him with a big majority.

The trouble is only that [the] little Jews who control the party in New York cannot do it—they lack *scope, vision* and *efficiency*. We never had half as good a chance in Milwaukee and we won out.

Well, sweetheart—tomorrow and Thursday I have to tend to my own business—*Leader* business. For Thursday evening I am invited to Hillquit's, Friday or Saturday I will go to Bridgeport, and Sunday I expect to leave for home,—expect to be in Milwaukee by Monday evening.

Seymour Stedman and his wife were here since Saturday—Stedy addressed a meeting on Sunday. He has left since but Irene is still here and is being entertained by Hillqits. They have a machine and a chauffeur now.

I don't want you to worry—no matter what they do in Washington. I can assure you, Schatzl, that I can take care of you and the babies, for a year or two, even if the Leader should be surpressed. On the other hand this will give the paper such an immense prestige that it will be three and four times as big the moment the war is over and war Legislation vanishes. Especially with the unprecedented growth of the party vote every where.

By-the-way, suggest to Miss Thomas to have Judd Wright[2] prepare a cartoon entitled "The Darling of the Gods"—Sam Gompers as the "darling" and the trusts, ammunition makers, mine owners and capitalists as the "gods". They are to look down upon him *approvingly* from some sort of an Olympas, and say nice things about him.

I expect to call up Arthur[3] tomorrow but since he is continuously traveling between here and Washington I have small hope of reaching him.

Don't worry about our girlies. There good stuff in them, especially also in Doris, and they will undoubtedly make good.

It is after 12 o'clock PM. and I am getting tired. Remember, all that I really must have from you in order to succeed is your love. Therefor, just love me, love me—I will do the rest.

Victor L.B.

1. Socialist Morris Hillquit finished third in the 1917 New York City mayoral election with 22 percent of the vote.

2. Jud Wright's cartoons ran in the *Milwaukee Leader* from November 9, 1915, through October 18, 1917. The cartoon suggested by Berger did not appear.

3. Arthur Brisbane.

Meta to Doris and Elsa

Milwaukee, Wisconsin
[October 7, 1917]

Dear Girls:—

This is Sunday & while papa is trying to ge[t] a nap I'm going to write first to you, then to Uncle Archie[1] & then my resignation to our suffrage board.[2]

My reasons you probably know. That bunch is too conservative too suspicious etc etc & not nearly courageous & radical enough to suit me. I am going to throw my efforts into more radical work. And the first thing I am going to do is to help get a conference here for the two women whom the Woman's Party is sending out here to Wis. namely Mrs. Lawrence Lewis of Phil. & Miss Mabel Vernon[3] of Nevada I think. The regular suffragists of Mil., Kenosha, Madison, Oshkosh etc are refusing to let them come to Wisconsin to tell their story of "Why we picketed in Washington." Now since I believe in hearing both sides of the story and am making a fight for free speech & free press I believe I ought to help them. Besides Frederick C Howe[4] gave them a most wonderful tribute. Now altho' the Madison Woman's Suffrage organization turned these ladies down I want very much to have the College Equal Suffrage Society let them come to Madison. So I had Carl Haessler telephone to Elsa Gluck[5] and I'm writing to you to ask you both to do what you can to induce the League to get up a meeting. Induce the Socialist Club to help if you can. Take this up with Bill Brokhausen[6] & others. Telephone Elsa Glück & see how else you can co operate. I believe your efforts will be well worth while. Let me know what Elsa Gluck & the socialists think about this. Don't stop to write for I shall see you Wed. sometime.

We are making plans here which are not yet completed but which if we succeed will keep us above water for a while but it will still be a terrific struggle. Sometimes my hopes are way up & then again they are all gone.

I may have to rent out Elsa's room to help out this winter. Also ask Arch to pay in full now. That is why I want to write him. Perhaps I'll get Franklin[7] back too. I'll have to decide this week just what I shall do.

In the meantime let me again caution you about discussing the war. No one is your friend now a days. So be reserved, dignified & quiet. That may be a little hard at times but it is wonderful training.

Inclosed also please find $4 of the $10 I borrowed. I'll send the other five next week.

Be good girls, study well. The knowledge that you both are making good is a wonderful help & stimulant to both your parents & they need your help in that way just now.

With loads of love to you

I am always your

devoted
Mother.

1. Archibald Anderson, the widower of Meta's sister, Paula.
2. Meta Berger resigned as first vice-president of the Wisconsin Woman Suffrage Association on October 8, 1917, to participate in the National Woman's Party. See Meta Berger to Executive Board, Records of the Wisconsin Woman Suffrage Organization, box 15, folder 1, SHSW.
3. Dora Kelly Lewis (1862–1928) served on the executive committee of the National Woman's Party, and Mabel Vernon (1883–1975) was its secretary. The National Woman's Party was a militant suffrage organization that gained national attention by picketing the White House throughout most of 1917, leading to the arrest of about 500 women and the jailing of 168. Lewis and Vernon spoke at the Bergers' Milwaukee residence on October 14, 1917, as part of a national tour.
4. Frederic C. Howe (1867–1940), a progressive lawyer and social reformer, served as commissioner of immigration at Ellis Island, 1914–1919. He resigned from the position because of his opposition to the Red Scare hysteria stirred up by the Wilson administration. He helped organize the Conference for Progressive Political Action and in 1924 actively supported the presidential candidacy of Robert M. La Follette Sr.
5. Elsie Glück was a student at the University of Wisconsin, where she received a B.A. (1920) and a Ph.D. (1929). She worked as a labor economist and served on the staff of the International Ladies' Garment Workers' Union.
6. William Emil Brockhausen (b. 1886), a student at the University of Wisconsin between 1913 and 1916, was the son of Frederick Brockhausen, a Milwaukee Socialist labor leader and former member of the Wisconsin Assembly.
7. Franklin Schweers, the stepson of Meta's sister, Hattie.

Meta to Doris and Elsa

Milwaukee, Wisconsin
[November 1, 1917]

Dear Doris & Elsa:—

This is Thursday night & I have just come home from the State Teacher's Convention, from 2 banquets, one at noon & one at night and I'm tired to death. Yet I feel that the day must not go by without my writing you tonight. I wish you could feel that way too; for while I haven't written, neither have you *two* girls.

Papa just left tonight to go to Dayton Ohio where he has gone to take part in the political campaign. I only hope the same thing that happened to Bigelow[1] will [not] happen to papa. I asked him to see that he had some sort of a body guard.

Hi[2] got his call to the army today. He is to report for a physical examination Nov. 6th at 8 A.M. I sent it right up to Shawano where he went with Uncle Ernie[3] for a week's hunting. I'm sorry as can be but I guess there is no help for him now. I wish this d—— war was over. It is on my nerves awfully.

Elsa must send his coat back and at once now. Don't borrow the things if you can't return them promptly.

I am holding my breath for Hillquits election. Even the administration is taking a hand in that campaign. Roosevelt, Root, etc etc are speaking against Hillquit & people sent by Wilson also. While on the other hand, Dudley Maloney, Amos Pinchot, Prof's Cattell & Beard & Rabbi Magnus[4] & several other Rev. gentlemen are speaking for him. Gee!

We'd get our second class mailing privilege back if Hillquit were elected. So pray for him girls. Pray for him.

And now I must say goodnight. I love you both dearly & devotedly. Be good girls, get your lessons well I hope all's well there. With devotion

I am always
Your Mama

1. On October 28, 1917, Cincinnati Congregational minister Herbert Seely Bigelow was kidnapped, stripped, and beaten after praying publicly for the "moral improvement" of the Kaiser.
2. Franklin Schweers, the stepson of Meta's sister, Hattie.
3. Ernst Schlichting, Meta's brother.
4. Dudley Field Malone (1882–1950) served as collector of the Port of New York from 1913 to 1917, when he resigned to protest the arrest of suffragists who picketed the White House. Amos Pinchot (1873–1944), a lawyer and the brother of conservationist Gifford Pinchot, helped to organize the Progressive Party in 1912, opposed American entry into World War I, and helped to found the National Civil Liberties Bureau. James McKeen Cattell (1860–1944) taught psychology at Columbia University from 1891 until 1917, when he was dismissed because of his opposition to the war. Historian Charles A. Beard (1874–1948) taught at Columbia University from 1907 until 1917, when he resigned to protest Cattell's firing. Judah L. Magnes (1877–1948), a New York City rabbi and Jewish community leader, was active in the antiwar and civil liberties movements and later became chancellor and president of the Hebrew University of Jerusalem.

Meta to Doris and Elsa

[Milwaukee, Wisconsin]
[November 3, 1917]

Dear Girls:

Do you realize that neither one of you have written home a single time this week? I begin to think that either you do not love me very much or that you are ill. But surely the two of you can hardly be sick at the same time. This won't do. I expect to hear regularly from you.

Tonight I am all alone. Papa has gone to Dayton Ohio, Jack & Josie are out. I am good & tired too after a hard hard week. We are cleaning house but as far as that is concerned I am not taking much interest in that. But I've been down at the office each day besides trying to hold up my end at the Teachers convention. I spoke twice but the best part of all was how I stole a march on Mrs. Youmans. It seems that she expected to introduce a suffrage resolution at the teachers convention & called upon Potter to permit her to do so. This I did not know however until yesterday after my own plans had been made. Neither Mrs. Youmans nor Mr. Potter took me into their confidences nor did Mrs Youmans show me any courtesy by coming to me as a member of the educational crowd & tell me she was going to do it. Well, dear girls Miss Rankin from Montana (congressman) came to Mil. Friday. I immediately called upon her at the hotel & asked her to be my guest & allow me to take her to the auditorium. She is very charming indeed, was quite at home at once & told me she was much more of a socialist (which is really true) than she was a Republican but not to give her away.

Then I had also received a letter from Ada James[1] of Richland Center who told me that the Woman's Party (Pickets) had secured 3 minutes from the Chairman of arrangements for the Teacher's Convention in which Miss James wanted *me* to introduce a suffrage resolution from the platform in the big convention hall just before Miss Rankin was to speak. So I went to Mr. Bussewitz[2] & showed him my letter & got the 3 minutes. In the meantime some one told Mrs. Youmans I am told, that I was going to do this whereupon she immediately called up Potter asking him as chairman of the evening not to permit me to do this as the resolution might not pass. Potter rang up Miss Rankin & ask[ed] her what she tho't about it & Miss R said "Why yes let Mrs. Berger do that."

Well so far so good. When we reached the Auditorium you can imagine that the place was packed. And in the front seat directly in front of the stage sat Mrs. Youmans, Mrs. Rogers & Mrs. Warfield.[3] Well that was really rich. A Mr. Slutz[4] of Ohio gave the first talk & it was a splendid talk. Then to my astonishment Potter calls upon a Mr. P. H. Martin[5] of Green Bay representing the Wisconsin Loyalty Legion. Then

I guessed that there might be uncomfortable moments for me who was on the stage with Miss Rankin. This Mr. Martin spoke for about 45 minutes uttering the most abusive & bitter tirade of abuse against the Pacifists, the Copperheads, the I.W.W.'s, the Socialists, the Bergerites, the Lafolletties etc etc. He denounced us as slimy snakes in the grass, copperheads & what not. Each & every time he mentioned Bergerism or Bergerites there was an awful Oh! whispered from the audience. This audience mind you was partly Milwaukee & partly state people. All of the Educators of the State, normal & university regents, Dr. Buckingham, L. D. Harvey, Mrs Runge[6] all were there. Well the best part of this speech was this; it was so abusive that the man over reached himself. I knew I had to follow him with my suffrage resolution & I couldn't imagine just how I would be received. I didn't know whether the patriots in the crowd would hiss me or what. But there was nothing to do except see it thro'. Potter whispered to me & asked me if I had rather postpone the resolution until the next day for the committee to handle but I said "No I'll take my chances." Where upon he got up and said "Ladies and Gentlemen I now introduce to you Mrs. *Victor L. Berger.*" Well I walked right to the front of the stage & with a smile started to speak when the whole house broke into a tremendous applause and each time the applause threatened to die down it broke forth greater than ever. Until I finally put up my hand asking them to stop & when I said Ladies & Gentlemen & *Friends* the applause broke forth with renewed vigor. It was the biggest ovation any woman ever got. Thank God all those state people were there now. Then I made my speech which was like this.

"We have listened to two very remarkable speeches this evening. The first gentleman calling upon us to make a conquest for our freedom & to contribute our services, & the 2nd speaker making a most wonderful plea for justice. (This was taken either sarcastically or otherwise.) I'll admit that these are stirring trying earnest times. These are the times when every man is expected to do his full duty towards his country.

These are the times when women are asked to make heroic sacrifice and they are cheerfully doing it.

These are the times when the right of citizenship is prized more highly than any other qualifications and because it *is just* that the right of citizenship should belong to all of the people of this country regardless of sex; I offer the following resolution,

Resolved that the Wis. Teachers Ass. in Convention assembled call upon Pres. Wilson & Congress to urge and secure the passage of the National Suffrage Amendment known as the Susan B Anthony Amendment & be it further

Resolved that a copy of these resolutions be sent to Pres. Wilson & the chairman of the suffrage committees of Each house.

Mr. Chairman I ask for the adoption of these resolutions as a matter of justice and as a complement to our distinguished guest of honor."

Well once more the house applauded and the resolution of course was passed.

After Miss Rankin spoke & she spoke very well indeed & the meeting adjourned, you should have seen the people flock about me to tell me what a splendid way I lived up to that tragical situation. Men came up to me to say "I want to shake you by the hand" & Mr. Slutz came up to me & said "Mrs Berger I shall go back to my state & tell them what a noble woman did nobly". So you see what might have been most painful turned out to be a real boomerang for Mr. Martin. All day today people are ringing me up to say nice things to me. And even Mrs. Potter rang me up to say how ashamed she & her husband were for this man etc. She had only the finest things to say today. Well neither papa nor my children were there. At first I was so glad & afterward I was sorry. I can't tell you how all the state people came & ask[ed] for introductions & tell me how much they admired my conduct.

And that Man Martin is a candidate for the U.S. Senate!!!! Well it is over with. Now I'll tell you about Miss Rankin. She is very charming, intellectual quite pretty when you are close to her; a good speaker and a good sport all round. After the meeting about 12 of us including Mabel Search, Alma Jacobus,[7] Etelka,[8] Maud,[9] Nettie,[10] Mary, Gertrude,[11] Mrs. Roberts, Mrs. Strachan,[12] Miss Ulbricht[13] & another lady whose name I don't remember all came with us to the Badger Room as Mabel Search's guests with Miss Rankin & staid with her until her train left again at 12.30 Midnight. Fortunately I had the car with me.

Well Mrs. Youmans was so furious she refused absolutely to speak to me. I know she thinks I did this to spoil her game but I didn't know she had any plans until after my plans were all made & then I felt I had as much [right] as she had. But none of them even stopped to speak to Miss Rankin, they went away furious. I am saving those letters tho' of Ada James & Miss Armstrong[14] of Washington in which she says Mr. Bussewitz promised the Woman's Party 3 minutes for I predict that some cattish work is going to be done.

I'll never forget their faces as they refused to bid me the time of day. And it really was fortunate I got the resolution in for the next day the resolutions committee decided to bar all resolutions except one pertaining to Loyalty. So if I hadn't done so it would not have been done at all.

Well, now I've written you a long long letter. So do like wise. Tell me all about the big game. In the meanwhile I hope & pray that papa will come home safe & sound & that he won't meet any pirates or Ku Klux Klan like Bigelow did. Poor Bigelow is still in a hospital suffering from the cut wounds & burns on his body. In closing girls let me caution you again & again about talking these days. Please be most guarded in what you say. In the University of Ill. at Urbana 8 Prof & teachers are grilled & even promised a whipping like Bigelow's.[15] So be careful I say again & again.

Elsa is to send Hi's[16] coat back & right away without fail. Don't forget to send your laundry & the box containing jelly glasses. I am getting tired writing. My fingers cramp up. So good night & write write write to your

Loving lonely
Mama

1. Ada James (1876–1952), a progressive Republican, was active in the women's suffrage, Prohibition, and peace movements. She served as president of the Wisconsin Political Equality League from 1911 until 1913, when it merged with the Wisconsin Woman Suffrage Association.

2. Maxillian A. Bussewitz (1867–1942) taught at Milwaukee State Normal School (later Milwaukee State Teachers College), 1898–1939, and served as secretary of the Wisconsin Teachers Association, 1911–1912 and 1913–1922.

3. Theodora Winton Youmans, Jane P. Rogers, and Lorna Hooper Warfield (1889–1986) were officers of the Wisconsin Woman Suffrage Association.

4. Frank D. Slutz (1882–1956) directed an experimental school in Dayton, Ohio, from 1917 to 1927.

5. Patrick Henry Martin (1862–1925) was a criminal lawyer from Green Bay, Wisconsin, who served as president of the state bar, 1919–1920. Although mentioned as a candidate for the U.S. Senate seat vacated by the death of Paul O. Husting on October 21, 1917, Martin did not run in the March, 1918, primary.

6. Burdette R. Buckingham (1876–1972) served as secretary to the Wisconsin Board of Education, 1916–1918. Lorenzo D. Harvey (1848–1922) was Wisconsin superintendent of schools, 1899–1903, and president of Stout Institute in Menomonie, Wisconsin, 1908–1922. Clara T. Runge (1860–1952) served on the Wisconsin Board of Regents of Normal Schools, 1916–1926, and the University of Wisconsin Board of Regents, 1926–1938.

7. Alma Jacobus (b. 1892?) worked as a librarian's assistant for the Milwaukee Public Library and as a librarian for the *Milwaukee Journal* and the *Milwaukee Leader*. In 1921 she accompanied Meta Berger on her trip to Asia.

8. Etelka Jacobi.

9. Maud McCreery.

10. Annette Rosenthal (Gould).

11. Gertrude Haessler Filtzer.

12. Ella N. Strachan (b. 1869?), the widow of Adam Strachan, a Milwaukee salesman.

13. Probably Elsa E. Ulbricht (1885–1980), who taught art at the Milwaukee State Normal School (later Milwaukee State Teachers College and Wisconsin State College, Milwaukee) from 1911 to 1955.

14. Meta Berger meant Virginia Arnold, a women's suffrage activist who served as president of the National Woman's Party. Copies of the letters from Arnold and James are in the Berger Papers, SHSW.

15. On October 31, 1917, a Department of Justice investigator met with several University of Illinois faculty members who had refused to buy war bonds. Within several days, newspapers around the nation reported that eight faculty members, some of them Socialists, were accused of disloyalty, but no formal charges were filed. All but one of the professors involved in the incident were forced from their positions by 1920.

16. Franklin Schweers, the stepson of Meta's sister, Hattie.

Victor to Doris

Milwaukee, Wisconsin
November 15, [1917]

My dear Dod:

Have received your special correspondence and as you may judge from the enclosed clipping—I have made good use of it.

I am glad you are very busy. You will find that your university life will mean a great deal more to you—and that you will even *enjoy* it *more*—if you *work hard,* than it meant to you last year when you wasted and wasted some valuable time by gossiping or visiting with insignificant Barnard Hall girls that mean nothing to you today. At the same time I don't want you to be so busy that it will would in any way interfere with either your good health or your studies.

First and *foremost* I want you to get proper and sufficient exercise for your body—rather a little more than a little less. I mean walking, skating etc.

That advise also holds good for Schnucks—as does all the other advise. In fact, I much prefer to have you take your walks, your enjoyments together—as sisters should that are so near together in age and studies.

If you, Dod, really mean to make a little money by writing, I can appoint you our correspondent in Madison at $3.00 per week to begin with—provided you send at least *two items per week,* long or short. Since you are working for the Cardinal that job should appeal to you—since you could use any news item that is of *general* interest.

If you do well, I will raise your salary to five dollars per week, after three months. But mark well, Dod—The Milwaukee Leader, not I, would pay the money, therefore, you must *actually earn* it, if you are appointed a correspondent.

There is another thing, my dear girl, about which I want to speak to you. Do *not* talk *about the war* to anybody—not even to your best friends. You will be misunderstood or misquoted—or your friend will tell it to somebody else, and that person will misunderstand or misquote.

And don't believe any of the innumerable lies which the newspapers tell about your father and even—about your mother. There seems to be a systematic *campaign* of lies waged against all prominent Socialists and particularly against *me*.

Now, do not worry about that Dod. If I did not amount to anything—they would not go to so much trouble. And you may rest assured that I shall do nothing but what is right and honorable—and for the best of all people, as I see it.

Therefore, even, if I should have to go to *prison* for my principles—you must not consider that a disgrace. On the other hand I will do all I can to *avoid* any catastrophe of that kind,—because at best, it is always a *misfortune* to the *family* and usually also a setback to the movement, at least, temporarily.

You can readily see that I do not believe in playing martyr, if martyrdom can be avoided without doing greater injury to one's better self or to the movement which a man represents.

As I see it, we will live through some very disagreeable days—in fact the barring of the Leader from the mail has made it very hard and disagreeable for us for some time—but since *Socialism* is a world-wide movement and the *natural outcome* and the *economic result* of *capitalism*—and since my political views are only the consistent expression of my economic views, and I have *at no time obstructed* the *activities* of the government after the laws were once passed—I refer to the war legislation, conscription laws, liberty loans etc.—the national administration has no legal handle of any kind against me.

The barring of the Leader was simply a piece of *stupid despotism* under special legislation of congress for that purpose.

Well, Dod, the letter is longer then I intended. Kiss my Schnuckie for me, and let her read this letter, of course—also *divide* the enclosed *ten dollar* check with her.

With the assurance of infinite love from both your sweet mother and me, I am always yours,

Papa.

Victor to Meta

Washington, D.C.
November 28, [1917]

My sweet Schatzl:

Two tedious and almost endless days in court—mainly taken up with legal technicalities and with the lawyers sparring for position.[1] The solicitor-general, Lamar,[2] with half a dozen attorneys represent the government—while Cochems and a very old lawyer, by the name of Charles Poe, who is full of terms, technicalities and legal lore—but knows nothing about Socialism—represents the Leader. So far Cochems has not at all come up to my expectation. The decisions of the judge have not favored us either—although Poe seems to be well satisfied with the case. One thing is very evident in the case—the government is repeating over and over again that we were *not barred from* the *mail* but that we have only lost our second class "privilege". The government also disclaims any intention of connecting us with the provision of the "Trading with the Enemy" act, according to which, we could not even print or distribute the paper in Milwaukee. It seems the government lawyers have no faith in that provision themselves—they practically admitted that it was *not* constitutional.

My editorials never sounded any better—or more convincing—than when read by one of the attorneys for the postal department. They evidently seem to have made an impression on the judge.

But with the servile atmosphere prevailing *here,* I do not know whether we can win the case in the lower court—I even have my doubts whether the Supreme Court will decide in our favor, although the administration seems to be getting ready to change its policy towards the Socialists.

News not only from Russia—but from France and Italy, is getting on Wilson's nerves. Coupled with that is the result of the last election in New York, Chicago and the Middle West. I suppose they will try "kind words" next.

Well, Sweetheart—I have so far seen nobody, not even Bob La Follette. Shall try to make an appointment for tomorrow, Thanksgiving day.

I feel very lonesome just now, and wish you were with me.

Kiss my Schnuckies for me. I shall try to see them when you go to Madison.

Lovingly your
V.L.B.

1. Berger appealed the loss of the *Milwaukee Leader*'s second-class mailing privileges to the Supreme Court of the District of Columbia on November 5, 1917. The court ruled against the *Leader* on January 16, 1918, and the U.S. Supreme Court upheld the lower court's decision on March 7, 1921.

2. William Harmong Lamar (1859–1928) served as assistant U.S. attorney general and solicitor for the Post Office Department, 1913–1921.

Victor to Meta

Washington, D.C.
November 29, [1917]

My sweet Schatzl:

Just a few lines—so as to keep up the continuity of thought.

Had a visit with Arthur[1] to-day. He told me that the administration was determined to carry out its policy—considering all opposition and especially every expression in favor of peace as "anti-American". A. himself was rather startled when I showed him that this policy led to a blind endorsement of everything Morgan, Schwab[2] and the Vanderbilts[3] demanded from the people. I also showed him that if they were so sure that 75 per cent of the American people were with Wilson—why did they everywhere combine with the Republicans against the Socialists? The Washington Star of *tonight* carried a big story on its first page to the effect that such will be done *nationally* "to keep the Socialists out", who *now* have *one measly representative* in congress—with the accent on the "measly", if you please.

In all probability he will bring about a meeting between Mr. Burleson and me, at which he will be present. As far as I am concerned I want to be on good terms with Burleson and the administration, if it can possibly be done without making me a traitor to principles, which I have preached and propagated for over 30 years.

I had a lonely day today. With so many acquaintances and "friends"—not even an invitation to a thanksgiving dinner. Several people tried to get me by telephone while I was away from the hotel—with Brisbane—I don't know who they were.

My friend Cochems slept until 12.30 P.M—a feat which I could not accomplish with the best of will.

Our case comes up tomorrow again. Hope it will be less tedious and less technical. I told Cochems to put it on a high plane—talk about the right of free speech, free press and "bill of rights" (the amendments) in the U.S. constitution. There is no constitution in Washington D.C. just now, however, and I don't know whether he will get the good will of the judge on such ground. I feel sure, nevertheless, that the action of the Postal department will never be set aside on a legal technicality, or on dozen of them.

Well, Schatzl, I hope you enjoy the company of your Schnuckies. Dod will not be there long enough to pick a quarrel and Schnucks will be so elated with the home "eats" that it will be a real "Thanks giving" vacation for her.

Kiss both of them for me—and ask Doris why she never even answered the business proposition I put up to her.

I will stay in Washington in all proba[bi]lity until Monday night.
With infinite love for my Mama Schatzl

V.L.B.

1. Arthur Brisbane.
2. Charles M. Schwab (1862–1939) served as chairman of the board of Bethlehem Steel Corporation from its founding in 1904 until his death. During World War I, Bethlehem Steel handled more than $500 million worth of war contracts and its net income grew from more than $5 million in 1913 to more than $43 million in 1916.
3. The Vanderbilt family owned extensive railroad holdings.

Meta to Doris and Elsa

[Milwaukee, Wisconsin]
[ca. March 9, 1918]

Dear Girls:—

I am writing tonight to reassure you if you need to be, that the indictment[1] against papa is a political move pure & simple. The charge is that literature, leaflets sent out from the Chicago office tend to discourage & hamper the government in its progress with the war. Papa doesn't even know what the leaflets are that are being circulated. He hasn't seen them. It may of course be charged that the St. Louis platform is one of them & possibly some of the editorials in the Leader. We do not know yet—Mr. Cochems just rang up to tell papa he had a talk with Mr. Sawyer[2] the district attorney (this must be very confidential so destroy this at once) & both agreed that it is done for political effect. The procedure will of course have to be gone thro' with. Monday Papa will go to the Federal Building & present himself. Whether they will formerly arrest him I do not know. Then we will have to submit bail & then await for the charges to be tried. This may be a matter of months. Germer was tried before & acquitted. Now he & the others are again indicted. It is strange that the authorities didn't include Stedman, Work,[3] Hillquitt & Anna Malley;[4] the other members of the National Executive Board. Papa's case will probably be similar to that of Eastman's.[5] So you girls keep up a stiff upper lip in the consciousness of knowing that papa is right & great & good. The inclosed cards are his campaign cards.[6] I think they are just splendid. Surely there is nothing seditious in them. Also his big posters are splendid. But we may have trouble getting them posted as the bill posting companies are also trying to refuse to do it as a matter of patriotism. Papa has the old parties scared to a frazzle. I am not much worried, at least for the present, about the indictment. I think that will come out O.K. Be good girls, work hard, & love

Your Mama & Papa.

1. On February, 2, 1918, a federal grand jury in Chicago indicted Berger, J. Louis Engdahl, Adolph Germer, William Kruse, and Irwin St. John Tucker with conspiracy to violate the Espionage Act. The indictments were announced on March 9, 1918.

2. Hiram Arthur Sawyer (1875–1946) served as district attorney for Washington County, Wisconsin, 1907–1915, and as federal district attorney for the Eastern District of Wisconsin, 1915–1923.

3. John M. Work (1869–1961), a lecturer and journalist, served as the Socialist Party's national secretary, 1911–1913, and as a member of its National Executive Committee during World War I. He ran the editorial page of the *Milwaukee Leader* (and its successor, the *Milwaukee Post*) from May, 1917, until 1942, when the paper stopped publishing. Work wrote most of the antiwar editorials that led to Berger's conviction under the Espionage Act.

4. Anna Agnes Maley (1873–1918), a Socialist journalist, served on the staff of the *Appeal to Reason*, the *New York Worker*, and the *New York Call*. She chaired the Woman's National Committee of the Socialist Party, 1909–1911, served as a member of the party's National Executive Committee, and ran unsuccessfully for governor of Washington in 1912.

5. Max Eastman (1883–1969), a radical journalist and the brother of Crystal Eastman, served as editor of the *Masses* from 1912 until its suppression in 1917 and as co-editor of the *Liberator* from 1918 until 1922. He was indicted under the Espionage Act, but two juries failed to reach a verdict. Between 1922 and 1924 Eastman lived in the Soviet Union, where he became allied with Leon Trotsky. After Eastman's return to America in 1927, he became a leader of the anti-Stalinist Left until 1940, when he renounced Marxism and socialism.

6. Berger was running in a special election for the U.S. Senate.

Meta to Doris and Elsa

Milwaukee, Wisconsin
[ca. March 23, 1918]

Dear dear girls:—

Please forgive me for not sitting down immediately & writing you my pleasure at receiving the pictures. You could have done nothing else that would have pleased me & papa better. When the box came I tho't it might contain a pair of silk something & I said, "I guess they tho't they had to give me something. I'll bet it is foolish." But papa saw first what it was & said, "That is *not* foolish." So you see that we both liked your thoughtfulness & appreciate your loving consideration. Now do I like the pictures; Yes because they are pictures of you; but I don't think the pictures do justice to either of you. Both are better looking. Everybody here says so. The artist did not pose you well. Of course I am glad the bangs are not in evidence but I know you are both better looking. Anyway I look at them the first thing in the morning & the last thing at night and am thankful that I have two lovely lovely girls. That at least no one can spoil for me.

These are bitter hard times & we all must try to bear what comes to us as best we may. I am trying to do my bit by helping papa just now. We haven't had a meal but breakfast at home since a week ago today. Last Sunday we went to Sheboygan to attend a meeting but found upon arrival there that the meeting was postponed due to the stormy weather as no car or train service could be had so we are going again tomorrow. On our way home we decided that papa's campaign committee needed push and energy as nothing was being done so Miss Thomas & I were appointed. We then got busy. We got volunteer & other help and addressed & mailed out more than 25,000 letters containing literature into the state. That was before primary literature. Now we will have to repeat that for after the primary.[1] You see they denied us advertising in country papers, refuse to post our poster on the bill-boards thro'-out the state; refuse to rent halls to us in small towns for our meetings so the only avenue open to us was the mail. Yesterday 10,000 letters went out. We kept one automobile busy taking them to the P.O. By Monday night I will have 10,000 addressed envelopes as a starter for the new work. So you see dearies I haven't wasted time this week. Up to the present moment the papers have not yet been served on papa. But we have enough men to go bond for him. At first it seemed a difficult problem to get bondsmen but we got them & not among our rich friends either. They were all afraid of the publicity they would get & so declined. I can tell you I have the utmost contempt for a rich man who is a coward. Stedy was up from Chicago & he told us not to worry as he could easily prove this to be a political trick. There is so much happening just now that it is impossible to write it all. I can understand what a skunk your prof. is who took the opportunity to talk against papa in your presence. All that happens in a life time. Be good girls, don't worry if you don't hear from me during [the] week. If any thing important happens I'll telephone you. And remember both papa & Mama need the inspiration of your love & devotion.

Lovingly
Mama.

1. Berger received 38,564 votes for U.S. senator in the uncontested Socialist Party primary held on March 19, 1918. His total represented 15 percent of all votes cast in the election. In the general election, held on April 2, 1918, Berger received 110,487 votes (26 percent of the vote) and carried eleven of the state's seventy-one counties, compared to 39 percent for Republican Irvine L. Lenroot and 35 percent for Democrat Joseph E. Davies.

Victor to Meta

Milwaukee, Wisconsin
August 2, 1918

My sweet Schatzl

It is late but I am still in my office trying to fix up copy for a few days in advance—because the meeting in Chicago will occupy two days for the National Executive Committee—and four more days for the meeting with the state secretaries.

I will have to be there Thursday morning. And I don't know whether it is more important for the movement (and for us) to attend that meeting (which will adopt some kind of a re-construction program) or to tend to business on the Leader and for my *district* (where I have received 21,570 votes last spring, against 15,147 for Davies[1] and 9,498 for Lenroot). If there are to be three candidates this fall—with Stafford and Carney in the field—it will be easy enough. But nobody knows what really is going to happen.

I have drafted a letter to the voters. Am also trying to fix up a card, similar to the one used this spring, of which card 50,000 are to be distributed *before* the Primary.

You see, it is of some importance to me to have a *good* Primary vote.[2] There is also this danger, however: unless the vote is so overwhelming at the Primary that it precludes any possibility of a defeat in the main election, the big vote may simply have the effect of driving the two old parties together, something for which the profiteers and the loyalists are praying night and day.

But never mind that, sweet Schatzl. I have accomplished what I went for (to Chicago) last Wednesday—as far as the Leader business is concerned; but I did not succeed in locating Mr. Brisbane during the few hours of my stay.

Was very sorry to read about the death of William Wallrich.[3] All the papers had the list of casualties, of course. Well, our capitalist patriots wanted this war—they got it. But please, darling, be careful about what you are saying, even in *private* conversation. Impress this also on our Doddie.

I have brought down the military blanket and Doris' night robe to the office. The parcel will be shipped tomorrow.

Phil. Wagner[4] of St Louis ("Rip Saw" and "Melting Pot" fame) was here today and took a large share of the afternoon. Rehfeld drove our car, and we showed Wagner the wonders of our town.

I expect Schnuckie here tomorrow. She wrote me a letter of very few lines (—she was just going to a "movie"—) telling me that the Belitzes[5] will bring her. Und sonst hast Du mich aber lieb, wie?[6]

With thousand kisses
V.L.B.

1. Joseph E. Davies (1876–1958), a prominent Wisconsin-born lawyer and Democratic politician, held a number of posts under Presidents Wilson and Franklin Roosevelt, including the chairmanship of the Federal Trade Commission, 1915–1916, and the ambassadorship to the Soviet Union, 1936–1938.

2. Berger received 8,552 votes for U.S. representative from Wisconsin's Fifth Congressional District in the uncontested Socialist Party primary held on September 3, 1918. Berger's total represented 30 percent of all votes cast in the election.

3. Lieutenant William Wallrich (1894–1918), the son of former Shawano, Wisconsin, mayor and businessman Michael J. Wallrich, died in France.

4. Phil Wagner of St. Louis published the socialist monthlies *National Rip-Saw* and *Melting Pot.*

5. Arthur F. Belitz (b. 1872) and his wife, Charlotte Ullrich Belitz (b. 1874?). Arthur, a Milwaukee lawyer who had moved to Madison to become assistant revisor of statutes, was Meta's first cousin.

6. And, otherwise, you do love me, don't you?

Victor to Meta

Chicago, Illinois
August 8, 1918

My sweet Schatzl:

I hope you made up your mind not to attend the conference.[1] The weather is hot and the new Executive Committee is impossible.

Stanley Clark—a former preacher and lawyer from the South, who has a very unsavory reputation in Oklahoma and Texas—was elected upon one nomination from some little local in Kentucky. His membership was *questioned* by the state secretary from Oklahoma and when I demanded proof of his membership, he declared that his word must [be] accepted as proof, and raised his chair threatening me—calling me all kinds of names. Stanley Clark was expelled from our party before—he is a drunkard and a defaulter—and just now he is on trial with the I.W.W., although not a member of the I.W.W.[2]

I have a good mind to go home and not take any further part in the deliberations.

Hillquit will not come to Chicago—he says that he is "not feeling well." Stedman has not attended any session as yet. Work is a *weak* sister and Goebel came here evidently as an emissary of the Appeal and of the Spargo-Simons-Walling[3] clique.

As for the rest, there is not much to them. Shiplakoff[4] is [a] little Jewish politician from New York, James O'Neill[5] (now with the Call) an old hanger-on of Mailly, Katterfeld, an impossibilist and Hogan,[6] a well meaning fool. Three of the others are in prison and Walter Thomas Mill's[7] seat is also protested. I have a good mind to cut loose and simply hold Wisconsin—which I could easily do—the trouble is, however, we cannot have a national party just in *one* state. But God knows, the whole bunch is not worth the sacrifice of a single *decent* and *strong* man.

Well, sweetheart, it is very unpleasant for me to tell you all this—but I must unfold my mind to somebody.

Do not come here, sweetheart. I may be going home myself by Monday or Tuesday and go up to Shawano.

With love to all and especially to my Schatzl

VL.B.

1. The Socialist Party held a joint conference of the National Executive Committee and the state party secretaries in Chicago on August 10–12, 1918. The meeting, intended to evaluate the party's war position, served only to highlight the differences between the party's right and left wings.

2. Stanley J. Clark, a Texas Socialist, was tried and convicted along with ninety-nine other defendants (mostly members of the IWW) for violating the Espionage Act. Judge Kenesaw Mountain Landis sentenced Clark to twenty-eight years in prison on August 31, 1918.

3. William English Walling (1877–1936), an independently wealthy Socialist, helped establish the National Association for the Advancement of Colored People and worked on behalf of the labor movement. Like John Spargo and Algie Simons, Walling left the party in 1917 because he disagreed with its opposition to the war.

4. Abraham I. Shiplacoff (1877–1934), a Russian-born Socialist, served as a New York assemblyman from 1916 to 1918.

5. James Oneal (1873–1962) worked as a Socialist Party speaker, writer, and editor from the party's founding until 1936, when he left to form the Social Democratic Foundation. Oneal edited or worked on the editorial staff of the *Worker,* the *New York Call,* and the *New Leader.* He served on the party's National Executive Committee and as secretary of the Indiana and Massachusetts Socialist Parties.

6. Dan Hogan edited the *Huntington Herald,* a Socialist newspaper in Arkansas, and served as secretary of the Arkansas Socialist Party, 1906–1910.

7. Walter Thomas Mills (1856–1942) was a political economist and author of *The Struggle for Existence,* a socialist textbook.

Victor to Meta

Milwaukee, Wisconsin
August 22, 1918

My sweet Schatzl:

I suppose you have read that the district attorney in Chicago has asked Judge Landis[1] that our case be hurried—i.e that it be put on trial when the court re-convenes in September. If the judge grants this request, which I believe he will—then our case will come up about the end of September and will take up the entire month of October—just before election.

While I was in *Shawano* last Saturday the Journal had a first page article (in a box) addressed to the U.S. district attorney in Milwaukee, asking him why he does not proceed against *me?*[2] Mr. L. W. Nieman was also appointed as a member of a "journalistic commission" of Seven, which is to proceed to France "to report" on conditions at the front. Of course, that "commission" is purely a junketing trip to reward Niemann and others for their loyalty to Wilson and the profiteers.

By-the-way, Schatzl, you would better send your letters to the house. They have held up our *entire mail* today.[3] I suppose, one of your letters is among the others. The letter which you sent to the *house*, however, containing the note from Mrs. Zachow, I have received.

The danger of all that "withholding of the mail" is that it ruins the *business* of the Leader. There is nothing in our mail that could ever hurt the Leader or me,—except possibly some letters from cranks, which I never publish or in any way consider, but simply throw away.

They can, therefore, never make out anything from our mail— unless they "would plant it" there—and that is *not* an easy matter. You see our paper was always the most conservative of the Socialist papers— so much so that for many years the Leader and its predessessor the Social Democratic Herald was simply a "by-word" and a "hiss" among the so-called "radical" socialists. Most all of these "radicals" are violent "patriots" today, willing to destroy the International Socialist movement and to kill or imprison its Leaders.

Well, let us talk about something more pleasant.

Dick[4] has sent his photo in his uniform as an officer of the Navy. He looks as proud and self-satisfied as if he were Woodrow Wilson's oldest son.

At times I feel very lonesome—especially in this hot weather. Since I must probably go to Chicago on Monday or Tuesday (money matters on account of the machinery we have bought, and want held back, until after the war)—therefore, I wish you folks would not come home until Wednesday or Thursday. Please let me know the time.

I don't want you to worry because I am *convinced* and *feel* it in *all my bones* that everything *will end well.*

I hope Doddie got a great [deal] of pleasure and satisfaction out of the letters I sent her—there was one from France.

Well, Schatzl, hast Du mich sonst lieb?[5] With oceans of love, as Schnuckie would say;

ever your
V.L.B.

1. Kenesaw Mountain Landis (1866–1944) served as a federal district judge, 1905–1922. He presided over the trials of Berger and his co-defendants and of William D. Haywood and other members of the IWW in 1918. Landis became commissioner of Major League Baseball in 1920, a position he held until his death.

2. "To the United States District Attorney," *Milwaukee Journal*, August 17, 1918. The article called for Berger's indictment because of his statements arguing that the United States went to war on behalf of commercial interests.

3. The post office refused to deliver first-class mail to the offices of the *Milwaukee Leader* from August 22, 1918, through June, 1921.

4. Richard G. Berger (1893–1977) was the son of Victor's sister, Rebecca, by her first marriage and was later adopted by Victor's parents. Richard worked as a research chemist for Thomas Edison for nine months prior to enlisting in the U.S. Navy in June, 1917. He later worked as a Bridgeport, Connecticut, stockbroker.

5. Little darling, do you otherwise love me?

Meta to Doris and Elsa

[Milwaukee, Wisconsin]
[October 29, 1918]

My Darling Girls:—

By this time you will have heard the news once more of the federal indictments.[1] Papa is charged on 86 counts in three charges that he conspired to influence boys of the army & navy & others of draft age against enlisting (This is not true). Secondly that he used mail unlawfully by—but what's the use. I'll enclose the page of the Free Press. You can get it all there.

I am very very sorry for you girls. Your college life has certainly been made hard thro' the events caused by the war. But I know you are made of the right kind of stuff & will meet the situation with a dignified calm which will only inspire respect for you from some of the patriotic peanuts out there. My chief concern now is to weather this storm. I guess it will be the last one. If the war closes soon I am hoping all this will be dropped. But without me, those men would not have had bondsmen enough. I got Morris Stern[2] who got his brother to put up half of a $60,000 bond. I really must pat myself on the back for that.

We are working hard in the campaign; harder than ever before. Somehow I hope that this last bit of persecution will be a boomerang. Those people surely have overreached themselves this time. Unless a man has an ax to grind, a normal man likes fair play in a fair fight. This campaign has gone on O.K. until these indictments were sprung.[3] I hope for [a] good reaction. We still have about 18,000 pieces of literature to get out besides the next Sunday's Voice of the People.

I saw Mildred Haessler[4] yesterday. She is up here for a day or two. She saw Carl at Leavenworth 2 days ago for 55 minutes. She went down taking a chance that she might see him altho' she had written him too that she was coming. Somehow that letter didn't get [to] him in time so she surprised him. She said however that she was weeping so hard that she didn't see him at all when he first came in. Later she saw that he was looking very well. He had broadened out a good deal & was more handsome than ever before. She said he even dignified his prison garb. He occupies a single cell which is good. He has reading privileges, is writing a book, was in good spirits (which of course he would be before Mildred) can receive letters & books but nothing to eat or smoke. He works in the office doing clericle work & has Sat. P.M. & Sun. off. The visit seemed to rejuvenate Mildred.

That's about all I know today. I shall stand by Papa always. He is the bravest man I know and is the most wholesome & educational influence in this City. Be good girls & you will help us both. With love I am

Mama

1. On October 28, 1918, Berger and five other Wisconsin Socialists were indicted in federal court in Milwaukee under the Espionage Act. Berger charged that the indictments were politically motivated because they came the week before the general election and were levied against the Socialist Party's congressional candidates in the Second (Oscar Ameringer), Fourth (Edmund Melms), Fifth (Berger), and Eighth (Leo Krzycki) Districts. In addition, charges were filed against the party's state secretary, Louis Arnold, and the head of the Milwaukee Social-Democratic Publishing Company, Elizabeth Thomas. The case never came to trial, and the charges were dropped on May 8, 1922.

2. Morris Stern (1878–1959), a Milwaukee attorney, served on the city's school board, 1915–1921, and was active in Socialist politics.

3. Berger won election to the U.S. House of Representatives on November 5, 1918, receiving 44 percent (17,920 votes) of the ballots cast versus 30 percent for Democrat Joseph P. Carney and 26 percent for incumbent Republican William H. Stafford.

4. Mildred Haessler (b. 1890), a schoolteacher, was the first wife of conscientious objector Carl Haessler.

Meta to Doris and Elsa

[Milwaukee, Wisconsin]
[November 14, 1918]

Dear Girls:—

Inclosed please find the check of $200.00. It was a long time coming. I think it is harder for papa to send you such big checks but we will see how he manages in the future. Use it sparingly.

I saw Eva[1] yesterday. We wanted her to take Edna Peters[2] place while Edna goes to the Rand School in New York on a scholarship. We tho't it might be a dandy experience for Eva. She however felt she owed it to Miss Buckley[3] to stick for a little while longer. Then too we couldn't exactly say what Eva was to do after the 6 mo were up. Papa tho't if she proved apt she might possibly work in as a Newspaper woman & thus gain a little world experience. But we will see about that later on. Eva couldn't act as his secretary in Washington. She lacks school etc. He needs some one upon whom he can depend for his correspondence but I've no doubt but what he would take her as a stenographer or assistant sec. if he ever gets his seat.

Now as to Chicago. The case comes up Nov. 25 unless it is again deferred. However Stedy filed an affidavit of prejudice against Judge Landis & it may be that if he acts favorably on that affidavit & decides to let some one else try it, another postponement might be had. Stedy said he would want you both there part of the time. Will let you know later.

We are now cleaning house. At present we are taking the books out in the Library. You know what a job that is. Edwin[4] was here Monday. I took both Edwin & Jack to the theatre Monday night. Jack has a job which he takes this morning at the Hawkes nursery in Wauwautosa. He likes that better than indoor work.

Take good care of your money. Don't lose the check. And be sure to get your money's worth of study & work as well as play.

With oceans of love to you from both of us I am Ever your loving

Mother

1. Eva Kurz (Filtzer).
2. Edna Peters was a reporter for the *Milwaukee Leader*.
3. Bessie E. Buckley (1878–1962) worked for the Milwaukee public school system from 1902 to 1948 as a teacher, truant officer, and principal.
4. Edwin Schweers (b. 1898) was the stepson of Meta's sister, Hattie. He later worked as a salesman in Oshkosh, Wisconsin.

Meta to Doris and Elsa

Milwaukee, Wisconsin
November 20, [1918]

Dear Girls:—

You can see by the paper[1] that I am not at home & that I have been busy you must be thinking for I haven't written you this week.

I'll begin at the beginning to tell you the news.

We left Madison about 3 P.M. for we went into the capitol to see the building. All went well, very well until we reached 3 miles or so within Pewaukee's distance. Then our troubles began once more. The lights all went out one after another. At Pewaukee we bought the only light a garage had left and a few minutes after that one went out. Then we took the dash board light & put it into the spot light & that also went out. So we had to travel from near Pewaukee to Mil in the dark, the moon even having deserted us by hiding behind a cloud. Both Hi[2] & I sweat blood for what seemed like hours. But eventually we struck the concrete pavement & then I felt better. We got home in spite of all our troubles by 7.30 P.M. At 8 P.M I was in bed, spent with nervous excitement.

Monday A.M. I took the car down & found I had a flat tire. So I raised cane at two places. Now the lighting system is fixed. A lo[o]se wire caused all the trouble. It is a pity Hi with his entire machinists knowledge couldn't discover that.

The solid tire man is putting in two new solid tires.

Monday I spent looking after the car, having company for supper, fitting dresses for Miss Heipp, interviewing teachers in trouble & calling for papa & the depot.

By the way, will you please tell Emma C. that I went to Bedells. They are not willing to send the coat on approval. But if she desires the coat, (which I saw & think pretty but a little too costly) she can send her check for it. Then if she doesn't like the coat, she can send it back & they will refund the money to her. They merely want to protect themselves. They seem to be too new here for the other way. I saw other coats that I tho't quite as good looking and wished very much that Emma could have been here.

Well papa had a most interesting tho' nerve racking experience. I can't write you about it as all our mail is opened & watched.[3] How do I know this? Two letters which papa wrote to me & which he himself mailed with 4 cts stamps & in which he told me of his mission & his experience together with his opinions on the administration and war were expressed, never reached me at all. But suffice it to say, you have a really truly wonderful papa.

Yesterday, Tuesday I again bothered with the car, took papa around, went to a dinner at the city Club to here Frederic C Howe, shopped for Miss Heipp, had Mr. Howe & Aunt Clara[4] for supper & went to a schoolboard meeting. The meeting was very exciting as members want to deprive the use of buildings because of alleged seditious remarks made at one meeting under the auspices of a People's Council meeting. I never have gotten to bed before Midnight.

Today, Wed. I again took papa out, attended a luncheon here & before running again for Miss Heipp I am stopping long enough to write my two sweet girls.

Papa tho't I was a little extravagent to drive out to see you so soon but realized that the expenses incidental to the car could have come at any time.

Please write all of your letters on the typewriter Doris & don't forget to number the pages so papa can enjoy reading them.

Remember too that your studies are your first object for going to the "U" & that the work while necessary should not crowd out your good standing.

I see by Elsa's letter that she went to a social & had company home. I do not object to that but Elsa dear remember not to permit liberties even in the name of courtesy. You are a real sensible girl & will I know be careful when you understand. Much begins under the guise of courtesy & ends in familiarities & they always breed contempt. Boys & men always respect those girls who are honest courageous & self respecting and I know both you & Doris are that. So be careful sweet schnuckie & Dudd I know will be so too.

I don't want to preach & I know I don't have to. Be good & love

your own
Mama & Papa.

1. Meta wrote the letter on City Club of Milwaukee stationery.
2. Franklin Schweers, the stepson of Meta's sister, Hattie.
3. Berger testified before a congressional committee that his personal mail had been opened as early as April, 1918. See *Hearings,* 1:536–537.
4. Clara Hipke.

Meta to Doris and Elsa

Chicago, Illinois
[December 12, 1918]

Darling Girls:—

The prosecution has begun.[1] They charge awful things; things of which we never heard before,—such as underground railway system etc to Mexico.[2] They certainly have worked hard to build up a case.

Stedy opens this morning with his remarks.

I am so excited all the time that my heart seems much to[o] big for my body. Papa says tho' that they can't prove anything. I hope so. Be good girls & love us both hard.

Ever your
Mother.

1. Berger and his four co-defendants were tried before Judge Kenesaw Mountain Landis between December 9, 1918, and January 8, 1919. The defendants were charged with violating the Espionage Act through the publication of materials that, by "persistently dwelling upon the evils and horrors of war and of said war without mentioning any consideration in favor thereof," encouraged "insubordination, disloyalty and refusal of duty" in the military and obstructed the military's recruitment efforts. Berger was charged with having published five antiwar editorials in the *Milwaukee Leader* between June 20 and August 24, 1917. For a transcript of the trial, see *Hearings,* vol. 2. The indictment appears on pages 17–35.
2. The prosecution attempted to show that the Socialist Party had established a system to help draft dodgers escape to Mexico. See *Hearings,* 2:86–90.

Meta to Doris and Elsa

Chicago, Illinois
December 13, 1918[1]

Darling girls:—

I wish I could say when if at all you are to come to the trial. Your coming will depend entirely on developments both Stedy & Cochems say.

You see, only today, the fourth day of the trial have they finished the opening arguments which are mere perfunctory statements as to what the charge is & what each side expects to prove.

Of course it is interesting & if it didn't cost so much of your school time (practically about 3 weeks) & so much money, I [would] like to have you here the whole time. This case they will still have to prove a conspiracy.

The federal authorities have co-erced & cajoled & threatened these soldiers with courtmartial if they don't tell these things (Destroy these letters without fail).

How far the gov. has gone to prove a *case of conspiracy against* papa I *can't tell yet.* One thing is sure they *will go the* limit, & yet they won't prove it because it didn't exist.

Papa was certainly surprised at the evidence & testimony today.

Now as to your coming; I'll let you know as soon as I can. Go ahead & make all arrangements any how. I mean packing etc & studying for your exam. You may not come until your vacation. I know you are anxious but I don't see how I can help it.

It is after midnight & I must try to get some sleep. I'll speak to Cochems again tomorrow. But we aren't beginning to produce evidence yet. And I think I'd rather have you here at the close of this beastly trial.

Your letters pleased us much. I am glad Doris is doing so well mighty glad. Also Elsa's chemistry mark is fine. Keep it up. Good night girls.

Lovingly
Mama

1. The letter was dated Thursday, December 13; it apparently was written in the early hours of Friday, December 13.

Meta to Doris and Elsa

Milwaukee, Wisconsin
February 5, 1919

Dear Girls:

The past two days were again spent in the court room.[1] The same setting and atmosphere but not very interesting was the argument. In the first place Stedy took up the legal technicalities which he tho't were errors & discussed those. He cited case after case & other decisions. Furthermore he addressed the judge [and] so much was said in a conversational tone & consequently lost to us. He talked until about 4 P.M. Then Cochems started in & he talked until 6.30 P.M. when the court adjourned until the next day. Tuesday he talked again until noon making points that to him & to us appeared as errors. He made a fine argument & became most eloquent again in his appeal for a new trial. After luncheon Fleming[2] talked only about an hour & a half devoting much of this time to say that Nixon[3] lied & that the evidence against us was overwhelming. At 4 P.M. the case was closed. The judge gave the attorneys one week to get their records in shape & to take under advisement the arguments for the appeal.

My impression is that he will not grant a new trial. It would be an admission on his part that the case tried in his court & before him was full of errors. One newspaper man however said he had been reporting in that court for years & that for the first time he tho't Judge Landis appeared to be thinking about the arguments. He tho't it was a hopeful sign but he also doubted whether a new trial would be granted. Hunter[4] lost his job because he reported the case too favorably for us.

Now several things may happen & I am writing you to inform you as well as prepare you.

Next Tuesday the motion for a new trial will be made & probable denied. Then a motion for a stay of execution will be made by our side. This I understand means that they will ask the Judge not to pronounce sentense during the appealing of the case. This too will be denied & then the five defendants will be asked why they ought not to be sentenced. Each will probable have a statement to make. After which the judge pronounces sentence. Then a motion to place them under new bond will be made. This is the dangerous part. The district Attorney is going to argue against bond because he says that they are still continuing their propaganda. To this our answer will be that our charge was to obstruct recruiting & to create disloyalty in the army. Now since the war is over & no recruiting is going on we cannot continue our propaganda. Of course if they mean socialist propaganda which they heretofore have denied we were charged with, that's a different matter.

However it will be up to the Judge alone to say whether or not bond will be permissible. In the case he refuses then the men will be in the custody of the marshall & held until the records for the appeal are ready for the higher court as I understand it. If that takes too long the men might be sent away for a time. This is the worst feature that can happen but I am hoping that Judge Landis will permit bond. I can hardly believe that he would dare to do otherwise especially that the war is over. I told you this because they told it to me. But all say it would be the first case except the I.W.W. case in the history of this country. And in the I.W.W. case the Judge did it right after the verdict was given.[5]

Next Tuesday we will be in Chicago again. I truly believe it will take the routine way of cases.

I shall write to Connie[6] but dearest I have much to do & cannot promise much of a letter. Don't out wear your welcome at Aarons.[7] And be discreet in your school work. Why doesn't Elsa write.

Lovingly
Mama

Number your pages for Papa's sake.

1. The jury, after nearly six hours of deliberation, found Berger and his co-defendants guilty of violating the Espionage Act on January 8, 1919. The defendants returned to court prior to sentencing and attempted to obtain a new trial.

2. Joseph B. Fleming (1881–1970), a Chicago attorney, served as special assistant to the U.S. attorney general in the prosecution of war dissenters during World War I.

3. Thomas C. Nixon (b. 1865?), a Chicago electrical engineer, served on the jury that convicted Berger. He later told the court that the bailiff, W. H. Streeter, had said in the presence of the jurors, "Every damn one of those fellows is guilty and if I had my way I would hang every one of them." Nixon also reported that Streeter had said, "Berger is a damn lying Dutchman and ought to be in Hell." Other jurors testified that they had not heard the remarks, and Judge Landis denied the defense request for a new trial. See *Hearings*, 2:57. See also 2:698–721 for testimony regarding the charge of jury tampering.

4. Kent A. Hunter (1892–1958) was a reporter for the *Chicago Examiner*, 1915–1917 and 1919–1921, and for the *Chicago Tribune* between his two stints with the *Examiner*. Hunter later worked as a journalist in Los Angeles, New York, and Washington, D.C.

5. On August 31, 1918, Judge Landis imposed severe sentences on eighty-three members of the IWW who had been convicted of violating the Espionage Act.

6. Constance Burnham (Reel) (1898–1967), a classmate of Doris and Elsa's at the University of Wisconsin.

7. Albert W. Aron (1886–1945), who taught German at the University of Wisconsin from 1911 to 1919, and his wife, Margarete Schenk Aron.

Meta to Doris and Elsa

[Milwaukee, Wisconsin]
[February 22, 1919]

[Dar]ling Girls:—

Well, that day of sentence has passed.[1] [It] was a hard hard day. You helped me much by being such fine brave girls in Madison. A thousand times a day I thought of you & said Well the girls understand & will hold their heads up. The sentence wasn't our surprise. It really doesn't make much difference whether the sentence is for 5, 10 or 20 years. But our shock came when they asked us to double the $25,000 on the first & on the second bond; thus making us schedule $100,000 on each defendant. For a few moments we were absolutely stunned. The men were held in the marshall's room in the custody of the marshalls. They couldn't get bond. So the women got busy. We had five telephones busy, 2 in the federal building, one in Betty's room, one in our room & one in Howe's office. We could not get calls for out of town out of the federal building. That was one reason we couldn't get you easily. Mabel[2] finally went to another phone to call you as ours were all busy getting bonds. Then Miss O'Reilly[3] & I got into a taxi & went to labor meetings & socialist meetings & ask people who had property to go home & get the legal description of their property & get down to the Federal Building by 9.30 P.M. It was a herculuian task by [*one word missing*] but we went "over the top at 9.30." Then [came] the recording of the bonds men & signing [documents] & calling of oaths & then waited for the judg[e.] He finally came at 11 P.M. or a little after. [He] enjoined the defendants not to talk or write anything violating the Esp. act or to repeat their alleged offense. Of course this bond can be revoked if they violate the agreement.

Now Papa is going to Washington either Monday or Tuesday & I think I shall go with him. I believe I ought to see all those Senators & Congress men as well as go to New York & see the amnesty people in New York. You see I am building for future action in the event that I need to act. It will cost money but this is not the time to let a matter of $150 or $200 stand in the way. So I believe you will approve of that won't you?

Furthermore I shall go to Sheboygan tomorrow to tell the story of the trial at a huge meeting there. I shall from this moment dedicate my life to get amnesty for all.

I feel too excited and too worried to allow myself to feel tired. Be good girls & get your work done well & you will help me immensely.

Also give us the name of your farmer friend so we will know how to get him in case we need him. Also Doris go down & see Evjue[4] & get Evjue to introduce you to Crownhart[5] & ask him to support the amnesty resolution[6] which comes up for a hearing March 4. Also see if Evjue can get Fitsgerald[7] or any one from Madison to go & speak.

I want to write more so will close. With the [most] devoted love I am always your

Mother.

1. On February 20, 1919, Judge Landis sentenced Berger and his co-defendants to twenty years in prison. The defendants immediately appealed to Judge Samuel Alschuler of the U.S. Court of Appeals, who set bail at $100,000 for each man. The U.S. Supreme Court, by a six to three vote, overturned the conviction on January 31, 1921.
2. Probably Mabel Search.
3. Probably Mary O'Reilly (1874?–1950), a Chicago teacher and one of the founders of the Chicago Teachers Federation.
4. William T. Evjue (1882–1970) was the founder and publisher of the *Capital Times,* a progressive Madison, Wisconsin, newspaper. He served in the Wisconsin Assembly, 1917–1919.
5. Charles H. Crownhart (1863–1940) was a progressive Republican attorney from Madison, Wisconsin, who managed Robert M. La Follette Sr.'s senatorial campaigns in 1910 and 1916. Crownhart served as chairman of the Wisconsin Industrial Commission, 1911–1915, and as a justice of the Wisconsin Supreme Court, 1922–1930.
6. Albert C. Ehlman, a Socialist from Milwaukee, introduced a resolution in the Wisconsin Assembly on February 6, 1919, calling for amnesty for all political prisoners in the United States and for repeal of the Espionage Act. The assembly defeated the resolution by a sixty-four to twenty vote on June 27, 1919.
7. Probably Milwaukee businessman William N. Fitzgerald, who served as the state's fuel administrator during World War I.

Meta to Doris and Elsa

[Milwaukee, Wisconsin]
[March 12, 1919]

Darling Girls:—

Papa has gone. He left yesterday but not before he got your "goodbye" letter. That was tho'tful & nice of you both. I will leave in 15 minutes to meet him in Chicago.

Since seeing you last I have had a conference with Cochems. We have decided that he is to go down to Washington too. You see—the Mil. Journal printed a news item yesterday in which the procedure to be followed in *preventing* papa from taking the *oath* of office was given. As soon as Wisconsin members are to take the oath a gentleman of the house is to say "I object to Mr. Berger taking the oath" where upon the clerk of the house[1] (who by the way has engineered the whole thing expecting to hold his job with the republican house altho' he is a democrate) will ask papa to step aside. Then a committee will be appointed with instructions to proceed with a hearing & a date set for final action.

I tho't possibly Cochems & La Follette etc. could find a way to prevent that in as much as I cannot see the right one member has to forbid another his taking the oath of office. Well we shall see! Also this same clerk of the House has held back papa's clerk line he having that matter in charge. Oh! we shall no doubt have an interesting time.

Be sure to destroy my letters. Don't leave them about for curious eyes to see. And there are many such, believe me. Not only curious eyes, but willing spies.

Now be good girls for me. I am so glad that I feel sure I do not need to worry about you at least.

Josie wants a letter. She says she will not send any more boxes (either of foods or hats) unless she hears from you. So you had better get busy quick.

I will write as often as possible. You are entitled to know what progress we make. I feel that papa is just going to make another period in the history of the socialist movement. I would much rather it would be a "dash" either in or out of Congress than a long deliberation. I'd like an election while the peace terms are still *warm.*

Be good & love us both as hard as you can. Ever your loving

Mother

1. South Trimble (1864–1946) served as clerk of the U.S. House of Representatives, 1911–1919 and 1931–1946, and as a Democratic congressman from Kentucky, 1901–1907. When the Republican-controlled House convened on May 19, 1919, it replaced Trimble with William Tyler Page.

Meta to Doris and Elsa

Milwaukee, Wisconsin
[April 5, 1919]

Dear Girls:—

Well this has been another rush week and so far every thing went according to schedule. Tuesday was the eventful election. You should have seen the women flock to the polls with the little pink "good government" slip in their hands. The priests & nuns did their share nobly also. The result was that on Tuesday 38,400 *women* alone voted. Heretofore only about 800 or 1,000 were interested enough to vote. But this time 38,400 came out.[1] Of this number the socialists had about 13,400 votes from women. That was not bad. But of course thro' the other 25,000 women we lost the election altho' our votes increased from 19,000 or 20,000 to 38,600 votes. We polled 42.5% of the school board vote at that; and 46.6% of the judicial vote. You can see the hand-writing on the wall can't you? And so do our opponents.

We always knew that if the women ever got the vote, we would receive a set-back. The poor dears haven't read much you see. Our work now is to educate our women at least.

The teachers also went back on us beautifully. If I wasn't so very tired nights I'd lie awake trying to think of how I could get even with them. But I can't, I always fall asleep.

Last night we had Buech's,[2] and Ameringers[3] up for supper. Mrs Ameringer is here from Rhinelander so I invited them & thus squared myself there. Wednesday I went to Chicago to see Germer & Barnes. I've asked them to start a nationwide protest movement against unseating papa & thus disfranchising the third political party in Congress. Let see how well they do it. Papa & I have not yet decided when he goes East but I hope it is soon.

Tomorrow, Nettie[4] entertains the Club at our house. So that fills the week pretty full doesn't it? Papa was most pleased with your letter. But I really think Doris is forgetting the little German she knew. You had better try to write oftener to keep up your practice.

I've been watching the Liberator to see if they printed your article. But nothing doing on that. Instead they printed one by Giovinetti[5] the Italian I.W.W. in which he takes a fearful wrap at papa. In the first place he lied & he made papa out a coward. I think the Eastman's horrid & mean & jealous. I would suggest that you read the article & then write them asking them to return your manuscript. We have pushed the Liberator until we ordered 150 for our newsstand, but yesterday we sent them all back with a letter. Tucker said that John Reed[6] called the two Eastmans "high class grafters". I guess they are that all right. Three years ago he support[ed] Wilson, now he helps knock Berger. Giovinetti also is a turn coat. He left this country at the beginning of he war & tried to enlist in the Italian army. They wouldn't have him because he was too fat & now he thinks he can square *himself* by knocking Berger. Well dears Elsa & Doris write often & love your

Mama

1. Beginning in 1901 Wisconsin permitted women to vote in school board elections. During the 1919 election, the *Milwaukee Journal* and the Good Government League launched a campaign encouraging women to vote against the Socialists.

2. Robert and Theresa Buech.

3. Oscar Ameringer (1870–1943), an editor and satirist, came to Milwaukee from Oklahoma in 1910 and worked as an organizer for the Socialist Party and as a writer for the *Milwaukee Leader*. He became one of Victor Berger's closest friends and ran as a Socialist for governor of Wisconsin in 1914 and for Congress in 1918. After World War I, Ameringer returned to Oklahoma City, where he published the *Oklahoma Leader* and later the *American Guardian*. Lulu Wood Ameringer (b. 1873?) was Oscar's first wife. The couple divorced during the 1920s.

4. Annette Rosenthal (Gould).

5. Arturo Giovannitti (1884–1959), an Italian immigrant, was an advocate of revolutionary syndicalism and the IWW prior to World War I. After the war,

Giovannitti worked as a labor organizer and writer for leftist periodicals. The April, 1919, issue of the *Liberator* printed Giovannitti's "Scott Nearing Reprieves Democracy," which criticized the way Berger disassociated himself from the IWW during his Chicago trial.

6. John Reed (1887–1920), a radical journalist, wrote for Max Eastman's *The Masses* and covered the Mexican revolution and World War I in eastern Europe. Reed lived in Russia in 1917–1918 and after his return to America published his account of the Russian Revolution in *Ten Days That Shook the World* (1919). Reed and other left-wingers split from the Socialist Party in August, 1919, and subsequently formed the Communist Labor Party. Indicted for sedition, Reed escaped to Russia, where he died.

Meta to Doris and Elsa

Milwaukee, Wisconsin
April 9, 1919

Dear Girls:—

That was an awfully mean thing for the house president or who ever it was to do. I mean to report you to the Dean. What in Heaven's name were you charged with having done. Write me the particulars. I am glad however that Miss Nardin[1] could understand your side too.

Why doesn't Elsa write? I do not even know her marks yet? Doesn't she think I am interested in her? Or doesn't she love me any more?

I have sent the books to Agnes's[2] brother but I have forgotten Connie's[3] address. So please send it to me again.

Papa & I spent 2 days in Chicago again. We want to have some one go to Washington to present our case to Mr Palmer[4] while he is reviewing Espionage cases. I do not believe that we ought to let the impression stand that Simons, Russell & Bloodgood gave about papa. So I am trying to get some one who knows the case & papa, preferably Cochems & some one else to go down to see Palmer. Stedy tho't it a good idea.

We are informed that the Wisconsin cases will not be tried until the Chicago case is settled.[5] I hope that is true. I saw it in the papers.

While in Chicago, Mr. Plummer[6] came up & shook hands with me. He seemed very friendly, told me he was the only one working on the case and that he wouldn't over work. (destroy this letter) That was a sort of a hint that he wasn't going to push the case. I was as friendly to him as I could be.

While in Chicago I bought a black silk dress. Now I am afraid I won't like it. It is so very black.

Papa and I expect to go East next week. We will be gone 10 days at least. I'll let you know definitely when we go etc.

A box of Keeley's came yesterday for Josie.

Franklin[7] also came yesterday. He is leaving for Shawano tomorrow. He looks fine. Talks more than he used to, but doesn't seem to know much more except of course his own experiences.

Please write me a letter telling me in detail about that report to Miss Nardin and Elsa you write & tell me your marks. Don't get out of the habit of writing home. With love to my two darling girls I am always your
Mother

1. F. Louise Nardin (1878–1970) served as dean of women at the University of Wisconsin, 1918–1931.
2. Agnes Ames Hiss of Lake Mills, Wisconsin, was a classmate of Doris and Elsa's at the University of Wisconsin.
3. Constance Burnham (Reel).
4. A. Mitchell Palmer ·(1872–1936), the U.S. attorney general, 1919–1921, vigorously prosecuted radicals during the Red Scare of 1919–1920. Palmer had previously served as a Democratic representative from Pennsylvania, 1909–1915.
5. Berger was indicted under the Espionage Act in Milwaukee on October 28, 1918, and in La Crosse, Wisconsin, on December 3, 1918. Neither case came to trial.
6. Lorenzo T. Plummer worked for the Bureau of Investigation, Department of Justice, beginning in April, 1917, and searched the Socialist Party headquarters in Chicago in September of that year. He appeared as a government witness at Berger's trial.
7. Franklin Schweers, the stepson of Meta's sister, Hattie, had returned from serving in World War I.

Meta to Doris and Elsa

Milwaukee, Wisconsin
April 22, 1919

My dear Girls:—

Josie & I are wondering whether or not you or Agnes called for a box of food which we sent you at Lake Mills. It was addressed to Agnes Hiss c/o Mrs. E Wegemann. Josie baked a cake specially for Easter and had boiled eggs, fresh tomatoes, olives, & cream cheese in it. The box itself weighed 7 lbs and cost quite a little to get up & to send. So let us know whether you did as I said & called at the Post Office for it. We had it sent insured and asked for a return receipt. This has not yet arrived therefore we have our doubts.

Inclosed is a copy of a letter sent to papa by Max Eastman.[1] The letter in itself is O.K. but Germer told us he had written quite a different letter, an angry letter to St John Tucker[2] in reply to Tucker's letter. To Tucker he blamed V.L.B. for repudiating Bill Haywood.

Now papa has never endorsed Haywood's policy & therefore couldn't repudiate him. However it is true Eastman & papa have always differed on I.W.W.ism. The inclosed letter does in a way make up for the nasty article and now I am anxious to see what the next Liberator will do.[3]

Sunday; Papa and I drove Ameringer, Betty & Emma Glaser[4] down to a meeting in Waukegan. The day was fine in the morning but in the afternoon we were frightfully cold all the way home. We found out that it is a bit too early for long cross-country drives. But the car ran perfectly.

Yesterday "Milwaukee's Own" 340th regiment returned from France. They were hero-ized to death & yet not any of them had been in battle anymore than had Franklin.[5] Walter Haessler[6] came home with this groupe.

Howard Eaton wants to organize for the socialist Party this summer. He put in his application with S. Ameringer.[7] I didn't know he was a Socialist before. I got a nice letter from Carl Haessler. He says a great many C.O's have already been released especially the Molakans.[8] They are the Russian C.O. I was astonished as to how well Carl was informed about world doings & events.

Last night when I got home for supper Mick, Frank, Hi. & Edwin[9] were at the house. They took 3 new cars with them to Shawano today. If it weren't for the fact that I am going to give a "coffee" tomorrow for the women who helped me in the campaign I might have gone along.

I am sending you also the inclosed clipping because I think Putnam sized the situation up about right. Tell me what you think of it & Eastman's letter.

Papa is in Chicago today. I hope he brings good news tomorrow. I think he went to see Arthur B——[10] & a certain Senator.

Write (*both* of you) & tell me how you enjoyed your 3 days at the lake & remember to love your

Own Mama.

Also write Aunt Matilda.[11]

1. Max Eastman wrote to Victor Berger on April 17, 1919, apologizing for a critical article by Arturo Giovannitti that appeared in the April issue of the *Liberator* (see Meta to Doris and Elsa, April 5, 1919, above). Eastman stated that he disagreed with the way Berger disassociated himself from the IWW but added, "so far as your personal courage and truth to your opinions on this stand goes, I do not question it." A copy of Eastman's letter is in the Berger Papers, SHSW.

2. Irwin St. John Tucker (1886–1982), an Episcopal minister since 1912, served as associate editor of the *Christian Socialist,* 1914–1916, and as literature director of the Socialist Party for six weeks in the summer of 1917. In 1919 Tucker was convicted with Berger and three others for violating the Espionage Act. He later served as the religion editor of the *Chicago Herald-American,* 1924–1954.

3. The May, 1919, issue of the *Liberator* ran an apology for Arturo Giovannitti's article criticizing Berger. The unsigned piece said, "It is a good deal to ask a man to be a martyr for his own beliefs. To ask him to be a martyr for the beliefs of those who have roasted him all their lives for disagreeing with them, is too much."

4. Emma Glaeser (b. 1888) worked as a cashier for the *Milwaukee Leader* between 1916 and 1930.

5. Franklin Schweers, the stepson of Meta's sister, Hattie.

6. Walter Haessler (1890–1973), the brother of Carl Haessler, headed his family's Milwaukee hardware company from the mid-1920s until his death.

7. Siegfried Ameringer (b. 1895?) was the son of Oscar and Lulu Ameringer.

8. Thirty-four Molokans (members of a pacifist sect also known as Spiritual Christians) from Arizona refused to register for the draft and were sentenced in August, 1917, to a year in prison. After ten months, twenty-eight of the men agreed to register and were released. The remaining six were inducted into the army as noncombatants and then were court-martialed and sentenced to prison terms ranging from fifteen to twenty-five years. The Wilson administration began to release conscientious objectors in January, 1919; the Molokans were freed in April.

9. Frank Schweers, Meta's brother-in-law, and his sons, Franklin ("Hi") and Edwin.

10. Arthur Brisbane.

11. Victor's sister, Mathilde Berger Weingarten.

Meta to Doris and Elsa

Milwaukee, Wisconsin
[April 26, 1919]

Dear Girls:—

Both Papa & I were so glad to hear from *both.*

The Socialist social must have been interesting according to Doris's account. Why doesn't Elsa also go to these affairs. It would help Elsa a lot to imbibe some tho'ts which she otherwise wouldn't get.

As to your childish quarrels:—Let me caution you girls about being too vehement in maintaining your point of view. Don't get into quarrels and thus endanger perfectly good friendships. Life is too short & too serious. It is hard to get good friends. If you have them make some efforts and sacrifices to keep them.

This week has been a rather dull and dreary one at home. Papa went to Chicago but brought no special news home with him. The so-called "left-wing" or bolshivik group here in the city threatens to make trouble. They are trying to organize a communist club here to correspond with the Lloyd, Ferguson,[1] & radical group in Chicago. Just at present the members of the Socialist party are voting on whether or not to hold a national party convention now or not.[2] Papa is opposed to this at this time because he says that a convention *must* be held next year anyway preparatory to a National presidential campaign. He furthermore says that no good would come by holding a convention now when the Espionage act is still in force. The trouble is these radicals do not believe in *political action* but want *direct* action at once. They think they can get hold of all industries by a revolution *now.* Poor fools! They can't even get a strike up much less a revolution.

The trouble is they are in the wrong party since the Socialist Party is a *political* party.

I suppose you will hear about that in Madison too.

While papa was in Chicago, I took Mable & Maud[3] out for a long ride & then they took me down town for a supper. We had quite a party.

Today I sent out Papa's letter to the Congressmen.[4] I will send you one when I get back to the office. I think it is quite good & certainly uncompromising. I wonder what kind of an impression it will make among the Congressmen.

Josie is sending another big box of food today. Tell me this; how much of Barnard Hall do we feed?

Next Wednesday we are invited to dinner at the Babcock's. Now I guess I've written all the news, at least I seem to think so.

Be good girls, & write often to me. I still do not know what Elsa's marks are. See if you can't find out.

With love to you from both papa & me I am always

Devotedly your
Mother.

Read the story of Kate R. O'Hare[5] in Saturday's Leader.

1. Isaac Ferguson (1888–1964), a Chicago attorney and personal secretary to William Bross Lloyd, served as secretary of the National Council of the Left Wing Section of the Socialist Party. In 1919 Ferguson and other members of his faction broke from the Socialist Party and helped form the Communist Party. Ferguson was indicted for criminal anarchy the same year and subsequently was convicted. He left the communist movement following his release from prison and returned to his law practice in Chicago.

2. Through much of 1919, the right and left wings of the Socialist Party fought bitterly over control of the organization, leaving it badly splintered. Despite Berger's opposition, the party called an emergency convention, which convened on August 30, 1919, in Chicago. After left-wing members failed to win control of the convention, they bolted and formed the Communist Labor Party. Other left-wingers who had previously broken with the party attended the convention of the Communist Party, which met in Chicago at the same time.

3. Mabel Search and Maud McCreery.

4. *Open Letter from Victor L. Berger Elected from the 5th District of Wisconsin to the National House of Representatives (66th Congress) Addressed to His Colleagues in Congress* (Milwaukee, 1919) was a twenty-two-page pamphlet written by Berger in which he argued that he was entitled to his seat in the House and that his trial and conviction resulted from an attempt to suppress the Socialist Party.

5. Kate Richards O'Hare (1876–1948) joined the Socialist Party in 1901 and lectured and organized on its behalf for a quarter century. She served on the party's National Executive Committee, chaired the committee that drafted the 1917 antiwar platform, and edited, with her husband Frank, the *National Rip-Saw*. She was convicted of violating the Espionage Act and served fourteen months of a five-year prison term in 1919–1920. Meta Berger was referring to "Meta Lilienthal Pays Tribute to Mrs. Kate O'Hare," *Milwaukee Leader*, April 26, 1919, which advocated O'Hare's release from prison.

Meta to Doris and Elsa

[Washington, D.C.]
May 20, 1919

Dear Girls:—

Yesterday's procedure went off according to schedule. Congressman Dallinger[1] of Mass. moved that Mr. Berger be not sworn in and that the question of seating him be referred to a committee. Papa tried several times to get the floor but was either told that was not the "proper time" or was not recognized when the time came. Gag rule was King yesterday. There was absolutely no demonstration except for a feeble effort of two democrats (probably from the south) who got off just two claps & then subsided.

The saddest thing of the whole affair was that not a *single voice* was raised in *protest*. Every body says the same thing even those who were there and didn't raise their own voices. But I believe every body was surprised with the quickness with which the Speaker put the question and it carried (by acclamation).

My impression is that papa hasn't a ghost of a chance. But of course I realize he must make the fight. The whole matter now rests with some committee & who is on that we do not know. The Speaker Mr. Gillette[2] told papa he [would] like to settle it at once, and Mr. Mondell[3] the floor leader of the Republicans says if he had his way he would defer action until after the Courts had rendered their decisions [and] in the meantime however get the facts of the case. If this committee goes into it thoroughly we will have another trial all over again.

We had another conference with the Senior Sen.[4] Also with Fred. C. Howe of New York. We will see them again tonight.

Mr. Doyle,[5] (Miss Hogarth's husband) is playing here & telephoned us to come to see him play & to go to dinner with him. We will do that Wednesday afternoon.

I expect to stay here until Friday or Sat. & then go up to New York for a few days to see what I can do there. Then I'll come back here. So address letters to either the House Office Building or the Congress Hall Hotel.

It is another case of "keep a stiff upper lip again."

Well one thing they cannot spoil for us & that is the love we have for one another.

Lovingly Mama.

1. Frederick William Dallinger (1871–1955) served as a Republican representative from Massachusetts, 1915–1925 and 1926–1932, and as a judge of the U.S. Customs Court, 1932–1942. Dallinger chaired the committee that investigated Berger's eligibility to sit in Congress.

2. Frederick H. Gillett (1851–1935) served as a Republican representative from Massachusetts, 1893–1925, as Speaker of the House, 1919–1925, and as a U.S. senator, 1925–1931.

3. Franklin Mondell (1860–1939) served as a Republican representative from Wyoming, 1895–1897 and 1899–1923, and as House majority leader, 1919–1923.

4. Robert M. La Follette Sr.

5. Leonard Doyle (1893?–1959), an actor, had a small role in Eugene Walter's *Poor Little Sheep*, a play about the love affair between the daughter of an affluent New England family and a wounded American aviator who found himself drawn into the impending class conflict on his return from the war.

Meta to Doris and Elsa

[Washington, D.C.]
[May 22, 1919]

Dear Girls:—

We have been here a week and a day & so far have not had a single line from you. What is the trouble? In my very first letter I asked [you] to address us c/o Congress Hall Hotel. Even if you address it House Office Building we would get it. Papa wanted to wire to see if all is well.

We are not making much progress here. Even papa's official status is not definitely settled. Although the rules of the House declare that during a contest over a seat the contested Congress man while he may not have a seat (voice & vote) he enjoys all other privileges. So far we haven't had any. Papa has an office assigned to him but a Mr. Ayres[1] of Kansas is still in it & doesn't seem to be in any hurry to move out. The clerks & door keepers here are very hostile & so far have refused us our requests unless ordered to do so by the Speaker. Now it is very embarrassing to have to go to the Speaker for everything. You know what effect that would have on Papa.

The papers here are also vicious. The Post says it is an "effrontary and an *indecency*" for Berger to ask the House to seat him. And so it goes on day after day.

We had, however a very pleasant evening at the Senior Senator's[2] home the other day. Fred. C. Howe of N.Y. was there. It was pleasant but we did not agree on a line of action.

I expect to go to New York tomorrow & leave papa here. I shall of course go to Bridgeport Sunday & see the folks. Will return to Washington by Wednesday of next week.

Mr. Doyle (Leona Hogarth's husband) is playing here this week. He invited us to come to the play Wed—Matinee. It is a Socialistic play giving the worst of course to the Socialists but not without putting some of our idealism in it. Also the capitalist politicians do not escape criticism. Not bad for this time of after war psychology. Write me a long long sweet loving letter so it will be here when I return from New York.

Lovingly
Mama

1. William Ayres (1867–1952) served as a Democratic representative from Kansas, 1915–1921 and 1923–1934, and as a member of Federal Trade Commission, 1934–1952.
2. Robert M. La Follette Sr.

Victor to Meta

Washington, D.C.
May 26, 1919

My sweet Schatzl:

I did not write any letter to you yesterday—because I did not know the address of the Rand School. You did not miss much however; since there is no news here at all.

I understand the election committee, which has my case will hold its first meeting tomorrow. I am not invited to that meeting. They will simply agree on the form of the complaint and on some mode of procedure.

I am trying to get some furniture into my office. The typewriter they gave me, is an old model and no good. They took out all the book cases, save one little one—and also the big filing case. The room looks, as if some (imaginary) Huns had ransacked it. I am trying to get some furniture from an unwilling and hostile set of underlings. By the time you get back I hope to be able to offer you a comfortable chair in my office.

Also made arrangements for a stenographer for two hours every day; i.e from 4–6 P.M. This is not a very convenient time because it is the time when they clean the offices. But Miss Kasemarck[1] (she is a Wisconsin girl and hails from Ashland) works in the War department—Miss Sasanli got her for me—cannot come any earlier. I pay her $10.00 per week to start with—so you see it is infinitely cheaper than to get work done by "the folio".

Have made arrangements also with the United press to carry about 300 words every day while "the case" is on. Must have the 300 words ready every day at 12 A.M. or rather at 12 M. Have not seen (or heard from) the Call correspondent as yet.

Had a letter from Rehfeld telling me that he had sent out a tracer for [the] bundle of Open Letters but has received no answer so far. He has sent another bundle.

There was a little trouble in our printing office i.e. the newspaper composing room, where the men led by Schurr and Milton[2] asked for considerable more wages than the other newspapers pay. They finally got an increase of about $2.00 per week above the scale—and since they work half an hour per day less in our office than in any other Milwaukee newspaper—you can readily see what we are up against.

Hope you had a pleasant time in Bridgeport—and that the folks (especially Grandpa and Mathilde)[3] enjoyed your visit.

Tried to find a report of the meeting held in the Madison Square Garden in this mornings New York papers—but did not see a line. Did you meet Dr. Magnes after the meeting?

Well, sweet Schatzl—this is about all—except that ich Dich imer noch unendlich lieb hab'.[4] You are the best and noblest part of

Victor L. Berger

1. Probably Mary Kazamek, a Washington, D.C., stenographer.
2. Probably John Schurr Jr., a machinist, and Ralph Milton, a linotype operator.
3. Victor's father, Ignatz, and his sister, Mathilde Berger Weingarten.
4. I still love you immensely.

Victor to Meta

Washington, D.C.
May 27, 1919

My sweet Schatzl:

The Open Letters came finally—and both packages came this morning—so that I am now abundantly supplied. Have made arrangements with the postmaster of the house office building to put a copy of my Open Letter into the box of every member.

Have sent you about two dozen Open Letters (under a special delivery stamp) to the Rand School.

The Clerk of the Election Contest Committee No 1 has just telephoned me that the first hearing of my case will be heard on June 11th and that I am to notify Cochems to that effect. Shall do so at once. The trouble is only that Cochems has the case of the man who ran over the woman and children on Wells & 12th street and that I cannot see how he can find the time to properly prepare himself for my case.[1] The committee notified me that the case will be taken up from the bottom *without any regard for the judicial end of it.* I don't know of course, what this is to mean. It may be that they are afraid to permit the courts to fix the elegibility of men to congress by indicting them or finding them guilty—and that the committee prefers to do "its own lynching" in this case.

Well, sweet Schatzl, my office—though still the most dilapidated in the building—is slowly getting into working condition. I now have the necessary stationary and it seems I shall be permitted even the use of my franking privilege—until the case is decided.

By the way while you are there—you might also look up the Public (122. E 37th), which has a very weak article on "Congress and Mr. Berger"[2]—give them a copy of my Open Letter and also a copy of the letter Mr. Shewalter[3] sent me from Indepen[den]ce Mo.—and with which not only Cochems, but every lawyer agrees—namely: that while the House of Representatives is the sole judge of the qualifications of its members—these qualifications are plainly stated in the constitution of the United States and the House can neither take from them nor add to them.

These qualifications are 25 years of age—a citizen for at least seven years—and citizen of the state from which I was elected.

The House is the *sole* judge whether I have complied with *these* qualifications—the rest is contained in my election certificate. Kindly make this plain to the editor of the Public.

Otherwise, there is not much news here. I may have to go home to get all the papers and documents in my case. I[t] would be a "flying trip." You might go home with me, Schatzl—and stay with the Leader, which, after all is the main important matter.

I was very glad to see that you are doing such good and important work in New York. Trachtenberg[4] invited me to speak in Madison Square Garden in New York on June 8th. As a rule I have declined all these invitations—this one I have accepted.

With infinite love for my sweet Schatzl, I am ever your

V.L.B.

1. See Victor to Meta, September 17, 1919, below.
2. *The Public,* a weekly liberal journal, ran an editorial favoring Berger's seating in the House (May 24, 1919, 536).
3. Joseph D. Shewalter (1856–1925), a Missouri attorney and constitutional historian, sent Berger a copy of his May 20, 1919, letter to Frederick Dallinger in which he argued that Berger's exclusion from the House was unconstitutional. For Shewalter's letter, see the enclosure in Berger to member of Congress, July, 1919, Berger Papers, SHSW.
4. Alexander Trachtenberg (1884–1966), a Russian immigrant, received a Ph.D. in economics from Yale University and taught at the Rand School. Although he welcomed the Bolshevik Revolution, he remained active in the Socialist Party until 1921, when he resigned to join the Workers Party. From 1924 until 1962, Trachtenberg ran International Publishers, the largest Marxist publishing house in the United States.

Meta to Doris and Elsa

Washington, D.C.
June 2, 1919

Dear Girls,

A new situation has arisen since I wrote you yesterday. We are going to proceed to New York as we had planned, but we may not be able to go home from there as we wanted to. The reason is this,—Mr. Gallenger[1] refuses to postpone the hearing which is set for June 11, and that means that we must return to Washington for that. We are however hoping that we may be able to secure some time between that hearing and the next one so that we [can] come west then. I do not know yet what is best for me to do, shall I stay here with papa or shall I go home.

This afternoon I am to see the Senior Senator[2] and ask him to come to Milwaukee to speak at a protest meeting. We want to get a Republican and a Democrat and a socialist if possible all to speak at the same meeting. If I succeed won't that be fine? I am going to do my best to try. Dudley F. Malone said he would come some time in the third week in June.

I spend most of my time in Washington in Papa's office while he is out on some business. I wait here to see people when they come and to do such things as he wants me to.

The weather continues beastly hot. We are going to change our room if we have to stay here. I have been telephoning all day to addresses given in the add columns.

Papa is disappointed at your apparent indifference as shown by your lack of writing. Please write more regularly. With much love from both of us and the hopes that your examines will go through all right I am always your own

Mother.

1. Thomas Gallagher (1850–1930), a Democratic representative from Illinois, 1909–1921.
2. Robert M. La Follette Sr.

Meta to Doris

Washington, D.C.
July 24, 1919

Dear Duddie,—

The fourth morning of the hearings has passed. So far the main question debated was the right of the House to take the action it did in denying Papa the right to take the oath. The committee has decided against us on that, i.e. it refuses to put the question up to the House itself as to the Constitutionality of the House in its act.

Now we are proceeding to the main question of disloyalty. Our plan is to show that the position of the Socialists the world over is the same and that Papa could not do differently and remain a Socialist. And that while he did not support the war with enthusiasm he did nothing to hinder the progress of the administration in the carrying out of its schemes.

The committee is very hostile as evidenced by the questions ask[ed] and by the kind way they are careful to see that McLogan,[1] Carny's lawyer, has every opportunity to answer or get his chance. The committee is very anxious to finish the hearings next week, whether they do this no one knows yet. You see the House is going to take a vacation for four weeks in August and they want to get through with this. If they do; then when they meet again they will probably be ready to report to the House and so deprive Papa of his seat. We will then have to plunge right into a campaign again. So you see there is a great chance that we shall be home in August.

Washington has been very much excited about the race riots here lately.[2] You see some time ago it is alledged that a colored man attacked several white women. This may be so. One woman is said to have died from the effects. The newspapers have been continuously printing sensational stuff about it until the white people are very much exercised about it. The result is that some of the soldiers; well fed and with nothing to do, came into town the other night looking for excitment and began to attack the colored men indiscrimintely. The colored people began to fight back and the result was a fine race riot with seven or eight dead and many more wounded. The next night the same thing occured with the same results. What those useless soldiers boys did, was to create a hatred among the colored people which will take years to overcome. And then they did not get the guilty one. It was very exciting here. White people as well as colored were asked not to come down town. But the town was full of young men and boys who just bristled with trouble.

Yesterday after the meeting in the morning we took a half day off and drove over to Baltimore. The ride was nice but the city of Baltimore certainly is the worst city I have ever been in. It is so unattractive and so un-beautiful. Why even Washington looked good to me even under the present circumstances.

You do not seem to write every day. Are you kept so busy that you cannot send us a daily message? In your next letter tell me something of your plans about Yellowstone and your return home.

Elsa also says that she has not had a word from you for weeks.[3] Please write to her.

I cannot tell how anxious I am to get home now. It takes almost a week for a letter to reach us here. So figure out that by the beginning of August or at least at the end of the first week in August we may possibly be home and direct your letters there after that. That is all for today. Be a good girl darling. And give my gratitude to your hostess for her great kindness to you.

With love from both Papa and myself I am your devoted

Mother.

1. Milwaukee attorney Harry R. McLogan (1881–1939) represented Democrat Joseph P. Carney during the hearings. Carney, who finished second in the general election, unsuccessfully claimed that he should be seated in Berger's

place. McLogan later served as a Milwaukee circuit court commissioner, 1921–1933, and as a member of the Wisconsin Industrial Commission, 1933–1939.

2. Spurred on by sensational news accounts warning of threats to white women, a race riot took place in Washington between July 19 and July 22. At least seven people died and nearly one hundred people sought hospital treatment.

3. Doris spent June–July, 1919, traveling in the American West with her friend, Agnes Hiss. Elsa had a summer teaching job in Milwaukee.

Victor to Meta

Washington, D.C.
September 15, 1919

My sweet Schatzl:

I arrived here Sunday morning—spending the day before on a smoky and dirty B & O train reading and clipping newspapers.

Got a room in Congress Hall hotel on the first floor, just above the kitchen, with one window and even that facing a brick wall in the court. I am glad for your sake that you are not with me. You are so sensitive about "smells"—and especially kitchen odors. The clerk promised to give me a better room as soon as one becomes vacant.

Spent all day Sunday until 12 o'clock (midnight) in my office practically re-writing my entire speech. Cochems came in for a few minutes with his friend Dr. Fowle,[1] both left and I saw nothing further of them all day.

All the members of the committee were present today except Eagle.[2] After a few preliminary skirmishes, I read my statement of which I will send you a copy. Cochems occupied the rest of the forenoon and all afternoon. He outdid himself in oratory, and if he could train himself to be a little more careful as to the *exactness* of his statements—which would be just as strong and even stronger if exact—he could not be equalled as a jury lawyer. As it was—that Democratic pinhead Welty[3] tripped him up once or twice. But on the whole—this was a record day for Henry.

Our friend Dallinger got the clerk of the Appealate court here from Chicago with some exhibits, and also the U.S. District attorney of the Northern district, Mr. Charles Kline[4] to explain and defend the Chicago trial. And all of this, after Dallinger had repeatedly declared that the Chicago trial would not be considered at all in these hearings. Well, Dallinger is evidently desparate.

Voight[5] told Cochems that he had it on good authority that we had five men of that committee. I don't believe it. I can see only three. Cole[6] is still doubtful, and Robinson,[7] to judge from his attitude today, is even more than doubtful. And positively hostile, with a sneering grin on his face and his back turned to the speaker—that was the position of Randall[8] of Kenosha. We may get *four* men—it would [be] nothing short of a miracle, if we did get Robinson also. We, therefore, better get ready for a re-election. They will never again try to unseat me, (even if I only get a minority report of that committee) in case I am re-elected.

I am rather worried about a secretary. I don't want Alma[9] to come here and spend all that money for railroad fare when I do not know how long I will stay.

On the other hand I cannot have Alma draw a salary for doing nothing in Milwaukee. She had three months at $120.00 "per"—which shows that I am a friend indeed.

Nevertheless I must have somebody here for a few hours every day. That will cost money. And if anybody is to draw money in Milwaukee on account of good intentions—it is going to be my Schatzl. Therefore, I will ask Alma to resign by October—and make you her regular heir and successor. Don't tell her—it is just barely possible that no one will ever find it out. Most all congressmen have their wives or daughters as secretaries—Voight and Mason[10] among others.

I intend to do positive missionary work among the congressmen—especially among the Republicans, although Gillette who is my main adversary, is a Republican. I will point out that during the entire war the Democratic party has succeeded in making the Republican party trail behind Wilson, and in doing the dirty work for Wilson. Of course, the fact is, the Republican party (before 1916) was as always the favorite mouth-piece of the trusts and high financiers. It was even more pro-war than the Democratic party. But "big business"—when it found out that with the help of House,[11] McAdoo,[12] Burleson etc. it could also have the Democrats—naturally—"played safe". It endorsed Wilson and made the "war cry" unanimous—so far as the capitalist parties are concerned. Wilson very soon outdid any Republican in war fervor and furnished all sorts of high sounding phrases for the profiteers on top of it.

That is the story of our participation in this war in a nutshell.

But enough of that.

I expected that the children would have some trouble with the "Lizzie." That doesn't matter—they get experience with machines that way.

And although Doris took a lot of books with her, I don't expect that she will read many. I don't care. I would rather have Doris and Elsa *row* two hours every day—than read two hours. I want them to become as athletic as possible. And in view of the operation[13] she is to undergo—I want Doris to get as much *fresh air* as possible.

And as for you, sweet Schatzl, I am almost ashamed to say, how *much* I miss you! Whenever I am not busy, I catch myself talking to myself—and I have a feeling of home-sickness (Heimweh) that I never had before. I am getting old, I suppose. And yet, everybody is telling me that I am acting with the same vigor and the same energy as in former days.

But I *miss* you more than ever. After I got through with my statement, Cochems told me—that it was a d—— good statement "very frank and full of teaching." Now I *know* you would have criticized me—and I would have gotten angry at the criticism—still, I missed it.

The truth of the matter is, Schatzl,—Most everything I have ever achieved—I have achieved by sheer *force*, in spite of great obstacles, in spite of a very "unpolitical" make-up. I had wonderful luck in *one* thing only, in getting the *best* and *sweetest* of wives—in getting my *Schatzl.*

With love to all, your

Papa

1. Probably either William C. Fowler (1864–1937), health officer for the District of Columbia, or Harry A. Fowler (b. 1872), a Washington, D.C., surgeon.

2. Joe Henry Eagle (1870–1963), a Democratic representative from Texas, 1913–1921 and 1933–1937.

3. Benjamin Franklin Welty (1870–1962), a Democratic representative from Ohio, 1917–1921.

4. Charles F. Clyne (1877–1965) served as U.S. attorney for the Northern District of Illinois, 1914–1923, and in that capacity prosecuted Berger during the Chicago trial. Clyne testified against Berger during the House hearings on September 15–16, 1919.

5. Edward Voigt (1873–1934), a Republican representative from Wisconsin, 1917–1927, and a Wisconsin circuit court judge, 1929–1934. Voigt was the only member of Congress to vote for Berger's seating in 1919.

6. Raymond Cole (1870–1957), a Republican representative from Ohio, 1919–1925.

7. Leonidas Robinson (1867–1941), a Democratic representative from North Carolina, 1917–1921.

8. Clifford Randall (1876–1934), a Republican representative from Wisconsin, 1919–1921.

9. Probably Alma Jacobus.

10. William Ernest Mason (1850–1921), a Republican representative from Illinois, 1887–1891 and 1917–1921, and a U.S. Senator, 1897–1903.

11. Colonel Edward House (1858–1938) served as a close adviser to President Wilson.

12. William Gibbs McAdoo (1863–1941), secretary of the treasury, 1913–1918, director general of railways, 1917–1919, an unsuccessful candidate for the Democratic presidential nomination in 1920 and 1924, and a U.S. senator from California, 1933–1938.

13. Doris had planned to have a tonsillectomy but later cancelled the operation.

Victor to Meta

Washington, D.C.
September 17, 1919

My sweet Schatzl:

Yesterday was the last day of the hearings—and since Henry Cochems had to go home in the evening in order to prepare the defence of the automobilist Montgomery[1] whose case will be tried next Monday,—the hearing practically *ended* with Charles Kline, the prosecuting attorney, having the last word. Very much as in Chicago.

And very much as in Chicago also that it mattered little what Cochems could have said any further—although the committee *invited him* to stay until Thursday to answer Kline's accusations, which undoubtedly created a vicious atmosphere. He dwelt mainly on three things: first, that I became an I.W.W. because I favored Germany and the Central powers. He made very much of the Wuori letter,[2] not because I gave the $10.00 but because I attacked Gompers who according to Kline did more than any other man "to win the war" by keeping labor quiet. Second, (and that was the reason why I should not be at large but be imprisoned for life) I am a "red" flagger, or rather I believed "in two flags"—the star spangled banner *and* the "red flag", and I had at one time said in a speech in Chicago that the red flag was "the bigger symbol" of the two, which clearly showed that I was an enemy of society. A man could not have two flags any more than he could have two wives, said Kline. Third: He, Kline was "morally" convinced that I was a pro-German, alright. He had other "proves" of my guilt, which he did not use and could not use at the trial in Chicago, because I was very "subtle" and "shrewd". But he, Kline, was "morally" convinced that I was a pro-German—and therefore it would be a disgrace and misfortune for the country to admit me to Congress. This was the substance of the five hour speech—as nearly as a man could get an idea out of it. But he pounded the table a great deal, and he praised Cochems' oratory and told the committee that he (Kline) liked to hear him himself, but that he never took any stock in what Cochems said.

Kline had the loving assistance of Dallinger and Welty all the time and he undoubtedly made an impression upon Robinson and Cole who were captivated by Kline's *patriotic* fervor.

Cochems begged him to stay 10 minutes to hear Cochems' answer but Kline declined contemptuously and left the room.

Cochems answer was undoubtedly weak. Kline's speech was a tissue of insinuations and falsehoods—not—a single fact or evidence was mentioned by him except the Wuori letter giving 10.00 to the defense fund for the I.W.W—the entire affair was carefully prepared, Kline having had sessions not only with Dallinger but with Mitchell Palmer and the "Department of Justice."

There were two very interesting matters brought out during his speech.

First, why I was indicted. He said there were many complaints against my writings and my activities, but he was slow to take action because I was a "very prominent" man and reputed to be very shrewd. He did not take action until a member of my staff—he did not remember her name—tipped off a proposed raid upon the I.W.W. headquarters in Milwaukee. Then he gathered all the material he could get from the Leader and went to Washington to lay the matter before the Attorney General Gregory[3] who told him to go ahead and indict me.

Second. That our case will be called up in the U.S. Court of Appeals on October 10th but that he does not expect any decision before next spring, since the documents in the case are very voluminous. And that would mean of course, even if the sentence should be confirmed, (which is hardly to expected in view of the change of atmosphere) no decision for at least *a year* from *next spring*, until the Supreme Court gets through with it. On the other hand, Kline thinks that there will be no amnesty for political offenders as far as Wilson is concerned,—Palmer, the Attorney General, told him so.

As a matter of fact I don't want any amnesty from that treacherous dog as far as I am concerned. I have committed no crime, and I am infinitely more honest than Woodrow Wilson ever dared to be during his entire rotten life. Therefore, I don't want any of that yellow dog's mercy.

As for the report of the Committee, I am positively certain of a minority report but I have good reasons to believe that the majority report will be adopted. That means an extra-campaign and a hot one at that.

By-the-way, today was the great "victory parade" of the "greatest of all generals" John Pershing.[4] I did not go. I telephoned to Bowie's and had Margaret Bowie[5] call for the tickets at the hotel office. I would not cross the street to witness a parade in honor of the greatest mass murder pulled off by our high financiers and munition makers and profiteers. As for Pershing—the only victory *he* ever won in his life was when he succeeded in winning the daughter of the U.S. senator and sheep king Warren[6] of Wyoming who was and is the chairman of the committee of military affairs of the Senate. In recognition of this great victory Theodore Roosevelt jumped the young officer 162 points over the heads of other officers and made a major of him, (in 1905 I believe).[7] There was a great deal of noise made in the opposition papers at that time, but, of course, it would be high treason and "interference with the success of the armed forces of the U.S." to mention the story now. John Pershing is a martinette and a conceited pin-head besides. May our capitalist class never have bigger generals than that fellow. He is being boomed as the "man on horseback" (the coming "imperator") and future nominee for president in the Washington papers.

Enclosed (—or rather pasted on the other side of this sheet) I send you a clipping from the Washington Post about the hearing on Monday—the papers reported nothing about yesterday.[8]

And now of other matters.

I shall have to stay here a few days to read the transcript very carefully. This time—my remarks are *not* in question. I read my speech. But Cochems spoke for several hours—besides introducing his brief of 100 pages as a whole into the record. Now the stenographer came to me last night—after the hearing—and told me that Cochems *speaks so fast* that there is no short hand expert in the country able to take down his language and "they have to guess at most of it". It would, therefore, require several days before they would be able to furnish a transcript. On the other hand, Cochems himself must have felt something of the kind because in parting, he asked me to look over his remarks *carefully*.

Under these conditions it will be practically impossible for me to attend the Freedom convention[9] (which should be held, of course, and boomed as much as possible) but I will try to be in Milwaukee about the 1st day of October[10] in order to install Costello.[11] By-the-way, I don't want anything said about Costello to any body until I get there.

This letter got to be much longer than I expected—but I am sure I did not tire you. Since you are my "Alter Ego"—my "other I"—you have to expect letters like this.

I was very sorry to hear of the unfortunate accident on Lake Shawano—it ought to be a warning to Doris and Elsa, *not to take chances.* Safety first!

As for my other affairs of interest to you Schatzl—they can all be expressed in three words: I love you!

V.L.B.

1. Cochems returned to Milwaukee to defend Judson Montgomery, a salesman who was being tried for second-degree murder resulting from an automobile accident.

2. Berger wrote to Abram Wouri (b. 1894?), a sign painter and secretary of the Milwaukee branch of the IWW, on May 6, 1918, and contributed ten dollars to the IWW defense fund. Although Berger stated that he did "not think much" of the IWW, he praised its "matchless spirit" and criticized Samuel Gompers and the AFL. The letter was published in *Hearings,* 1:796.

3. Thomas Watt Gregory (1861–1933), U.S. attorney general, 1914–1919.

4. John Joseph Pershing (1860–1948) served as commander of the American Expeditionary Forces in World War I. On September 17, 1919, Pershing led a five-mile-long victory parade in Washington, D.C., in front of 400,000 spectators.

5. Probably Margaret Bowie, the daughter of Edward Hall Bowie, who served as national forecaster for the U.S. Weather Bureau from 1909 to 1924.

6. Francis Emroy Warren (1844–1929), a U.S. senator from Wyoming, 1890–1893 and 1895–1929.

7. Pershing married Frances Warren, the daughter of Senator Warren, in 1905. In the following year, Pershing was promoted from the rank of captain to brigadier general, rising over eight hundred of his superiors.

8. Berger enclosed an article entitled "Berger's Plea Bitter" from the *Washington Post,* September 16, 1919. The article summarized Berger's closing remarks to the House committee.

9. Meta Berger served as a delegate to the American Freedom Convention held on September 25–28, 1919, in Chicago. The convention called for the lifting of wartime limits on freedom of the press, speech, and assembly and for the immediate release of political prisoners.

10. The rest of this paragraph was later crossed out in pencil.

11. Edward J. Costello (b. 1879?) appeared on the masthead of the *Milwaukee Leader* as its managing editor from October 13, 1919, through March 30, 1920, while Berger was on a leave of absence. Costello also succeeded Berger as editor of the *Leader,* serving from 1929 to 1932.

Victor to Meta

Washington, D.C.
September 20, 1919

My own sweet Schatzl:

I hope that you have received both of the letters in which I described the hearing of Monday and Tuesday.

It was against all precedent—and especially against what they claimed at the outset that the hearing would be—to get the U.S. *prosecuting attorney* whose business is of a *criminal* nature from Chicago to testify against me. It proved the bitterness of the chairman Friedrich Wilhelm Dallinger—and also that there is really nobody in that committee to take up the cudgel for me openly.

At any rate I am glad now that Mr Klein (or Clyne) did come because he made a most miserable impression and according to (—at least two—) members helped my case considerably. As the case stands now—at the close of the hearing and with all the so-called "evidence" in—I believe that I have the *majority* of the committee standing in my favor.

Mr. Dallinger remained hostile to the last moment. He did not give me sufficient time to revise the transcript—which especially Henry Cochems' speech needed very badly. Under the pretext that he Dallinger was going to leave the same day for Boston he forbade that the manuscript leave his room, and what little corrections I could make I had to make right in his room. If you consider that Cochems speaks so fast that the stenographers claim they cannot follow him—that the subject matter was unfamiliar to the stenographers—and that that we had four extra-long sessions in two days (the transcript of which the stenographers could not deliver until two days later because of the Pershing holiday)—then you will appreciate Dallinger's *pettyness.*

Well, it is over with—although Mr. Dallinger (in order to make sure that nobody shall take the trouble to read the report of the hearings, I suppose) wants to embody the two big volumes of 1,700 pages containing the Chicago trial in the report.

A country that could spend 32 billions in order to collect one billion and a half for Morgan & Co—can easily spend a few hundred dollars on a report of that kind. I suspect Morgan & Co. would be willing that the U.S. should spend a million dollars to keep me out of congress. Why not?

Enough of that affair, however. Monday and Tuesday I will see a few of my friends and then I expect to go to New York to see a few of them there—especially Villard[1] and Littell.[2]

I expect to return here Saturday and on Sunday take the train for home. I may stay home a month or so. And when I return to Washington you may have to return with me—that will depend entirely, of course, in what shape my case will be by that time.

And now, how about Dod? When is she going to have her tonsils tended to? Or will the little operation be over by the time this letter will reach you? At any rate, I wish (even though I may be in New York towards the end of the week) to be informed *at once.* Just send your letters or telegrams to the House Office as usual. I expect to have somebody here for a few hours every day.

I do hope that they do sell bonds for the Leader for a while. Because with the immensely growing expense-account I cannot see how they will make it go. Peace will not be declared for some months to come—and even then, the additional advertising that we get from Gimbel's for instance will hardly make up for the additional costs. And we don't want to drown just when we are about reaching the shore—and *such* a shore!

During the next six months I expect such fearful labor troubles that Rehfeld must be prepared with white paper. And that requires very much capital at the present time.

I have no idea how the national party is getting along at present. The new executive board contains one or two *good workers,* like O'Neil and Brand,[3] but it does not have a single big man. And this is the time when they need one. Well, we can go it alone for a while in Wisconsin, if absolutely necessary.

Sonst aber hast Du mich lieb? Hast Du Schatzl? Ich hab' Dich sehr lieb![4]

With love to all and especially the two Schnuckies whom I will not see until I get to Madison, I suppose, I am ever *your*

V.L.B.

1. Oswald Garrison Villard (1872–1949), a liberal New York journalist, was president and owner of the *New York Evening Post* from 1900 until 1918. He controlled the weekly *Nation* from 1900 until 1935 and served as its editor between 1918 and 1932. An opponent of American entry into World War I, Villard successfully fought the banning of the *Nation* from the mails in 1918.

2. Philip Littell (1868–1943) was a writer and editor who served on the staff of the *Milwaukee Sentinel*, 1890–1901, and of the *New Republic*, 1914–1923.
3. William M. Brandt (1868–1942), a St. Louis Socialist and labor leader, served as secretary of the party in Missouri and as a vice-president of the Cigar Makers' International Union.
4. But otherwise you still love me? Do you, little darling? I love you very much!

Victor to Meta

Washington, D.C.
September 21, 1919

My sweet Schatzl

Well, sometimes, I begin to think as you do i.e. that I am a fool who to a certain extent has thrown his life away on a "mirage."

Now just look at the steelworkers? Who is their attorney and chosen mouth-piece? W. B. Rubin, the man who only a few months ago was in danger of being disbarred and jailed in connection with crooked deals with the Kroeger Bros department-store—, of which he was the attorney—and in which he bought $2,000,000 "worth of stock" for $50,000—, of which $50,000, he kept $10,000 as a "commission". Cochems saved Rubin.

Rubin, of course will sell out the Iron & Steel Workers at the first opportunity. But he is the kind of a man that Sam Gompers has always favored and patronized. I am willing to bet dollars to doughnuts that the steel workers will either lose their strike entirely or win a barren victory—it cannot be otherwise with a bunch of Judases at their head to start with. I am not in a position to say anything however—nor can you even hint without risking the claim of the mass that you are throwing cold water on their movement and that you are their enemy.

Moreover I am disgusted with what is going on in Europe. The world was divided up by a lot of highway robbers sitting in Versailles and these brigands had the blessing and benediction of that vainglorious liar and hypocrite Woodrow Wilson.

But that isn't what I have in mind just now. I am not as cock-sure as I used to be about *my own belief* in Socialism. Burleson gave us a good taste of the all-powerful state—of the politician in control of opinions. I am absolutely certain that I would not want to trust William Bross Lloyd or Wagenknecht[1] in the same position in a Socialist Commonwealth either. Capitalism is bad and is daily becoming more impossible—but Fraina's[2] Communism would mean a new form of *slavery*.

In practice, of course, as I have often told my friends, Lenin and Trotsky[3] did not establish collective ownership (or even less so communistic ownership) in Russia. What they really did accomplish was to take the agricultural land of Russia away from the large owners (and without compensation to the owner) and to parcel it out to the peasants who consider it their property, although *nominally* the title rests in the Russian commonwealth. (the same was done during the great French Revolution). And since these farmers in Russia form over 80 per cent of the population there is now a serious question in my mind whether this small peasant ownership has not closed Russia to Socialism for several hundred years. Thus the Bolsheviks may prove the greatest bulwark against "Socializing the means of production."

I understand that similar measures were passed in Czecho-Slovakia and in Poland—only there is less land to go around in these densely populated countries than in Russia. However in these two Slavonic countries also there will be a strong Roman-Catholic land-owning peasantry *opposed* to Socialism—and it will take generations to overcome that opposition.

I don't know as yet how they will arrange matters in Germany and Austria—these poor, beaten and half-devoured and starved countries. I trust to the German genius that a sensible way will be found, which will make *gradual socialization* of all industries possible and at the same time guaranty certain *fundamental liberties* for every *individual.*

As for our own country—I have the least hopes and the greatest fears. Our working class is more ignorant than the corresponding classes in Central and Western Europe. Moreover, our working class is lead by corrupt and venal leaders and it has no press to amount to anything.

On the other hand—in no country is the capitalist class so strong, so well organized and so ruthless as in our country.

And in no country is the middle class so completely under the leadership of the *plutocracy* as in America.

Thus we have a right to expect all kinds of "Hail Columbia" during the next 30 years.

And if possible I want for myself a little fruit farm—say of 40 acres—either in Wisconsin or Michigan as a "retreat" for *your old age* and *mine.* And also as a last resort for both children—if any of them, or both of them, should ever get tired of the insane strife.

Let's work for that, sweet Schatzl. In about four or five years—I may be ready to retire, provided I am still with the living. And your nature will surely hanker for peace—five years from now.

This is a queer letter. Aber ich hab' Dich sehr lieb' gute Mama.[4]

V.L.B.

1. Alfred Wagenknecht (1881–1956), a left-wing member of the Socialist Party's National Executive Committee, helped form the Communist Labor Party with William Bross Lloyd in 1919 and served as the new party's executive secretary. Wagenknecht later served as executive secretary of the United Communist Party and as a member of the executive board of the Workers Party.

2. Louis Fraina (1892–1953), a journalist and communist theoretician, had been a member of the Socialist Labor Party until 1914 and joined the Socialist Party in 1917. He helped to found the Communist Party in 1919 and served as its international secretary. Disillusioned with communism in the 1920s, he subsequently worked as a writer, editor, and economist under the name Lewis Corey.

3. Soviet leaders Vladimir Ilyitch Lenin (1870–1924) and Leon Trotsky (1879–1940).

4. But I love you very much, good Mama.

Meta to Victor

Milwaukee, Wisconsin
September 22, 1919

My dearest Lover,

Just got your special delivery letter & altho' it is nearly midnight I will write so you will hear from me in New York.

I got both your letters & your telegram before leaving Shawano. I do not believe your mail is being tampered with at the present time. Those in authority have gotten what they wanted & have done the "dirty" work.

What discourages me so, is the fact that the amnesty for political prisoners is not being talked of as yet. Furthermore no one seems to have the courage to come out & make a fight for it. That is why the convention in Chicago is so important. However I think you may be right in not taking part altho' I got your name on the programe on request if you recall.

I have agreed however to substitute in a sort of a way & tell the story of the Leader case. That surely cannot do any harm.

I think Dallinger must have felt his case almost lost when he resorted to getting that cur from Chicago. He certainly is the limit for pettiness & vindictiveness. Oh! how I crave for the time to come when these people will be made to suffer. My whole soul cries for retribution. I am much more hurt I believe than you are altho' I know what you feel too. But you take it all in such a philosophical way.

When you go to New York, I advise you to go to Bridgeport & see your old father if only for an hour or two. He is on the brink of the grave. You will not regret the time you spend that way now.

Doris's throat looks much improved after receiving a treatment from Dr. Heebe.[1] He seems to understand his business pretty well. He will treat her throat each day this week except Friday & Sat when Doris wants to attend the Freedom Convention. So that you will not be surprised let me tell you that Elsa also wants to go. Both girls will use their own money. I tho't this best for them. Thus they will see that they can't spend it & keep it too.

I have been in the office all day today doing things for Okla. Leader.[2]

So far not much money has come in from the men who are out. Zumach[3] however has hopes for several thousand within a week or two—

I told Reh——[4] what you said about supply of paper. He agreed it was necessary to put in a supply but said he could not do so until he had money much more money.

He also informed me that the Grandfather Falls Mills cannot supply Okla. He said that the Kuryer Polski[5] did not sign up its contract quick enough with the Grandfather Mills & they consequently refused to sell the Kuryer paper. The Kuryer has engaged Cochems & Wolfe to force the Mill to sell paper. That is a peculiar situation but should be a warning for us to be on the look-out for ourselves in the future.

Well darling, otherwise there is no news from here that is important. You knew of course that Siegfried[6] is gone. Also two nice dresses came for the girls from the East.

Next Monday Duddie is 21 years old. I wish you might be home before they leave for the U. They leave Monday for Madison.

You are the inspiration for my love dearest & I even enjoy loving you when you are not here. Of course I just enjoy thinking of our love. But you come home & I'll enjoy loving you really. I count the days until then. Ever your

Meta.

1. Dr. Harry J. Heeb (1882–1976) was a Milwaukee eye, ear, nose, and throat specialist.

2. The Bergers and the Milwaukee Social-Democratic Publishing Company assisted Oscar Ameringer and Freda Hogan (Ameringer) in establishing the *Oklahoma Leader*, a daily socialist newspaper in Oklahoma City. In June, 1918, the Milwaukee company authorized its business manager to purchase land and equipment in Oklahoma, eventually acquiring more than $50,000 in assets there, and the following year the land and equipment were exchanged for stock in the Oklahoma Leader Publishing Company, which the Milwaukee Social-Democratic Publishing Company held until 1929. See the Minutes of the Milwaukee Social-Democratic Publishing Company, SHSW.

3. William C. Zumach (1887–1981), a Milwaukee labor organizer, served as a Socialist member of the Wisconsin Senate, 1917–1921.

4. Ferdinand Rehfeld.

5. An anticlerical Polish-language newspaper in Milwaukee.

6. Probably Siegfried Ameringer.

Meta to Victor

[Milwaukee, Wisconsin]
September 24, 1919

My dearest Lover,

Tonight I happened to attend the County Central Committee. My! It was a hot meeting. The discussion arose when the 6th ward branch demanded that the Liberator[1] be placed on the Leader news stand. Richter[2] got up to say that the Leader Corporation a private corporation dictated not only the policy of the Leader a private corporation supported by party members etc, but that the M.S.D.P. Co also presumed to dictate what the comrades shall or shall not read. He was emphatic & bitter & much opposed to the private ownership of the Leader etc.[3] Criticized Miss Thomas. Buech jumped up & called a spade a spade & then the fight was on. He said just about 1½ years ago when Richter joined the Party, spies came into the party & always since then have these spies stabbed the older comrades in the back & injected poison in the minds of the comrades. These spies he said had gone from meeting to meeting denouncing the Leader & so it went on at a fierce rate for more than 2 hours or more. Hoan[4] also resented the charge that the Leader was a private capitalist paper & challenged them to change the board of directors just to show them that the control was in the hands of the stock-holders. Where upon Hampel[5] derisively laughed & asked Hoan how this could be done with one man holding all the stock. . .

They also called Buech an enemy of the paper because he made 5 or 6 thousand dollars out of the Leader when it was going down. Sam Rubin made that charge. But Betty told them that Buech & Ameringer saved the Leader at that time & that Rubin was one of those who also took commission.

It was a nasty meeting. You are right that one is a fool to make too great a sacrifice for this or any other crowd.

Yes I too was astonished that W. B. Rubin was the Steel Workers employee. That is where Rubin again pulled one over on them. They knew not what they did. Dearest it is 1.30 A.M. & I am tired but I love you more tonight than ever.

Your Meta.

1. The *Milwaukee Leader* stopped selling Max and Crystal Eastman's *Liberator,* a magazine sympathetic to the Russian Revolution, after it printed Arturo Giovannitti's article criticizing Berger in the April, 1919, issue. For the controversy surrounding the article, see Meta to Doris and Elsa, April 5, 1919, and April 22, 1919, above.

2. Probably Arthur W. Richter (1884–1952), a Milwaukee lawyer known for his advocacy of civil rights and organized labor. Richter later left the Socialist Party to join the Progressive Party.

3. Berger incorporated the Milwaukee Social-Democratic Publishing Company in 1906, and he and Elizabeth Thomas were among the company's major stockholders. Thomas served as the company's president and Berger as its vice-president. The company published the *Social-Democratic Herald,* the *Vorwärts,* the *Naprzod,* and the *Milwaukee Leader* as well as other Socialist literature.

4. Daniel Webster Hoan (1881–1961), a lawyer and Socialist politician, served as Milwaukee city attorney, 1910–1916, and mayor, 1916–1940. Hoan left the Socialist Party in 1941 and later helped revitalize the Wisconsin Democratic Party, running as its candidate for governor in 1944 and 1946 and for the U.S. Congress in 1948.

5. Probably George Hampel (1885–1954), a Socialist politician who served as Milwaukee County clerk, 1919–1920, state assemblyman, 1931–1933, and state senator (as a member of the Progressive Party), 1937–1945.

Meta to Doris and Elsa

Milwaukee, Wisconsin
[October 31, 1919]

My darling Girls:—

Haven't I been short some letters this week? It seems to me a long time between "drinks". Tonight I talked in a *church* to about 500 people. It was a wonderful chance & I think I made some new friends. At any rate people were very sympathetic. It was an intensely religious crowd & the meeting was something like revivals are, all praying aloud & calling on the Lord Jesus etc.

Pap[a] went to the German theatre on my suggestion. You see the American Legion has asked the Pabst Theatre Co. to stop & they threatened all sorts of acts to force the Co. to stop. They even placed a machine gun on the City Hall Sq pointing it towards the Pabst Theatre for a bluff.[1] One man, Dr. Pfister,[2] told me that the action of this American Legion was making plenty of votes for V.L.B. So I tho't he ought to go. Now I am waiting for his return and I am anxious to see what he has to say.

The inclosed clippings I cut out of the Sentinel & the Journal to show you what these papers consider news.[3] I sometimes think Dudd doesn't know how to get news. I would suggest that she visit the office at the Capitol every now & then. There is the Industrial Commission, The RR commission, & the other Commissions besides the Gov. office, Cary's[4] office, Fitzpatrick,[5] the Labor Leaders, Mrs. Turner[6] & a lot of other places. If only one story a day or an average of one a day comes I know that papa would be satisfied.

Did you see that the Gov. is doubtful as to when he should call the special election for Papa?[7] The truth of the matter is that the politicians here are frightened stiff because there is so much Berger sentiment. They do not want the election now or in the spring either because they fear the socialists then. They suggest that the elections be held one year from now thus leaving this district with out representation all this time. They figure that by that time sentiment will have cooled off & goodness knows what the new issues might be. That is political strategy. Well, we will see!

I suppose you will be so busy with your guests this week that you will only half pay attention to the clippings & work but please darling, take this seriously. It helps me so much.

I am a bit tired so will close. Send me a nice loving letter, both of you. Your letters are like a tonic to me & I need that kind of a tonic. Please! Lovingly

Mama.

I shall send you a copy of Lit. Digest. It contains an account of Washington Labor Conference.[8]

1. On October 31, 1919, members of the American Legion demanded that Milwaukee's Pabst Theater cancel its German-language plays. When the theater's management refused, the legionnaires attempted to intimidate playgoers by placing a machine gun on City Hall Square aimed at the theater. The plan backfired, and *Der G'wissenswurm*, a comedy by Ludwig Anzengruber (1839–1889), was performed with police and sheriff's protection before a sold-out crowd, an additional two thousand patrons were turned away, and a second performance was scheduled.

2. Probably Franz Pfister (1862–1952), an Austrian-born Milwaukee physician.

3. Meta enclosed clippings from Milwaukee newspapers about homecoming events, traffic rules, and the Thanksgiving holiday at the University of Wisconsin.

4. Charles P. Cary (1856–1943), a Republican, served as Wisconsin's superintendent of public instruction, 1903–1921.

5. Edward A. Fitzpatrick (1884–1960) served as secretary of the Wisconsin Board of Education, 1919–1923.

6. Jennie McMullin Turner (1885–1967) served as a research assistant at the Wisconsin Legislative Reference Bureau, 1914–1920.

7. Although the U.S. House of Representatives did not adopt the committee report recommending Berger's exclusion until November 10, 1919, Wisconsin politicians expected his seat to be declared vacant and speculated about whether Wisconsin governor Emanuel L. Philipp would call an immediate election, set the election for April, 1920, or leave the seat vacant for the remainder of the term. See, for example, "Socialists Will Back Berger," *Milwaukee Journal,* October 25, 1919.

8. "The Split on Collective Bargaining," *Literary Digest,* November 1, 1919, 11–13. President Wilson called representatives of business, labor, and the public together for an industrial conference, which was held in Washington, D.C., on October 4–23, 1919. The conference failed to develop any plans for cooperation between management and labor.

Above: *North side of State Street, Milwaukee, ca. 1914. The second build-ing from the right housed the offices of the* Social-Democratic Herald. Below: *Poster for Populist rally, Madison, 1894.*

Above: *Early home of the* Social-Democratic Herald *and* Wisconsin Vorwärts, *614 State Street, Milwaukee, ca. 1902. Victor Berger is standing at left.* Below: Milwaukee Leader *newsboys, ca. 1915.*

The Milwaukee Leader

HOME EDITION

Milwaukee News

"UNAWED BY INFLUENCE AND UNBRIBED BY GAIN"

Vol. 9—No. 12.　　Weather—Fair and Warmer.　　SATURDAY EVENING, DECEMBER 20, 1919.　　PRICE TWO CENTS

PEOPLE'S RULE UPHELD IN BERGER VICTORY

VICTORY MARKS BRILLIANT PAGE IN U.S. HISTORY, STATES BERGER

"Vote Is Fair Warning to Powers That Be."

WORM IS TURNING

WARNING IS URGED.

BLUE INTERPRET VOTE.

THANKS THE VOTERS.

A USEFUL SENATE.

A successful man.

WARMER WEATHER HERE PREDICTED BY STEWART

SHERIFF LOSES TWO SPARE MARMON TIRES

THE TRACK IS CLEARED

SOCIALISM

COMMITTEE OK'S PEACE RESOLUTION BY 7 TO 3 BALLOT

Senator Lodge Immediately Starts to Senate With Report on Bill.

IRISH INDEPENDENCE DRIVE SHORT $125,000

CITY SEEKS TO BUY LOCAL STOCK YARDS UNDER PALMER RULE

U. S. PEACE COMMISSION MEMBERS BACK SUNDAY

NAME WILSON'S COAL COMMISSIONERS TONIGHT

COMPARATIVE WARD TOTALS

Wards and Totals			
First	571	2178	296	2975
Second	1004	997	648	1382
Sixth	1482	835	1856	1187
Seventh	2459	791	1452	1282
Ninth	1729	768	1261	1101
Tenth	1495	520	998	842
Thirteenth	1654	1167	1051	1662
Fifteenth	886	1326	611	1669
Seventeenth	509	2954	573	2295
Nineteenth	1714	1663	1291	1965
Twentieth	1789	1138	2122	1719
Twentyfirst	2270	998	1696	1473
Twentysecond	2555	2100	1749	2493
Twentyfifth	2719	417	2090	1148
Sherwood	103	461	51	337
North Milwaukee	211	142	137	202
Whitefish Bay	65	105	31	86
Town Granville	191	112	207	144
Town Milwaukee	300	87	306	136
Total	24367	18561	17822	22848

TO DEFER COLLECTION OF INTEREST ON LOANS TO FOREIGN COUNTRIES

ORGANIZE IN OCONTO

VOTE ON CUMMINS RAILROAD BILL SET FOR 3:30 SATURDAY

La Follette to Continue Attack on Measure Until Ballot Time.

BOB IN JOB.

WILL SPEAK ENTIL VOTE.

HERE'S HOW THEY'LL MOVE TO BAR BERGER

THE CRY OF THE AGES
BY OSCAR AMERINGER

HEADLINE: "BERGER WINS, WILL NOT BE SEATED?" Who cares?

AND now in impotent rage the gray wolves howl, "Jail him?"

FOOLS that you are, you cannot jail nor murder thought.

DISTRICT RETURNS SOCIALIST TO SEAT CONGRESS REFUSED

Socialists Ready for 3rd Campaign

Big Business Routed by 4,806 Votes, as Balloting Shows Gain of 6,548 for Socialist Party.

GENUINE AMERICANISM WINS DECISIVE VICTORY

RACINE MAYOR PLANS FIGHT FOR ABOLITION OF RATE COMMISSION

THE WEATHER FORECAST

Front page of the Milwaukee Leader, *December 20, 1919, announcing Berger's reelection to the House of Representatives after that body had already refused to seat him once.*

Above: *Bindery at the* Milwaukee Leader, *1914.* Below: *The* Leader *newsroom, 1924.*

Above: *Eugene V. Debs speaking in Milwaukee, ca. 1908. Victor Berger and Frederic Heath are seated at left.* **Below:** *Caucus of Milwaukee Socialist city officials, 1910.* Standing, left to right: *Harry Briggs, August W. Strehlow, Ferdinand W. Rehfeld, Charles Weiley, Gilbert H. Poor, Max Grass, Jacob Rummel.* Seated: *Albert Welch, Charles B. Whitnall, Carl D. Thompson, Daniel W. Hoan, Albert F. Giese, John Hassman, Martin Gorecki, John L. Reisse, Martin Mikkelson, William Coleman, Edmund T. Melms.*

WHi(X3)39609

Milwaukee mayor Emil Seidel, reformist lawyer Frederic C. Howe, and Victor Berger, 1910.

Standing, left to right: *Frederick Brockhausen, James Graham Phelps Stokes, Victor Berger, Frederic Heath, unknown, unknown.* Seated: *Rose Pastor Stokes, Elizabeth Thomas, unknown. The Stokeses were in Milwaukee for a Socialist Party fund-raiser, July, 1907.*

Victor Berger and Frederic Heath in Berger's residence, Milwaukee, 1897.

Above: *Berger's senatorial campaign poster, 1918.* Below: *Socialist Party national executive committee, May, 1911. Standing, left to right: Victor Berger, George Goebel, Robert Hunter. Seated: Morris Hillquit, John Spargo, Lena Morrow Lewis, James F. Carey, and party secretary J. Mahlon Barnes.*

Milwaukee at the turn of the century. Above: *City Hall.* Below: *A view of Chestnut Street (later Juneau Avenue). Victor Berger's office was located on Chestnut Street beginning in 1911.*

Victor L. Berger, ca. 1910.

Meta Berger, ca. 1910.

Above: *Oscar Ameringer, Socialist journalist and friend of the Bergers, ca. 1920s.* Below: *Daniel W. Hoan, Milwaukee city attorney and later mayor, in his office, 1914.*

Inez Milholland, prominent Socialist and suffragist, ca. 1912.

Arthur Brisbane, Hearst columnist and financial supporter of the Leader, *ca. 1890s.*

Seymour Stedman, Berger's attorney during the Espionage Act trial, ca. 1920s.

Morris Hillquit, New York Socialist and Berger's political ally, ca. 1920.

WHi(X3)48948

Above: *980 First Street, Milwaukee, the Bergers' residence beginning in 1912.* Below: *Berger at his farm at Thiensville, Wisconsin, ca. 1925.* (Photo courtesy Polly Keusink.)

WHi(X3)48227

Victor and Meta Berger in Europe, 1923.

Jennie Goessling (Meta's cousin), Deborah and Polly Welles (Doris and Colin's daughters), Doris Berger Welles, Meta Berger, and Elsa Berger Edelman, ca. 1933.

Meta to Doris and Elsa

[Washington, D.C.]
[November 10, 1919]

Darling girls,—

This day like all other days finally is over. I think it was the hardest day I have ever spent. I will try to tell you just what happened. The first order of business was papa's case. Mr. Dallinger had complete control of the thing. He asked the house for unanimous consent to permit Papa to speak at all. The House voted to grant this only one vote against it. Papa was given 1½ hours time. Then Dallinger stated the case from his point of view and of course was very bitter and patriotic. Papa came next and read his speech. He was frequently interrupted by members who said he was saying seditious things and was preaching revolution and desecrating the flag and the memory of the dead soldiers in France. Really a tame speech too. You can imagine the strain on Papa and on me. His talk took about five minutes over the hour & half. As soon as he was through dozens of members jumped to their feet to ask questions. Of course these questions were impudent, catchy, and patriotic and intended to show Papa up. After that the different members of the committee had the time all divided up between them and no time allotment was made for any one who might wish to say a word for Papa. Each speaker then proceeded to denounce Papa to his heart's content. They tried to make a German out of him, a liar, a coward, a traitor and I cannot say what not. They took the record of the Chicago trial and quoted the St. Louis Platform, the Price we Pay, Why you should fight, the articles of the Chicago Socialist especially the one about the woman who uses their sex to help enlistment and thus became worse than a prostitute etc. etc. etc.[1] The thing that appealed most to these men was all the sentimental slush about Americanism, women, the flag, etc. The whole procedure lasted more than seven hours. After Papa was through some man moved that his whole speech be striken from the record because he said it was so revolutionary, and slammed the administration so much that it was most insulting. Well the vote was taken and all but one man voted to unseat Papa and that one man was Voigt of Sheboygan.[2] All the other Wisconsin men voted against us. Voigt told me that Brown did so very reluctantly and would probably not have done so if several more had only stood with him. Such is the courage of some of them.

Tomorrow we leave for New York. I hope I can get some rest after I get home as I am very very tired. Mr Lunde[3] was here with us today and that was very nice. Otherwise we were alone. Be good girls and work hard so that some day you may be able to get even with this rotten bunch and system.

I love you and Papa more and more each day. I think trouble binds us more closely together. Don't you? Lovingly your own

Mother.

1. "The Price We Pay" and "Why You Should Fight" were Socialist Party pamphlets by Irwin St. John Tucker that described the horrors of war and characterized the war as being fought to protect capitalism. "Women and War" appeared in the *American Socialist*, April 14, 1917, and stated that women who worked in army recruitment efforts "are only a step higher than women who solicit for the sale of their bodies." These items were part of the government's evidence against Berger and the other defendants. See *Hearings*, 2:120–125, 148–149, 151.

2. The House voted 311 to 1, with 119 absent, against seating Berger.

3. Theodore H. Lunde was president of the American Industrial Company in Chicago. He was active in the antiwar movement during World War I and supported the amnesty movement after the conflict ended.

Meta to Doris and Elsa

[Milwaukee, Wisconsin]
December 8, [1919]

My darling Children,

This is the end of a hard working day. The results of the primary at this hour with two precincts missing is

| Bodenstab[1] | Berger |
| 8,444 | 13,830. |

That is a fine vote & it is obtained without the Socialists making an effort to *get* the *vote out.*

Now for the home run! Here's hoping! Wishing! almost Praying!

The checks will be welcome won't they! With best of love always

your Mother.

1. Henry H. Bodenstab (1874–1948), a Republican attorney, served as a state senator, 1909–1913, Milwaukee assistant district attorney, 1913–1914, and Milwaukee County court commissioner, 1934–1941. Bodenstab ran as a fusion candidate for the U.S. House of Representatives against Berger in the December, 1919, special election. Berger received 13,892 votes in the uncontested Socialist primary on December 8, 1919, compared to Bodenstab's 9,270 votes in the uncontested Republican primary. Berger won the general election on December 19, with 24,350 votes (55 percent) to Bodenstab's 19,566 (45 percent).

Victor to Meta

New York, New York
January 4, 1920

My sweet Schatzl:

Was late in Boston owing to a freight wreck near Worcester, Mass.— the crowd waited, however. A number of policemen and Birak,[1] the law-partner of Geo. Roewer,[2] waited for me at the station, but owing to the headless arrangements, I had encountered every-where—there was no machine to take me over to the hall, and we had to walk about a dozen blocks, policemen, committee and speaker—a fine procession. It was late and cold and few people on the street—the parade must have looked funny, however, with some of the committee carrying my heavy bags, surrounded by a strong guard of police.

And I had hardly alighted from the sleeper when Birak took a hold of my arm and with terror in his face cautioned me not to mention the war, or the American Legion or president Wilson in my speech. I told him, these were the issues on which I won and it would [be] cowardly and silly to avoid mentioning them. He told me, I did not understand the situation in Boston—the American Legion had met the same day and had "forbidden" the meeting. I answered, it was up to the Socialist party to protect its own meeting. Entering the hall we met James F. Carey who repeated the warning, and suggested that I should just make "the regular Socialist speech" and not enter upon the "questions of the day" at all. I laughed at the suggestion. And before introducing me, the chairman, Geo. Röwer also admonished me—sutto voce—not to mention the war because there were "any number of secret service men and American Legion fellows in the hall".[3] I started out by telling how high a valuation the national administration put upon "me" and by reading the extract of our St. Louis war program and the quotation from Wilson's speech characterizing this war as a capitalist war—and I had the audience at once. It was overwhelmingly a *non-Socialist* audience. Our movement in Boston was largely Russian, Lettish, Jewish etc.—and that crowd has gone over bag and baggage to the Communists and the Communist Labor party.

Ameringer did not appear in Boston until the day after the meeting. He missed no less than *three* connections between Erie and Boston. This shows again how *wise* "I" was to miss him at the depot in Milwaukee—the chances are that if I had gone to Erie with him, we would *both* have missed the very interesting Boston meeting—interesting, because I was "heckled" by David Goldstein,[4] the Socialist-killer, and others.

By-the-way, please, do not forget to have Zummach telephon to Merlin Hull[5] in Madison, about the sending of my election certificate to Washington.

When this letter reaches you the children will be back in Madison, I suppose. Bank the check you receive from the East and send them the money *immediately*—it is their money and we have no right to use it at all.[6]

I have two meetings today—one in the afternoon down-town on 4th street—and one in the evening, up-town. It is now after two o'clock P.M. and I have to close. Will write you more tomorrow. I intend to call upon half a dozen influential radicals and liberals including Mr. Villard.

Letzte Nacht habe ich fortwährend an Dich gedacht—ich konnte nicht schlafen.[7] With love

Ever your
V.L.B.

1. Joseph Bearak (1890?–1939), a Boston labor lawyer.
2. George Edward Roewer Jr. (b. 1885) was a Boston lawyer who joined the Socialist Party in 1901 and served several terms on the party's National Executive Committee.
3. The *New York Times*, January 3, 1920, reported that ten uniformed policemen were present at Berger's Boston speech and that fifty others were held in readiness in case of disturbances. The American Legion had successfully blocked Berger from speaking in Cambridge, Massachusetts, and Providence, Rhode Island, and a group of Legionnaires gathered outside the hall when Berger spoke in Boston.
4. David Goldstein (1870–1958) was a Boston organizer and candidate of the Socialist Labor Party and Socialist Party before he renounced socialism in 1903. He converted from Judaism to Catholicism in 1905 and subsequently traveled throughout the country as an antisocialist lecturer.
5. As Wisconsin secretary of state, Merlin Hull (1870–1953) certified Berger's election to Congress.
6. Beginning in the fall, 1917, Victor's sisters contributed funds to help pay for Doris and Elsa's education at the University of Wisconsin.
7. Last night I thought of you constantly—I could not sleep.

Victor to Meta

New York, New York
January 6, 1920

My sweet Schatzl:

Sunday it did look for a while as if I was going to [be] arrested—at least the police captain of the district claimed that I would be arrested immediately if I should attempt to take the platform. For a while we spent our energy in getting a lawyer and making sure of bondsmen in case of an arrest—when I appeared in the hall, however, at about 4 P.M. and mounted the platform nothing happened except incredible applause although two policemen were on the platform (behind the wings) and any number of policemen "plain clothesmen" and government "secret service" men were scattered about the hall.

The same performance was repeated in the evening. Last night there was banquett in my honor with 800 covers and several hundred guests in the gallery. I am a poor subject for *veneration*, but any other man, E. V. Debs for instance, would have enjoyed the occassion immensely. The only thing that pleased me a little was that Charles Ervin[1] of the N.Y. Call had to pay me compliments—which I was convinced, he hated to do. We collected a little over $1,100 at the banquet for the national office which after all is the object of our trip.

I don't know whether I shall be able to speak in Jersey city tonight. According to the papers the commissioners will meet today and pass a special ordinance to bar me "and all men of the Berger class", whatever that may mean.[2]

You have read about James R. Mann. He is undoubtedly the most influential Republican in the House of Representatives today—but I dont know of course, how many men he can sway this time, in view of the "white terror" and the insanity of the war profiteers and their press. I am glad now that I did not see [him] on the case—and that he can truthfully state that he has never spoken a word to me about it.

There is a committee from Jersey City coming to see me now and I must close this letter. Will keep you posted, of course, as events will develop.

Under the circumstances hold back the printing of my speech, until further orders.

Give my love to all, but keep the best always for *yourself.* I wish you were with me—I know *you* would enjoy the incredible enthusiasm manifested in all our meetings.

Ever your
V.L.B.

1. Charles W. Ervin (1865–1953), a member of the Socialist Party since 1906, served as editor of the Socialist *New York Call* from 1917 to 1922.
2. The Jersey City, New Jersey, police prohibited Berger from speaking on the evening of January 6, 1920, and escorted him out of the city.

Victor to Meta (telegram)

WASHINGTON, D.C.
JANUARY 10, 1920

CRUCIFIED ONCE MORE.[1] THEY DID NOT EVEN HAVE THE DECENCY TO GRANT ME TEN MINUTES FOR MY DEFENSE. MANN SHERWOOD[2] AND VOIGHT WANTED ME SEATED AND SISSON[3] PROTESTED AGAINST THE INJUSTICE OF PROCEDURE. I WILL HAVE TO FIGHT AGAIN AND BE REELECTED ARRIVE HOME MONDAY NIGHT LOVINGLY

VICTOR BERGER

1. The House voted 330 to 6, with 91 members absent, to exclude Berger from Congress. Anthony J. Griffin (D-N.Y.), John W. Harreld (R-Okla.), James R. Mann (R-Ill.), Isaac R. Sherwood (D-Ohio), Thomas U. Sisson (D-Miss.), and Edward Voigt (R-Wis.) voted to seat Berger.
2. Isaac R. Sherwood (1835–1925), a Republican representative from Ohio, 1873–1875, and a Democratic representative from Ohio, 1907–1921 and 1923–1925.
3. Thomas Upton Sisson (1869–1923), a Democratic representative from Mississippi, 1909–1923.

Meta to Doris and Elsa

Milwaukee, Wisconsin
January 11, 1920

Darling girls:—

Well the expected even came off according to schedule & papa is excluded again. I got a nice telegram from him in which he is. "Don't worry Schatzl we are fighting a world's fight and are winning every step of the way. We will win completely eventually."[1] Can you beat that for faith. He will be back home tomorrow night.

Ameringer just telephoned me that he was fighting mad & that he would not proceed directly to Oklahoma but would stay on here until papa came back & then lay plans for further work. I am glad of that for Ameringer has a sort of tonic affect on papa.

We are planning among other things a big mass meeting at which we want that ousted N.Y. assembly man Claessens[2] here. He will make a hit if he comes.

Last night I was so tired that I went to bed at 8 P.M. and this morning I have done nothing but read the papers & write to Aunt Hattie & to you. The Sentinel & Journal have a great many news items on the University this week. Among others is one by Goodnight[3] on "why Freshman fail" Another on a class on Americanization by some other professors & several more.

Phyllis Schleip's engagement is also announced.

It seems kind of strange, that while the newspapers all carried big headlines on Berger's exclusion not a single person has telephoned me about it yet. I do not quite understand it.

I will send the chess game in next weeks laundry bag. It is awkward to send separately. Well, I guess this is all the news for today. But you write even if the letters are not all equally news, like this one for instance, still it is great to hear often.

With loads of love I am always

Your devoted
Mother

1. Meta misquoted Victor's telegram of January 11, 1920, which actually read: "DONT WORRY SCHATZL WE ARE FIGHTING THE WORLDS GREATEST BATTLE AND WE CANNOT LOSE WE ARE ALREADY WINNING." Berger Papers, SHSW.

2. August Claessens (1885–1954) was a New York assemblyman who had first been elected in 1917. He and four other Socialists were refused their seats in January, 1920, on the basis of their party affiliation. Claessens won a special election in September, 1920, but the assembly again refused to admit him. He was finally seated in March, 1922, following his election in 1921. Claessens resigned from the Socialist Party in 1936 and was active in the American Labor Party until 1944, when he joined the Liberal Party.

3. Scott Holland Goodnight (1875–1972) served as dean of men at the University of Wisconsin, 1916–1945.

Victor to Meta

[Milwaukee, Wisconsin]
[September 8, 1920]

My dear Schatzl:

Well,—the primary is over and compared with the primary of 1918 the Republican party has gained 50 percent. The Democratic party was practically *wiped out* and the Socialist party has gained 60 percent compared with the primary of two years [ago].

Enclosed please find a few clippings that will tell the story. Our gains would have been very much larger, if it was not for two conditions.

First. The women's vote. In the 18th Ward where I visited almost every precinct during the afternoon—the women had regular knitting parties in the booths and near the booths. They seemed to have tally sheets of all the voters—and the women's vote was almost as large as the men's vote—in one precinct, it was even larger.

In the Socialist wards however not only was the vote light, but the women's vote amounted only to 20 per cent of the total.

More over, so many of our Socialists voted the Republican ticket—in order to nominate "weak men". Thus Edward Ziegler for instance voted the Republican ticket to nominate Wilcox[1] and Stafford[2]—and many others did the same foolish stunt.

Under these conditions it is rather surprising that we received over 22,000 votes.[3] Of course, we needed only a little over 2,000 to get our ticket on the ballot for the election.

Well, Schatzl, I am glad, it is over so far, at least. If it had not been for the letters we sent out, the vote at the primary would hardly been greater than two years ago.

In one way, I wish you could stay there another two weeks—until I get back from Oklahoma. You need a vacation.

On the other hand, I am afraid that with a house full of people and no maid, you do not get so much of a vacation after all.

How about that girl? As things look here, I may postpone my trip South for another week.

There is a letter here for Colin[4] but I believe I shall hold it until he gets here. With love to all and especially to my Mamma

V.L.B.

1. Roy P. Wilcox (1873–1946), an Eau Claire attorney, unsuccessfully ran for governor in the Republican primaries of 1918 and 1920. He served in the Wisconsin Senate, 1917–1921.

2. William H. Stafford won the Republican nomination for Congress in the Fifth Congressional District and went on to beat Berger in the general election, 55 percent to 45 percent.

3. Socialist William C. Coleman received 22,495 votes in Milwaukee County in the 1920 Wisconsin gubernatorial primary.

4. Colin Welles (1896–1962) married Doris Berger on July 17, 1920; the couple divorced in March, 1935. Welles taught at the University of the Philippines in Manila in 1921 and 1922 while doing research on plant pathology, and he received a Ph.D. in botany from the University of Wisconsin in 1923. He taught science at the Milwaukee Vocational School from 1925 to 1950 and in 1935 was elected the first president of the Wisconsin Federation of Teachers.

Victor to Meta

Oklahoma City, Oklahoma
December 3, 1920

My sweet Schatzl:

Arrived here safely on Wednesday—being recognized on the train before I was there five minutes—which made it a bit uncomfortable because the crowd did not seem sympathetic, except the train crew, which was very much so.

O. Ameringer waited for me at the station and took me to the Hotel Egbert kept by Fred Holt[1] who is a director and the vice-president of our publishing company.[2] Needless to say that I would not go there if I had to cho[o]se a hotel myself. I got the best room of the 75 in the house but it is full of cockroaches and (judging from the queer sensations that I experienced during the last two nights) I am prone to suspect some more ferocious domestic animals. Like Oscar—I may nilli-willi—shed my blood for the cause. However, before coming home I may take the necessary precaution of putting enough "sachet powder" into my suit case to prevent any unwelcome importation into our home.

So much for the personal side and for "the roof over my head".

As for the business end—be prepared for the greatest surprise.

The paper makes four times as big a deficit as we ever made in Milwaukee. On the face of it—the news simply staggered me.

I went to work at once on Wednesday noon and kept at it continuously until last night. I got the figures of every department in detail and all I could really see that could be cut out—was about $235.00 a week, which was only a drop in the bucket—and that cut would to a certain extent interfere with the efficiency of the paper.

On the other hand—they have done remarkably well. They now have a paid-up circulation of over 15,000,—a wonderful showing in a town and a state like this. And they are on the *upward* path. So much I could see at once.

What is against them—is the air-tight boycott of the Chamber of Commerce and of the businessmen in general. And Oklahoma City being essentially a Southern town (led by Northern business adventurers) is virtually at least 50 years behind Milwaukee. Yet, our people here have one element of strength that we never had until the world war:

our people here have thousands of *farmers* ready and willing to invest a couple of hundred dollars (and even a thousand or two thousand) in the Leader. The trouble is only that these farmers have been hit hard by the recent slump in cotton and many of them are also holding their wheat for better prices. Thus until I get a more intimate view of their "hinterland"—the country back of them, I am not even ready to give them any advice.

Tomorrow (Saturday) I shall go with Ameringer to Tulsa—the great oil center—about a hundred miles north-east of here. We expect to return by Monday.

Knowing what I know now—I will probably not stay here longer than two weeks this time. Under *no* circumstances will I go with Oscar to see farmers for the purpose of selling stock—and I also vetoed the idea of inviting a few hundred to town and have me address them in behalf of the Leader. Oscar and Freda[3] are in a position to sell the stock as a *business proposition* to anybody who is in sympathy with the general trend of the movement.

Oscar, however, just came in this moment and insists that such a meeting be called—even if it should include only the main pillars of the movement. Will tell you more about it, next time.

I thought a great deal of you and the girls between acts—especially of Elsa, because Doris really does not worry me. I think Colin will be well able to take care of her, even if she should need it, which I do not believe that she ever will.

I am not so sure about Elsa. And therefore, we must insist that she does finish her studies and get her diploma—*by all means.* She is very young and it really does not matter whether it takes a year more or less, but I want her to get her diploma.

Rehfeld has not sent the papers—I mean copies of the Milwaukee Leader containing considerable advertising—to me, care of Oklahoma Leader. *Ask him, please, to do so at once.*

I hope the parting of Doris and Colin from Mama was not too tear-ful.[4] They have a wonderful chance to see the world and ought to be congratulated.

I suppose Hattie is with you, now. Give her my love and ask her to stay as long as possible.

Now this is the longest letter I have written in "long hand" in a year. And the main thing in this long letter is that you know that business may be good or bad and the movement may advance or recede—but as far as I am concerned the *only* fixed and valuable thing in my hard life was the knowledge that you love me—and this I want to keep to my dying day. Hast Du mich verstanden, Schatzl?[5]

Ever your
V.L.B.

1. Fred Holt had been an official with the United Mine Workers in Arkansas, Oklahoma, and Texas.

2. The Oklahoma Leader Publishing Company, publisher of the *Oklahoma Leader*. For Berger's involvement in the company, see Meta to Victor, September 22, 1919.

3. Freda Hogan (Ameringer) (1892–1988), the daughter of Arkansas Socialist Dan Hogan, served as state secretary of the Arkansas Socialist Party and on the Socialist Party's National Women's Committee. She helped Oscar Ameringer establish the *Oklahoma Leader* and married him in 1930.

4. Colin Welles had obtained an appointment at the University of Manila, and Doris and Colin had departed for the Philippines.

5. Did you understand me, little darling?

Victor to Meta

Milwaukee, Wisconsin
October 17, 1921

My sweet Schatzl

Have written you a 10 page letter in care of the American Express office at Tokyo, Japan—expecting that you will by all means take a trip to the capital of Japan, if you stop over in Japan at all.[1] In order to make sure of it—I also send you this note.

Everybody is well here—and things are going on in the usual fashion. It is hardly necessary for me to tell you that I miss you very much—miss you practically every hour.

Economic conditions are getting rather worse than better—and a big railroad strike is looming up today.[2] I expect, however, that in case of a strike the government will take over the management of the railroads. This may be a shrewd maneuver or scheme of the railroad magnates to sell their property to the government at advantageous terms, while they still own and control the government.

Nevertheless I have ordered two extra-carloads of paper,—and have bought ½ barrel of flour and a ham for ditto canned goods (sardines & salmon) and some breakfast foods. Now there!

I may have to go East in the near future and spend a day with our Schnuckie[3]—expect to go to Washington at the same time and make a strenuous effort to get Debs[4] out of the clutches of a reactionary and stupid government.

Mrs. Rehfeld[5] has started to work here today. She is in Toohey's[6] department.

The rest of the news you will get in the 10 page letter addressed in charge of the American Express in Tokyo.

Here I can only wish again that you will enjoy your trip as much as you deserve. And that you think of me often—thus blessing me by telepathy.

With best regards for Alma[7] and thousand kisses for you—

always your

V.L.B.

1. Meta Berger left Milwaukee around September 27, 1921, to visit Doris and Colin Welles, who were then living in the Philippines. Before her return to the United States on April 25, 1922, Meta also toured China, Japan, and Korea.

2. On October 15, 1921, the "Big Four" railroad brotherhoods called for a general strike of 750,000 railway workers to begin on October 30. A settlement was reached before the strike deadline.

3. After receiving a B.S. in medicine from the University of Wisconsin in 1921, Elsa Berger enrolled in medical school at the University of Pennsylvania in Philadelphia.

4. Eugene V. Debs entered federal prison in April, 1919, to serve a ten-year sentence following his conviction for antiwar activities under the Espionage Act.

5. Mary Rehfeld (b. 1877) was the widow of *Milwaukee Leader* business manager Ferdinand Rehfeld, who died on August 12, 1921.

6. Harry H. Toohey (b. 1882) was the circulation manager for the *Milwaukee Leader*.

7. Alma Jacobus, who accompanied Meta on the trip.

Meta to Victor

[Tokyo, Japan]

October 31, 1921

My dear Honorable Husband:—

We are in Tokyo & stopping at the Imperial Hotel. It is an awful place. They have tried to build an addition which was to be different & new & the result is it is a freak & awful. However we only expect to stay here 2 days so we can stand that.

Our bill at the Grand was $16. (each) for 2 nights all meals & the cartage of our trunks. Not so much as I tho't.

Tokyo is an immense city with much wider streets in the business section of the city but none are paved except between Streetcar tracks. Every thing else is mud. It rained & consequently it was *mud*.

Some day when the Japs get a public spirit Tokyo (down town) will really be a modern city. At present the Ginza (Their Broadway) is one heap of sink holes & torn up street with venders of all kinds of junk lined up on the sidewalk—It looks much like the East Side of N.Y.

We must take rickishaws here for the distances are very long. Yesterday we drove thro' two beautiful parks filled with Japs. In one of these Shiba Park was the first Temple that I saw that impressed me at all. It was huge, carved wood, highly colored & very very grotesque. A student priest took us thro' & explained various dragons lions & other figures. I was for the moment transfered to another age. It was of course interesting.

Then we drove thro' another park called Hibiya Park which has the largest public play ground I ever saw. Here were thousands & thousands of children & young men playing. There must be millions & millions of Japanese & no wonder they are looking for a place to expand. *They must.* It will be a case of "A place under the Sun" all over again.

Then we passed the Emperor's grounds. These are in the center of the city almost, situated high & lovely over looking the bay and are surrounded by three different moats so no one can approach.

In the evening Mr. Steindorf[1] who came over on the Empire State & who represents Home here, & a friend of his Mr. Scott, in the same dep't, took us to a real Japanese tea house for chow. This house had a pretty garden in the center, rooms encircling the garden. All rooms were typically Japanese, matting on floor, no furniture or decorations. Cushions were brought in to us after we had removed our shoes & so we sat on cushions & had a girl cook our chow (beef, rice, & onions) right before us in a little hole of a stove in the center of a low table. The fire consisted of live charcoal. The chow was very good, saki went with it. Saki is plain alcohol made of rice & must be taken hot to be at all palatable. We also had a bottle of beer, beer made in China. This was an interesting & pleasant experience.

Before coming to Tokyo, we went to Kamakura a small village on the beautiful bay. Here were numerous temples & the big bronze Buddahs. The bronze Buddah came up to expectations.

Today we are going to see the big shopping district of Tokyo 2 more parks & temples. I do not care to see any more narrow alley-way streets for they all look alike.

Will finish this letter later. But I wouldn't have written this without telling you again how much I love you & how much dearer you seem to me as I go farther away.

October 31 7. A.M.

Have just come in from another strenuous day. Tokyo is an immense city. The distances are great & one gets very tired going from place to place.

Today is the Emperor's birthday & therefore a holiday. All shops except a few first class ones are open for business but the crowds are out in the streets nevertheless.

We went out to see two parks in which are famous temples & tombs. It is most remarkable that these huge richly but grotesquely carved buildings are in as good a state of preservation as they are considering their ages & the fact that no repairing & painting is done. Some of those buildings are 300 & 400 years old & the tombs are still older. Both Mr. Steindorf & his friend Mr. Scott came to the hotel at noon today & surprised us. They offered their services which are accepted with much gratitude for it is very very hard to get around this city when you don't know the language & cannot read the signs. Mr. Scott has been here a year & has studied Japanese & therefore was a great help to us. We never could have done it alone & seen so much. Both of these men are college boys from Washington University Georgetown.

I cannot describe these temples nor give you any kind of an idea of Tokyo except its size. It has 2,800,000 inhabitants. Some streets are no more than 8 or 10 ft wide & very very dirty & smelly. In fact the white folks here ask you if you are familiar with the national air & you get familiar with it before you are in the place 5 minutes.

Tomorrow we leave for Nikko. They tell me nothing I have seen so far compares with Nikko. I am all expectant.

Tokyo reminds me of a world's fair midway.

Sweetheart, goodnight. Ich hab Dich zum sterben lieb.[2]

Always your own
Meta

1. Paul P. Steintorf (1894–1957) served in Tokyo with the Far Eastern Division of the Bureau of Foreign and Domestic Commerce beginning in 1920 and eventually became trade commissioner, a post he held from 1926 to 1937.
2. I love you to death.

Victor to Meta

Washington, D.C.
December 8, 1921

My sweet Schatzl:

I am in Washington (on my way to New York tomorrow)—but trying to make an appointment with the President in the Debs matter. Senator Lenroot is trying to bring it about—he is now getting the Leader every day—and to my dismay Irvin Lenroot pointed out an editorial attack upon him in the Leader just while I was asking him for a favor. My friend John M. Work did it, of course.

Just at present it looks as if I will have to return here next week for the appointment,—probably next Saturday—since all his time is taken up with the so-called Arms Conference and the incumbent "social affairs." We ought to have two Presidents—one for business and another for "social functions."

Under the circumstances I have wired to Schnuckie to meet me at the Broad street station in Philadelphia tomorrow at 4 P.M.—and go to New York with me on the next train. At the end of next week—I intended to spend a day with Elsa in the City of Brotherly Love, but it seems I shall have to go [to] Washington directly, because that is more important.

I have an idea that I will be successful—especially since both Lenroot and Guy D. Goff[1] told me that the President wants to see me.

In New York we will give Saturday and Sunday to our relatives—Elsa to return to Philadelphia on Monday morning. This will give me only 5 days at best in New York, (may be only 4½) but I shall try to make the best of my time, especially as to advertising contracts for our paper.

Must see also Hillquit, the Rand School, Lee etc., of course—all of which will require time.

I am writing these lines in Meyer London's office—expecting word from the Wisconsin senator as to the exact date of the appointment.

I am stopping at the Congress Hall Hotel, which is very much the same place as it was, when we were there. The women there make me sick, although some of them, Mrs. Rose, Mrs Adair[2] and one or two others came up and wanted to be remembered to you.

Met Dallinger on the street. He told that personally he always was "friendly to me." With a rather sheepish face he also admitted that it would have been only fair to defer the decision of the case until the Supreme Court had taken action. Cole, Rose[3] and Welty told me the same thing yesterday.

And Welty—who is now an "ex" but on some business in Washington—also explained that they—Cole, Rose, Welty and Luehring[4]—had an agreement with Rodenberg[5] to sign his report to that effect, which would make it a majority report. But owing to the absence of "Bill" they did not dare to do so. But they did dare to make rotten speechs against me in order to prove their "100 per cent patriotism" and to "kow-tow" to the war-hysteria.

Rodenberg—after telling me that I was the most daring (or one of the most daring) men he has ever met—a man rather "fool-hardy", he said—explained that his absence from the House just at that time was caused by the sickness of his aged mother who afterwards died. He claimed that he had the promise of the other 4 men to sign his report but Randall (of Kenosha) succeeded in scaring them out of it, while Rodenberg was absent. I believe that Randall did not have to frighten them very much; they were pretty well scared by the "general atmosphere" prevailing in Congress and in the press at that time.

But enough of that.

I hope that you enjoy your trip, Schatzl—if you don't then you would be wasting money badly.

Therefore I want [you] to take in everything and see everything that a reasonable and respectable tourist can,—but above all I want to take good care of your health and your comfort. Under no circumstances over-do anything. I want a new and healthy Mama when you return—and a Mama as good as she was in every other respect.

Give my love to my kids and to Alma[6] and don't permit Dudd to worry in any way.

With many kisses
Your V.L.B.

1. Guy Despard Goff (1866–1933) served as U.S. district attorney for the Eastern District of Wisconsin, 1911–1915, as assistant U.S. attorney general, 1917 and 1920–1923, and as a Republican U.S. senator from West Virginia, 1925–1931.

2. Probably Fannie Slick Rose, the wife of Republican representative John Marshall Rose of Pennsylvania, and Grace Johnson Adair, the wife of John A. M. Adair, a former Democratic representative from Indiana.

3. John Marshall Rose (1856–1923), a Republican representative from Pennsylvania, 1917–1923.

4. Oscar Raymond Luhring (1879–1944), a Republican representative from Indiana, 1919–1923.

5. William August Rodenberg (1865–1937), a Republican representative from Illinois, 1899–1901, 1903–1913, and 1915–1923. As a member of the committee that considered Berger's eligibility for the House in 1919, Rodenberg issued a minority report that recommended postponing the decision on Berger's seating until the courts acted on his appeal.

6. Alma Jacobus.

Victor to Meta

Philadelphia, Pennsylvania
December 16, 1921

My sweet Schatzl:

You will probably be surprised to get a letter from me from Philadelphia—but I have spent the last 2 weeks in the east. Was rather successful in landing advertisements—three contracts in New York, with prospects of a few more. And what is of greater importance still, had a heart-to-heart talk with President Harding[1] yesterday, in which I told him that they kept the wrong man in prison, since E. V. Debs was not present in St. Louis when the famous War Program was framed and was even almost ready to repudiate it—when he was arrested on account of a speech where he was intoxicated with his own words and carried away by the applause, this often happens to orators, actors and lawyers. I told him that nobody could have swayed the St. Louis Socialist Convention at that time—but that I did not even try.

The President was seemingly impressed—asked many questions—expressed his regrets at the end of the interview that he could [not] stay any longer because there was a meeting of the cabinet—and in the end invited me to come to see him as often as I am in Washington.

Now while a good deal of this may be "senatorial courtesy" and plain "politics", there is no doubt that he is convinced that the Socialists are not wolves but human beings after all. At any rate he seemed to be anxious to keep in touch with the movement and its spokesmen. As to Debs—I have no doubt that he will be a free man before this letter reaches you.

And now to our Schnuckie! She is a "Nixnutz"[2] who is trying to play the "popularity stunt"—and going out with ½ dozen different boys to theaters, dances and parties. As long as she keeps her head and her health—and does not lose any time from her studies, I don't mind it a bit. But Elsa is very apt to over-do these things, therefore I suggest that you issue a solemn warning.

At any rate I had Elsa, Margaret Doer and Ardis Hess[3] out to dinner last night and they almost ate me out of house and home. Their boarding house is simply wretched—a ramshackle old place where they still use gas—and the food is as poor as the house. Next year Elsa will have to change it.

Elsa went with me to Bridgeport last Sunday where she was lionized no little. We also went to see Edith and Rose[4]—who just bought a house lately—had dinner at Lee's and visited with Hillquits. Elsa was considered "wonderful" wherever we went. She can be very nice when she wants to be.

Just now she wants me to buy Christmas presents for a number of people—among them Ora R. McMurry[5]—and also to pay some debts for her, (she said she had to pay a duty of $13.75 on the Kimona you sent her and which I could have gotten for about that sum in some Jap shop in Chicago.)

Which again proves that you should not buy expensive things in the Far East, if you love me. I buy you nothing because I love you. But Schnucks is right behind me and she is very anxious to go shopping, since we have not much time because I leave for home this evening.

Take good care of yourself, sweetheart—With thousand kisses

Your V.L.B.

1. President Warren G. Harding (1865–1923) announced on December 23, 1921, that Debs and twenty-three other political prisoners would be freed on Christmas Day.
2. a little good-for-nothing.
3. Margaret Doerr (Muendel) (1899–1976) and Ardis Marie Hess (Kaufman) (1899–1972) were classmates of Elsa's in medical school at the University of Pennsylvania. Muendel later worked as a physician in New York; Kaufman practiced medicine in Pennsylvania.
4. Victor's sister, Rose Berger Morganstern, and her daughter, Edith Morganstern Lehman, who were living in Hoboken, New Jersey.
5. Ora Richard McMurry (1894–1974) received a B.S. from the University of Wisconsin in 1922 and an M.D. from the University of Pennsylvania in 1924; he later practiced medicine in Eagle River, Wisconsin. Elsa and McMurry were engaged to be married from 1921 until November, 1922.

Victor to Meta

Milwaukee, Wisconsin
February 12, 1922

My dear Schatzl:—

Did not want to write to you unless I could enclose a draft. After some hard thinking and hustling, I succeeded in providing a New York draft for $1,000—which I was told was better than gold.

As conditions are in Europe and Asia now—New York exchange commands a larger premium than gold. By-the-way, the draft would really mean gold, if you should insist on it.

This money I sent in a *registered* letter on January 7th 1922—expecting it would reach Los Banos sometime early in February.

Moreover, to save you some anxiety, I sent a cable message to Colin on Jan. 25th telling you of the draft.

Still I had a certain feeling that everything was not as it should be. Therefore, in the early part of last week I went to the postmaster and had the letter traced, which was easy enough, since it had been registered.

And then I found that the druggist where I had registered it on Jan. 7th (Saturday) did not send it to the post office until the *next* day (Sunday) and that on that occassion a substitute-clerk handled the mail, who believing that the shortest route to Los Banos and the Philippines was via New York—sent the letter east, instead of west.

That meant a delay of at least 5 days and possibly more, if the letter missed a boat.

I was worried and tried to cable again yesterday but was told that I could not cable, except by way of England, (which would mean *double* cost) because the *Pacific* cable or wire-less was out of order.

Since I could not do much good by sending the few words, and knowing that Alma[1] would have enough money to help you out until the draft reached you, I did not cable again.

I am very glad that you are enjoying your trip, because the extra-expense is not an easy matter for me. The interest on my debts are *very high*. I paid $656.15 in taxes alone this year (i.e. last month)—with the Federal income tax still coming. Then there is my life-insurance. Elsa is also costing a lot of money this year, and M.S. is getting his 50.00 a month (on account) automatically. Surely this is no picnic for me, this year.

But I made it all right so far—and I hope to live long enough to pay off the mortgage on the house, pay off the farm and pay off what we owe on our shares in the Leader—I am willing to sell and liquidate everything else. But it is a very hard job.

Colin's idea of starting an agricultural paper may be all right. I would prefer, of course, to see him in the business department of the

Leader but if he wants to be an agriculturist I am with him. Doris can be in the Leader.

By the way—Doris promised (and offered) to write various articles for me, but I did not see any. The tropical climate (and the worry about her work) is taking the starch out of the girl, I suppose.

At any rate, I am also glad for *her sake* that you went to the Philippines.

On your way home—look out for that robber's roost Cairo. I see from reports in the newspapers that they are taking every advantage of travelers there—and especially of Americans—all of whom are supposed to be multi millionaires, particularly if they are "globe-trotters". They are the favorite prey.

The same will hold good (in a somewhat lesser degree) of Italy, France and Switzerland.[2]

In Austria, Germany and England you will have the advantage of knowing the language and also of the "valuta";—you will learn the present value of the dollar. But the war has made all Europeans—and especially all Germans—desparately poor and they look upon every tourist as a "golden goose" that must lay "golden eggs".

The Leader is making good. We have considerable Schuster and Gimbel advertising—and I also hope to get *more* Boston copy in the near future. The *circulation* of the paper is holding out very well.

Slowly but surely, we are getting back our outside advertising. The Leader will be a wonderful newspaper some of these days—also from a business point of view.

I may have to give up the New Day,[3] however and I shall surely send no more money to the Oklahoma paper.

There is to be an annual stockholder's meeting in Oklahoma City next Wednesday and I will leave for that point tonight. It is really surprising that the Oklahoma paper is still in existence. It prints only 4 pages now and wants to give up even its press service and use Milwaukee plates—(or rather matrices) in order to survive. It still has about 14,000 daily—mainly mail subscribers.

I expect to return by the end of the week because I want to observe a meeting called by railroad men, miners, machinists etc. in Chicago. While they *disclaim* the formation of a new party—such may be the outcome.[4]

Mac[5] came in a week ago Friday (Feb 3rd) to spend the "week end". He seems to like me very much more than he used to.

Elsa wrote me that she wants to spend the summer in some hospital in the east as an "interne". Nothing doing! She must come home and spend the summer with you in Shawano.

At any rate she writes rarely, and very unsastisfactory notes. Her last "letter" was the scribbling of three different days on a little sheet of paper telling me that she is busy and that Ardis Hess has an attack of the "flu". Told Elsa to take care of her health. I may go East again in March or April.

The dogs I have returned—temporarily at least. Anna was going to strike on account of the muss they made. Moreover, they ran away quite frequently, since there [was] nobody at home to play with them—and then I had to pay "ransom". When you are back we shall decide what to do with them—may be we will have the boys build a dog house for them.

Hattie and Frank[6] were at the house for about a week during the auto-show. Hattie looks as usual i.e. good.

The car is at Abresch again. While we use it very little—not once in 2 weeks—the *paint cracked* off the *radiator* during the extreme cold we had for a few days. Will have that fixed and also a new coat of varnish for the entire car.

I dont get my sweat-baths as I used to, which is a bad thing for me. I now have a touch of rheumatism, something I never had before.

I go to the German theater rather frequently—and whenever I cannot I give the ticket to Ziegler's.

Gretchen[7] is working for the Co-operative Printery now. When Oscar Trazewitz[8] left on Jan 1st—(he had been a secret partner in the Atlas printery for some time—throwing all the business he could that way—and is now blossoming out as its "president")—his assistant, Miss Eleanor Somers, (who did the figuring on the small jobs and had a salary of $30.00 per week) informed us that she expected 45.00 in future, or she would leave. I promptly told her to leave, and put Gretchen in her place.

It will also interest you that two weeks ago, we had the fire department busy in your corner flat on the South Side. The damage will be between $500.00 and $600.00 and Gustav Schmidt, the carpenter, is busy repairing it. The insurance companies will have to pay for the loss, of course.

Well, this is about all the local home news I can think of, at the present moment. The bigger things you undoubtedly got from the Leader while you were with Doris.

I cannot meet you in Egypt—I would not have the money, even if I could get the passport.

As for my case—while my interview with the President was very cordial, I did not mention my case (or rather my various cases) at all, of course. I was not begging for any mercy, nor did I ask for any pardon for myself. From all sides I have the positive assurance that my "cases" are dead absolutely.

On the other hand, the lawyers warn me "not to wake any sleeping dogs"—if "the department" wanted to, it could "select" jurors in Chicago, Milwaukee or anywhere even now—in very much the same fashion as some years ago, and with similar results. The lawyers advise me to let the affair die a *natural death*. It may be the wisest thing to do so. Moreover, I have no money for more troubles. I am still in debt for the past.

And therefore, sweet Schatzl, I would appreciate it, if you could get along with the $1,000 draft I mailed on Jan. 7th. However I want you to travel in comfort, and if you need it, I shall have to send you $500.00 more, I suppose, in order to get my Schatzl home. Above all I want you *to enjoy* your trip—only it is really extremely hard sometimes to get the money—and still harder to pay it back. However, I don't want you to worry about that.

And now Schatzl, I will close. Miss Thomas is coming to dinner today—Edwin[9] is here already—and I have not as yet taken my weekly "abolution".

It is unneccesary for me to tell you that I *love you*—I am proving it, I believe. No man in *my economic sphere,* and with circumstances as they are, would send his wife to a trip like yours—unless he *loved her* and believed that it would *do* her *a lot of good.* I sincerely hope it will.

With thousand kisses
Your V.L.B.

1. Alma Jacobus.
2. Meta Berger did not visit Europe and North Africa on her tour; rather, she returned to the United States via the Pacific.
3. The Socialist Party published the weekly *New Day* in Chicago from June, 1920, until April, 1921, when the Milwaukee Social-Democratic Publishing Company assumed control of the paper and moved it to Milwaukee under the editorship of Frederic Heath. Berger discontinued the paper in July, 1922.
4. The organizational meeting of the Conference for Progressive Political Action, which brought together labor leaders, Socialists, Farmer-Laborites, and other progressives, eventually led to the 1924 presidential candidacy of Robert M. La Follette Sr. but never resulted in the creation of a labor party as desired by Berger and other Socialists.
5. Ora McMurry.
6. Hattie and Frank Schweers, Meta's sister and brother-in-law.
7. Gretchen Ziegler, the daughter of former *Milwaukee Leader* business manager Edward Ziegler, later became manager of the Co-operative Printery. Berger established the business in 1905 to do printing for the Socialist Party and for the Milwaukee Social-Democratic Publishing Company.
8. Oscar Traczewitz had been manager of the Co-operative Printery.
9. Edwin Schweers, the stepson of Meta's sister, Hattie.

Victor to Meta

Milwaukee, Wisconsin
July 12, 1922

My sweet Schatzl:

Your letter and Doris' letter received. I want to send them a steamer letter and a telegram—but I have forgotten the name of the steamer of the Admiral line—on which they arrive.[1] I asked Mable[2] to find out from the post-office, but nobody seems to [know] anything there. If I cannot learn the name from the American Express Co. I shall have to telephon to the agency in Chicago.

Have sent you a Fisk tire (35-by 4½) by express. Also some fruit. Hope you will receive everything in good condition.

It is wrong for you, sweetheart to gage my love for you by the number of letters I am writing. I was never much of a letter writer.

> My love is as deep as the ocean,
> > My love is as strong as the sea—
> It is foolish to judge my devotion
> > By the letters I am writing to thee!

So there, young woman of 49! You are driving [me] into poetry. And poetry I have always considered a mild and beautiful form of insanity.

At any rate I have paid a certain Mr. Calligan who has made the cement steps on your alley house $45.00, which I consider a big sum for that kind of work. He claimed that you ordered the job.

Next Sunday is the state picnic—and at the same time I should be in Buffalo where the National Executive Committee holds its session. I moved to postpone the meeting but that was voted down. I will stay home and attend the state picnic.

By the way—the picnic-committee, (made up of a lot of big overgrown minors), has made a contract with a negro jazz-band—the one that made the noise for the minstrel show—to furnish the music. Now those negroes danced with the white girls at the minstrel show and even took some of them home. Some women protested in writing—and with farmers coming in from everywhere to the state-picnic, I can see trouble ahead, if these colored people should take any liberties. Well, I suggested to Seidel to ask these musical "bandits" not to try to dance themselves—but only to furnish the music for [the] rest.

Well, darling, there is not much news. I am at work every day, as usual trying to do as much as I can.

With much love,

Your
Papa

1. Doris and Colin Welles returned from the Philippines in July, 1922.
2. Probably Mabel Search.

Victor to Meta

[Milwaukee, Wisconsin]
July 27, 1922

My dear Schatzl:

It is extremely hot here—and I am very glad for your sake and for the children—that you are in Shawano.

Miss Thomas has returned, but I cannot possibly leave here for another week—on account of financial matters in connection with my trip to Europe. I expect my pass to arrive by the end of next week.

In connection with any action of the Department of Injustice, I was told that even *if* they tried any "funny" business—it would be impossible before December. As the matter stands now the Appelleate court has not as yet rendered its decision, which of course, it cannot until vacation is over. The decision must be a reversal since the Supreme Court has so ruled.

Now then, even if the decision should come as the first business after the vacation and the Republican administration would decide on another trial at once—they would have to give the lawyers 90 days or more time to prepare—, which would make it impossible for the case to come up this year. Moreover, when in Washington Guy D. Goff told me that the case was as dead as a door-nail—the only thing I worried about was—that they *might* call up the case while I was in Europe, but that cannot be done.

Therefore, if I can get the money I shall go.

In the midst of this letter I was interrupted by a noisy quarrel between Tuohy and Mabel.[1] It seems that our friend Beitz[2] has sent in a news item about the newly founded Loan and Building association expecting an extra-boom, which he did not get. Tuohy is one of the original charter-members and raised a fearful howl, which was answered by cynical and scornful remarks on the part of Mable. I finally pacified them.

I enclose a letter from Mrs Lee and an editorial from the Milwaukee Journal. You will be interested in both. Now don't worry and don't work!

With love to all

Papa.

1. Mabel Search.
2. William R. Beitz (1870–1929) was secretary of the Home Mutual Building and Loan Association in Milwaukee and served on the board of directors of the Milwaukee Social-Democratic Publishing Company.

Victor to Meta

Milwaukee, Wisconsin
July 31, 1922

My sweet Schatzl:

There is really no news—except that it is very warm here and that I got angry at the ice-man because he came so late to the house this morning.

Tonight I am going to the circus with Tom Duncan.[1] Have invited him to a bachelor supper at the house and then he will take me over in the machine, if a Ford deserves that title. However, if I had to use the street car—I would rather not go at all, there will be too much of a jam going home.

Tomorrow I am going to Chicago—I haven't been there in a long time. But there is not much foreign business now—although it will begin in August i.e. that is the time when some of the newspaper lists are made up by the "ad" agencies.

If Doris positively wants to go to Scotia I shall get the money for her, of course. Would prefer that she waits until the 12th. It would also be a nice thing for Colin and her to accompany us on our trip through the northern woods—which will take 4 or 5 days next week.

I can readily understand, however that a person with Doris' temperament is not very happy in Shawano after the novelty has worn off in the first 3 days. Neither would she like it in Scotia, however, for any lenght of time.

But for you, Schatzl, the peace of Shawano is real tonic for your nerves—provided the kids let you have much peace.

The newspapers are still keeping up their attacks upon me—linking me up with La Follette—or even hyphenating our names. Especially the Sentinel editorials are the acme of silliness. Unless our people in Wisconsin are not only crazy but also idiotic—Bob ought to be nominated 3 to 1.[2] Since the Journal and the Sentinel have made the war the issue, no other result should be possible.

With the trend of public opinion among Radicals in Milwaukee just now, there is even great danger that our people by taking part in the Republican primary, will weaken our own battle line to such a degree— as to endanger our own nominations. We must send out at least one strong letter before the primary—showing that the La Follette affair is a "one man" affair—and that the success of the La Follette agitation depends very largely on the existence of a strong and lively party in Wisconsin. The La Follette "idea" surely cannot expect much support from either the Republican or the Democratic organization.

Well, sweetheart, I don't want to talk so much politics to you.

What I want you to do—is to take a good long rest and to bother about nothing.

Alles was ich von Dir noch verlang ist, daß Du mich sehr lieb hast.[3]
With love to all

Papa.

1. Thomas M. Duncan (1893–1959), a Socialist from Milwaukee, served as
secretary to Mayor Daniel Hoan, 1920–1929, as a state assemblyman, 1923–
1929, and as a state senator, 1929–1932. Duncan resigned from the Socialist
Party in 1931 and served as Governor Philip F. La Follette's chief aide, 1931–
1933 and 1935–1938. He served as director of the AFL-CIO Committee on
Political Action, 1947–1958.
2. Robert M. La Follette Sr. won renomination to the U.S. Senate with 72
percent of the vote and carried the general election with 81 percent. Wisconsin's Socialists did not nominate a senatorial candidate in 1922, causing the
press to link Berger with La Follette.
3. All that I am still asking of you is, that you love me very much.

Victor to Meta

Washington, D.C.
November 21, 1922

My dear Schatzl:

We spent a most profitable day in Washington. I went to see Rodenberg and met Nic. Longworth[1] there—both assured me that there was
not the slightest danger of my being unseated[2]—in fact they did not
believe that anybody would raise the question now, since the cases are
knocked out. James R. Mann, Speaker Gillette and a few others were of
the same opinion. And more than that—the clerk of the House Wm
Tyler Page[3] consulted Mann about the pay checks and was told that all
he had to do is to make sure that he got the election certificate from
the secretary of the state—that puts me automatically upon the pay roll.
Any other steps would be the business of the House and not of the
clerk. Mr. Page so informed me with a sweet sour smile, and also that
he hoped that the House would not be called into extra-session next
April. (The interview with the clerk I want you to keep quiet because I
don't want the profiteer press to set up a howl). Tomorrow I shall try to
see a few prominent Democratic leaders and on Thursday we may drop
in on Harding. By Friday we will be ready to leave Washington for New
York and Philadelphia.

Just as a matter of pre-caution I shall have interviews with the editors of the Times, World, Nation, Freeman, New Republic etc—as the
situation is now that is hardly necessary.

M[a]y stay over for Edna's[4] wedding—provided I can profitably
employ my time to get advertising for the Leader.

Well, sweet Schatzl—so far so good! There is another worry that
you may just as well dismiss.

We came down in the same sleeper from Chicago with Mr. & Mrs William La Follette[5] who formerly represented a district in the state of Washington. Both send their best regards to you. Their daughter[6] is one o[f] the editors of the Freeman in New York.

There is nothing else to write about—except that I do not want you to work or to worry. If seated I shall not run for Congress again—unless they insisted to make me a U.S. Senator and the election was absolutely sure.

With many kisses and loving thoughts

Your V.L.B.

1. Nicholas Longworth (1869–1931), a Republican representative from Ohio, 1903–1913 and 1915–1931. Longworth served as Republican floor leader, 1923–1925, and as Speaker of the House, 1925–1931.

2. Berger had been elected to Congress earlier in the month, winning 53 percent of the vote against 47 percent for incumbent Republican William H. Stafford.

3. William Tyler Page (1868–1942), clerk of the House of Representatives, 1919–1931, served that body in various capacities from 1881 until his death.

4. Edna Weingarten (1894–1992), the daughter of Victor's sister, Mathilde, married Arthur B. Weiss (1895–1966) in Bridgeport, Connecticut, on November 30, 1922.

5. William Leroy La Follette (1860–1934), a Republican representative from Washington, 1911–1919, and his wife, Mary Tabor La Follette (b. 1865).

6. Suzanne Clara La Follette (1893–1983), a feminist writer, served as assistant editor of the *Freeman*, 1920–1924. She later wrote and edited for the *American Mercury* and served as a founding editor of the *National Review*.

Victor to Meta

New York, New York
November 25, [1922]

My sweet Mama:

You have not had a letter from me since Thursday—and, therefore, I owe you both a letter and a night message, which I am going to send here-with.

Well Thursday we saw the President. Lenroot's secretary, who arranged for the interview—since the Senator is in Wisconsin at present—could not locate us, we missed our regularly allotted half-an-hour, and were only switched in before lunch—and that did not make for a satisfactory interview. There were hordes waiting outside "to shake hands with him". Moreover, he had the Ship Subsidy bill on his mind and a lot of Senators in the ante-room. And thus all I could do was to tell him that I appreciated the fact that according to published statements in the press the Harding administration did not oppose my being seated—while the Wilson regime had opposed me most venemously. He said I need not thank him for that—because I evidently represented my people and my people had a right to be represented by me. Then I told them that our country was the only one which still had political prisoners—except Ireland where the political prisoners were really prisoners of a war still going on. I suggested that in view of the recent election it would not only be the right thing—but also the *wisest* thing to let them go. He answered by asking me whether fellows who advocated arson and sabotage were political prisoners? I frankly said *no*—but told him that these men were not put into prison because they were I.W.Ws but *ostensibly* at least because they were opposed to the War. And they were found guilty of violating the Espionage act. He answered that he is letting some go every day and that all of them would be liberated "in due time". The interview while exceedingly *friendly*—was not as satisfactory as it should be, or would have been, if we had had more time.

Goff has resigned his job and we were trying to see Dougherty[1]—but he wasn't in. We shall try to make an appointment on our way back home,—since we intend to stop over in Washington again in order to see Finis Garrett[2] who wants to find out the sentiment of the Democratic members in the mean time. Garrett who used to live in the Farragut appartments when we also lived there—is now acting as the Democratic floor leader.

We left Washington Friday afternoon (late) for New York.

Friday morning we had some very satisfactory interviews with Don Seitz[3] the business manager of the N.Y. World—and especially also with Frank Cobb[4] its chief editorial writer. They promised that this very important Democratic paper would absolutely and unqualifiedly *demand* that I am to be seated.

We went to lunch with Wilfred Bates[5] of our agency in New York. And from there went up to the Times but found that all the men we wanted to see were either out or to lunch.

Half in despair I finally went up to Adolf Och's[6] sanctum and sent in my card. He was also to lunch, but the secretary of the company—a Mr. Frank[7]—asked us to come into his office and sent my card to the private room where Adolf Ochs, the proprietor of the N.Y. Times,—Rollo Ogden,[8] his editor-in-chief,—Phelps Dodge[9] of the Mergenthaler Typesetting Machine Co. and of the U.S. Print Paper Co.—young H. Selfridge,[10] a department store owner from London, England—and half a dozen other invited guests whose names I do not remember had their lunch. We were invited to take part but thanked because we just came from the restaurant.

Now followed about 2 hours of the most interesting—and in all probability also—the most effective and profitable time—of this whole trip. I evidently made a great hit. After they all left Mr. Ochs invited us to stay a little longer and finally asked me to state my position in an article of about 3,000 words for next Sunday's Times (Dec. 3rd), since the issue for November 25th was virtually already in print.[11]

I shall take a few hours off on Monday to dictate the article—but make it shorter than 3,000 words because few people like to read such long articles. Mr. Ochs was very sarcastic and almost hostile at first—his invitation was evidently prompted by the curiosity of his entire company—but he surely became friendly enough before we got through. I even invited him to come to see us in Milwaukee, if he should ever come as near as Chicago. He promised to do so.

In the evening we went to see Morris Hillquit who had been attending a conference of the Committee of Fifteen,[12] which is to call the convention for December 11th. As I predicted to you, that affair is rather hopeless. The members of the railroad brotherhoods who were very much inclined towards independent action—are very cocky just now and claim that they had put over La Follette, Brookhart,[13] Frazier[14] and a number of others. They are *very willing* to stay in the old parties and to capture the nominations. It is nonsense of course,—because the old parties are the machines of capitalism and cannot serve the working class any more than a reaper could be used as a typewriter. But the railroadmen will try it again—and William Johnston,[15] the president of the Machinists who had fathered "independent action" last year is meekly seconding them now.

And Morris Hillquit to my immense surprise is now even willing that the Socialists should go in with them, and vote the old party tickets in the primaries in order "to capture them". When I told him that he would be fired out, if he should try to run on a Tammany ticket in New York he laughingly informed that unless he fired me or I fired him— there was nobody else who could fire either of us out of the Socialist party. With the exception of Milwaukee and very little in New York— there was nothing left, he said.

The seance at Hillquit's was very unsatisfactory to me.

This morning (Saturday) Mrs. Liess[16] called up from the Commodore Hotel. I went up there and found a very much changed woman. Her features have become hardened and her hair very gray— or rather very gray in spots. She is slow, lifeless and tired—and does not seem to take any interest in anything in particular, except to buy some things for her grand-children. You are about 50 years younger, sweet Schatzl, and incomparably more active and alert.

She is not at all sure that she will come to Milwaukee because she seems to be very anxious to make some date in Denver, Col.

Tomorrow, Sunday, I shall spend with Schnuckie—but come back in the evening. We will make our plans, however, about attending

Edna's[17] wedding. I am not quite sure whether I can be there, since I must be in Washington Friday morning.

Well, Schatzl—this got to be a rather lenghty and "gossippy" letter—read it in instalments, if it is too much for one sitting.

Give my love to the children and remember—as much as I may differ in my make-up and my character from the average man—you differ infinitely more from most women; you are certainly way above all the women I know. I certainly was a lucky man when I got you. Just take the best of care of yourself, sweetheart,—for *my sake at least.* Therefore, don't worry and don't over-work!

But love me—
V.L.B.

1. Harry M. Daugherty (1860–1941) served as U.S. attorney general from 1921 until 1924, when he was dismissed amid charges of corruption.

2. Finis James Garrett (1875–1956), a Democratic representative from Tennessee, 1905–1929. Garrett served as Democratic floor leader in the House, 1923–1929.

3. Don Carlos Seitz (1862–1935) served as business manager of Joseph Pulitzer's *New York World,* 1898–1923, and as manager of the *New York Evening World,* 1923–1926.

4. Frank Irving Cobb (1869–1923) was responsible for the editorial page of the *New York World* from 1904 until his death, holding the title of editor in chief beginning in 1911.

5. Wilfred G. Bates (1876?–1946) was a partner in Fralick and Bates, a newspaper advertising agency with offices in New York and Chicago.

6. Adolph S. Ochs (1858–1935) was the owner and publisher of the *New York Times* from 1896 until his death.

7. Benjamin C. Franck (1856–1932), a first cousin of Adolph Ochs, served as secretary of the New York Times Company from 1896 until his death.

8. Rollo Ogden (1856–1937) served on the editorial staff of the *New York Evening Post,* 1891–1920, and as associate editor, 1920–1922, and editor, 1922–1937, of the *New York Times.*

9. Berger meant Philip T. Dodge (1851–1931), a New York City lawyer and businessman.

10. Harry Gordon Selfridge Jr., the son of the founder of an English department store chain.

11. "Berger Defends His War Record; Sees New Fascisti in Ku Klux Klan," *New York Times,* December 3, 1922.

12. The Committee of Fifteen carried on the work of the Conference for Progressive Political Action between conventions.

13. Smith Wildman Brookhart (1869–1944), a Republican U.S. senator from Iowa, 1922–1926 and 1927–1933.

14. Lynn Frazier (1874–1947) was a Republican who served as governor of North Dakota, 1917–1921, and as a U.S. senator, 1923–1941.

15. William H. Johnston (1874–1937), a Socialist, served as president of the International Association of Machinists, 1912–1926. Johnston advocated political action by labor, helped to organize the Conference for Progressive Political Action, and presided over the convention that nominated Robert M. La Follette Sr. for president in 1924.

16. Frieda Liess (b. 1876?) was the widow of Emil Liess (1864–1917), a San Francisco attorney.

17. Victor's niece, Edna Weingarten (Weiss).

Meta to Victor

[Milwaukee, Wisconsin]
February 18, 1923

Dearest.

I have just returned from the Muehlenberg Unit No. 36 of the Steuben Society's[1] meeting.

They had an immense crowd. The entire lower floor, all the boxes, and the entire first balcony of the *entire* auditorium was *filled* with a sprinkling in the upper gallery. I didn't believe they could do it.

The crowd—well it wasn't our crowd. True here & there I saw a familiar workingman's socialist face. But almost the entire audience was made up of spiesbürger[2] & petty business men, old & gray. There were few young people there. More gray heads & bald heads & the vast majority were men.

If the Steuben Society has reached the strength this audience would indicate, then it will be a power in the body-politic. I surely was amazed.

Hoan spoke. He also was delegated to read the telegrams from Voigt, Beck[3] & Lampert[4] as well as your statement.

Unterman[5] prepared a statement which was a splendid editorial but which in my judgement didn't represent you nor your vigor or pep. It had no teeth in it. I told Unterman it lacked something upon which he replied that I could supply the adjectives. Then I took it up to Miss Thomas who tho't it was good but not sufficiently *"arousifying"*. So we tried to doctor it up. Finally I laid it aside entirely, got a Leader of Feb 8 & took your resolutions, fixed them over to read like a statement leaving the wording the same & handed that in. It got more applause than any of the others of course. In fact *it* got as much applause as any of the speakers did.

Several times when Speakers referred to La Follette & Borah[6] some one in the audience would yell "And Berger" always calling for some applause. I am sorry you could not have been a speaker too. Also sorry I didn't speak even tho' it would have been hard on my nerves. We have paid the price in nerves so often that one more time wouldn't have hurt. George W. Bruce[7] called for the most vigorous applause when he told that he himself had seen thousands of colored troupes in the Rhine District & then called Clemenceau a "damned liar".[8]

Other speakers were Hoan, F. X Bodden,[9] Bomrich.[10]

The programe was well arranged for the band played a popular peppy German air between each speaker like "Oh Lauterbach" Mädel

rück zur meiner grüne Seite[11] etc etc thus working on German sentiment all the more so much for that.

Now I am waiting for Betty to come for supper.

This morning Anna didn't get up until 10 A.M. She was at the
masked ball of the Freie Gemeinde[12] until 4 A.M. Yesterday I took care
of that statement, called on Nettie R.[13] who is ill & in bed & then went
to the Club meeting. This morning I wrote letters to the tenants, to
Doris, Elsa & Hattie. This is my 13th letter today. I haven't wasted a
minute since I got up this A.M. I want Betty to mail this this evening.

Please be careful of yourself. And when you see Elsa in Philadelphia, urge her to take care of the sciatica & her teeth. She must be tired
at this season of the year or she wouldn't have so many things the matter with her. But don't scold her. Talk nicely to her. Tell her I worry
about her etc etc.

Besides all this tell her how much I love her.

I hate so to see you always go away & yet I know it must be done.

Best luck & most devoted love to you always.

Meta

1. The Steuben Society was a German-American patriotic organization
founded in 1919. The Milwaukee meeting was held to protest French occupation of the Ruhr.

2. comfortable, narrow-minded, middle-class people.

3. Joseph David Beck (1866–1936), a Republican representative from Wisconsin, 1921–1929, and a member of the Wisconsin Industrial Commission,
1911–1917.

4. Florian Lampert (1863–1930), a Republican representative from Wisconsin, 1918–1930.

5. Ernest Untermann (1864–1956), a German-born Socialist theoretician,
writer, and artist, served on the editorial staff of the *Milwaukee Leader* from 1915
to 1916, when he resigned because of Berger's complaints about the pro-
German tone of his writings. Untermann worked for the *Leader* again during
the 1920s and later became director of Milwaukee's Washington Park Zoo.

6. William E. Borah (1865–1940), a Republican senator from Idaho,
1907–1940.

7. Meta Berger meant William George Bruce (1856–1949), a journalist
and publisher who served as president of the Milwaukee Harbor Commission,
1913–1945.

8. Georges Eugène Benjamin Clemenceau (1841–1929) served as French
premier, 1906–1909 and 1917–1920. The use of Senegalese troops to occupy
Germany immediately after World War I provoked complaints from the German government. During his visit to the United States in late 1922,
Clemenceau declared that there were no longer any black troops in Germany, a
statement that U.S. Senator Gilbert Hitchcock (D-Nebr.) called a lie.

9. Frank X. Bodden (1869–1934) was the vice-president of a Milwaukee
bank and insurance company.

10. Louis G. Bohmrich (1855–1925) was a German-born Milwaukee lawyer
who ran for governor of Wisconsin in 1900 as a Democrat.

11. Lass, come close to me.
12. The Frei Gemeinde (Free Congregation) was a liberal German social organization founded in Milwaukee in 1851.
13. Annette Rosenthal (Gould).

Victor to Meta

New York, New York
February 26, 1923

My sweet Schatzl:

Although my night messages by wire kept you fairly well informed of my movements and doings—I feel that I owe you a good long letter.

I shall begin with Washington. There the atmosphere was decidedly friendly—with the single exception of Dallinger. I did not see him but London told me that he says that the House would "stultify" itself, if it did seat me now, after I had been refused a seat twice. I replied to London that in my opinion the House "stultified" itself when it *refused* to seat me, since I was legally elected every time.

When I called on the Attorney General, he asked me to return later in the day in order to give me the exact "status" of my various cases.

That the Wisconsin cases have been "nolled"[1] you know, of course. But I have been surprised to learn that Charlie Cline had been ordered on September 16th 1922 to "nolle" my Chicago case, that he acknowledged a letter received a month later by the Department of Justice the receipt of the order. In November 1922 he asked the Department whether that meant that he should *also* "quash" the cases against the other 4 defendants? And in December he admitted receiving the order to *also* annul the cases of the others.

Since then the Department has heard nothing from Charlie—but the Attorney-General asked me whether my attorney, a man by the name of Seymour Stedman was asleep? When I get to Chicago I shall ask Stedy the same question. But remember, we were always afraid to wake up the sleeping dogs.

While in Washington I looked up the Clerk of the House (Mr. Page) and received the blanks for the appointment of my secretaries. I labored under a misapprehension in that respect. I thought the salary was $3,200 for one clerk—it is really the *total* sum allowed for clerk hire, the congressman is permitted to divide it up as he cho[o]ses. Only in case he divides it among 2 persons—*each* person appointed is entitled to a *"bonus"* of $20.00 a month additional. Thus if I appoint one secretary with $2,000 and the other with $1,200,—the first one will have $2,240 and the other $1,440 annually.

We will talk this over when I get home.

As for my salary—I have signed my pay-checks for the *first year* at the office of the Sergeant-at-Arms.

I stopped over in Philadelphia for 2 days. Found my Schnuckie an expensive proposition. Had to buy slippers ($10.00) and had to take out her friends—the girls and the boys—to dinners and suppers, which cost me a lot of money. Schnucks and her two girl friends came with me to New York for 2 days. I could not give them much attention, (since I was in session) but Schnuck managed to get $15.00 out of me for shirt-waists and gloves. Schnuck is a bad Racker[2]—I shall not invite her to go to New York with me any more.

While in Philadelphia I went to see the Saturday Evening Post. It so happened that Lorimer,[3] the editor is still in California and not expected to return until March 5th—but the assistant editors seemed to think that it would be very interesting to have my point of view represented as to the conditions prevailing in Europe today. They suggested that I write a letter to Lorimer as soon as he returns.

The meeting of the National Executive Committee was of special interest to me this time, because it revealed to me the fact that Hillquit was utterly at sea and hopeless as far as the Socialist party is concerned—and he also seemed to have given up hope to get anything worth while out of the Chicago-Cleveland conferences.[4] Well, I am not quite as dejected as he is—but the party will have hard sledding for some time to come. The stupidity and ignorance of both the capitalist parties (*and* of the "reformers") however, will build us up again and make us much bigger than ever before. At the meeting you were elected an *"alternate"*—and so was Vera Hillquit. This will give you a badge, a seat in the convention, and the admission to all the "festivities". You have even the right to speak but have no vote.

I am trying to get our tickets to Europe and return—on an advertising contract. It is *hardly ever done,* but I have set the wheels in motion and hope to succeed. Don't tell anything to anybody, please.

Thank you for your congratulatory letter and for tending to the tax matter so promptly, Darling.

And get ready for the trip to New York—Schatzl. Let us hope that apart from the serious and solemn occassion—and the condition of the people of Germany—the trip to Europe will prove to us *personally* a most interesting and pleasant one.

Expect to return to Milwaukee on Monday. Will stop over to see Stedy for a few hours.

Well, sweetheart—this is about all the important news—and it is probably enough for one letter.

I have not called up my people—shall leave that for the end of the week.

Brisbane is out of town—but I shall try to see "Moe" Annenberg[5]—his man-Friday.

Shall also make the rounds among some of our advertisers and those that we intend to get.

Hope you received the two night letters, which I sent to Madison.

And now, sweet Schatzl, remember that it was you—and you only—who made it possible for me to stay in the movement and build up whatever has been build up, especially as to the paper. And it was *you* especially who had to sacrifice—and for that matter is still sacrificing, Schatzl.

Auf baldiges Wiedersehen![6] With thousand kisses

Your
V.L.B.

Post Scriptum:

By-the-way, Schatzl—*Don't* reproach my Schnuckie about bringing her friends to dinners and suppers. *I do the inviting*, you know.

Moreover, any letter like that might get into the hands of her friends—they have a common household, you know—and create bad blood.

With love

Papa

1. *Nolle prosequi* is a declaration by a prosecutor that a case will not be pursued. Berger's indictments in Wisconsin under the Espionage Act had been dropped on May 8, 1922. The federal attorney for the Northern District of Illinois announced on January 8, 1923, that he would not prosecute the Chicago indictments again, although Berger and the *Milwaukee Leader* did not learn of the dismissal of these charges until late February, 1923. See "Last Charges Against Berger Are Dropped," *Milwaukee Leader*, February 27, 1923.

2. rascal.

3. George Horace Lorimer (1867–1937) served as editor of the *Saturday Evening Post*, 1899–1936.

4. The February, 1922, Chicago meeting and the December, 1922, Cleveland meeting of the Conference for Progressive Political Action.

5. Moses Louis "Moe" Annenberg (1878–1942) served as circulation director for Hearst publications from 1920 to 1924. After leaving the Hearst organization in 1926, Annenberg made a fortune through his newspapers and his racing news services, although he spent his final years in federal prison because of tax fraud. From 1907 until 1920 Annenberg lived in Milwaukee, where he established a newspaper distribution agency and briefly served as publisher of the Hearst-owned *Wisconsin News*.

6. See you soon!

Victor to Meta

New York, New York
February 27, 1923

My sweet Schatzl:

I spent a busy day today. Was hot at the trail of Mr. Rosenfeld (who is Viereck's business manager)[1] to make arrangements for tickets—can get the best "cabin de luxe" for a *minimum* first class payment—about $840.00 for a round trip ticket, but I sent the man back to the manager offering an advertising arrangement. Will know more about it by tomorrow evening.

Also got the solicitor of Fralick & Bates on the same mission to other companies. I shall succeed someway, I hope.

Had a very impressive and confidential talk with Roger Baldwin[2] the head of that "million dollar" Foundation.[3] Told him that we had the only successful daily Radical paper in the English speaking world, and that I would let the Foundation continue it—since I had no son or son-in-law willing to shoulder the burden—if the Foundation would give me $250,000 to get the majority of the stock and pay some of my personal debts. He seemed to be very much impressed, but he did not know whether the other directors—Norman Thomas[4]—and a few more, would take to it.

By the way, Norman Thomas or Harry Laidler[5] will be in Milwaukee next Monday—and will undoubtedly show up at the Leader. They do not know anything about my plans, of course, but be friendly tell them that I will be home late in the afternoon.

Had also a talk with Don Seitz business manager of the N.Y. World. That trail leads nowhere.

Was at the Rand school and Bertha Mailly[6]—my bosom enemy of old·standing—was so friendly that she called me "Victor" all the time.

Part of the afternoon I spent to find out why we had not received a Price Baking Powder ad—which I had been promised last Christmas. I was told that we are on the list but that internal difficulties of the concern had prevented any and all copy from going out.

Invited Morris Hillquit to go out to lunch with me—and then forgot all about it. I shall hear about that for a long time.

Late in the afternoon I went to visit the Vorwaerts people and Abe Cahan[7] offered me $300 for 12 articles, which they of course, would have to translate. That sum is the maximum they pay. I will not accept the mission, but I appreciate the spirit.

For tomorrow—which happens to be my birthday—the Vorwaerts bunch (under the leadership of Vladeck)[8] has arranged a luncheon in my honor—at the Hotel LaFayette, where you and I had dinner once, which did not impress us particularly, although it was expensive enough.

Tonight I was to speak in Brooklyn at a Ruhr protest meeting—i.e. I told them that I could not come, yet they advertised me and boomed me in all the papers. Seeing this I sent them a telegram to be read at the meeting. It contained about 200 words and cost me $5.00. I hope the message will do some good—it is expensive enough.

By-the-way, Schatzl I have all the income-tax reports of the last 4 years—including those of last year reporting for 1921—in a very large envelope in the wide drawer of the old black walnut book-case. Look them over when you have time—but dont lose any of them.

Well, darling—this developed into a chatty and gossippy letter, but I know that you will enjoy this for a change. At any rate you can see from this that I am getting around New York fast enough—in fact I had to use a taxi twice today.

You will also appreciate the fact that I am not only trying to make the European trip possible—but also comfortable and less burdensome.

Well, Sweetheart, I hope everything in going on all right at home and in our paper. You cannot expect many more letters, because they could not reach you much sooner than I.

But think of me lovingly Darling—it adds to my vigor, to my resilliance and to my determination. Ich hab' Dich lieb![9] Don't worry!

With many kisses

V.L.B.

1. Harry Rosenfeld served as secretary-treasurer of George Sylvester Viereck's Fatherland Corporation. Viereck (1884–1962), a journalist and German propagandist, defended German policies during World War I but was not prosecuted. Viereck wrote sympathetically about the Nazis during the 1930s and went to prison in 1943 as a foreign agent.

2. Roger Nash Baldwin (1884–1981), a peace and civil liberties advocate, founded the National Civil Liberties Bureau in 1917 (renamed the American Civil Liberties Union in 1920) and directed the organization until his retirement in 1949.

3. The American Fund for Public Service, established by Charles Garland in 1920, distributed more than $2 million over twelve years for working-class causes. Roger Baldwin served as secretary of the fund's board.

4. Norman Thomas (1884–1968), a Presbyterian minister and pacifist, joined the Socialist Party in 1918, became its leading spokesman after the death of Eugene Debs in 1926, and ran as the party's presidential candidate in every election from 1928 through 1948. During World War I, Thomas worked on behalf of conscientious objectors and helped to found the National Civil Liberties Bureau.

5. Harry W. Laidler (1884–1970), a Socialist since 1903, served as executive secretary of the Intercollegiate Socialist Society (called the League for Industrial Democracy after 1921) from 1910 to 1957. He joined the American Labor Party in 1937 and the Liberal Party in 1944.

6. Bertha Howell Mailly (1869–1960), the widow of former Socialist Party secretary William Mailly, served as executive secretary of the Rand School, 1912–1925, and remained affiliated with the institution until 1941.

7. Abraham Cahan (1860–1951), a Socialist journalist and author, edited the *Jewish Daily Forward* from 1903 until his death.

8. Baruch Charney Vladeck (1886–1938), a Russian-born Jewish Socialist, worked for the *Jewish Daily Forward* as manager of the Philadelphia edition, 1912–1916, as New York city editor, 1916–1918, and as general manager, 1918–1938. Vladeck served as a Socialist alderman in New York City, 1917–1921. In 1936 he helped to found the American Labor Party.

9. I love you!

Meta to Doris and Colin

Essen, Germany
July 11, 1923

My blessed Children—

We are in the occupied territory.[1]

There are so many interesting things to tell you that I know I shall forget some of the most important ones.

In the first place, the Germans are scared to death. I know they must have good reasons, for the fear is quite general. The highest official and richest capitalist has become a trembling scared individual. The organized worker, doesn't talk of fear so much as he talks of the danger to himself and to his country if the passive resistance breaks down.

But I'll have to go back a bit and begin at the beginning. When we first told of our intention of going to the Ruhr, all raised their eyebrows, and many said it was dangerous and that in all probability we couldn't get thro'.

All warned us not to ride on trains seized by the French and run by the French as it was very dangerous to do so. And no German would think of riding on that train anyway. Nevertheless, we bought our ticket thro' to Duesseldorf which is occupied territory & we shipped our baggage by train. We did not reach Duesseldorf as connections could not be made due to occupation. We changed 3 times & finally landed at Köln instead of Duesseldorf.

Men on the train in the same compartment, told us we would probably have difficulty in getting to D. as we would have to go partway by train & partway by streetcar & perhaps we would have to walk. Papa said he would get an auto, whereupon they replied that automobiles were forbidden & that no German was permitted to travel by auto, furthermore, no German could be induced to take us as all feared the French & the seizure of the auto. Anyway no gasoline would be sold to a German without a permit from a French man.

Also these men, (one a manufacturer of Kölnisches Toilette water and the other a publisher) told us of the outrages the French perbetrated on the Germans. They declared that the Germans had become virtual slaves of the soldiers of France. Not only are the Germans ordered out of their homes at midnight, wife & babies together, and deported, but that hardly enough time is given them to gather the necessary clothes to take with them. They must leave all furniture etc behind & the French as a rule destroy the belongings. They do these things to intimidate the Germans & scare them into submission.

Also we were told, that if German citizens sit quietly in a Cafe drinking coffee & a soldier suddenly appears & pounds the tables with his riding whip, & orders them all out, they must go or suffer arrest. If by chance they brush against a French man on the street (& streets & sidewalks are narrow in these mining towns) then the German is likly to get the whip-lash across his face.—These are some of the things we were told.

Also that Englishmen had been quartered in their homes with utter ruin to their furniture. It is true that the England promised to reemburse the German for the ruination of carpets etc, but so far no payment had been made.

After we arrived at Cologne we discovered an American Consul was located in that city. This was Saturday at 1 P.M. We immediately proceeded to pay our respects to him. He had locked his office it being a few minutes after 1 o'clock. Fortunately we found the Partiere who opened the door for us and admitted us into the office & presence of Mr Sauer[2] the Am. Consul.

He was very cordial & offered to assist us after we told him what we wanted, he sent for his Driver & ordered him to make arrangements for an automobile. This was done.

The next day at 10 A.M. The automobile was at our disposal. We also received a letter written in French asking the free passage of Hon V. L. Berger et femme travelling in auto IX 9538. Thus armed, we set out for Duesseldorf.

After travelling about an hour, we saw our first French soldier in the middle of the road, armed to the teeth. The auto drew up to the side. Papa showed his letter, the soldier smiled & told us to proceed. This happened once more before we entered the town.

Arriving at noon & being hungry we proceeded to what was once the best hotel in Duesseldorf, the Breidenher hof. This was in the possession of the French who occupied it. But they permitted friends to eat their. So we proceeded to the dining room. Here we found high French & British officers & their ladies enjoying the best of things all at the expense of the Germans. The Germans had to build whole colonies of brick villas so that the French & British families could live in comfort. I was quite aroused when I saw them drinking the best of wines & gourging themselves generally. They seized the wine cellars. They rob folks of their coal etc etc.

Before coming to Duesseldorf, we chanced to meet an American a Mr. Stimson who has business associations here & with the Krupps.[3] Mr. Stimson told us that the French are more brutal by far here in peace times, than were the Germans in Belgium during the war. Mr. Stimson

also recommended that we do not stop in Duesseldorf but proceed on
to Essen and make that our headquarters, which we did.

We left Duesseldorf & went on to Essen stopping here at the
Essener hof, first because Stimson told us to, & secondly because all
other hotels in Essen are occupied by the French. The only reason this
one isn't is because it is the home of the Interallied commission composed of one Englishman, one Italian, one Frenchman. And they say
the Englishman cannot be trifled with.

When we got here, we found the Essener hof was the private hotel
belonging to the Krupps & used generally by them to entertain their
business friends. But under present conditions they permit others to
enter upon the payment of hotel rates. So now we are stopping at this
very famous hotel. Isn't fate a capricious thing.

Queer as it may seen we also found the editor[4] of the Avanti the
Socialist paper of Italy stopping here. He too couldn't find a room else
where.

Essen has hundreds of French soldiers here, and Oh! how the Germans hate & smart under them.

The French are quartered in all hotels, city hall & school houses.
The German children are therefore without schools & education
except such as they can get in abbreviated form.

All telephones are cut off. Mail goes but only letters and all letters
are open to censorship. No packages can be delivered & telegraphic
connection is also cut off. If the Germans wish to communicate they
must do so under cover or by courrier.

Mr. Stimson (the American, who had heard all about Papa) gave us
letters of introduction to the Directors of Krupps. These received us
with open arms & told us quite freely all the things we wanted to know.
Also they introduced us to their workingmen's council or the leaders of
the Workers connected with Krupp or the Coal Industries. These workingmen told us that at present, all factions within their organizations
were united in their passive resistance against the Ruhr invasion. Also
they said they recognize that their stand does not only mean a resistance against the French, but a fight for liberties & rights which it has
taken centuries to obtain & thirdly their resistance means the preservation of the German nation. Their one hope & prayer is that their funds
may be replenished & that hunger will not make them break down.

The directors of the institute complained more bitterly about the
infringement of their personal liberties. For instance, no German can
leave the occupied territory without a passport, visaed by the French.
Now there are about 5,000,000 people in this territory. And here in
Essen (250,000) there are only two offices which issue the French
stamp & these offices only open up at 9 A.M. So the Germans, come &
stand in line before day-breake waiting patiently. Finally a French sol-

diers takes a handful of papers on which are numbers & throws them out on the waiting Germans. These poor devils make a free for all scramble trying to capture one of these numbers so that he may have the right to travell[in]g from one district to another. All these districts are within the occupied territory. While the Germans scramble for a number, a movie picture man takes their picture to show the world what wild beasts the Germans are.

Or an officer gives a young girl money & orders her to go into a florist & buy a bouquet of flowers and as she comes out & hands the flowers to the officer her picture is taken to show how the German girl tries to captivate the soldier etc etc. In short, one hears of brutalities and propaganda methods all the time.

While at Duesseldorf we looked for our baggage. We found that it had not reached D. as the Germans send nothing into territory controlled by French. We were told it was at Gerresheim, the last station free before reaching occupied territory. So we motored to Gerresheim. Here we found a temporary station hurriedly built by Germans & there were our things. We got the man to recheck them to Stuttgart. This he was willing enough to do. But he told us to inquire at a station at Vohwinkle to see if the French let them thro'. We were to wait until the train had passed Vohwinkle. This we did & then went to Vohwinkel. Sure enough, the French had ordered them off the German train & held for inspection. We again showed our letters & finally the officer OK'd them & now we hope they are on their way to Stuttgart. We will drive out again to make sure.

This afternoon, we drove to Gelsenkirchen, a town held by the communists for three days & then on to Bochum another town in which great disturbances had taken place. At both these places the same stories were told. The communist up raising was due largely to a hunger revolt.[5] The worker earned about 12,000 marks a day or 25 cts. It has been said the Communists are support[ed] by the French. This we believe is true, notwithstanding the weak denial by the communists. In many places the police men are armed (they are the only ones allowed to carry arms) & they are under the control of the French. That appears to be what the communists are negotiating for.

Tomorrow we are to go thro' Krupps big industry. They manufacture every thing from hair springs to locomotives. I am not permitted to go thro' there so they will show me thro' their welfare dep't. After that we will go to Duesseldorf & then back to Koln. War is hell, but occupation such as this is worse. I'll have to tell you the rest. I am pretty tired. I admire the solidarity of the workers here beyond expression. If *American* working class had had the intelligence & the organization & unity that these folks have, we never would have entered the war and much present misery here could have been avoided.

Good night dear dearest ones.

Remail this letter to dear Miss Thomas after you both get thro with it. Send it to Doris & Dudd to Betty.

Papa is quite well I think. He has a ravinous appetite & I sometimes wonder if he will get another attack but so far so good. I am O.K. I feel much better than I did; but still get awfully tired. I don't even stop to spell or write correctly.

Any way I love you all. So far I've had 1 letter from Elsa, 2 from Dudd & 2 from Betty. That doesn't seem like quite enough for 6 weeks does it?

Be good children.

Mama

1. Meta and Victor toured Austria, Germany, Hungary, Switzerland, France, Belgium, and the Netherlands between May and August, 1923, and spent ten days in the Ruhr district, which had been occupied by France since January, 1923. Victor was a delegate to the congress of the Second International, held in Hamburg, Germany, May 21–25, 1923. The meeting led to the creation of the new Labor and Socialist International.

2. Emil Sauer (1881–1949) served as U.S. consul in Cologne, 1915–1917 and 1919–1925.

3. The Krupp family was Germany's major munitions manufacturer.

4. Pietro Nenni (1891–1980) served as editor of *Avanti!*, the paper of the Italian Socialist Party, from 1923 until 1926, when he fled to France as a result of his opposition to Mussolini. After World War II, he held a number of posts in the Italian government, including foreign minister.

5. Workers in the Ruhr went on strike for wage increases on May 16, 1923. The Communist Party supported the strike and promised a general strike if the workers' demands were not met. Street fighting broke out in a number of cities, including Bochum and Gelsenkirchen. The labor dispute was settled by May 28, and most of the strikers returned to work by the end of the month.

Victor to Meta

Washington, D.C.
December 2, 1923

My dear Schatzl:

I have been straining my eyes so much during the last 2 weeks that they hurt me. I shall have to be careful.

My trip to New York was for the purpose of interesting some people in a bill[1] which I am going to introduce to have our government aid Germany and the re-construction of Europe by doing the following:

The United States to guaranty a *credit* of one billion dollars by certain American industrial groups having raw materials such as cotton, wool, hides, copper, zink etc. for sale—to certain German manufacturers; and also guaranty the credit extended by other commercial groups in America in selling food and victuals such as wheat, rye, flour, beef, pork, bacon lard, cotton-seed oil etc, to the corresponding groups in Germany—; the debt to be paid within 10 years with 6% interest.

An American commission (both in the United States and in Germany) is to watch the regularity of the business, to prevent profiteering and to protect the interest of the debtors as well as that of the creditors. The various plants, factories and real estate of the Germans connected with the transaction are to furnish the security—the debt to be considered the first mortgage on all these properties.

Our government is not to advance any money—and not to spend any money—except to pay the salary of the commissioners,—and I am convinced that the Germans in their present plight would be glad to pay even that.

And it might be even an easier and simpler way, if America would simply guaranty the issuing of bonds to that amount ie. a billion. That would be the first real "liberty loan" ever issued. The danger is only that the French would grab the cash, if they could lay their thievish hands on it. And the main argument *against* my proposition even *now* is—that France would simply take everything the Germans could produce and make it impossible for the Germans to repay even the first instalment.

I took up the proposition with Hillquit first. He received it very coldly. Then I had him make an appointment for me with Samuel Untermeyer[2] and Oswald G. Villard.

Villard was very friendly at first—and seemed to take to the idea. He was to accompany me to Paul Warburg[3] and another banker for their advice. When I came to see him in the afternoon, however, he was a changed man. He said I should not introduce it because I am suspected of being "pro-German,"—La Follette and a congressman from Illinois ("with a German name") are going to do something similar. When I told him that La Follette and the congressman from Illinois "with the German name" would also be suspected of being "pro-German"—he had no answer. The truth is, that meanwhile Oswald Garrison Villard "had been seen" by somebody—by Charlie Ervin, I suppose—who is now working for The Nation as promotion-manager. "Charlie" looked somewhat guilty when I greeted him.

At any rate, Villard went with me to Untermeyer and told him also that he had in vain tried to persuade me to *drop* the matter. I had a long talk with Untermeyer, however, after Villard left, with the result that Untermeyer promised to send me the draft of such a bill carefully worked out in detail—to be introduced before Christmas. I asked him to "keep mumm" about it—and he agreed to do so. He would consult only *one* person, a banker, who is very friendly to Germany *now*. Whom do you think? Otto H. Kahn[4] of Kuhn, Loeb & Co.

On my return to Washington, I tried to sound some Senators, who are to introduce a corresponding bill in the Senate.

I tried Lenroot, I pointed out to him that there was his chance to expiate for his sinful position during the War—to get solid again not only in Wisconsin, but through the Middle West.

But Lenroot could not see the thing in the same light. He told me the bill would have no chance to pass. French sentiment is very strong in America and in Congress. Even i[f] the bill did pass and we did lend the money (or the raw material and the food) to Germany—the French would grab the finished products and the United States would surely not declare war against France on that account.

He also told me that there was a German broker in New York (by the name of Brauer) who had proposed a similar loan two years ago—and it afterwards turned out that he was to receive an immense commission, if the deal went through.

In short Lenroot is not willing to help.

I may try Borah or Reed.[5] And if I cannot get anybody in the Senate—, I shall simply introduce my bill in the House of Representatives anyway—under the constitution all bills pertaining to finance must originate in the lower house. It will be good propaganda.

As to my seating—there is no doubt about it this time. I don't believe that even Blanton[6] will chirp.

Elsa had a bad cold and had to stay in bed for a few days. Coming up to see her—I found that she smoked although she had a very sore throat. Whereupon, I played the doctor, and gave the cigarettes to the colored man who happened to be there. Elsa got very "huffy" because these cigarettes had been bought with "her" money. But since I had given her a twenty dollar bill just the day before (to pay her dressmaker for a party dress)—my conscience does not bother me. But it may bother me when she brings me the bill for the material from which the dress was made.

As for my job here—I like it less than I ever liked it before; and you may rest assured that since they are not going to bother me I shall never run for the seat in the House of Representatives again.

And I also feel more lonesome this time. May be I am getting old.

Elsa surely is not much company for me. This morning she came to the hotel and had breakfast with me. She looked bad and was still coughing considerably. This afternoon she went out riding with "Bill"—a Dr. William Morgan[7] whom I have never met—and Elsa is not very anxious that I should meet him. But she wants me to invite Dexter[8] to a dinner before he leaves for Honolulu, and I will have to do it, I suppose. I am glad he is going.

Mrs Putnam is here. Had her to dinner at the hotel on Friday and also at Keith's vaudeville, where Breitbart[9] (the iron bending Samson we saw on the Hans Ballin) and a trained crow were the main attractions. Spent a dreary evening. She told me all about the big money she was going to make in Florida—selling building lots. Frank Putnam will also be here tomorrow. He is allright.

That is about all the news I know. And I also know that I have written *twice* as many letters as you. *How is the farm?*[10]

With love to all.

Ever Your V.L.B.

1. Berger introduced a bill calling for a billion-dollar revolving-credit fund to allow Germany to purchase raw materials and food, but the measure died in committee.

2. Samuel Untermyer (1858–1940) practiced law in New York from 1879 to 1924 and made a fortune representing business interests. Untermyer backed Germany at the outbreak of World War I but became a outspoken supporter of the Allied cause after the United States entered the war.

3. Paul Warburg (1868–1932) emigrated from Germany in 1902 and became a prominent New York banker. He served on the Federal Reserve Board, 1914–1918, and on the board's advisory council, 1921–1926.

4. Otto H. Kahn (1867–1934), a native of Germany, came to New York in 1893 and became a successful banker and a patron of the arts. During World War I, Kahn actively supported the Allied cause.

5. Probably James A. Reed (1861–1944), a Democratic senator from Missouri, 1911–1929.

6. Thomas Lindsay Blanton (1872–1957), a Democratic representative from Texas, 1917–1929 and 1930–1937. During the debate over Berger's seating in 1920, Blanton objected to Berger's being allowed ten minutes to speak.

7. William Arthur Morgan (b. 1891), a Washington, D.C., physician specializing in the ear, nose, and throat.

8. Dexter Bullard (1898–1981), a medical student at the University of Pennsylvania, secretly married Elsa Berger on April 23, 1923. Elsa informed her sister, Doris, of the marriage six months later and told her that she and Bullard planned to divorce. Elsa also asked Doris not to tell their parents about the marriage. See Elsa to Doris, November 11, 1923, Berger Papers, SHSW. Bullard served as the medical director of a Maryland psychiatric hospital from 1931 to 1969.

9. Sigmund Breitbart (1883?–1925) was a vaudeville strongman billed as the "Iron King."

10. Victor bought a forty-acre farm in Ozaukee County, north of Milwaukee, in November, 1921, and purchased an adjoining thirty-six acres in June, 1922. Doris and Colin Welles moved to the property in March, 1924, and established a fox farm.

Victor to Meta

Washington, D.C.
December 7, 1923

My sweet Schatzl:

Enclosed, please, find a check for $300.00 which I hope will help out a little on some of the necessities for the farm. I cannot do more just at present. I don't want you to worry. We shall make things meet in the end—we have always done so in the past—and we always will in the future.

I have received the draft of the bill from Untermeyer with a letter strongly urging that I should not introduce it but let somebody who was strongly in favor of the war do so. He wants to give the bill to the press and also find the man. I wired back that he has not the right view of the situation. Just now I seem to be very popular with both sides of the House and it is only natural that I should introduce it, since everything I have predicted as the outcome of the War has come to pass.

Now it is up to me to get a Senator of high standing to introduce the bill in the other House. I have three of them in view: Pepper of Pennsylvania, Norris of Nebraska and Spencer of Missouri.[1]

Will see the President[2] next Monday for the political prisoners. I believe I can get him to let them all go unconditionally—since he is a candidate for nomination and election.

I am not hard on Elsa—only I want her to have some dignity, especially since she is an M.D.—and "dignity" forms a considerable part of the stock of that trade.

Under separate cover I send you and Dr. & Mrs. Wells[3] the i[n]vitations to the Presidents reception next Wednesday. Dr. Schnucks also has an invitation—has accepted it—and is going.

Dan Hoan and G. W. Bruce had lunch with me to-day. They have attended a River & Harbor Congress.

I have not done much work for the Leader this week. Shall begin again tonight—because it is really of more importance than any other work I can do here.

I agree with you that under the circumstances you must send the money to Ebert[4]—wait however until you have at least $5,000. Don't hesitate to ask Oscar Greenwald or Nathan Stone or Carl Herzfeld or Theodore Kronshage.[5] Tell them that you will send it directly to Ebert and print his receipt—or a *photograph* of it—in the Milwaukee Leader.

But above all—don't work hard. Let somebody else do the talking and telephoning. Doris ought to help you.

Everybody is very friendly—but after the harrowing experiences I had, I do not fully trust anybody. I am here "with good-will to all and ill-will to none"—but the best that is in me I shall tell or expose to no one, except to my Schatzl,—and to my children when they grow up, if they ever do.

It is very hard to keep diet when you are invited by people—or you invite them. I am getting stout again and I really hate myself. Moreover, I am getting physically lazy.

There is not much other news here than what you read in the papers. I am gratified that the English Labor Party has made such headway at the recent election. That will influence the situation in Europe in great shape.

With love to all and especially to my Schatzl

Ever your V.L.B.

1. George Wharton Pepper (1867–1961), a Republican U.S. senator from Pennsylvania, 1922–1927; George W. Norris (1861–1944), a Republican representative from Nebraska, 1903–1913, and a U.S. senator, 1913–1943; and Selden Palmer Spencer (1862–1925), a Republican U.S. senator from Missouri, 1918–1925.

2. Calvin Coolidge (1872–1933) served as U.S. president from Warren Harding's death on August 2, 1923, until 1929.

3. Colin and Doris Welles.

4. Friedrich Ebert (1871–1925), a German Social Democrat, served as president of Germany from 1919 until his death. According to the *Milwaukee Leader,* December 12, 1923, Meta Berger sent $2,000 for German hunger relief to Ebert.

5. Oscar J. Greenwald (1872–1941), Nathaniel Stone (1866–1931), and Carl Herzfeld (1866–1930) were Milwaukee department store executives. Theodore Kronshage Jr. (1869–1934), a progressive Milwaukee lawyer, served on the University of Wisconsin Board of Regents, 1921–1927, and as chairman of the Wisconsin Public Service Commission, 1931–1934.

Victor to Meta

Washington, D.C.
December 10, 1923[1]

My dear Schatzl:

I think you are *right* in sending the money you have collected to President Ebert—since you have promised to send it to him. But I believe the money would have done *more* good (and we would incidentally have gotten some prestige out of your hard work) if you had sent it to Otto Wells[2] (or Wels) for the S.D party, which cannot pay its editors and type-setters.

This morning I had a rather friendly and encouraging interview with President Coolidge, on the bill which I want to introduce to grant Germany a credit of $1,000,000,000 in raw material and food stuff. He seemed to agree with everything I said and was pleased that I consulted him. I left the bill there for his perusal. The trouble is only he will consult a half dozen Wall street politicians—some of whom may have a financial interest in grabbing the Ruhr (and letting Germany die) and who are in partnership with the "maitres des forges"—with the great iron magnates—that dictate the French foreign policy.

At any rate, I will not have an easy job to find an *influential* Senator to introduce the bill in the Senate. If it is introduced in the House only—then it is remains simply a propaganda measure.

To make a long story short—I don't like my job here. When I came here 12 or 13 years ago—the party was swinging upward, now it is going down. Then I was considered a "coming man" and received considerable attention. Now everybody considers the Socialist party of America dead (outside of Wisconsin)—and they simply give me credit of having a great *personal* following in Milwaukee, and some in the State.

This is bad, because it makes me impotent in a situation where everything hinges on a party. I begin to understand why La Follette is hanging on to the Republican party for dear life. But I don't understand why they don't kick him out,—since he really is no Republican, if there is any meaning at all to the term "Republican".

You ask me, how I spend my evenings? I stay in my office until midnight and read and clip. How I spend my Sundays? I stay in my office all day and read and clip. I don't like my room in the hotel. It is clean—but it is small, dark and not at all home-like. And it faces on an alley.

I shall hunt for an appartment the next few days but I don't know whether we can find something suitable. The country—i.e. the large cities of our country are a million houses short. There is only one large city in the country that has more houses than it needs—Bridgeport, Conn.[3]

Schnuck is no company for me at all. I only see her when she wants a good steak—and then she leaves me instantly. She always has some appointments with this or the other doctor—and so far she has never had any time for me. I suppose, such is the fate of all parents. Our children are nice and good children—as children go—but if I should leave this world tomorrow, they would never miss me,—provided, I left an ample fortune for each of them.

May be that is my own fault. And let's hope that they will repay to the next generation—to their children—what they owe us.

As to the well on the farm—I don't understand why that should be 210 feet, far below the level of the lake. But since you have gone so far—you must drill *far enough* to get a *sufficient flow* of *water,*—sonst ist die ganze Geschichte für die Katz'.[4]

[*Remainder of letter missing*]

1. Victor dated the letter Monday, December 9, 1923, although December 9 was a Sunday. From context, it appears he meant Monday, December 10, 1923.
2. Otto Wels (1873–1939) served as chairman of the Majority German Social Democratic Party.
3. Berger's parents and siblings had substantial real estate holdings in Bridgeport, Connecticut.
4. otherwise the whole business is a total waste.

Victor to Meta

Washington, D.C.
December 14, 1923

My dear Schatzl:—

With the House still unorganized—as far as committees are concerned—and with all sorts of other affairs pending—I cannot see how I will be able to get away [from] here in the early part of next week.

As for my bill to open up a credit of one billion for Germany—the prospects that it will be adopted are not very bright of course. Senator Spencer of Missouri who acted as he wanted to introduce in the Senate last Tuesday—told me yesterday to go ahead and introduce it in the House first. Hoover[1] does not favor it, nor does Hughes. Both of them want some arrangement with France first, because they fear that the French would take everything the Germans would manufacture.

And both of them said—as did also President Coolidge—that the United States would lose the money because the German manufacturers could not pay for either the food or the raw material, unless France would permit them to pay, or we would send an army over to fight France, which is out of question, of course.

Thus France has virtually become the dictator, not only of Europe but of the entire world—, since we "won the war to make the world safe for democracy", for Poincarè.[2]

And Mellon[3] looks at the matter simply from a banker's point of view. They all live in the past. *Not* one of them is as yet willing to admit that our participation in the War was a crime and a blunder—although Hoover *almost* admitted it. Hughes, the old ass, even said that if we "had not entered the War we would today be the vassal's of some German prince"—although he could not keep a straight face when he said it. He evidently did not believe the nonsense himself. There is one thing certain, however, they all were very apologetic—all seemed to be on the defensive—the moment one discussed the War with them.

Well, Schatzl, I am not going to fill this letter with politics—shall only tell you that I renewed with all those that I knew here before and also with some of the new "big guns"—and found everywhere a friendly reception. My stand against the War has evidently not injured my reputation among the "big men". I am beginning to despise politics, however, and I dislike my job. A politician must be a smooth, oily and dishonest man. I was never cut out for it. You are right, when you say, that I succeed in spite of myself. And I am not such a great success, after all.

Elsa and I went to the reception at the White House last night. It was the biggest and most "colorful" function in many years—the diplomatic corps of so many new countries in brand-new gold-braided uniforms—the army and navy—the judiciary—and last but not least,

Congress. Elsa enjoyed it hugely, but I was bored. For once, I was glad you weren't there—because I did not have my dress-suit and in the entire crowd I could only detect one or two others who did not wear one. I didn't mind it. I am used to being pointed out, although as a rule not on account of my clothes. But I am afraid Schnuckie was embarrassed—a little anyhow. She made the best of it, however, and in real Schnuckie-fashion struck up an acquaintance with the wife of some South American diplomat who proposed to teach her French, if she in turn would [teach] the other English. Get Schnuck among people and she is some Schnuck, I tell you.

And now, how about the farm? I believe now that Doris and Co will not be able to go out there before March 1st and that is only 2½ months from now. I am afraid that if they try to *force* the matter and go now— Doris will get tired of the whole business before they ever get really started.

What do you think of the idea of having Doris and Co stay in our house this winter? And using the next two months to prepare their future house and business in a deliberate and thoro fashion? It may be the *best* and *safest* way. Talk this over with the children, Schatzl.

After all, however, I will most assuredly stand by them, to the best of my ability, no matter what they decide. I believe that Doris—the moment she learns to concentrate (and I believe that her lack of concentration is based on the lack of physical exercise) has the elements of a great woman in her. And the farm life, which will compel physical exercise for Dud, will also be a Godsend for Co. It will take the malaria out of him and make a new man of him. Thus I look upon the farm as the best investment I've ever made, from every point of view.

Well, Schatzl—this is enough for one letter, especially since I hope to see you by Wednesday. Give my love to all and always think of me as your own, old, loving

V.L.B.

1. Herbert Hoover (1874–1964) served as U.S. secretary of commerce, 1921–1928, and as U.S. president, 1929–1933.
2. Raymond Poincaré (1860–1934) served as the president of France, 1913–1920, and as the country's premier, 1912–1913, 1922–1924, and 1926–1929.
3. Andrew W. Mellon (1855–1937), a financier and one of the wealthiest men in America, served as U.S. secretary of the treasury, 1921–1932.

Victor to Meta

Washington, D.C.
January 25, 1924

My sweet Schatzl:

There is not much news—except that I went to see Hoover again on my German "Revolving Credit" bill, and also Col. Hill[1] on a bill which I intend to introduce for the purpose of returning private property of Germans that is held now by the Enemy Property Custodian to their rightful owners.

Hoover was extremely cool—even more so than last time. The victory of the English Labor party seemed to have frightened them all. Tonight's Star has a long interview with me on the editorial page, but I am never referred to by name—always as a "prominent Socialist."

By the way, Schatzl—in one or two of the *drawers* of the East side book-case, which stands near the one you used to call your own—you find some *speeches,* which I delivered in the 62nd Congress (1911–1913) on the Old Age Pension bill, also some speeches on other questions; kindly bring me (or still better, *send* me) a couple of each. I forgot to take some when home.

I do not remember the time when I was so *little satisfied* with my work. I get tired very easily and I am drowsy often. While I sleep tolerably well—when I sleep—it is the usual thing for me to wake-up at 1 or 2 o'clock A.M. and then read for an hour or two. It will be very hard on you—if both of us will have to live in one room.

Moreover, I have a deep rooted contempt for Congress and particularly for the House of Representatives. I intend to bring in a bill to change the make-up of Congress—so as to have one house elected by geographical lines, and the other house according to occupations.

Not that [I] have any hopes that the bill will pass—nothing can pass except measures on which Wall street and the descendants of the Southern (ex)-slave-barons agree, but I might thus give some guiding lines for the future. I suppose that kind of a bill will raise the howl of "soviet" rule from every cornfield lawyer in the country and particularly from those in Congress.

I have chosen as my subject for the lecture in John Haynes Holmes'[2] church—The War and Since. It is a theme near my heart—but you need not fear. I shall treat it calmly.

I was told that I made quite a hit with the Face-the Facts delegation from Wisconsin, although I refused to go up to the speaker's table as a "guest of honor".[3]

Tomorrow (Saturday) the so-called Progressives have a dinner to which I am invited. I shall go. If they call on me, I will tell them my opinion.

On one hand—Bob La Follette and his press agents (especially William Hard)[4] are trying to tie up in some mythical manner with Ramsay McDonald[5] and the Labor party in England. On the other hand they are continuously proclaiming how they detest Socialists and Socialism. They don't seem to know or don't want to know that the British Labor party is a regular member of the Second Socialist International, in fact its main member.

These Progress-ifs make me tired—I very much prefer an honest reactionary to such political swindlers.

Well, sweet Schatzl, I don't care to excite myself. 'Nuff said. Tell me all about the farm and the children next time. I can readily see that you will stay over for the next school-board meeting (Feb. 5th) and that you will not be in Washington for 2 weeks, to make it mild.

Well, I have paid my life-insurance, which is something—however I owe some interest and will have to pay a big income tax. I cannot see just now how I will make it all.

That's about all—the rest you see in the newspapers.

With love to all and especially to my Schatzl

Ever your
V.L.B.

1. John Boynton Philip Clayton Hill (1879–1941) served as a Republican representative from Maryland, 1921–1927.

2. John Haynes Holmes (1879–1964), a social gospel activist and pacifist, served as pastor of New York City's Unitarian Church of the Messiah (renamed the Community Church of New York in 1919) from 1907 to 1949.

3. On January 21, 1924, the Association Against the Prohibition Amendment sponsored a "Face the Facts" conference in Washington, D.C., at which more than a thousand delegates met to urge the modification of the Volstead Act.

4. William Hard (1878–1962), a muckraking journalist, regularly wrote for periodicals such as *Everybody's Magazine, Collier's Magazine,* the *New Republic,* and the *Nation.* During the 1930s he became a radio broadcaster.

5. J. Ramsay MacDonald (1866–1937), the leader of the British Labour Party, served as a member of Parliament, 1906–1918, 1922–1935, and 1936–1937, and as prime minister of Great Britain, 1924 and 1929–1935.

Victor to Meta

Washington, D.C.
February 1, 1924

My sweet Schatzl:

Elsa went to Philadelphia this noon, after lunching with me at the Capitol.

Developements are coming thick and fast from all angles in the Teapot Dome oil lease affair.[1] Within about a week or so I expect to take the floor—to sum up the situation.

The Democratic party is now as deeply in the mire as the Republican party.

Gregory (Wilson's Attorney General), Stimson[2] (Wilson's Secretary of War) and McAdoo (Wilson's Secretary of Treasury and son-in-law) have been named by the multi-millionaire, E. L. Doheny, (oil magnate) as being in his pay, even at the present time. Daniel[3] (Wilson's Secretary of the Navy), Edward House (Wilson's friend and adviser) have at least been named in connection with the leases.

In short the Democrats have not even the shadow of a right to make political capital out of Roosevelt, Fall, Denby, and Daugherty[4] on the Republican side.

It will be easy enough for me to prove that since the last period of the Roman empire—money has not played the important part it is playing now. And also that we are "enjoying" the most corrupt government on the face of the globe since the Czar's government has disappeared in Russia in a river of blood.

And the same fate is awaiting our own ruling class, unless real and thorough going reforms are carried out. All the lawlessness of the Ku Kluxers, Mobs and Lynchers are simply preparing the mind of the people for a violent change.

But the worst aspect from my point of view is—that our American working class, (if there is such a thing) is also corrupt. Our American workers are willing to select as leaders, and to support as such, the most despicable thieves and hold-ups, so long as these gangsters "get results"—i.e. a dollar or two more per day in wages for the "rank and vile."

And this is very discouraging for the Socialists and especially for me. It makes one almost despair of the future. Socialism pre-supposes and requires an honest and aimful working class.

Everywhere in Europe—and especially in England, Germany and in the Germanic countries, the working-class is essentially honest, or was so, in normal times, before the war. Corrupt leaders of labor are even now impossible in Europe—with the exception of France. Here such leaders are the rule.

But our thievish politicians are trying to keep immigrants away from this country under the pretext that the "quality" of the American people might suffer. Just think the *"quality"* of foremost flower of our population, Doheny, Stillman,[5] Sinclair, Gould[6]—or Fall, McAdoo, Daugherty—"suffering" from the influx of the European foreigners.

Well, sweet Schatzl—I did not want to write this letter for any other purpose than to have you get a message from me on Sunday.

With love to all and especially to my sweet Schatzl

Ever your
V.L.B.

1. Oil operators Harry Sinclair (1876–1956) and Edward Doheny (1856–1935) bribed Secretary of the Interior Albert Fall to obtain a secret lease for the Teapot Dome oil reserve in Wyoming and the Elk Hills reserve in California. The Teapot Dome scandal came to symbolize the graft and corruption of the Harding administration.

2. Henry L. Stimson (1867–1950), U.S. secretary of war, 1911–1916 and 1940–1945.

3. Josephus Daniels (1862–1948), U.S. secretary of the navy, 1913–1921.

4. Assistant Secretary of the Navy Theodore Roosevelt Jr. (1887–1944), former Secretary of the Interior Albert Fall (1861–1944), Secretary of the Navy Edwin Denby (1870–1929), and Attorney General Harry Daugherty (1860–1941).

5. James A. Stillman (1873–1944) was a New York banker involved in a highly publicized divorce case marked by charges of marital infidelity.

6. George Jay Gould (1864–1923), a financier and railroad executive, was the subject of a number of lawsuits charging him with mismanagement.

Victor to Meta

Washington, D.C.
February 14, 1924

My sweet Schatzl:—

Tell Hoan not to let the peanut politicians worry him, but to go right ahead with his campaign.[1] The platform is somewhat unusual in its form for a *Socialist* platform but that may be in its favor, considering that it is to serve a local purpose and at one election only.

The poster should contain as little reading matter as possible—and Dan should send out at least 2 letters—one early in March and another about a week before election. I think I better dictate a letter to him myself, however, and not bother you with these things. Will send at once a check for $253.75 to the West Side Bank to cover the payment due Feb. 16th. I have borrowed the money to make my first payment of $1,000 on the stock, which I bought from Fralick & Bates.

Tell R. F. Borchardt[2] (308 Hendricks street Merrill, Wis) whose land contract and note for $2,200.00 becomes due April 8th 1924—to pay down $500.00 and the interest on the note—and you will extend the remaining $1,700 for another 3 years at 6% interest. We need the money, otherwise I would extend the entire sum.

I wired you that I want you to stay in Milwaukee until the end of this month, since it is uncertain whether I can get away for the 28th of February and the Leader meeting. And you or I must be there Schatzl, or there would be no quorum present. Tell Louis[3] to use only as much of your stock as is necessary to make a quorum.

Make it a point to let the stock holder's meeting know (a sort of offhand and incidentally) that the Fralick and Bates stock has been acquired by Doris Berger Welles.

If I should be unable to get away here to make that meeting,—the debate on the Mellon Income Tax Bill[4] started today—I shall surely try to be there as soon as possible early in March. I owe it to the movement and the Leader to lend a helping hand in the campaign. It would be a hard knock for the paper, if Hoan should lose out, and I cannot see any reason why he should. The Wilson incident[5] ought to help him, not to hurt him. And it will help him—as soon as I get home.

By-the-way, Schatzl—order all the coal you need. If there is any left over, it will be good next year.

Had a nice letter from Doris and it made me feel good, especially since I needed some cheering-up, in view of the bad cold, which I have contracted. Elsa is still coughing also, and it is worrying me much more than my own, which is already disappearing.

Elsa is waiting anxiously for you to come—she wants to buy her summer—or rather her spring apparel.

Otherwise there is not much news that I can tell. I feel that I am neglecting the Leader shamefully, but I do not seem to have any energy and I do my work rather automatically. My "pep" will come back when my cold is gone—I suppose.

At this rate, you and I, (and some who will want to see Washington in spring) may drive down in the auto, after all. Today and yesterday we had some snow here, however.

But after all is said and done—die Hauptsache ist daß Du mich lieb hast.[6] Lovingly

Your
V.L.B.

1. Socialist Daniel Hoan won reelection as Milwaukee's mayor on April 1, 1924, with more than 56 percent of the vote.

2. Richard F. Borchardt (1896–1973) worked for a paper company in Merrill, Wisconsin.

3. Louis Baier (1872–1934) began working as an assistant to Victor Berger on the *Vorwärts* in 1895 and later served as an auditor and bookkeeper for the Milwaukee Social-Democratic Publishing Company, a position he held until his death.

4. Secretary of the Treasury Andrew Mellon proposed a plan to substantially cut federal income taxes.

5. Following the death of former president Woodrow Wilson on February 3, 1924, Mayor Hoan refused to send a message of condolence to the Wilson family. The Milwaukee Common Council tried to override Hoan and passed a message of condolence, which Hoan refused to sign.

6. the main thing is that you love me.

Victor to Meta

Washington, D.C.
February 15, 1924

My sweet Schatzl:

By the time this letter reaches you, I shall have made my first big speech of this season, having been granted some time on the Mellon bill (so-called) for tomorrow night—after the house is tired out after a 3 days deluge of oratory, and nobody cares to listen to anybody. Moreover, so many of them *read* their long speeches (for instance Frear[1] of Wisconsin who acts as a sort of leader for the La Follette group in the House, very much to the dismay of John Nelson) which makes them twice as tiresome.

But I feel it in my bones that I am going to make a big hit and I am not going to read my speech either. I have prepared one tonight, which will take about 40 minutes to deliver, I believe.

I show that according to the official figures there are only 4,361,000 individual income tax schedules expected in 1924—which means that in this rich country and in the richest nation on earth ⅘ of the people do not earn enough to pay any income tax, which begins with an income of $2,000. (We have more than 22,000,000 families in the United States.) It also means that about 18,000,000 families are even in the so-called good times below the level of the lowest subsistence, since it takes about $1,980 to keep a family of five supplied with necessities and the great majority does not earn that.

I also show that of those paying taxes 83 per cent pay on incomes of less than $5,000—while on the other hand 351 were paying taxes (in 1921) on incomes of more than $300,000 annually—and 21 on incomes of more than $1,000,000 annually.

Therefore many things are more important than income tax revision to ⅘ of the American people.

Our main fight ought to be to fight poverty—the utter poverty of ⅘ of the nation. Poverty, the mother of ignorance, crime, disease,—of dirt and of misery. We ought to have an old age pension bill—do something to help the housing situation—about child labor which is increasing on an enormous scale—amend the Volstead act—and prepare for the next industrial crisis etc. I also say a few things about the War—about the necessity of calling a constitutional convention to frame a new constitution adapted to the 20th century—and show how little difference there is really between the two old parties (to which the so-called Progressives still adhere) and try to bring it home to them to leave the oil-soaked preserves and join a movement for a new third party.

This is the outline of my speech—I have given it to you because I have written you a letter so there is not much news that I could tell you, in this letter which is intended for your Sunday dessert.

However, Mr & Mrs. Berger are invited to Justice Brandeis[2] for tea next Wednesday at 7.15 P.M—I will take Schnuckie instead—; and you are also to assist informally Mrs. La Follette on Washington's birthday, as per enclosed card.

Wenn Du mich nur sonst lieb hast![3]

Ever your V.L.B.

1. James Archibald Frear (1861–1939), a Republican representative from Wisconsin, 1913–1935.
2. Louis D. Brandeis (1856–1941) served as an associate justice of the U.S. Supreme Court, 1916–1939. Brandeis was one of two judges who dissented from the Supreme Court's decision to deny the *Milwaukee Leader* its mailing privileges. He had previously voted with the majority to overturn Berger's conviction under the Espionage Act.
3. If only you love me anyhow!

Meta to Doris and Colin

Washington, D.C.
[April 13, 1924]

My beloved blessed children:—

Just a few lines to urge you to go to the Bertrand Russell lecture. Drive in from Mequon no matter if you are tired. You will feel repaid I am sure. Papa & I heard him last night.[1] He spoke to a large audience of high-brows & rich folks here & he gave them a fine talk on the British Labor Gov. & chaos in Europe touching on future wars. I couldn't help but feel rebellious when I tho't of the future wars & the possibility that you may also be sacrificed.

So go to the lecture.

This week Ameringer & Hillquit were in Washington attending [a] conference which we hoped might lead to a third party. After the conclusion of the week & the conference we were all more or less discouraged because after all, the so called liberal crowd, is merely a crowd of old party politicians interested primarily in getting this or that office. And that is correct, most of those liberals are no good. But this is the auspicious time for the formation of a new political alignment & they will go ahead until the national convention called at Cleveland July 4.[2] I met in this work a most charming person by the name of Isabelle Kendig, other wise Mrs. Howard Gill;[3] the mother of 3 boys 2, 3½ & 4½ years of age. She is the executive secretary of the Woman's Committee for Political Action. I think we both fell in love with each other & some day I hope you will meet her.

Last night I met Miss Cramm at the Russell dinner & thro' her I got H. D. Schwartz telephone number. So this week some time I'll get in touch with Dr. Schwartz.

Elsa has been offered the Assistant Residenceship at the hospital by the Chief Resident. He will propose her name to the Board of Directors. They of course must vote on her. But it was fine to be offered it for it shows she has made good. She works very hard & is often too tired to eat evenings. She doesn't know yet whether she will take that new honor or go some where else for next year.

Inclosed find a check of $20. for which Papa wants Coie to order from the State Forestry Department, in Madison trees like black locusts for the bluff or bank & cedars for your yard or whatever trees you want for the yard. I think it might be well to take care of the bluff as soon as possible. Papa says that this check has this string to it. He wants you to use it for trees.

Now be sure to go to the Russell lecture. You will enjoy it hugely. Also I am so glad the house is so fine. Have you heard from Fromms?[4] And are you considering the remodelling of the Reuter house? And are there any puppies? And Oh! we want to know all about you & every thing. Best luck & best & most devoted love from

Papa & Mama

1. Bertrand Russell (1872–1970), a British philosopher, author, and mathematician, delivered an address to the League for Industrial Democracy and the Penguin Club in Washington, D.C., in which he predicted that another war would break out unless changes were made in the world's economic system. He delivered an antiwar address in Milwaukee on April 22, 1924.
2. The Conference for Progressive Political Action met on July 4, 1924, and nominated Robert M. La Follette Sr. for the presidency.
3. Isabelle V. "Sally" Kendig (1889–1974) served as legislative and membership secretary of the National Woman's Party, 1922–1923, and as research secretary of the National Council for the Prevention of War, 1923–1924. During the 1930s she started a long career as a Washington, D.C., psychologist. Her husband, Howard B. Gill (1889–1989), opened an industrial and commercial research office in Washington, D.C., in 1924. Gill later became a noted prison reformer and headed the Norfolk Prison Colony in Massachusetts.
4. Arthur Fromm (1884–1945) and his wife, Della Plumb Fromm (1884–1964), operated the Shorecliffe Silver Fox Farm with Doris and Colin Welles in Thiensville, Wisconsin.

Meta to Doris and Colin

Washington, D.C.
May 9, 1924[1]

My blessed children:—

The passed 10 days have been so very crowded with visitors & conventions, that I did not take the time to write, altho' I've wanted to do it dozens of times. This morning I could not sleep so after tossing about for some time, I've decided to get up early, before 6 o'clock, & get a letter off to you before the day begins.

I believe I told you of the large delegation from Wisconsin that attended the Woman's International League for Peace & Freedom (W.I.L. for short). There were Mrs. Roberts, Strachan, Duncan,[2] Padway,[3] Levine, Shutkin,[4] Polacheck,[5] Misses Soik, Roche,[6] Sabin[7] & finally Mrs La Follette & myself. Later on Mrs. Haessler & Dorothy;[8] besides two more school teachers one from Madison & one from Chicago. also Lotta Abbott appeared. All these people looked to me for guidance about arranging their sight seeing at least.

The W.I.L. was a large convention composed of representatives from 43 different countries Jane Addams being the international president. Their topic was Peace & how to get it. Of course they will not achieve their end by merely talking "understanding one another", "abolish tariffs which cause wars" & the "doctrine of love instead of the doctrine of hate". A few were there who touched upon the economic imperialism & a change in the system but generally speaking, its a conservative groupe, well meaning but not courageous. To declare war illegal even on the statute books will not prevent war.

There were a large percentage of Quakers present among them Caroline Wood,[9] the sister of Hollingsworth Wood[10] who did so much good during the war. Also Mrs. Gannett[11] the mother of Louis Gannett[12] whom Coie admires so much. all thro' the convention, I wished Coie's mother[13] could have been with us.

The only countries not represented were Spain, Portugal & Russia.

All the Americans were at a great disadvantage; for all the foreign delegates were the master of from 2 to 3 languages. It was a joy to see some Swedish, Czek or German or English woman get up, make her speech in her native tongue & then turn around & translate her own speech into English or French as the case might be. We in this country are a stupid lot. Well the Wisconsin [women] made such a big groupe that we decided to get together for a dinner inviting Mrs. La follette & Miss Sabin to be the guests of honor. Both ladies accepted the invitation which I issued. There were 15 of us present. Elsa was absent as she got off duty too late.

The girls that stopped in this hotel presented me with a beautiful corsage bouquet to wear to the President's reception of the W.I.L. The girls th[at] stayed in the Hotel Washington sent me a huge box of flowers & the book "The life of Ghandi." Nellie Roche sent me a beautiful silk night dress & so they showed their appreciation for my small efforts.

Yesterday the National section of the W.I.L. held its national convention to adopt or amend its constitution & to elect a new national board. Some one wanted to nominate a teacher but didn't know of anyone present so jokingly I said, "I am as good as a teacher, nominate me." This was said in a joke & only Mrs Polacheck heard it. In fact I hadn't taken the floor nor been active at all, merely attending the two conventions as an observer. But Mrs Polacheck got up & nominated me & to my surprise that nomination was applauded. But of course no one expected I would be elected since I knew so very few of the women present. In fact I left the convention to attend another conference for the Woman's Committee for Political Action. Late last night, I was telephoned to that I was elected on the National Board. The vote was a preferential ballot & since 11 had to be elected out of a list of 25 or 30, it took several hours to count the vote. But I cannot tell you how surprised I am. Many people came to me & said "I voted for you Mrs Berger but I cannot believe you will be elected" so you see I was not alone in that tho't.

Well, the other convention of the Woman's Committee for Political Action started yesterday. My socialist & school board training in parliamentary law has come into an excellent stand by. I cannot tell you how inefficient some of the most intellectual women are. I shall be most happy if this conference gets even a slight showing of success. We are looking forward to the formation of a third political party & this committee hopes to be instrumental in starting the liberal, radical & progressive women along that line.

I was glad Papa brought me some news of you. He told me of having stayed at your home 2 nights & I think he thoroughly enjoyed himself. He also said that he & Dudd got on to a chummier bases than ever before. He told me about the new car etc etc. My suggestion is that you get Winnie washed up & mended so that you can sell her for something rather than have her deteriorate completely.

I've spent two days with Mrs Haessler but each day we've been in some group so she hasn't talked to me of personal affairs. I rather think tho' that she will talk to me sooner or later about Bob & Gertrude.[14] Somehow I hope she won't.

I haven't seen Elsa in two days. She was invited out some where both evenings but I expect to see her tonight. I'd give a whole lot if Elsa would come home with me for the summer & even decide to locate there. I know that she would be a lot happier where we could all be together than she ever will be down here or any where else unless of course she settles down. She is getting a bit tired herself but says she has no friends in Mil. But she hasn't friends in any new place that she may go to. She is not sure yet of staying on here for next winter & I am sort of hoping she won't.

Please write me & tell me how many puppies you have, & when you expect the Fromm's back. And tell me more about yourselves & Eva & Bob[15] etc.

The weather here has been ideal. We have had only one real hot sultry day but we have had considerable rain. I expect the hot weather any moment. Now I wish we had a car here too. Best of luck to you my blessed two, & lots & lots of most devoted love

Always,
Mama.

1. Meta Berger mistakenly dated the letter April 9, although she wrote it on May 9, during the convention of the Women's International League for Peace and Freedom, a peace organization created in 1919 from other women's pacifist and suffrage groups.

2. Catherine M. Duncan (1893–1987), the wife of Socialist Wisconsin assemblyman Thomas Duncan, was active in women's suffrage, peace, and civil liberties organizations.

3. Lydia Rose Paetow Padway (1891–1981), the wife of Milwaukee Socialist politician and labor lawyer Joseph Padway.

4. Susie Shutkin (1886–1926), the wife of Milwaukee Socialist alderman Arthur Shutkin, was active in the Zionist movement.

5. Probably Hilda Salt Polacheck (1886–1967), the wife of Milwaukee businessman William Polacheck.

6. Nellie D. Roche (b. 1884) was a Milwaukee public school teacher.

7. Ellen C. Sabin (1850–1949) served as president of Downer College (after 1895 called Milwaukee-Downer College) from 1891 to 1921.

8. Lina Haessler (1864–1952), the mother of Carl Haessler, and her daughter, Dorothy Haessler (Todd) (1899–1975).

9. Carolena Morris Wood (1871–1936) was a Quaker social worker and women's suffrage activist.

10. L. Hollingsworth Wood (1873–1956) helped to found the American Friends Service Committee and served as president of the National Urban League, 1915–1941.

11. Mary Thorn Lewis Gannett.

12. Lewis Gannett (1891–1966) served on the editorial staff of the *Nation*, 1919–1928, and of the *New York Herald-Tribune*, 1928–1956.

13. Cornelia Bell Welles (b. 1857).

14. Robert L. Filtzer (1893–1983), an engineer, and Gertrude Haessler Filtzer (1894–1975), a social activist and sister of Carl Haessler, spent the early 1920s in the Soviet Union, where he worked as an engineer and she as a translator. Gertrude did not accompany Robert when he returned in January, 1924, to Milwaukee, where he worked for the city planning commission, and the couple divorced in 1925. Gertrude settled in New York and married American communist leader William Weinstone.

15. Eva Kurz and Robert L. Filtzer, who married in 1927.

Meta to Doris and Colin

Cleveland, Ohio
[July 6, 1924]

My blessed Children:—

The Conference for Progressive Political Action has ended & with it the surrender of the Socialist Party has virtually taken place.[1]

There was no alternative. But for such men as Papa, Hillquit, Hoehne,[2] Lee etc etc, it was as hard a time as ever existed within the history of the socialist movement. Of course the socialists are going to try to keep their organization in tact especially where they have one. But the fact of the matter is that only in Mil. County, there existed anything like a real party.[3] Every where else it seems to have dwindled down to a mere hundred or two hundred to states.

I sat for two days in this Conference for Political Action with my soul weeping. The Progressives were merciless & selfish & yielded practically nothing. We however forced them to pledge themselves to issue a call next Nov. with the express purpose of starting a bona fide Third Party. La follette is practically pledge[d] to that. La follette's statement you undoubtedly read. He wanted to run on a sort of namby-pampy Wisconsin platform. The Socialists however forced a real socialist platform upon him & he will have to stand upon it.

His sons Bob & Phil[4] were much in evidence as was the son-in-law.[5] Nepatism was in evidence truly.

There were practically all the parlor socialists, progressives & liberals in the country present besides the socialists. But without doubt, the only people who showed any thing like an intelligent constructive programe & by far the ones with the greatest ability were the socialists.

Miss Kendig & Mrs. Burch are both subscribing to the Leader because they said, after seeing & hearing all the folks here, they emerged from this conference as socialists.

The Lafollette progressives of Wis. were of course here in full force. Cong. J. M. Nelson, Ed. Brown, J. Schaeffer,[6] Ada James (who is O.K.), Ekern,[7] Crownhart, Lutie Stearns, Mrs Patzer,[8] Mrs Kannenberg[9] & others were all here. There were over 50 Wisconsin delegates. I'll have to tell you more about it as the story is too long to put on paper.

And evidently word had gone out to *sit* on the *Socialists* & especially *V.L.B.* The managers kept aloof from him & yet his name was the only one applauded when it was read on a committee.

Now we are holding the Socialist convention. Fireworks will begin tomorrow morning. I expect the walls will tremble with the oratory let lo[o]se on the Leaders i.e. Hillquit who was the spokesman for the party.

One thing happened which made Miss Stearns & Mrs Patzer sick. I was chosen & not either one of them to represent Wis. on the first meeting to discuss the national campaign.[10] Oh! you should have seen their faces. Chester Platt,[11] Ada, Irma,[12] & Mr. Ekern arranged that.

Now there are many many interesting things to tell & you will have to wait for them until I get home. However a things will interest you right now.

Mrs. Ruth Stewart[13]
606 Temple—Detroit Mich,

says she sent you to the P.O. a 5 lb box of candy & often wondered why you did not respond. Will you not sit down *at once* & write her a nice letter. She is worth while & is awfully sweet to me too. Please do that at once. I explained that of course you never got the box etc. But you write any how. *Do it.*

Then Gaz Davidow was here. He is really a fine looking man. He has developed wonderfully. He is no longer a member of the Socialist Party but is running for Congress on the Republican Ticket. I was so amazed at his fine appearance that I didn't know him.

Of course I saw the Lee's,[14] Bermann's,[15] Hillquits, Miss Kendig & all the rest.

By the way—Nina Hillquit[16] is coming west with us. She will stop in Chicago one day & then come to Mil. for 3 days. Will you help me entertain her & let me bring her to the farm? And will you sort of plan & programe for her? I know you will just love to do that for me & for her.

I must stop altho' I'd like to go for a long time yet. But they are waiting for me. Best love dearest two, I love you both so much. I don't even feel so sorry now Coie wasn't here. We Papa & I did not have a very happy time letting go even a little bit.

Your Mama

1. The Conference for Progressive Political Action, meeting in Cleveland on July 4, 1924, nominated Robert M. La Follette Sr. for president but failed to create a new political party, as desired by many Socialists. The Socialist Party held its convention in Cleveland on July 6–8, 1924, and endorsed La Follette's independent candidacy.

2. Gottlieb A. Hoehn (1865–1951), a St. Louis labor leader and one of the founders of the Social Democratic Party, edited the *St. Louis Arbeiter-Zeitung* and *St. Louis Labor.*

3. Despite the absence of a Socialist presidential ticket in the November election, the party won seven of twenty Wisconsin Assembly seats in Milwaukee County (down from ten) and retained one of three open state senate seats in the county. Berger won reelection to Congress with 42 percent of the vote against 41 percent for Republican Ernst A. Braun and 17 percent for Democrat Raymond Moore.

4. Robert M. La Follette Jr. (1895–1953) and Philip F. La Follette (1897–1965) were the sons of Robert M. La Follette Sr. Robert La Follette Jr. served as his father's private secretary, 1919–1925, and succeeded him in the U.S. Senate, serving 1925–1947. Philip La Follette served as governor of Wisconsin, 1931–1933 and 1935–1939.

5. Ralph Gunn Sucher (b. 1895), a journalist and attorney, worked as a secretary for Robert M. La Follette Sr., 1919–1921, and married the senator's daughter, Mary, in 1921. The couple divorced in 1935.

6. John Charles Schafer (1893–1962), a Republican representative from Wisconsin, 1923–1933 and 1939–1941.

7. Herman L. Ekern (1872–1954), an attorney and progressive Republican politician, served as a Wisconsin state assemblyman, 1903–1909, commissioner of insurance, 1910–1915, attorney general, 1923–1927, and lieutenant governor, 1938–1939.

8. Margaret Patzer (1859–1926) was a prominent Wisconsin progressive activist.

9. Louise Kanneberg (1879–1931) was the wife of Wisconsin railroad commissioner Adolph Kanneberg.

10. Meta Berger was one of two Wisconsin members of the national campaign planning committee for the Conference for Progressive Political Action.

11. Chester C. Platt Sr. (1857–1934) served as editor of the *(Madison) Wisconsin Leader,* 1920–1926.

12. Irma E. Hochstein (1887–1974) worked for the Wisconsin Legislative Reference Library, 1914–1925.

13. Ida Ruth Stewart (b. 1874?) was the wife of Arthur J. Stewart (b. 1869?), a partner in a Detroit real estate company and in an automobile repair and storage business.

14. Rand School educational director Algernon Lee and his wife, Dr. Matilda S. Lee (1872?–1953), one of the first women dentists in the United States.

15. Morris Berman (1865?–1945) headed a chain of New York clothing stores and served as president of the People's Educational Camp Society, which ran the Rand School's Camp Tamiment, from 1929 until his death.

16. Nina Hillquit (1895?–1958), the daughter of Morris Hillquit, served as her father's secretary and later worked on the staff of the International Confederation of Free Trade Unions.

Meta to Doris and Colin

Washington, D.C.
December 13, 1924

My blessed Children,—

We have had three days of sessions. First the Woman's Committee for Political Action met and resumed its work which had practically been dropped for campaign work. We found quite a disposition to criticize us for being a paper organization. But after some lively discussions we showed the ladies led by Mrs. Plumb[1] that they were absolutely wrong. The next day the Committee of one hundred met and there again an attack was made on us by Mrs. Plumb. This time I jumped into the argument and showed these women that we were not only the first but also the only national organization in existence today that represented the progressive and radical women of the country. That all the ladies that did campaign work might belong to various local affairs but that they were not tied up nationally and that it would be a crime to start a second and competing organization thus doing what the liberals had always done, namely keep the progressive element divided. After some heated discussions I showed that Mrs. Plumb herself was a product of the Woman's Committee and probably never would have had the opportunity to serve in the capacity that she did if she had not been first a member of our organization and thus become a delegate to the Cleveland Convention representing us. Well the result was that they all finally agreed not to start a dual league or club.

Then yesterday I sat in as a delegate to the national C.P.P.A. and saw the work of the Railroad Brotherhoods and the way they tried to destroy the chance for the creation of a third party. You see they never were quite with us even last July. They merely accepted Lafollette because their candidate McAdoo did not succeed in getting the nomination. Now they do not want a third party because they are really hide bound democrats and are waiting for four years to pass by, to wipe out the memory of oil and then hope to put over their idol McAdoo. That is the hope of the labor leaders. I saw how obviously crooked they are and it is no wonder Papa is so disgusted with the labor leaders.

Then today the Socialists held their executive committee meeting. So you see we had three full days. It was real fun both at the woman's meeting of one hundred and at the C.P.P.A. meeting. In each of these two meetings our side won.

The date set for the third party convention is Feb 21 at Chicago.[2] I hope you will be able to go to that convention. Feb. 21 falls on Friday. But seldom is the important business done on the first day. It will undoubtedly run over to Saturday Feb 22 when I believe the real event will come off. So plan by all means to go. Both of you, if possible. Through Melms or Miss Koenen you can secure tickets to attend. This is a long time ahead but I may be in Panama and not be able to tell you all about it then.

Debs is here as are Hillquit, Maurer and others. There is a banquet arranged for this evening by the local socialists. Miss Kendig has been permitted to sit in at the socialist meeting and both she and her husband are coming to the dinner. They are being introduced to Socialist thought and tactics.

We may have to change our date for Panama or give up the trip if Papa and I wish to attend that convention. Papa hasn't decided yet whether he wants to give up his trip.

I am glad that you finally answered Howard Gill's letter. Elsa I do not see as often as I wish. Either I have had dates or she has had. This week I have only seen her for about two hours altogether. We haven't had her friends for luncheons or dinners because we are so infernally hard up. After Xmas I would like to help her get even with her friends for all the kindnesses they have shown her.

I will write more tomorrow. I am pretty tired now and besides I must be getting ready to go to that dinner. You haven't written me very much lately. Please write more about yourselves and in detail.

Best love to you both always.

Mama

1. Marie Coyle Plumb (b. 1881?) served as Midwest director of the women's section of the Conference for Progressive Political Action. She was the widow of Chicago lawyer Glenn Plumb (1866–1922), who had developed a plan for government ownership of the railroads.

2. The convention of the Conference for Progressive Political Action, which opened in Chicago on February 21, 1925, failed to create a third party, largely because of the opposition of participating labor unions.

Meta to Doris and Colin

Washington, D.C.
December 21, 1924

My beloved Children:—

I am imagining all sorts of things and wondering just what sort of preperations Doris is making for a Xmas celebration. I know that if given full reign that you are all going to have the jolliest & the best & happiest of evenings. Elsa & I will be with you in love & in spirit even if we cannot be there in person. Just what we do & how we shall spend our evening is still a problem but it will have to be doing something rash & jolly too if I am to be happy.

Elsa isn't much of a hand in creating situations, so I guess it will be up to me. I never know tho' just where I am at here, for I can never tell before hand whether we shall be just us two, or whether Bill Morgan must be counted in too.

Neither does Elsa. It's a queer friendship & situation. Certainly her friendship for Bill restricts her friendship for others whether she knows it or not.

Elsa has finished her shopping. She had quite a few people to remember here. She got Mrs. Henning[1] some good linen handker-chiefs, Bill a leather bill-fold & then I made her get Dr. Carl[2] some thing so that the effect wouldn't be so marked. She got Carl a cigarette holder. She placed these all in one box. Therefore it just appears now as it should that she remembers them all as good friends. For Mrs. Tri-ble[3] she got a silk vest & for the baby a box of wood-beads. Then nurses etc got small things. But you have no idea how the money goes. I've sent Mrs Henning a Xmas floral-piece & a basket of fruit for Sally & Howard Gill.

I feel a little concerned about Howard Gill. He is frail as can be & is so thin. He has had a cold which has lasted for weeks with temperature every evening. They are venturing into a new field as you probably guessed from the card you sent them. And I'm very much afraid they are headed for some very hard times. Cost of living is fearful down here. They have to wait for clients & pay house rent & office rent besides pay for house keeper & private schools. I asked her whether she had a big bank account to tide them over & she said "No, I've borrowed $500 from father & that will last us until some time in January." I feel sorry for them for they will have to give up their wonderful ideals & cope with a hard mercenary world. They think you & Colin are so fortunate to be able to build up a business on the side, while you are still doing what you want to do.

Sally invited me out to spend Sunday or Xmas Day with them. She is very sweet.

We called on Mrs. Shipstead[4] together & have her tentative promise to go on our Woman's Committee Ex. Board. But the Senator, may prevent her doing it. He is so afraid Mrs Shipstead may do or say something which may injure his political future.

You have no idea how bound & cowardly all these folks down here are. They fear for their jobs with every breath they draw.

The Progressives here are the worst of all. They are sort of angry with Papa because he says the Republicans are right in excluding them from the Republican Party. They too fear they will be ousted & then they will be all dressed up but no party to go to. Just the same Papa is right. I understand Lafollette is the only one ready to go ahead, & he is that, because he cannot help himself. Young Bobby[5] told Hillquit [h]is father was for a third party; but why doesn't the Senator say so to the world.—Just waiting to see if its safe.

Politics makes cowards out of most men. As socialists we certainly are free-er than the others.

Schafer—is acting like a Boob too. He goes belly aching around here because the Leader didn't support him or take his adds.

To change the subject—I've been reading some very delightful books. One by Mrs Snowden[6] is especially pleasant reading. She has an easy chatty style & very fascinating. The book is "The Political Pilgrim in Europe".[7] She describes the Conference of the Second International, the Women's Peace Meeting etc etc. No wonder she is capable & bright. The folks with opportunities can do things. She talks about so many of the folks we have met or know thro our party connections or thro reading. Elsa is reading it now & enjoys it quite as much as I do. I'll have her send it on to you when she is thro'. Then I am reading Roosevelts letters to his sister.[8] They too are interesting & charming. He too has had exceptional opportunities. No wonder he became the President. He too talks of so many many people we know of or know personally. I wish you'd get them from the library & read them. I shall go home & read his "Winning the West"[9] now. He was the tenderest man with his friends & family but uncompromising in his political policies. And he loved to *kill*,—anything from a grouse to a bear & his fellow beings if they were in his way. Try to get that book if you can.

Then I've read "Marie Antoinette" by Hilaire Belloc.[10] Poor Marie— she was such a victim & so much abused. You'd enjoy reading that too.

I sort of dread the next week. Living so all alone when I'm such a family person is going from one extreme to another. The Radio is just fine company. Last night I had an especially fine concert. Good artists sang all the things Papa is so fond of.

And now my blessed dear Ones, just have the jolliest of jolly times. Don't over eat, drink moderately and think of Elsa & me a little. We shall think of you much & with the most unselfish devotion, only we shall wish every minute we were all with you. Give Pepper a nice bone for Xmas too. Best of love to you all are your friends there & where is Bill Koch.

Lovingly
Mama.

1. Nina Henning (b. 1883), the wife of Dr. Carl Henning.
2. Carl Henning (1880–1956) was a physician with whom Elsa Berger worked at the Episcopal Hospital in Washington, D.C.
3. Nina Trible (b. 1878) was the wife of Dr. George B. Trible (b. 1883), a physician with whom Elsa Berger worked at the Episcopal Hospital in Washington, D.C.
4. Lula Anderson Shipstead (b. 1886), the wife of U.S. Senator Henrik Shipstead (1881–1960) of Minnesota. Henrik Shipstead served in the U.S. Senate as a member of the Farmer-Labor Party, 1923–1941, and as a Republican, 1941–1947.
5. Robert M. La Follette Jr.
6. Ethel Snowden (1881–1951), a British women's suffrage and temperance activist, was a prominent member of the Labour Party.
7. Ethel Snowden (Mrs. Philip Snowden), *A Political Pilgrim in Europe* (New York, 1921).
8. Theodore Roosevelt, *Letters from Theodore Roosevelt to Anna Roosevelt Cowles, 1870–1918* (New York and London, 1924).
9. Theodore Roosevelt, *The Winning of the West: An Account of the Exploration and Settlement of Our Country from the Alleghanies to the Pacific*, 6 vols. (New York, 1889).
10. Hilaire Belloc, *Marie Antoinette* (New York, 1909).

Meta to Victor

Washington, D.C.
December 23, 1924

Beloved Wonder-Man:—

Just to show you how good I am, you are going to get a letter before you write one I am sure.

After you left, I walked to the Episcopal Hospital which took just 50 minutes. I was somewhat tired but none the worse for wear. Elsa & I spent the afternoon and early evening together after which I came back to the hotel & listened to a very wonderful concert on the radio. Roxy's[1] programe was exceptionally fine for their were fine artists from the Metropolitan Opera Co singing. The Evening Star[2] was so fine that I was just a bit homesick for you for I know how fond you are of it.

Yesterday, I spent the morning with Schnucks, in the afternoon I wrote three long family letters, one to Betty, one to Dudd & Coie & the third to Mildren.[3] Then I walked to the office, got the mail, talked with Marx Lewis[4] & his friend Sigmund[5] etc. Sigmund, Schneider's Secretary nominated me as a good candidate for U.S. Senator to break Blaine's[6] machine. He said it was in the air & fashionable now to elect women & he tho't progressives would take more kindly to me than to you. I told him he didn't know the psychology of the German farmer who was anti woman in everything except the three K.K.K.[7]

We are getting many cards & I'm sure we are getting some from folks we have over looked. Helen Sumner Woodbury[8] for one & there are others.

Last night Butler Walsh, a young attorney & friend of Elsa's came over & we three spent the evening listening to the radio again. This young lawyer told me that a check made out by anyone who died, could not be cashed as the banks wouldn't pay out any money in a case of that kind. So please don't die, don't over eat, don't indulge too much New Year's Eve, where ever you are but have just the jolliest kind of a time with the children & your friends.

I think Elsa & I will go to the theatre Xmas Eve. It will be about the pleasantest way we can spend the evening & not think too much of home & Papa & Dudd & Coie.

I shall go out now & see if I can get tickets & then walk down to the office again.

Best love darling Papa always.

May our next years be full of health happiness & less cares.

Always devotedly your
Meta

Gov Blaine sent us a Xmas card.

1. Samuel L. "Roxy" Rothafel (1881–1936) was a New York theater manager and film and radio pioneer. From 1920 to 1927 he served as master of ceremonies of a popular radio program, "Roxy and His Gang."
2. "O Du, Mein Holder Abendstern" (Hymn to the Evening Star) from act 3 of Richard Wagner's opera, *Tannhäuser*.
3. Mildred Calkins (b. 1904?) worked as a maid for the Bergers in 1924–1925 and later worked as a maid and nanny for Doris and Colin Welles.
4. Marx Lewis (1897–1990) served as congressional secretary to New York Socialist Meyer London, 1917–1919 and 1921–1923, and to Victor Berger, 1923–1929. After Berger left office, Lewis worked as a New York City tax collector and as a union official.
5. Samuel Sigman (1899–1976) served as secretary to Republican Congressman George J. Schneider (1877–1939) of Wisconsin. Sigman later became involved in Progressive Party politics and served as Outagamie County, Wisconsin, district attorney, 1935–1936.

6. John J. Blaine (1875–1934), a progressive Wisconsin Republican, served as state attorney general, 1919–1921, governor, 1921–1927, and U.S. senator, 1927–1933.

7. *Kinder, Kirche, Küche* (Children, Church, Kitchen).

8. Helen Laura Sumner Woodbury (1876–1933), a Socialist economist, worked with the U.S. Children's Bureau, 1913–1924, and with the Institute of Economics, 1924–1926.

Meta to Doris and Colin

Washington, D.C.
January 8, 1925

Blessed Children:—

There isn't an hour of the day but what I think of you & wish we could all be together again. I wish so much too that Elsa could & would locate in Milwaukee. At present I cannot see what chance there is of that, but I wish it just the same.

I got a letter from Mildred[1] yesterday in which she told me that you had taken the punch-bowl & glasses in preparation for your big party. Did you have a good time? I hope so. Write & tell me all about it.

Mildred said you looked all tired out. I hope you did not over due altho' I don't believe this vacation did you much good in the way of a rest.

I've been helping Sally[2] get out some circular letters. They are all out now. We do hope that we will be able to start the National Woman's Organization, altho' its hard hard work. And no money coming in at all.

Papa has joined the Penguin Club here. Its a Club of liberals from all over the country. They have rented a charming old residence here for their club house. The lower floor consists of reception hall & 4 immense parlors is given over for entertainments & reading rooms. The upper 4 stories are rented to permanent club members or to associate members. Darrow spoke there the other evening to a crowded house. We did not go, just because Papa wouldn't. But last night I went over alone & heard a discussion by Villard, Shipstead, Arthur Hayes,[3] & Edw. Keating,[4] on the subject "Shall we proceed to organize a third party." All but Keating who is the Irish Editor of "Labor"—the Railroad Brotherhood's Journal were in favor of a Third Party. I spent a fine evening and was with Helen Hoy Greeley[5] all evening. She had called me up asking me to go with her.

Yesterday she & I spent the day together in the Senate listening to the debate on the Postal Salary Bill & the President's Veto.[6] There were some very sarcastic speeches aimed at the "Lame ducks" who were completely reversing themselves. Before election they voted for the Salary increases, hoping thereby to advance their chances for election, & now, these Lame Ducks voted to sustain the Veto, because they hope the President will recognize their *loyalty* to *him* & appoint them to some Lame Duck commission.

Really—politics make cowards & cringing beings of men.

The galaries were so crowded that Mrs. Greeley & I couldn't get in, So we went to Lafollette's office & asked young Bobby[7] to get us into the reserved gallery, which he did.

Last night we had dinner with Lawrence Todd & his wife[8] at their home at Chevy Chase. At one time the Todds were not friendly to us; quite the contrary. He was communistically inclined & so was she. We met them in Berlin while we were in Europe. They were then on their way to Russia.

Their attitude has changed very much towards us. Now they are quite friendly. Last night we discovered the reason we think. In the first place, to do them justice, I think they are changing towards the communistic theory; secondly—he used to represent the Federated Press here & I think he got much of his impression about us thro' Carl Haessler;—thirdly—Todd knows us better now—fourthly, the Federated Press is dying. The people who are executors of the Garland Fund, which had subsidized the Federated Press, have withdrawn their financial support & fifthly (this isn't fair I know, but seems to have some truth to it) Todd is out of a job & wants to represent labor papers in Washington.

Well, anyway, he is a very modest quiet unassuming young man, with an aggressive wife. He is most interesting however because he knows so many many people & facts.

He told us that while he was in Russia he met Haywood, Gertrude, Bob[9] & of course many others. Papa told him that Bob & Gertrude were divorced now & they were very much surprised but later remembered several things Gertrude had said to them in Moscow which took the first edge off their surprise. Mrs Todd asked me whether the other man in the case was Albert Ryse Williams.[10] But of course I didn't know. Gertrude had told Mrs. Todd that she had had several opportunities for new alliances but that she had always rejected them because she didn't wish to give up Bob.

Tonight we are all going to the White House Reception. I had Marx Lewis telephone over for an invitation for Dr. Wm. Morgan. So he is going with us. I tho't Elsa would like that & besides it would give her a chance to dance once in the East Room. It will probably be the only opportunity we will have this winter. I guess Bill Morgan was sort of pleased but I can never tell.

Mildred writes that she *thinks* she has enough coal for the winter. I don't think she has. So will you please call & speak to her about it & if necessary you order 3 more tons at the Arthur Kuesel Coal Co. You will need stove size I think. Tell the Kuesel Coal Co to send the same size & grade that they last supplied us with.

Then when you are there please remember to take the box of jam down to the Leader Office & have Walter Otto *express* it to us. Mark it "handle with care." I promised that to Marx Lewis who gets many of his own meals.

Next Tuesday—we are throwing a dinner party for Elsa's friends. The Tribles, Hennings etc. Papa expects to be in Milwaukee Jan 22 to attend a Leader Stockholders meeting. So you will see him again.

I am expecting Mrs. Schmelkes here some time soon.

There—now I've written you all the news; except that I love you both & always have a longing in my heart for you. This life is easy—lazy—has some charm, but I sort of miss my active home life with all its interests & ups & downs. But most of all I miss you all the time. So write me oftener & make me happy.

Devotedly
Mama.

1. Mildred Calkins.
2. Isabelle V. Kendig.
3. Arthur Garfield Hays (1881–1954) was a New York lawyer and civil liberties activist who served as the state's chairman for the 1924 La Follette campaign.
4. Edward Keating (1875–1965) served as a Democratic representative from Colorado, 1913–1919, and as editor of *Labor,* 1919–1953.
5. Helen Hoy Greeley (b. 1879) was a Washington, D.C., lawyer.
6. The Senate failed to override President Coolidge's veto of a bill raising the pay of postal workers.
7. Robert M. La Follette Jr.
8. Laurence Todd (1882–1957) and his first wife, Constance Leupp Todd. A member of the Socialist Party from 1904 to 1920, Laurence Todd worked as a journalist for various newspapers and news services. He served as secretary to Socialist Congressman Meyer London, 1915–1916, and worked for Tass, the Soviet news agency, 1923–1952. He married Dorothy Haessler, the sister of Carl Haessler, in 1938.
9. Gertrude Haessler Filtzer and Robert Filtzer.
10. Albert Rhys Williams (1883–1962), a Congregational minister and former Socialist Party member, lived in Russia between 1917 and 1918 and for much of the time between 1922 and 1931. He wrote extensively on behalf of the Soviet government.

Meta to Doris and Colin

Ancon, Panama Canal Zone
February 14, 1925

My dear Children:—

We arrived in the Canal Zone yesterday, none the worse for wear. Our trip was perfect from a weather point of view and the little freighter never rolled once nor did she pitch enough to speak of it.

The sun shown every day. Again I say—from a weather point of view it was perfect.

Papa however was attacked with either lumbago or a stretched ligament in his back & had to go to bed for a day on board & now has to lie down whenever there is an attack. It must be most painful for he makes a terrible fuss each time. He cannot put on shoes or stoop at all.

The tropics here remind me so much of Los Banios. We are of cours[e], surrounded with hills & for all the world I can see Banahai(?) each time I look out. The air is the soft hot house kind. So far it hasn't been hot because the trade winds blow a beautiful breeze all the time. This is trade wind time down here.

All houses are screened so that we do not sleep under a net. And last night we sat out on the hotel porch enjoying the loveliest evening and not a mosquito around.

The U.S. health Dep't has almost conquored that pest. There is hope for the P.I. Here malaria is almost wiped out but when it does come or attack, it seems to be of a specially vicious type.

I want to go back & tell you of our stop at Port Au Prince Haiti. At the port Papa was addressed by a man who knew him in Washington & who is a business companion & boon friend of former Congressman Bill Rodenberg. Mr. Rodenberg was the only friendly Congressman on the Committee of Representatives who tried our case before the House. He put in a sort of weak minority report. Mr. Cochran & Mr. McCrosson whom Papa knew too in Washington took us in tow and placed their auto and themselves at our disposal. They took us up to their home for dinner. Treated us first to a wonderful French Sautern wine, then a cock-tail & finally champagne. It was the first, eatable meal we had since we left N.Y.

Port Au Prince is very very crude & primitive. Instead of Phillipinos there were negroes & it seems much poorer & more diseased than any Phillipino I ever saw. They had something like a city at Port Au Prince. Low house's made of brick & mud & thatched covered. Also a wonderful church (cathedral) quite new. Wherever the Americans lived there was the semblance of civilization but there & there only. I'll have [to] tell you about the history of Haiti when I get home. Apparently years ago when the French possessed the island there was some culture there, but the 2,000,000 negroes were slaves to the French & still live in terror of the treatment they received. Revolution after revolution finally made a law-breaking mad vicious criminally inclined people of them. It is small wonder that they resented American occupation in the beginning. Apparently a better & more friendly relationship exists now. Their market-place in the large square in front of the white cathedral was indeed a sight to behold. There were thousands & thousands of negroes there, poor, black beasts of burden who had travelled, some of them some 20 or 30 miles to sell a few products that they pick growing wild.

No cultivation is undertaken at all by the natives.

The market scene reminded me very much of the scene in Baguio only this one is much larger & more congested.

Open sewers every where & the usual tropical stench. The shops in Port Au Prince are very crude & there is nothing there any American wants except good drinks & French perfumes.

The Scot[1] Congressional party of whose divorce we have been reading at home, took with them from Haiti 504 *cases* of the best stuff Haiti had. How about trying to enforce the 18th Amendment with our law makers?

The McCrossen's & Mr. Cochran gave us a royal time for the 7 or 8 hours we were in Haiti.

We met some very delightful Canal Zone officials who did everything possible to make our travelling on the Isthmus easy. Passes on the R.R. were provided for us & our baggage was attended to.

The hotels at either end of the Zone are large & spacious. This one The Tivoli, is the older of the two, larger, more crowded but not as nice as the Washington Hotel at Cristobal & Colon. However they say the city here is far more interesting.

So far I've seen nothing of cities except for a 2 block walk to the R.R. Station. The shops are just like those on the Escolta Manila except that the goods look cheaper & more tawdry. Most of the shops I've seen are in the hands of Hindu's.

More later.—Let Betty read this & then send it on to Aunt Hattie.

Best of best love to you all. I shall be happy if Papa gets back home & takes care of his back.

—Lovingly
Mama

1. Frank Douglas Scott (1878–1951) served as a Republican representative from Michigan, 1915–1927. Scott and his wife, Edna James Scott, were involved in an acrimonious divorce suit in which he was accused of smuggling a truck-load of liquor into the United States following a 1921 congressional tour of Panama.

Victor to Meta

New York, New York
July 29, 1925

My sweet Schatzl:—

And now I have to say "good bye" to my dear good Momma—and for some reason I do so more reluctantly than ever before.[1] I know, if nothing unforseen happens it is only for two months—and I have been away for much longer periods in the past. Moreover, apparently we are both in pretty fair health—considering our age and the various mishaps, to which we were subject. I believe it is just my conscience that is troubling me—I have no business to go on such a long trip without you. And I shall never again do so.

And New York never looked so dreary to me as this time. So many of the folks that I wanted to see were out of town. Saw Vladeck, of course, and some of Forward[2] crowd—they were very friendly but they all seemed to be much worried about their *local* situation. The Communists (or "left wingers")—as they still insist on calling them in this city—are taking away the "Yiddish" trades unions—which are the back-bone of the paper. And whenever they (the Communists) do not succeed in getting the upper hand in the organization, they simply go to work and *ruin* it. The Communists seem to be well supplied with money, which they evidently get from Russia. I try to impress it upon the leaders of the "right wing"—that the most valuable asset of the movement today,—in fact the *only* asset—is the Milwaukee Leader. And that it is their duty to preserve it for the future—if I should pass away. Moreover that the only way to do so, is to get a hold of it, while I am still vigorous and in good health, and can furnish "a bridge". I have to say all these things very carefully—and I must take good care not to arouse the suspicion that I want to sell them something that they do not want—and that they would not know what to do with, after they got it. They are Jews, you know. And the Forward is a closed corporation with less than a 150 members—and I can talk to very few of them *only*. So much for that.

Have not seen Brisbane. He gave me a sort of a send-off in his column, however,—saying that I have "a better education by 80% than 80 per cent of the other members of Congress". He means to get even for the 90% that I marked him a few weeks ago—when I caught hem not being posted on Christian theology. He claims that I "slipped" on the "sons of great fathers" in history. The fact is, however, that he was wrong again when he tried to correct me. But that is nothing, of course—mere pleasantry.

Have neither seen nor heard anything of Duncan. Will meet him on the Thuringia, tomorrow. I went to the boat today to make sure that my trunk was there. It is much smaller than the Christobal, but much newer and cleaner. And while it had nothing of the elegance of the Reliance or of the Hans Ballin,—there is an air of German cleanliness and homeliness about it, which is refreshing. The chief steward came up and told me that the captain asked for the honor to have me sit at his table. And he also showed the list of the others that were to sit there—and whether I had any objection to any of them. I told him that

I could not object to people that I did not know, but that I wanted Tommy there. Well, Tom's name went on the list.

Gretchen Ziegler was here with a girl friend of hers. They spent 2 days in the city and I invited them to breakfast and to a dinner at the Alamac. They were very happy—although I did not bother with them at all during day time.

Howard Gill called me up by telephon to wish me a "bon voyage"— but I was not at the hotel when the message came and the telephon girl did not ask for his number, so that I could not thank him.

"Mine host" of Washington D.C.—Mr. & Mrs. Bahrse—called up and invited me to dinner, but I could not accept the invitation, since my time was taken up.

Today (Wednesday) however I had lunch with Mrs. Stuart from Detroit. She read my interview in the N.Y. Times[3] and sent in a telegram from Montclair N.J. where she stays with a niece—inviting *you* and *me* to have lunch with her at the Waldorf-Astoria. She was under the impression that you were with me. Stuart made a great deal of money in Detroit real estate during the last 10 years and they are going to live in New York or thereabout in the future. They have no children and I suggested to her to leave their wealth to me. She is still a Socialist although she has no use for the party here, for which I cannot blame her much.

Now this is the sum and substance of my doings and "entertainings" since I left Milwaukee. And isn't this a gossipy letter, such as you would never expect from me?

As for the fur coat for Elsa—I don't care what you select and how much you pay, so long as you use good judgement. A fur coat must last at least 3 or 4 years, in order to be worth while. I have no doubt that you have done the best you could under the circumstances.

All of these things, however, are of minor importance. The main thing is that you, sweet Schatzl, keep your health and your good nature. Because, you may not know—but I know—that the light would go out of my life, if something happened to you. For me there is no other woman as *good*, as *noble*, and as *pure* as you.

With love to all

—your V.L.B.

Au Revoir—auf Wiedersehen![4]

1. Berger took a two-month tour of Europe with Thomas Duncan, a Wisconsin Socialist assemblyman, and served as a delegate to the Congress of the Labor and Socialist International, which met in Marseilles, France, August 22–27, 1925.

2. The *Jewish Daily Forward.*

3. In the interview, Berger announced that he would not run in the upcoming U.S. Senate election to fill the vacancy created by the death of

Robert M. La Follette Sr. "Berger Not After La Follette's Post," *New York Times*, July 27, 1925.
    4. Goodbye—goodbye!

Victor to Meta

Marseilles, France
August 28, 1925

My sweet Schatzl:

The International Socialist and Labor Congress closed last night— and I cannot say that it was worth coming for, a distance of more than 4,000 miles. The main value of these international meetings consists in meeting the leaders of the various countries—and I may claim a very wide acquaintance just at the present time.

As to my resolution[1]—they "meaning the statesmen" were prepared for it this time and determined that it should not come up. When I introduced it in the "commission I"—which had to treat with the prevention of war and general disarmament—and of which commission I became a member, very much to the disgust of even some of our own delegates—for the simple reason that we were entitled to *two* members in that "Commission" and no one dared to question my title—my resolution was simply *referred* to the "sub-commission" evidently with the intention that it should never come to light again. When the full "commission" met and brought in a report as long as perdition, containing thousands of words but really saying nothing—I simply re-introduced my resolution as a "substitute for the whole". The chairman ruled it out of order at the request of Hilferding[2] (of the German delegation) and of the French and Belgian delegation—without permitting the resolution to be read. And when I appealed from that rotten decision—speaking especially to Arthur Henderson[3] and the English members (as coming from a country where modern parliamentarism originated), Henderson tried to hide behind the subterfuge that the resolution had been considered by the sub-committee—, which by-the way was not true. The chairman then put the *motion*, whether the *substitute* should be permitted to be *read at all*. The French, Belgian, British and *Germans* and Poles voted against even permitting the reading of the substitute.

Then I exploded, of course. I held up the entire proceedings for about 10 minutes—told them that this International would go the way of the previous Internationals—if the Socialist leaders would continue to be cheap politicians looking for big jobs, instead of becoming pioneers blazing the trail for new ideas—if these leaders would continue to do the work of the big financiers and war makers, instead of facing the truth and telling it. I called them also a few hard names like "miserable cowards"—and wound up by telling them to go to certain warm place. Then I took my hat and left the meeting.

Hillquit knowing what was coming—had gone out on the porch when the trouble began. There were a half dozen cabinet ministers—past and present in the commission—and they sat there dumbfounded. I left. And the meaningless report was then adopted unanimously without a change, of course.

Well, the next morning, Henderson and some of the others came up and said that they were all very tired the night before and that the discussion of my substitute would have taken up all night, if read and brought before the Commission. Various speakers in Congress referred to my resolution, as "well meant" but as too early for "practical politics." We all became friends again.

I am disgusted with the whole crowd. Only party members representing party papers were permitted at meetings of the commissions—and thus these gentlemen believe themselves safe. But they are mistaken. I understood that the *Manchester Guardian* got the story and the main points of my resolution—and will print both very prominently. Pat Nolan, a delegate from the Clyde, (Scotland), and one of the most radical of the English crowd, was present at the meeting of the Commission. He made a copy of the resolution—said, it was excellent—and the rest I can guess.

I am very thankful for your letters, sweetheart, and for keeping me informed about home matters. But I am very much disturbed about your *health,* darling;—now, if you feel better lying down, than walking or sitting; why don't you lie down every day *until you are thoroughly rested?*

Doris is undoubtedly home by this time and after her siege at Scotia, she ought to be very good to the best mamma that ever lived. If Colin wants to stay a whole month at one stretch with his old parents, he ought to do so—but I do not think that it is necessary for Doris to go along.

I am sorry that you had so much trouble to keep the farm going while the children were away. Now, why were not the Fromm's there? I understood that it was a part of the agreement that they were to be there during the summer vacation.

Nothing else here—that is nothing of any importance. Only, I shall never again go on a long trip without you. If you cannot go along, I will not go either.

I am no "wonder man". I am a plain "damfool", as Artemus Ward[4] would say. But you are the crown of all women and even getting better as you are getting older.

With love to all, ever your

Papa.

1. Berger introduced a resolution calling for the abrogation of the Treaty of Versailles.
2. Rudolf Hilferding (1877–1941), a Social Democrat, served as the German minister of finance, 1923–1929.
3. Arthur Henderson (1863–1935) served as secretary of the British Labour Party, 1911–1934, and as a member of Parliament, 1903–1931.
4. Artemus Ward was the pen name of American humorist Charles Farrar Browne (1834–1867).

Victor to Meta

Berlin, Germany
September 13, [1925]

Sweet Schatzl:

This is the last letter I address to you from Europe—I am more than willing to go home. The Germans are terrible "spongers"—and Germany today is the most expensive country in the world, it is even more expensive than Switzerland. Austria is very much cheaper—but even there Elsa will have to look for a "pension" as quickly as possible.

I have not seen anything of Tom[1] since last Thursday. Inquiries at his hotel showed that he had left there about 2 days ago without leaving his address. I suspect that Alma Schlesinger[2] invited him to her home and that Tom is saving money twofold,—by not paying hotel-fare, and by being shown the town. I am very glad of it. Tom should have telephoned his whereabouts, however.

The Germans are an extremely disappointing people. They do not seem to have any great outstanding figures at the present time. The upper classes—especially the yunkers,[3] the big land-owner[s] and some of the office-holders—would have a monarchy tomorrow, if they could. The middle class has been ruined by the war and the inflation of the money two years ago—and nobody seems to trust the future, everybody spends everything he gets. The working class, which was a little better-of[f] than the other classes during the inflation, although the working also suffered severely—is now in a very bad predicament, with wages ranging from 30–40 mark per week—, which means $7½ to $10—and meat bread and clothing more expensive than in America. Just now the Germans are the most poorly dressed people in Europe—although their women are much better looking than the Irish, English or French.

As for the German Social Democratic party—it lacks real leadership and while it still is the largest single political party in Germany, its *spirit* is *gone*. I was told by leading members that the German workingmen are "Spiessbürgers"[4] with a red label, however.

In short, sweet Mamma,—every thing was disappointing. It may also be—that the fault lies within me—I am getting old and dissatisfied.

After this Schatzl—I shall concentrate entirely on my family, the Leader and my immediate friends. I may be a big man—they all tell me

I am—but I am not big enough to change things in any appreciable manner. Although my heart aches when I talk to some of them and they tell me of their home conditions—I have not even power enough to alleviate some individual cases.

As I understand now: the great International Congress of the Socialist parties of the world held at Marseille did not even create a ripple in the European press. Had my resolution been adopted—or even publicly discussed—the whole world would have been in a commotion because the Socialists are the leading—or the next to the leading—party in most of the European countries. But what's the use about that now. They are cowards.

Well, sweet Schatzl—I hope to find a letter in Hamburg. You need not call for me in New York—and we might just as well save the money.

I hope that the people in Milwaukee are missing me. At any rate sweet Mamma, I know *you* do—because I miss you, you who in so many ways is bigger and in every way better than

your V.L.B

1. Thomas Duncan.
2. Alma Schlesinger Haensel (b. 1888) was a Milwaukee social worker who moved to Berlin after her marriage in the early 1920s.
3. junkers, members of the Prussian landed aristocracy.
4. comfortable, solid, and narrow-minded middle-class people.

Meta to Victor

Milwaukee, Wisconsin
September 26, 1925

My Darling!

Oh, you cannot know how welcome, how very very welcome you are. These have been a long 10 weeks or more for me. Nothing I had planned could be carried out. I just had to fit myself in as circumstances provided.

After Doris & Coie came back, I expected I'd have a sort of a vacation myself, but nothing came of it.

Mrs. Greeley visited me for 3 or 4 days after which I thought I'd go on a long auto trip thro' upper Michigan with Hattie & Frank[1] on their anniversary trip, but that too had to be abandoned, due to a miserable boil which developed on my knee. I had to stay at home & poultice. That's over with now. In a way I guess it was fortunate that I didn't leave the city.

As you know Blaine called the special election[2] for Sept 15 & 29; just the time I would have been gone. Well, the socialists, were sitting down on their quarters twirling their thumbs & feeling helpless. Finally John M. Work telephoned me, asking me to come to the office for a conference with him. At this conference, he appealed to me to talk with Coleman[3] & Melms. This was 3 or 4 days before the Sept 15 primary. I immediately went upstairs & found that Weber,[4] Louis Arnold, Melms & Coleman had constituted themselves a temporary campaign committee in lieu of the absence from town of the members of the State Committee. And this temporary campaign committee had decided that they would not go into debt for the Senatorial campaign & since they had but $270, or something like that, the[y] couldn't conduct much of a campaign & were therefore depending on the good will of small papers thro'out the state to print such messages as John Work mailed out to them.

They hadn't even appointed a committee to get money.

So I started right in & scolded with the result that we had a call issued for another committee for the next Sat. at noon when Hoan was to return to the city. At this committee meeting, 3 days before the primary we started a campaign for Work. Why those boobs upstairs didn't have pep enough to *take* the *really fine* suggestions Marx Lewis offered nor did they accept his offer to work every afternoon & evening for the campaign.

Well—we got a finance committee started, we planned out a very small & useless distribution of literature thro' out the state. That will be like a drop of water on a hot griddle.

No factory meetings had been scheduled until I went over to the city hall & had Hoan call up Melms & read a riot act to him. And so on & on. In fact no one in Milwaukee seemed to know who our candidate was, altho' they knew that the Socialists didn't endorse young Bobby. And the primary vote showed it. We polled about 6,000 votes in the entire state. In Mil. County about 5,700 votes were cast.

Since the primary however, we have conducted a much better campaign & the socialists have taken a little heart.

We had a Debs meeting; hired two small halls down stairs, but needed only *one*. Filled that one hall. Then I pledge[d] $50 for you. I don't know whether that is too much or not. But I believe we needed to do it, for the sake of the party, the Leader & the future.

Ameringer with one exception, refused to write for Work in the Findings.[5] His reason is, that he who prints the Carmen's Journal in Oklahoma, which lives on the revenue derived from that job contract, couldn't come out against young Lafollette, when the Brotherhoods endorse Bobby. Ameringer was afraid of losing that printing contract. In the meantime Work, Miss Thomas & I sent him telegrams urging him to write for a united Socialist front without saying anything about the specific candidate. Even this he did not do. And so, here too, in America, we do not fight like we used to.

Then here's another piece of news which distressed Betty T. very much. The federal income tax dep't. sent a man over to study the books. He was there one and one half days. He was especially interested in exemptions claimed for the Oklahoma Leader. I think if he had stayed longer—Betty would have died.

The hard months for the Leader were passed without borrowing, altho' I am told the rent isn't paid & some bills for features are not paid.

Otherwise, things are as usual.

I am terribly hard up. You were right, when you expressed doubt as to the amount of money you left and its capacity to go far. So you had better be prepared to finance some important jobs.

I just received your letter from Berlin saying you do not receive many letters from me. That's quite true. I didn't write as often as I was inclined to as I didn't exactly know where & *when* to send letters to the Am. Ex. offices everywhere. But I did have a letter for you at every stopping place you were at.

I hope you got the one I sent to Hamburg too.

I have been getting facts & figures on oil burners & have quite a bit of data to submit. The gas company also is in the house *heating* game now. The cost of installation is about the same as installing oil burners, & the cost of consumption of fuel is also about the same. They will submit figures to you also when you return. I will let no contract until you come back & we can talk things over.

Our home affairs are as usual. Doris loves her work on The Leader. Coie is back at school. Elsa writes cheerful letters. She takes charge of the Episcopal Hospital from Oct 1. Will you stop to see her enroute home?

Lewis wants very much to go to Washington to attend to some of his affairs & also some congressional cases. I've kept him here however to help Miss Thomas during your absence & during the campaign. Miss Thomas thinks he is a jewel & wishes we could keep him.

The only disgruntled person is your wife and I am sure that she will be all right again once she has her husband back again. It's strange & fearful how I do miss you darling. You certainly are a part of me & my whole happy existence depends on you & on our love for each other as well as the beautiful & wonderful close companionship we enjoy. So don't stay in N.Y. or Washington too long but hurry home. You arrive in N.Y. on Duddie's birthday, so I shall have two reasons for rejoicing on that day.

It is also election day for U.S. Senator. I am fearful about results however. I do hope our vote won't slump too much. Send me a wire, or night letter as soon as you arrive. And be assured again of the warm & full of love welcome awaiting you at home. God! how I do love you still.

Your

Meta.

1. Hattie and Frank Schweers, Meta's sister and brother-in-law.
2. Robert M. La Follette Jr. was elected to the U.S. Senate in a special election held in September, 1925. John M. Work, the Socialist candidate, received 3 percent of the vote statewide and 14 percent in Milwaukee County.

3. William Coleman (1878–1933), a Milwaukee labor leader and Socialist politician, served as a city alderman, 1910–1914, 1916–1922, and 1932–1933, state assemblyman, 1925–1929, and secretary of the state Socialist Party, 1923–1928 and 1931–1932.

4. Frank Weber (1849–1943), a Socialist, organized the Milwaukee Federated Trades Council in 1887, served as its secretary, 1902–1934, and headed the Wisconsin Federation of Labor, 1893–1917. Weber served in the Wisconsin Assembly, 1907–1911, 1915–1917, and 1923–1927.

5. "Findings" was a column by Oscar Ameringer that appeared daily on the front page of the *Milwaukee Leader*.

Meta to Doris

Washington, D.C.
April 28, 1926

My Darling,—

The best I could do yesterday was to send you Elsa's nice letter. I had no time to write myself. The annual meeting of the W.I.L.[1] took place here for the past two days and I attended that. Am again elected on the Board altho' to tell the truth it is not a very inspiring groupe. The women are very fine women but only with a Quaker vision. Nevertheless it seems to be the only groupe in Wisconsin that I can join and the only one that does not make the already hard work for the Socialists still harder.

There was a conference of ten different Peace organizations here before our own W.I.L. met. At this conference one could see the line of cleavage very clearly between the old ladies and the more energetic and impulsive younger element who make up the other and more advanced groupes. I really belong with them as far as sympathy and tactics go but it is not in accordance with the policy of the Socialist party. We met the Ohmsteds[2] etc. I also tried to get a job for Sally[3] in the office of the W.I.L. but Dorothy Detzer[4] at once bristled and said very emphatically "I won't work with her for a moment" and since Dorothy Detzer is the Executive Secretary I guess Sally can't get even a summer job there. Wonder why there is that animosity there.

Elsa is really learning to write better letters isn't she? The last one even passed Papa's critical attitude. He brought it up to me with the remark "Here is a lovely letter from our nix nutxigen[5] Schnucks." It is the first letter over which we did not have an argument.

At the meeting yesterday I met a young girl who is so wonderfully attractive and bright and full of poise and charm that she beats any one I have ever seen including Sally or any one else. She is about your age, a college graduate, by the name of Edith Hilles. She is a Quaker and when she addresses her Quaker Friends she addresses them with the charming "thee" and "thou". I went up to her and ask[ed] her to tell about all herself etc. etc. She is a farmer. She has a fruit farm about 20 miles from Philadelphia which she runs herself. I want very much that you two meet some day. I think you will agree that she is very wonderful. I also want Sally to meet her.

The inclosed literature came to me from one of the advanced Peace organization[s]. Will you please give it to Miss Thomas and ask her to give it such publicity as she thinks wise. It is very remarkable that Senator Frasier consented to introduce it.

We missed your letter today very much. I don't want to urge you to write when I know that you are so busy but I do ardently hope that you are all right. You see I have very special reasons to always wonder if you are O.K. and when I do not hear from you I have all the more reason to wonder.

Mrs. Pauly is here now. I will not continue altho there is nothing that I would rather do than talk to you. Mr. Durand also came to see us this week. So we do see Milwaukee folks once in a while.

Be a dear sweet good girl and try to be as happy as I try to be and as I pray that you will be. Goodbye for the present my dear dear Dudd. My love to Co and approval for sending the publications.

Mama.

1. Women's International League for Peace and Freedom.
2. Mildred Scott Olmsted (1890–1990), a suffragist and Women's International League leader after World War II, and Allen Seymour Olmsted (1888–1977), a Pennsylvania attorney and judge, were Quaker peace activists.
3. Isabelle V. Kendig.
4. Dorothy Detzer (1893–1981) served as executive secretary of the U.S. section of WILPF, 1924–1946. She worked in relief missions in Austria, 1920–1922, and in Russia, 1922–1924.
5. good for nothing.

Victor to Jan

Milwaukee, Wisconsin
July 28, 1926

My dear Mr. Edelman:—[1]

It is unnecessary for me to tell you that your letter, asking for the hand of Elsa, was a great surprise to both Mrs. Berger and to me—and not a pleasant surprise.

We have sent our daughter to Europe to become more proficient in the knowledge of medicine, but not to choose a husband in any of the old countries.

Elsa is free and of age and at liberty, of course, to marry any man her heart desires.

Nevertheless, if you are an honest and an intelligent man, please put yourself in our position.

We have a nice and healthy—a physically and mentally exceptionally well developed child. We gave her the best education America has to offer. She decided to study medicine.

Very well.

We sent her for four years to the University of Wisconsin and for two years to the University of Pennsylvania, where she graduated as a doctor of medicine. After that she interned for nearly three years at the Emergency and Episcopal Hospitals at Washington, D.C. And then the young doctor went to Europe to get more perfect in her chosen specialty at various old universities.

And lo and behold! Now comes a letter from a young man whom we do not know and of whom we have not heard—asking for her hand in marriage.

We do not know anything about his age—his family—his physical or mental qualities—his education—his ability to support a family—we know nothing except that his name is Jan Edelman, that he is a Dutchman and that he says he met Elsa on the boat crossing the Atlantic and that he loves her.

Now Mr. Edelman, I am a man who has seen considerable of the world. As the editor of a daily paper and as a member of the Congress of the United States, I have had many chances to study and to learn the ways of human beings. From frequent observations I know that love making and falling in love is a common pastime for young people who cross the Atlantic. I consider it a very poor place to choose a mate because the social atmosphere on such a boat is artificial, though bewitching at times. The infatuations of the boat usually and properly end with the landing of passengers on terra firma.

Is this to be different in your case and why? Now do not misunderstand me. We have nothing against you—we simply do not know you.

If fate has decreed that it is to be a son-in-law from Europe—I would probably prefer a Hollander. From my study of history and ethnography, I have acquired a liking for Holland and the Hollanders.

But you must remember this: Mrs. Berger and I have sacrificed a great deal for Elsa and we naturally want to see her happy and secure in the future.

Before we say "yes" therefore, we must first learn to know you. We must know the whence and whereto. We must know your antecedents and your prospects.

You say in your letter that you lived in our country for three years and that you expect to be here this fall.

Well and good. Come over here and let us get acquainted. This is the country where Elsa was born—whose language she speaks and where she must live and practice her profession.

Moreover, you hardly know each other. You don't know much about each others temperaments and whether your respective sympathies will stand the test of time.

Therefore, I suggest that you try yourselves out first. Do not bind yourselves—simply be good friends. Correspond with each other. Learn to know each other and if your love can stand the test of time and the test of closer acquaintance and if Elsa then still wants to marry you, you may have our blessing.

Yours for better acquaintance in the future,

[Victor L. Berger]

1. Jan Edelman (1900–1963) met Elsa Berger in January or February, 1926, while she was traveling to Europe to study medicine in Austria. The couple married in Milwaukee on February 1, 1927. A native of the Netherlands, Edelman received a B.S. from the University of Wisconsin in 1935 and worked as an electrical engineer in Milwaukee.

Meta to Jan

Milwaukee, Wisconsin
September 28, 1926

My dear Jan:—

May I be so informal as to call you Jan?

I want very much to clear up an impression you seem to have regarding Mr. Berger's & my "displeasure." But before going on to that subject, permit me to say that both Mr. Berger and I are very deeply concerned about the health of your good father.

Elsa told us of his illness & a very high blood pressure etc, but we really didn't realize how very seriously ill he is. We know what anxious hours you, your mother & sisters are living now and we ardently hope that when the crisis is passed, the report will be that Mr. Edelman has a chance for recovery.

Please convey my sincere & warm regards to both of your parents.

Now as to any "displeasure." We were so surprised at the news & as Mr. Berger stated in his letter to you, such surprises are not pleasure exactly, not knowing any thing about the case. Elsa had written that there was only one person who might interest her at all & that was a young Hollander, & that all the other European men she had met, meant nothing to her. But that was about the extent of our knowledge concerning this new friendship.

Now, I assure you we have sort of accustomed ourselves to the idea and after all, what we want most of all is that Elsa should be happy & that the man she marries shall be equally happy.

We have never interfered with the girl's choice. Doris was very lucky. I feel certain now, that if you love Elsa & she loves you, that she too will be lucky. As far as Mr. Berger & I are concerned, I can assure you, Jan, that you will find a warm welcome when you do come.

Elsa tells me that she knows I shall love you as much as I love Colin Welles. I wrote back to her & said I was prepared to do just that sort of thing provided you two young people had decided the question between you. I shall be looking forward with very pleasant anticipation to your coming.

Thank you also for writing again. Your letters justify Mr. Berger's opinion of the Hollanders.

Very cordially yours
Meta Berger.

Victor to Meta

Washington, D.C.
December 2, 1926

My sweet Schatzl:

Here goes a letter—although I have very little to tell. I have just looked over the mail, which is largely routine. Marx Lewis is not here, he left before I came—to be present in New York at the trial of a case in which he is concerned.

I have a rather nice room at the Wardman Park Hotel. The building was put up in wings (five of them I believe) and all rooms are outside rooms, i.e. they face a rather large wooded lot. The hotel has 1500 rooms (so I am told) and has the longest lobby I have ever seen—and a "sun parlor" of almost the same size as the lobby. Only the *lower* two floors are used as a hotel in the old accepted sense—the rest is rented out in suites and appartements, some of which have as many as nine rooms. There are a member of foreign ministers in the place—also some statesmen and ex-statesmen whom I know, for instance A. Mitchell Palmer.

Everybody is "putting on the dog" heavily, except your papa—who nevertheless is getting considerable attention, as you may well imagine. When Elsa comes, she will have a room in the place also, I must get something for our advertising, you know,—cannot afford to give it away.

I am still in a quandary about meeting that Schnuck. As the enclosed clipping will tell you, she arrives on Monday,—I don't know at what time of the day. On Monday, at 12 o'clock at noon, the Congress opens[1] and I hate to miss the first roll-call—although I don't care much, whether I hear the Presidents message read or not, since I will have to read it in the newspaper any how. If I make up my mind to meet her at the dock, I shall leave here on Sunday afternoon;—or I may wire her to meet me at the Astor Hotel, if I decide to answer to my name, before I go to New York on Monday.

The situation is awkward—I wish the boat would arrive either a day sooner, or a day later. At any rate I shall think it over.

As for the work in Congress I don't believe—this short session will do much of importance.

The German property seized during the war—i.e. as much as there is still left after the various Alien Property Custodians had their way—will be returned to the various private owners, because our capitalists are afraid of the odium of "confiscating private property", although as a matter of fact, Palmer and Garvan[2] stole about 2,000 German patents, i.e. "sold" them to the Chemical Foundation, which they and their friends own. And the Supreme Court has upheld robbery because in 1918 in the bill creating the Alien Property Custodian A. Mitchell Palmer had the words inserted giving the Custodian the power to act "as though he were the absolute owner."

Well, so much for that.

But the President's suggestion of a "refund" to the taxpayer's because there is a 400 million dollar surplus in the treasury—which means that the multi-millionaires would get most of the refund—, has struck a snag. The leaders of the Republican party informed him, that he could not get even half of the Republicans to vote for that proposition. So it appears that the surplus will be applied to the payment of the national debt—but I hope that they will at least abolish the "nuisance taxes", as for instance the tax of theater tickets.

All of this "statesman business" may interest you very little, and I only tell it to you, because I have nothing else to tell.

I hope, however, that there will be no extra-session this summer. The Republicans would be foolish to permit it, since it would give the Democrats a good chance to play politics without doing anything themselves.

Well, I don't want a special session either—for many reasons.

This letter is getting too long, however. Therefore I just want to tell you to take that 2 hours *rest every day* that the physicians prescribed for you—and don't forget the pills either—if you love me and the children. Otherwise I am

as always—ever your
V.L.B.

1. Berger was in Washington to attend the opening of the second session of the Sixty-ninth Congress. On November 2, he had been elected to the

Seventieth Congress, winning 49 percent of the vote compared to 45 percent for Republican William Stafford and 6 percent for Democrat Rose Horwitz.

2. Francis P. Garvan (1875–1937), a New York attorney, managed the New York office of the alien property custodian from November, 1917, until March, 1919, when he became alien property custodian and assistant U.S. attorney general. In this role, Garvan oversaw the sale of German dye and chemical patents to the Chemical Foundation, Inc., which he had founded. On October 11, 1926, the U.S. Supreme Court upheld the legality of Garvan's actions.

Victor to Meta

Washington, D.C.
December 12, 1926

My sweet Schatzl:

With all the attention to our various kids we are apt to neglect the best part of the family and that is our mamma. I have sent you mainly night-letters last week.

Well, Elsa is here and making the rounds. For this afternoon and evening (Sunday)—the poor thing is sadly neglected—after having lunch with me at the Occidental (Buchholz on Pennsy ave) she has only four (4) engagements, among them a dinner with Henry Simon, the French attachè who used to bring us champagne last year.

The scheme to have her take the place of Bill Morgan in the Walker[1] firm looks not promising, however. Dr. Walker returned from his trip this morning and told Morgan that he would let Elsa know by letter about the engagement. The fact is that Bill was away for several months on account of illness and Dr. Walker and his assistant found that they could attend to all the business without Bill—and now Dr. Walker wants to save that salary.

In a way I am glad of that. If Elsa has to take a *temporary* position for a few months until she gets married and permanently located somewhere—I prefer to have her do so in Milwaukee, if possible. You and she will have to make some preparations, if she is to get married in March, as planned.

I have also taken up the matter of Jan's entrance into our country and his future citizenship with the Secretary of Labor, Mr. James J. Davis[2] and have found a very sympathetic reception, although the matter is not so simple, since our Ku Klux legislation[3] is still in full force. Where there is a will, there is a way, I suppose, and we will arrange it, in some way.

I am glad to hear that your "cold" is getting better. As for Coie— our children ought to let the *fresh air in* and *keep* the *dog* and the *cat out;* and they would surely be healthier. "La Grippe" is simply a *disease of filth,* which became especially epidemic during the World War, because there was more filth, and more different kinds of filth, piled up during that war than there had been in a hundred years. But if Co and Doris will play and handle dogs and cats much—and not wash their hands a hundred times a day, they are liable to catch all kinds of filth-diseases and they may call them "grippe" or what not, just as they like.

You showed your good sense, Schatzl, by not driving the car on the icy pavement.

Elsa will leave here Monday afternoon; and I must put a special delivery stamp on this letter, so that you get it before her arrival. I expect her to arrive in Milwaukee about noon on Tuesday—12.30 P.M, to be more exact.

I have not had any music, since I left home. I have been in Voight office only once, for a minute or so, on some business. He told me then that they would come to see me, and he and the little girl came down yesterday to my office—but since I have not been invited to their home I didn't go.

There is only one more Sunday left before Xmas—next Sunday. I shall be in New York then—attending a meeting of the National Executive Committee. I have spent all of my evenings in my hotel room—unless I am in the office—I never go down to the lobby, where everything is full dress, shoddy-aristocracy and dancing to jazz music. I detest the place.

Have had a very friendly reception in the House—but I do not feel at home in Congress, now less than ever. I feel that our "parliament" and our democracy is a fake—and that most of us are simply a stage decoration. It is a colossal waste of time for anybody who really wants to accomplish something.

Our "progressives" are tragi-comical figures. Their "leaders"— Frear, Nelson, etc. are trying hard to become stand-patters again.

The Farmer-Labor party—was reduced to two members in the House and one in the Senate. Although their convention has decided that they are to affiliate with the Democratic party—I expect that Henrik Shipstead will become a *full-fledged Republican,* if they should promise to put him up for re-election on their ticket. American "politics"—is a dirty game.

Now, I don't know how much all of that will interest you,—nor why I am telling that to you. Especially, considering the fact that things are not any more honest in Europe, where Dawes, Chamberlain and Briand got the Nobel prize[4] for their activities and achievements during the World War? No, the prize for peace!

I have trouble with my right knee. At times I can hardly walk. This has been going on for some weeks—as you know—and I seriously intend to take a cure either in Waukesha or at Battle Creek.

I hope you take your pills regularly—and especially the two hours rest, which the Washington physicians prescribed for you. Elsa also thinks that it is very important for you to obey literally.

That is about all that is on my mind at the present moment.

Give my love to the children. And remember that after all you are *everything* to your

V.L.B.

1. Dr. Reginald R. Walker (b. 1877), a Washington, D.C., physician.
2. James John Davis (1873–1947), a Republican, served as secretary of labor, 1921–1930, and as a U.S. senator from Pennsylvania, 1930–1945.
3. The Immigration Act of 1924 placed restrictions on the number of immigrants that could be admitted to the United States. The Ku Klux Klan claimed partial credit for the legislation and, according to some accounts, spent more than $1 million to help secure its passage.
4. Charles G. Dawes (1865–1951), U.S. vice-president, 1925–1929, won the Nobel Peace Prize in 1925 for his role in developing the Dawes plan, a program for the economic and industrial reorganization of Germany. Dawes shared the prize with British Foreign Secretary Sir Austen Chamberlain (1863–1937). Aristide Briand (1862–1932), French premier during much of World War I, won the Nobel Peace Prize in 1926 for his role in the 1925 Treaty of Locarno.

Meta to Victor

Milwaukee, Wisconsin
January 7, [1927][1]

My Darling:—

Let me see—you left for Washington last Sunday;—this is Friday night 11. P.M. & so far I've had just one night letter from you & no other word.—All right, if you have lived up to your promise of going to Drs. Clark, King[2] etc and are following their advice. Are you?—Sure?

I've kept my promise to you & have rested daily, altho' many times I've a lot of other things I could spend my time doing. So write me the news I want to hear most, that you are taking care of yourself.

Yesterday Glenn Frank[3] was in the city to address an all high school students convention. He asked if you were in the city & said he'd like to see you if you were. He is great! Did you see how fearlessly & strongly he came out for academic freedom for "U" professors in answer to Blaine's attack on Prof McCrory's[4] taxation leaflet? Frank certainly doesn't intend to let the governor or senator or any political body intimidate him. Now more than ever I'd like to be a "U" regent. And in this respect I wonder if it would be wise to take Ada James into our confidence or Comings[5] & ask them also to see the Gov. What do you think of that? Ada James, the papers say is slated for some political job because she supported Zimmerman.[6] Write me about the suggestion to see Ada?

Will you also send the Muqdilianie article[7] back?

Tonight I had Nettie & Lucius Gould[8] & Fr. & Mabel Putnam in to dinner. They left a few moments ago. Elsa & Doris went to the Chicago Civic Opera & Coie & I are home alone. Coie is sleeping & I'm writing.

Jan cabled Elsa today. He is on the way having left Holland Jan 6. The cable came from Southampton.

Did you notice a new column called "Politics" in the Capital Times written by Wm. T. Evjue? I tho't it would be a fine idea if Doris could write such a newsy chatty column about local politics in the Leader. Thus she'd get thoroughly interested in the political problems, & eventually be the best informed person on local politics besides being a power & a unique person being a woman.

A little later they (Welles's) might change their *legal* residence back to Mil. for political purposes. What do you think of such a column. Look up Evjue's Column in the Times. And please dear Papa take care of yourself & love me as I love you. That's enough.

Your Meta.

1. Meta misdated this letter 1926.
2. William Earl Clark (b. 1879) and Clapham P. King (1889–1968) were Washington, D.C., physicians.
3. Glenn Frank (1887–1940) served as president of the University of Wisconsin, 1925–1937.
4. Meta meant MacGregor rather than McCrory. Ford H. MacGregor, a professor of political science at the University of Wisconsin, 1909–1935, wrote *A Taxation Catechism*, which criticized the state's tax system. Glenn Frank issued a statement defending academic freedom after Wisconsin Governor John J. Blaine demanded that MacGregor either retract his statements or resign.
5. George F. Comings (1848–1942), a progressive Republican, served as lieutenant governor of Wisconsin, 1921–1925.
6. Fred R. Zimmerman (1880–1954), a Republican, served as Wisconsin's governor, 1927–1929, and secretary of state, 1923–1927 and 1939–1954.
7. Meta was probably referring to an unidentified article by or about Giuseppe Emanuele Modigliani (1872–1947), an Italian socialist leader and anti-Fascist who fled Italy for Paris in 1925.
8. Lucius Gould (1863–1935) taught geography at the University of Wisconsin Extension in Milwaukee. He had recently married Meta's friend, Annette "Nettie" Rosenthal.

Victor to Meta

Washington, D.C.
January 8, 1927

My sweet Schatzl:

I am always exceedingly glad to get your lovely and loving letters— only I do not get enough of them to satisfy me. My life here is very drab and monotonous.

Have made an appointment with Drs. Clark, King & Co for Monday morning 9 A.M. and shall, of course, religiously follow any professional advice they may give me. Had so much *pain* with reumathisms in my knee of late that I could not sleep at night—and it seems to me that the pain is spreading.

Dossie[1] is not in Washington. Her mother is sick, and Dossie has not returned since Xmas.

I have not called up Sally[2] as yet—may do so next week.

We had some lively times in the House about the additional cruisers. The President wanted the building of the 3 cruisers authorized by the law of 1924 postponed (temporarily) until the outcome of *his next* disarmament conference is known. This is only a "gesture", of course, since these cruisers could not be ready for *some* years and, therefore, would neither add to nor detract from our naval strenght at the present time. The Presidents point of view was upheld by a small majority. The Socialist party voted unanimously with the President in this case.[3]

Considering the position of the President and his administration in Nicaragua and also his threats against Mexico—that "pacifist" gesture does not amount to much.[4]

So much for Washington.

As for home affairs—I am glad to hear that you are beginning to buy an "outfit"—Ausstattung heisst das auf deutsch[5]—for Schnucks.

I expected the gas bill for December to be very high—since we had an extremely cold month.

Before buying a fur coat at Gimbels—look over fur coats and prices in several stores like Reel, Hansen, etc. I am inclined to believe, however, that you will find in the end that you can do as well at Gimbel's as in any place. Only sometimes you are apt to strike a bargain at some furrier's for a high priced coat like an Alaska seal, however, because they do not sell many coats of that type—after the main season is over. Get a long coat, while you are at it—45 inches or even 50 inches long. In case you should decide to buy a fur coat at Gimbel's, I shall make arrangements to pay the Gimbel bill or a large share of it, *before* you get the coat.

What you are saying about the Sentinel's method of reporting the school board, and especially your activity—is aggravating, of course. John Work ought to take up the matter some time, for the sake of our party.

I hope Doris will pass the bar examination this time—but if she does not I shall love her just as much.

The appointment of Ralph Smith—son of Socialist director Smith[6]—must be made either by Schafer or by one of the U.S. Senators. I cannot do it under the law, since he lives in the 4th district.

This answers all of your questions, Schatzl. Take good care of yourself. Remember, you'r the apple of the eye of your

V.L.B.

1. Dorothy "Dossie" Rigg, a friend of Elsa Berger's, worked as a secretary for Dr. William Earl Clark.

2. Isabelle V. Kendig.

3. President Coolidge had asked Congress in December, 1926, to postpone construction of three cruisers authorized by the Butler Cruiser Act of 1924. The House voted 183 to 161 on January 7, 1927, not to build the cruisers, with Berger voting with the majority. The House reversed itself on February 28, 1927, on a 208 to 172 vote; Berger again opposed building the cruisers.

4. The U.S. sent marines into Nicaragua in May, 1926, following the outbreak of civil war. President Coolidge charged that Mexico was supplying weapons to Nicaraguan revolutionaries, and Secretary of State Frank B. Kellogg warned against the danger of a communist takeover of Latin America. Nicaraguan rebel leader Augusto Sandino refused to agree to the American-mediated settlement of May, 1927, and subsequently led his forces against U.S. troops.

5. that is called Ausstattung in German.

6. William L. Smith (1878–1964) was a barber who served on the Milwaukee School Board, 1923–1927. His son, Ralph W. Smith (b. 1907), worked as a clerk for an insurance company and was seeking an appointment to the U.S. Naval Academy at Annapolis.

Meta to Victor

Milwaukee, Wisconsin
January 10, 1927

Darling!

Today you are to have your session with the doctors. I hope that the reports will be favorable. Be sure to follow orders.

We at home are going along normally. Your letter just came. I cannot quite understand your sustaining Coolidge on his Cruiser request.[1]

Here at home I am urging the Peace groupe to call a meeting & to pass some drastic resolutions against our butting in on Nicaragua at all. I think its quite outrageous to send cruisers marines etc to help either side down there. Tell me if you think we can be duped into a war with Mexico via Nicaragua? If the situation becomes more tense, you may have an extra session won't you?

Elsa wants me to go to Chicago with her to meet Jan. I'd like to go too, because there will be a dinner given by the Women's International League Women for Jane Adams Jan 20, which will be just the time Jan is expecting to be in Chicago. I will not go however unless we have a hotel which I can use. Please write me whether or not we still have a contract. I do not want to spend money because I'm always at the ragged edge of bankruptcy. I paid Coie the $35 for the typewriter. You see sums of that size & the $92 gas bill take an awful bite out of my pay envelope.

I want to get 4 tickets for the Opera when Jan is here. So you see I've got to be saving.

I shall not get any fur coat this winter. I just wrote you about the coat at Gimbels because they are sort of "laying for me" and I had to make a gesture of interest because I wanted them to reline Elsa's coat.

Doris & Co stayed in town last night. It has been blizzarding for 24 hours & they feared the roads are impassable. Miss Thomas asked Doris to write an editorial on the inocuousness of Pacifist groups on the Nicaraguan situation.[2] Doris was quite proud of it—the request I mean. Please, my Lover—take care of yourself before its too late.

Devotedly M.

1. Meta misunderstood Victor's vote because she mistakenly believed that Coolidge supported the building of the cruisers. See Victor to Meta, January 8, 1927, above.

2. Doris probably wrote an unsigned editorial entitled "Act Now!" that appeared in the *Milwaukee Leader* on January 11, 1927. It urged peace groups to protest U.S. involvement in Mexico and Central America and warned that if "the condition which confronts us now does not stir them into an effective and nation-wide protest, then their propaganda is less important than their prayers, their pledges more futile for peace than their parades during the last cataclysm."

Victor to Meta

Washington, D.C.
January 13, 1927

My sweet Schatzl:

Of course—nobody in our family is as good as our Mamma, that's admitted without discussion. Papa surely isn't, nor are the kids. I will say in my defense, however, that during the 10 days that I am away from home, you have received 3 or 4 letters by wire and 2 by mail, which kept you fairly well posted as to my whereabouts and my doings.

And now to begin with, please, find my check for $100.00. Use it sparingly and carefully but I don't want you to be hard-up when a future son-in-law of our's comes to see us. Also ask the due-bill for the *Hotel Atlantic* from *Elmer Krahn*.[1] He has it. I have the Sherman Hotel but that is *not valid* during September, October, January and February. The Hotel Atlantic is a pretty fair place, however.

I expect to be home during the last week of January for the annual meeting of the Leader—and thus I will have a chance to get acquainted with Mr. Edelmann, I hope.

Please, tell Doris to get me the tax bills for our property in Merill and also the tax bill for the farms and lots in Ozaukee Co. She has the *old receipts,* which I gave her when I was home. All she has to do to send them to the resp. town treasurer and get the bills for 1926.

I paid the taxes for our house and for the lots on Humboldt ave. The receipts will be sent to you, Schatzl. Please, put them *aside* and *give them to me* when *I get home.*

Do the same with the receipt from the Northwestern Mutual Life Insurance Co., which I have also directed to be sent to the house.

What you say about Frank's "brave stand" in defense of Prof. McCrory[2] and against Gov. Blaine—is not entirely to the point. Blaine is not the Governor any longer—Zimmermann is. And Zimmermann was elected by the "Stalwarts" of Wisconsin, whose tax-views Prof. McCrory was defending. Thus President Frank selected the right moment for the defense of "academic freedom". He defends it at a time when those who attacked "academic freedom" and every other freedom—needed a defense in *their own* behalf.

On the other hand, Blaine's behavior shows how much the so-called "Progressives" believe in freedom—or free speech—when the opinions expressed are not to their liking and whenever [they] believe that they (the Progressives) have the power to *surpress* such opinions.

The Capital Times does not come to our office in Washington. I am going to tell Evjue to send it.

I have always had in mind that Doris *should have* a column. And if she would promise to cut out some of her company, I would let her have it. A column requires a lot of reading and a *continuously fresh mind,* one that is *rested.* The editorial she wrote was pretty good.[3]

I shall not know until tomorrow what the doctors say—and I will obey, of course, their medical advice.

Get a fur coat, if you can get it at a good reduction. And have the bureau in Elsa's room fixed up, especially the mirror.

This is about all, that is on my mind at this moment—except that you are the best Mamma that ever lived. With love your

V.L.B.

1. Elmer A. Krahn (1890–1967) began working in the business office of the *Milwaukee Leader* in 1916 and became its business manager in 1930. He served as editor of the *Milwaukee Post,* successor to the *Leader,* from 1939 to 1942.
2. Berger meant MacGregor. See Meta to Victor, January 7, 1927, above.
3. See Meta to Victor, January 10, 1927, above.

Meta to Victor

Milwaukee, Wisconsin
February 17, 1927

Darling Papa,—

Three days have gone by without my getting a moment's time to write letters. I've been out to Madison, my first visit as a regent on the normal board.[1] It was a very strenuous meeting lasting from 9 A.M. until midnight with only short periods for food. The budget for the nine schools was gone over so carefully that it was almost niggardly and the big state of Wisconsin has no reason to be proud of its generosity or lack of it as far as these schools are concerned. I finally told the board that I personally didn't believe that by figuring so closely that we positively allowed the schools to deteriorate was poor public policy and that instead of trying to shield the poor legislators by not being too hard on them in our requests for money that I for one would go before them and put the responsibility squarely upon their shoulder. If we maintain a fire-trap then the refusal for the money to repair such conditions must be theirs. I told them that I was appointed to administer to the needs of the schools and that the members of the legislature are going to know what our problems were and that they were going to face the responsibility of conditions in the schools over which they had some jurisdiction. Well,—I guess I threw a bomb alright enough. The whole board was up in arms at once and didn't know just what to do with such an unruly member. We reached an agreement whereby the joint finance committee of the legislature accepted the invitation to visit the schools themselves and see first hand the conditions and then we could present our needs for money. So we still have one part of the budget to work for. But my reception by every member of the board and by many other folks out at Madison exceeded even my wildest imagination for its warmth and cordiality. I seemed to be introduced and pointed out in the hotel lobby and in the capitol and everywhere.

Tommy Duncan was especially nice to me. He invited me to dinner with him at the hotel Lorraine and during the dinner in the main dining room he always brought all the Senators and Assembly men over to our table and introduced them to me. This made a wonderful impression on the members of the Board of Normal Regents as well as on all the nine Normal school presidents. My standing went up and up. Now I'll have to live up to their opinion of me.

Tonight Doris & Co are attending a dinner at the Athletic club given by the Alumni of the University where Glenn Frank is speaking on the policy of the University. They didn't want to go and spend the money but I urged them to go. If ever they want to take a part in the life of this community they must take that part by being one of the crowd. I wanted them to be seen. They are also changing their legal residence to 980 First st. I want them to be able to do things here in the city. They can wait a long time before those farmers out there at Mequon will be jarred into activity or before they would recognize the children.

Elsa writes that she and Jan are buying furniture.[2] So far they have bought twin beds, chest of drawers, table, two chairs, two rugs, dishes, and a day-bed instead of a couch. They are paying $55, a month for a two room apartment like the one we had in the Chastleton except that their rooms are a bit larger. Also they are two blocks from Harvard square and in the latin students quarters. I guess that that is about as reasonable a rent as they could expect in Cambridge.

I wrote to Elsa giving her George Roewer's name and asked her to call on him and see if he could help her in anyway either to get her acquainted with doctors or labor organizations or schools to see if she couldn't find some kind of social medical service.

If you go to New York after adjournment you probably will not be at home until the second week in March. That seems a long way off. Is there any danger of a special session? Or is Coolidge anxiously waiting for Congress to adjourn before he will venture to move in the Mexican situation?

I read your speech on the McNary Haugen bill. That is I read the extract in the Leader.[3] It was pretty good except I didn't like the "charity" touch you gave for the reason you supported the measure.

I just came home from addressing a Mothers and Daughters banquet at a public school and since I am very tired I guess I'll stop although I'd like to talk a long long time with you. I think Doris should do some political reporting and she should be sent on that kind of a run if ever she is to become familiar and conversant with local politics. Also she should do court reporting and if Leo[4] or Miss Thomas do not send her on that work you will have to do it when you come home. I really mean this.

Too tired to continue? Goodnight my Dear Dear.

Always your devoted
Meta.

1. In February, 1927, Governor Fred R. Zimmerman appointed Meta Berger to a five-year term on the Wisconsin Board of Regents of Normal Schools. She resigned from the board in February, 1928, to accept an appointment to the University of Wisconsin Board of Regents.

2. Following their marriage, Jan and Elsa Berger Edelman moved to Cambridge, Massachusetts, where Elsa practiced medicine.

3. In a speech on February 14, 1927, Berger said that he would support the McNary-Haugen farm bill because it would help atone for American interference in World War I by making low-cost food available to Europeans. He called it a measure of "charity to the European workers, and justice to the American farmers." See "Benefits of Farm Aid Bill Told by Berger," *Milwaukee Leader,* February 16, 1927.

4. Leo Wolfsohn (1889?–1956) joined the *Milwaukee Leader* in 1914 as a copyreader and rose to the rank of managing editor in 1936. He left the *Leader* in 1938 and moved to Washington, D.C., to take a job with the federal government.

Victor to Meta

Washington, D.C.
May 24, [1927]

My dear Schatzl:

This morning I saw Kellogg,[1] who was very friendly. He at once sent for the chief of the visa department and told him in my presence to do everything possible under the law to get Jan in. And do it right a way.

Now this is—as the case stands now. Jan's application was filed with the department of Labor on March 22nd. It was approved on the same day, because I happened to be there when it was done.

The State department received the application on April 26th and sent the same with its endorsement to the Consul at Montreal on April 27th, to be put on the preference quota for the Netherlands.

The preferential quota of the Netherlands is rather favorable at the present time,—there are still about 67 places (& persons) left. The chances that Jan will soon come in are *very good*.

All he has to do is—to *write* to the *Consul General* in Montreal, Can. and ask for further *instructions*.

I shall go to see the children and tell them all about it—besides wiring them tonight.

It is almost unnecessary for me to see Davies. He has done all he could and the case is really out of his hands. I shall simply go there to keep my appointment and as a matter of policy.

Got your telegram, Schatzl—and I am very sorry that you did not get the right kind of a maid. Keep her until you get a better one.

Above all—take care of your health don't worry and don't work too hard.

> With love to all, ever your
> V.L.B.

1. Frank B. Kellogg (1856–1937) served as U.S. secretary of state, 1925–1929. He had previously served as a Republican U.S. senator from Minnesota, 1917–1923, and as U.S. ambassador to Great Britain, 1923–1925.

Victor to Meta

> Washington, D.C.
> December 6, 1927

My dear Schatzl:

I do hope that you will take good care of yourself. You don't realize how much we all depend on you—and especially how much I depend on you. Take your t[h]yroid pills regularly and try to get used to the *resting period* which the Washington physicians have prescribed for you.

There is not much news here. I broke into the Congressional Record on the first day—when the case of James M. Beck[1] of Pennsylvania came up. He was a 1,000 per center during the war and is now the personal attorney of William Vare[2] of Pennsylvania who bought his seat to the U.S. Senate—but is almost certain of being rejected, since *not one* of the Senators who voted for Newberry[3] some years [ago] was returned. Vare is the boss of Philadelphia. He ordered the newly elected congressman[4]—one of his tools to resign—and had Beck nominated and elected and thus has his personal attorney in Congress.

The Democrats however claim that Beck *never* was a resident of Philadelphia or of Pennsylvania which he *must be,* in order to be elegible under the U.S. constitution.

Beck simply rented an appartment in P[h]iladelphia 3 months before election—visited there once or twice and then claimed that he was a voter.

Garett, the Democratic leader, moved to *bar* Beck from taking his oath and to send his case to the election committee. The chairman of the committee on rules (Snell,[5] Republican) had the audacity to claim that there *never* had been a *precedent* for such a procedure.

Well, I got up and gave them *two* precedents, and told them that both precedents had happened to me. I most assuredly had both sides of the house with me—but the Republican majority went ahead with its programm and voted to let Beck take the oath. His case was then referred to the committee on elections—(Snell turned to me privately that my contention was right—but he added that the House *had not* treated me fairly.)

Well, it was once more a sort of a good-natured vindication. I am disgusted with the crowd, however.

With love to all, and especially my Schatzl and Debby[6]

V.L.B.

1. James Montgomery Beck (1861–1936) served as a Republican representative from Pennsylvania, 1927–1934. Although Beck did not establish residency in Philadelphia until 1927, the effort to deny him his seat failed.
2. William Scott Vare (1867–1934), the head of the Republican Party machine in Philadelphia, served as a U.S. representative from Pennsylvania, 1912–1927. In the 1926 Republican primary for the U.S. Senate, Vare defeated incumbent Senator George Wharton Pepper and Gifford Pinchot and won the general election in the fall. Because of Vare's excessive campaign spending, the Senate appointed an investigative committee after the primary, refused to seat him when he presented his credentials in December, 1927, and declared his seat vacant in 1929.
3. Truman H. Newberry (1864–1945) defeated Henry Ford in the 1918 Republican primary for the U.S. Senate in Michigan in a campaign marked by heavy spending. Newberry then beat Ford, who ran as a Democrat, in the general election. Newberry was convicted of corrupt election practices in 1920, but the U.S. Supreme Court overturned his conviction the following year. In 1922 the Senate voted forty-six to forty-one that Newberry was entitled to his seat but expressed disapproval about the amount of campaign spending. Facing increasingly heavy criticism, Newberry resigned.
4. James Miller Hazlett (1864–1941), the Philadelphia recorder of deeds, 1915–1936, was elected to Congress as a Republican in 1926 but resigned on October 20, 1927, before the Seventieth Congress convened.
5. Bertrand Hollis Snell (1870–1958), a Republican representative from New York, 1915–1939, and House minority leader, 1931–1939.
6. Doris Berger Welles gave birth to the Bergers' first grandchild, Deborah, on November 2, 1927.

Meta to Victor

[Milwaukee, Wisconsin]
December 8, 1927

Darling Papa:—

I haven't been out of the house but once (& that was Monday Morning) since last Friday. I'm just staying here resting & getting my balance so to speak. Today I'm feeling fairly well altho' the night wasn't so good. I think I'll see Hipke this afternoon. Mrs Whitnall[1] says that her husband had symptoms like mine & that his doctors pronounced it nerve-exhaustion. Anyway; you know I've always complained of dizziness at night & head aches at night. I am taking the thyroid & the strychnine regularly as I've had sort of a lesson. I *do not* get up nights with the baby.

She is very very lovely. Yesterday for instance she slept all day long except for feeding periods and she only was restless a little bit during the night-time (before midnight) & then slept the rest of the night except for a feeding period. And today—with sub-zero weather out of doors, she is sleeping in the serving room with the door wide open. She feels warm & seems comfortable. We have a hot water bottle at her feet & a little fur robe covering her.

The whole town is interested & shocked at the death of Wm. Polacheck.[2] This was the second time he was found in the garage, but what is still worse is that the doctors claim he didn't die of monoxide gas but of cyanide which he took first. All of his friends maintain that he must have taken it by mistake, but they will have a hard time to prove that to the satisfaction of the insurance companies. They think he has forfeited his $20,000 insurance. If he did take poison & then went to the garage & started his car to cover up his deed, he was a cad or insane. The two funerals are today but I shall not go. I've sent flowers.

Bob Filtzer wants to send a letter to Bobby Lafollette about restitution for you by Congress. We asked him to with hold the letter for a few days until I could write to you. We believe it would be better to have Robert Filtzer write to a conservative but fair leader of the Republican Party than to a Progressive who only would aggravate the old party leaders & get you nothing. So I said I'd write you & have you suggest the name of some one whom you think would be a good person & then Bob could send a letter to him & send young La follette or others a copy of such letter. Now please don't turn a cold shoulder on this. It is surely worth an effort in *this Congress* & it may be your last chance. And besides, at present you have the good will of many. You may be able to get the Leaders on your side early in this session. Now please think this over. It is taking no chance whatever for you & may *bring you* about $12,000 + to which you are entitled. This, to me, seems the psychological time. So let's start it now.[3]

Your case *isn't like Beck's at all* & there should be *no comparison with it, especially not by you.* And now you have Snell's opinion that you were not treated fairly. So if you have courage—you will lay the foundation of getting what the government owes you & we will help if possible. That's all for today. Our dearest dear love to you always.

Your, Meta

Answer this! And don't compare your case with Beck's Vare or any one else. You should stand out as a shining example of having gone down on principle only.

1. Marie Kottnauer Whitnall (1874–1957), the second wife of Socialist Charles Whitnall, was active in the Socialist Party and served on the Milwaukee school board, 1923–1929.
2. William Polacheck (1890–1927) was president of Milwaukee's Polly Manufacturing Company.
3. On February 28, 1929, Senator Guy D. Goff of West Virginia proposed that the federal government pay Berger $15,000 as compensation for the period when he was denied his seat in the House. Goff's motion, which was offered as an amendment to a bill before the Senate, was ruled out of order on a point of order raised by Senator Francis Warren of Wyoming. In 1934 Congress appropriated $9,586 for Berger's estate as full settlement of claims for back pay.

Victor to Meta

Washington, D.C.
December 14, 1927

My sweet Schatzl:

The House voted to adjourn on Dec. 22nd—and I have at once reserved my sleeping car ticket for that day. If possible however I shall try to run away a day earlier. It all depends on the debate on the tax question[1] and how soon afterwards the Alien Property Bill[2] can be voted on. Since the bill has passed the House before—there will be no trouble about passing it, I want to be here however to vote for it.

Went to see the President this morning about getting a pardon for Edward Grieb.[3] Had a lenghty interview and evidently made out a good case. I believe Grieb will be a free man before Christmas.

Had also occassion to see Jim Davis about legislative matters. Told him that Jan would probably look him up during his visit in this city. Jan will be welcome.

Also spoke to Davis about the muskrat farm. He seemed to be interested, wants to see a prospectus and said he might invest a few thousand dollars in the venture.

The salary case, which you want Bob Filzer to take up, we will thoroughly discuss, when I get home next week.

I am very glad to hear that your health is improving. Sleep as much as possible—take walks in the fresh air as much as you can—and don't neglect to take the pills in a single instance.

A hundred dollars is a lot of money for me just now—but I believe little Debby is surely worth it.

With love to all and especially to my Mama

Papa

1. The House passed a tax reduction bill on December 15, 1927, by a vote of 366 to 24, with Berger voting against the bill. The Senate passed the bill, and President Coolidge signed it into law in May, 1928.

2. The Alien Property Bill settled World War I claims of the United States and Germany as well as those of their nationals. The House approved the bill on December 20, 1927, without a roll call, and President Coolidge signed an amended version of the bill in March, 1928.

3. Edward Grieb (1866–1939), a real estate salesman and member of the Milwaukee Public Land Commission, 1919–1922 and 1930–1939, was convicted of stock fraud in 1924 and sentenced to five years in prison. President Coolidge pardoned Grieb in 1928.

Meta to Victor

[Milwaukee, Wisconsin]
[ca. January 18, 1928]

Dearest!

Here's the big piece of news! Mrs. Gov. Zimmerman[1] called me up this morning from the Executive Mansion to ask me if I would like to be a "U" Regent in the place of Leola Hirschman.[2] I said quite off-hand "I'd love it." Whereupon she replied, "That's fine. I know the Governor will be pleased about that." So I suppose he will appoint me some time before Feb. or whenever Miss Hirschman's term expires.

Now what do you think I'd better do? I sometimes feel like deserting a sinking ship when I stop to think of the state of affairs the Normal Schools are in. I believe I ought to stay with them until after the legislative disposal of that matter before I take on any new jobs.[3]

However, I also feel that for myself, for you & for the party, I ought to enjoy the recognition of being the "U" regent.

What will be the reaction of folks in Milwaukee? That's the big question to ask.

I'm sending this by air mail together with letters from Elsa & Jan. I couldn't trust the gossip over the wires as perhaps the Gov. may change his mind, altho' I don't think he would have commissioned his wife to call up long distance unless he meant it.

You can wire me but wire discreetly.

Every body hear sends heaps of love to you especially Debby.

Always your

Meta

P.S. Oscar[4] writes—3 more gas wells within 1½ miles of our property.

P.P.S. Jan sold 7 fox furs for $1,075 & these furs were not best. Jan earns $125 commission. Elsa gets 100 which she loaned Dudd in Paris.

1. Amanda Freedy Zimmerman (1882–1960) was the wife of Wisconsin Governor Fred R. Zimmerman.

2. Leola Hirschman (Shure) (1883–1941), secretary to Milwaukee labor lawyer William B. Rubin, served on the University of Wisconsin Board of Regents, 1922–1928. Governor Zimmerman appointed Meta Berger as Hirschman's replacement on the board, and she served from February, 1928, to February, 1934.

3. On January 11, 1928, Governor Zimmerman called a special session of the Wisconsin legislature to consider appropriations for the state's normal schools.

4. Oscar Ameringer.

Meta to Victor

Madison, Wisconsin

January 20, 1928

Darling:

I've had sort of an exciting time. I've had to decline 3 invitations from Mrs. Zimmerman to dinner & luncheons because of other & previous dates.

However today I went in to see him[1] personally at his request. He said he had a telegram from you which he read.

He said he really wanted to appoint me today, but seeing that Leola Hirschman is to be married next week, he tho't he wouldn't spoil her happiness at this time & would like to wait for another week. I said "That's all right Mr. Zimmerman & suits me also, seeing that a special session is on for next week and since I don't like to have folks think I'm deserting my ship, I'd just as soon wait until the matter of Normal schools is settled if he had no objections." He said "That's all right with me Mrs. Berger." Then he asked me whether I wanted the change & I replied "I always wanted that 'U.' job & it was one of my pet ambitions." He read me the provisions of the law which provide that I would have to represent some manual trade; but he said, he had inquired from some lawyers who said they tho't that house work would be considered a manual trade. Mr. Z. said he wasn't looking for any one challenging my qualifications on that score & that he had a *right* to *appoint* the *wife* of a *Socialist* if he wanted to. With that—we left it.

So its to happen in the future. I hope nothing will interfere.

I told him Miss Hirschman wasn't expecting him to re appoint her which information came to me. That's all.

I must hurry to catch the train.

Love
Meta

1. Governor Fred R. Zimmerman.

Victor to Meta

Washington, D.C.
January 26, 1928

My dear Schatzl:

I always claimed that you are better than I am—especially also in writing letters. And there isn't much news here, except such news as you get in the papers.

Just at present your appointment to the Board of Regents of the University of Wisconsin interests *me most*. For a number of reasons. And also that Evjue inquired about the Leader. Next week Tuesday, however, I shall go to New York again, see certain men and incidentally promote our foreign advertising.

Fred Zimmerman sent me a letter in answer to mine—but asking me, not to tell anybody and not to have anything in the Leader, until he makes the appointment. I think that's sensible and wired you today (Thursday) for that reason.

I am sounding various men about my back salary. While everyone that I have spoken to—is friendly, and everyone seems to agree with me that I am morally and fairly entitled to it, no one seems to know of a law or a precedent for my case. And no one has volunteered to put in a bill. It must be either a very prominent Republican or a very prominent Democrat, if the bill is to pass Congress in this session. No Progressive in either House or Senate will dare to vote against it, of course. I may try to get either Begg[1] of Ohio who is now a candidate for governor— or Coneally[2] of Texas who wants to become a U.S. Senator, to help me.

Have written Voigt offering my assistance. He thanked me and told me that he would call on me later in the campaign. The Leader is to boom him, without over-doing it—put special stress on his courageous vote in my case and on his judicial temperament.[3]

If Schallitz[4] is to be the only candidate against Hoan, the latter will be elected by a majority of 30,000. It is necessary, however, to get out a *big vote* at the *Primary* and, therefore, these Socialist politicians ought to work their heads off, to increase the circulation of the Milwaukee Leader. Please, tell Hoan that I shall send him the revised platform by the end of this week.

Tell Dudd—when I say in a letter that Grandma and Debby represent the "sweet elements" in my family, then that is meant to be a figure of speech, of course.[5] She holds a diploma from some school of rhetorics, I believe, and ought to appreciate and understand "them beautiful sentiments". There is no gainsaying the fact that Grandma is the oldest, and Debby is the youngest female member of the Victor-Berger tribe (—may it grow, increase and multiply)—and that they both hold the center of the stage, whether they are in the spotlight or not. This is no reflection on Doris or even on Elsa. And the mere fact that I picked Doris as my chief successor—and as the "heir of my policies" and ambitions (and I do not at all mean the Socialist party)— ought be sufficient testimony as to what I think of her. It is very unfortunate (and was always a source of a great deal of grieve to me) that she never got as close to me as she should. If she had—she would have achieved wonderful success, even by this time; since she has many advantages that I never had. But then, she is still very young and has a life full of opportunities before her. And she surely has my greatest good will and my blessing!

So—am I getting "pious" now?

I have written a letter to Elsa this week. Jan and Elsa act, as if [I] did not exist for them.

And so does Coie act, as if I didn't exist. Have written and wired begging him to inquire whether the taxes on the farm, on which he is supposed to live—have been paid for 1927. I have neither my check stubs here, nor my receipts, and I do not remember whether I paid these particular taxes or not. They may sell the taxes by February first— and at any rate they will make me pay 12% interest, if the bill is not paid by that time. Coie can inquire at the town treasurer's by telephon. Do I not deserve *that much* consideration?

I lead a very dreary life here—no fun at all. My routine is: hotel, house office, committee room (I'm on many busy committees this session), House of Representatives, house office, hotel—a dismal circle. I have not attended more than *one* show in this town, since November; and not a single reception of the President. And I have no social intercourse with anybody. But I don't want to complain—I'm simply stating a fact.

Otherwise I am all right. I hope you are taking the prescribed rest every day. With love to all, and especially to Grandma, Duddie and Debby;

Always the same old
Papa.

1. James Thomas Begg (1877–1963), a Republican representative from Ohio, 1919–1929.

2. Tom Connally (1877–1963), a Democratic representative from Texas, 1917–1929, and U.S. senator, 1929–1953.

3. Former Congressman Edward Voigt, a Republican, won election as a Wisconsin circuit court judge in April, 1928. Voigt was the only member of Congress to vote for Berger's seating in 1919.

4. Charles Schallitz (1882–1937), a Republican, served as Milwaukee County sheriff, 1927–1929. In the primary election for Milwaukee mayor held on March 13, 1928, Socialist incumbent Daniel Hoan received 42,713 votes to 28,969 for Schallitz and 7,246 for Edward Schubert. In the general election on April 3, 1928, Hoan defeated Schallitz, 64,874 to 46,657.

5. In a letter dated January 22, 1928, Victor wrote to Meta that "You and Debby represent now all that is sweet in the family." In her reply of January 24, 1928, Meta stated that Doris was hurt by the remark: "She is quite quite sensitive & looks so anxiously & eagerly for an endearing word or encouragement from you especially. She would value that far more than any thing I say, because you say them so seldomly or not at all while I'm doing it all the time." Berger Papers, SHSW.

Victor to Meta

Washington, D.C.
February 2, 1928

My sweet Schatzl:

There isn't much news to tell—except that I get very tired at times and suffer from a slight head-ache, which story is no news to you.

The extremely poor showing of our advertising department also worries me. I agree with you in wishing that Evjue take over the paper. If it were possible, I would pack up my things and go to Milwaukee, but that is not possible, nor would my mere staying there for a while, change anything.

I may go to New York tomorrow (Friday) while the bill to appropriate for the War department is before the House. I am going to vote against the bill anyway, but I don't want to miss the roll call. The trouble is only that the week-end is a very poor time for business, unless I simply go to play "good fellow" with certain people.

Hoan's so-called platform draft was simply impossible. It did not even contain the old well-worn and axiomatic *Socialist* promise of Public Ownership of Public Utilities, as soon as legislation and city finances would permit. Well, I rehashed the "document" and put the old plank in. All that Hoan "promised" was that the office holders would be "polite" when dealing with citizens. I also corrected his wretched English. He has my letter by this time.

But never mind—Hoan will be re-elected. He is a good hand-shaker, his idiotic wife[1] goes to "an early mass" every morning, he appoints all kinds of Babbits to all kinds of commissions, and both he and his wife are to be found at all public gatherings. Moreover, he proves his radicalism by eating with his knife,—and by stamping with his foot, whenever he wants emphasis,—what more can the proletariat expect?

Politics in our country has become a stupid farce, and often a criminal swindle.

Let's talk of something more pleasant. Doris probably works too much or worries too much—that's the reason her milk supply runs low. I hope she keeps the right diet. Debby should *double* her birthweight after 3 months, especially since she was such a small baby when she arrived.

From the Bureau of Standards I have secured a report on "Ultra Violet Transmission of Various Glasses", which Lewis will send you under separate cover, please, watch out for it—and let the children read it.

Have also written to the Bureau for a *list* of the manufacturers of the various glasses mentioned in the report. Shall send it to you, of course.

Coie ought to be very careful about the grip. The malaria is not quite out of his system and he has not very much power of resistance. Open air and sunshine are *his* best medicine also.

Wisconsin is surely going backward—but I'm glad that *you* at least will be in a position of great usefulness for the next five years. Hope the appointment will come before the end of the week.

By the way, Joe Beck, the La Follette candidate, asked me for a list of names of Progressives (not Socialists) in the 5th district, to whom he wants to send some literature.[2] Pick out a number of names of men and women who *under no circumstances would* ever *vote our state ticket*—when you find time. You need not be in any great hurry about it—because I am not so sure whether this would be very fair to Fred Zimmerman, who after all tries to be very fair to us—fairer than the La Follette bunch ever was.

Well, that's about all I know, except that you are my best and sweetest Schatzl.

Papa.

1. Agnes Bernice Magner Hoan (1883–1941) married Daniel Hoan in October, 1909. A devout Catholic, she was active in her husband's political campaigns and in many women's organizations, including the Women's International League for Peace and Freedom.
2. Congressman Joseph Beck, who had the endorsement of the La Follettes, lost the Republican gubernatorial primary to businessman Walter J. Kohler. Fred R. Zimmerman, the incumbent governor, finished third.

Meta to Victor

Madison, Wisconsin
February 7, 1928

My Darling:—

Did the flapjacks taste good? And was it worth while and interesting? Sometimes celebrities are criticized severely for partaking of syrup

& cakes, especially Vermont syrup.[1] That was the reason for sending you the telegram of warning.

I've made a mistake. A big mistake in taking the "U" regents job. I'm being criticized by a good many folks, but especially Normal school people. I came to Madison today to attend the meeting of the Normal Board tomorrow at Dempsey['s][2] request to the Governor. For some reason or other my conscience bothers because I accepted the other job. The Milwaukee State Normal school faculty refuses to be pacified or consoled. They say they had placed their faith in me so implicitly & their confidence was so great that they feel I've thrown them over especially since the Normal Schools are in such dire need of friends. The inclosed note from Mr. Gates[3] is typical & speaks for itself. I hate to go down stairs for fear I shall meet the other regents today.

And Milwaukee people are not expressive of joy. I've had congratulatory letters only from two—Judge Aarons & Dr. Dearholt.[4] One or two teachers have telephoned me, but that is all. Politically speaking I think I've make a mistake.

The University people haven't written either. Mrs Frank[5] & the Otto's[6]—and that's all there. Judge Backus[7] told me not to pay any attention to the attitude of the Normal school teachers as they will get over it soon.

I don't think Zimmerman will make a good appointment as my successor as he seems determined to appoint a woman. And in all of Milwaukee, there isn't another woman who is qualified except possibly Gertrude Sherman[8] & she is impossible. Gov. Z. did mention Hattie Tegtmeyer over the long distance telephone to me. If he appoints her—he is trying to repay Archie Tegtmeyer[9] for supporting the Governor. Hattie is sweet, good, nice & conscientious but doesn't know much about school administration. Pres. Baker[10] is in despair.

Well, I'll write you again tomorrow or next day & tell you of my last meeting. You see, I made good & the talk was that I was to be the next president of the Normal Board. Also Tom Duncan said I made a fine speech to the joint-finance committee and a wonderful impression on all the legislators. That coming from Tom, was going some.

Debby is darling. She weighs 12 lb. 6 ounces now. But she is a frightfully restless child whenever she is awake. She sleeps well at night however and that helps a whole lot. Duddie is cute. She always watches Debby to see if she smiles more at me than at Doris and strange to say—I get most of the smiles. Duddie is quite envious.

I shall be glad when you come home the end of this month. You are needed everywhere. And as time goes on, I feel more & more certain that we ought to get rid of our big house and its terrific cost. Perhaps the spring will find a solution. Also the work & responsibility is heavy. I really don't do any house work, with those two girls there;—and the house looks it. But at night time I'm exhausted.

Last night at the Mil. School Board meeting I succeeded in stopping the Mil. Journal from using the public school organization to boost that national spelling & oratory contest. The board by refusing to move the suspension of the rules, placed the communication on file. It would have been a dandy 100% circulation stunt. All parochial schools children and all public schools children subscribing for the paper because they were in the national contest. One of the Journal's representatives came to see me first. I told him the stand I'd take & tho't he ought not ask for favors & then he wouldn't be turned down. But he asked anyway & was turned down.

Goodnight Papa Darling—take care of yourself for my sake. I feel as tho' I needed you tonight. I hate to go to the Board meeting tomorrow. Write oftener—please please. Your devoted

Meta.

1. A reference to Victor's breakfast with President Calvin Coolidge, a Vermont native, scheduled for the morning of February 8, 1928. See Victor to Meta, February 8, 1928, below.

2. Edward J. Dempsey (1878–1956), an attorney, served on the Wisconsin State Board of Education, 1917–1923, and as president of the Wisconsin Board of Regents of Normal Schools, 1924–1949.

3. Clough Gates (1877–1965), a newspaperman from Superior, Wisconsin, served on the Wisconsin Board of Regents of Normal Schools, 1912–1931, and the University of Wisconsin Board of Regents, 1936–1939.

4. Hoyt Dearholt (1879–1939), a Milwaukee physician.

5. Mary Smith Frank (1884–1975), the wife of University of Wisconsin President Glenn Frank.

6. Max Otto (1876–1968), a University of Wisconsin professor of philosophy, and his wife, Rhoda Owen Otto.

7. August C. Backus (1877–1952) served as a Milwaukee municipal judge, 1910–1924, publisher of the *Milwaukee Sentinel*, 1924–1930, and a regent of the University of Wisconsin, 1929–1939.

8. Gertrude Sherman (1877–1978) served on the Milwaukee school board, 1919–1937.

9. Archie Tegtmeyer (1869–1946) and Hattie Tegtmeyer (1872–1964) were Milwaukee jewelers. Archie served on the Milwaukee Public Library Board from about 1915 until 1944.

10. Frank E. Baker (1877–1961) served as president of Milwaukee State Teachers College (previously Milwaukee State Normal School), 1923–1944.

Victor to Meta

Washington, D.C.
February 8, 1928

My sweet Schatzl:

Just a few lines in answer to your welcome letter and your telegram.

The breakfast with the President was a very tame affair—and had absolutely *no political* significance. Eight Republicans, six Democrats and the lone Socialist had the honor of "breaking bread" with Calvin Coolidge. The President tried to be particularly friendly to me—probably because I was the "odd one"—but after all, the real "comradeship" is surely not in him.

Enclosed, please, find a check for $50.00, Sweetheart, since you complain that you are hard-up. I cannot send you more at the present moment. If you must have more, get it from Emma.[1] I have also given Jan and Elsa $25.00 as a gift for their wedding anniversary.

You folks must be careful with little Debby. Don't show her off. Don't perambulate her more than you have to. Don't do anything that might excite or over-develop that young baby-brain.

On the other hand, you cannot possibly give her too much fresh air—so long as you keep her reasonably warm. And you cannot possibly give her too much sun-shine—so long as you reasonably protect her eyes against the direct rays. And do not overdress her or smother her with blankets. The baby's covering ought to be as *light* and as warm and as soft—as possible. If you follow my advise you will raise a wonderful child—if nothing unforseen happens which will not happen, I hope.

I also enclose the letter from the Bureau of Standards giving the addresses of manufacturers of some ultraviolet glasses. Doris or Colin ought to write at once for price lists and information. I will stand *half* of the *cost* because Debby is my first grand child—and because I really believe that she *is* a *grand* child.

Getting my "back pay" will not be so easy. The Republican party does not depend on my vote, as that party depended on La Follette's vote in the Senate because the margin was so close some years ago. On the other hand, I am a Socialist—and was excluded for my unpatriotic stand in the World War—which the Democrats claim was *their* war. They are asses, of course; it was the war of Big Financiers and Big Profiteers who used the Southern asses because they happened to be in power; but one cannot tell them this unpalatable truth. Nevertheless I believe I will get my "back pay."

Don't worry! And don't work too hard! Remember that after all, you also belong to me, not only to the Kids and Debby.

With love to all and especially to my Schatzl and to Doris

Papa.

1. Emma Glaeser.

Meta to Victor

[Milwaukee, Wisconsin]
February 12, 1928

Darling Papa:—

I don't think I've written you since I've been in Madison. I feel much better about the whole transfer of jobs since it's all over with.

The members of the Normal Board & the nine presidents of the schools were all there and they were perfectly lovely to me. They made farewell speeches which were most complimentary & laudatory. In the evening I went to spend the time with Mrs. Zimmerman who had called on me & left her card at the hotel. The Governor came in later & we sat & chatted over non essentials for a time & then they took me back to the hotel. On the way he asked me what I tho't of Fred Dorner,[1] an engineer and a Shriner. I replied that I tho't he would make a pretty good regent because he understood building needs. The Governor said he tho't that perhaps an engineer's point of view might be better than another lawyer's or doctor's or business man's point of view. That would indicate that he has given up the idea of appointing a woman. But no one knows. If some one else see's the Governor later, he will again change his mind.

I came back Friday & yesterday the Peace society ran a big card party. There were more than 400 women present. We made about $150. It was held at the new Schroeder Hotel. This hotel is a regular New York style of hotel.

Socialists & others here want to know what you have done about the Nicaraguan War. Have you done anything so far? Also the communists are circulating leaflets criticizing you for not acting in the Nic. Situation.

Debby is cute & well but frightfully restless all the time that she is awake. I think you will find quite a change in her this time. Elsa wrote that you sent her $25 for a wedding gift. That was fine. I couldn't send her any this month so I'm twice glad you did it.

The inclosed card came from Max C. Otto of Madison. We sent them one of the new regent going up to 1155 Edgewood with her hands stretched out crying "Help! Help!"

Oh Dear! I am tired tonight & cannot write more. I wish I were twenty instead of 55. Isn't it a pity that we must grow old & thro' so many symptoms see the hand writing on the wall. It just seems to me I'm prematurely old. But like wine, age improves my love for you. Doris & I talked of my love for you today—I agreed heartily that if I had a chance I'd marry you all over again.

Your Meta.

1. Fred H. Dorner (1881–1942), an engineer, served on the Milwaukee Sewerage Commission, 1921–1923.

Victor to Meta

Washington, D.C.
February 17, 1928

My sweet Schatzl:

Whenever I don't send letters by mail—I send them by wire, but I always keep you informed.

Was in New York and had lunch with Carl Bickel,[1] President of the United Press, which is closely affiliated with the Scripps-Howard concern. Bickel told me *confidentially* that the Scripps-Howard people are rather badly tied-up at present—losing more than a million dollars last year on the Telegram in New York and over half a million on their paper in Denver, Col. They own 28 daily papers, however, and some of them are great money makers, especially those in Cleveland, Pittsburg and Cincinnati. And Milwaukee is a city of the same type. Nevertheless, Roy Howard[2] will entertain no new proposition at present or in the near future—since he has trouble in financing what he has. The man turned gray during the last few months. So much for that.

Carl Bickel gave me an entirely new lead also. Of this I shall tell you more, as soon as I know more.

I see that Evjue is printing enormous papers nowadays. Sorry I did not take the one third interest when I had a chance.[3]

By this time you probably know that Milwaukee will get a *Bureau* of *Foreign Commerce* by the first of July. I don't know whether I am entitled to all the credit in this—because I have a notion that "Bobby" LaFollette lent a helping hand. That's the reason why I did not crow too hard in the papers. If Bobby helped, however—he did not tell me about it, and the letter from the Department of Commerce *gives me* the *credit* for *helping*. At any rate: here is something worth while for exporting manufacturers of Milwaukee and Wisconsin. They cannot claim after this, that I am solely interested in the welfare of the proletariat and neglect the business interest of the city. Nor can they claim that I have no influence whatsoever that is of any value to them.

You have never informed me, Schatzl, whether you have received the check for $50.00, which I sent you about a week ago.

I am very sorry that Duddie ever went into this bar affair—very sorry, on account of her nerves—especially since she is not going to *practice* law anyway. But now we shall have to see the matter through, of course, although I will not cry, if she should fail again. The trouble with her is that on account of her nervousness she is a poor subject for an examination, even when she knows her subject "thoroly".

And now I must close this letter because I want it to go by *air-mail*—so that you have money to go to Chicago, if you care to go. Get the hotel contract from Elmer.[4]

With best wishes and lots of love

Your V.L.B.

1. Karl August Bickel (1882–1972) served as president of the United Press, 1923–1935.

2. Roy W. Howard (1883–1964), an editor and publisher, served as president of the United Press wire service, 1912–1921, and as chairman of the board (1921–1936) and president (1936–1953) of the Scripps-McRae (after 1925, Scripps-Howard) newspaper chain.

3. The Bergers owned 10 percent of William T. Evjue's *Capital Times,* a progressive Madison, Wisconsin, newspaper. See Victor to Meta, February 19, 1929, below.

4. Elmer A. Krahn.

Meta to Victor

Milwaukee, Wisconsin
February 17, 1928[1]

Darling Papa.

Your letters are as scarce as hen's teeth. The only news I get from you I have to get from the papers. Fortunately one paper in Milwaukee carries news about my husband. Otherwise I couldn't stay home & have you in Washington.

We are all anxious to hear what you have to say about Duddies oil-letter.[2] The kids are so anxious about it. From all reports coming from the west, the prospects loom up fine.

Tonight Doris & Colin went to the opening of the new Schroeder Hotel. They went on the press tickets. It will be a gala occasion for Milwaukee I understand. Covers at $10 a piece.

The hotel is very gorgeous. More like a jazzy New York hotel. Well, I'm afraid Milwaukee is over staffed as far as hotels are concerned but we certainly needed one like this one for a long long time. It has a beautiful parlor where one can meet people besides the lobby & any number of other attractions.

Have you been watching the Wisconsin papers on the news about refusing to let Dora Russell,[3] Mrs. Bertrand Russell speak in Madison. She was to have spoken before the "U Student forum." Upon the advice of Glenn Frank their contract was canceled. He is said to have told the students her talks are inadvisable & altho' he didn't insist he hoped they would withdraw the contract. Then she attempted thro' Ernie Meyer[4] to get the Labor Temple. Labor voted unanimously to refuse their hall, whereupon C. B. Ballard[5] gave her the assembly chamber. The Women's Clubs then got busy & finally he refused to give her the Assembly Chamber. Now the minister of the Unitarian Church gave her his church & so I guess she will talk in Madison after all unless the good folks of the congregation withdraw their consent. In view of all this publicity several young men whom you know got together and rented a hall at the Auditorium & invited her here to speak Monday night hoping thereby not only to serve free speech but also to make a little money if possible. Now I am anxious to see how many Milwaukeeans will go to hear the famous free-lover. Papa Darling—if you realized how tired I am nights when I write you, you would really appreciate my noble efforts with such poor results & you would respond by writing oftener to me. Yes! you would!

Helen Hoyer[6]—Clara Hipke's sister died yesterday. Funeral is tomorrow.

Good night, I must stop & take a bath & go to bed. Goodnight Lover!

Mama.

1. Meta dated this letter February 18, 1928, but it was actually written a day earlier.
2. Doris Berger Welles wrote to Victor about Senate Bill 767, introduced by Senator Francis Warren of Wyoming, which would have given Standard Oil control over certain western oil reserves and would have excluded a company in which Colin Welles had invested. She told her father that "we all think this might be quite an opportunity for you to expose a sensational bit of graft." Warren's bill died in committee. See Doris to Victor, February 14, 1928, Berger Papers, SHSW.
3. Dora Winifred Black Russell (b. 1894) was the wife of British philosopher Bertrand Russell from 1921 until 1935, when the couple divorced. Dora Russell gave an address entitled "Should Women Be Protected?" at a Madison, Wisconsin, Unitarian church on February 17, 1928, after being barred from speaking at the University of Wisconsin, the Madison Labor Temple, and the state capitol as a result of controversy over her views on free love and birth control. On February 20, she gave a talk in Milwaukee called "Can We Be Happy?"
4. Ernest L. Meyer (1892–1952) worked for the *Madison (Wisconsin) Capital Times* for most of the period from 1920 to 1934, rising to the post of managing editor. After leaving Madison, he served on the editorial staffs of the *New York Post* and the *New York Daily News*. In 1918 the University of Wisconsin expelled Meyer because of his opposition to World War I, and he later served four months in military prisons because of his conscientious objector status.
5. Clinton B. Ballard (1860–1946), a progressive Republican who joined the Socialist Party in 1934, served as state superintendent of public property, 1927–1929, and as a state assemblyman, 1909–1913, 1915–1917, and 1919–1921. Governor Fred R. Zimmerman ordered Ballard to rescind permission for Russell to use the state capitol building for her speech because her views were "subversive of everything which a Christian civilization holds to be sacred in the family relation."
6. Helen Belitz Hoyer (1855–1928) was Meta's first cousin.

Victor to Meta

Washington, D.C.
February 19, 1928

My sweet Schatzl:

There is nothing new to write, of course. Nothing of importance has happened since a day before yesterday when I wrote my last letter. The House was not even in session yesterday.

I have sent 35,000 speeches to Vogt—I hope they will be sent out promptly—since it is my intention to send out *a speech* every two weeks for some months to come. Tell Miss Thomas and Emma[1] to charge up to my account the working time of the girls necessary to send the literature.

Hoan has written me a letter telling me that he and Tom[2] have worked out a plan by which the party could pay one-half salary of a cartoonist as well as part of the salary of a man who would go out to gain subscriptions for the Leader and at the same time secure names of voters and get them registered in the wards. He suggests that at all campaign meetings the importance of the Leader should be emphasized, subscribers to the paper solicited. He also wants us to solicit campaign subscriptions in the Leader.

Now I am, of course, absolutely in *favor* of the *Leader* and the *party* working in *harmony*—only the party must also do its share. So many of the Socialist politicians seem to have the idea that the paper is there only for the purpose to give unlimited space to the booming and boosting of idiotic (and sometimes even crooked) ninnies who happen to have the Socialist label to cover their "activities". This continuous "blah" about Socialist politicians had a great deal to do with stopping the growth of the Leader.

The Leader must print the news of all the parties and all the candidates—only print the news of our party more fully.

As a matter of fact, we always had more politics in the Leader than the bulk of the readers could digest. And most of it was idiotic repetition.

And as for asking campaign-contributions in the paper—well, Hoan had $20,000 for his election last time, and he wants *more now,* and he will get it from the *city contractors* and *similar sources.* But our readers can subscribe only very little, thus this will be used mainly as a "smoke screen". Keep this quiet!

Not taking any sweat baths, I am bothered with rheumatism very much. I walk like a lame man often. And I also suffer from head aches—and this accounts for this stupid letter. Aber ich hab' Dich sehr lieb und das ist die Hauptsache.[3] And you have heard from me anyhow.

With love to all, especially Grandma and Doris.

Papa.

1. Emma Glaeser.
2. Thomas M. Duncan.
3. But I love you very much and that is the main thing.

Meta to Victor

Milwaukee, Wisconsin
[February 20, 1928]

Darling Papa:

Under separate cover I am sending you one day's clippings about Mrs. Russel's case in Wisconsin. These clippings are from the three Milwaukee papers—Sentinel, Wis. News & Journal.

The whole state is in a furor because she was denied the right to speak at Madison. Glenn Frank has made a mistake because by his refusal, he has merely added to her importance. I do not think she ought to preach her doctrine to the half baked co-eds at Madison. I think Pres. Frank is right about that. But by so deliberately refusing her a forum, the whole mess takes on too much importance. I'm sending you the clippings because I expect the matter to be brought up in the Board of Regents & I just don't know how I stand. Frank has a responsibility to the parents whose children go to the "U". To condone a philosophy of free-love, several trial marriages, or affairs etc. isn't exactly what a "U" President ought to stand for. And yet there is the question of "free speech" with you fighting for the teeth in the 1st Amendment.

So read the clippings & give me your reactions.

Debby is sick. She has a sore throat & a slight fever. We think she is a little better today. But she is very hard to take care of. We are all tired out!

Isn't it too bad about the death of Vincent Schoenecker.[1] He was only 60 years old.

The Mrs. Russel meeting was held tonight. About 856 people were inveigled into going. The young people who arranged it made $75 on the venture but this has to be split 3 ways. Well Goodnight. I'm too tired to be careful or even very loving even tho I love you more & more each year. Be good to yourself by taking care of yourself.

Your
Meta

1. Vincenz J. Schoenecker Jr. (1867–1928), a Milwaukee Democrat and president of a local shoe company, finished second in the 1910 mayoral race behind Socialist Emil Seidel.

Victor to Meta

Washington, D.C.
March 21, 1928

My sweet Schatzl:

Enclosed you will find two clippings of the *same date* containing Arthur Brisbanes "Today" column. One is from the N.Y. American, the other from the Milwaukee Sentinel of last Sunday.

Brisbane said some complimentary things about me—as you will see from the N.Y. American—the Milwaukee Sentinel very *carefully cut out every word that referred to me.* Otherwise the columns are identical.[1] And only a little more than a week ago "the Judge"—A.C. Backus—told me, how much he thought of me, and what he was going to do for me. He also implored me to get into touch with the correspondent of the Milw. Sentinel—one Timmons[2]—and have him get news at my office regularly. My secretary has called him several times, in order to give him news, of which we always have more than any other congressman but Mr. Timmons has not showed up, so far.

Just keep these clippings for me please—at the proper time I shall show them to Mr. Backus.

So much of that.

Well, sweet Schatzl—I want you to get ready to come to Washington. Unless something entirely unforseen happens, I will call for [you] at the beginning of April. And I want you to be *well dressed*—since I am very much in the public eye and receive many invitations. We shall accept one or two—but in the main keep to ourselves, as we did in the past.

Getting my back pay is slow work—yet I feel that I will get it, since there can be no doubt that I am entitled to it.

Went up with Charles Lindbergh[3] this afternoon. Sat in the cockpit with him. He gave me his card—wrote his name and todays date on it, and afterwards I had my picture taken with him and the whole crowd, including a lot of fat and old Congressional women, who pushed themselves between us, although the N.E.A had arranged (and intended) to have only "Lindy" and me on the picture. Es geht auch so.[4]

Hope the family and especially *you* keep well—and that you obey the prescription of the physician at least as to the tablets, I know that you do *not* take the prescribed daily rest. I hope however that you will do so when you are in Washington.

Have you heard from Jennie?[5] And when do you expect her to take up her job?

Marx Lewis could not confer with all the New York folks, since most of them were not there. He only spoke to Hillquit and to Gillis,[6] the lame fellow, you know. Vladeck was out of town.

And I wish you would write more often. I have sent this week two night letters and one day letter by wire—and this is the second message

you get by mail. You must tell me more about Doris, Colin and Debby—
and also what the Bostonians[7] are doing, they never seem to notice me.

Moreover, I am still bothered with rheumatism.

With love to all, but especially to my sweet old Schatzl

Papa.

1. The *Milwaukee Sentinel,* March 18, 1928, omitted five paragraphs from
Arthur Brisbane's syndicated column as it appeared in the *New York American* of
the same date. Brisbane praised Berger's remarks in Congress on behalf of
workers who were too poor to pay federal income taxes. Brisbane concluded,
"Congressmen don't agree with Berger, but listen to him, laugh at his good
points and applaud him. THEY KNOW HE IS HONEST."

2. Bascom N. Timmons (1890–1987) operated a Washington, D.C., news
service between 1917 and 1976. In 1911 Timmons worked in Milwaukee as a
Sentinel reporter.

3. Charles A. Lindbergh (1902–1974) had completed his famous solo
flight across the Atlantic the previous year and was in Washington, D.C., to
receive the Congressional Medal of Honor. During his visit he took hundreds of
representatives and senators on flights to promote commercial aviation.

4. It works also this way.

5. Jennie Schlichting Goessling (1869–ca. 1937) was Meta's widowed
cousin. She lived with Colin and Doris Berger Welles after April, 1928, and
helped with household chores.

6. Meyer Gillis (1865–1940) helped to found the *Jewish Daily Forward* and
worked in the paper's advertising department from 1902 until 1939.

7. Jan and Elsa Berger Edelman.

Victor to Meta

Washington, D.C.
April 18, [1928]

My sweet Schatzl:

Enclosed, please, find my check for twenty-five dollars—I hope that
will get you to Washington in good shape, otherwise wire me and I shall
send you more. You undoubtedly have some money still left.

I came back in time to hear Norman Thomas make his speech of
acceptance—and also in time to enable me to *second* the nomination of
both Thomas and Maurer,[1] which I did in a rather humorous and good-
natured fashion. Got the usual "ovation", of course.

In the evening, however, I met with disaster. The committee—
which adopted my platform draft on the whole with very slight changes,
refused to report my plank for "light wines and beer under strict supervision"—and was upheld by the Convention. The vote was 60 to 30—
many delegates not voting at all. The convention also refused to vote
the delegations according to voting strenght by states, as is costumary in
all conventions, and was also done in Socialist conventions in the past.
Thus the state of Wisconsin, for instance, which is entitled to 36 votes—

could only vote the *4 delegates present,* while New York and Massachussetts and New Jersey could vote their full strenght. So much for that.

Found a letter from Hans Koenig of the Northwestern Saengerbund, which has invited the President of the United States to come to the Saengerfest in Milwaukee.[2] Explained to Mr. Coolidge that this was his chance to show his appreciation of the German element—which numbers about 25 millions of our population. He told me that he had waited for some time for an occassion of that kind, but could not give me any *positive answer* on account of the sickness of his mother-in-law who is dying from cancer of the stomach. The President was extremely friendly—got up and shook both of my hands when I left. The Socialists would lynch me, if they had seen it. I have not given anything about the invitation to the press. Don't you say anything to anybody.

I agree with you that Elsa and Jan are "darling children". Kiss them both for me. But the most darling of all—as a matter of fact a darling beyond comparison—is the *sweet Mamma* of this

Papa.

1. The Socialist Party nominated Norman Thomas for the presidency and James H. Maurer as his running mate in their convention held April 13–17, 1928, in New York City.
2. Hans A. Koenig (1877–1948) served as mayor of Wauwatosa, Wisconsin, 1916–1920, and as that city's assessor, 1928–1934. Koenig was president of the Milwaukee Saengerfest Association, which hosted a German music festival in Milwaukee on June 14–16, 1928. President Coolidge declined to attend, although he was vacationing in Wisconsin during the Saengerfest.

Victor to Meta

Washington, D.C.
December 4, 1928

My sweet Schatzl:

There isn't much to write. I met Carss[1] of Minnesota (another "lame duck")[2] on the train who "sympathized" with me, until I was almost dizzy. He was one of the two Farmer-Laborites in the House and is very sore. Shipstead, who has gone over to the Republicans, is his special "bête noir."

Today, however, is the 31st anniversary of our marriage, and were I [a] pious man I should naturally spend the day in giving thanks to the Good Lord for the blessing. As it is, I can only promise you to do all I can to make the rest of your life as happy and care-free as is within my power. On the other hand, I want you to use all of *your* will-power—and every medical devise—to become all well again as soon as possible.

The Hotel Raleigh—for which I have a due-bill of $150.00 is on 12th & Pennsylvania ave, which means that it is a very noisy place. I have a room near the corner and pay $4.00 per day—a reduction of $1.00 for Congressmen. They seem to have good meals, but the "eats" are very expensive, therefore I shall not patronize the dining room.

The reception in the House was very friendly. Everybody—including the Republican leaders—expressed the wish and the hope that I would return in 2 years. Will Woods,[3] the chairman of the Republican Congressional Committee said, that he was sorry that in my case the Republican Party "won too much"—more than (he thought) was good for the welfare of the country. Others wanted me to go through with the *recount.* Judge Kading[4] (Watertown, Wis.) even offered to hand me a check of $50.00 towards defraying the expenses. I thanked them all— and simply smiled. I am through with politics, and I want no sympathy. And don't you say anything to anybody.

There will not be very much chance to do things in the short session—even if I had the inclination to work hard. I shall take up a few matters, however, so as to keep up my reputation.

I am curious to know, how Coie will come out with the sale of his fox-pelts, this year. The telegram from Frank did not sound very encouraging;—how many were sent to Boston? Do you know?

The main thing, however, after all, is that my Schatzl should get well as quickly as possible, because we want to take that trip that you planned. With love to the whole tribe—but especially to Grandma and Debby,

Papa

1. William Leighton Carss (1865–1931) served as a Minnesota congressman, 1919–1921 and 1925–1929, and was elected on the Union Labor ticket for his first term and on the Farmer-Labor ticket for his second and third terms.

2. On November 6, 1928, Republican William H. Stafford defeated Berger in his bid for reelection to Congress by 729 votes out of 106,113 cast. Stafford received 38.9 percent to 38.2 percent for Berger and 22.7 percent for Democrat Thomas O'Malley. The election was marked by ballot shortages, a new method of ticket splitting, and rumors of election fraud.

3. William Wood (1861–1933) served as a Republican representative from Indiana, 1915–1933, and as chairman of the Republican National Congressional Committee, 1920–1933.

4. Charles A. Kading (1874–1956) served as a Republican representative from Wisconsin, 1927–1933.

Victor to Meta

Washington, D.C.
December 8, 1928

My dear Mamma-Schatzl:

Evidently the heavy Christmas mail is interfering with the prompt delivery of the letters—but by this time you must have received a considerable number of them.

Enclosed you will find 4 items. Two of them are checks of one dollar each from "Workmens circles"—while one them is made out to the Leader, the letter states that it is a contribution to my *campaign*. Please, tell Miss Thomas so.

Then there is the official report, which I received from the Secretary of State, as to the result of the vote in the 5th district. It gives Stafford just 729 plurality. This only proves that we should have gone through with the recount. That talk about "2500 majority for Stafford" was evidently engineered by some election commissioner—presumably Ed. Buer[1]—in order to *discourage* a recount. The commissioners naturally hated to do the tedious work, and Buer (who had heavy bets against me) was financially interested in seeing Stafford elected.

There is also a clipping from a paper telling that traveling by automobile is the most dangerous way of travel. And since our children are compelled by conditions to use the automobile continuously, I want to impress it upon them, to be as careful as possible—and *never* to take any chance whatsoever.

And upon you, my dear Schatzl, I must imbue the idea of serenity—of a hopeful outlook—which you seem to lack entirely of late. You have no reason to fear the poor house—or even penury in your old age. Even if I should die tonight, or soon (which we will not hope), there would be enough left for you to live in reasonable comfort, without dependence on the children, or touching the farm. But if the Good Lord lets me keep my health for a few years longer, we shall both be alright and carry out most of your beautiful plans.

Therefore, don't worry! Be cheerful! Practice a little "new thought"! Enjoy the children and Debby, and *take care of your health* above everything else.

Tell Doris to write to me also—especially the news from the fox farm, in which I am interested to the tune of 10 per centum.

Lovingly
Papa

---

1. Edward R. Buer (1889–1958), an attorney, had been expelled from the Socialist Party for unethical conduct in 1927 but remained the party's representative on the Milwaukee County Election Commission, a position he had held since 1918. Berger had asked for a recount after losing the congressional election by a small margin, but after Buer announced to the press that Berger was losing by more than 2,100 votes, Berger dropped his request. Buer later claimed to be surprised when the official figures showed that Berger lost by only 729 votes. The *Milwaukee Leader,* December 11–12, 1928, charged that Buer had bet heavily against Berger in the election.

Meta to Victor

Milwaukee, Wisconsin
December 11, 1928

Dearest Mine!

Inclosed are the clippings relating to your case. For your information *only* Quick[1] went up to the inspector in the 11th precinct 15th ward where the evidence showed that crosses had been placed after your name in a pencil different from the ones on top of the Republican column, and questioned the socialist inspector there & got a confession from him that he & the policeman up there had actually done that trick. And the poor boobs did it so clumsily that in the entire precinct they didn't give Stafford a single straight vote. Of course we are not saying a *word* about this to anyone as we don't want to get either the policeman or the S. inspector into trouble. Quick says we ought to go ahead on the recount as the ballots in the 15th ward will have to speak for themselves. Buer is getting nervous now.

We're immensely proud of your statement altho' Doris says it's libelous.[2] Miss Thomas was too afraid in the beginning to permit any thing stronger to creep into the Leader than what you see on our clipping. But Doris exclaimed when your statement came "Oh, Papa is still young & full of fight. I'm so proud of him."

The results may not change anyway

Now family news—The Welles family i.e. Jennie[3] & Debby moved in today. Coie's quite sick with the Grippe. Temp. 102 last night. I sent Dr. Dollert[4] out & he ordered Debby away so they moved into town. I hope Co will throw this off like a regular cold, but he certainly was sick last night. He's been dieting a little too strenuous, working too hard both night & day & not getting enough sleep, so he's a fit subject for grippe. I'll keep you informed.

Bless you Darling. You deserve better luck than you've had these past few months. If we will only all keep our health we will yet triumph over our difficulties. Our best love to you from all. Your

Meta.

1. William F. Quick (1885–1966), a Milwaukee attorney and a Socialist, served as a state senator, 1923–1926, civil court judge, 1926–1927, and assistant city attorney, 1932–1936.
2. "Count Would Have Gone On, Berger Says," *Milwaukee Leader,* December 11, 1928. In his statement, Berger charged that election commissioner Edward Buer was financially interested in seeing Berger defeated and "not only violated the law, but all rules of decency and honesty" by betting on the outcome of the race in the Fifth Congressional District.
3. Jennie Schlichting Goessling.
4. Frederick F. Dollert was a Milwaukee physician.

Victor to Meta

Washington, D.C.
December 17, 1928

My dear Schatzl:

Glad to hear that Coie is better—hope he will be up and his own self by the end of the week. The news about Mildred[1] is also cheering.

Don't worry about Dufenhorst.[2] Would have paid the note, if the notice had reached me. As it is, I shall take care of it when I get home.

Do not fear a libel suit from Buer. He is in no position to start libel suits—especially after the editorial he got in the Journal last Saturday.[3]

Duddie must not mind what those vulgar "sports" say about her being "yellow". Most of the court house gang ought to be in the *penitentiary*. *She* is not to say it, but *I* will say it when the time comes. And Eugene Warnimont[4] is one of the crookedest of the gang. Tell Duddie to take good care of the affidavits.

Sorry that fox pelts are quoted at so low a price *this* winter already. As you know I expected that sooner or later such would be the case, since they have started miriads of silver fox farms all over the country and in Canada. Muskrat farms will be the staple and paying line, henceforth, in the fur farm business.

Went to see the President this morning about restoring the citizenship to Ed. Grieb. Had a very friendly reception. Coolidge did not remember much about the case any more—except that last year I had "asked him to release somebody from prison as a Christmas present". Had to repeat the entire story again. But I had no papers with me, not even an application from Grieb to have his citizenship restored. Moreover, Coolidge told me that it was his rule in all such cases to have 3 years go by—before he acted on the application. To which I answered that I had told Grieb's family and everybody else— that he (Coolidge) didn't do things by halfs, and that he had meant to pardon him. Also, that Grieb was hampered in making a living by not being a citizen. Finally, he told me that he was probably going to make an exception in this case. Since he had no papers before him, however, would I see to it that Grieb make the formal application? And that the mayor and the priest of Grieb's congregation also send in a petition to that effect. I wired both Hoan and Grieb to send in the petitions at once.

Tomorrow I will also introduce a bill in the House to restore the citizenship *to all those* who *lost* it during *the war* for one reason or another.[5] A measure of that kind is being urged by the Civil Liberties Union.

I don't know whether these things interest you much—especially now when you have Schnuckie and Jan and Debby in the house. I suppose, you are in clover just now. Only don't let them tire you out. For

you, Dr. Rogers[6] is a much bigger doctor than Dr. Berger-Edelman—
don't forget that, please.

Kiss the whole tribe for me. And don't worry! Take it easy! "And if
you can't take it easy, take it as easy as you can"—as the Irish say.

With love to all, especially to my sweet Grandma

Papa.

1. Mildred Calkins, a maid and nanny working for Doris and Colin Welles.
2. Probably Edward L. Dufenhorst, a Milwaukee advertising agent.
3. "Election Commission Needs a Shaking-Up," *Milwaukee Journal,* December 15, 1928. The editorial criticized the county election commission for committing "a flagrant error" in miscounting the votes in Berger's congressional race and for then adding an "affront to the public" and "injury to Mr. Berger" for failing to announce the corrected figures.
4. Eugene Warnimont (1885–1950) served on the Milwaukee County Board, 1914–1950.
5. On December 19, 1928, Berger introduced a resolution calling for a full pardon and amnesty for political prisoners. The resolution was referred to the Committee on the Judiciary, where it died.
6. Malcolm F. Rogers (1891–1962) was a Milwaukee cardiologist.

Victor to Meta

Washington, D.C.
January 10, 1929

My sweet Mamma-Schatzl:

This is a sinful pen to write with—but the other is worse—and I
must send you a letter.

Well, the first greeting I got was from Edgar Howard[1] of
Nebraska—a long haired freakish "Bryan Democrat", who once-upon-a-
time was Bryan's secretary. He informed me that all the Wisconsin "Progressives" are getting ready "to jump through the hoop"—i.e. to join
the "stand pat" band wagon. Well, not even Bill Evjue will have any reason to put on any mourning.

Was also told that I was missed by my friends in the House, but otherwise *I* didn't miss much, except a few roll calls. And I did not vote on
the question of seating that great war-patriot, James Beck, who in 1916
wrote a book justifying the case of the All-Lies,[2] which brought him a
great deal of praise and recognition in England and France, even
before *we* got into the War. Beck had himself elected in Philadelphia,
where he was born—but he had not lived there for 25 years or longer,
and his seat was contested for that reason and because he virtually had
been *appointed* to the House by Bill Vare, the corrupt Philadelphia
"boss", whose case he is conducting before the election committee of
the Senate.

But then what is the House of Representatives anyhow? It is getting
to be a sort of a "Wittwen-Sitz"[3] for the wives of deceased members.

Enclosed, please find clipping. If this continues much longer, we shall have to appoint sets of bridge-tables, instead of committees. Our parliamentarism is even more of a joke than our democracy.

The clipping about the fox farm scheme, which is the subject of a trial before the U.S. Supreme Court, will not only interest you but also Doris and Coie, because it resembles the plan on which the Nieman-Fromm fox farms were built up.

There isn't any news here otherwise. I again have exactly the same type of room in the Hotel Raleigh,—near the corner of 12th & Pennsylvania—but this time on the 5th floor.

Tomorrow, we shall vote on the reapportionment bill. It is questionable whether it will pass—although the present representation is the House is clearly unconstitutional.[4]

I hope you are well, sweetheart,—and getting better every day. Just obey the orders of Dr. Rogers religiously.

Kiss all the children for me—and this includes not only Debby, but also Jan and Coie. But, please, don't let even Debby tire you.

With love to all, and especially to my Schatzl

Papa.

1. Edgar Howard (1858–1951), a Democratic representative from Nebraska, 1923–1935.

2. Beck's widely read *The Evidence in the Case* (New York, 1914; revised edition, 1916) supported the Allied cause in World War I. Beck also published a sequel entitled *The War and Humanity* (New York, 1916).

3. "home for widows." Pearl Oldfield (1876–1962), a Democrat from Arkansas, became the fifth woman elected to the Seventieth Congress when she won a January 9, 1929, special election held to fill the vacancy caused by the death of her husband. Three of the five women were widows of former members of Congress and one was the wife of a former member who was still alive.

4. Congress had failed to reapportion the House of Representatives following the 1920 census, as mandated by the Constitution. The House passed a reapportionment bill on January 11, 1929, with Berger voting with the majority, although the Senate failed to act on the measure before Congress adjourned.

Meta to Victor

Milwaukee, Wisconsin
January 23, 1929

Darling Papa:—

After you left yesterday, we tried to get back to some sort of normalcy here, but Debby was so cross that all we could do for some hours was to try to find out what was the trouble. She must have missed you when you left & took that means of letting us know. In the afternoon, we finally took her for an auto ride, in all that drizzle so that we could get her out. She fell asleep in my arms so we kept on driving for

another hour. When we got back she was ready for her orange juice &
cod-liver oil, took her milk later in the day & was quite all right again.
And last night she slept the night thro' which gave us all a good sleep.

Last night Norman Hapgood spoke. Duddie & I didn't go, but Coie
& Bob[1] did. Neither liked Norman Hapgood but Coie was absolutely
withering in his criticism. He wrote a letter to the Leader which I hope
you will see. I'm glad I didn't make the effort to go out & Doris surely
was in no condition to go.

The day is bright, sunny & cold & the streets & sidewalks are covered
with frightfully smooth ice. The winter has been sort of hard so far. Yesterday Mr. Sivyer[2] was killed by two skidding cars on the icy pavements.

Augustyn was advanced to the President of the National Exchange
Bank. Well—he was a faithful servant these many many years. Now—he
too is a Hollander & I wonder if when next you come home, we couldn't
have a talk with him too about Jan.

Doris had a talk with Quick this A.M. Quick is of the opinion that
the Judges all would grant a writ of mandamus, but since any false
reports given out to the press by Buerr would not have changed the
result of the election according to the count as it stood when you
stopped the recount, but that these false reports only affected your attitude towards continuing the recount. Quick said that the judges (*for he
talked with every judge*) would be on the side of Stafford which would not
be so good for you in the end. Quick said the writ of mandamus would
be temperary until the arguments were made & then the judges would
deny the writ because there was no law to cover such a case. In short,
I've tried to make you see it as I understand it. And with all the doubts
etc etc I believe it to be good policy to finish a fight. It may be that the
party however will not again want to vote the necessary funds. And of
course the results will not be changed in as much as Stafford has a lead
& an election certificate.

I've been feeling first-rate & like working again. All I want is to get
the "pep" I used to have.

I want the mail man to take this letter so good-bye for the present.
You know I haven't much news to write.

Every one here sends you loads of love including your very
adorable grand-daughter.

Devotedly your
Meta.

1. Robert Filtzer.
2. Frederick L. Sivyer (1879–1929) was president of Sivyer Steel Casting
Company in Milwaukee.

Victor to Meta

Washington, D.C.
January 29, 1929

My sweet Mamma-Schatzl:

Had lunch in New York yesterday with the third member of the Forward board—with Meyer Gillis. The three men (Vladeck, Held[1] and Gillis) with whom I had separate conferences, are supposed to be able to swing the board, but they want first to look over the matter privately and learn all the details.

Vladeck and Held are, therfore, to come to Milwaukee as soon as the session ends. It is, of course, not to the interest of the enterprise that the Forward shall be known as the owner—at least not for some years to come. If the deal goes through, the stock will remain in my name, or in the name of some one they may select later—Therefore, in order to give them an inside into the business, I am going to bring *home* one book at a time and they will look it over at their leisure.

They told me that the deficit of $20,000 a year means nothing to them. Any small business in N.Y. has occassionally a deficit like that. Their little scientific *monthly*—the Zukunft—which they publish as a side issue, has an annual deficit of $20,000 annually. Besides, they all know that the Forward is doomed, since immigration has been stopped. Even this *last year* their income was *$200,000 less* than *the year before*, I was told by Gillis. Five or ten more years more—may put them on the rocks.

All three men are very much in *favor* of my proposition.

My proposition however is still somewhat hazy. I have not told them the facts about the circulation. I don't want to scare them, until they are impressed with the magnitude of the thing, which is still *alive* and *going*, and capable of immense expansion, if money is put behind it.

I told them that I am willing to turn over my stock and get a majority ownership for them. But what I owe on the stock will have to be paid, of course, and also the money furnished to acquire a majority. This, with the bank debts that I have—I figured would require about $30,000, (right-away) which they did not consider a big sum at all. I want Miss Thomas to be paid for her stock—about $3,700. Don't mention anything about the matter to her, however, I shall tell her all she needs to know. She is so fidgety and nervous—as you are aware, and might drop a word to Teddy.[2]

I told her that I was going to see the Forward people (—when I was in Milwaukee last week—) and she explained that she had enough money to live on, and that she was willing to turn over her stock *without* a *cent*, for any new deal.

As for myself—well, they want me and *must* have me, of course. I am to hold the rank of editor-in-chief but will not be expected to do much *actual* work, other than that of general supervision. Tentatively they have agreed to pay me a salary, somewhat like Cahan gets, for 10 years. But I shall prefer an agreement, which we will *not* call a salary but a *fixed payment*, for—let's say $20,000 the first year, and $10,000 the following nine years annually, which is to be paid to my wife or my children (in case of my untimely "departure")—so as to be on the safe side. Vladeck, Held and Gillis may not always be there in the future, and I don't want to be at the mercy of any kind of a mob. Nor do I want to have any law suits.

The entire proposition looks very good and very probable—so far. As the matter stands now, it is not only *my* neccessity, but it is also theirs. They *must* change *their* paper into an English paper within the next few years—and there is no place where they can try themselves out with better prospects and *less risk* than by taking over ours—which is alive and going proposition, with an advertising patronage, which alone would cost them infinite labor and hundreds of thousand dollars to get. And if they put in $100,000 a year for improvement and promotion—and they intend to do that, of course—they can make the paper a very profitable property in a very short time.

Now, you know all I know about the deal. Let *Doris* read this letter, but impress it upon her that the proposition and the paper would cease, if the story got out. In all such deals the utmost secrecy is very essential—in our case it is the *first* requisit.

And remember, sweet Schatzl—in all this I have you, and almost entirely you, in mind. I want you to have a sunny, safe and care-free old age—such as you deserve. And I am convinced that you will get it, if Providence keeps me alive a short while longer.

But you must take care of your *health* Mamma-Darling. That is your end of it—and that is what *you owe us.*

Give my love to the children and tell Doris not to work so hard. Also ask Doris and Coie whether they have taken out accident insurance—for $12,000 each—as they have promised me.

Kiss Debby for me, and remember, sweet Mamma that *you* are the guiding light, of your

Papa.

1. Adolph Held (1885–1969) served as the city editor, 1906–1912, and business manager, 1912–1917, of the *Jewish Daily Forward* and held the presidency of the Forward Association (the paper's publisher), from 1925 to 1962. He served as a Socialist New York City alderman, 1917–1919.

2. Theodore N. Sweers (1888–1968), a Milwaukee Social-Democratic Publishing Company stockholder, worked in the pressroom of the *Social-Democratic Herald* and later the *Milwaukee Leader* from 1904 until 1929, serving as the *Leader's* production manager, 1928–1929. He subsequently became business manager for the Web Pressman's Union, a position he held until his retirement in 1957.

Victor to Meta

New York, New York
February 2, 1929

My sweet Mamma!

Another meeting of the National Executive Committee and not a pleasant one. About two days of wrangling. Hillquit occupied about ⅔ of the time with speeches. He is bright fellow but he has constituted himself as the party pope. As for the others, well we have four *lawyers* on the committee, but Roewer resigned today; he didn't give any reason, he is very much disgruntled about Henry,[1] however. More over, Roewer is rich now. He has established a good practice, mainly with the help of the Finns, and he has also inherited money, or rather his wife[2] has inherited it.

What got me sore was that Maurer told us that I had no business to spend so much money for myself—that the party in Reading spent all the money necessary for his election, after he gave *his* contribution. I was so angry that I *didn't* even *think* it *worth while* to tell him—that without knowing what sum he contributed in Reading, I gave at least *3 times as much* in cash this year in Milwaukee, not counting the money I spent in literature which naturally helped the entire ticket. Nevertheless, the party machinery of Milwaukee headed by the candidate for sheriff concentrated all its power and all its money in a futile effort to elect a sheriff.[3]

Well, I didn't say it. What's the use?

But the fact is that I feel like a sinner at times—since I had the natural ability to make money in any business, and thus having had the gift easily to secure a comfortable and care-free old age for my wonderful wife and for myself—and to leave some wealth for my children—that I missed these opportunities by spending my life in a thankless movement.

Now I am almost 70 years old. And I have made up my mind that if the deal I am negotiating should fall through for any reason whatsoever—I shall use my wits in a rather *ruthless fashion* to dispose of that property, and secure our old age.

Well, sweet Schatzl—this a rather disgruntled note, which really should not be addressed to you—especially since I do believe that the Forward deal will come through. And, therefore, instead of mailing this letter to my Mamma I shall send it to Doris. She ought to know all of these things.

I am very glad that our little Debby is making such good progress. But I am *very anxious* to know *exactly* what the doctors in Madison *said* about *Mamma* and I want Duddie to write me *all about it.*

I shall stay here tomorrow (at least part of the day) and try to meet Held once more. I don't want the thing to cool off.

With best love to the entire family but especially to our sweet Grandma and Debby—the same old

Papa

1. William H. Henry served as executive secretary of the Socialist Party from 1926 through 1929. He later became a party organizer in Wisconsin.
2. Rosa Roewer (b. 1885) was the wife of George Roewer Jr.
3. Milwaukee's Socialists fared poorly in the 1928 election. In addition to losing Berger's congressional seat, Socialists failed to win a single county office and carried only one out of three open state senate seats and three out of twenty seats in the state assembly. The Socialist candidate for sheriff, Al Benson, received 27 percent of the vote and finished third.

Victor to Meta

Washington, D.C.
February 8, 1929

My sweet Mamma-Darling:—

Have not had many letters from you of late—and there is not much news here, other than what you read in the papers but I must send you a few lines so that you get a message from me for Sunday.

Well, many members have asked me to make a speech in the House before I leave, and I have consented.[1] The steering committee is willing to give me an hour (out of the regular order) and John Tilson,[2] the Republican floor leader, even wants to announce it two days ahead, in order to secure a big crowd, which is not an easy matter now.

My mind is entirely occupied with the Leader matter, however, and I really have no idea what I am going to say. I don't want to make a philosophical and learned Socialist speech, in fact I would not have the time to prepare one. Nevertheless I don't want "to fall down" on this occassion and therefore, I shall have to buckle up tomorrow and Sunday and get the material.

So much for that.

Went to call on Prittwitz,[3] the German Ambassador, this morning— and spent a rather interesting hour with him discussing the situation in Germany, the Dawes plan etc. He asked me to come often—that he wanted to see me often. I explained however, that in the near future he would have to come to Milwaukee, if he wanted to meet me. He seemed somewhat disappointed. Before I left, he told me that he had the pleasure of meeting you and that he wants to be remembered.

Well, Schatzl—I may not stay here until the end of the session. If I can get Vladeck and Held to come west with within 2 weeks I am willing to leave by the 26th. The trouble is only that I don't know whether I can get these men to come *this month*. Also, they made speaking dates for me in various cities, including Boston and Springfield between the 6th and 12th of March and that would include a lot of traveling, if I went home first. Well, I shall write to Vladeck and get his version.

There is nothing else that I can tell you—except to beg you again and always to take the *best possible care* of *your health.* Compared with that—nothing else counts.

Tell Doris and Coie *not* to work so hard—and to *sleep* as much as possible, especially since they have no chance at all to walk a lot. And they are *not* to try to make a *learned person* out of *Debby* at the present time—because she is really to[o] young for that. And kiss her for her Grandpa, and have *her* kiss *Grandma,* for your

Papa.

1. Berger delivered parting remarks on February 21, 1929, in a lengthy speech discussing Anglo-American relations and calling for efforts to prevent future wars.
2. John Quillin Tilson (1866–1958), a Republican representative from Connecticut, 1909–1913 and 1915–1932, and House majority leader, 1925–1931.
3. Friedrich von Prittwitz und Gaffron (1884–1955) served as German ambassador to the United States, 1928–1933.

Victor to Meta

Washington, D.C.
February 19, 1929

My sweet Mamma-Schatzl:

For a few days I have not written you a letter—because I was busy organizing my speech—and night wires are not very satisfactory.

Now I have spread your last (3) daily letters before me, and shall answer all your questions.

But before I do so, I must tell you how glad I am that you are evidently improving as far as your health is concerned. It may take some time, of course, before you get *all well* again—and you must have patience and strictly obey the orders of your phy[si]cian. I was told of cases where persons having similar heart troubles—not only regained their health but lived to be 90 years old. Let's hope you will do the same.

Take special care of your "cold", however. On account of the unusually cold season, you probably do not get enough *fresh air*—and since you cannot move about much, it is also probable that your bowels are not in the proper condition. Watch out for all that, Schatzl.

As to the Hamilton stock—well, I may sell that whenever I have a chance to make a reasonable profit. Small stockholders don't count in big concerns. The Hamilton company did not start like Ford's with a small capital, which grew to immense proportions. The Hamilton had a considerable capitalization from the start. We count for so much in the Madison Times[1] because we have not only 10 percent of all the stock that was sold—but by circumstances our stock holds the balance of power.

You say that you hate Wisconsin winters and yearn for a warmer climate. If the Leader deal goes through—I firmly believe it will—I shall buy 40 acres in Florida, which have been offered to me by a big landowner at a very small price because he admits that the bottom has fallen out of the Florida land boom. The man who wants to sell it to me is very wealthy—is the state chairman of the Republican party of Florida,[2] which he carried for Hoover last fall. The land is heavily wooded, is situated on the west coast and is right on the Mexican Golf. A little city, with a harbor, is near by. He says he has known of me and has admired me for 30 years and will be proud to have me as a neighbor—in fact, he thinks it will advertise the place. He wants you and I to take an automobile trip down to Florida this summer, and if we like the proposition, to build a little house (he said "shack") and spend the winters there—boating, fishing and bathing. Besides we can grow oranges, figs and grapefruits on the farm, if we care to do so. Now, what do you say to this, Schatzl?

I am sorry that my "Valentine" was not a success. This year also I have ordered 70 plants from the Botanical Garden to be sent to us (32 trees, 38 shrubs)—the trouble is only that these things do not seem to thrive in our climate.

It is too late to introduce a bill to make Lincoln's birthday a national holiday—the 70th Congress is about to close. Moreover, the idea is not new, several such bills have been introduced before. Nevertheless, I shall send Conrad Schroeder[3] a letter of thanks for suggesting it.

Well, I may leave here by Tuesday noon. And since it takes always 2 days (and often even 3 days) for a letter to get here, I will suggest that you mail your last letter to reach me here, no later than *Saturday morning*, unless you put a "special delivery" stamp on. I have written to Vladeck but he says, neither he nor Held, could come to Milwaukee before March 4th. Thus I shall have a little time to prepare.

Enclosed you will find a letter from the Woman's International League. It seems you will have to send your acceptance for a nomination to the national board to Miss Elizabeth D. Fry,[4] 836 Rose Building, Cleveland, O.

What more news can I tell you? I often feel very lonesome and I am glad to get home now. My farewell address I shall make Thursday.

Tell Doris and Coie not to work too hard. If they take good care of their *health*—and use their brains normally and get sufficient sleep—and if they don't spend their money foolishly—they will be very well off financially, and will not need to worry about their old age, by the time

they are 50 years old. And they will be in a good position to take care of
Debby and of any sisters or brothers that Debby may have. Therefore,
let them use "common sense".

And since you cannot kiss Debby for me on account of your cold—
have Doris do so. But cold or no cold—*you* can by telepathy kiss, your
loving old

Papa

1. In 1932, after Victor's death, Meta sold her 5,750 shares of the *Madison
(Wisconsin) Capital Times* for $12,000. See memorandum of sale, William T.
Evjue Papers, SHSW.
2. Glenn B. Skipper was a businessman who headed the Florida Republican Party from 1928 to 1932.
3. Conrad Schroeder was a superintendent at a Milwaukee brewery.
4. Elisabeth D. Fry served as head of the nominating committee of the
Women's International League for Peace and Freedom in 1928–1929.

Meta to Victor

Richland Center, Wisconsin
June 26, 1929

Darling Papa:—
The ride over hear from Madison was beautiful beyond all expectations. I want so much that you & I come this way at the end of September when the leaves are colored. We drove thro' a valley all the
way with hills (irregular clumps) on each side & farms down in the
valley. This place reminded me much of the Black Forest region
except that the hills here are covered with elm, oaks & other trees
instead of the stately pines. It was a miniature Schwartz wald[1]—only
not so sublime.

Ada,[2] of course is just lovely and her home is simple & spacious. An
old old house, large rooms, many windows & simply furnished mostly
with furniture older than Ada herself and some of it built by her great
grandfather.

I'm sort of eaten with remorse Dear Papa because I cause you even
a moment's aggravation & concern. I'm sorry that we have arguments
over trifling things & I know that you mean the best for all of us & for
me particularly. I'm going to try to make our few years more tranquil by
conforming. Surely we ought not to get excited nor out of patience
with each other in this evening of our lives. Please forget my nervousness—I'm nervous for the first time in my life. I really want to live comfortably & without so many restrictions but I'm going to meet you half
way here after if possible.

I'll wire you care of the office some time Thursday what my plans
are for coming home. All my love to you & Debby & Doris & Coie.
Always devotedly and faithfully your

Meta

1. Black Forest.
2. Ada James.

* * *

*Victor L. Berger was injured in a streetcar accident in Milwaukee on July 16,
1929, and died the following August 7. Berger's body lay in state in Milwaukee's City Hall, and more than 100,000 people came to pay their respects.*

Index

417